One World, Many Cultures

Fifth Edition

D0209467

STUART HIRSCHBERG

Rutgers: The State University of New Jersey, Newark

TERRY HIRSCHBERG

PEARSON
Longman

New York • San Francisco • Boston
London • Toronto • Sydney • Tokyo • Singapore • Madrid
Mexico City • Munich • Paris • Cape Town • Hong Kong • Montreal

E pluribus unum

Senior Vice President, Publisher: Joe Opiela
Vice President, Publisher: Eben W. Ludlow
Executive Marketing Manager: Ann Stypuloski
Senior Supplements Editor: Donna Campion
Production Manager: Charles Annis
Project Coordination, Text Design, and Electronic Page Makeup: Pre-Press Co., Inc.
Cover Designer/Manager: Wendy Fredericks
Cover Art: Illustration© Joel Nakamura; Background texture:© GettyImages, Inc./Artville
Manufacturing Manager: Roy Pickering
Printer and Binder: R.R. Donnelley and Sons Company
Cover Printer: Coral Graphic Services, Inc.

For permission to use copyrighted material, grateful acknowledgment is made to the copyright holders on pp. 577–582, which are hereby made part of this copyright page.

Library of Congress Cataloging-in-Publication Data
One world, many cultures / [compiled by] Stuart Hirschberg, Terry Hirschberg.
--5th ed.
    p. cm.
  Includes bibliographical references and index.
  ISBN 0-321-16401-6 (alk. paper)
    1. College readers. 2. Pluralism (Social sciences)--Problems, exercises, etc.
  3. Ethnic groups--Problems, exercises, etc. 4. English language--Rhetoric.
  5. Readers--Social sciences. I. Hirschberg, Stuart. II. Hirschberg, Terry.

PE1417.O57 2004
808'.0427--dc21   2002043859

Please visit our website at http://www.ablongman.com

ISBN 0-321-16401-6
1 2 3 4 5 6 7 8 9 10—DOH—06 05 04 03

Contents

2   *Coming of Age*   85

4 *How Work Creates Identity*   241

5 *Class and Caste*   310

6   *The Individual in Society*   *372*

7 *Strangers in a Strange Land*   439

8   *Customs, Rituals, and Entertainment*   **514**

Preface

This fifth edition of *One World, Many Cultures* is a global, contemporary reader whose international and multicultural selections offer a new direction for freshman composition courses.

In eight thematic chapters, consisting of sixty-three readings, twenty-five of which are new to this series, by internationally recognized writers from thirty-two countries, we explore cultural differences and displacement in relation to race, class, gender, region, and nation. *One World, Many Cultures* also reflects the emphasis on cultural studies and argumentation that has become an integral part of many college programs since the fourth edition.

The selections challenge readers to see similarities between their own experiences and the experiences of others in radically different cultural circumstances. Compelling and provocative writings by authors from the Caribbean, Africa, Asia, Europe, South America, and Central America reflect the cultural and ethnic heritage of many students.

The forty-seven nonfiction selections include diaries, essays, interviews, autobiographies, and prison memoirs. These and the sixteen short stories encourage readers to perceive the relationship between a wide range of experiences in different cultures and corresponding experiences of writers within the United States. The fifth edition of *One World, Many Cultures* continues to provide a rich sampling of accounts by writers who are native to the cultures that they describe, allowing the reader to hear authentic voices rather than filtered journalistic reports.

New to This Edition

- Twenty-five selections are new to this edition. Many have never been previously anthologized.
- Six new short works of fiction represent a wide variety of cultural and ethnic backgrounds.

Hanan al-Shaykh	"The Persian Carpet"
Albert Camus	"The Guest"
Kate Chopin	"Désirée's Baby"
Catherine Lim	"Paper"
Tayeb Salih	"A Handful of Dates"
Wakako Yamauchi	"And the Soul Shall Dance"

- Half the readings are by women writers.
- Prompts ("Before You Read") precede each selection.
- More information on the lives of the Maasai, Iban, and Mbuti has been added.

Chapter Descriptions

The eight chapters move from the most personal sphere of family life through adolescent turning points, questions of sexual identity, the responsibilities of work, and conflicts of class and race to the more encompassing dimensions of citizenship, immigration, and social customs.

Chapter 1, "Family and Cultural Ties," introduces families in India, Morocco, Japan, China, the Sudan, the Congo, and within the United States, an African-American family and a Mexican-American family, among others. These selections illustrate that the "family," however defined (as a single-parent household, a nuclear family, or the extended family of an entire community), passes on the mores and values of a particular culture to the next generation.

Chapter 2, "Coming of Age," provides insights into both formal and informal rites of passage, initiation ceremonies, and moments of discovery in the lives of a Chinese-American girl, an Egyptian physician, a girl of the !Kung tribe in Botswana, a Japanese-American girl, a young woman in Lebanon, a Maasai warrior, a young boy in Ireland, and an adventurer in Borneo.

Chapter 3, "How Culture Shapes Gender Roles," explores the role of culture in shaping sexual identity. Readers can gain insight into how gender roles are culturally conditioned rather than biologically determined. The extent to which sex role expectations, both heterosexual and homosexual, differ from culture to culture can be seen in societies as diverse as those of Puerto Rico, Nigeria, Saudi Arabia, India, the Hispanic community in Miami, and turn-of-the-century Louisiana.

Chapter 4, "How Work Creates Identity," explores work as a universal human experience through which we define ourselves and others. The role of culture in shaping attitudes toward work can be seen in the different experiences of a minimum-wage service worker and a Mexican-American rock blaster. We can share the work experiences of a disillusioned Japanese corporate employee, an American student exchanging English lessons for martial arts instruction in China, a firefighter reporting for duty on September 11, 2001, a maid's daughter in Argentina who must come to terms with her place in society, and a Brazilian, self-proclaimed ornithologist who becomes obsessed by his work.

Chapter 5, "Class and Caste," takes up the crucial and often unrecognized relationships between race, identity, and social class through readings that explore positions of power and powerlessness. Selections include Mahdokht Kashkuli's story of a family in modern-day Iran who must place one of their children in an orphanage. The voices heard are those of men and women of many races in several nations, including Antonio, a teenage contract killer in Colombia's drug capital, Medellín. Unusual perspectives on class issues are provided by Mary Crow Dog's account of her experiences in a government-run school for Native Americans, Viramma's account of her life as an "untouchable" in south India, Raymonde Carroll's investigation of the different cultural values that determine success in France and America, Anita Gates's analysis of class values in "Frasier," and Catherine Lim's bittersweet fable of a couple who speculate in the Singapore Stock Exchange, drawn by the lure of becoming wealthy overnight.

Chapter 6, "The Individual in Society," looks at the resilience and courage of ordinary citizens in the Balkans, and state tyranny in the China of Mao Tse-Tung during the Cultural Revolution, and recent forms of repression in contemporary China. We hear the voices of writers of conscience and survivors of oppressive regimes in Chile, in Kenya, in Cyprus during British colonial rule, and in contemporary Pakistan.

Chapter 7, "Strangers in a Strange Land," explores the condition of exiles—whether refugees, immigrants, or travelers—who are caught between two cultures, but are at home in neither. The need of those who have left "home" to make sense of their lives in a new place is a theme explored by Gloria Anzaldúa, Jesse W. Nash, Palden Gyatso, David R. Counts, Itabari Njeri, George Carlin, Poranee Natadecha-Sponsel, and Albert Camus.

Chapter 8, "Customs, Rituals, and Entertainment," focuses on the role that ritual, religion, and popular culture, East and West, play in shaping social behavior. The decisive influence of cultural values is explored through an analysis of foot-binding practices in ancient China, the wearing of the kimono in Japan, how the importance of good teeth differs between the United States and East Europe, the meaning of fiestas in Mexico, and the role of voodoo in Haitian society. We gain insight into the role rituals play in forming a pop-culture icon, the place of revenge in Bedouin culture, and how a family in Botswana resorted to an outlawed tribal ritual to produce rain.

Editorial Apparatus

A fifteen-page introduction covers the important aspects of critical reading, keeping a journal, and responding to the text, and includes a sample selection by Edward T. Hall ("Hidden Culture") for students to annotate. Chapter introductions discuss the theme of each chapter as related to the individual selections. Biographical sketches preceding each selection give background information on the writer's life and identify the cultural, historical, and personal context in which the selection was written. Prompts ("Before You Read") that precede each selection alert students to an important cultural idea expressed in the selection. Relevant background information is provided for all countries before the selections.

The questions that follow each selection are designed to encourage readers to discover relationships between personal experiences and ideas in the text, to explore points of agreement and areas of conflict sparked by the viewpoints of the authors, and to provide ideas for further research and inquiry.

The first set of questions, "Evaluating the Text," asks readers to think critically about the content, meaning, and purpose of the selections and to evaluate the author's rhetorical strategy, voice projected in relationship to his or her audience, evidence cited, and underlying assumptions.

The questions in "Exploring Different Perspectives" focus on relationships between readings within each chapter that illuminate differences and similarities between cultures. These questions encourage readers to make connections between diverse cultures, to understand the writer's values and beliefs, to enter into the viewpoints of others, and to understand how culture shapes perception and a sense of self.

The questions in "Extending Viewpoints through Writing" invite readers to extend their thinking by seeing wider relationships between themselves and others through writing of many different kinds, including personal or expressive as well as expository and persuasive writing and more formal research papers.

Following each chapter, "Connecting Cultures" challenges readers to make connections and comparisons among selections within the chapter and throughout the book. These questions provide opportunities to consider additional cross-cultural perspectives on a single issue or to explore a particular topic in depth.

A pronunciation key to author's names, a rhetorical index, a geographical index, an index of authors and titles, and a map of the world identifying countries mentioned in the selections are included to allow the text to accommodate a variety of teaching approaches.

Instructor's Manual

An *Instructor's Manual* provides guidelines for using the text including teaching short works of fiction, supplemental bibliographies of books and periodicals, suggested answers to discussion questions in the text, relevant Websites and films, and additional activities, which include optional discussion questions and, in some cases, suggested answers as well as classroom activities.

Acknowledgments

Once again, we want to acknowledge our appreciation for the encouragement and enthusiasm of our editor, Eben W. Ludlow, and our gratitude to all those teachers of composition who offered their thoughtful comments and gave this fifth edition the benefit of their scholarship and teaching experience. We would very much like to thank Beth Freedman, Washington and Jefferson College; Catherine H. Houghton, Point Park College; and Kim Stanley, McPherson College who suggested changes for this edition.

For their dedication, skill, and good humor, we owe much to Longman's able staff, especially Bill Russo, Assistant Editor, and Robin Gordon, Project Manager at Pre-Press Company.

Introduction

$\blacklozenge$

Critical Reading for Ideas and Organization

One of the most important skills to have in your repertoire is the ability to survey unfamiliar articles, essays, or excerpts and to come away with an accurate understanding of what the author wanted to communicate and how the material is organized. On the first and in subsequent readings of any of the selections in this text, especially the longer ones, pay particular attention to the title, look for introductory and concluding paragraphs (with special emphasis on the author's statement or restatement of central ideas), identify the headings and subheadings (and determine the relationship between these and the title), and identify any unusual terms necessary to fully understand the author's concepts.

As you work your way through an essay, you might look for cues to enable you to recognize the main parts of the argument or help you perceive the overall organization of the article. Once you find the main thesis, underline it. Then work your way through fairly rapidly, identifying the main ideas and the sequence in which they are presented. As you identify an important idea, ask yourself how this idea relates to the thesis statement you underlined or to the idea expressed in the title.

Finding a Thesis

Finding a thesis involves discovering the idea that serves as the focus of the essay. The thesis is often stated in the form of a single sentence that asserts the author's response to an issue that others might respond to in different ways. For example, the opening paragraphs of "The Little Emperors" presents Daniela Deane's assessment of an important aspect of contemporary Chinese society:

> The one-child campaign, a strict national directive that seeks to limit each Chinese couple to a single son or daughter, has other dramatic consequences: millions of abortions, fewer girls and a generation of spoiled children.

1

This thesis represents the writer's view of a subject or topic from a certain perspective. Here, Deane states a view of China's one-child policy that will serve as a focus for her essay. Writers often place the thesis in the first paragraph or group of paragraphs so that the readers will be able to perceive the relationship between the supporting evidence and this main idea.

As you read, you might wish to underline the topic sentence or main idea of each paragraph or section (since key ideas are often developed over the course of several paragraphs). Jot it down in your own words in the margins, identify supporting statements and evidence (such as examples, statistics, and the testimony of authorities), and try to discover how the author organizes the material to support the development of important ideas. To identify supporting material, look for any ideas more specific than the main idea that is used to support it. Also look for instances where the author uses examples, descriptions, statistics, quotations from authorities, comparisons, or graphs to make the main idea clearer or prove it to be true.

Pay particular attention to important transitional words, phrases, or paragraphs to better see the relationships among major sections of the selection. Noticing how certain words or phrases act as transitions to link paragraphs or sections together will dramatically improve your reading comprehension. Also look for section summaries, where the author draws together several preceding ideas.

Writers use certain words to signal the starting point of an argument. If you detect any of the following terms, look for the main idea they introduce:

> since, because, for, as, follows from, as shown by, inasmuch as, otherwise, as indicated by, the reason is that, for the reason that, may be inferred from, may be derived from, may be deduced from, in view of the fact that

An especially important category of words is that which includes signals that the author will be stating a conclusion. Words to look for are these:

> therefore, hence, thus, so, accordingly, in consequence, it follows that, we may infer, I conclude that, in conclusion, in summary, which shows that, which means that, and which entails, consequently, proves that, as a result, which implies that, which allows us to infer, points to the conclusion that

You may find it helpful to create a running dialogue with the author in the margins, posing and then trying to answer the basic questions *who, what, where, when,* and *why,* and to note observations on how the main idea of the article is related to the title. These notes can later be used to evaluate how effectively any specific section contributes to the overall line of thought.

Responding to What You Read

When reading an essay that seems to embody a certain value system, try to examine any assumptions or beliefs the writer expects the audience to share. How is this assumption related to the author's purpose? If you do not agree with these assumptions, has the writer provided sound reasons and evidence to persuade you to change your mind?

You might describe the author's tone or voice and try to assess how much it contributed to the essay. How effectively does the writer use authorities, statistics, or examples to support the claim? Does the author identify the assumptions or values on which his or her views are based? Are they ones with which you would agree or disagree? To what extent does the author use the emotional connotations of language to try to persuade his or her reader? Do you see anything unworkable or disadvantageous about the solutions offered as an answer to the problem the essay addresses? All these and many other ways of analyzing someone else's essay can be used to create your own. Here are some specific guidelines to help you.

When evaluating an essay, consider what the author's purpose was in writing it. Was it to inform, explain, solve a problem, make a recommendation, amuse, enlighten, or achieve some combination of these goals? How is the tone or voice the author projects toward the reader related to his or her purpose in writing the essay?

You may find it helpful to write short summaries after each major section to determine whether you understand what the writer is trying to communicate. These summaries can then serve as a basis for an analysis of how successfully the author employs reasons, examples, statistics, and expert testimony to support and develop his or her main points.

For example, if the essay you are analyzing cites authorities to support a claim, assess whether the authorities bring the most timely opinions to bear on the subject or display any obvious biases, and determine whether they are experts in that particular field. Watch for experts described as "often quoted" or "highly placed reliable sources" without accompanying names, credentials, or appropriate documentation. If the experts cited offer what purports to be a reliable interpretation of facts, consider whether the writer also quotes equally trustworthy experts who hold opposing views.

If statistics are cited to support a point, judge whether they derive from verifiable and trustworthy sources. Also, evaluate whether the author has interpreted them in ways that are beneficial to his or her case, whereas someone who held an opposing view could interpret them quite differently. If real-life examples are presented to support the author's opinions, determine whether they are representative or whether they are too atypical to be used as evidence. If the author relies on hypothetical examples or analogies to dramatize ideas that otherwise would be hard to grasp, judge whether these examples are too farfetched to back up the claims being made. If the essay depends on the stipulated definition of a term that might be defined in different ways, check whether the author provides clear reasons to indicate why one definition rather than another is preferable.

As you list observations about the various elements of the article you are analyzing, take a closer look at the underlying assumptions and see whether you can locate and distinguish between those assumptions that are explicitly stated and those that are implicit. Once the author's assumptions are identified, you can compare them with your own beliefs about the subject, determine whether these assumptions are commonly held, and make a judgment as to their validity. Would you readily agree with these assumptions? If not, has the author provided sound reasons and supporting evidence to persuade you to change your mind?

Marking as You Read

The most effective way to think about what you read is to make notes as you read. Making notes as you read forces you to go slowly and think carefully about each sentence. This process is sometimes called annotating the text, and all you need is a pen or a pencil. There are as many styles of annotating as there are readers, and you will discover your own favorite technique once you have done it a few times. Some readers prefer to underline major points or statements and jot down their reactions to them in the margin. Others prefer to summarize each paragraph or section to help them follow the author's line of thinking. Other readers circle key words or phrases necessary to understand the main ideas. Feel free to use your notes as a kind of conversation with the text. Ask questions. Express doubts. Mark unfamiliar words or phrases to look up later. If the paragraphs are not already numbered, you might wish to number them as you go to help you keep track of your responses. Try to distinguish the main ideas from supporting points and examples. Most importantly, go slowly and think about what you are reading. Try to discover whether the author makes a credible case for the conclusions he or she reaches. One last point: take a close look at the idea expressed in the title before and after you read the essay to see how it relates to the main idea.

Distinguishing between Fact and Opinion

As you read, distinguish between statements of fact and statements of opinion. Statements of fact relate information that is widely accepted and objectively verifiable; facts are used as evidence to support the claim made by the thesis. By contrast, an opinion is a personal interpretation of data or a belief or feeling that however strongly presented should not be mistaken by the reader for objective evidence. For example, consider the following claim by Edward T. Hall in "Hidden Culture":

> Each culture and each country has its own language of space, which is just as unique as the spoken language, frequently more so. In England, for example, there are no offices for the members of Parliament. In the United States, our congressmen and senators proliferate their offices and their office buildings and simply would not tolerate a no-office situation.

The only statement that could be verified or refuted on the basis of objective data is "In England . . . there are no offices for the members of Parliament." All the other statements, *however persuasive they may seem*, are Hall's interpretations of a situation (multiple offices and office buildings for U.S. government officials) that might be interpreted quite differently by another observer. These statements should not be mistaken for statements of fact.

A reader who could not distinguish between facts and interpretations would be at a severe disadvantage in understanding Hall's essay. Part of the difficulty in separating fact from opinion stems from the difficulty of remaining objective about statements that match our own personal beliefs.

Take a few minutes to read and annotate the following essay. Feel free to "talk back" to the author. You can underline or circle key passages or key terms. You can make observations, raise questions, and express your reactions to what you read.

A SAMPLE ESSAY FOR STUDENT ANNOTATION

Edward T. Hall

Hidden Culture

◆

1   A few years ago, I became involved in a sequence of events in Japan that completely mystified me, and only later did I learn how an overt act seen from the vantage point of one's own culture can have an entirely different meaning when looked at in the context of the foreign culture. I had been staying at a hotel in downtown Tokyo that had European as well as Japanese-type rooms. The clientele included a few Europeans but was predominantly Japanese. I had been a guest for about ten days and was returning to my room in the middle of an afternoon. Asking for my key at the desk, I took the elevator to my floor. Entering the room, I immediately sensed that something was wrong. Out of place. Different. I was in the wrong room! Someone else's things were distributed around the head of the bed and the table. Somebody else's toilet articles (those of a Japanese male) were in the bathroom. My first thoughts were, "What if I am discovered here? How do I explain my presence to a Japanese who may not even speak English?"

2   I was close to panic as I realized how incredibly territorial we in the West are. I checked my key again. Yes, it really was mine. Clearly they had moved somebody else into my room. But where was my room now? And where were my belongings? Baffled and mystified, I took the elevator to the lobby. Why hadn't they told me at the desk, instead of letting me risk embarrassment and loss of face by being caught in somebody else's room? Why had they moved me in the first place? It was a nice room and, being sensitive to spaces and how they work, I was loath to give it up. After all, I had told them I would be in the hotel for almost a month. Why this business of moving me around like someone who has been squeezed in without a reservation? Nothing made sense.

3   At the desk I was told by the clerk, as he sucked in his breath in deference (and embarrassment?) that indeed they had moved me. My particular room had been reserved in advance by somebody else. I was given the key to my new room and discovered that all my personal ef-

fects were distributed around the new room almost as though I had done it myself. This produced a fleeting and strange feeling that maybe I wasn't myself. How could somebody else do all those hundred and one little things just the way I did?

4   Three days later, I was moved again, but this time I was prepared. There was no shock, just the simple realization that I had been moved and that it would now be doubly difficult for friends who had my old room number to reach me. *Tant pis,* I was in Japan. One thing did puzzle me. Earlier, when I had stayed at Frank Lloyd Wright's Imperial Hotel for several weeks, nothing like this had ever happened. What was different? What had changed? Eventually I got used to being moved and would even ask on my return each day whether I was still in the same room.

5   Later, at Hakone, a seaside resort where I was visiting with friends, the first thing that happened was that we were asked to disrobe. We were given *okatas,* and our clothes were taken from us by the maid. (For those who have not visited Japan, the okata is a cotton print kimono.) We later learned, when we ventured out in the streets, that it was possible to recognize other guests from our hotel because we had all been equipped with identical okatas. (Each hotel had its own characteristic, clearly recognizable pattern.) Also, I noted that it was polite to wave or nod to these strangers from the same hotel.

6   Following Hakone, we visited Kyoto, site of many famous temples and palaces, and the ancient capital of Japan.

7   There we were fortunate enough to stay in a wonderful little country inn on the side of a hill overlooking the town. Kyoto is much more traditional and less industrialized than Tokyo. After we had been there about a week and had thoroughly settled into our new Japanese surroundings, we returned one night to be met at the door by an apologetic manager who was stammering something. I knew immediately that we had been moved, so I said, "You had to move us. Please don't let this bother you, because we understand. Just show us to our new rooms and it will be all right." Our interpreter explained as we started to go through the door that we weren't in that hotel any longer but had been moved to *another* hotel. What a blow! Again, without warning. We wondered what the new hotel would be like, and with our descent into the town our hearts sank further. Finally, when we could descend no more, the taxi took off into a part of the city we hadn't seen before. No Europeans here! The streets got narrower and narrower until we turned into a side street that could barely accommodate the tiny Japanese taxi into which we were squeezed. Clearly this was a hotel of another class. I found that, by then, I was getting a little paranoid, which is easy enough to do in a foreign land, and said to myself, "They must think we are very low-status people indeed to treat us this way."

8   As it turned out, the neighborhood, in fact the whole district, showed us an entirely different side of life from what we had seen before, much more interesting and authentic. True, we did have some communication problems, because no one was used to dealing with foreigners, but few of them were serious.

9   Yet, the whole matter of being moved like a piece of derelict luggage puzzled me. In the United States, the person who gets moved is often the lowest-ranking individual. This principle applies to all organizations, including the Army. Whether you can be moved or not is a function of your status, your performance, and your value to the organization. To move someone without telling him is almost worse than an insult, because it means he is below the point at which feelings matter. In these circumstances, moves can be unsettling and damaging to the ego. In addition, moves themselves are often accompanied by great anxiety, whether an entire organization or a small part of an organization moves. What makes people anxious is that the move usually presages organizational changes that have been coordinated with the move. Naturally, everyone wants to see how he comes out vis-à-vis everyone else. I have seen important men refuse to move into an office that was six inches smaller than someone else's of the same rank. While I have heard some American executives say they wouldn't employ such a person, the fact is that in actual practice, unless there is some compensating feature, the significance of space as a communication is so powerful that no employee in his right mind would allow his boss to give him a spatial demotion—unless of course he had already reached his crest and was on the way down.

10   These spatial messages are not simply conventions in the United States—unless you consider the size of your salary check a mere convention, or where your name appears on the masthead of a journal. Ranking is seldom a matter that people take lightly, particularly in a highly mobile society like that in the United States. Each culture and each country has its own language of space, which is just as unique as the spoken language, frequently more so. In England, for example, there are no offices for the members of Parliament. In the United States, our congressmen and senators proliferate their offices and their office buildings and simply would not tolerate a no-office situation. Constituents, associates, colleagues, and lobbyists would not respond properly. In England, status is internalized; it has its manifestations and markers—the upper-class received English accent, for example. We in the United States, a relatively new country, externalize status. The American in England has some trouble placing people in the social system, while the English can place each other quite accurately by reading ranking cues, but in general tend to look down on the importance that Americans attach to space. It is very easy and very natural

to look at things from one's own point of view and to read an event as though it were the same all over the world.

11 I knew that my emotions on being moved out of my room in Tokyo were of the gut type and quite strong. There was nothing intellectual about my initial response. Although I am a professional observer of cultural patterns, I had no notion of the meaning attached to being moved from hotel to hotel in Kyoto. I was well aware of the strong significance of moving in my own culture, going back to the time when the new baby displaces older children, right up to the world of business, where a complex dance is performed every time the organization moves to new quarters.

12 What was happening to me in Japan as I rode up and down elevators with various keys gripped in my hand was that I was reacting with the cultural part of my brain—the old, mammalian brain. Although my new brain, my symbolic brain—the neocortex—was saying something else, my mammalian brain kept repeating, "You are being treated shabbily." My neocortex was trying to fathom what was happening. Needless to say, neither part of the brain had been programmed to provide me with the answer in Japanese culture. I did have to put up a strong fight with myself to keep from interpreting what was going on as though the Japanese were the same as I. This is the conventional and most common response and one that is often found even among anthropologists. Any time you hear someone say, "Why *they* are no different than the folks back home—they are just like I am," even though you may understand the reasons behind these remarks you also know that the speaker is living in a single-context world (his own) and is incapable of describing either his world or the foreign one.

13 The "they are just like the folks back home" syndrome is one of the most persistent and widely held misconceptions of the Western world, if not the whole world. There is very little any outsider can do about this, because it expresses views that are very close to the core of the personality. Simply talking about "cultural differences" and how we must respect them is a hollow cliché. And in fact, intellectualizing isn't much more helpful either, at least at first. The logic of the man who won't move into an office that is six inches smaller than his rival's is *cultural* logic; it works at a lower, more basic level in the brain, a part of the brain that synthesizes but does not verbalize. The response is a total response that is difficult to explain to someone who doesn't already understand, because it is so dependent on context for correct interpretation. To do so, one must explain the entire system; otherwise, the man's behavior makes little sense. He may even appear to be acting childishly—which he most definitely is not.

14 It was my preoccupation with my own cultural mold that explained why I was puzzled for years about the significance of being

moved around in Japanese hotels. The answer finally came after further experiences in Japan and many discussions with Japanese friends. In Japan, one has to "belong" or he has no identity. When a man joins a company, he does just that—joins himself to the corporate body—and there is even a ceremony marking the occasion. Normally, he is hired for life, and the company plays a much more paternalistic role than in the United States. There are company songs, and the whole company meets frequently (usually at least once a week) for purposes of maintaining corporate identity and morale.

15   As a tourist (either European or Japanese) when you go on a tour, you *join* that tour and follow your guide everywhere as a group. She leads you with a little flag that she holds up for all to see. Such behavior strikes Americans as sheeplike; not so the Japanese. The reader may say that this pattern holds in Europe, because there people join Cook's tours and the American Express tours, which is true. Yet there is a big difference. I remember a very attractive young American woman who was traveling with the same group I was with in Japan. At first she was charmed and captivated, until she had spent several days visiting shrines and monuments. At this point, she observed that she could not take the regimentation of Japanese life. Clearly, she was picking up clues, such as the fact that our Japanese group, when it moved, marched in a phalanx rather than moving as a motley mob with stragglers. There was much more discipline in these sightseeing groups than the average Westerner is either used to or willing to accept.

16   It was my lack of understanding of the full impact of what it means to belong to a high-context culture that caused me to misread hotel behavior at Hakone. I should have known that I was in the grip of a pattern difference and that the significance of all guests being garbed in the same okata meant more than that an opportunistic management used the guests to advertise the hotel. The answer to my puzzle was revealed when a Japanese friend explained what it means to be a guest in a hotel. As soon as you register at the desk, you are no longer an outsider; instead, for the duration of your stay you are a member of a large, mobile family. *You belong.* The fact that I was moved was tangible evidence that I was being treated as a family member—a relationship in which one can afford to be "relaxed and informal and not stand on ceremony." This is a very highly prized state in Japan, which offsets the official properness that is so common in public. Instead of putting me down, they were treating me as a member of the family. Needless to say, the large, luxury hotels that cater to Americans, like Wright's Imperial Hotel, have discovered that Americans do tenaciously stand on ceremony and want to be treated as they are at home in the States. Americans don't like to be moved around; it makes them anxious. Therefore, the Japanese in these establishments have learned not to treat them as family members.

Keeping a Reading Journal

The most effective way to keep track of your thoughts and impressions and to review what you have learned is to start a reading journal. The comments you record in your journal may express your reflections, observations, questions, and reactions to the essays you read. Normally, your journal would not contain lecture notes from class. A reading journal will allow you to keep a record of your progress during the term and can also reflect insights you gain during class discussions and questions you may want to ask, as well as unfamiliar words you intend to look up. Keeping a reading journal becomes a necessity if your composition course will require you to write a research paper that will be due at the end of the semester. Keep in mind that your journal is not something that will be corrected or graded, although some instructors may wish you to share your entries with the class.

TURNING ANNOTATIONS INTO JOURNAL ENTRIES

Although there is no set form for what a journal should look like, reading journals are most useful for converting your brief annotations into more complete entries that explore in depth your reactions to what you have read. Interestingly, the process of turning your annotations into journal entries will often produce surprising insights that will give you a new perspective. For example, a student who annotated Edward T. Hall's "Hidden Culture" converted them into the following journal entries:

- Hall's personal experiences in Japan made him realize that interpreting an action depends on what culture you're from.
- Hall assumes hotels should treat long-term guests with more respect than overnight guests. "Like someone who had been squeezed in without a reservation" shows Hall's feelings.
- What does having your clothes replaced with an okata—cotton robe—have to do with being moved from room to room in a hotel? The plot thickens!
- The hotel in Hakone encourages guests—all wearing the same robes—to greet each other outside the hotel in a friendly, not formal, manner.
- Hall says that in America, size of office = personal value and salary. Hall compared how space works in the United States in order to understand Japanese attitudes toward space.
- Thesis—"culturally defined attitudes toward space are different for each culture." Proves this by showing how unimportant space is to members of Parliament in England when compared

with the great importance office size has for U.S. congresspersons and senators.

- Hall is an anthropologist. He realizes his reactions are instinctual. Hall wants to refute the idea that people are the same all over the world. Says that which culture you are from determines your attitudes and behavior.
- He learns from Japanese friends that workers are hired for life and view their companies as family. Would this be for me? In Japan, group identity is all-important.
- Hall describes two tour groups, one Japanese and one American, as an example of Japanese acceptance of regimentation, whereas Americans go off on their own.
- The answer to the mystery of why he was being moved: moving him meant he was accepted as a member of the hotel family. They were treating him informally, as if he were Japanese: a compliment, not an insult. Informality is highly valued because the entire culture is based on the opposite—regimentation and conformity.

SUMMARIZING

Reading journals may also be used to record summaries of the essays you read. The value of summarizing is that it requires you to pay close attention to the reading in order to distinguish the main points from the supporting details. Summarizing tests your understanding of the material by requiring you to restate, concisely, the author's main ideas in your own words. First, create a list composed of sentences that express in your own words the essential idea of each paragraph, or each group of related paragraphs. Your previous underlining of topic sentences, main ideas, and key terms (as part of the process of critical reading) will help you follow the author's line of thought. Next, whittle down this list still further by eliminating repetitive ideas. Then formulate a thesis statement that expresses the main idea behind the article. Start your summary with this thesis statement, and combine your notes so that the summary flows together and reads easily.

Remember that summaries should be much shorter than the original text (whether the original is one page or twenty pages long) and should accurately reflect the central ideas of the article in as few words as possible. Try not to intrude your own opinions or critical evaluations into the summary. Besides requiring you to read the original piece more closely, summaries are necessary first steps in developing papers that synthesize materials from different sources. The test for a good summary, of course, is whether a person reading it without having read the original article would get an accurate, balanced, and complete account of the original material.

Writing an effective summary is easier if you first compose a rough summary, using no more than two complete sentences to summarize each of the paragraphs or group of paragraphs in the original article. A student's rough summary of Hall's essay might appear as follows. Numbers show which paragraphs are summarized from the article.

1–3 Hall describes how a seemingly inexplicable event that occurred while he was staying in a Tokyo hotel, frequented mostly by Japanese, led him to understand that the same action can have a completely different significance from another culture's perspective. Without telling him, the hotel management had moved his personal belongings to a new room and had given his room to another guest.

4 Three days later when Hall is again moved without warning, he is less startled but begins to wonder why this had never happened during his stay at Frank Lloyd Wright's Imperial Hotel in Tokyo.

5 At another hotel in Hakone, Hall is given an *okata*, a kind of cotton robe, to wear instead of his clothes and is encouraged to greet other guests wearing the same *okata* when he sees them outside the hotel.

6–7 At a third hotel, a country inn near Kyoto, Hall discovers that he has been moved again, this time to an entirely different hotel in what he initially perceives to be a less desirable section of town. Hall interprets this as an insult and becomes angry that the Japanese see him as someone who can be moved around without asking his permission.

8 The neighborhood he had initially seen as less desirable turns out to be much more interesting and authentic than the environs of hotels where tourists usually stay.

9 Hall relates his feelings of being treated shabbily ("like a piece of derelict luggage") to the principle that in the United States, the degree of one's power and status is shown by how much control one has over personal space, whether in the Army or in corporations, where being moved to a smaller office means one is considered less valuable to the company.

10–11 Hall speculates that the equation of control over space with power may pertain only to the United States, since in England, members of Parliament have no formal offices, while their counterparts in the United States—congressmen and senators—attach great importance to the size of their offices. Hall begins to realize that he has been unconsciously applying an American cultural perspective to actions that can be explained only in the context of Japanese culture.

12 Hall postulates the existence of an instinctive "cultural logic" that varies from culture to culture, and he concludes that it is necessary to understand the cultural context in which an action takes place in order to interpret it as people would in that culture.

13–14 Once Hall suspends his own culturally based assumption that one's self-esteem depends on control over personal space, he learns from conversations with Japanese friends that in Japan one has an identity only as part of a group. Japanese workers are considered as family by the companies that hire them for life.

15 The emphasis Japanese society places on conforming to a group is evident in the behavior of Japanese tourists, who move as a coordinated group and closely follow their guide, while American tourists refuse to accept such discipline.

16 Hall realizes that wearing an *okata* and being moved to different rooms and to another, more authentic, hotel means that he is being treated in an informal manner reserved for family members. What Hall had misperceived as an insult—being moved without notice—was really intended as an honor signifying he had been accepted and was not being treated as a stranger.

Based on this list, a student's formulation of a thesis statement expressing the essential idea of Hall's essay appears this way:

> Every society has a hidden culture that governs behavior that might seem inexplicable to an outsider.

The final summary should contain both this thesis and your restatement of the author's main ideas without adding any comments that express personal feelings or responses to the ideas presented. Keep in mind that the purpose of a summary or concise restatement of the author's ideas in your own words is to test your understanding of the material. The summary would normally be introduced by mentioning the author as well as the title of the article:

> Edward T. Hall, writing in "Hidden Culture," believes every society has a hidden culture that governs behavior that might seem inexplicable to an outsider. In Japan, Hall's initial reactions of anger to being moved to another room in a hotel in Tokyo, having his clothes replaced by a cotton kimono or *okata* in Hakone, and being relocated to a different hotel in Kyoto led him to search for the reasons behind such seemingly bizarre events. Although control over space in America is related to status, Hall realizes that in other cultures, like England, where members of Parliament have no offices, this is not the case. Hall discovers that, rather than being an insult, being treated informally meant he was considered to be a member of the hotel "family."

Although some features of the original essay might have been mentioned, such as the significance of office size in corporations in the United States, the student's summary of Hall's essay is still an effective one. The summary accurately and fairly expresses the main ideas in the original.

USING YOUR READING JOURNAL TO GENERATE IDEAS FOR WRITING

You can use all the material in your reading journal (annotations converted to journal entries, reflections, observations, questions, rough and final summaries) to relate your own ideas to the ideas of the person who wrote the essay you are reading. Here are several different kinds of strategies you can use as you analyze an essay in order to generate material for your own:

1. What is missing in the essay? Information that is not mentioned is often just as significant as information the writer chose to include. First, you must have already summarized the main points in the article. Then, make up another list of points that are not discussed, that is, missing information that you would have expected an article of this kind to have covered or touched on. Write down the possible reasons why this missing material has been omitted, censored, or downplayed. What possible purpose could the author have had? Look for vested interests or biases that could explain why information of a certain kind is missing.

2. You might analyze an essay in terms of what you already know and what you didn't know about the issue. To do this, simply make a list of what concepts were already familiar to you and a second list of information or concepts that were new to you. Then write down three to five questions you would like answered about this new information and make a list of possible sources you might consult.

3. You might consider whether the author presents a solution to a problem. List the short-term and long-term effects or consequences of the action the writer recommends. You might wish to evaluate the solution to see whether positive short-term benefits are offset by possible negative long-term consequences not mentioned by the author. This might provide you with a starting point for your own essay.

4. After clearly stating what the author's position on an issue is, try to imagine other people in that society or culture who would view the same issue from a different perspective. How would the concerns of these people be different from those of the writer? Try to think of as many different people, representing as many different perspectives, as you can. Now, try to think of a solution that would satisfy both the author and at least one other person who holds a different viewpoint. Try to imagine that you are an arbitrator negotiating an agreement. How would your recommendation require both parties to compromise and reach an agreement?

1

Family and Cultural Ties

────────────◆────────────

The family has been the most enduring basis of culture throughout the world and has provided a stabilizing force in all societies. The complex network of dependencies, relationships, and obligations may extend outward from parents and children to include grandparents, cousins, aunts and uncles, and more distantly related relatives. In other cultures, the entire community or tribe is seen as an extended family. The unique relationships developed among members of a family provide a universal basis for common experiences, emotions, perceptions, and expectations. At the same time, each family is different, with its own unique characteristic relationships and bonds. Family relationships continue to exert a profound influence on one's life long after childhood. In the context of the family we first learn what it means to experience the emotions of love, hope, fear, anger, and contentment. The works in this chapter focus on parent–child relationships, explore the connections between grandparents and grandchildren, and depict the impact of cultural values on these relationships.

The structure of the family is subject to a wide range of economic and social influences in different cultures. For example, childrearing in Morocco is a vastly different enterprise from what it is in America because of the enormous differences in economic circumstances and political systems. The variety of family structures depicted by writers of many different nationalities offers insight into how the concept of the family is modified according to the constraints, beliefs, and needs of particular societies.

For many families, the family history is inseparable from the stories told about a particular member of the family, which define the character of the family and its relationship to the surrounding society. These stories can be told for entertainment or education and often explain old loyalties and antagonisms. Some are written and some are part of an oral history related by one generation to the next. The complex portraits of family life offered in this chapter allow us to share, sympathize, and identify with writers from diverse cultures and more completely understand your own family experiences in the light of theirs.

Daniela Deane reports on the unanticipated results of China's mandatory one-child policy in "The Little Emperors." The current Maharani of Jaipur, Gayatri Devi, recalls the opulent splendor of her childhood home in "A Princess Remembers." Fatima Mernissi, in "Moonlit Nights of Laughter," relates how privacy was a rare commodity in the Moroccan harem where she was raised. Pat Mora, in "Remembering Lobo," recalls the integral part her aunt played in her Mexican-American family's life. The African-American writer Gayle Pemberton, in "Antidisestablishmentarianism," describes how her no-nonsense grandmother taught her to think for herself. Based on his fieldwork in the Congo, Colin Turnbull, in "The Mbuti Pygmies," describes the importance of rituals in shaping the behavior of children in Mbuti society.

The delicacy known as fugu fish symbolizes the deadly nature of some family relationships in Kazuo Ishiguro's story, "A Family Supper." Last, the Sudanese writer, Tayeb Salih, tells the story, "A Handful of Dates," of a moment during the harvest of date palms that permanently alters the relationship between a boy and his grandfather.

Daniela Deane

The Little Emperors

◆

Daniela Deane is a staff writer who specializes in real estate for the Washington Post. *"The Little Emperors," which first appeared in the* Los Angeles Times Magazine, *July 26, 1992, describes the consequences of China's population management program that encourages couples to marry late and have only one child. Faced with a staggering doubling of the population during Mao Zedong's (Tse-tung's) rule, China, the world's most populous country, with 1.16 billion people, has strictly enforced this one-child policy, and as of 1999 prenatal care became compulsory.*

The People's Republic of China is ruled by a government established in 1949 after the victory of Mao Zedong and his communist forces against the Nationalist forces of Chiang Kai-shek, who fled to Taiwan and set up a government in exile. Under Mao's leadership, industry was nationalized and a land reform program, based on collectivization, was introduced. China entered the Korean War against United Nations forces between 1950 and the Armistice of 1953. China's modern history has been characterized by cycles of liberalization followed by violent oppression. In 1957, reaction against the so-called let a hundred flowers bloom period led to a crackdown against intellectuals. In 1966, Mao launched the Cultural Revolution to purge the government and society of liberal elements. After Mao's death in 1976, a backlash led to the imprisoning of Mao's wife, Jiang Qing, and three colleagues (the "Gang of Four"). A period of liberalization once again followed, as Deng Xiaoping came to power in 1977 and adopted more conciliatory economic, social, and political policies. The United States recognized the People's Republic of China as a valid government on January 1, 1979. The pattern re-emerged in June 1989, when government troops were sent into Tiananmen Square to crush the prodemocracy movement. Zhao Ziyang, who had shown sympathy toward the students, was ousted and replaced by hardliner Jing Zemin. The June events, in which thousands are reported to have died, led to a crackdown and execution of sympathizers throughout China, despite widespread international condemnation. A behind-the-scenes power struggle in 1992 by Deng Xiaoping has led to some economic market style reforms although political liberalization still is not allowed. In 2002, Hu Jintao was elevated to the top level of Chinese leadership.

Before You Read

As you read this article, underline what you consider to be the key points in Deane's analysis. In the margins, note your responses to what she says, including examples that illustrate or contradict her position. Consider the various reasons that Deane offers for her thesis.

———————————◆———————————

1   Xu Ming sits on the worn sofa with his short, chubby arms and legs splayed, forced open by fat and the layers of padded clothing worn in northern China to ward off the relentless chill. To reach the floor, the tubby 8-year-old rocks back and forth on his big bottom, inching forward slowly, eventually ending upright. Xu Ming finds it hard to move.

2   "He got fat when he was about 3," says his father, Xu Jianguo, holding the boy's bloated, dimpled hand. "We were living with my parents and they were very good to him. He's the only grandson. It's a tradition in China that boys are very loved. They love him very much, and so they feed him a lot. They give him everything he wants."

3   Xu Ming weighs 135 pounds, about twice what he should at his age. He's one of hundreds of children who have sought help in the past few years at the Beijing Children's Hospital, which recently began the first American-style fat farm for obese children in what was once the land of skin and bones.

4   "We used to get a lot of cases of malnutrition," says Dr. Ni Guichen, director of endocrinology at the hospital and founder of the weight reduction classes. "But in the last 10 years, the problem has become obese children. The number of fat children in China is growing very fast. The main reason is the one-child policy," she says, speaking in a drab waiting room. "Because parents can only have one child, the families take extra good care of that one child, which means feeding him too much."

5   Bulging waistlines are one result of China's tough campaign to curb its population. The one-child campaign, a strict national directive that seeks to limit each Chinese couple to a single son or daughter, has other dramatic consequences: millions of abortions, fewer girls and a generation of spoiled children.

6   The 10-day weight-reduction sessions—a combination of exercise, nutritional guidance and psychological counseling—are very popular. Hundreds of children—some so fat they can hardly walk—are turned away for each class.

7   According to Ni, about 5% of children in China's cities are obese, with two obese boys for every overweight girl, the traditional preference toward boys being reflected in the amount of attention lavished on the child. "Part of the course is also centered on the parents. We try to teach them how to bring their children up properly, not just by spoiling them," Ni says.

8   Ming's father is proud that his son, after two sessions at the fat farm, has managed to halve his intake of *jiaozi*, the stodgy meat-filled

dumplings that are Ming's particular weakness, from 30 to 15 at a sitting. "Even if he's not full, that's all he gets," he says. "In the beginning, it was very difficult. He would put his arms around our necks and beg us for more food. We couldn't bear it, so we'd give him a little more."

9   Ming lost a few pounds but hasn't been able to keep the weight off. He's a bit slimmer now, but only because he's taller. "I want to lose weight," says Ming, who spends his afternoons snacking at his grandparents' house and his evenings plopped in front of the television set at home. "The kids make fun of me, they call me a fat pig. I hate the nicknames. In sports class, I can't do what the teacher says. I can run a little bit, but after a while I have to sit down. The teacher puts me at the front of the class where all the other kids can see me. They all laugh and make fun of me."

10   The many fat children visible on China's city streets are just the most obvious example of 13 years of the country's one-child policy. In the vast countryside, the policy has meant shadowy lives as second-class citizens for thousands of girls, or, worse, death. It has made abortion a way of life and a couple's sexual intimacy the government's concern. Even women's menstrual cycles are monitored. Under the directive, couples literally have to line up for permission to procreate. Second children are sometimes possible, but only on payment of a heavy fine.

11   The policy is an unparalleled intrusion into the private lives of a nation's citizens, an experiment on a scale never attempted elsewhere in the world. But no expert will argue that China—by far the world's most populous country with 1.16 billion people—could continue without strict curbs on its population.

12   China's communist government adopted the one-child policy in 1979 in response to the staggering doubling of the country's population during Mao Tse-tung's rule. Mao, who died in 1976, was convinced that the country's masses were a strategic asset and vigorously encouraged the Chinese to produce even-larger families.

13   But large families are now out for the Chinese—20% of the world's population living on just 7% of the arable land. "China has to have a population policy," says Huang Baoshan, deputy director of the State Family Planning Commission. With the numbers ever growing, "how can we feed them, house them?"

14   Dinner time for one 5-year-old girl consists of granddad chasing her through the house, bowl and spoon in hand, barking like a dog or mewing like a cat. If he performs authentically enough, she rewards him by accepting a mouthful of food. No problem, insists granddad, "it's good exercise for her."

15   An 11-year-old boy never gets up to go to the toilet during the night. That's because his mother, summoned by a shout, gets up instead

and positions a bottle under the covers for him. "We wouldn't want him to have to get up in the night," his mother says.

16   Another mother wanted her 16-year-old to eat some fruit, but the teen-ager was engrossed in a video game. Not wanting him to get his fingers sticky or daring to interrupt, she peeled several grapes and popped one after another into his mouth. "Not so fast," he snapped. "Can't you see I have to spit out the seeds?"

17   Stories like these are routinely published in China's newspapers, evidence that the government-imposed birth-control policy has produced an emerging generation of spoiled, lazy, selfish, self-centered and overweight children. There are about 40 million only children in China. Dubbed the country's "Little Emperors," their behavior toward their elders is likened to that of the young emperor Pu Yi, who heaped indignities on his eunuch servants while making them cater to his whims, as chronicled in Bernardo Bertolucci's film *The Last Emperor*.

18   Many studies on China's only children have been done. One such study confirmed that only children generally are not well liked. The study, conducted by a team of Chinese psychologists, asked a group of 360 Chinese children, half who have siblings and half who don't, to rate each other's behavior. The only children were, without fail, the least popular, regardless of age or social background. Peers rated them more uncooperative and selfish than children with brothers and sisters. They bragged more, were less helpful in group activities and more apt to follow their own selfish interests. And they wouldn't share their toys.

19   The Chinese lay a lot of blame on what they call the "4-2-1" syndrome—four doting grandparents, two overindulgent parents, all pinning their hopes and ambitions on one child.

20   Besides stuffing them with food, Chinese parents have very high expectations of their one *bao bei,* or treasured object. Some have their still-in-strollers babies tested for IQ levels. Others try to teach toddlers Tang Dynasty poetry. Many shell out months of their hard-earned salaries for music lessons and instruments for children who have no talent or interest in playing. They fill their kids' lives with lessons in piano, English, gymnastics and typing.

21   The one-child parents, most of them from traditionally large Chinese families, grew up during the chaotic, 10-year Cultural Revolution, when many of the country's cultural treasures were destroyed and schools were closed for long periods of time. Because many of that generation spent years toiling in the fields rather than studying, they demand—and put all their hopes into—academic achievement for their children.

22   "We've already invested a lot of money in his intellectual development," Wang Zhouzhi told me in her Spartan home in a tiny village of Changping country outside Beijing, discussing her son, Chenqian, an only child. "I don't care how much money we spend on him. We've bought him an organ and we push him hard. Unfortunately, he's only a mediocre student," she says, looking toward the 10-year-old boy.

Chenqian, dressed in a child-sized Chinese army uniform, ate 10 pieces of candy during the half-hour interview and repeatedly fired off his toy pistol, all without a word of reproach from his mother.

23   Would Chenqian have liked a sibling to play with? "No," he answers loudly, firing a rapid, jarring succession of shots. His mother breaks in: "If he had a little brother or sister, he wouldn't get everything he wants. Of course he doesn't want one. With only one child, I give my full care and concern to him."

24   But how will these children, now entering their teen-age years and moving quickly toward adulthood, become the collectivist-minded citizens China's hard-line communist leadership demands? Some think they never will. Ironically, it may be just these overindulged children who will change Chinese society. After growing up doing as they wished, ruling their immediate families, they're not likely to obey a central government that tells them to fall in line. This new generation of egotists, who haven't been taught to take even their parents into consideration, simply may not be able to think of the society as a whole—the basic principle of communism.

25   The need for family planning is obvious in the cities, where living space is limited and the one-child policy is strictly enforced and largely successful. City dwellers are slowly beginning to accept the notion that smaller families are better for the country, although most would certainly want two children if they could have them. However, in the countryside, where three of every four Chinese live—nearly 900 million people—the goal of limiting each couple to only one child has proved largely elusive.

26   In the hinterlands, the policy has become a confusing patchwork of special cases and exceptions. Provincial authorities can decide which couples can have a second child. In the southern province of Guangdong, China's richest, two children are allowed and many couples can afford to pay the fine to have even a third or fourth child. The amounts of the fines vary across the country, the highest in populous Sichuan province, where the fine for a second child can be as much as 25% of a family's income over four years. Special treatment has been given to China's cultural minorities such as the Mongolians and the Tibetans because of their low numbers. Many of them are permitted three or four children without penalty, although some Chinese social scientists have begun to question the privilege.

27   "It's really become a two-child policy in the countryside," says a Western diplomat. "Because of the traditional views on labor supply, the traditional bias toward the male child, it's been impossible for them to enforce a one-child policy outside the cities. In the countryside, they're really trying to stop that third child."

28   Thirteen years of strict family planning have created one of the great mysteries of the vast and remote Chinese countryside: Where

have all the little girls gone? A Swedish study of sex ratios in China, published in 1990, and based on China's own census data, concluded that several million little girls are "missing"—up to half a million a year in the years 1985 to 1987—since the policy was introduced in late 1979.

29   In the study, and in demographic research worldwide, sex ratio at birth in humans is shown to be very stable, between 105 and 106 boys for every 100 girls. The imbalance is thought to be nature's way of compensating for the higher rates of miscarriage, stillbirth and infant mortality among boys.

30   In China, the ratio climbed consistently during the 1980s, and it now rests at more than 110 boys to 100 girls. "The imbalance is evident in some areas of the country," says Stirling Scruggs, director of the United Nations Population Fund in China. "I don't think the reason is widespread infanticide. They're adopting out girls to try for a boy, they're hiding their girls, they're not registering them. Throughout Chinese history, in times of famine, and now as well, people have been forced to make choices between boys and girls, and for many reasons, boys always win out."

31   With the dismantling of collectives, families must, once again, farm their own small plots and sons are considered necessary to do the work. Additionally, girls traditionally "marry out" of their families, transferring their filial responsibilities to their in-laws. Boys carry on the family name and are entrusted with the care of their parents as they age. In the absence of a social security system, having a son is the difference between starving and eating when one is old. To combat the problem, some innovative villages have begun issuing so-called girl insurance, an old-age insurance policy for couples who have given birth to a daughter and are prepared to stop at that.

32   "People are scared to death to be childless and penniless in their old age," says William Hinton, an American author of seven books chronicling modern China. "So if they don't have a son, they immediately try for another. When the woman is pregnant, they'll have a sex test to see if it's a boy or a girl. They'll abort a girl, or go in hiding with the girl, or pay the fine, or bribe the official or leave home. Anything. It's a game of wits."

33   Shen Shufen, a sturdy, round-faced peasant woman of 33, has two children—an 8-year-old girl and a 3-year-old boy—and lives in Sihe, a dusty, one-road, mud-brick village in the countryside outside Beijing. Her husband is a truck driver. "When we had our girl, we knew we had to have another child somehow. We saved for years to pay the fine. It was hard giving them that money, 3,000 yuan ($550 in U.S. dollars), in one night. That's what my husband makes in three years. I was so happy when our second child was a boy."

34   The government seems aware of the pressure its policies put on expectant parents, and the painful results, but has not shown any flexibility. For instance, Beijing in 1990 passed a law forbidding doctors to tell

a couple the results of ultrasound tests that disclose the sex of their unborn child. The reason: Too many female embryos were being aborted.

35 And meanwhile, several hundred thousand women—called "guerrilla moms"—go into hiding every year to have their babies. They become part of China's 40-million-strong floating population that wanders the country, mostly in search of work, sleeping under bridges and in front of railway stations. Tens of thousands of female children are simply abandoned in rural hospitals.

36 And although most experts say female infanticide is not widespread, it does exist. "I found a dead baby girl," says Hinton. "We stopped for lunch at this mountain ravine in Shaanxi province. We saw her lying there, at the bottom of the creek bed. She was all bundled up, with one arm sticking out. She had been there a while, you could tell, because she had a little line of mold growing across her mouth and nostrils."

37 Death comes in another form, too: neglect. "It's female neglect, more than female infanticide, neglect to the point of death for little girls," says Scruggs of the U.N. Population Fund. "If you have a sick child, and it's a girl," he says, "you might buy only half the dose of medicine she needs to get better."

38 Hundreds of thousands of unregistered little girls—called "black children"—live on the edge of the law, unable to get food rations, immunizations or places in school. Many reports are grim. The government-run China News Service reported last year that the drowning of baby girls had revived to such an extent in Guangxi province that at least 1 million boys will be unable to find wives in 20 years. And partly because of the gender imbalance, the feudalistic practice of selling women has been revived.

39 The alarming growth of the flesh trade prompted authorities to enact a law in January that imposes jail sentences of up to 10 years and heavy fines for people caught trafficking. The government also recently began broadcasting a television dramatization to warn women against the practice. The public-service message shows two women, told that they would be given high-paying jobs, being lured to a suburban home. Instead, they are locked in a small, dark room, and soon realize that they have been sold.

40 Li Wangping is nervous. She keeps looking at the air vents at the bottom of the office door, to see if anyone is walking by or, worse still, standing there listening. She rubs her hands together over and over. She speaks in a whisper. "I'm afraid to get into trouble talking to you," Li confides. She says nothing for a few minutes.

41 "After my son was born, I desperately wanted another baby," the 42-year-old woman finally begins. "I just wanted to have more children, you understand? Anyway, I got pregnant three times, because I wasn't using any birth control. I didn't want to use any. So, I had to

have three abortions, one right after the other. I didn't want to at all. It was terrible killing the babies I wanted so much. But I had to."

42   By Chinese standards, Li (not her real name) has a lot to lose if she chooses to follow her maternal yearnings. As an office worker at government-owned CITIC, a successful and dynamic conglomerate, she has one of the best jobs in Beijing. Just being a city dweller already puts her ahead of most of the population.

43   "One of my colleagues had just gotten fired for having a second child. I couldn't afford to be fired," continues Li, speaking in a meeting room at CITIC headquarters. "I had to keep everything secret from the family-planning official at CITIC, from everyone at the office. Of course, I'm supposed to be using birth control. I had to lie. It was hard lying, because I felt so bad about everything."

44   She rubs her hands furiously and moves toward the door, staring continuously at the air slats. "I have to go now. There's more to say, but I'm afraid to tell you. They could find me."

45   China's family-planning officials wield awesome powers, enforcing the policy through a combination of incentives and deterrents. For those who comply, there are job promotions and small cash awards. For those who resist, they suffer stiff fines and loss of job and status within the country's tightly knit and heavily regulated communities. The State Family Planning Commission is the government ministry entrusted with the tough task of curbing the growth of the world's most populous country, where 28 children are born every minute. It employs about 200,000 full-time officials and uses more than a million volunteers to check the fertility of hundreds of millions of Chinese women.

46   "Every village or enterprise has at least one family-planning official," says Zhang Xizhi, a birth-control official in Changping county outside Beijing. "Our main job is propaganda work to raise people's consciousness. We educate people and tell them their options for birth control. We go down to every household to talk to people. We encourage them to have only one child, to marry late, to have their child later."

47   China's population police frequently keep records of the menstrual cycles of women of childbearing age, on the type of birth control they use and the pending applications to have children. If they slip up, street committees—half-governmental, half-civilian organizations that have sprung up since the 1949 communist takeover—take up the slack. The street committees, made up mostly of retired volunteers, act as the central government's ear to the ground, snooping, spying and reporting on citizens to the authorities.

48   When a couple wants to have a child—even their first, allotted one—they must apply to the family-planning office in their township or workplace, literally lining up to procreate. "If a woman gets pregnant without permission, she and her husband will get fined, even if it's their first," Zhang says. "It is fair to fine her, because she creates a burden on the whole society by jumping her place in line."

49   If a woman in Nanshao township, where Zhang works, becomes pregnant with a second child, she must terminate her pregnancy unless she or her husband or their first child is disabled or if both parents are only children. Her local family-planning official will repeatedly visit her at home to pressure her to comply. "Sometimes I have to go to people's homes five or six times to explain everything to them over and over to get them to have an abortion," says Zhang Cuiqing, the family-planning official for Sihe village, where there are 2,900 married women of childbearing age, of which 2,700 use some sort of birth control. Of those, 570 are sterilized and 1,100 have IUDs. Zhang recites the figures proudly, adding, "If they refuse, they will be fined between 20,000 and 50,000 yuan (U.S. $3,700 to $9,500)." The average yearly wage in Sihe is 1,500 yuan ($285).

50   The lack of early sexual education and unreliable IUDs are combining to make abortion—which is free, as are condoms and IUDs—a cornerstone of the one-child policy. Local officials are told not to use force, but rather education and persuasion, to meet their targets. However, the desire to fulfill their quotas, coupled with pressure from their bosses in Beijing, can lead to abuses by overzealous officials.

51   "Some local family-planning officials are running amok, because of the targets they have to reach," a Western health specialist says, "and there are a bunch of people willing to turn a blind eye to abuses because the target is so important."

52   The official *Shanghai Legal Daily* last year reported on a family-planning committee in central Sichuan province that ordered the flogging of the husbands of 10 pregnant women who refused to have abortions. According to the newspaper, the family-planning workers marched the husbands one by one into an empty room, ordered them to strip and lie on the floor and then beat them with a stick, once for every day their wives were pregnant.

53   "In some places, yes, things do happen," concedes Huang of the State Family Planning Commission. "Sometimes, family-planning officials do carry it too far."

54   The young woman lies still on the narrow table with her eyes shut and her legs spread while the doctor quickly performs a suction abortion. A few moments, and the fetus is removed. The woman lets out a short, sharp yell. "OK, next," the doctor says.

55   She gets off the table and, holding a piece of cloth between her legs to catch the blood and clutching her swollen womb, hobbles over to a bed and collapses. The next patient gets up and walks toward the abortion table. No one notices a visitor watching. "It's very quick, it only takes about five minutes per abortion," says Dr. Huang Xiaomiao, chief physician at Beijing's Maternity Hospital. "No anesthetic. We don't use anesthetic for abortions or births here. Only for Cesarean sections, we use acupuncture."

56   Down the hall, 32-year-old Wu Guobin waits to be taken into the operating room to have her Fallopian tubes untied—a reversal of an earlier sterilization. "After my son was killed in an accident last year, the authorities in my province said I could try for another." In the bed next to Wu's, a dour-faced woman looks ready to cry. "She's getting sterilized," the nurse explains. "Her husband doesn't want her to, but her first child has mental problems."

57   Although it's a maternity hospital, the Family Planning Unit—where abortions, sterilizations, IUD insertions and the like are carried out—is the busiest department. "We do more abortions than births," says Dr. Fan Huimin, head of the unit. "Between 10 and 20 a day."

58   Abortions are a way of life in China, where about 10.5 million pregnancies are terminated each year. (In the United States, 1.6 million abortions are performed a year, but China's population is four to five times greater than the United States'.) One fetus is aborted for about every two children born and Chinese women often have several abortions. Usually, abortions are performed during the first trimester. But because some women resist, only to cave in under mental bullying further into their terms, abortions are also done in the later months of pregnancy, sometimes up till the eighth month.

59   Because of their population problem, the Chinese have become pioneers in contraceptive research. China will soon launch its own version of the controversial French abortion pill RU-486, which induces a miscarriage. They have perfected a non-scalpel procedure for male sterilization, with no suture required, allowing the man to "ride his bicycle home within five minutes." This year, the government plans to spend more than the $34 million it spent last year on contraception. The state will also buy some 961 million condoms to be distributed throughout the country, 11% more than in 1991.

60   But even with a family-planning policy that sends a chill down a Westerner's spine and touches every Chinese citizen's life, 64,000 babies are born every day in China and overpopulation continues to be a paramount national problem. Officials have warned that 24 million children will be born in 1992—a number just slightly less than the population of Canada. "The numbers are staggering," says Scruggs, the U.N. Population Fund official, noting that "170 million people will be added in the 1990s, which is the current population of England, France and Italy combined. There are places in China where the land can't feed that many more people as it is."

61   China estimates that it has prevented 200 million births since the one-child policy was introduced. Women now are having an average of 2.4 children as compared to six in the late '60s. But the individual sacrifice demanded from every Chinese is immense.

62   Large billboards bombard the population with images of happy families with only one child. The government is desperately trying to convince the masses that producing only one child leads to a wealthier,

healthier and happier life. But foreigners in China tell a different story, that the people aren't convinced. They tell of being routinely approached—on the markets, on the streets, on the railway and asked about the contraceptive policies of their countries. Expatriate women in Beijing all tell stories of Chinese women enviously asking them how many sons they have and how many children they plan to have. They explain that they only have one child because the government allows them only one.

63

"When I'm out with my three children on the weekend," says a young American father who lives in Beijing, "people are always asking me why am I allowed to have three children. You can feel when they ask you that there is envy there. There's a natural disappointment among the people. They just want to have more children. But there's a resigned understanding, an acceptance that they just can't."

✧ Evaluating the Text

1. How has the one-child policy affected the ratio of the sexes of children? What Chinese cultural values and economic forces are responsible for the preference for boys?

2. How do the experiences of the parents help explain the kinds of expectations and hopes they have attached to their "little emperors"?

3. In your view, what will be the effects on Chinese society when this new generation of "little emperors" becomes adult? How does the way in which they have been raised create a potential conflict with the collectivist value system underlying Chinese society?

✧ Exploring Different Perspectives

1. Discuss the influences on family structure of growing up in communal societies like those in China and Morocco (see "Moonlit Nights of Laughter" by Fatima Mernissi).

2. Compare and contrast the effects on children in indulgent environments such as those described by Deane and by Gayatri Devi in "A Princess Remembers."

✧ Extending Viewpoints through Writing

1. What picture do you get of the extent to which the government in China intrudes into the everyday life of the Chinese citizen?

2. If you are an only child, to what extent have you been treated similarly to the only children in China? Have you wished that you had brothers and/or sisters? Why or why not? If you have siblings, would you have preferred to be an only child? Explain your reactions.

Gayatri Devi, with Santha Rama Rau

A Princess Remembers

———————◆———————

Gayatri Devi was born in 1919 in London and raised in West Bengal, India, as the daughter of the Maharajah of Cooch Behar and the Princess of Baroda. She married the Maharajah of Jaipur in 1940 and has had a distinguished career as a member of the Indian Parliament from 1962 to 1977. As the Maharani of Jaipur, she is the founder of the Gayatri Devi Girl's Public School in Rajasthan. The following chapter is drawn from her autobiography A Princess Remembers: The Memoirs of the Maharani of Jaipur *(1976), written with Santha Rama Rau, who is herself the author of eleven books, including* Home to India *(1945) and numerous magazine articles that have appeared in* The New Yorker, The New York Times Sunday Magazine, *and* Reader's Digest. *In this account, Devi recreates the palatial splendor of her childhood home and reveals the close ties she had with her mother.*

India is a republic in southern Asia whose 800 million people make it the second most populous country in the world, after China. Although Indian civilization dates back more than 5,000 years, European traders discovered it only in the sixteenth century. By 1757, Britain had gained control of India from the maharajas (ruling princes). In 1919, Mohandas "Mahatma" (great souled) Gandhi, a lawyer who had worked for Indians in South Africa, launched the movement for India's independence from Britain, using techniques of passive resistance and civil disobedience. His dream was realized in 1947 with the dissolution of the British Raj. India was then partitioned into India and Pakistan with hopes of ending the civil war between Hindu and Muslim communities. Gandhi was assassinated the following year. In 1984, Prime Minister Indira Gandhi (no relation to Mohandas) was assassinated by Sikh members of her own bodyguard. She was succeeded by her son, Rajiv Gandhi, who resigned in 1989, and was assassinated himself less than two years later, during a bid for re-election. Congress party leader P.V. Narasimha Rao became prime minister in 1991. The destruction by Hindus of a Muslim mosque in 1992 led to riots and calls for government investigations. In July of 1997, K.R. Narayanan became the first Dalit (Untouchable) to be elected president. The nation celebrated its fiftieth anniversary of independence on August 14, 1997. Since then, hostilities with Pakistan led to the deployment of troops on the Kashmir border.

Before You Read

As you read, notice how Devi uses her personal experiences to raise the broader theme of the responsibilities that members of royalty had in traditional Indian society.

✦

1   During our childhood, our family often journeyed the two thousand miles from our home, the palace in Cooch Behar State, tucked into the north-east corner of India, right across the country to my grandparents' palace in the state of Baroda, on the shores of the Arabian Sea. All five of us children had watched with excited anticipation the packing of mountains of luggage. We seemed to be preparing for the most unlikely extremes of heat and cold, not to mention more predictable occasions such as a state visit or a horse show. On the day of our departure the station was a bedlam, what with all the luggage and staff that accompanied us wherever we went. But by the time we arrived everything was checked and on board, thanks to the efforts of our well-trained staff.

2   Nonetheless, my mother invariably had a deluge of instructions and questions as soon as we arrived. Where was the dressing-case that she wanted in her compartment? she would ask, in her slightly husky, appealing voice. Well, then, unload the baggage and find it. What about her *puja* box, which contained the incenses and powders necessary for the performance of her morning prayers? Ah, there it was. Fortunately, that meant that no one need hurry back to the palace to fetch it.

3   When she did actually leave, telegrams were sent in all directions: PLEASE SEND MY GOLD TONGUE-SCRAPER, or, HAVE LEFT MY SPOON AND LITTLE ONYX BELL BEHIND, or, IN THE LEFT-HAND CUPBOARD IN THE THIRD DRAWER DOWN YOU'LL FIND MY GREEN SILK DRESSING-GOWN. Then came the supplementaries: NOT THE DARK GREEN, THE LIGHT GREEN, or, IN THAT CASE LOOK IN THE DRESSING-ROOM.

4   Anyway, once we got started, those week-long journeys were among the most cherished memories of my childhood. As a child it seemed to me that we occupied the whole train. We had at least three four-berth first-class compartments. My mother, elder sister, and a friend or relation occupied one; my younger sister, a governess, and myself were in another; my two brothers and their companion with an aide in another. Then the aides and secretaries would have a couple of second-class compartments, while the maids, valets, and butlers travelled third class.

5   In the twenties, a train trip by even the most plain-living Indian was reminiscent of a Bedouin migration, for everything in the way of bedding, food, and eating utensils had to be taken along. In those days most Indian trains had no dining-cars and did not provide sheets, blankets, pillows, or towels, although there were proper bathrooms where you

could take a shower. We always travelled with our personal servants to cope with the daily necessities of living on the long journey to Baroda.

6   First there was the overnight trip from Cooch Behar to Calcutta, and we broke our journey for a couple of days in our house there. Then we set off again for the longest part of the trip. The cooks prepared "tiffin-carriers," a number of pans, each holding different curries, rice, lentils, curds, and sweets. The pans fitted into each other, and a metal brace held them all together so that you could carry in one hand a metal tower filled with food. But those tiffin-carriers were intended to supply us with only our first meal on the train. From then on we were in the hands of a chain of railway caterers. You could give your order to the railway man at one stop and know that instructions would be wired ahead to the next stop and that your meal would be served, on the thick railway crockery, as soon as the train came into the station. More often than not we hadn't finished before the train left the station—but that didn't matter. Another waiter would be ready to pick up empty containers, glasses, cutlery, and plates at any further stop that the train made.

7   For us children the excitement of travelling across India by train was not so much in the ingenious arrangements for meals and service as in the atmosphere of the station platforms themselves. As soon as the train pulled in to any station, our carriage windows were immediately besieged by vendors of sweets, fruit, hot tea, and—my favourites—by men selling the charming, funny, painted wooden toys that I have seen nowhere except on Indian station platforms: elephants with their trunks raised to trumpet, lacquered in grey and scarlet, caparisoned in gold with floral designs picked out in contrasting colours; horses decked out as though for a bridegroom; camels, cheetahs, tigers, and dozens of others, all stiff and delightful, with wide, painted eyes and endearing, coquettish smiles. I wanted them all, but my mother said, "Nonsense, nonsense! You children have too many toys as it is." But she could never resist bargaining, so she had a lovely time with the fruit-, flower-, and sweets-vendors, and afterwards our compartment was filled with clinging tropical scents from all her purchases. I don't really know whether she was as good a bargainer as she thought—she was, by nature, very generous—and the vendors always went away looking appropriately bereaved, although with a secret air of satisfaction.

8   In any case, it didn't matter. All of us had the fun of chasing each other about the platforms, and when the train stayed in a station for an hour or more, we ate in the railway dining-room, ordering what we used to call "railway curry," designed to offend no palate—no beef, forbidden to Hindus; no pork, forbidden to Muslims; so, inevitably, lamb or chicken curries and vegetables. Railway curry therefore pleased nobody. Long before the train was due to leave we were summoned by our aides or governess or tutor, telling us to hurry, not to dawdle over our meal in the station restaurant; the train was leaving in five minutes. Of course it didn't, and we soon learned to trust the

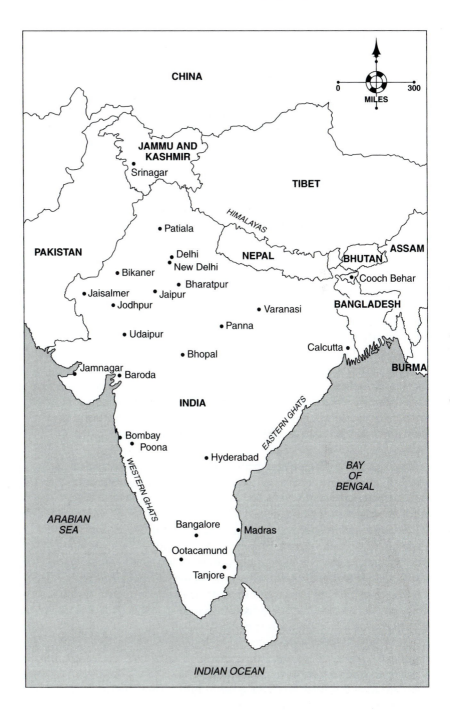

railway personnel, who let us loiter till the last possible moment before bustling us back to our compartments.

9 Finally we would arrive in Baroda to be met at the station by a fleet of Baroda State cars and driven to Laxmi Vilas, the Baroda Palace and my mother's girlhood home. It is an enormous building, the work of the same architect who built our own palace in Cooch Behar in the mid-nineteenth century. In Baroda, he had adopted what I believe architects describe as the "Indo-Saracenic" style. Whatever one calls it, it is certainly imposing. Marble verandas with scalloped arches supported by groups of slender pillars bordered the building. Impressive façades were topped by onion-shaped domes. Outside the main entrance were palm trees standing like sentries along the edges of perfectly kept lawns that were watered daily. Tall and rather municipal-looking street lights with spherical bulbs illuminated the grand approach. And always on duty were the splendid household guards, dressed in white breeches with dark blue jackets and black top-boots. Because we were the grandchildren of the Maharaja, the ruler of the state, every time we went in or out of the front gate they played the Baroda anthem.

10 Inside, the palace was a strange blend of styles, partly Victorian, partly traditional Indian, with here and there a touch of antique English or French. There were courtyards with little pools surrounded by ferns and palms. Persian carpets flowed down interminable corridors. The halls were filled with displays of shields, swords, and armouries of spears. The sitting-rooms overflowed with French furniture, with photographs in silver frames, with ornaments and knickknacks on occasional tables. The palace also contained a gymnasium and a dispensary. Two doctors were permanently in residence, and one of them used to travel with my grandfather wherever he went.

11 Throughout the palace silent formality reigned, and there always seemed to be a number of anonymous, mysterious figures around— two or three sitting in every room. They must have had some proper place in the design of things, but we children never found out who they were or what they were doing. Waiting for an audience with our grandfather? Visiting from some other princely state? Guarding the many precious objects that were scattered throughout the palace? True to our training, we knew that we must pay our respects to our elders, so we may well have folded our hands in a *namaskar*, the traditional Indian greeting, or obeisance, to maidservants and companions as well as to distinguished guests.

12 In sharp contrast to our own decorous behaviour and the general standard of proper courtesy in the palace were the huge longtailed monkeys which roamed everywhere. They were easily aroused to anger and would often follow us down the passages, chattering and baring their teeth in a most terrifying manner.

13 As with all old Indian palaces and family residences, our grandparents' home was divided into two parts, and each of them had its

separate entrance. This tradition of special zenana quarters for the women, and their keeping of purdah, literally "a curtain," to shield them from the eyes of any men other than their husband or the male members of their immediate family, was introduced into India at the time of the Muslim invasions during the twelfth century. At first only Muslims kept these customs, but later, during the rule of the Mogul emperors of India, which lasted from the sixteenth century until the Indian Mutiny of 1857 when the British took over sovereign command, most of the princely states of India as well as the families of the nobles and the upper classes adopted a number of Muslim customs ranging from styles of architecture to a rich and varied cuisine. Among these borrowings was the tradition of keeping their womenfolk carefully segregated from the view of outside eyes.

14   In Baroda the full tradition of purdah no longer existed; both my grandparents were too liberal to allow it. Strict purdah would have required the women to stay entirely within the zenana quarters and, if they had any occasion to venture outside, to travel well chaperoned, only in curtained or shaded vehicles. But my grandparents treated the custom relatively loosely—women could go about fairly freely as long as they were chaperoned and had nothing to do with men outside their family circle. If, for instance, there was a cheetah hunt or a polo match, the ladies would all go together, separately from the men. They didn't have to be veiled; they just stayed on their side of the grounds and the men stayed on the opposite side. For us children, there were no restrictions at all. We wandered freely all over the palace, even to the billiard-room, which in Edwardian days was considered forbidden territory to any female.

15   My grandmother, a formidable lady, had grown up totally accepting the idea of purdah. Following the custom of her time and the tradition of her family, she had, through her early years, observed the strictest purdah, never appearing in public, and in private only before women, close male relatives, and her husband. When she was only fourteen, a marriage was arranged for her to the ruler of Baroda. Her family, like his, was Maratha, members of the Kshatriya caste, which included many warriors and rulers. Like other Indian communities, Marathas traditionally married among themselves. She was, besides, of the right noble background, and he, after the untimely death of his first wife, the Princess of Tanjore, wanted to marry again.

16   My grandfather, well ahead of his time in many of his attitudes and actions, hired tutors for my grandmother, first to teach her to read and write (she was illiterate when she was married), then to expand her education. Later still, he encouraged her to free herself from suffocating Indian traditions and to pursue a role in public life. It was owing to his liberal views that my grandmother emerged as an important leader in the women's movement in India. She became the president of the All-India Women's Conference, the largest women's organization in the world and one which concerns itself with women's rights

as well as with the spread of education and the loosening of the constricting ties of orthodox Indian society on its women. She was not just a figure-head in this important office but a very effective spokeswoman for the emancipation of Indian women. Eventually she even wrote a book, now a standard reference work, on the position of Indian women in their society. After all, she could draw amply on her own experience, first as a sheltered, obedient daughter of a conservative family and later as a free and progressive wife.

17   But it wasn't for her—or for any of us, her three granddaughters or our mother—a total transformation. Within the family in the Baroda Palace she still retained much of the conventional manners and the severe sense of propriety of all upper-class Indian households. All of us always touched her feet as a sign of respect when we first arrived in Baroda, again before we left, and also on all ceremonial occasions. (This custom, still observed in most Hindu families, applied not only to our grandmother but to all close relatives who were our seniors, even brothers, sisters, and cousins who might be just a few months older.)

18   It was at public functions that my grandparents made it most clear that they had more or less dispensed with the rules of purdah, for they always appeared together. Although they still maintained separate kitchens and separate household staffs, my grandfather came to take his meals with the rest of us, and with whatever visitors happened to be staying in Baroda, in my grandmother's dining-room. There she served the most marvellous food in the Indian way, on *thals*, round silver trays loaded with small matching silver bowls containing quantities of rice pilau, meat, fish and vegetable curries, lentils, pickles, chutneys, and sweets. She was a great gourmet and the food from her kitchen was delicious, whether it was the Indian chef who was presiding or, when she was unsure of the tastes of foreign visitors, the cook for English food who was in charge. She spent endless time and trouble consulting with her cooks, planning menus to suit the different guests she invited. It was dangerous to be even faintly appreciative of any dish, for if you took a second helping, she noticed and thrust a third and a fourth upon you, saying, "Come on, come on, you know you like this." Her kitchen was particularly well known for the marvellous pickles it produced and for the huge, succulent prawns from the estuary. Only when there were a large number of outside guests, and on ceremonial occasions like my grandfather's Diamond Jubilee, were meals served from his kitchen and in the banqueting hall on his side of the palace.

19   On religious and ceremonial occasions, durbars were held in his great audience hall. These were very elaborate affairs, something like holding court. The nobility and other important families came formally to offer their allegiance to their rulers—usually a token of a single gold coin.

20   Often we went duck shooting, sometimes we watched the falconing, and then there were the special thrills of elephant fights and, better

yet, the tense and gripping cheetah hunts, a speciality of Baroda, when carefully trained cheetahs, hooded and chained, were taken out to the scrub land in shooting-brakes. There they were unhooded and let loose into a herd of black buck. With foot full down on the accelerator, one could just manage to keep pace with the astonishing speed of the animals during the chase.

21   My own favourite entertainment as a child came from the relatively tame performances of my grandfather's trained parrots. They used to ride tiny silver bicycles, drive little silver cars, walk tightropes, and enact a variety of dramatic scenes. I remember one in particular in which a parrot was run over by a car, examined by a parrot doctor, and finally carried off on a stretcher by parrot bearers. The grand climax of their performance was always a salute fired on a tiny silver cannon. It made the most amazing noise for a miniature weapon, and the parrots were the only ones to remain unperturbed.

22   While my grandmother approved of all these innocent diversions for the children, she wanted us to retain the traditional skills of Indian girls. She wanted us, for instance, to learn how to cook proper Maratha food. My sisters, Ila and Menaka, showed talent and profited by the lessons, while I never seemed able to grasp even the rudiments of cooking.

23   Because almost every princely Indian family put strong emphasis on sports—and also because we ourselves were sports-mad—we used to get up at daybreak and go riding. By the time we returned, my grandmother's side of the palace was already bustling with activity, with maids preparing for the day, women waiting for an audience, and countless arrangements being made. We used to go in to say our required "Good morning" to her before we went to our rooms to settle down to lessons with our tutors. The floors of her apartments were covered, in the traditional Indian fashion, with vast white cloths. We had to take off our shoes before entering, and everyone except my grandmother sat on the floor.

24   I remember her from those days as an admirable, remarkable, and somewhat terrifying woman. She must have been beautiful when she was young. Even to my childish eyes, at that time, she was still handsome and immensely dignified. She wasn't tall, though she gave the impression of height partly because her manner was so very regal. But she had a sour sense of humour.

25   My grandfather was an impressive though kindly figure in our lives, and I remember how his eyes were always laughing. We often took our morning ride with him on the four-mile bridle-path around the Baroda Palace grounds. It was difficult to keep up with him because he liked strenuous exercise and had his favourite horse specially trained to trot very fast.

26   When we returned to the palace he would leave us and spend the rest of the morning dealing with work that he lumped under the

comprehensive heading of "matters of state." Though I didn't know the details at the time, the ruler of an Indian princely state had important functions to fulfil and was a real sovereign to his people. The British, as they gradually took over the major role in India during the nineteenth century, made varying agreements with the different princes defining the division of responsibilities, although much was also left to evolving custom. One major point of all the agreements was that the princes could have relations with foreign powers only through the British. Each of the more important states—and Baroda was one of the most important—had a British Resident who was the voice of the British Government of India. But the states had their own laws, their own courts of justice, their own taxes, and in many cases their own military forces, so that the people of each state looked towards the prince, and not towards anyone else, as the real governmental authority in their lives. My grandfather had, therefore, to confer with his ministers (who were responsible only to him) and to decide many things that affected the lives of millions of people.

27   I knew him, however, not as a statesman but as a man and a grandfather. One conversation with him lives clearly in my memory. I had gone to say good night to him. He was, as always at that time of day, at the billiard table. He stopped his game and said, in a friendly way, "Ah, I see you're off to bed. I hope you have a good sleep."

28   I explained to him that there was no question of sleep for some time to come as I had to think about all that had happened during the day.

29   "No, no," he said, gently but emphatically. "If you go to bed, you should sleep. If you are reading, you should read. If you are eating, you should eat. And if you are thinking, then you should think. Never mix the different activities. No good ever comes of it, and what's more, you can't enjoy—neither can you profit from—any of them."

30   Then, because he was playing billiards, he turned back to the table and gave the game his undivided attention once more. He lived by the clock all his life and did everything in strict order: up at sunrise, walk or ride, work until lunch, brief rest, work until tea, recreation, evening work, supper, reading. It had been the same for fifty years.

31   My grandfather was known as the Gaekwar of Baroda, Gaekwar being both a family name and a title. Most of the Indian princes had the hereditary titles of Maharaja ("Great King") or Raja (simply, "Ruler," or "King"), depending on the size, importance, and history of their states. I always knew that my grandfather was a special person but it was only years later, when I knew the full range of his background and accomplishments, that I realized what an extraordinary man he was.

32   He had spent the first twelve years of his life in a village about two hundred miles south of Baroda City. His father, a distant relative of the ruling family, was village headman and earned only a modest living

from farming. However, when the previous ruler of Baroda was deposed by the British for misrule, someone from the family had to be chosen as a successor. My grandfather, along with one of his brothers and a cousin, was brought to the capital of the state and presented to the Dowager Maharani of Baroda, the widow of the deposed ruler's father. She was asked by the British to select one of the boys to be the new ruler, and her choice fell upon my grandfather.

33   Since he had been brought up in a village where a sound practical grasp of farming was considered the only necessary knowledge, he could neither read nor write, so the six years following his arrival at the palace were devoted exclusively to his education, and habits were instilled that lasted all his life. He always rose at six o'clock and went to bed at ten, and with the exception of two hours' riding (considered an essential princely skill), one hour of games of various kinds suitable to his rank, and breaks for meals, the entire day was devoted to work. He learned to read and write in four languages: Marathi, the language of his princely ancestors; Gujarati, the language of the bulk of the population in Baroda; Urdu, the language of his Muslim subjects, employing the Arabic script; and, of course, English. India was still the "brightest jewel" in the British imperial crown, so he had to study English history as well as Indian; beyond that, he received intensive tuition in arithmetic, geography, chemistry, political economy, philosophy, Sanskrit, and something that his tutor called "conversations on given subjects," which was, I suppose, designed to fill any gaps in the small-talk of royal social life.

34   It is astonishing, when I think back on it, that these two people, brought up in such a tradition-ridden atmosphere, married in the customary way by an arrangement between their elders, should have become leaders of change and reform, encouraging new and more liberal ideas in an orthodox society. My grandfather devoted his life to modernizing the state of Baroda, building schools, colleges, libraries, and an outstanding museum and providing an admirable and just administration. He took an enthusiastic interest in everything from commissioning a special translation of *Alice in Wonderland* into Marathi to working for Hindu women's emancipation, even to the point of introducing the revolutionary concept of divorce in Baroda. (My mother used to tease my grandmother, undaunted by her rectitude, about having a husband who was so warm an advocate of divorce. My grandmother tried to be dignified and huffy but was soon overcome by that wonderful silent laugh of hers, her face contorted, her body shaking like a jelly, and not a sound out of her mouth.)

35   My grandfather felt particularly strongly about the inequalities and abuses that had evolved in Indian society and were protected by the caste system. Hindus are born into one of four castes, which are, in descending order, the Brahmins (originally the scholars and priests),

the Kshatriyas (warriors and often, as a result of skill in conquest or a reward for success, rulers and large landowners), Vaisyas (usually businessmen, traders, artisans), and Sudras (usually the peasants, though all peasants are not Sudras). In a separate group were those Hindus who were excluded from the ordinary social and religious privileges of Hinduism and were known as Untouchables. They performed the most menial tasks—sweeping streets, cleaning latrines—and thus were thought to carry pollution to caste Hindus.

36   Mahatma Gandhi, in the emotional battle for the acceptance of the Untouchables by Hindu society, acted as their champion, changing their name to Harijans (Loved Ones of God) and insisting that they be allowed access to temples from which they had always been excluded. Their legal battles were fought for them by one of the most brilliant men in Indian politics, Dr. Bhimrao Ramji Ambedkar, himself a Harijan. Dr. Ambedkar was one of my grandfather's special protégés, encouraged and educated by him when he was a penniless boy. After his long crusade for the advancement of his community, Dr. Ambedkar was appointed chairman of the committee that drafted the Constitution of free India.

37   My grandmother played a strong though less conspicuous part in the life of Baroda State. I can see her so plainly in the mornings, coping with her personal affairs—choosing saris, making up her mind about lengths of silk or cloth of gold that her maids held up, listening attentively to the cooks with menus for the day, giving orders to the tailor, asking about domestic details; in short, supervising the running of an enormous household—and still giving her alert attention to the grievances and complaints of any of her women subjects, whether it was the illness of a child or a dispute in a family about the inheritance of land.

38   This was all part of a maharani's duty, and so were the more ceremonial occasions, as when she presided over formal durbars in the women's apartments of the Baroda Palace. I especially remember the first one I saw, her birthday durbar. All the wives and womenfolk of the nobility and the great landowners were assembled in their richest clothes and jewellery to pay homage to my grandmother. She was seated on a *gaddi*, a cushioned throne, and wore a sari made of rose-pink cloth of gold, draped in the Maratha way with a pleated train between the legs.

39   Along with her dazzling sari, my grandmother wore all the traditional jewellery for this occasion, including heavy diamond anklets and a wealth of diamond rings on her fingers and toes. The noble ladies paid their respects to her with a formal folding of hands in a *namaskar* and offered her the traditional gold coin to signify their allegiance. At the end of the hall was a troupe of musicians and dancers from Tanjore in south India. Like many Indian princes, my grandfather

maintained the troupe as palace retainers, and they always gave a performance of the classical south Indian dancing called *bharata natyam* at any important palace occasion. At such festive times, the family all ate off gold *thals,* while everyone else ate off silver. (This distinction always used to embarrass me.)

40   My mother, Princess Indira Gaekwar of Baroda, was the only daughter of these two extraordinary people. Because of their advanced views on education, she was one of the first Indian princesses to go to school and to graduate from Baroda College. She also accompanied her parents on their trips to England. One of the earliest stories I know about her tells how she and her four brothers, all quite small and dressed identically in white pyjama trousers and brocade jackets, with gold-embroidered caps, were taken to Buckingham Palace to be presented to Queen Victoria. As they stood before her, the elderly Queen-Empress asked which one was the little girl. Five pairs of dark brown eyes stared back at her, and then, because they all enjoyed fooling grown-ups, one of the boys stepped forward. But they underestimated Queen Victoria, who, sensing that something was wrong, walked around to the back of the row of solemn children, and there a long black pigtail betrayed my mother.

41   It is difficult to describe my mother without slipping into unconvincing superlatives. She was, quite simply, the most beautiful and exciting woman any of us knew. Even now, when I have travelled widely and have met many famous beauties from all levels of society, she remains in my memory as an unparalleled combination of wit, warmth, and exquisite looks. She was photographed and painted many times, but while those pictures show the physical charm—the enormous eyes, the lovely modelling of her face, the slightly drooping mouth that made you want to make her smile, the tiny fragile figure—none of them captures the electric vitality that made her the focus of attention wherever she went. Her own passionate interest and concern for others made her both special and accessible to anybody. She was always called "Ma," not only by us but by friends and even by the peasants of Cooch Behar. As a child I was fascinated by her—what she said, what she did, what she wore. With her, nothing was ever dull and one felt that at any moment anything might happen.

42   She herself was oddly unaware of the impression she created, and this, I suppose, was due to her mother's fear, during her childhood, that she might become spoiled—an only daughter, adored by her father, loved and cherished by her brothers. If anyone commented favourably on my mother's looks, my grandmother would immediately counter the admiration with some deprecating comment like, "Her nose is too lumpy at the end—just look," or, "Her hair hasn't a trace of a curl to it."

43   My mother once told me that she had no idea that she was even passably good-looking until one day when her brothers were discussing some attractive girl they had met. Seeing their sister looking a bit dejected, one of them said, with true brotherly enthusiasm, "You know, you're not all that bad yourself."

44   For the first time she really *looked* at herself in the mirror and thought, Well, he may be right. I'm *not* all that bad.

✧ *Evaluating the Text*

1. What features of Devi's account give you the clearest idea of what her life was like in the privileged surroundings in which she was raised? What role do the different cultural customs reflected in her account play in Devi's life at the palace?

2. What kinds of things provided her with the most enjoyment? How was she educated and how was she made aware of the special responsibilities that she would have to assume as a member of royalty?

3. What impressions do you get of her grandparents and mother and their influence on her life?

✧ *Exploring Different Perspectives*

1. In what respects is Devi's childhood similar and dissimilar to that of Fatima Mernissi's (in a harem in Morocco) in terms of the self-enclosed worlds in which they were raised?

2. How do the games Gayatri Devi played as a child compare with those of the Mbuti children, as described by Colin Turnbull, and what do these games suggest about important cultural values?

✧ *Extending Viewpoints through Writing*

1. Contained in the panoramic sweep of Devi's description are innumerable fascinating aspects of her everyday life that she touches on but does not explore in depth. Choose one of these and, after doing some research, write a short essay that explains its function in Indian culture.

2. What is the most exotic place you have ever visited? Describe the architecture, everyday rituals, and customs that will bring your reader into this world.

Fatima Mernissi

Moonlit Nights of Laughter

◆

Fatima Mernissi was born in Fez, Morocco. She is a distinguished scholar whose approach is one of a feminist sociologist. Mernissi currently teaches at the University of Mohammed V in Rabat, Morocco. Among her published works are Islam and Democracy: Fear of the Modern World *(1992) and* Dreams of Trespass: Tales of a Harem Girlhood *(1994), from which the following chapter is drawn. In it, Mernissi recalls her childhood as an inhabitant of a harem (from an Arabic word meaning "forbidden"), which she characterizes as a domain in which women—spouses and daughters—are almost completely isolated from the world. Yet, within this confinement, she describes how her strong-willed mother managed to create the rarest of all events, private family dinners. Most recently, she has written* Scheherazade Goes West: Different Cultures, Different Harems *(2001).*

The kingdom of Morocco is situated in northwest Africa, bounded by the Atlantic Ocean on the west, the Mediterannean Sea on the north, Algeria to the southeast, and the western Sahara to the southwest. As a result of Arab conquest in the seventh century, most Moroccans are Muslims. Originally, the country was inhabited by Berber tribespeople, who today still form a large minority living mostly in the mountains. In 1912, most of Morocco became a French protectorate, and in 1956 it became an independent nation under a traditional monarchy. Fez, the city in Mernissi's account, is located in north-central Morocco and is noted for its Muslim art and handicrafts, particularly the brimless felt hat (the fez), which was formerly a characteristic item of dress in the Middle East. The city of nearly a million has more than 100 mosques. Following elections in 1998, the socialist, Abderr el Youssoufi, became prime minister. Hassasn II (who held the throne since 1961) was succeeded by his son, Moham, in 1999.

Before You Read

As you read, pay particular attention to Mernissi's word choices and how they express her personal feelings toward the institution of the harem. How do you think you would react to the lack of privacy that defines harem life?

◆

1   On Yasmina's farm, we never knew when we would eat. Sometimes, Yasmina only remembered at the last minute that she had to feed me, and then she would convince me that a few olives and a piece of her good bread, which she had baked at dawn, would be enough. But dining in our harem in Fez was an entirely different story. We ate at strictly set hours and never between meals.

2   To eat in Fez, we had to sit at our prescribed places at one of the four communal tables. The first table was for the men, the second for the important women, and the third for the children and less important women, which made us happy, because that meant that Aunt Habiba could eat with us. The last table was reserved for the domestics and anyone who had come in late, regardless of age, rank, or sex. That table was often overcrowded, and was the last chance to get anything to eat at all for those who had made the mistake of not being on time.

3   Eating at fixed hours was what Mother hated most about communal life. She would nag Father constantly about the possibility of breaking loose and taking our immediate family to live apart. The nationalists advocated the end of seclusion and the veil, but they did not say a word about a couple's right to split off from their larger family. In fact, most of the leaders still lived with their parents. The male nationalist movement supported the liberation of women, but had not come to grips with the idea of the elderly living by themselves, nor with couples splitting off into separate households. Neither idea seemed right, or elegant.

4   Mother especially disliked the idea of a fixed lunch hour. She always was the last to wake up, and liked to have a late, lavish breakfast which she prepared herself with a lot of flamboyant defiance, beneath the disapproving stare of Grandmother Lalla Mani. She would make herself scrambled eggs and *baghrir,* or fine crêpes, topped with pure honey and fresh butter, and, of course, plenty of tea. She usually ate at exactly eleven, just as Lalla Mani was about to begin her purification ritual for the noon prayer. And after that, two hours later at the communal table, Mother was often absolutely unable to eat lunch. Sometimes, she would skip it altogether, especially when she wanted to annoy Father, because to skip a meal was considered terribly rude and too openly individualistic.

5   Mother dreamed of living alone with Father and us kids. "Whoever heard of ten birds living together squashed into a single nest?" she would say. "It is not natural to live in a large group, unless your objective is to make people feel miserable." Although Father said that he was not really sure how the birds lived, he still sympathized with Mother, and felt torn between his duty towards the traditional family and his desire to make her happy. He felt guilty about breaking up the family solidarity, knowing only too well that big families in general, and harem life in particular, were fast becoming relics of the past. He even prophesied that in the next few decades, we would become like the Christians, who hardly ever visited their old parents. In fact, most of

my uncles who had already broken away from the big house barely found the time to visit their mother, Lalla Mani, on Fridays after prayer anymore. "Their kids do not kiss hands either," ran the constant refrain. To make matters worse, until very recently, all my uncles had lived in our house, and had only split away when their wives' opposition to communal life had become unbearable. That is what gave Mother hope.

6   The first to leave the big family was Uncle Karim, Cousin Malika's father. His wife loved music and liked to sing while being accompanied by Uncle Karim, who played the lute beautifully. But he would rarely give in to his wife's desire to spend an evening singing in their salon, because his older brother Uncle Ali thought it unbecoming for a man to sing or play a musical instrument. Finally, one day, Uncle Karim's wife just took her children and went back to her father's house, saying that she had no intention of living in the communal house ever again. Uncle Karim, a cheerful fellow who had himself often felt constrained by the discipline of harem life, saw an opportunity to leave and took it, excusing his actions by saying that he preferred to give in to his wife's wishes rather than forfeit his marriage. Not long after that, all my other uncles moved out, one after the other, until only Uncle Ali and Father were left. So Father's departure would have meant the death of our large family. "As long as [my] Mother lives," he often said, "I wouldn't betray the tradition."

7   Yet Father loved his wife so much that he felt miserable about not giving in to her wishes and never stopped proposing compromises. One was to stock an entire cupboardful of food for her, in case she wanted to discreetly eat sometimes, apart from the rest of the family. For one of the problems in the communal house was that you could not just open a refrigerator when you were hungry and grab something to eat. In the first place, there were no refrigerators back then. More importantly, the entire idea behind the harem was that you lived according to the group's rhythm. You could not just eat when you felt like it. Lalla Radia, my uncle's wife, had the key to the pantry, and although she always asked after dinner what people wanted to eat the next day, you still had to eat whatever the group—after lengthy discussion—decided upon. If the group settled on couscous with chick-peas and raisins, then that is what you got. If you happened to hate chick-peas and raisins, you had no choice but to shut up and settle for a frugal dinner composed of a few olives and a great deal of discretion.

8   "What a waste of time," Mother would say. "These endless discussions about meals! Arabs would be much better off if they let each individual decide what he or she wanted to swallow. Forcing everyone to share three meals a day just complicates things. And for what sacred purpose? None of course." From there, she would go on to say that her whole life was an absurdity, that nothing made sense, while Father would say that he could not just break away. If he did, tradition would vanish: "We live in difficult times, the country is occupied by foreign armies, our culture is

threatened. All we have left is these traditions." This reasoning would drive Mother nuts: "Do you think that by sticking together in this big, absurd house, we will gain the strength we need to throw the foreign armies out? And what is more important anyway, tradition or people's happiness?" That would put an abrupt end to the conversation. Father would try to caress her hand but she would take it away. "This tradition is choking me," she would whisper, tears in her eyes.

9   So Father kept offering compromises. He not only arranged for Mother to have her own food stock, but also brought her things he knew she liked, such as dates, nuts, almonds, honey, flour, and fancy oils. She could make all the desserts and cookies she wanted, but she was not supposed to prepare a meat dish or a major meal. That would have meant the beginning of the end of the communal arrangement. Her flamboyantly prepared individual breakfasts were enough of a slap in the face to the rest of the family. Every once in a long while, Mother *did* get away with preparing a complete lunch or a dinner, but she had to not only be discreet about it but also give it some sort of exotic overtone. Her most common ploy was to camouflage the meal as a nighttime picnic on the terrace.

10   These occasional tête-à-tête dinners on the terrace during moonlit summer nights were another peace offering that Father made to help satisfy Mother's yearning for privacy. We would be transplanted to the terrace, like nomads, with mattresses, tables, trays, and my little brother's cradle, which would be set down right in the middle of everything. Mother would be absolutely out of her mind with joy. No one else from the courtyard dared to show up, because they understood all too well that Mother was fleeing from the crowd. What she most enjoyed was trying to get Father to depart from his conventional self-controlled pose. Before long, she would start acting foolishly, like a young girl, and soon, Father would chase her all around the terrace, when she challenged him. "You can't run anymore, you have grown too old! All you're good for now is to sit and watch your son's cradle." Father, who had been smiling up to that point, would look at her at first as if what she had just said had not affected him at all. But then his smile would vanish, and he would start chasing her all over the terrace, jumping over tea-trays and sofas. Sometimes both of them made up games which included my sister and Samir (who was the only one of the rest of the family allowed to attend our moonlit gatherings) and myself. More often, they completely forgot about the rest of the world, and we children would be sneezing all the next day because they had forgotten to put blankets on us when we had gone to sleep that night.

11   After these blissful evenings, Mother would be in an unusually soft and quiet mood for a whole week. Then she would tell me that whatever else I did with my life, I had to take her revenge. "I want my daughters' lives to be exciting," she would say, "very exciting and filled

with one hundred percent happiness, nothing more, nothing less." I would raise my head, look at her earnestly, and ask what one hundred percent happiness meant, because I wanted her to know that I intended to do my best to achieve it. Happiness, she would explain, was when a person felt good, light, creative, content, loving and loved, and free. An unhappy person felt as if there were barriers crushing her desires and the talents she had inside. A happy woman was one who could exercise all kinds of rights, from the right to move to the right to create, compete, and challenge, and at the same time could feel loved for doing so. Part of happiness was to be loved by a man who enjoyed your strength and was proud of your talents. Happiness was also about the right to privacy, the right to retreat from the company of others and plunge into contemplative solitude. Or to sit by yourself doing nothing for a whole day, and not give excuses or feel guilty about it either. Happiness was to be with loved ones, and yet still feel that you existed as a separate being, that you were not there just to make them happy. Happiness was when there was a balance between what you gave and what you took. I then asked her how much happiness she had in her life, just to get an idea, and she said that it varied according to the days. Some days she had only five percent; others, like the evenings we spent with Father on the terrace, she had full-blown one hundred percent happiness.

12   Aiming at one hundred percent happiness seemed a bit overwhelming to me, as a young girl, especially since I could see how much Mother labored to sculpt her moments of happiness. How much time and energy she put into creating those wonderful moonlit evenings sitting close to Father, talking softly in his ear, her head on his shoulder! It seemed quite an accomplishment to me because she had to start working on him days ahead of time, and then she had to take care of all the logistics, like the cooking and the moving of the furniture. To invest so much stubborn effort just to achieve a few hours of happiness was impressive, and at least I knew it could be done. But how, I wondered, was I going to create such a high level of excitement for an entire lifetime? Well, if Mother thought it was possible, I should certainly give it a try.

13   "Times are going to get better for women now, my daughter," she would say to me. "You and your sister will get a good education, and you'll walk freely in the streets and discover the world. I want you to become independent, independent and happy. I want you to shine like moons. I want your lives to be a cascade of serene delights. One hundred percent happiness. Nothing more, nothing less." But when I asked her for more details about how to create that happiness, Mother would grow very impatient. "You have to work at it. One develops the muscles for happiness, just like for walking and breathing."

14   So every morning, I would sit on our threshold, contemplating the deserted courtyard and dreaming about my beautiful future, a cascade of serene delights. Hanging on to the romantic moonlit terrace evenings,

challenging your beloved man to forget about his social duties, relax and act foolish and gaze at the stars while holding your hand, I thought, could be one way to go about developing muscles for happiness. Sculpting soft nights, when the sound of laughter blends with the spring breezes, could be another.

15   But those magical evenings were rare, or so they seemed. During the days, life took a much more rigid and disciplined turn. Officially, there was no jumping around or foolishness allowed in the Mernissi household—all that was confined to clandestine times and spaces, such as late afternoons in the courtyard when the men were out, or evenings on the deserted terraces.

✧ Evaluating the Text

1. What features of communal life in the harem did Mernissi's mother find most restrictive?

2. What compromises were invented to offset these limitations?

3. In light of Mernissi's mother's experiences in the harem, discuss the wishes or desires she projected onto her daughter. What do you think she meant by the phrase "one hundred percent happiness"?

✧ Exploring Different Perspectives

1. In what ways are both Gayle Pemberton's (see "Antidisestablishmentarianism") grandmother and Mernissi's mother critical of prevailing social values?

2. Compare and contrast the phenomenon of the extended family in both Mernissi's and Pat Mora's (see "Remembering Lobo") narratives.

✧ Extending Viewpoints through Writing

1. Imagine living in a communal setting of the kind described by Mernissi. How do you think you would react to the lack of privacy at mealtimes and the need to arrange your schedule to conform to that of the group? What positive features might offset these disadvantages?

2. To what extent has privacy become an increasingly rare luxury in modern culture? In a short essay, explore the reasons for this.

Pat Mora

Remembering Lobo

◆

Pat Mora was born in El Paso, Texas, in 1942. She received a bachelor's degree in 1963 from Texas Western College and earned a master's degree from the University of Texas at El Paso in 1967. Her two collections of poems, Chance *(1984) and* Waters *(1986), celebrate the Southwest and the desert. Mora's third volume of poetry,* Communion *(1991), explores basic questions of Hispanic identity as she travels to Cuba, New York, and central India. Mora has written books for children, including* A Birthday Present for Tia *(1992) and* Pablo's Tree *(1993). Her 1997 memoir is titled* House of Houses. *In the same year she also published a book of poetry,* Aunt Carmen's Book of Practical Saints. *Her commentaries are collected in* Nepantla: Essays from the Land in the Middle *(1993), in which "Remembering Lobo" first appeared. Evoking the image of her aunt, this essay addresses the theme of what it means to be a Chicana in American society and celebrates Mora's cultural identity.*

Before You Read

Pay particular attention to Mora's tone. How would you characterize her attitude toward her aunt and the values of Hispanic culture she embodied?

◆

1   We called her *Lobo.* The word means "wolf" in Spanish, an odd name for a generous and loving aunt. Like all names it became synonymous with her, and to this day returns me to my childself. Although the name seemed perfectly natural to us and to our friends, it did cause frowns from strangers throughout the years. I particularly remember one hot afternoon when on a crowded streetcar between the border cities of El Paso and Juarez, I momentarily lost sight of her. "Lobo! Lobo!" I cried in panic. Annoyed faces peered at me, disappointed at such disrespect to a white-haired woman.

2   Actually the fault was hers. She lived with us for years, and when she arrived home from work in the evening, she'd knock on our front door and ask, "*¿Dónde están mis lobitos?*" "Where are my little wolves?"

3   Gradually she became our *lobo,* a spinster aunt who gathered the four of us around her, tying us to her for life by giving us all she had. Sometimes to tease her we would call her by her real name. "*¿Dónde está Ignacia?*" we would ask. Lobo would laugh and say, "She is a ghost."

49

4   To all of us in nuclear families today, the notion of an extended family under one roof seems archaic, complicated. We treasure our private space. I will always marvel at the generosity of my parents, who opened their door to both my grandmother and Lobo. No doubt I am drawn to the elderly because I grew up with two entirely different white-haired women who worried about me, tucked me in at night, made me tomato soup or hot *hierbabuena* (mint tea) when I was ill.

5   Lobo grew up in Mexico, the daughter of a circuit judge, my grandfather. She was a wonderful storyteller and over and over told us about the night her father, a widower, brought his grown daughters on a flatbed truck across the Rio Grande at the time of the Mexican Revolution. All their possessions were left in Mexico. Lobo had not been wealthy, but she had probably never expected to have to find a job and learn English.

6   When she lived with us, she worked in the linens section of a local department store. Her area was called "piece goods and bedding." Lobo never sewed, but she would talk about materials she sold, using words I never completely understood, such as *pique* and *broadcloth*. Sometimes I still whisper such words just to remind myself of her. I'll always savor the way she would order "sweet milk" at restaurants. The precision of a speaker new to the language.

7   Lobo saved her money to take us out to dinner and a movie, to take us to Los Angeles in the summer, to buy us shiny black shoes for Christmas. Though she never married and never bore children, Lobo taught me much about one of our greatest challenges as human beings: loving well. I don't think she ever discussed the subject with me, but through the years she lived her love, and I was privileged to watch.

8   She died at ninety-four. She was no sweet, docile Mexican woman dying with perfect resignation. Some of her last words before drifting into semiconsciousness were loud words of annoyance at the incompetence of nurses and doctors.

9   "*No sirven.*" "They're worthless," she'd say to me in Spanish.

10   "They don't know what they're doing. My throat is hurting and they're taking X rays. Tell them to take care of my throat first."

11   I was busy striving for my cherished middle-class politeness. "Shh, shh," I'd say. "They're doing the best they can."

12   "Well, it's not good enough," she'd say, sitting up in anger.

13   Lobo was a woman of fierce feelings, of strong opinions. She was a woman who literally whistled while she worked. The best way to cheer her when she'd visit my young children was to ask for her help. Ask her to make a bed, fold laundry, set the table or dry dishes, and the whistling would begin as she moved about her task. Like all of us, she loved being needed. Understandable, then, that she muttered in annoyance when her body began to fail her. She was a woman who

found self-definition and joy in visibly showing her family her love for us by bringing us hot *té de canela* (cinnamon tea) in the middle of the night to ease a cough, by bringing us comics and candy whenever she returned home. A life of giving.

14   One of my last memories of her is a visit I made to her on November 2, *El Día de los Muertos,* or All Souls' Day. She was sitting in her rocking chair, smiling wistfully. The source of the smile may seem a bit bizarre to a U.S. audience. She was fondly remembering past visits to the local cemetery on this religious feast day.

15   "What a silly old woman I have become," she said. "Here I sit in my rocking chair all day on All Souls' Day, sitting when I should be out there. At the cemetery. Taking good care of *mis muertos,* my dead ones.

16   "What a time I used to have. I'd wake while it was still dark outside. I'd hear the first morning birds, and my fingers would almost itch to begin. By six I'd be having a hot bath, dressing carefully in black, wanting *mis muertos* to be proud of me, proud to have me looking respectable and proud to have their graves taken care of. I'd have my black coffee and plenty of toast. You know the way I like it. Well browned and well buttered. I wanted to be ready to work hard.

17   "The bus ride to the other side of town was a long one, but I'd say a rosary and plan my day. I'd hope that my perfume wasn't too strong and yet would remind others that I was a lady.

18   "The air at the cemetery gates was full of chrysanthemums: that strong, sharp, fall smell. I'd buy tin cans full of the gold and white flowers. How I liked seeing aunts and uncles who were also there to care for the graves of their loved ones. We'd hug. Happy together.

19   "Then it was time to begin. The smell of chrysanthemums was like a whiff of pure energy. I'd pull the heavy hose and wash the gravestones over and over, listening to the water pelting away the desert sand. I always brought newspaper. I'd kneel on the few patches of grass, and I'd scrub and scrub, shining the gray stones, leaning back on my knees to rest for a bit and then scrubbing again. Finally a relative from nearby would say, *'Ya, ya, Nacha,'* and laugh. Enough. I'd stop, blink my eyes to return from my trance. Slightly dazed, I'd stand slowly, place a can of chrysanthemums before each grave.

20   "Sometimes I would just stand there in the desert sun and listen. I'd hear the quiet crying of people visiting new graves; I'd hear families exchanging gossip while they worked.

21   "One time I heard my aunt scolding her dead husband. She'd sweep his gravestone and say, *'¿Porqué?* Why did you do this, you thoughtless man? Why did you go and leave me like this? You know I don't like to be alone. Why did you stop living?' Such a sight to see my aunt with her proper black hat and her fine dress and her carefully polished shoes muttering away for all to hear.

22   "To stifle my laughter, I had to cover my mouth with my hands."

✧ Evaluating the Text

1. How does Mora's account of her aunt emphasize attributes that make Lobo an apt name? What qualities does Mora's aunt possess that provide a valuable counterbalance to the narrator's own personality?

2. What is the significance of the Mexican custom of visiting the cemetery on All Souls' Day?

3. Why is the shift from the narrator's account to Lobo's own words effective? Why do you think Mora structures her account in this fashion?

✧ Exploring Different Perspectives

1. Compare the influence of Gayle Pemberton's grandmother (see "Antidisestablishmentarianism") with that of Pat Mora's aunt.

2. How do religious rituals solidify ties between Mora and her Aunt Lobo and undermine them between the boy and his grandfather in Tayeb Salih's story?

✧ Extending Viewpoints through Writing

1. Create a one-page vignette about a relative whom you think of as unusual or striking in some way. Provide descriptive details and examples that will help the reader visualize this person.

2. In what way do you embody the coming together of two diverse ethnic and cultural traditions from your mother's and father's sides of the family? Tell what you know about the past histories of both sides of your family.

Gayle Pemberton

Antidisestablishmentarianism

———————◆———————

*Gayle Pemberton is currently William R. Kenan Professor of the Human-
ities at Wesleyan University. Born in 1948, she spent her childhood in
Chicago and Ohio. She received a Ph.D. in English and American Literature at Harvard University and has taught at Smith, Reed, and Bowdoin
Colleges.* The Hottest Water in Chicago: On Family, Race, Time, and
American Culture *(1992) is part memoir, part social analysis, and part
literary criticism. Pemberton focuses on her experiences growing up as
an African-American female in mid-twentieth-century America. The title
derives from her father's experience in 1954 as an organizer with the Urban League who had the dubious honor of integrating a Chicago hotel. As
Pemberton recounts, it was a desperately dirty establishment for tran-
sients whose owner had shamelessly boasted of offering "the hottest water
in Chicago." The chapter from this book, "Antidisestablishmentarianism," describes the influential role played by Pemberton's grandmother
in shaping her outlook.*

Before You Read

As you read this memoir, consider how the attitude of Pemberton's grandmother offers insight into the social forces that shaped the responses of
blacks during that era.

———————◆———————

1   Okay, so where's Gloria Lockerman? I want to know. Gloria Lockerman was partially responsible for ruining my life. I might never have
ended up teaching literature if it had not been for her. I don't want to
"call her out." I just want to know how things are, what she's doing.
Have things gone well, Gloria? How's the family? What's up?

2   Gloria Lockerman, in case you don't recall, won scads of money on
"The $64,000 Question." Gloria Lockerman was a young black child, like
me, but she could spell anything. Gloria Lockerman became my nemesis
with her ability, her a-n-t-i-d-i-s-e-s-t-a-b-l-i-s-h-m-e-n-t-a-r-i-a-n-i-s-m.

3   My parents, my sister, and I shared a house in Dayton, Ohio, with
my father's mother and her husband, my stepgrandfather, during the
middle fifties. Sharing is an overstatement. It was my grandmother's
house. Our nuclear group ate in a makeshift kitchen in the basement;

my sister and I shared a dormer bedroom, and my parents actually had a room on the main floor of the house—several parts of which were off-limits. These were the entire living room, anywhere within three feet of Grandma's African violets, the windows and venetian blinds, anything with a doily on it, the refrigerator, and the irises in the backyard.

4   It was an arrangement out of necessity, given the unimpressive state of our combined fortunes, and it did not meet with any one's satisfaction. To make matters worse, we had blockbusted a neighborhood. So, for the first year, I integrated the local elementary school—a thankless and relatively inhuman experience. I remember one day taking the Sunday paper route for a boy up the block who was sick. It was a beautiful spring day, dewy, warm. I walked up the three steps to a particular house and placed the paper on the stoop. Suddenly, a full-grown man, perhaps sixty or so, appeared with a shotgun aimed at me and said that if he ever saw my nigger ass on his porch again he'd blow my head off. I know—typical American grandfather.

5   Grandma liked spirituals, preferably those sung by Mahalia Jackson. She was not a fan of gospel and I can only imagine what she'd say if she were around to hear what's passing for inspirational music these days. She also was fond of country singers, and any of the members of "The Lawrence Welk Show." ("That Jimmy. Oh, I love the way he sings. He's from Iowa.") She was from Iowa, Jimmy was from Iowa, my father was from Iowa. She was crazy about Jimmy Dean too, and Tennessee Ernie Ford, and "Gunsmoke." She could cook with the finest of them and I wish I could somehow recreate her Parkerhouse rolls, but I lack bread karma. Grandma liked flowers (she could make anything bloom) and she loved her son.

6   She disliked white people, black people in the aggregate and pretty much individually too, children—particularly female children—her daughter, her husband, my mother, Episcopalianism, Catholicism, Judaism, and Dinah Shore. She had a hot temper and a mean streak. She also suffered from several nagging ailments: high blood pressure, ulcers, an enlarged heart, ill-fitting dentures, arteriosclerosis, and arthritis—enough to make anyone hot tempered and mean, I'm sure. But to a third grader, such justifications and their subtleties were ultimately beyond me and insufficient, even though I believe I understood in part the relationship between pain and personality. Grandma scared the daylights out of me. I learned to control my nervous stomach enough to keep from getting sick daily. So Grandma plus school plus other family woes and my sister still predicting the end of the world every time the sirens went off— Grandma threatened to send her to a convent—made the experience as a whole something I'd rather forget, but because of the mythic proportions of family, can't.

7   I often think that it might have been better had I been older, perhaps twenty years older, when I knew Grandma. But I realize that she

would have found much more wrong with me nearing thirty than she did when I was eight or nine. When I was a child, she could blame most of my faults on my mother. Grown, she would have had no recourse but to damn me to hell.

8   Ah, but she is on the gene. Grandma did everything fast. She cooked, washed, cleaned, moved—everything was at lightning speed. She passed this handicap on to me, and I have numerous bruises, cuts, and burns to show for it. Watching me throw pots and pans around in the creation of a meal, my mother occasionally calls me by my grandmother's first name. I smile back, click my teeth to imitate a slipping upper, and say something unpleasant about someone.

9   Tuesday nights were "The $64,000 Question" nights, just as Sundays we watched Ed Sullivan and Saturdays were reserved for Lawrence Welk and "Gunsmoke." We would all gather around the television in what was a small, informal family section between the verboten real living room and the mahogany dining table and chairs, used only three or four times a year. I don't remember where I sat, but it wasn't on the floor since that wasn't allowed either.

10   As we watched these television programs, once or twice I sat briefly on Grandma's lap. She was the world's toughest critic. No one was considered worthy, apart from the above-mentioned. To her, So-and-So or Whosits could not sing, dance, tell a joke, read a line—nothing. In her hands "Ted Mack's Amateur Hour" would have lasted three minutes. She was willing to forgive only very rarely—usually when someone she liked gave a mediocre performance on one of her favorite shows.

11   I must admit that Grandma's style of teaching critical thinking worked as well as some others I've encountered. My father had a different approach. Throughout my youth he would play the music of the thirties and forties. His passion was for Billie Holiday, with Ella Fitzgerald, Peggy Lee, Sarah Vaughan, and a few others thrown in for a touch of variety. He enjoyed music, and when he wanted to get some musical point across, he would talk about some nuance of style that revealed the distinction between what he called "really singing" and a failure. He would say, "Now, listen to that there. Did you catch it? Hear what she did with that note?" With Grandma it was more likely to be:

12   "Did you hear that?"

13   "What?" I might ask.

14   "That. What she just sang."

15   "Yes."

16   "Well, what do you think of it?"

17   "It's okay, I guess."

18   "Well, that was garbage. She can't sing a note. That stinks. She's a fool."

19   Message across. We all choose our own pedagogical techniques.

20   Game shows are, well, game shows. I turned on my television the other day, and as I clicked through channels looking for something to

watch I stopped long enough to hear an announcer say that the guest contestant was going to do something or other in 1981. Reruns of game shows? Well, why not? What difference does it make if the whole point is to watch people squirm, twist, sweat, blare, weep, convulse to get their hands on money and gifts, even if they end up being just "parting gifts"? (I won some of them myself once: a bottle of liquid Johnson's Wax, a box of Chunkies, a beach towel with the name of a diet soda on it, plus a coupon for a case of the stuff, and several boxes of Sugar Blobs—honey-coated peanut butter, marshmallow, and chocolate flavored crispies, dipped in strawberry flavoring for that special morning taste treat!)

21   Game shows in the fifties were different, more exciting. I thought the studio sets primitive even when I was watching them then. The clock on "Beat the Clock," the coat and crown on "Queen for a Day"—nothing like that mink on "The Big Payoff" that Bess Meyerson modeled—and that wire card flipper on "What's My Line" that John Charles Daly used—my, was it flimsy looking. The finest set of all, though, was on "The $64,000 Question." Hal March would stand outside the isolation booth, the door closing on the likes of Joyce Brothers, Catherine Kreitzer, and Gloria Lockerman, the music would play, and the clock would begin ticking down, like all game show clocks: *TOOT-toot-TOOT-toot-TOOT-toot-BUZZZZZZ.*

22   There were few opportunities to see black people on television in those days. I had watched "Amos 'n' Andy" when we lived in Chicago. But that show was a variation on a theme. Natives running around or jumping up and down or looking menacing in African adventure movies; shuffling, subservient, and clowning servants in local color movies (or any other sort); and "Amos 'n' Andy" were all the same thing: the perpetuation of a compelling, deadly, darkly humorous, and occasionally laughable idea. Nonfictional blacks on television were limited to Sammy Davis, Jr., as part of the Will Mastin Trio and afterward, or Peg Leg Bates on "The Ed Sullivan Show" on Sunday, or the entertainers who might show up on other variety shows, or Nat King Cole during his fifteen-minute program. Naturally, the appearance of Gloria Lockerman caused a mild sensation as we watched "The $64,000 Question," all assembled.

23   "Look at her," Grandma said.

24   I braced myself for the torrent of abuse that was about to be leveled at the poor girl.

25   "You ought to try to be like that," Grandma said.

26   "Huh?" I said.

27   "What did you say?"

28   "Yes, ma'am."

29   I was shocked, thrown into despair. I had done well in school, as well as could be hoped. I was modestly proud of my accomplishments, and given the price I was paying every day—and paying in silence, for

I never brought my agonies at school home with me—I didn't need Gloria Lockerman thrown in my face. Gloria Lockerman, like me, on television, spelling. I was perennially an early-round knockout in spelling bees.

30   My sister understands all of this. Her own story is slightly different and she says she'll tell it all one day herself. She is a very good singer and has a superb ear; with our critical training, what more would she need? Given other circumstances, she might have become a performer herself. When she was about eleven Leslie Uggams was on Arthur Godfrey's "Talent Scouts" and was soon to be tearing down the "Name That Tune" runway, ringing the bell and becoming moderately famous. No one ever held Leslie Uggams up to my sister for image consciousness-raising. But my sister suffered nevertheless. She could out-sing Leslie Uggams and probably run as fast; she knew the songs and didn't have nearly so strange a last name. But, there she was, going nowhere in the Middle West, and there was Leslie Uggams on her way to "Sing Along With Mitch." To this day, my sister mumbles if she happens to see Leslie Uggams on television—before she can get up to change the channel—or hears someone mention her name. I told her I saw Leslie Uggams in the flesh at a club in New York. She was sitting at a table, just like the rest of us, listening with pleasure to Barbara Cook. My sister swore at me.

31   Grandma called her husband "Half-Wit." He was a thin, small-boned man who looked to me far more like an Indian chief than like a black man. He was from Iowa too, but that obviously did not account for enough in Grandma's eyes. He had a cracking tenor voice, a head full of dead straight black hair, reddish, dull brown skin, and large sad, dark brown eyes. His craggy face also reminded me of pictures I'd seen of Abraham Lincoln—but, like all political figures and American forefathers, Lincoln, to my family, was fair game for wisecracks, so that resemblance did Grandpa no good either. And for reasons that have gone to the grave with both of them, he was the most thoroughly henpecked man I have ever heard of, not to mention seen.

32   Hence, domestic scenes had a quality of pathos and high humor as far as I was concerned. My sister and I called Grandpa "Half-Wit" when we were alone together, but that seemed to have only a slight effect on our relations with him and our willingness to obey him—though I cannot recall any occasions calling for his authority. Grandma was Grandma, Half-Wit was Half-Wit—and we lived with the two of them. I have one particularly vivid memory of Grandma, an aficionada of the iron skillet, chasing him through the house waving it in the air, her narrow, arthritis-swollen wrist and twisted knuckles turning the heavy pan as if it were a lariat. He didn't get hurt; he was fleet of foot and made it out the back door before she caught him. My father's real father had been dead since the thirties and divorced from Grandma since the teens—so Half-Wit had been in place for quite some years and was still around to tell the story, if he had the nerve.

33   Grandma had a glass menagerie, the only one I've seen apart from performances of the Williams play. I don't think she had a unicorn, but she did have quite a few pieces. From a distance of no less than five feet I used to squint at the glass forms, wondering what they meant to Grandma, who was herself delicate of form but a powerhouse of strength, speed, and temper. I also wondered how long it would take me to die if the glass met with some unintended accident caused by me. Real or imagined unpleasantries, both in the home and outside of it, helped develop in me a somewhat melancholic nature. And even before we had moved to Ohio I found myself laughing and crying at the same time.

34   In the earlier fifties, in Chicago, I was allowed to watch such programs as "The Ernie Kovacs Show," "Your Show of Shows," "The Jackie Gleason Show," "The Red Skelton Show," and, naturally, "I Love Lucy." I was continually dazzled by the skits and broad humor, but I was particularly taken with the silent sketches, my favorite comedians as mime artists: Skelton as Freddy the Freeloader, Caesar and Coca in a number of roles, thoroughly outrageous Kovacs acts backed by Gershwin's "Rialto Ripples." My father was a very funny man and a skillful mime. I could tell when he watched Gleason's Poor Soul that he identified mightily with what was on the screen. It had nothing to do with self-pity. My father had far less of it than other men I've met with high intelligence, financial and professional stress, and black faces in a white world. No, my father would even say that we were all poor souls; it was the human condition. His mimicking of the Gleason character—head down, shoulders tucked, stomach sagging, feet splayed—served as some kind of release. I would laugh and cry watching either of them.

35   But my absolute favorite was Martha Raye, who had a way of milking the fine line between tragedy and comedy better than most. I thought her eyes showed a combination of riotous humor and terror. Her large mouth contorted in ways that seemed to express the same two emotions. Her face was a mask of profound sadness. She did for me what Sylvia Sidney did for James Baldwin. In *The Devil Finds Work*, Baldwin says, "Sylvia Sidney was the only American film actress who reminded me of a colored girl, or woman—which is to say that she was the only American film actress who reminded me of reality." The reality Raye conveyed to me was of how dreams could turn sour in split-seconds, and how underdogs, even when winning, often had to pay abominable prices. She also could sing a jazz song well, with her husky scat phrasing, in ways that were slightly different from those of my favorite singers, and almost as enjoyable.

36   There were no comedic or dramatic images of black women on the screen—that is, apart from Sapphire and her mother on "Amos 'n' Andy." And knowing Grandma and Grandpa taught me, if nothing else suggested it, that what I saw of black life on television was a gross burlesque—played to the hilt with skill by black actors, but still lacking reality.

37   Black female singers who appeared on television were, like their music, sacrosanct, and I learned from their styles, lyrics, and improvisations, lessons about life that mime routines did not reveal. Still, it was Martha Raye, and occasionally Lucille Ball and Imogene Coca at their most absurd, that aligned me with my father and his Poor Soul, and primed me to both love and despise Grandma and to see that in life most expressions, thoughts, acts, and intentions reveal their opposite polarities simultaneously.

38   Grandma died in 1965. I was away, out of the country, and I missed her funeral—which was probably a good idea since I might have been tempted to strangle some close family friend who probably would have launched into a "tsk, tsk, tsk" monologue about long-suffering grandmothers and impudent children. But, in another way, I'm sorry I didn't make it. Her funeral might have provided some proper closure for me, might have prompted me to organize her effect on my life sooner than I did, reconciling the grandmother who so hoped I would be a boy that she was willing to catch a Constellation or a DC-3 to witness my first few hours, but instead opted to take the bus when she heard the sad news, with the grandmother who called me "Sally Slap-cabbage" and wrote to me and my sister regularly, sending us the odd dollar or two, until her death.

39   I remember coming home from school, getting my jelly sandwich and wolfing it down, and watching "The Mickey Mouse Club," my favorite afternoon show, since there was no afternoon movie. I had noticed and had been offended by the lack of black children in the "Club," but the cartoons, particularly those with Donald Duck, were worth watching. On this particular episode—one of the regular guest act days—a group of young black children, perhaps nine or ten of them, came on and sang, with a touch of dancing, "Old MacDonald Had a Farm," in an up-tempo, jazzy version. In spite of the fact that usually these guest days produced some interesting child acts, I became angry with what I saw. I felt patronized, for myself and for them. Clearly a couple of them could out-sing and out-dance any Mouseketeer—something that wasn't worth giving a thought to—but this performance was gratuitous, asymmetrical, a nonsequitur, like Harpo Marx marching through the Negro section in *A Day at the Races*, blowing an imaginary horn and exciting the locals to much singing, swinging, and dancing to a charming ditty called "Who Dat Man?"

40   I must have mumbled something as I watched the group singing "Old MacDonald." Grandma, passing through, took a look at what was on the screen, and at me, turned off the television, took my hand, led me to her kitchen, and sat me down at the table where she and Half-Wit ate, poured me some milk, and without so much as a blink of her eye, said, "Pay no attention to that shit."

✧ *Evaluating the Text*

1. What impression do you get of the circumstances surrounding Pemberton's early life? How do they help explain why her grandmother was so influential in shaping her outlook on life?

2. How would you characterize the voice that you hear in Pemberton's essay? What personality traits does she possess as a writer? Why is it important to know that the narrator's family was the only black family in that neighborhood? What can you infer about her experiences at school?

3. In what ways was the media's presentation of African Americans in the 1950s stereotyped? How does this help explain Pemberton's grandmother's reaction to Gloria Lockerman?

✧ *Exploring Different Perspectives*

1. Compare and contrast the effects of living in an extended family as described by Pemberton with Fatima Mernissi's narrative, "Moonlit Nights of Laughter."

2. Compare the effects on Pemberton and Pat Mora (see "Remembering Lobo") of growing up with a free-thinking, independent female relative.

✧ *Extending Viewpoints through Writing*

1. To what extent did one of your grandparents or relatives exert a shaping influence on your outlook, personality, and expectations? Describe one or two key incidents that illustrate this.

2. In your view, what television shows either reflect or fail to reflect African-American life in the United States today?

Colin Turnbull

The Mbuti Pygmies

◆

*Born in 1924 in Harrow, England, Colin Turnbull received a B.A.
(1947) and an M.A. (1949) from Magdalen College, Oxford, and his
Ph.D. in Social Anthropology from Oxford University in 1964. Turnbull served as curator of the American Museum of Natural History in
New York, taught at Virginia Commonwealth University, Hunter College, Vassar College, and was a professor of anthropology at George
Washington University. He wrote extensively about various peoples in
Africa based on years of anthropological field research. His published
works include* The Mountain People *(1972), an influential study of the
Ik of northern Uganda,* Tradition and Change in African Life *(1966),
and several studies on the pygmies of the Ituri Forest of the Congo with
whom he spent four years. His work on the pygmies includes* The Forest People *(1961),* The Mbuti Pygmies: An Ethnographic Survey
(1965), Wayward Servants: The Two Worlds of the African Pygmies *(1965),* In a Pygmy Camp *(1969), and* The Mbuti Pygmies:
Change and Adaptation *(1983), from which the following selection is
taken. Turnbull found the pygmies to be a wise people whose society has
developed remarkably effective methods for fostering conflict resolution
and cooperation. Turnbull died in 1994.*

*The Mbuti are nomadic hunters and gatherers who live within the
Ituri rain forest of Zaire. Parts of the Congo River run through the forest
and the ground receives no direct sunlight because of the broad-leafed
evergreen trees, which reach 100 to 200 feet. The average temperature is
88 degrees and the rain forest receives seventy-five inches of rain per year.
The Mbuti, whose total population is between twenty and fifty thousand,
are thought to have lived in this location for 4,500 years. They live in
small bands of ten to twenty-five families and are mainly farmers and
fishermen. They speak Bira, which is a fusion of Arabic and indigenous
African languages. They call themselves "the children of the forest" and
share their territory with many animals, including antelopes, elephants,
leopards, hogs, buffalo, peacocks, and monkeys, which they hunt. They
also eat berries, nuts, vegetables, snails, grubs, termites, ants, larvae, and
occasionally, fresh-water crabs. The most highly sought food is honey,
which must be gathered by men climbing the tall trees. The Mbuti have a
very closely-knit social structure and ceremonies in which art, music, and
dance are practiced mark significant stages in the life of the Mbuti.*

*The People's Republic of the Congo, in West Central Africa, achieved
its independence from France in 1960. Because of its location, the Congo
has always played an important role as a center of commerce and transportation connecting inland areas of Africa with the Atlantic Ocean. After a series of coups, a new military regime following socialist policies, led
by Colonel Sassou-Nguesso, was installed in 1979. A multiparty system
was introduced in 1991, but hyperinflation and government corruption
brought about successive civil wars throughout the late 1990s. The pre-
sumptive head of government, as of 2002, is Laurent Kabila.*

Before You Read

Consider how the games the Mbuti play define important cultural values
in their society and how this differs from Western values.

The Educational Process

1   . . . In the first three years of life every Mbuti alive experiences almost total security. The infant is breast-fed for those three years, and is
allowed almost every freedom. Regardless of gender, the infant learns to
have absolute trust in both male and female parent. If anything, the
father is just another kind of mother, for in the second year the father formally introduces the child to its first solid food. There used to be a beautiful ritual in which the mother presented the child to the father in the
middle of the camp, where all important statements are made (anyone
speaking from the middle of the camp must be listened to). The father
took the child and held it to his breast, and the child would try to suckle,
crying "ema, ema," or "mother." The father would shake his head, and
so "no, father . . . eba," but like a mother (the Mbuti said), then give the
child its first solid food.

2   At three the child ventures out into the world on its own and enters
the *bopi*, what we might call a playground, a tiny camp perhaps a hundred yards from the main camp, often on the edge of a stream. The *bopi*
were indeed playgrounds, and often very noisy ones, full of fun and high
spirits. But they were also rigorous training grounds for eventual economic responsibility. One entry to the *bopi*, for one thing, the child discovers the importance of age as a structural principle, and the relative
unimportance of gender and biological kinship. The *bopi* is the private
world of the children. Younger youths may occasionally venture in, but if
adults or elders try, as they sometimes do when angry at having their afternoon snooze interrupted, they invariably get driven out, taunted, and
ridiculed. Children, among the Mbuti, have rights, but they also learn
that they have responsibilities. Before the hunt sets out each day it is the
children, sometimes the younger youths, who light the hunting fire.

3   Ritual among the Mbuti is often so informal and apparently casual
that it may pass unnoticed at first. Yet insofar as ritual involves sym-

bolic acts that represent unspoken, perhaps even unthought, concepts or ideals, or invoke other states of being, alternative frames of mind and reference, then Mbuti life is full of ritual. The hunting fire is one of the move obvious of such rituals. Early in the morning children would take firebrands from the *bopi*, where they always lit their own fire with embers from their family hearths, and set off on the trail by which the hunt was to leave that day (the direction of each day's hunt was always settled by discussion the night before). Just a short distance from the camp they lit a fire at the base of a large tree, and covered it with special leaves that made it give off a column of dense smoke. Hunters leaving the camp, both men and women, and such youths and children as were going with them, had to pass by this fire. Some did so casually, without stopping or looking, but passing through the smoke. Others reached into the smoke with their hands as they passed, rubbing the smoke into their bodies. A few always stopped for a moment, and let the smoke envelop them, only then almost dreamily moving off.

4   And indeed it *was* a form of intoxication, for the smoke invoked the spirit of the forest, and by passing through it the hunters sought to fill themselves with that spirit, not so much to make the hunt successful as to minimize the sacrilege of killing. Yet they, the hunters, could not light the fire themselves. After all, they were already contaminated by death. Even youths, who daily joined the hunt at the edges, catching any game that escaped the nets, by hand, if they could, were not pure enough to invoke the spirits of forestness. But young children were uncontaminated, as yet untainted by contact with the original sin of the Mbuti. It was their responsibility to light the fire, and if it was not lit then the hunt would not take place, or, as the Mbuti put it, the hunt *could* not take place.

5   In this way even the children in Mbuti society, at the first of the four age levels that dominate Mbuti social structure, are given very real social responsibility and see themselves as a part of that structure, by virtue of their purity. After all, they have just been born from the source of all purity, the forest itself. By the same reasoning, the elders, who are about to return to that ultimate source of all being, through death, are at least closer to purity than the adults, who are daily contaminated by killing. Elders no longer go on the hunt. So, like the children, the elders have important sacred ritual responsibilities in the Mbuti division of labor by age.

6   In the *bopi* the children play, but they have no "games" in the strict sense of the word. Levi-Strauss has perceptively compared games with rituals, suggesting that whereas in a game the players start theoretically equal but end up unequal, in a ritual just the reverse takes place. All are equalized. Mbuti children could be seen every day playing in the *bopi*, but not once did I see a game, not one activity that smacked of any kind of competition, except perhaps that competition that it is necessary for us all to feel from time to time, competition with our own private and personal inadequacies. One such pastime (rather than

game) was tree climbing. A dozen or so children would climb up a young sapling. Reaching the top, their weight brought the sapling bending down until it almost touched the ground. Then all the children leapt off together, shrieking as the young tree sprang upright again with a rush. Sometimes one child, male or female, might stay on a little too long, either out of fear, or out of bravado, or from sheer carelessness or bad timing. Whatever the reason, it was a lesson most children only needed to be taught once, for the result was that you got flung upward with the tree, and were lucky to escape with no more than a few bruises and a very bad fright.

7   Other pastimes taught the children the rules of hunting and gathering. Frequently elders, who stayed in camp when the hunt went off, called the children into the main camp and enacted a mock hunt with them there. Stretching a discarded piece of net across the camp, they pretended to be animals, showing the children how to drive them into the nets. And, of course, the children played house, learning the patterns of cooperation that would be necessary for them later in life. They also learned the prime lesson of egality, other than for purposes of division of labor making no distinction between male and female, this nuclear family or that. All in the *bopi* were *apua'i* to each other, and so they would remain throughout their lives. At every age level—childhood, youth, adulthood, or old age—everyone of that level is *apua'i* to all the others. Only adults sometimes (but so rarely that I think it was only done as a kind of joke, or possibly insult) made the distinction that the Bira do, using *apua'i* for male and *amua'i* for female. Male or female, for the Mbuti, if you are the same age you are *apua'i*, and that means that you share everything equally, regardless of kinship or gender.

Youth and Politics

8   Sometimes before the age of puberty boys or girls, whenever they feel ready, move back into the main camp from the *bopi* and join the youths. This is when they must assume new responsibilities, which for the youths are primarily political. Already, in the *bopi*, the children become involved in disputes, and are sometimes instrumental in settling them by ridicule, for nothing hurts an adult more than being ridiculed by children. The art of reason, however, is something they learn from the youths, and it is the youths who apply the art of reason to the settlement of disputes.

9   When puberty comes it separates them, for the first time in their experience, from each other as *apua'i*. Very plainly girls are different from boys. When a girl has her first menstrual period the whole camp celebrates with the wild *elima* festival, in which the girl, and some of her chosen girl friends, are the center of all attention, living together in a special *elima* house. Male youths sit outside the *elima* house and wait for the girls to come out, usually in the afternoon, for the *elima* singing. They sing in antiphony, the girls leading, the boys responding. Boys come from neigh-

boring territories all around, for this is a time of courtship. But there are always eligible youths within the camp as well, and the *elima* girl may well choose girls from other territories to come and join her, so there is more than enough excuse for every youth to carry on several flirtations, legitimate or illegitimate. I have known even first cousins to flirt with each other, but learned to be prudent enough not to pull out my kinship charts and point this out—well, not in public anyway.

10   The *elima* is more than a premarital festival, more than a joint initiation of youth into adulthood, and more than a rite of passage through puberty, though it is all those things. It is a public recognition of the opposition of male and female, and every *elima* is used to highlight the *potential* for conflict that lies in that opposition. As at other times of crisis, at puberty, a time of change and uncertainty, the Mbuti bring all the major forms of conflict out into the open. And the one that evidently most concerns them is the male/female opposition.

11   The adults begin to play a special form of "tug of war" that is clearly a ritual rather than a game. All the men are on one side, the women on

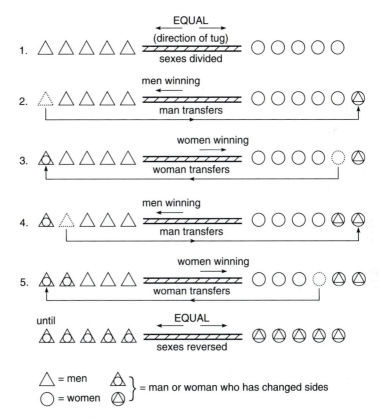

Tug of War. This is one of the Mbuti's many techniques of conflict resolution, involving role reversal and the principle of opposition without hostility.

the other. At first it looks like a game, but quickly it becomes clear that the objective is for *neither* side to win. As soon as the women begin to win, one of them will leave the end of the line and run around to join the men, assuming a deep male voice and in other ways ridiculing manhood. Then, as the men begin to win, a male will similarly join the women, making fun of womanhood as he does so. Each adult on changing sides attempts to outdo all the others in ridiculing the opposite sex. Finally, when nearly all have switched sides, and sexes, the ritual battle between the genders simply collapses into hysterical laughter, the contestants letting go of the rope, falling onto the ground, and rolling over with mirth. Neither side wins, both are equalized very nicely, and each learns the essential lesson, that there should be *no* contest. . . .

✦ Evaluating the Text

1. What values do the first rituals in which the child takes part communicate?

2. In what ways is the concept of the age of the peer group the most important determinant of identity for the growing child?

3. Explain the significance of why only young children are allowed to light the fire preceding each day's hunt.

4. What values is the "tug of war" game designed to communicate?

✦ Exploring Different Perspectives

1. What factors explain why the children, described by Daniela Deane, although raised in the communal society of China, might become individualistic in a way that Mbuti children would not?

2. How are the values that Mbuti children are encouraged to learn strikingly similar to the ideals expressed in the Koran, as portrayed in Tayeb Salih's story, "A Handful of Dates"?

✦ Extending Viewpoints through Writing

1. What games did you play when you were a child? Which, if any, were not competitive? If none were noncompetitive, what can you infer from this?

2. Are you aware of rituals in which the youngest child present performs a role determined solely by his or her age? Describe the ritual, its purpose, and the role the child plays.

Kazuo Ishiguro

A Family Supper

◆

Kazuo Ishiguro was born in Nagasaki, Japan, in 1954 and moved to England in 1960 where he spent most of his life. As a young man, he had a variety of jobs, including being the grouse beater for the Queen Mother at Balmoral Castle in Aberdeen, Scotland. Because his parents had intended to return to Japan, they raised him as both Japanese and English, a bicultural emphasis that underlies "A Family Supper" (from Firebird 2, *1982). His novels include* A Pale View of Hills *(1982),* An Artist of the Floating World *(1986), and* The Remains of the Day *(1989), which won Britain's highest literary award, the Booker Prize, and was later made into a 1993 film starring Anthony Hopkins and Emma Thompson. More recently, he has published* The Unconsoled *(1995), and* When We Were Orphans *(2001), which was shortlisted for the prestigious Booker Prize.*

Known historically as the "land of the rising sun," symbolized in the national flag, Japan is made up of four main islands off the coast of east Asia: Honshu (the largest, where the capital Tokyo and major cities are located), Hokkaido, Shikoku, and Kyushu. Two-thirds of Japan's terrain is mountainous, including the most famous peak, Mount Fuji. Earth tremors are a frequent occurrence. Because Japan has few natural resources, and such a small percentage of land is suitable for cultivation, the country must import almost half its food supply and almost all raw materials required for industrial production. Despite this, Japan is one of the most productive industrial nations; its exports of automobiles, electronic equipment, televisions, textiles, chemicals, and machinery have made it an economic superpower. Education is free and compulsory to the age of fifteen, and Japan has an extraordinarily high literacy rate of 99 percent.

According to legend, Japan was founded by Emperor Jimmu in 660 B.C. and has had a line of emperors that continues into the present. The current emperor, Akihito, succeeded to the throne in 1989 following his father, Hirohito, who was emperor from 1926. Actual political control of the country from the twelfth to the late nineteenth century was held by feudal lords, called Shoguns. *In 1854, Commodore Matthew Perry reopened contact with Japan after the Shoguns had expelled all foreigners from the country in the seventeenth century. Subsequently, the Shoguns lost power to the emperor, and with the defeat of China in 1895 and victory over Russia in the Russo–Japanese War ending in 1905, Japan became a global power.*

In 1999 the Japanese Diet voted to recognize the rising-sun flag and the imperial hymn as the nation's offical flag and national anthem, a decision that caused concern because it evoked memories of Japan's imperial and militaristic past.

Before You Read

Consider how Ishiguro's story dramatizes a clash between the American emphasis on self-determination and the importance the Japanese place on obedience, traditional family values, and self-sacrifice.

1   Fugu is a fish caught off the Pacific shores of Japan. The fish has held a special significance for me ever since my mother died after eating one. The poison resides in the sex glands of the fish, inside two fragile bags. These bags must be removed with caution when preparing the fish, for any clumsiness will result in the poison leaking into the veins. Regrettably, it is not easy to tell whether or not this operation has been carried out successfully. The proof is, as it were, in the eating.

2   Fugu poisoning is hideously painful and almost always fatal. If the fish has been eaten during the evening, the victim is usually overtaken by pain during his sleep. He rolls about in agony for a few hours and is dead by morning. The fish became extremely popular in Japan after the war. Until stricter regulations were imposed, it was all the rage to perform the hazardous gutting operation in one's own kitchen, then to invite neighbors and friends round for the feast.

3   At the time of my mother's death, I was living in California. My relationship with my parents had become somewhat strained around that period and consequently I did not learn of the circumstances of her death until I returned to Tokyo two years later. Apparently, my mother had always refused to eat fugu, but on this particular occasion she had made an exception, having been invited by an old school friend whom she was anxious not to offend. It was my father who supplied me with the details as we drove from the airport to his house in the Kamakura district. When we finally arrived, it was nearing the end of a sunny autumn day.

4   "Did you eat on the plane?" my father asked. We were sitting on the tatami floor of his tearoom.

5   "They gave me a light snack."

6   "You must be hungry. We'll eat as soon as Kikuko arrives."

7   My father was a formidable-looking man with a large stony jaw and furious black eyebrows. I think now, in retrospect, that he much resembled [Chinese Communist leader] Chou En-lai, although he would not have cherished such a comparison, being particularly proud of the pure samurai blood that ran in the family. His general presence was not one that encouraged relaxed conversation; neither were things helped much by his odd way of stating each remark as if it were the conclud-

ing one. In fact, as I sat opposite him that afternoon, a boyhood memory came back to me of the time he had struck me several times around the head for "chattering like an old woman." Inevitably, our conversation since my arrival at the airport had been punctuated by long pauses.

8   "I'm sorry to hear about the firm," I said when neither of us had spoken for some time. He nodded gravely.

9   "In fact, the story didn't end there," he said. "After the firm's collapse, Watanabe killed himself. He didn't wish to live with the disgrace."

10   "I see."

11   "We were partners for seventeen years. A man of principle and honor. I respected him very much."

12   "Will you go into business again?" I asked.

13   "I am . . . in retirement. I'm too old to involve myself in new ventures now. Business these days has become so different. Dealing with foreigners. Doing things their way. I don't understand how we've come to this. Neither did Watanabe." He sighed. "A fine man. A man of principle."

14   The tearoom looked out over the garden. From where I sat I could make out the ancient well that as a child I had believed to be haunted. It was just visible now through the thick foliage. The sun had sunk low and much of the garden had fallen into shadow.

15   "I'm glad in any case that you've decided to come back," my father said. "More than a short visit, I hope."

16   "I'm not sure what my plans will be."

17   "I, for one, am prepared to forget the past. Your mother, too, was always ready to welcome you back—upset as she was by your behavior."

18   "I appreciate your sympathy. As I say, I'm not sure what my plans are."

19   "I've come to believe now that there were no evil intentions in your mind," my father continued. "You were swayed by certain . . . influences. Like so many others."

20   "Perhaps we should forget it, as you suggest."

21   "As you will. More tea?"

22   Just then a girl's voice came echoing through the house.

23   "At last." My father rose to his feet. "Kikuko has arrived."

24   Despite our difference in years, my sister and I had always been close. Seeing me again seemed to make her excessively excited, and for a while she did nothing but giggle nervously. But she calmed down somewhat when my father started to question her about Osaka and her university. She answered him with short, formal replies. She in turn asked me a few questions, but she seemed inhibited by the fear that her questions might lead to awkward topics. After a while, the conversation had become even sparser than prior to Kikuko's arrival. Then my father stood up, saying: "I must attend to the supper. Please excuse me for being burdened by such matters. Kikuko will look after you."

25   My sister relaxed quite visibly once he had left the room. Within a few minutes, she was chatting freely about her friends in Osaka and

about her classes at university. Then quite suddenly she decided we should walk in the garden and went striding out onto the veranda. We put on some straw sandals that had been left along the veranda rail and stepped out into the garden. The light in the garden had grown very dim.

26 "I've been dying for a smoke for the last half hour," she said, lighting a cigarette.

27 "Then why didn't you smoke?"

28 She made a furtive gesture back toward the house, then grinned mischievously.

29 "Oh, I see," I said.

30 "Guess what? I've got a boyfriend now."

31 "Oh, yes?"

32 "Except I'm wondering what to do. I haven't made up my mind yet."

33 "Quite understandable."

34 "You see, he's making plans to go to America. He wants me to go with him as soon as I finish studying."

35 "I see. And you want to go to America?"

36 "If we go, we're going to hitchhike," Kikuko waved a thumb in front of my face. "People say it's dangerous, but I've done it in Osaka and it's fine."

37 "I see. So what is it you're unsure about?"

38 We were following a narrow path that wound through the shrubs and finished by the old well. As we walked, Kikuko persisted in taking unnecessarily theatrical puffs on her cigarette.

39 "Well, I've got lots of friends now in Osaka. I like it there. I'm not sure I want to leave them all behind just yet. And Suichi . . . I like him, but I'm not sure I want to spend so much time with him. Do you understand?"

40 "Oh, perfectly."

41 She grinned again, then skipped on ahead of me until she had reached the well. "Do you remember," she said as I came walking up to her, "how you used to say this well was haunted?"

42 "Yes, I remember."

43 We both peered over the side.

44 "Mother always told me it was the old woman from the vegetable store you'd seen that night," she said. "But I never believed her and never came out here alone."

45 "Mother used to tell me that too. She even told me once the old woman had confessed to being the ghost. Apparently, she'd been taking a shortcut through our garden. I imagine she had some trouble clambering over these walls."

46 Kikuko gave a giggle. She then turned her back to the well, casting her gaze about the garden.

47 "Mother never really blamed you, you know," she said, in a new voice. I remained silent. "She always used to say to me how it was

their fault, hers and Father's, for not bringing you up correctly. She used to tell me how much more careful they'd been with me, and that's why I was so good." She looked up and the mischievous grin had returned to her face. "Poor Mother," she said.

48   "Yes. Poor Mother."

49   "Are you going back to California?"

50   "I don't know. I'll have to see."

51   "What happened to . . . to her? To Vicki?"

52   "That's all finished with," I said. "There's nothing much left for me now in California."

53   "Do you think I ought to go there?"

54   "Why not? I don't know. You'll probably like it." I glanced toward the house. "Perhaps we'd better go in soon. Father might need a hand with the supper."

55   But my sister was once more peering down into the well. "I can't see any ghosts," she said. Her voice echoed a little.

56   "Is Father very upset about his firm collapsing?"

57   "Don't know. You never can tell with Father." Then suddenly she straightened up and turned to me. "Did he tell you about old Watanabe? What he did?"

58   "I heard he committed suicide."

59   "Well, that wasn't all. He took his whole family with him. His wife and his two little girls."

60   "Oh, yes?"

61   "Those two beautiful little girls. He turned on the gas while they were all asleep. Then he cut his stomach with a meat knife."

62   "Yes, Father was just telling me how Watanabe was a man of principle."

63   "Sick." My sister turned back to the well.

64   "Careful. You'll fall right in."

65   "I can't see any ghost," she said. "You were lying to me all that time."

66   "But I never said it lived down the well."

67   "Where is it then?"

68   We both looked around at the trees and shrubs. The daylight had almost gone. Eventually I pointed to a small clearing some ten yards away.

69   "Just there I saw it. Just there."

70   We stared at the spot.

71   "What did it look like?"

72   "I couldn't see very well. It was dark."

73   "But you must have seen something."

74   "It was an old woman. She was just standing there, watching me."

75   We kept staring at the spot as if mesmerized.

76   "She was wearing a white kimono," I said. "Some of her hair came undone. It was blowing around a little."

77   Kikuko pushed her elbow against my arm. "Oh, be quiet. You're trying to frighten me all over again." She trod on the remains of her

cigarette, then for a brief moment stood regarding it with a perplexed expression. She kicked some pine needles over it, then once more displayed her grin. "Let's see if supper's ready," she said.

78   We found my father in the kitchen. He gave us a quick glance, then carried on with what he was doing.

79   "Father's become quite a chef since he's had to manage on his own," Kikuko said with a laugh.

80   He turned and looked at my sister coldly. "Hardly a skill I'm proud of," he said. "Kikuko, come here and help."

81   For some moments my sister did not move. Then she stepped forward and took an apron hanging from a drawer.

82   "Just these vegetables need cooking now," he said to her. "The rest just needs watching." Then he looked up and regarded me strangely for some seconds. "I expect you want to look around the house," he said eventually. He put down the chopsticks he had been holding. "It's a long time since you've seen it."

83   As we left the kitchen I glanced toward Kikuko, but her back was turned.

84   "She's a good girl," my father said.

85   I followed my father from room to room. I had forgotten how large the house was. A panel would slide open and another room would appear. But the rooms were all startlingly empty. In one of the rooms the lights did not come on, and we stared at the stark walls and tatami in the pale light that came from the windows.

86   "This house it too large for a man to live in alone," my father said. "I don't have much use for most of these rooms now."

87   But eventually my father opened the door to a room packed full of books and papers. There were flowers in vases and pictures on the walls. Then I noticed something on a low table in the corner of the room. I came nearer and saw it was a plastic model of a battleship, the kind constructed by children. It had been placed on some newspaper; scattered around it were assorted pieces of gray plastic.

88   My father gave a laugh. He came up to the table and picked up the model.

89   "Since the firm folded," he said, "I have a little more time on my hands." He laughed again, rather strangely. For a moment his face looked almost gentle. "A little more time."

90   "That seems odd," I said. "You were always so busy."

91   "Too busy, perhaps." He looked at me with a small smile. "Perhaps I should have been a more attentive father."

92   I laughed. He went on contemplating his battleship. Then he looked up. "I hadn't meant to tell you this, but perhaps it's best that I do. It's my belief that your mother's death was no accident. She had many worries. And some disappointments."

93   We both gazed at the plastic battleship.

94 "Surely," I said eventually, "my mother didn't expect me to live here forever."

95 "Obviously you don't see. You don't see how it is for some parents. Not only must they lose their children, they must lose them to things they don't understand." He spun the battleship in his fingers. "These little gunboats here could have been better glued, don't you think?"

96 "Perhaps. I think it looks fine."

97 "During the war I spent some time on a ship rather like this. But my ambition was always the air force. I figured it like this: If your ship was struck by the enemy, all you could do was struggle in the water hoping for a lifeline. But in an airplane—well, there was always the final weapon." He put the model back onto the table. "I don't suppose you believe in war."

98 "Not particularly."

99 He cast an eye around the room. "Supper should be ready by now," he said. "You must be hungry."

100 Supper was waiting in a dimly lit room next to the kitchen. The only source of light was a big lantern that hung over the table, casting the rest of the room in shadow. We bowed to each other before starting the meal.

101 There was little conversation. When I made some polite comment about the food, Kikuko giggled a little. Her earlier nervousness seemed to have returned to her. My father did not speak for several minutes. Finally he said:

102 "It must feel strange for you, being back in Japan."

103 "Yes, it is a little strange."

104 "Already, perhaps, you regret leaving America."

105 "A little. Not so much. I didn't leave behind much. Just some empty rooms."

106 "I see."

107 I glanced across the table. My father's face looked stony and forbidding in the half-light. We ate on in silence.

108 Then my eye caught something at the back of the room. At first I continued eating, then my hands became still. The others noticed and looked at me. I went on gazing into the darkness past my father's shoulder.

109 "Who is that? In that photograph there?"

110 "Which photograph?" My father turned slightly, trying to follow my gaze.

111 "The lowest one. The old woman in the white kimono."

112 My father put down his chopsticks. He looked first at the photograph, then at me.

113 "Your mother." His voice had become very hard. "Can't you recognize your own mother?"

114 "My mother. You see, it's dark. I can't see it very well."

115   No one spoke for a few seconds, then Kikuko rose to her feet. She took the photograph down from the wall, came back to the table, and gave it to me.

116   "She looks a lot older," I said.

117   "It was taken shortly before her death," said my father.

118   "It was dark. I couldn't see very well."

119   I looked up and noticed my father holding out a hand. I gave him the photograph. He looked at it intently, then held it toward Kikuko. Obediently, my sister rose to her feet once more and returned the picture to the wall.

120   There was a large pot left unopened at the center of the table. When Kikuko had seated herself again, my father reached forward and lifted the lid. A cloud of steam rose up and curled toward the lantern. He pushed the pot a little toward me.

121   "You must be hungry," he said. One side of his face had fallen into shadow.

122   "Thank you." I reached forward with my chopsticks. The steam was almost scalding. "What is it?"

123   "Fish."

124   "It smells very good."

125   In the soup were strips of fish that had curled almost into balls. I picked one out and brought it to my bowl.

126   "Help yourself. There's plenty."

127   "Thank you." I took a little more, then pushed the pot toward my father. I watched him take several pieces to his bowl. Then we both watched as Kikuko served herself.

128   My father bowed slightly. "You must be hungry," he said again. He took some fish to his mouth and started to eat. Then I, too, chose a piece and put it in my mouth. It felt soft, quite fleshy against my tongue.

129   The three of us ate in silence. Several minutes went by. My father lifted the lid and once more steam rose up. We all reached forward and helped ourselves.

130   "Here," I said to my father, "you have this last piece."

131   "Thank you."

132   When we had finished the meal, my father stretched out his arms and yawned with an air of satisfaction. "Kikuko," he said, "prepare a pot of tea, please."

133   My sister looked at him, then left the room without comment. My father stood up.

134   "Let's retire to the other room. It's rather warm in here."

135   I got to my feet and followed him into the tearoom. The large sliding windows had been left open, bringing in a breeze from the garden. For a while we sat in silence.

136   "Father," I said, finally.

137   "Yes?"

138 "Kikuko tells me Watanabe-san took his whole family with him."

139 My father lowered his eyes and nodded. For some moments he seemed deep in thought. "Watanabe was very devoted to his work," he said at last. "The collapse of the firm was a great blow to him. I fear it must have weakened his judgment."

140 "You think what he did . . . it was a mistake?"

141 "Why, of course. Do you see it otherwise?"

142 "No, no. Of course not."

143 "There are other things besides work," my father said.

144 "Yes."

145 We fell silent again. The sound of locusts came in from the garden. I looked out into the darkness. The well was no longer visible.

146 "What do you think you will do now?" my father asked. "Will you stay in Japan for a while?"

147 "To be honest, I hadn't thought that far ahead."

148 "If you wish to stay here, I mean here in this house, you would be very welcome. That is, if you don't mind living with an old man."

149 "Thank you. I'll have to think about it."

150 I gazed out once more into the darkness.

151 "But of course," said my father, "this house is so dreary now. You'll no doubt return to America before long."

152 "Perhaps. I don't know yet."

153 "No doubt you will."

154 For some time my father seemed to be studying the back of his hands. Then he looked up and sighed.

155 "Kikuko is due to complete her studies next spring," he said. "Perhaps she will want to come home then. She's a good girl."

156 "Perhaps she will."

157 "Things will improve then."

158 "Yes, I'm sure they will."

159 We fell silent once more, waiting for Kikuko to bring the tea.

✧ Evaluating the Text

1. Discuss the relationship between the lethal effects of the *fugu* fish, the suicide of Watanabe, the fact that he murdered his family, and the family supper described in the title. What possibilities do these juxtapositions create in the reader's mind?

2. There are a number of unsolved questions in this story, such as whether the narrator would return to the United States or move back to Japan to live with his family or whether the narrator's mother died accidentally or killed herself. At what points in the story does the imagery of the descriptions magnify ambiguity and create suspense?

3. To what extent does the narrator react to the assumption that would be typical for the Japanese—that a son would live with his family and provide for them? What part does this theme play in the story?

✧ Exploring Different Perspectives

1. To what extent do the relationships between the narrator and his father in this story and between Gayatri Devi and her mother transcend the respective cultures of Japan and India?

2. Discuss how the fugu fish in Ishiguro's story and dates in Tayeb Salih's story are used to symbolize the relationships between family members?

✧ Extending Viewpoints through Writing

1. When the son in the story says "surely my mother didn't expect me to live here forever," Ishiguro states an idea that transcends cultures. In your opinion, is the father's expectation that both his children will live with him even after they are adults an unreasonable assumption? Why or why not?

2. What unsolved mysteries are part of your family folklore? To what extent do they overshadow family get-togethers?

Tayeb Salih

A Handful of Dates

◆

Tayeb Salih was born in the northern province of the Sudan in 1929. He was head of drama in the BBC's Arabic Service and now works for UNESCO in Paris. His writings include Season of Migration to the North, *translated by Denys Johnson-Davies (1969), and the collection of a short novel and stories titled* The Wedding of Zein *(1978), from which "A Handful of Dates" (translated from Arabic into English by Denys Johnson-Davies) was taken. This story describes a boy's reaction to the discovery that his grandfather's business practices conflict with the teachings of the Koran, the sacred book of Islam, which Muslims believe contain the divine teachings revealed to the prophet Muhammed.*

    Sudan, the largest country on the African continent, is a republic in the northeast, bordered on the north by Egypt; on the east by the Red Sea and Ethiopia; on the south by Kenya, Uganda, and Zaire; and on the west by Chad and Libya. The population (24.5 million) of the Sudan is divided into three main groups—northerners, who speak Arabic and are Muslims (70 percent); peoples from West Africa; and southerners, who follow traditional animistic beliefs (20 percent). Animism is the belief that natural objects such as rivers and rocks possess a soul or spirit and are alive. Independence from British control was achieved in 1956, although a bloody civil war between Muslims and those who follow animistic beliefs lasted seventeen years and ended only in 1972, after 1.5 million had died. The period of time during which "A Handful of Dates" was written corresponded with a movement that sought to impose Islamic law (sharia) on the whole country. Reaction against this triggered a civil war between Muslims in the north and the members of the Sudan People's Liberation Movement—who desire a secular democratic state, free from control by Islamic law—in the south. In 1999, President Omar Hassan Ahmad al-Bashir took dramatic steps to end the continuing conflict.

Before You Read

As you read Salih's story, pay particular attention to how the boy's reactions illuminate important tenets in Islam.

◆

1   I must have been very young at the time. While I don't remember exactly how old I was, I do remember that when people saw me with my grandfather they would pat me on the head and give my cheek a pinch—things they didn't do to my grandfather. The strange thing was that I never used to go out with my father, rather it was my grandfather who would take me with him wherever he went, except for the mornings when I would go the mosque to learn the Koran. The mosque, the river and the fields—these were the landmarks in our life. While most of the children of my age grumbled at having to go to the mosque to learn the Koran, I used to love it. The reason was, no doubt, that I was quick at learning by heart and the Sheikh always asked me to stand up and recite the *Chapter of the Merciful* whenever we had visitors, who would pat me on my head and cheek just as people did when they saw me with my grandfather.

2   Yes, I used to love the mosque, and I loved the river too. Directly we finished our Koran reading in the morning I would throw down my wooden slate and dart off, quick as a genie, to my mother, hurriedly swallow down my breakfast, and run off for a plunge in the river. When tired of swimming about I would sit on the bank and gaze at the strip of water that wound away eastwards and hid behind a thick wood of acacia trees. I loved to give rein to my imagination and picture to myself a tribe of giants living behind that wood, a people tall and thin with white beards and sharp noses, like my grandfather. Before my grandfather ever replied to my many questions he would rub the tip of his nose with his forefinger; as for his beard, it was soft and luxuriant and as white as cotton-wool—never in my life have I seen anything of a purer whiteness or greater beauty. My grandfather must also have been extremely tall, for I never saw anyone in the whole area address him without having to look up at him, nor did I see him enter a house without having to bend so low that I was put in mind of the way the river wound round behind the wood of acacia trees. I loved him and would imagine myself, when I grew to be a man, tall and slender like him, walking along with great strides.

3   I believe I was his favourite grandchild: no wonder, for my cousins were a stupid bunch and I—so they say—was an intelligent child. I used to know when my grandfather wanted me to laugh, when to be silent; also I would remember the times for his prayers and would bring him his prayer-rug and fill the ewer for his ablutions without his having to ask me. When he had nothing else to do he enjoyed listening to me reciting to him from the Koran in a lilting voice, and I could tell from his face that he was moved.

One day I asked him about our neighbour Masood. I said to my grandfather: 'I fancy you don't like our neighbour Masood?'

4   To which he answered, having rubbed the tip of his nose: 'He's an indolent man and I don't like such people.'

5   I said to him: 'What's an indolent man?'

6   My grandfather lowered his head for a moment, then looking across at the wide expanse of field, he said: 'Do you see it stretching out from the edge of the desert up to the Nile bank? A hundred feddans. Do you see all those date palms? And those trees—sant, acacia, and sayal? All this fell into Masood's lap, was inherited by him from his father.'

7   Taking advantage of the silence that had descended upon my grandfather, I turned my gaze from him to the vast area defined by his words. 'I don't care,' I told myself, 'who owns those date palms, those trees or this black, cracked earth—all I know is that it's the arena for my dreams and my playground.'

8   My grandfather then continued: 'Yes, my boy, forty years ago all this belonged to Masood—two-thirds of it is now mine.'

9   This was news to me for I had imagined that the land had belonged to my grandfather ever since God's Creation.

10   'I didn't own a single feddan when I first set foot in this village. Masood was then the owner of all these riches. The position has changed now, though, and I think that before Allah calls to Him I shall have bought the remaining third as well.'

11   I do not know why it was I felt fear at my grandfather's words—and pity for our neighbour Masood. How I wished my grandfather wouldn't do what he'd said! I remembered Masood's singing, his beautiful voice and powerful laugh that resembled the gurgling of water. My grandfather never used to laugh.

12   I asked my grandfather why Masood had sold his land.

13   'Women,' and from the way my grandfather pronounced the word I felt that 'women' was something terrible. 'Masood, my boy, was a much-married man. Each time he married he sold me a feddan or two.' I made the quick calculation that Masood must have married some ninety women. Then I remembered his three wives, his shabby appearance, his lame donkey and its dilapidated saddle, his djellaba with the torn sleeves. I had all but rid my mind of the thoughts that jostled in it when I saw the man approaching us, and my grandfather and I exchanged glances.

14   'We'll be harvesting the dates today,' said Masood. 'Don't you want to be there?'

15   I felt, though, that he did not really want my grandfather to attend. My grandfather, however, jumped to his feet and I saw that his eyes sparkled momentarily with an intense brightness. He pulled me by the hand and we went off to the harvesting of Masood's dates.

16   Someone brought my grandfather a stool covered with an oxhide, while I remained standing. There was a vast number of people there, but though I knew them all, I found myself for some reason, watching Masood: aloof from the great gathering of people he stood as though it were no concern of his, despite the fact that the date

palms to be harvested were his own. Sometimes his attention would be caught by the sound of a huge clump of dates crashing down from on high. Once he shouted up at the boy perched on the very summit of the date palm who had begun hacking at a clump with his long, sharp sickle: 'Be careful you don't cut the heart of the palm.'

17   No one paid any attention to what he said and the boy seated at the very summit of the date palm continued, quickly and energetically, to work away at the branch with his sickle till the clump of dates began to drop like something descending from the heavens.

18   I, however, had begun to think about Masood's phrase 'the heart of the palm'. I pictured the palm tree as something with feeling, something possessed of a heart that throbbed. I remembered Masood's remark to me when he had once seen me playing about with the branch of a young palm tree: 'Palm trees, my boy, like humans, experience joy and suffering.' And I had felt an inward and unreasoned embarrassment.

19   When I again looked at the expanse of ground stretching before me I saw my young companions swarming like ants around the trunks of the palm trees, gathering up dates and eating most of them. The dates were collected into high mounds. I saw people coming along and weighing them into measuring bins and pouring them into sacks, of which I counted thirty. The crowd of people broke up, except for Hussein the merchant, Mousa the owner of the field next to ours on the east, and two men I'd never seen before.

20   I heard a low whistling sound and saw that my grandfather had fallen asleep. Then I noticed that Masood had not changed his stance, except that he had placed a stalk in his mouth and was munching at it like someone surfeited with food who doesn't know what to do with the mouthful he still has.

Suddenly my grandfather woke up, jumped to his feet and walked towards the sacks of dates. He was followed by Hussein the merchant, Mousa the owner of the field next to ours, and the two strangers. I glanced at Masood and saw that he was making his way towards us with extreme slowness, like a man who wants to retreat but whose feet insist on going forward. They formed a circle round the sacks of dates and began examining them, some taking a date or two to eat. My grandfather gave me a fistful, which I began munching. I saw Masood filling the palms of both hands with dates and bringing them up close to his nose, then returning them.

21   Then I saw them dividing up the sacks between them. Hussein the merchant took ten; each of the strangers took five. Mousa the owner of the field next to ours on the eastern side took five, and my grandfather took five. Understanding nothing, I looked at Masood and saw that his eyes were darting about to left and right like two mice that have lost their way home.

22   'You're still fifty pounds in debt to me,' said my grandfather to Masood. 'We'll talk about it later.'

23   Hussein called his assistants and they brought along donkeys, the two strangers produced camels, and the sacks of dates were loaded on to them. One of the donkeys let out a braying which set the camels frothing at the mouth and complaining noisily. I felt myself drawing close to Masood, felt my hand stretch out towards him as though I wanted to touch the hem of his garment. I heard him make a noise in his throat like the rasping of a lamb being slaughtered. For some unknown reason, I experienced a sharp sensation of pain in my chest.

24   I ran off into the distance. Hearing my grandfather call after me, I hesitated a little, then continued on my way. I felt at that moment that I hated him. Quickening my pace, it was as though I carried within me a secret I wanted to rid myself of. I reached the river bank near the bend it made behind the wood of acacia trees. Then, without knowing why, I put my finger into my throat and spewed up the dates I'd eaten.

✦ Evaluating the Text

1. What is the role of the "Chapter of the Merciful" of the Koran in the child's reaction to the ensuing events in this story? What inferences might you draw about Salih's view of the Koran from this story?

2. Why does the boy so drastically change his attitude toward his grandfather?

3. Why does the boy wish "my grandfather wouldn't do what he said"? What is it that the grandfather is going to do? What values seem to motivate the boy's wishes, and how do they contrast with those of his grandfather? How does the boy bring a very different set of assumptions to the situation from that of the grandfather? How does this contrast in underlying assumptions explain the boy's disillusionment?

4. How do you know that Salih intends to show that the boy sympathizes with Masood and not with his grandfather?

5. How does the boy's reaction (in making himself vomit the dates he had eaten) relate to his reluctance to become the kind of person his grandfather would wish him to be?

✦ Exploring Different Perspectives

1. How does the grandfather's view of women in "A Handful of Dates" confirm what Fatima Mernissi suggests is a prevailing social view toward women in the harem in Morocco?

2. In what way does Daniela Deane's description of the shortages of resources in China contrast with Salih's description of the abundance found on the date farms in the Sudan?

✧ Extending Viewpoints through Writing

1. Has your attitude ever changed toward a member of your family or a close friend based on a business practice that showed you a side of their nature you had not known existed? Did you react as strongly as the boy in Salih's story? Did this event permanently alter your relationship? If so, in what way?

2. Has any major religious text (the Koran, the Old Testament, the New Testament, the Bhagavad Gita, etc.) had as profound an impact in shaping your ideals and attitudes as the Koran did for the boy in "A Handful of Dates"? Discuss your experiences.

Connecting Cultures

◆

Daniela Deane, "The Little Emperors"

Compare and contrast the childrearing practices in China, as described by Deane, with those of the !Kung in Botswana (see Marjorie Shostak's "Memories of a !Kung Girlhood," Chapter 2).

Gayatri Devi, "A Princess Remembers"

Contrast the very different life experiences and perspectives offered by Gayatri Devi and Viramma in "A Pariah's Life" (Chapter 5) at the extremes of society in India.

Fatima Mernissi, "Moonlit Nights of Laughter"

To what extent do Fatima Mernissi's and Elizabeth W. Fernea and Robert A. Fernea's accounts (Chapter 3) illustrate the restrictions Middle Eastern Moslem cultures place on women?

Pat Mora, "Remembering Lobo"

In what way does the idea of work well done connect with a successful adaptation to American society, for both Pat Mora's aunt, and Victor Villaseñor's father in "Rain of Gold" (Chapter 4)?

Gayle Pemberton, "Antidisestablishmentarianism"

In what ways do the grandmothers of Gayle Pemberton and Mary Crow Dog (see "Civilize Them with a Stick," Chapter 5) offer advice and a historical perspective on racism in American culture?

Colin Turnbull, "The Mbuti Pygmies"

What role do games that teach hunting and gathering skills play in both the Mbuti culture and in !Kung society (see Majorie Shostak's "Memories of a !Kung Girlhood," Chapter 2).

Kazuo Ishiguro, "A Family Supper"

The son obviously identifies with American cultural values that bring him into conflict with his father's traditional Japanese values. How does this issue enter into both this story and into Poranee Natadecha-Sponsel's analysis (see "Individualism as an American Culture Value," Chapter 7)?

Tayeb Salih, "A Handful of Dates"

How do both Salih's story and Hanan al-Shaykh's ("The Persian Carpet," Chapter 2) reach crisis points in which children see the actions of adults in a realistic light?

2

Coming of Age

◆

In virtually every society, certain rites or ceremonies are used to signal adulthood. Although many of these occasions are informal, some are quite elaborate and dramatic. This chapter offers a range of perspectives that illustrate how such turning points are marked by informal and formal rituals across a broad spectrum of cultures. These moments of insight may be private psychological turning points of ceremonies that initiate the individual into adulthood within a community. These crucial moments in which individuals move from childhood innocence to adult awareness often involve learning a particular society's rules governing what should or should not be done under different circumstances, values, knowledge, and expectations as to how one should present oneself in a wide variety of situations.

Coming of age often occurs during adolescence, when we explore the limits of what society will and will not allow us to do. This is the time when rebellion and defiance against society's rules take place. We acquire societal norms through imitation, identification, and instruction into what behavior patterns our society deems acceptable or unacceptable. From internalizing these values we get a sense of personal and social identity. This is often the time when we form our first voluntary associations or friendships and discover our capacity to trust and develop relationships, whether strong or fragile, that can lead to reward or disappointment.

In some cases, belonging to a group, association, fraternity, or sorority involves passing some initiation or test to gain acceptance. Because this chapter is rich in a wide variety of perspectives, it invites you to make discoveries about the turning points in your own life.

The essays and stories in this chapter focus on the psychological and cultural forces that shape the identity of those who are about to be initiated into their respective communities. From Ireland, we read the moving narrative of Christy Brown, who, in "The Letter 'A,'" describes his struggles to communicate signs of intelligence by drawing the letter *A* with his left foot after having been diagnosed as hopelessly retarded by cerebral palsy. The Chinese-American writer Sucheng Chan describes with honesty and humor her struggle to confront her disabilities, in "You're Short, Besides!" The renowned Egyptian feminist writer, Nawal El Saadawi, in "Circumcision of Girls," analyzes the cultural prejudices that still encourage the archaic and damaging practice of female circumcision in many countries of the Middle East. The international French explorer, Douchan Gersi, offers a hair-raising account appropriately titled "Initiated into an Iban Tribe of Headhunters," a firsthand narrative based on his experiences in modern-day Borneo. In the first autobiographical account ever written by a Maasai, Tepilit Ole Saitoti, in "The Initiation of a Maasai Warrior," describes the circumcision ceremony that served as his rite of passage into adulthood. Marjorie Shostak relates an account by Nisa, of the !Kung tribe in Botswana, who describes the stages she went through before accepting her role as a woman, in "Memories of a !Kung Girlhood."

The Lebanese writer Hanan al-Shaykh, tells a story, "The Persian Carpet," of a moment of discovery that permanently alters the relationship between a girl and her mother. Last, Wakako Yamauchi in "And the Soul Shall Dance," offers unparalleled insight into the harsh lives of Japanese immigrant families in California.

Christy Brown

The Letter "A"

◆

Christy Brown (1932–1981) was born in Dublin, the tenth child in a family of twenty-two. Brown was diagnosed as having cerebral palsy and being hopelessly retarded. An intense personal struggle and the loving attention and faith of his mother resulted in a surprising degree of rehabilitation. Brown's autobiography, My Left Foot *(1954), describing his struggle to overcome his massive handicap, was the basis for the 1989 Academy Award–winning film. Brown is also the author of an internationally acclaimed novel,* Down All the Days *(1970). "The Letter 'A,'" from his autobiography, describes the crucial moment when he first communicated signs of awareness and intelligence.*

The Republic of Ireland occupies all but the northeast corner of the island of Ireland, in the British Isles, and has a population of 3.5 million. Cork, founded in the seventh century, is the second-largest city in the Republic of Ireland. A treaty with Great Britain in 1922 partitioned Ireland into the Irish Free State and the six counties of Ulster in the northeast (whose population now numbers 1.5 million) and precipitated a civil war. The anti-treaty forces were identified with the Irish Republican Army (IRA), a nationalist organization that was defeated at the time but has continued to fight for the unification of Ireland. The ongoing conflict between Irish Roman Catholics and Ulster's Protestants stems from Henry VIII's attempt in 1541 to impose the Protestant Church of Ireland on the predominantly Catholic population. To this day, Ulster's Protestants and Catholics are divided over whether to remain under British rule or join the Republic of Ireland. In 1937, a new constitution was put forward, establishing the sovereign state of Ireland within the British Commonwealth. In 1949, the Republic of Ireland was proclaimed, and the country withdrew from the Commonwealth. Discussions with British authorities over the issue of returning Northern Ireland to Irish sovereignty have produced little progress. A high unemployment rate and a poor economy led to the collapse of Ireland's coalition government in 1992. A new coalition was formed under Albert Reynolds, who served as prime minister until 1994. Following his resignation, a new government was formed in April 1995, with John Bruton serving as prime minister until he was replaced by Bertie Aherne in 1997. The Good Friday Agreement of 1998 proposed a comprehensive settlement allowing for release of paramilitary prisoners and the decommissioning of IRA weapons. In 1999, Ireland adopted the Euro as its currency.

Before You Read

Notice how Brown draws on his own experiences to raise the larger issue of how children with disabilities should be treated.

———————◆———————

1   I was born in the Rotunda Hospital,[1] on June 5th, 1932. There were nine children before me and twelve after me, so I myself belong to the middle group. Out of this total of twenty-two, seventeen lived, but four died in infancy, leaving thirteen still to hold the family fort.

2   Mine was a difficult birth, I am told. Both mother and son almost died. A whole army of relations queued up outside the hospital until the small hours of the morning, waiting for news and praying furiously that it would be good.

3   After my birth Mother was sent to recuperate for some weeks and I was kept in the hospital while she was away. I remained there for some time, without name, for I wasn't baptized until my mother was well enough to bring me to church.

4   It was Mother who first saw that there was something wrong with me. I was about four months old at the time. She noticed that my head had a habit of falling backward whenever she tried to feed me. She attempted to correct this by placing her hand on the back of my neck to keep it steady. But when she took it away, back it would drop again. That was the first warning sign. Then she became aware of other defects as I got older. She saw that my hands were clenched nearly all of the time and were inclined to twine behind my back; my mouth couldn't grasp the teat of the bottle because even at that early age my jaws would either lock together tightly, so that it was impossible for her to open them, or they would suddenly become limp and fall loose, dragging my whole mouth to one side. At six months I could not sit up without having a mountain of pillows around me. At twelve months it was the same.

5   Very worried by this, Mother told my father her fears, and they decided to seek medical advice without any further delay. I was a little over a year old when they began to take me to hospitals and clinics, convinced that there was something definitely wrong with me, something which they could not understand or name, but which was very real and disturbing.

6   Almost every doctor who saw and examined me labeled me a very interesting but also a hopeless case. Many told Mother very gently that I was mentally defective and would remain so. That was a hard blow to a young mother who had already reared five healthy children. The doctors were so very sure of themselves that Mother's faith in me seemed almost an impertinence. They assured her that nothing could be done for me.

[1]Rotunda Hospital, a hospital in Dublin, Ireland.

7   She refused to accept this truth, the inevitable truth—as it then seemed—that I was beyond cure, beyond saving, even beyond hope. She could not and would not believe that I was an imbecile, as the doctors told her. She had nothing in the world to go by, not a scrap of evidence to support her conviction that, though my body was crippled, my mind was not. In spite of all the doctors and specialists told her, she would not agree. I don't believe she knew why—she just knew, without feeling the smallest shade of doubt.

8   Finding that the doctors could not help in any way beyond telling her not to place her trust in me, or, in other words, to forget I was a human creature, rather to regard me as just something to be fed and washed and then put away again, Mother decided there and then to take matters into her own hands. I was *her* child, and therefore part of the family. No matter how dull and incapable I might grow up to be, she was determined to treat me on the same plane as the others, and not as the "queer one" in the back room who was never spoken of when there were visitors present.

9   That was a momentous decision as far as my future life was concerned. It meant that I would always have my mother on my side to help me fight all the battles that were to come, and to inspire me with new strength when I was almost beaten. But it wasn't easy for her because now the relatives and friends had decided otherwise. They contended that I should be taken kindly, sympathetically, but not seriously. That would be a mistake. "For your own sake," they told her, "don't look to this boy as you would to the others; it would only break your heart in the end." Luckily for me, Mother and Father held out against the lot of them. But Mother wasn't content just to say that I was not an idiot: she set out to prove it, not because of any rigid sense of duty, but out of love. That is why she was so successful.

10   At this time she had the five other children to look after besides the "difficult one," though as yet it was not by any means a full house. They were my brothers, Jim, Tony, and Paddy, and my two sisters, Lily and Mona, all of them very young, just a year or so between each of them, so that they were almost exactly like steps of stairs.

11   Four years rolled by and I was now five, and still as helpless as a newly born baby. While my father was out at bricklaying, earning our bread and butter for us, Mother was slowly, patiently pulling down the wall, brick by brick, that seemed to thrust itself between me and the other children, slowly, patiently penetrating beyond the thick curtain that hung over my mind, separating it from theirs. It was hard, heartbreaking work, for often all she got from me in return was a vague smile and perhaps a faint gurgle. I could not speak or even mumble, nor could I sit up without support on my own, let alone take steps. But I wasn't inert or motionless. I seemed, indeed, to be convulsed with movement, wild, stiff, snakelike movement that never left me, except in sleep. My

fingers twisted and twitched continually, my arms twined backwards and would often shoot out suddenly this way and that, and my head lolled and sagged sideways. I was a queer, crooked little fellow.

12   Mother tells me how one day she had been sitting with me for hours in an upstairs bedroom, showing me pictures out of a great big storybook that I had got from Santa Claus last Christmas and telling me the names of the different animals and flowers that were in them, trying without success to get me to repeat them. This had gone on for hours while she talked and laughed with me. Then at the end of it she leaned over me and said gently into my ear:

13   "Did you like it, Chris? Did you like the bears and the monkeys and all the lovely flowers? Nod your head for yes, like a good boy."

14   But I could make no sign that I had understood her. Her face was bent over mine hopefully. Suddenly, involuntarily, my queer hand reached up and grasped one of the dark curls that fell in a thick cluster about her neck. Gently she loosened the clenched fingers, though some dark strands were still clutched between them.

15   Then she turned away from my curious stare and left the room, crying. The door closed behind her. It all seemed hopeless. It looked as though there was some justification for my relatives' contention that I was an idiot and beyond help.

16   They now spoke of an institution.

17   "Never!" said my mother almost fiercely, when this was suggested to her. "I know my boy is not an idiot; it is his body that is shattered, not his mind. I'm sure of that."

18   Sure? Yet inwardly, she prayed God would give her some proof of her faith. She knew it was one thing to believe but quite another thing to prove.

19   I was now five, and still I showed no real sign of intelligence. I showed no apparent interest in things except with my toes—more especially those of my left foot. Although my natural habits were clean, I could not aid myself, but in this respect my father took care of me. I used to lie on my back all the time in the kitchen or, on bright warm days, out in the garden, a little bundle of crooked muscles and twisted nerves, surrounded by a family that loved me and hoped for me and that made me part of their own warmth and humanity. I was lonely, imprisoned in a world of my own, unable to communicate with others, cut off, separated from them as though a glass wall stood between my existence and theirs, thrusting me beyond the sphere of their lives and activities. I longed to run about and play with the rest, but I was unable to break loose from my bondage.

20   Then, suddenly, it happened! In a moment everything was changed, my future life molded into a definite shape, my mother's faith in me rewarded, and her secret fear changed into open triumph.

21   It happened so quickly, so simply after all the years of waiting and uncertainty, that I can see and feel the whole scene as if it had hap-

pened last week. It was the afternoon of a cold, gray December day. The streets outside glistened with snow, the white sparkling flakes stuck and melted on the windowpanes and hung on the boughs of the trees like molten silver. The wind howled dismally, whipping up little whirling columns of snow that rose and fell at every fresh gust. And over all, the dull, murky sky stretched like a dark canopy, a vast infinity of grayness.

22 Inside, all the family were gathered round the big kitchen fire that lit up the little room with a warm glow and made giant shadows dance on the walls and ceiling.

23 In a corner Mona and Paddy were sitting, huddled together, a few torn school primers before them. They were writing down little sums onto an old chipped slate, using a bright piece of yellow chalk. I was close to them, propped up by a few pillows against the wall, watching.

24 It was the chalk that attracted me so much. It was a long, slender stick of vivid yellow. I had never seen anything like it before, and it showed up so well against the black surface of the slate that I was fascinated by it as much as if it had been a stick of gold.

25 Suddenly, I wanted desperately to do what my sister was doing. Then—without thinking or knowing exactly what I was doing, I reached out and took the stick of chalk out of my sister's hand—with my left foot.

26 I do not know why I used my left foot to do this. It is a puzzle to many people as well as to myself, for, although I had displayed a curious interest in my toes at an early age, I had never attempted before this to use either of my feet in any way. They could have been as useless to me as were my hands. That day, however, my left foot, apparently by its own volition, reached out and very impolitely took the chalk out of my sister's hand.

27 I held it tightly between my toes, and, acting on an impulse, made a wild sort of scribble with it on the slate. Next moment I stopped, a bit dazed, surprised, looking down at the stick of yellow chalk stuck between my toes, not knowing what to do with it next, hardly knowing how it got there. Then I looked up and became aware that everyone had stopped talking and was staring at me silently. Nobody stirred. Mona, her black curls framing her chubby little face, stared at me with great big eyes and open mouth. Across the open hearth, his face lit by flames, sat my father, leaning forward, hands outspread on his knees, his shoulders tense. I felt the sweat break out on my forehead.

28 My mother came in from the pantry with a steaming pot in her hand. She stopped midway between the table and the fire, feeling the tension flowing through the room. She followed their stare and saw me in the corner. Her eyes looked from my face down to my foot, with the chalk gripped between my toes. She put down the pot.

29 Then she crossed over to me and knelt down beside me, as she had done so many times before.

30   "I'll show you what to do with it, Chris," she said, very slowly and
in a queer, choked way, her face flushed as if with some inner excitement.

31   Taking another piece of chalk from Mona, she hesitated, then very
deliberately drew, on the floor in front of me, *the single letter "A."*

32   "Copy that," she said, looking steadily at me. "Copy it, Christy."

33   I couldn't.

34   I looked about me, looked around at the faces that were turned towards me, tense, excited faces that were at that moment frozen, immo-
bile, eager, waiting for a miracle in their midst.

35   The stillness was profound. The room was full of flame and
shadow that danced before my eyes and lulled my taut nerves into a
sort of waking sleep. I could hear the sound of the water tap dripping
in the pantry, the loud ticking of the clock on the mantel shelf, and the
soft hiss and crackle of the logs on the open hearth.

36   I tried again. I put out my foot and made a wild jerking stab with
the chalk which produced a very crooked line and nothing more.
Mother held the slate steady for me.

37   "Try again, Chris," she whispered in my ear. "Again."

38   I did. I stiffened my body and put my left foot out again, for the
third time. I drew one side of the letter. I drew half the other side. Then
the stick of chalk broke and I was left with a stump. I wanted to fling it
away and give up. Then I felt my mother's hand on my shoulder. I
tried once more. Out went my foot. I shook, I sweated and strained
every muscle. My hands were so tightly clenched that my fingernails
bit into the flesh. I set my teeth so hard that I nearly pierced my lower
lip. Everything in the room swam till the faces around me were mere
patches of white. But—I drew it—*the letter "A."* There it was on the
floor before me. Shaky, with awkward, wobbly sides and a very uneven center line. But it *was* the letter "A." I looked up. I saw my
mother's face for a moment, tears on her cheeks. Then my father
stooped and hoisted me onto his shoulder.

39   I had done it! It had started—the thing that was to give my mind
its chance of expressing itself. True, I couldn't speak with my lips. But
now I would speak through something more lasting than spoken
words—written words.

40   That one letter, scrawled on the floor with a broken bit of yellow
chalk gripped between my toes, was my road to a new world, my key
to mental freedom. It was to provide a source of relaxation to the tense,
taut thing that was I, which panted for expression behind a twisted
mouth.

✧ *Evaluating the Text*

    1. What unusual signs alerted Christy's mother that he might be
physically impaired? What did her response to the doctors' diag-
nosis reveal about her as a person and her attitude toward Christy?

2. What did Christy's mother hope to achieve by showing him pictures of animals and flowers? How did her friends and relatives react to her decision to treat Christy as if he were capable of mental development? How would Christy's day-to-day treatment have differed if his mother had not treated him as a member of the family?

3. Why does the narrative shift from Christy's mother's perspective to Christy's recollection of the day he was able to form the letter *A* with his left foot?

4. From the point of view of Christy's mother, father, and siblings, how did they know that his forming the letter *A* was a sign of intelligence and not merely an imitative gesture? How does the conclusion of this account suggest that this moment had deeper meaning for Christy than it did even for his family? What did this mean to him?

✧ Exploring Different Perspectives

1. In what way can Brown be considered to be just as courageous in meeting the challenge he faced as Tepilit Ole Saitoti was in exhibiting bravery during his initiation as a Maasai warrior (see "The Initiation of a Maasai Warrior")?

2. What similarities in coping with a disability can you discover in this account by Christy Brown and that of Sucheng Chan in "You're Short, Besides!"?

✧ Extending Viewpoints through Writing

1. On any given day, how do you think Christy would have been treated if his mother had not made the decision to treat him as a member of the family? Write two brief accounts analyzing why over a period of time the difference in the way he was treated might have been capable of producing the unexpected development Christy describes. Include in your account such everyday events as meals and visits from friends.

2. Rent a copy of the 1989 Academy Award–winning film *My Left Foot,* based on Christy Brown's autobiography of the same name, and discuss which treatment, film or written word, more effectively dramatized the issues at stake and the feelings of Christy and his family at the moment when he drew the letter *A*.

3. If you have ever been temporarily physically incapacitated or have a disability, write an essay that will help your audience understand your plight and the visible and subtle psychological aspects of discrimination that the disabled must endure every day.

Sucheng Chan

You're Short, Besides!

————◆————

Sucheng Chan graduated from Swarthmore College in 1963 and received an M.A. from the University of Hawaii in 1965. In 1973 she earned a Ph.D. from the University of California at Berkeley, where she subsequently taught for a decade. She is currently professor of history and chair of Asian-American studies at the University of California at Santa Barbara. Her works include Quiet Odyssey: A Pioneer Korean Woman in America *(1990) and the award-winning* The Asian Americans: An Interpretive History *(1991). "You're Short, Besides!" first appeared in* Making Waves: An Anthology of Writing by and about Asian-American Women *(1989). In recent years, she has served as the editor of numerous collections, including* Hmong Means Free: Life in Laos and America *(1994),* Major Problems in California History, *with Spencer C. Olin (1997), and* Claiming America: Constructing Chinese American Identities During the Exclusion Era, *with K. Scott Wong (1998).*

Before You Read

Consider to what extent culture shapes concepts of normalcy and disability and the ways in which Asian cultures in Chan's view differ from Western ones.

————◆————

1   When asked to write about being a physically handicapped Asian American woman, I considered it an insult. After all, my accomplishments are many, yet I was not asked to write about any of them. Is being handicapped the most salient feature about me? The fact that it might be in the eyes of others made me decide to write the essay as requested. I realized that the way I think about myself may differ considerably from the way others perceive me. And maybe that's what being physically handicapped is all about.

2   I was stricken simultaneously with pneumonia and polio at the age of four. Uncertain whether I had polio of the lungs, seven of the eight doctors who attended me—all practitioners of Western medicine—told my parents they should not feel optimistic about my survival. A Chinese fortune teller my mother consulted also gave a grim prognosis, but for an entirely different reason: I had been stricken be-

cause my name was offensive to the gods. My grandmother had named me "grandchild of wisdom," a name that the fortune teller said was too presumptuous for a girl. So he advised my parents to change my name to "chaste virgin." All these pessimistic predictions notwithstanding, I hung onto life, if only by a thread. For three years, my body was periodically pierced with electric shocks as the muscles of my legs atrophied. Before my illness, I had been an active, rambunctious, precocious, and very curious child. Being confined to bed was thus a mental agony as great as my physical pain. Living in war-torn China, I received little medical attention; physical therapy was unheard of. But I was determined to walk. So one day, when I was six or seven, I instructed my mother to set up two rows of chairs to face each other so that I could use them as I would parallel bars. I attempted to walk by holding my body up and moving it forward with my arms while dragging my legs along behind. Each time I fell, my mother gasped, but I badgered her until she let me try again. After four nonambulatory years, I finally walked once more by pressing my hands against my thighs so my knees wouldn't buckle.

3   My father had been away from home during most of those years because of the war. When he returned, I had to confront the guilt he felt about my condition. In many East Asian cultures, there is a strong folk belief that a person's physical state in this life is a reflection of how morally or sinfully he or she lived in previous lives. Furthermore, because of the tendency to view the family as a single unit, it is believed that the fate of one member can be caused by the behavior of another. Some of my father's relatives told him that my illness had doubtless been caused by the wild carousing he did in his youth. A well-meaning but somewhat simple man, my father believed them.

4   Throughout my childhood, he sometimes apologized to me for having to suffer retribution for his former bad behavior. This upset me; it was bad enough that I had to deal with the anguish of not being able to walk, but to have to assuage his guilt as well was a real burden! In other ways, my father was very good to me. He took me out often, carrying me on his shoulders or back, to give me fresh air and sunshine. He did this until I was too large and heavy for him to carry. And ever since I can remember, he has told me that I am pretty.

5   After getting over her anxieties about my constant falls, my mother decided to send me to school. I had already learned to read some words of Chinese at the age of three by asking my parents to teach me the sounds and meaning of various characters in the daily newspaper. But between the ages of four and eight, I received no education since just staying alive was a full-time job. Much to her chagrin, my mother found no school in Shanghai, where we lived at the time, which would accept me as a student. Finally, as a last resort, she

approached the American School, which agreed to enroll me only if my family kept an *amah* (a servant who takes care of children) by my side at all times. The tuition at the school was twenty U.S. dollars per month—a huge sum of money during those years of runaway inflation in China—and payable only in U.S. dollars. My family afforded the high cost of tuition and the expense of employing a full-time *amah* for less than a year.

6   We left China as the Communist forces swept across the country in victory. We found an apartment in Hong Kong across the street from a school run by Seventh-Day Adventists. By that time I could walk a little, so the principal was persuaded to accept me. An *amah* now had to take care of me only during recess when my classmates might easily knock me over as they ran about the playground.

7   After a year and a half in Hong Kong, we moved to Malaysia, where my father's family had lived for four generations. There I learned to swim in the lovely warm waters of the tropics and fell in love with the sea. On land I was a cripple; in the ocean I could move with the grace of a fish. I liked the freedom of being in the water so much that many years later, when I was a graduate student in Hawaii, I became greatly enamored with a man just because he called me a "Polynesian water nymph."

8   As my overall health improved, my mother became less anxious about all aspects of my life. She did everything possible to enable me to lead as normal a life as possible. I remember how once some of her colleagues in the high school where she taught criticized her for letting me wear short skirts. They felt my legs should not be exposed to public view. My mother's response was, "All girls her age wear short skirts, so why shouldn't she?"

9   The years in Malaysia were the happiest of my childhood, even though I was constantly fending off children who ran after me calling, *"Baikah! Baikah!"* ("Cripple! Cripple!" in the Hokkien dialect commonly spoken in Malaysia). The taunts of children mattered little because I was a star pupil. I won one award after another for general scholarship as well as for art and public speaking. Whenever the school had important visitors my teacher always called on me to recite in front of the class.

10   A significant event that marked me indelibly occurred when I was twelve. That year my school held a music recital and I was one of the students chosen to play the piano. I managed to get up the steps to the stage without any problem, but as I walked across the stage, I fell. Out of the audience, a voice said loudly and clearly, "Ayah! A *baikah* shouldn't be allowed to perform in public." I got up before anyone could get on stage to help me and, with tears streaming uncontrollably down my face, I rushed to the piano and began to play. Beethoven's "Für Elise" had never been played so fiendishly fast before or since,

but I managed to finish the whole piece. That I managed to do so made me feel really strong. I never again feared ridicule.

11   In later years I was reminded of this experience from time to time. During my fourth year as an assistant professor at the University of California at Berkeley, I won a distinguished teaching award. Some weeks later I ran into a former professor who congratulated me enthusiastically. But I said to him, "You know what? I became a distinguished teacher by *limping* across the stage of Dwinelle 155!" (Dwinelle 155 is a large, cold, classroom that most colleagues of mine hate to teach in.) I was rude not because I lacked graciousness but because this man, who had told me that my dissertation was the finest piece of work he had read in fifteen years, had nevertheless advised me to eschew a teaching career.

12   "Why?" I asked.

13   "Your leg . . ." he responded.

14   "What about my leg?" I said, puzzled.

15   "Well, how would you feel standing in front of a large lecture class?"

16   "If it makes any difference, I want you to know I've won a number of speech contests in my life, and I am not the least bit self-conscious about speaking in front of large audiences. . . . Look, why don't you write me a letter of recommendation to tell people how brilliant I am, and let *me* worry about my leg!"

17   This incident is worth recounting only because it illustrates a dilemma that handicapped persons face frequently: those who care about us sometimes get so protective that they unwittingly limit our growth. This former professor of mine had been one of my greatest supporters for two decades. Time after time, he had written glowing letters of recommendation on my behalf. He had spoken as he did because he thought he had my best interest at heart; he thought that if I got a desk job rather than one that required me to be a visible, public person, I would be spared the misery of being stared at.

18   Americans, for the most part, do not believe as Asians do that physically handicapped persons are morally flawed. But they are equally inept at interacting with those of us who are not able-bodied. Cultural differences in the perception and treatment of handicapped people are most clearly expressed by adults. Children, regardless of where they are, tend to be openly curious about people who do not look "normal." Adults in Asia have no hesitation in asking visibly handicapped people what is wrong with them, often expressing their sympathy with looks of pity, whereas adults in the United States try desperately to be polite by pretending not to notice.

19   One interesting response I often elicited from people in Asia but have never encountered in America is the attempt to link my physical condition to the state of my soul. Many a time while living and traveling

in Asia people would ask me what religion I belonged to. I would tell them that my mother is a devout Buddhist, that my father was baptized a Catholic but has never practiced Catholicism, and that I am an agnostic. Upon hearing this, people would try strenuously to convert me to their religion so that whichever God they believed in could bless me. If I would only attend this church or that temple regularly, they urged, I would surely get cured. Catholics and Buddhists alike have pressed religious medallions into my palm, telling me if I would wear these, the relevant deity or saint would make me well. Once while visiting the tomb of Muhammad Ali Jinnah in Karachi, Pakistan, an old Muslim, after finishing his evening prayers, spotted me, gestured toward my legs, raised his arms heavenward, and began a new round of prayers, apparently on my behalf.

20   In the United States adults who try to act "civilized" toward handicapped people by pretending they don't notice anything unusual sometimes end up ignoring handicapped people completely. In the first few months I lived in this country, I was struck by the fact that whenever children asked me what was the matter with my leg, their adult companions would hurriedly shush them up, furtively look at me, mumble apologies, and rush their children away. After a few months of such encounters, I decided it was my responsibility to educate these people. So I would say to the flustered adults, "It's okay, let the kid ask." Turning to the child, I would say, "When I was a little girl, no bigger than you are, I became sick with something called polio. The muscles of my leg shrank up and I couldn't walk very well. You're much luckier than I am because now you can get a vaccine to make sure you never get my disease. So don't cry when your mommy takes you to get a polio vaccine, okay?" Some adults and their little companions I talked to this way were glad to be rescued from embarrassment; others thought I was strange.

21   Americans have another way of covering up their uneasiness: they become jovially patronizing. Sometimes when people spot my crutch, they ask if I've had a skiing accident. When I answer that unfortunately it is something less glamorous than that they say, "I bet you *could* ski if you put your mind to it!" Alternately, at parties where people dance, men who ask me to dance with them get almost belligerent when I decline their invitation. They say, "Of course you can dance if you *want* to!" Some have given me pep talks about how if I would only develop the right mental attitude, I would have more fun in life.

22   Different cultural attitudes toward handicapped persons came out clearly during my wedding. My father-in-law, as solid a representative of middle America as could be found, had no qualms about objecting to the marriage on racial grounds, but he could bring himself to comment on my handicap only indirectly. He wondered why his son, who had dated numerous high school and college beauty queens, couldn't

marry one of them instead of me. My mother-in-law, a devout Christian, did not share her husband's prejudices, but she worried aloud about whether I could have children. Some Chinese friends of my parents, on the other hand, said that I was lucky to have found such a noble man, one who would marry me despite my handicap. I, for my part, appeared in church in a white lace wedding dress I had designed and made myself—a miniskirt!

23   How Asian Americans treat me with respect to my handicap tells me a great deal about their degree of acculturation. Recent immigrants behave just like Asians in Asia; those who have been here longer or who grew up in the United States behave more like their white counterparts. I have not encountered any distinctly Asian American pattern of response. What makes the experience of Asian American handicapped people unique is the duality of responses we elicit.

24   Regardless of racial or cultural background, most handicapped people have to learn to find a balance between the desire to attain physical independence and the need to take care of ourselves by not overtaxing our bodies. In my case, I've had to learn to accept the fact that leading an active life has its price. Between the ages of eight and eighteen, I walked without using crutches or braces but the effort caused my right leg to become badly misaligned. Soon after I came to the United States, I had a series of operations to straighten out the bones of my right leg; afterwards though my leg looked straighter and presumably better, I could no longer walk on my own. Initially my doctors fitted me with a brace, but I found wearing one cumbersome and soon gave it up. I could move around much more easily—and more important, faster—by using one crutch. One orthopedist after another warned me that using a single crutch was a bad practice. They were right. Over the years my spine developed a double-S curve and for the last twenty years I have suffered from severe, chronic back pains, which neither conventional physical therapy nor a lighter work load can eliminate.

25   The only thing that helps my backaches is a good massage, but the soothing effect lasts no more than a day or two. Massages are expensive, especially when one needs them three times a week. So I found a job that pays better, but at which I have to work longer hours, consequently increasing the physical strain on my body—a sort of vicious circle. When I was in my thirties, my doctors told me that if I kept leading the strenuous life I did, I would be in a wheelchair by the time I was forty. They were right on target; I bought myself a wheelchair when I was forty-one. But being the incorrigible character that I am, I use it only when I am *not* in a hurry!

26   It is a good thing, however, that I am too busy to think much about my handicap or my backaches because pain can physically debilitate as well as cause depression. And there are days when my spirits get

rather low. What has helped me is realizing that being handicapped is akin to growing old at an accelerated rate. The contradiction I experience is that often my mind races along as though I'm only twenty while my body feels about sixty. But fifteen or twenty years hence, unlike my peers who will have to cope with aging for the first time, I shall be full of cheer because I will have already fought, and I hope won, that battle long ago.

27   Beyond learning how to be physically independent and, for some of us, living with chronic pain or other kinds of discomfort, the most difficult thing a handicapped person has to deal with, especially during puberty and early adulthood, is relating to potential sexual partners. Because American culture places so much emphasis on physical attractiveness, a person with a shriveled limb, or a tilt to the head, or the inability to speak clearly, experiences great uncertainty—indeed trauma—when interacting with someone to whom he or she is attracted. My problem was that I was not only physically handicapped, small, and short, but worse, I also wore glasses and was smarter than all the boys I knew! Alas, an insurmountable combination. Yet somehow I have managed to have intimate relationships, all of them with extraordinary men. Not surprisingly, there have also been countless men who broke my heart—men who enjoyed my company "as a friend," but who never found the courage to date or make love with me, although I am sure my experience in this regard is no different from that of many able-bodied persons.

28   The day came when my backaches got in the way of having an active sex life. Surprisingly that development was liberating because I stopped worrying about being attractive to men. No matter how headstrong I had been, I, like most women of my generation, had had the desire to be alluring to men ingrained into me. And that longing had always worked like a brake on my behavior. When what men think of me ceased to be compelling, I gained greater freedom to be myself.

29   I've often wondered if I would have been a different person had I not been physically handicapped. I really don't know, though there is no question that being handicapped has marked me. But at the same time I usually do not *feel* handicapped—and consequently, I do not act handicapped. People are therefore less likely to treat me as a handicapped person. There is no doubt, however, that the lives of my parents, sister, husband, other family members, and some close friends have been affected by my physical condition. They have had to learn not to hide me away at home, not to feel embarrassed by how I look or react to people who say silly things to me, and not to resent me for the extra demands my condition makes on them. Perhaps the hardest thing for those who live with handicapped people is to know when and how to offer help. There are no guidelines applicable to all situations. My advice is, when in doubt, ask, but ask in a way that does not

smack of pity or embarrassment. Most important, please don't talk to us as though we are children.

30   So, has being physically handicapped been a handicap? It all depends on one's attitude. Some years ago, I told a friend that I had once said to an affirmative action compliance officer (somewhat sardonically since I do not believe in the head count approach to affirmative action) that the institution which employs me is triply lucky because it can count me as non-white, female and handicapped. He responded, "Why don't you tell them to count you four times? . . . Remember, you're short, besides!"

✧ Evaluating the Text

1. What insight into cross-cultural perceptions of disabilities do you get from Chan's account? Specifically, how do Asian perceptions of disabilities differ from those in America?

2. To what extent did Chan have to overcome the well-meaning advice of family and friends and discount their perception of her diminished potential?

3. Chan has very strongly developed views; that is, she is an agnostic, doesn't believe in affirmative action, is uninhibited about sex, and has an unusual attitude toward the debilitating nature of her handicap. Which of her responses toward events made you aware of her unique personality?

✧ Exploring Different Perspectives

1. What personal attributes link Sucheng Chan with Christy Brown in confronting disabilities? (See "The Letter 'A.'")

2. How do the accounts by Sucheng Chan and Nawal El Saadawi, in "Circumcision of Girls," reveal stereotyped attitudes toward girls in the traditional cultures of China and the Middle East?

✧ Extending Viewpoints through Writing

1. To what extent are attitudes toward disability conditioned by cultural forces?

2. Do you know anyone who has a sense of irony and detachment similar to Chan's toward a disability or ailment? Write a short account of how this attitude enables him or her to cope with circumstances that might devastate another person.

Nawal El Saadawi

Circumcision of Girls

◆

Nawal El Saadawi is an Egyptian physician and feminist writer whose work publicizing the injustices and brutalities to which Arab women are subject is well known throughout the world. Born in the village of Kafr-tahla on the banks of the Nile, in 1931, she began her medical practice in rural areas, then in Cairo, and finally became Egypt's Director of Public Health. The publication of her first nonfiction book, Women and Sex *(1972), resulted in her dismissal from her post by Anwar Sadat, imprisonment, and censorship of her books on the status, psychology, and sexuality of women. Her works are now banned in Egypt, Saudi Arabia, and Libya. The following chapter, "Circumcision of Girls," is from* The Hidden Face of Eve: Women in the Arab World *(1980, translated and edited by Saadawi's husband, Dr. Sherif Hetata), a work depicting the hitherto unpublicized but culturally accepted procedure of female circumcision, a practice to which she herself was subjected at the age of eight.* A Daughter of Isis: The Autobiography of Nawal El Saadawi *was translated into English from the Arabic in 1999.*

Egypt is an Arab republic in northeastern Africa, bordered by the Mediterranean in the north, Israel and the Red Sea to the east, the Sudan to the south, and Libya to the west. Egypt was the site of one of the earliest civilizations that developed in the Nile valley over 5,000 years ago and flourished until it became part of the Roman Empire in 30 B.C. As always, Egypt depends on the Nile River for maintaining arable lands, and its economy, although weakened in the 1980s by earlier Arab–Israeli wars, remains primarily agricultural. Under the leadership of Anwar Sadat, in 1979, Egypt became the first Arab nation to sign a peace treaty with Israel. In 1981, Sadat was assassinated by Muslim fundamentalists, and his successor, Hosni Mubarak, has faced the difficult task of dealing with the resurgence of Islamic fundamentalism while moving Egypt into a position of leadership in the Arab world. Egypt joined the United States and other nations in sending troops to Saudi Arabia after the August 1990 invasion of Kuwait by Iraq. Saadawi's analysis reveals the extent to which women's lives in the Middle East are constrained by age-old Islamic laws and customs. In October of 1993, Hosni Mubarak was sworn in for a third six-year term as president.

Before You Read

Consider how El Saadawi is careful to present herself as a physician articulating and supporting a claim, and not as someone who is simply a victim.

1   The practice of circumcising girls is still a common procedure in a number of Arab countries such as Egypt, the Sudan, Yemen and some of the Gulf states.

2   The importance given to virginity and an intact hymen in these societies is the reason why female circumcision still remains a very widespread practice despite a growing tendency, especially in urban Egypt, to do away with it as something outdated and harmful. Behind circumcision lies the belief that, by removing parts of girls' external genital organs, sexual desire is minimized. This permits a female who has reached the 'dangerous age' of puberty and adolescence to protect her virginity, and therefore her honour, with greater ease. Chastity was imposed on male attendants in the female harem by castration which turned them into inoffensive eunuchs. Similarly female circumcision is meant to preserve the chastity of young girls by reducing their desire for sexual intercourse.

3   Circumcision is most often performed on female children at the age of seven or eight (before the girl begins to get menstrual periods). On the scene appears the *daya* or local midwife. Two women members of the family grasp the child's thighs on either side and pull them apart to expose the external genital organs and to prevent her from struggling—like trussing a chicken before it is slain. A sharp razor in the hand of the *daya* cuts off the clitoris.

4   During my period of service as a rural physician, I was called upon many times to treat complications arising from this primitive operation, which very often jeopardized the life of young girls. The ignorant *daya* believed that effective circumcision necessitated a deep cut with the razor to ensure radical amputation of the clitoris, so that no part of the sexually sensitive organ would remain. Severe hemorrhage was therefore a common occurrence and sometimes led to loss of life. The *dayas* had not the slightest notion of asepsis, and inflammatory conditions as a result of the operation were common. Above all, the lifelong psychological shock of this cruel procedure left its imprint on the personality of the child and accompanied her into adolescence, youth and maturity. Sexual frigidity is one of the after-effects which is accentuated by other social and psychological factors that influence the personality and mental make-up of females in Arab societies. Girls are therefore exposed to a whole series of misfortunes as a result of outdated notions and values related to virginity, which still remains the fundamental criterion of a girl's honour. In recent years, however, educated

families have begun to realize the harm that is done by the practice of
female circumcision.

5   Nevertheless a majority of families still impose on young female
children the barbaric and cruel operation of circumcision. The research
that I carried out on a sample of 160 Egyptian girls and women showed
the 97.5% of uneducated families still insisted on maintaining the custom, but this percentage dropped to 66.2% among educated families.[1]

6   When I discussed the matter with these girls and women it tran-
spired that most of them had no idea of the harm done by circumcision, and some of them even thought that it was good for one's health
and conducive to cleanliness and 'purity.' (The operation in the common language of the people is in fact called the cleansing or purifying
operation.) Despite the fact that the percentage of educated women
who have undergone circumcision is only 66.2%, as compared with
97.5% among uneducated women, even the former did not realize the
effect that this amputation of the clitoris could have on their psychological and sexual health. The dialogue that occurred between these
women and myself would run more or less as follows:

7   'Have you undergone circumcision?'

8   'Yes.'

9   'How old were you at the time?'

10   'I was a child, about seven or eight years old.'

11   'Do you remember the details of the operation?'

12   'Of course. How could I possibly forget?'

13   'Were you afraid?'

14   'Very afraid. I hid on top of the cupboard [in other cases she would
say under the bed, or in the neighbour's house], but they caught hold
of me, and I felt my body tremble in their hands.'

15   'Did you feel any pain?'

16   'Very much so. It was like a burning flame and I screamed. My
mother held my head so that I could not move it, my aunt caught hold
of my right arm and my grandmother took charge of my left. Two
strange women whom I had not seen before tried to keep me from
moving my thighs by pushing them as far apart as possible. The *daya*
sat between these two women, holding a sharp razor in her hand
which she used to cut off the clitoris. I was scared and suffered such
great pain that I lost consciousness at the flame that seemed to sear me
through and through.'

17   'What happened after the operation?'

18   'I had severe bodily pains, and remained in bed for several days,
unable to move. The pain in my external genital organs led to retention
of urine. Every time I wanted to urinate the burning sensation was so
unbearable that I could not bring myself to pass water. The wound
continued to bleed for some time, and my mother used to change the
dressing for me twice a day.'

19   'What did you feel on discovering that a small organ in your body had been removed?'

20   'I did not know anything about the operation at the time, except that it was very simple, and that it was done to all girls for purposes of cleanliness, purity and the preservation of a good reputation. It was said that a girl who did not undergo this operation was liable to be talked about by people, her behaviour would become bad, and she would start running after men, with the result that no one would agree to marry her when the time for marriage came. My grandmother told me that the operation had only consisted in the removal of a very small piece of flesh from between my thighs, and that the continued existence of this small piece of flesh in its place would have made me unclean and impure, and would have caused the man whom I would marry to be repelled by me.'

21   'Did you believe what was said to you?'

22   'Of course I did. I was happy the day I recovered from the effects of the operation, and felt as though I was rid of something which had to be removed, and so had become clean and pure.'

23   Those were more or less the answers that I obtained from all those interviewed, whether educated or uneducated. One of them was a medical student from Ein Shams School of Medicine. She was preparing for her final examinations and I expected her answers to be different but in fact they were almost identical to the others. We had quite a long discussion which I reproduce here as I remember it.

24   'You are going to be a medical doctor after a few weeks, so how can you believe that cutting off the clitoris from the body of a girl is a healthy procedure, or at least not harmful?'

25   'This is what I was told by everybody. All the girls in my family have been circumcised. I have studied anatomy and medicine, yet I have never heard any of the professors who taught us explain that the clitoris had any function to fulfill in the body of a woman, neither have I read anything of the kind in the books which deal with the medical subjects I am studying.'

26   'That is true. To this day medical books do not consider the science of sex as a subject which they should deal with. The organs of a woman worthy of attention are considered to be only those directly related to reproduction, namely the vagina, the uterus and the ovaries. The clitoris, however, is an organ neglected by medicine, just as it is ignored and disdained by society.'

27   'I remember a student asking the professor one day about the clitoris. The professor went red in the face and answered him curtly, saying that no one was going to ask him about this part of the female body during examinations, since it was of no importance.'

28   My studies led me to try and find out the effect of circumcision on the girls and women who had been made to undergo it, and to

understand what results it had on the psychological and sexual life. The majority of the normal cases I interviewed answered that the operation had no effect on them. To me it was clear that in the face of such questions they were much more ashamed and intimidated than the neurotic cases were. But I did not allow myself to be satisfied with these answers, and would go on to question them closely about their sexual life both before and after the circumcision was done. Once again I will try to reproduce the dialogue that usually occurred.

29   'Did you experience any change of feeling or of sexual desire after the operation?'

30   'I was a child and therefore did not feel anything.'

31   'Did you not experience any sexual desire when you were a child?'

32   'No, never. Do children experience sexual desire?'

33   'Children feel pleasure when they touch their sexual organs, and some form of sexual play occurs between them, for example, during the game of bride and bridegroom usually practised under the bed. Have you never played this game with your friends when still a child?'

34   At these words the young girl or woman would blush, and her eyes would probably refuse to meet mine, in an attempt to hide her confusion. But after the conversation had gone on for some time, and an atmosphere of mutual confidence and understanding had been established, she would begin to recount her childhood memories. She would often refer to the pleasure she had felt when a man of the family permitted himself certain sexual caresses. Sometimes these caresses would be proffered by the domestic servant, the house porter, the private teacher or the neighbour's son. A college student told me that her brother had been wont to caress her sexual organs and that she used to experience acute enjoyment. However after undergoing circumcision she no longer had the same sensation of pleasure. A married woman admitted that during intercourse with her husband she had never experienced the slightest sexual enjoyment, and that her last memories of any form of pleasurable sensation went back twenty years, to the age of six, before she had undergone circumcision. A young girl told me that she had been accustomed to practise masturbation, but had given it up completely after removal of the clitoris at the age of ten.

35   The further our conversations went, and the more I delved into their lives, the more readily they opened themselves up to me and uncovered the secrets of childhood and adolescence, perhaps almost forgotten by them or only vaguely realized.

36   Being both a woman and a medical doctor I was able to obtain confessions from these women and girls which it would be almost impossible, except in very rare cases, for a man to obtain. For the Egyptian woman, accustomed as she is to a very rigid and severe upbringing built on a complete denial of any sexual life before marriage, adamantly refuses to admit that she has even known, or experienced, anything re-

lated to sex before the first touches of her husband. She is therefore ashamed to speak about such things with any man, even the doctor who is treating her.

37   My discussions with some of the psychiatrists who had treated a number of the young girls and women in my sample, led me to conclude that there were many aspects of the life of these neurotic patients that remained unknown to them. This was due either to the fact that the psychiatrist himself had not made the necessary effort to penetrate deeply into the life of the woman he was treating, or to the tendency of the patient herself not to divulge those things which her upbringing made her consider matters not to be discussed freely, especially with a man.

38   In fact the long and varied interchanges I had over the years with the majority of practising psychiatrists in Egypt, my close association with a large number of my medical colleagues during the long periods I spent working in health centres and general or specialized hospitals and, finally, the four years I spent as a member of the National Board of the Syndicate of Medical Professions, have all led me to the firm conclusion that the medical profession in our society is still incapable of understanding the fundamental problems with which sick people are burdened, whether they be men or women, but especially if they are women. For the medical profession, like any other profession in society, is governed by the political, social and moral values which predominate, and like other professions is one of the institutions which is utilized more often than not to protect these values and perpetuate them.

39   Men represent the vast majority in the medical profession, as in most professions. But apart from this, the mentality of women doctors differs little, if at all, from that of the men, and I have known quite a number of them who were even more rigid and backward in outlook than their male colleagues.

40   A rigid and backward attitude towards most problems, and in particular towards women and sex, predominates in the medical profession, and particularly within the precincts of the medical colleges in the Universities.

41   Before undertaking my research study on 'Women and Neurosis' at Ein Shams University, I had made a previous attempt to start it at the Kasr El Eini Medical College in the University of Cairo, but had been obliged to give up as a result of the numerous problems I was made to confront. The most important obstacle of all was the overpowering traditionalist mentality that characterized the professors responsible for my research work, and to whom the word 'sex' could only be equated to the word 'shame.' 'Respectable research' therefore could not possibly have sex as its subject, and should under no circumstances think of penetrating into areas even remotely related to it. One of my medical colleagues in the Research Committee advised me not to refer at all to

the question of sex in the title of my research paper, when I found my-self obliged to shift to Ein Shams University. He warned me that any such reference would most probably lead to fundamental objections which would jeopardize my chances of going ahead with it. I had ini-tially chosen to define my subject as 'Problems that confront the sexual life of modern Egyptian women,' but after prolonged negotiations I was prevailed to delete the word 'sexual' and replace it by 'psycholog-ical.' Only thus was it possible to circumvent the sensitivities of the professors at the Ein Shams Medical School and obtain their consent to go ahead with the research.

42   After I observed the very high percentages of women and girls who had been obliged to undergo circumcision, or who had been ex-posed to different forms of sexual violation or assault in their child-hood, I started to look for research undertaken in these two areas, ei-ther in the medical colleges or in research institutes, but in vain. Hardly a single medical doctor or researcher had ventured to do any work on these subjects, in view of the sensitive nature of the issues in-volved. This can also be explained by the fact that most of the research carried out in such institutions is of a formal and superficial nature, since its sole aim is to obtain a degree or promotion. The path of safety is therefore the one to choose, and safety means to avoid carefully all subjects of controversy. No one is therefore prepared to face difficulties with the responsible academic and scientific authorities, or to engage in any form of struggle against them, or their ideas. Nor is anyone pre-pared to face up to those who lay down the norms of virtue, morals and religious behaviour in society. All the established leaderships in the area related to such matters suffer from a pronounced allergy to the word 'sex,' and any of its implications, especially if it happens to be linked to the word 'woman.'

43   Nevertheless I was fortunate enough to discover a small number of medical doctors who had the courage to be different, and therefore to examine some of the problems related to the sexual life of women. I would like to cite, as one of the rare examples, the only research study carried out on the question of female circumcision in Egypt and its harmful effects. This was the joint effort of Dr. Mahmoud Koraim and Dr. Rushdi Ammar, both from Ein Shams Medical College, and which was published in 1965. It is composed of two parts, the first of which was printed under the title *Female Circumcision and Sexual Desire*,[2] and the second, under the title *Complications of Female Circumcision*.[3] The con-clusions arrived at as a result of this research study, which covered 651 women circumcised during childhood, may be summarized as follows:

44   1. Circumcision is an operation with harmful effects on the health of women, and is the cause of sexual shock to young girls. It reduces the capacity of a woman to reach the peak of her sexual pleasure (i.e., or-gasm) and has a definite though lesser effect in reducing sexual desire.

45   2. Education helps to limit the extent to which female circumcision is practised, since educated parents have an increasing tendency to refuse the operation for their daughters. On the other hand, uneducated families still go in for female circumcision in submission to prevailing traditions, or in the belief that removal of the clitoris reduces the sexual desire of the girl, and therefore helps to preserve her virginity and chastity after marriage.

46   3. There is no truth whatsoever in the idea that female circumcision helps in reducing the incidence of cancerous disease of the external genital organs.

47   4. Female circumcision in all its forms and degrees, and in particular the fourth degree known as Pharaonic or Sudanese excision, is accompanied by immediate or delayed complications such as inflammations, haemorrhage, disturbances in the urinary passages, cysts or swellings that can obstruct the urinary flow or the vaginal opening.

48   5. Masturbation in circumcised girls is less frequent than was observed by Kinsey in girls who have not undergone this operation.

49   I was able to exchange views with Dr. Mahmoud Koraim during several meetings in Cairo. I learnt from him that he had faced numerous difficulties while undertaking his research, and was the target of bitter criticism from some of his colleagues and from religious leaders who considered themselves the divinely appointed protectors of morality, and therefore required to shield society from such impious undertakings, which constituted a threat to established values and moral codes.

50   The findings of my research study coincide with some of the conclusions arrived at by my two colleagues on a number of points. There is no longer any doubt that circumcision is the source of sexual and psychological shock in the life of the girl, and leads to a varying degree of sexual frigidity according to the woman and her circumstances. Education helps parents realize that this operation is not beneficial, and should be avoided, but I have found that the traditional education given in our schools and universities, whose aim is simply some certificate, or degree, rather than instilling useful knowledge and culture, is not very effective in combating the long-standing, and established traditions that govern Egyptian society, and in particular those related to sex, virginity in girls, and chastity in women. These areas are strongly linked to moral and religious values that have dominated and operated in our society for hundreds of years.

51   Since circumcision of females aims primarily at ensuring virginity before marriage, and chastity throughout, it is not to be expected that its practice will disappear easily from Egyptian society or within a short period of time. A growing number of educated families are, however, beginning to realize the harm that is done to females by this custom,

and are therefore seeking to protect their daughters from being among its victims. Parallel to these changes, the operation itself is no longer performed in the old primitive way, and the more radical degrees approaching, or involving, excision are dying out more rapidly. Nowadays, even in upper Egypt and the Sudan, the operation is limited to the total, or more commonly the partial, amputation of the clitoris. Nevertheless, while undertaking my research, I was surprised to discover, contrary to what I had previously thought, that even in educated urban families over 50% still consider circumcision as essential to ensure female virginity and chastity.

52   Many people think that female circumcision only started with the advent of Islam. But as a matter of fact it was well known and widespread in some areas of the world before the Islamic era, including in the Arab peninsula. Mahomet the Prophet tried to oppose this custom since he considered it harmful to the sexual health of the woman. In one of his sayings the advice reported as having been given by him to Om Attiah, a woman who did tattooings and circumcision, runs as follows: 'If you circumcise, take only a small part and refrain from cutting most of the clitoris off . . . The woman will have a bright and happy face, and is more welcome to her husband, if her pleasure is complete.'[4]

53   This means that the circumcision of girls was not originally an Islamic custom, and was not related to monotheistic religions, but was practised in societies with widely varying religious backgrounds, in countries of the East and the West, and among peoples who believed in Christianity, or in Islam, or were atheistic . . . Circumcision was known in Europe as late as the 19th century, as well as in countries like Egypt, the Sudan, Somaliland, Ethiopia, Kenya, Tanzania, Ghana, Guinea and Nigeria. It was also practised in many Asian countries such as Sri Lanka and Indonesia, and in parts of Latin America. It is recorded as going back far into the past under the Pharaonic Kingdoms of Ancient Egypt, and Herodotus mentioned the existence of female circumcision seven hundred years before Christ was born. This is why the operation as practised in the Sudan is called 'Pharaonic excision.'

54   For many years I tried in vain to find relevant sociological or anthropological studies that would throw some light on the reasons why such a brutal operation is practised on females. However I did discover other practices related to girls and female children which were even more savage. One of them was burying female children alive almost immediately after they were born, or even at a later stage. Other examples are the chastity belt, or closing the aperture of the external genital organs with steel pins and a special iron lock.[5] This last procedure is extremely primitive and very much akin to Sudanese circumcision where the clitoris, external lips and internal lips are completely excised, and the orifice of the genital organs closed with a flap of sheep's intestines leaving only a very small opening barely sufficient to let the tip of the finger in, so that the menstrual and urinary flows

are not held back. This opening is slit at the time of marriage and widened to allow penetration of the male sexual organ. It is widened again when a child is born and then narrowed down once more. Complete closure of the aperture is also done on a woman who is divorced, so that she literally becomes a virgin once more and can have no sexual intercourse except in the eventuality of marriage, in which case the opening is restored.

55   In the face of all these strange and complicated procedures aimed at preventing sexual intercourse in women except if controlled by the husband, it is natural that we should ask ourselves why women, in particular, were subjected to such torture and cruel suppression. There seems to be no doubt that society, as represented by its dominant classes and male structure, realized at a very early stage that sexual desire in the female is very powerful, and that women, unless controlled and subjugated by all sorts of measures, will not submit themselves to the moral, social, legal and religious constraints with which they have been surrounded, and in particular the constraints related to monogamy. The patriarchal system, which came into being when society had reached a certain stage of development and which necessitated the imposition of one husband on the woman whereas a man was left free to have several wives, would never have been possible, or have been maintained to this day, without the whole range of cruel and ingenious devices that were used to keep her sexuality in check and limit her sexual relations to only one man, who had to be her husband. This is the reason for the implacable enmity shown by society towards female sexuality, and the weapons used to resist and subjugate the turbulent force inherent in it. The slightest leniency in facing this 'potential danger' meant that woman would break out of the prison bars to which marriage had confined her, and step over the steely limits of a monogamous relationship to a forbidden intimacy with another man, which would inevitably lead to confusion in succession and inheritance, since there was no guarantee that a strange man's child would not step into the waiting line of descendants. Confusion between the children of the legitimate husband and the outside lover would mean the unavoidable collapse of the patriarchal family built around the name of the father alone.

56   History shows us clearly that the father was keen on knowing who his real children were, solely for the purpose of handing down his landed property to them. The patriarchal family, therefore, came into existence mainly for economic reasons. It was necessary for society simultaneously to build up a system of moral and religious values, as well as a legal system capable of protecting and maintaining these economic interests. In the final analysis we can safely say that female circumcision, the chastity belt and other savage practices applied to women are basically the result of the economic interests that govern society. The continued existence of such practices in our society today signifies that these economic interests are still operative. The thousands of

dayas, nurses, paramedical staff and doctors, who make money out of female circumcision, naturally resist any change in these values and practices which are a source of gain to them. In the Sudan there is a veritable army of *dayas* who earn a livelihood out of the series of operations performed on women, either to excise their external genital organs, or to alternately narrow and widen the outer aperture according to whether the woman is marrying, divorcing, remarrying, having a child or recovering from labour.[6]

57   Economic factors and, concomitantly, political factors are the basis upon which such customs as female circumcision have grown up. It is important to understand the facts as they really are, the reasons that lie behind them. Many are the people who are not able to distinguish between political and religious factors, or who conceal economic and political motives behind religious arguments in an attempt to hide the real forces that lie at the basis of what happens in society and in history. It has very often been proclaimed that Islam is at the root of female circumcision, and is also responsible for the under-privileged and backward situation of women in Egypt and the Arab countries. Such a contention is not true. If we study Christianity it is easy to see that this religion is much more rigid and orthodox where women are concerned than Islam. Nevertheless, many countries were able to progress rapidly despite the preponderance of Christianity as a religion. This progress was social, economic, scientific and also affected the life and position of women in society.

58   That is why I firmly believe that the reasons for the lower status of women in our societies, and the lack of opportunities for progress afforded to them, are not due to Islam, but rather to certain economic and political forces, namely those of foreign imperialism operating mainly from the outside, and of the reactionary classes operating from the inside. These two forces cooperate closely and are making a concerted attempt to misinterpret religion and to utilize it as an instrument of fear, oppression and exploitation.

59   Religion, if authentic in the principles it stands for, aims at truth, equality, justice, love and a healthy wholesome life for all people, whether men or women. There can be no true religion that aims at disease, mutilation of the bodies of female children, and amputation of an essential part of their reproductive organs.

60   If religion comes from God, how can it order man to cut off an organ created by Him as long as that organ is not diseased or deformed? God does not create the organs of the body haphazardly without a plan. It is not possible that He should have created the clitoris in woman's body only in order that it be cut off at an early stage in life. This is a contradiction into which neither true religion nor the Creator could possibly fall. If God has created the clitoris as a sexually sensitive organ, whose sole function seems to be the procurement of sexual pleasure for women, it follows that He also considers such pleasure for

women as normal and legitimate, and therefore as an integral part of mental health. The psychic and mental health of women cannot be complete if they do not experience sexual pleasure.

61   There are still a large number of fathers and mothers who are afraid of leaving the clitoris intact in the bodies of their daughters. Many a time they have said to me that circumcision is a safeguard against the mistakes and deviations into which a girl may be led. This way of thinking is wrong and even dangerous because what protects a boy or a girl from making mistakes is not the removal of a small piece of flesh from the body, but consciousness and understanding of the problems we face, and a worthwhile aim in life, an aim which gives it meaning and for whose attainment we exert our mind and energies. The higher the level of consciousness to which we attain, the closer our aims draw to human motives and values, and the greater our desire to improve life and its quality, rather than to indulge ourselves in the mere satisfaction of our senses and the experience of pleasure, even though these are an essential part of existence. The most liberated and free of girls, in the true sense of liberation, are the least preoccupied with sexual questions, since these no longer represent a problem. On the contrary, a free mind finds room for numerous interests and the many rich experiences of a cultured life. Girls that suffer sexual suppression, however, are greatly preoccupied with men and sex. And it is a common observation that an intelligent and cultured woman is much less engrossed in matters related to sex and to men than is the case with ordinary women, who have not got much with which to fill their lives. Yet at the same time such a woman takes much more initiative to ensure that she will enjoy sex and experience pleasure, and acts with a greater degree of boldness than others. Once sexual satisfaction is attained, she is able to turn herself fully to other important aspects of life.

62   In the life of liberated and intelligent women, sex does not occupy a disproportionate position, but rather tends to maintain itself within normal limits. In contrast, ignorance, suppression, fear and all sorts of limitations exaggerate the role of sex in the life of girls and women, and cause it to swell out of all proportion and to end up by occupying the whole, or almost the whole, of their lives.

REFERENCES

1. This research study was carried out in the years 1973 and 1974 in the School of Medicine, Ein Shams University, under the title: *Women and Neurosis.*
2. *Female Circumcision and Sexual Desire*, Mahmoud Koraim and Rushdi Ammar (Ein Shams University Press, Cairo, 1965).
3. *Complications of Female Circumcision*, the same authors (Cairo, 1965).
4. See *Dawlat El Nissa'a*, Abdel Rahman El Barkouky, first edition (Renaissance Bookshop, Cairo, 1945).
5. Desmond Morris, *The Naked Ape* (Corgi, 1967), p. 76.
6. Rose Oldfield, 'Female genital mutilation, fertility control, women's roles, and patrilineage in modern Sudan,' *American Ethnologist*, Vol. II, No. 4, November 1975.

✧ *Evaluating the Text*

1. How does the fact that El Saadawi herself is a physician who has treated girls suffering the medical complications of circumcision enhance the credibility of her analysis?

2. Why does El Saadawi find it so distressing that, even among the educated (of whom two-thirds have undergone the operation), few women have given up the cultural programming that female circumcision is a purifying or cleansing procedure?

3. What are the psychological and economic objectives of female circumcision? How, in El Saadawi's view, does it function as one of the main methods by which the countries of Sudan, Yemen, Saudi Arabia, and Libya keep their social structure intact and ensure the transmission of property from one generation to the next?

4. Do you believe that the 160 interviews she conducted would be a sample sufficiently large to form the basis for generalizations? Why was the interview with the medical student particularly significant? What harmful psychological effects of female circumcision did El Saadawi discover from the interviews she conducted?

5. What prevailing beliefs did Koraim and Ammar's study about the supposed medical efficacy of circumcision disclose to be baseless? How does El Saadawi use the results of their study in her analysis?

6. How does El Saadawi's reference to Mahomet's comment support her claim that female circumcision was not originally an Islamic custom? How is this phase of her argument intended to undercut claims by religious leaders that they are simply upholding Islamic religious values?

✧ *Exploring Different Perspectives*

1. How is circumcision intended to physically and psychologically restrict girls in Middle Eastern cultures described by El Saadawi and to empower and confer authority onto boys among the Maasai in East Africa (see Tepilit Ole Saitoti's "The Initiation of a Maasai Warrior")? Discuss the different culturally defined values attached to circumcision.

2. How are the cultural values attached to circumcision of girls in Maasai culture (see Tepilit Ole Saitoti's "The Initiation of a Maasai Warrior") similar to, yet different from, the corresponding procedure performed on girls in Middle Eastern countries? How would you distinguish between the underlying social objectives of both cultures?

✧ *Extending Viewpoints through Writing*

1. Compare and contrast the value placed on female virginity in the cultures El Saadawi is describing with contemporary American society. What factors do you think explain the differences, and how do these differences reflect the different ways women are viewed in these two cultures?

2. Is there any outdated custom or practice that you would like to eliminate in contemporary society? Formulate your response as an argument, making sure that you cite evidence and give cogent reasons to support your views. You should also attempt to anticipate the objections opponents to your views might raise and think of responses to each of these possible objections.

3. Drawing on El Saadawi's essay, explore the relationship between law and custom and women's freedom of choice. How is the societal practice of female circumcision intended to take the power of choice out of the woman's hands as to what she will do with her body? Discuss possible similarities between this practice and issues arising from the continuing abortion debate in America.

Douchan Gersi

Initiated into an Iban Tribe of Headhunters

◆

*Douchan Gersi is the producer of the National Geographic television series
called* Discovery. *He has traveled extensively throughout the Philippines,
New Zealand, the Polynesian and Melanesian Islands, the Sahara Desert,
Africa, New Guinea, and Peru. "Initiated into an Iban Tribe of Headhunters," from his book* Explorer *(1987), tells of the harrowing initiation
process he underwent to become a member of the Iban Tribe in Borneo.*

*The Iban are a friendly and hospitable people who are a majority of
the Sarawak population of northwest Borneo. They are well known for
their textile weaving, woodcarving, and weaving of intricate mats and
baskets. An accomplished Iban man not only would be proficient in argument and courageous in hunting, but also would be skillful in woodcarving. The traditional Iban dwelling is the longhouse (which is nearly
always built by the bank of a navigable river) a semipermanent structure
housing twenty or more families in separate apartments. The longhouse
is decorated with drums, gongs, weavings, and hanging skulls from days
gone by. The area in which they live is also prized for its orangutan population, a protected species that has resulted in a burgeoning tourism
trade. The Iban have many festivals through which they maintain their
cultural identity and heritage. Superstitions abound and the carved wood
charms (often symbolized by crocodile and python figures) play a crucial
role in protecting families from malevolent spirits.*

*Borneo, the third largest island in the Malay archipelago, is situated
southwest of the Philippines and north of Java. The indigenous people of
Borneo, or Dyaks, number over 1 million and occupy the sparsely populated interior, a region of dense jungles and rain forests. The northern
portion of the island is Malaysian territory; the southern portion is part
of the Republic of Indonesia. Gersi's account introduces us to the mode of
life of the Iban, a people whose customs, including intertribal warfare and
headhunting, have remained unchanged for centuries.*

Before You Read

Consider the ways in which rites of passage provide a means by which
cultures divide "us" from "them."

◆

116

The hopeful man sees success where others see shadows and storm.

—O. S. Marden

1   Against Tawa's excellent advice I asked the chief if I could become a member of their clan. It took him a while before he could give me an answer, for he had to question the spirits of their ancestors and wait for their reply to appear through different omens: the flight of a blackbird, the auguries of a chick they sacrificed. A few days after the question, the answer came:

2   "Yes . . . but!"

3   The "but" was that I would have to undergo their initiation. Without knowing exactly what physical ordeal was in store, I accepted. I knew I had been through worse and survived. It was to begin in one week.

4   Late at night I was awakened by a girl slipping into my bed. She was sweet and already had a great knowledge of man's morphology. Like all the others who came and "visited" me this way every night, she was highly skilled in the arts of love. Among the Iban, only unmarried women offer sexual hospitality, and no one obliged these women to offer me their favors. Sexual freedom ends at marriage. Unfaithfulness—except during yearly fertility celebrations when everything, even incest at times, is permitted—is punished as an offense against their matrimonial laws.

5   As a sign of respect to family and the elders, sexual hospitality is not openly practiced. The girls always came when my roommates were asleep and left before they awoke. They were free to return or give their place to their girlfriends.

6   The contrast between the violence of some Iban rituals and the beauty of their art, their sociability, their kindness, and their personal warmth has always fascinated me. I also witnessed that contrast among a tribe of Papuans (who, besides being headhunters, practice cannibalism) and among some African tribes. In fact, tribes devoted to cannibalism and other human sacrifices are often among the most sociable of people, and their art, industry, and trading systems are more advanced than other tribes that don't have these practices.

7   For my initiation, they had me lie down naked in a four-foot-deep pit filled with giant carnivorous ants. Nothing held me there. At any point I could easily have escaped, but the meaning of this rite of passage was not to kill me. The ritual was intended to test my courage and my will, to symbolically kill me by the pain in order for me to be reborn as a man of courage. I am not sure what their reactions would have been if I had tried to get out of the pit before their signal, but it occurred to me that although the ants might eat a little of my flesh, the Iban offered more dramatic potentials.

8　　Since I wore, as Iban do, a long piece of cloth around my waist and nothing more, I had the ants running all over my body. They were everywhere. The pain of the ants' bites was intense, so I tried to relax to decrease the speed of my circulation and therefore the effects of the poison. But I couldn't help trying to get them away from my face where they were exploring every inch of my skin. I kept my eyes closed, inhaling through my almost closed lips and exhaling through my nose to chase them away from there.

9　　I don't know how long I stayed in the pit, waiting with anguish for the signal which would end my ordeal. As I tried to concentrate on my relaxing, the sound of the beaten gongs and murmurs of the assistants watching me from all around the pit started to disappear into a chaos of pain and loud heartbeat.

10　　Then suddenly I heard Tawa and the chief calling my name. I removed once more the ants wandering on my eyelids before opening my eyes and seeing my friends smiling to indicate that it was over. I got out of the pit on my own, but I needed help to rid myself of the ants, which were determined to eat all my skin. After the men washed my body, the shaman applied an herbal mixture to ease the pain and reduce the swellings. I would have quit and left the village then had I known that the "pit" experience was just the hors d'oeuvre.

11　　The second part of the physical test started early the next morning. The chief explained the "game" to me. It was Hide and Go Seek Iban-style. I had to run without any supplies, weapons, or food, and for three days and three nights escape a group of young warriors who would leave the village a few hours after my departure and try to find me. If I were caught, my head would be used in a ceremony. The Iban would have done so without hate. It was simply the rule of their life. Birth and death. A death that always engenders new life.

12　　When I asked, "What would happen if someone refused this part of the initiation?" the chief replied that such an idea wasn't possible. Once one had begun, there was no turning back. I knew the rules governing initiations among the cultures of tradition but never thought they would be applied to me. Whether or not I survived the initiation, I would be symbolically killed in order to be reborn among them. I had to die from my present time and identity into another life. I was aware that, among some cultures, initiatory ordeals are so arduous that young initiates sometimes really die. These are the risks if one wishes to enter into another world.

13　　I was given time to get ready and the game began. I ran like hell without a plan or, it seemed to me, a prayer of surviving. Running along a path I had never taken, going I knew not where, I thought about every possible way I could escape from the young warriors. To hide somewhere. But where? Climb a tree and hide in it? Find a hole and squeeze in it? Bury myself under rocks and mud? But all of these seemed impossible. I had a presentiment they would find me anyway. So I ran straight ahead, my head going crazy by dint of searching for a way to safely survive the headhunters.

14   I would prefer staying longer with ants, I thought breathlessly. It was safer to stay among them for a whole day since they were just simple pain and fear compared to what I am about to undergo. I don't want to die.

15   For the first time I realized the real possibility of death—no longer in a romantic way, but rather at the hands of butchers.

16   Ten minutes after leaving the long house, I suddenly heard a call coming from somewhere around me. Still running, I looked all around trying to locate who was calling, and why. At the second call I stopped, cast my gaze about, and saw a woman's head peering out from the bushes. I recognized her as one of my pretty lovers. I hesitated, not knowing if she were part of the hunting party or a goddess come to save me. She called again. I thought, God, what to do? How will I escape from the warriors? As I stood there truly coming into contact with my impossible situation, I began to panic. She called again. With her fingers she showed me what the others would do if they caught me. Her forefinger traced an invisible line from one side of her throat to the other. If someone was going to kill me, why not her? I joined her and found out she was in a lair. I realized I had entered the place where the tribe's women go to hide during their menstruation. This area is taboo for men. Each woman was her own refuge. Some have shelters made of branches, others deep covered holes hidden behind bushes with enough space to eat and sleep and wait until their time is past.

17   She invited me to make myself comfortable. That was quite difficult since it was just large enough for one person. But I had no choice. And after all, it was a paradise compared to what I would have undergone had I not by luck crossed this special ground.

18   Nervously and physically exhausted by my run and fear and despair, I soon fell asleep. Around midnight I woke. She gave me rice and meat. We exchanged a few words. Then it was her turn to sleep.

19   The time I spent in the lair with my savior went fast. I tried to sleep all day long, an escape from the concerns of my having broken a taboo. And I wondered what would happen to me if the headhunters were to learn where I spent the time of my physical initiation.

20   Then, when it was safe, I snuck back to the village . . . in triumph. I arrived before the warriors, who congratulated and embraced me when they returned. I was a headhunter at last.

21   I spent the next two weeks quietly looking at the Iban through new eyes. But strangely enough, instead of the initiation putting me closer to them, it had the opposite effect. I watched them more and more from an anthropological distance: my Iban brothers became an interesting clan whose life I witnessed but did not really share. And then

suddenly I was bored and yearned for my own tribe. When Tawa had to go to an outpost to exchange pepper grains for other goods, I took a place aboard his canoe. Two days later I was in a small taxi-boat heading toward Sibu, the first leg in civilization on my voyage home.

22   I think of them often. I wonder about the man I tried to cure. I think about Tawa and the girl who saved my life, and all the others sitting on the veranda. How long will my adopted village survive before being destroyed like all the others in the way of civilization? And what has become of those who marked my flesh with the joy of their lives and offered me the best of their souls? If they are slowly vanishing from my memories, I know that I am part of the stories they tell. I know that my life among them will be perpetuated until the farthest tomorrow. Now I am a story caught in a living legend of a timeless people.

✦ Evaluating the Text

1. What do the unusual sexual customs of hospitality bestowed upon outsiders suggest about the different cultural values of the Iban? Do these customs suggest that the initiation would be harsher or milder than Gersi expected? Interpret this episode as it relates to the probable nature of Gersi's forthcoming initiation.

2. In a paragraph, explain the nature of the "hide and go seek" game that constituted the main test for a candidate. Explain why the use of the lighthearted term *game* is ironic in this context.

3. How does the reappearance of one of the girls who had earlier paid a nocturnal "visit" to Gersi result in his finding a safe hiding place? What does the nature of the hiding place reveal about the tribe's taboos?

4. Explain in what way the initiation resulted in Gersi feeling quite different than he had expected. That is, instead of feeling he was now part of the tribe, he actually felt more distant from them than he had felt before the initiation. To what factors do you attribute the unexpected sense of alienation? What did he discover about his own preconceptions during the initiation that stripped away certain romantic ideas he had about the Iban and the ability of any outsider to truly become a member of the tribe?

✦ Exploring Different Perspectives

1. Contrast how the experience Gersi describes is intended to empower the initiate with the quite opposite result produced by the operation described by Nawal El Saadawi in "Circumcision of Girls."

2. What similarities can you discover between Tepilit Ole Saitoti's experiences in "The Initiation of a Maasai Warrior" and those of Gersi? What might explain their very different reactions after being initiated?

✧ *Extending Viewpoints through Writing*

1. If you have ever been initiated into a fraternity or sorority or any other organization, compare the nature of Gersi's initiation with the one you experienced. In particular, try to identify particular stages in these initiations that mark the "death" of the outsider and the "rebirth" of the initiated member.

2. Examine any religious ritual, such as confirmation in the Catholic Church, and analyze it in terms of an initiation rite. For example, the ceremony of the Catholic Church by which one is confirmed as an adult member follows this pattern. A period of preparation is spent the year before confirmation. The ceremony has several stages, including confession, communion, and subsequent confirmation. Candidates are routinely quizzed prior to communion about their knowledge of basic theology and must be sponsored by a member in good standing of the Catholic community. For example, what is the significance of the newly chosen confirmation name? What responsibilities and obligations do candidates incur who complete the confirmation ceremony?

3. What was your reaction to learning that the culture Gersi describes is one that exists today (in Borneo) two days away from taxi-boats and civilization? Would you ever consider undertaking a journey to such a place? Describe the most exotic place you want to visit, and explain why you would want to go there.

Tepilit Ole Saitoti

The Initiation of
a Maasai Warrior

◆

Named for the language they speak—Maa, a distinct, but unwritten
African tongue—the Maasai of Kenya and Tanzania, a tall, handsome,
and proud people, still live much as they always have, herding cattle,
sheep, and goats in and around the Great Rift Valley. This personal nar-
rative is unique—the first autobiographical account written by a Maasai,
which vividly documents the importance of the circumcision ceremony
that serves as a rite of passage into warrior rank. Tepilit Ole Saitoti stud-
ied animal ecology in the United States and has returned to Kenya, where
he is active in conservation projects. His experiences formed the basis for
a National Geographic Society film, Man of Serengeti *(1971). This ac-*
count first appeared in Saitoti's autobiography, The Worlds of a Maasai
Warrior *(1986).*

The Maasai are a nomadic pastoral people of East Africa. Massai soci-
ety is patrilineal; polygyny (having two or more wives at the same time) is
practiced. Boys are initiated into a warrior age-group responsible for herd-
ing and other tribal labors. Only after serving as a warrior may a man
marry. The Maasai traditionally live in the kraal, a compound within
which are mud houses (eight to fifteen huts per kraal). The settlements are
surrounded by a thorn bush fence and in the evening, cattle, goats, and
other domestic animals are brought inside the kraal for protection against
wild animals. The Maasai drink cow's milk every day and when they do not
have enough, they mix cow's blood with the milk (the Massai believe the
blood makes them strong). The wealth of the Maasai is measured by the
number of cattle they have acquired and they believe that God has entrusted
his cattle with them. As young boys reach fifteen, they are initiated into
manhood in a ceremony in which they wear headdresses of ostrich plumes
and eagle feathers, shave their heads, are circumcised, and become morani
or warriors. They then color their skin red and braid their ocher-colored hair
and with their fellow initiates learn survival skills. The image most people
have of these warriors is of a tall, thin man holding a spear in one hand with
a red cloth wrapped around his waist or thrown over his shoulders.

The United Republic of Tanzania was formed in 1964 by the union of
Tanganyika and Zanzibar. It is bordered on the north by Kenya, Lake Vic-
toria, and Uganda. Fossils discovered by British anthropologist Louis B.
Leakey at Olduvai Gorge in northeastern Tanzania have been identified

as the remains of a direct ancestor of the human species from 1.75 million years ago. Tanzania contains the famed Mount Kilimanjaro, which at 19,340 feet is the highest point in Africa. Tanzania also boasts the highest literacy rate in Africa. In May 1992 multiparty democracy was introduced into what had been a one-party state.

In 1999, bills were introduced that, if they become law, will return land to Maasai cattle-herding communities, secure their rights to land that they have inhabited for centuries, and gain them a fair share of the money raised from tourists. The Maasai are also trying to gain legal control over sacred sites to protect them from commercial exploitation.

Before You Read

Consider what rituals in our society signify a person has left childhood behind and how those differ from those of the Maasai.

◆

1   "Tepilit, circumcision means a sharp knife cutting into the skin of the most sensitive part of your body. You must not budge; don't move a muscle or even blink. You can face only one direction until the operation is completed. The slightest movement on your part will mean you are a coward, incompetent and unworthy to be a Maasai man. Ours has always been a proud family, and we would like to keep it that way. We will not tolerate unnecessary embarrassment, so you had better be ready. If you are not, tell us now so that we will not proceed. Imagine yourself alone remaining uncircumcised like the water youth [white people]. I hear they are not circumcised. Such a thing is not known in Maasailand; therefore, circumcision will have to take place even if it means holding you down until it is completed."

2   My father continued to speak and every one of us kept quiet. "The pain you will feel is symbolic. There is a deeper meaning in all this. Circumcision means a break between childhood and adulthood. For the first time in your life, you are regarded as a grownup, a complete man or woman. You will be expected to give and not just to receive. To protect the family always, not just to be protected yourself. And your wise judgment will for the first time be taken into consideration. No family affairs will be discussed without your being consulted. If you are ready for all these responsibilities, tell us now. Coming into manhood is not simply a matter of growth and maturity. It is a heavy load on your shoulders and especially a burden on the mind. Too much of this—I am done. I have said all I wanted to say. Fellows, if you have anything to add, go ahead and tell your brother, because I am through. I have spoken."

3   After a prolonged silence, one of my half-brothers said awkwardly, "Face it, man . . . it's painful. I won't lie about it, but it is not the end. We all went through it, after all. Only blood will flow, not milk." There was laughter and my father left.

4   My brother Lellia said, "Men, there are many things we must acquire and preparations we must make before the ceremony, and we will need the cooperation and help of all of you. Ostrich feathers for the crown and wax for the arrows must be collected."

5   "Are you *orkirekenyi?*" One of my brothers asked. I quickly replied no, and there was laughter. *Orkirekenyi* is a person who has transgressed sexually. For you must not have sexual intercourse with any circumcised woman before you yourself are circumcised. You must wait until you are circumcised. If you have not waited, you will be fined. Your father, mother, and the circumciser will take a cow from you as punishment.

6   Just before we departed, one of my closest friends said, "If you kick the knife, you will be in trouble." There was laughter. "By the way, if you have decided to kick the circumciser, do it well. Silence him once and for all." "Do it the way you kick a football in school." "That will fix him," another added, and we all laughed our heads off again as we departed.

7   The following month was a month of preparation. I and others collected wax, ostrich feathers, honey to be made into honey beer for the elders to drink on the day of circumcision, and all the other required articles.

8   Three days before the ceremony my head was shaved and I discarded all my belongings, such as my necklaces, garments, spear, and sword. I even had to shave my pubic hair. Circumcision in many ways is similar to Christian baptism. You must put all the sins you have committed during childhood behind and embark as a new person with a different outlook on a new life.

9   The circumciser came the following day and handed the ritual knives to me. He left drinking a calabash of beer. I stared at the knives uneasily. It was hard to accept that he was going to use them on my organ. I was to sharpen them and protect them from people of ill will who might try to blunt them, thus rendering them inefficient during the ritual and thereby bringing shame on our family. The knives threw a chill down my spine; I was not sure I was sharpening them properly, so I took them to my closest brother for him to check out, and he assured me that the knives were all right. I hid them well and waited.

10   Tension started building between me and my relatives, most of whom worried that I wouldn't make it through the ceremony valiantly. Some even snarled at me, which was their way of encouraging me. Others threw insults and abusive words my way. My sister Loiyan in particular was more troubled by the whole affair than anyone in the whole family. She had to assume my mother's role during the circumcision. Were I to fail my initiation, she would have to face the consequences. She would be spat upon and even beaten for representing the mother of an unworthy son. The same fate would befall my father, but

he seemed unconcerned. He had this weird belief that because I was not particularly handsome, I must be brave. He kept saying, "God is not so bad as to have made him ugly and a coward at the same time."

11   Failure to be brave during circumcision would have other unfortunate consequences: the herd of cattle belonging to the family still in the compound would be beaten until they stampeded; the slaughtered oxen and honey beer prepared during the month before the ritual would go to waste; the initiate's food would be spat upon and he would have to eat it or else get a severe beating. Everyone would call him Olkasiodoi, the knife kicker.

12   Kicking the knife of the circumciser would not help you anyway. If you struggle and try to get away during the ritual, you will be held down until the operation is completed. Such failure of nerve would haunt you in the future. For example, no one will choose a person who kicked the knife for a position of leadership. However, there have been instances in which a person who failed to go through circumcision successfully became very brave afterwards because he was filled with anger over the incident; no one dares to scold him or remind him of it. His age-mates, particularly the warriors, will act as if nothing had happened.

13   During the circumcision of a woman, on the other hand, she is allowed to cry as long as she does not hinder the operation. It is common to see a woman crying and kicking during circumcision. Warriors are usually summoned to help hold her down.

14   For women, circumcision means an end to the company of Maasai warriors. After they recuperate, they soon get married, and often to men twice their age.

15   The closer it came to the hour of truth, the more I was hated, particularly by those closest to me. I was deeply troubled by the withdrawal of all the support I needed. My annoyance turned into anger and resolve. I decided not to budge or blink, even if I were to see my intestines flowing before me. My resolve was hardened when newly circumcised warriors came to sing for me. Their songs were utterly insulting, intended to annoy me further. They tucked their wax arrows under my crotch and rubbed them on my nose. They repeatedly called me names.

16   By the end of the singing, I was fuming. Crying would have meant I was a coward. After midnight they left me alone and I went into the house and tried to sleep but could not. I was exhausted and numb but remained awake all night.

17   At dawn I was summoned once again by the newly circumcised warriors. They piled more and more insults on me. They sang their weird songs with even more vigor and excitement than before. The songs praised warriorhood and encouraged one to achieve it at all costs. The songs continued until the sun shone on the cattle horns clearly. I was summoned to the main cattle gate, in my hand a ritual

cowhide from a cow that had been properly slaughtered during my naming ceremony. I went past Loiyan, who was milking a cow, and she muttered something. She was shaking all over. There was so much tension that people could hardly breathe.

18   I laid the hide down and a boy was ordered to pour ice-cold water, known as *engare entolu* (ax water), over my head. It dripped all over my naked body and I shook furiously. In a matter of seconds I was summoned to sit down. A large crowd of boys and men formed a semicircle in front of me; women are not allowed to watch male circumcision and vice versa. That was the last thing I saw clearly. As soon as I sat down, the circumciser appeared, his knives at the ready. He spread my legs and said, "One cut," a pronouncement necessary to prevent an initiate from claiming that he had been taken by surprise. He splashed a white liquid, a ceremonial paint called *enturoto*, across my face. Almost immediately I felt a spark of pain under my belly as the knife cut through my penis' foreskin. I happened to choose to look in the direction of the operation. I continued to observe the circumciser's fingers working mechanically. The pain became numbness and my lower body felt heavy, as if I were weighed down by a heavy burden. After fifteen minutes or so, a man who had been supporting from behind pointed at something, as if to assist the circumciser. I came to learn later that the circumciser's eyesight had been failing him and that my brothers had been mad at him because the operation had taken longer than was usually necessary. All the same, I remained pinned down until the operation was over. I heard a call for milk to wash the knives, which signaled the end, and soon the ceremony was over.

19   With words of praise, I was told to wake up, but I remained seated. I waited for the customary presents in appreciation of my bravery. My father gave me a cow and so did my brother Lellia. The man who had supported my back and my brother-in-law gave me a heifer. In all I had eight animals given to me. I was carried inside the house to my own bed to recuperate as activities intensified to celebrate my bravery.

20   I laid on my own bed and bled profusely. The blood must be retained within the bed, for according to Maasai tradition, it must not spill to the ground. I was drenched in my own blood. I stopped bleeding after about half an hour but soon was in intolerable pain. I was supposed to squeeze my organ and force blood to flow out of the wound, but no one had told me, so the blood coagulated and caused unbearable pain. The circumciser was brought to my aid and showed me what to do, and soon the pain subsided.

21   The following morning, I was escorted by a small boy to a nearby valley to walk and relax, allowing my wound to drain. This was common for everyone who had been circumcised, as well as for women who had just given birth. Having lost a lot of blood, I was extremely weak. I walked very slowly, but in spite of my caution I fainted. I tried

to hang on to bushes and shrubs, but I fell, irritating my wound. I came out of unconsciousness quickly, and the boy who was escorting me never realized what had happened. I was so scared that I told him to lead me back home. I could have died without there being anyone around who could have helped me. From that day on, I was selective of my company while I was feeble.

22   In two weeks I was able to walk and was taken to join other newly circumcised boys far away from our settlement. By tradition Maasai initiates are required to decorate their headdresses with all kinds of colorful birds they have killed. On our way to the settlement, we hunted birds and teased girls by shooting them with our wax blunt arrows. We danced and ate and were well treated wherever we went. We were protected from the cold and rain during the healing period. We were not allowed to touch food, as we were regarded as unclean, so whenever we ate we had to use specially prepared sticks instead. We remained in this pampered state until our wounds healed and our headdresses were removed. Our heads were shaved, we discarded our black cloaks and bird headdresses and embarked as newly shaven warriors, Irkeleani.

23   As long as I live I will never forget the day my head was shaved and I emerged a man, a Maasai warrior. I felt a sense of control over my destiny so great that no words can accurately describe it. I now stood with confidence, pride, and happiness of being, for all around me I was desired and loved by beautiful, sensuous Maasai maidens. I could now interact with women and even have sex with them, which I had not been allowed before. I was now regarded as a responsible person.

24   In the old days, warriors were like gods, and women and men wanted only to be the parent of a warrior. Everything else would be taken care of as a result. When a poor family had a warrior, they ceased to be poor. The warrior would go on raids and bring cattle back. The warrior would defend the family against all odds. When a society respects the individual and displays confidence in him the way the Maasai do their warriors, the individual can grow to his fullest potential. Whenever there was a task requiring physical strength or bravery, the Maasai would call upon their warriors. They hardly ever fall short of what is demanded of them and so are characterized by pride, confidence, and an extreme sense of freedom. But there is an old saying in Maasai: "You are never a free man until your father dies." In other words, your father is paramount while he is alive and you are obligated to respect him. My father took advantage of this principle and held a tight grip on all his warriors, including myself. He always wanted to know where we all were at any given time. We fought against his restrictions, but without success. I, being the youngest of my father's five warriors, tried even harder to get loose repeatedly, but each time I was punished severely.

25   Roaming the plains with other warriors in pursuit of girls and adventure was a warrior's pastime. We would wander from one settlement to another, singing, wrestling, hunting, and just playing. Often I was ready to risk my father's punishment for this wonderful freedom.

26   One clear day my father sent me to take sick children and one of his wives to the dispensary in the Korongoro Highlands. We rode in the L.S.B. Leakey lorry. We ascended the highlands and were soon attended to in the local hospital. Near the conservation offices I met several acquaintances, and one of them told me of an unusual circumcision that was about to take place in a day or two. All the local warriors and girls were preparing to attend it.

27   The highlands were a lush green from the seasonal rains and the sky was a purple-blue with no clouds in sight. The land was overflowing with milk, and the warriors felt and looked their best, as they always did when there was plenty to eat and drink. Everyone was at ease. The demands the community usually made on warriors during the dry season when water was scarce and wells had to be dug were now not necessary. Herds and flocks were entrusted to youths to look after. The warriors had all the time for themselves. But my father was so strict that even at times like these he still insisted on overworking us in one way or another. He believed that by keeping us busy, he would keep us out of trouble.

28   When I heard about the impending ceremony, I decided to remain behind in the Korongoro Highlands and attend it now that the children had been treated. I knew very well that I would have to make up a story for my father upon my return, but I would worry about that later. I had left my spear at home when I boarded the bus, thinking that I would be coming back that very day. I felt lighter but now regretted having left it behind; I was so used to carrying it wherever I went. In gales of laughter resulting from our continuous teasing of each other, we made our way toward a distant kraal. We walked at a leisurely pace and reveled in the breeze. As usual we talked about the women we desired, among other things.

29   The following day we were joined by a long line of colorfully dressed girls and warriors from the kraal and the neighborhood where we had spent the night, and we left the highland and headed to Ingorienito to the rolling hills on the lower slopes to attend the circumcision ceremony. From there one could see Oldopai Gorge, where my parents lived, and the Inaapi hills in the middle of the Serengeti Plain.

30   Three girls and a boy were to be initiated on the same day, an unusual occasion. Four oxen were to be slaughtered, and many people would therefore attend. As we descended, we saw the kraal where the ceremony would take place. All those people dressed in red seemed from a distance like flamingos standing in a lake. We could see lines of other guests heading to the settlements. Warriors made gallant cries of

happiness known as *enkiseer*. Our line of warriors and girls responded to their cries even more gallantly.

31 In serpentine fashion, we entered the gates of the settlement. Holding spears in our left hands, we warriors walked proudly, taking small steps, swaying like palm trees, impressing our girls, who walked parallel to us in another line, and of course the spectators, who gazed at us approvingly.

32 We stopped in the center of the kraal and waited to be greeted. Women and children welcomed us. We put our hands on the children's heads, which is how children are commonly saluted. After the greetings were completed, we started dancing.

33 Our singing echoed off the kraal fence and nearby trees. Another line of warriors came up the hill and entered the compound, also singing and moving slowly toward us. Our singing grew in intensity. Both lines of warriors moved parallel to each other, and our feet pounded the ground with style. We stamped vigorously, as if to tell the next line and the spectators that we were the best.

34 The singing continued until the hot sun was overhead. We recessed and ate food already prepared for us by other warriors. Roasted meat was for those who were to eat meat, and milk for the others. By our tradition, meat and milk must not be consumed at the same time, for this would be a betrayal of the animal. It was regarded as cruel to consume a product of the animal that could be obtained while it was alive, such as milk, and meat, which was only available after the animal had been killed.

35 After eating we resumed singing, and I spotted a tall, beautiful *esiankiki* (young maiden) of Masiaya whose family was one of the largest and richest in our area. She stood very erect and seemed taller than the rest.

36 One of her breasts could be seen just above her dress, which was knotted at the shoulder. While I was supposed to dance generally to please all the spectators, I took it upon myself to please her especially. I stared at and flirted with her, and she and I danced in unison at times. We complemented each other very well.

37 During a break, I introduced myself to the *esiankiki* and told her I would like to see her after the dance. "Won't you need a warrior to escort you home later when the evening threatens?" I said. She replied, "Perhaps, but the evening is still far away."

38 I waited patiently. When the dance ended, I saw her departing with a group of other women her age. She gave me a sidelong glance, and I took that to mean come later and not now. With so many others around, I would not have been able to confer with her as I would have liked anyway.

39 With another warrior, I wandered around the kraal killing time until the herds returned from pasture. Before the sun dropped out of

sight, we departed. As the kraal of the *esiankiki* was in the lowlands, a place called Enkoloa, we descended leisurely, our spears resting on our shoulders.

40   We arrived at the woman's kraal and found that cows were now being milked. One could hear the women trying to appease the cows by singing to them. Singing calms cows down, making it easier to milk them. There were no warriors in the whole kraal except for the two of us. Girls went around into warriors' houses as usual and collected milk for us. I was so eager to go and meet my *esiankiki* that I could hardly wait for nightfall. The warriors' girls were trying hard to be sociable, but my mind was not with them. I found them to be childish, loud, bothersome, and boring.

41   As the only warriors present, we had to keep them company and sing for them, at least for a while, as required by custom. I told the other warrior to sing while I tried to figure out how to approach my *esiankiki*. Still a novice warrior, I was not experienced with women and was in fact still afraid of them. I could flirt from a distance, of course. But sitting down with a woman and trying to seduce her was another matter. I had already tried twice to approach women soon after my circumcision and had failed. I got as far as the door of one woman's house and felt my heart beating like a Congolese drum; breathing became difficult and I had to turn back. Another time I managed to get in the house and succeeded in sitting on the bed, but then I started trembling until the whole bed was shaking, and conversation became difficult. I left the house and the woman, amazed and speechless, and never went back to her again.

42   Tonight I promised myself I would be brave and would not make any silly, ridiculous moves. "I must be mature and not afraid," I kept reminding myself, as I remembered an incident involving one of my relatives when he was still very young and, like me, afraid of women. He went to a woman's house and sat on a stool for a whole hour; he was afraid to awaken her, as his heart was pounding and he was having difficulty breathing.

43   When he finally calmed down, he woke her up, and their conversation went something like this:

44   "Woman, wake up."

45   "Why should I?"

46   "To light the fire."

47   "For what?"

48   "So you can see me."

49   "I already know who you are. Why don't *you* light the fire, as you're nearer to it than me?"

50   "It's your house and it's only proper that you light it yourself."

51   "I don't feel like it."

52   "At least wake up so we can talk, as I have something to tell you."

53   "Say it."

54 "I need you."

55 "I do not need one-eyed types like yourself."

56 "One-eyed people are people too."

57 "That might be so, but they are not to my taste."

58 They continued talking for quite some time, and the more they spoke, the braver he became. He did not sleep with her that night, but later on he persisted until he won her over. I doubted whether I was as strong-willed as he, but the fact that he had met with success encouraged me. I told my warrior friend where to find me should he need me, and then I departed.

59 When I entered the house of my *esiankiki*, I called for the woman of the house, and as luck would have it, my lady responded. She was waiting for me. I felt better, and I proceeded to talk to her like a professional. After much talking back and forth, I joined her in bed.

60 The night was calm, tender, and loving, like most nights after initiation ceremonies as big as this one. There must have been a lot of courting and lovemaking.

61 Maasai women can be very hard to deal with sometimes. They can simply reject a man outright and refuse to change their minds. Some play hard to get, but in reality are testing the man to see whether he is worth their while. Once a friend of mine while still young was powerfully attracted to a woman nearly his mother's age. He put a bold move on her. At first the woman could not believe his intention, or rather was amazed by his courage. The name of the warrior was Ngengeiya, or Drizzle.

62 "Drizzle, what do you want?"

63 The warrior stared her right in the eye and said, "You."

64 "For what?"

65 "To make love to you."

66 "I am your mother's age."

67 "The choice was either her or you."

68 This remark took the woman by surprise. She had underestimated the saying "There is no such thing as a young warrior." When you are a warrior, you are expected to perform bravely in any situation. Your age and size are immaterial.

69 "You mean you could really love me like a grownup man?"

70 "Try me, woman."

71 He moved in on her. Soon the woman started moaning with excitement, calling out his name. "Honey Drizzle, Honey Drizzle, you *are* a man." In a breathy, stammering voice, she said, "A real man."

72 Her attractiveness made Honey Drizzle ignore her relative old age. The Maasai believe that if an older and a younger person have intercourse, it is the older person who stands to gain. For instance, it is believed that an older woman having an affair with a young man starts

to appear younger and healthier, while the young man grows older and unhealthy.

73　　　The following day when the initiation rites had ended, I decided to return home. I had offended my father by staying away from home without his consent, so I prepared myself for whatever punishment he might inflict on me. I walked home alone.

✧ *Evaluating the Text*

1. How is the candidate's life, reputation, and destiny dependent on the bravery he shows during the ceremony? What consequences would his family have to suffer if he were to flinch or shudder? What is the function of the relentless taunting by warriors and those who are newly circumcised prior to the ceremony?

2. What is Tepilit's attitude toward his father? What assumptions about a son's responsibilities account for how Tepilit's father treats him?

3. Several Maasai customs reveal the profound symbiotic relationship they have with nature and the animal world. For example, what is the rationale behind their practice of not eating milk and meat together? Why is Tepilit careful not to allow the blood from his wound to spill onto the ground as he lies on his bed bleeding from the surgery?

4. What responsibilities does Tepilit assume and what privileges is he allowed upon successful completion of the ceremony?

✧ *Exploring Different Perspectives*

1. Compare the very different objectives that circumcision is designed to achieve among the Maasai and in Middle Eastern countries, as described by Nawal El Saadawi in "Circumcision of Girls."

2. Compare the kinds of courage exhibited by Saitoti and Christy Brown in "The Letter 'A'" despite all that separates them.

✧ *Extending Viewpoints through Writing*

1. Every culture or society has some form of initiation that its members must undergo to become part of that society. In what way is the Maasai ritual Tepilit describes intended to deepen the bond between the community and the initiate in ways that are quite similar, allowing for cultural differences, to the Bar or Bat Mitzvah in Judaism and the confirmation ceremony in Christianity? In an essay, explore how any of these rites of passage affirm the culture, unite the candidate with his or her community, and ensure the continuation of traditions.

2. Despite obvious differences between the Maasai society and contemporary American culture, Tepilit's interactions with his friends and the opposite sex are quite typical of those of any teenage boy. Write an essay exploring these similarities.

3. If you had to choose between being initiated as a warrior into the Maasai in East Africa or into the Marine Corps, which would you choose and why? Keep in mind the great differences in the length of time over which the initiation takes place, the respective penalties for not successfully completing the rite of passage, and the privileges and responsibilities that ensue from a successful completion.

Marjorie Shostak

Memories of a !Kung Girlhood

———————◆———————

Marjorie Shostak initially spent two years, from 1969 to 1971, living and working among the !Kung San of Botswana, as a research assistant on the Harvard Kalahari Desert Project. The !Kung or !Kung bushmen live in southwestern Africa in isolated areas of Botswana (where they make up only 3 percent of the population), Angola, and Namibia. The ! is meant to represent a clicking sound in their language made by the tongue breaking air pockets in different parts of the mouth. Anthropologists have studied this nomadic community with great interest because they are one of the few peoples who live by hunting and gathering rather than by some form of agriculture. After gaining fluency in the language of the !Kung, Shostak returned to Botswana in 1975 for six months to complete the life histories of several women in the tribe. The results of her fieldwork first appeared in Kalahari Hunter–Gatherers: Studies of the !Kung San and Their Neighbors, *edited by Richard B. Lee and Irven De Vore (1976), and later in* Human Nature, *as "Memories of a !Kung Girlhood" (1978). Shostak's research also served as the basis for the 1983 book* Nisa: The Life and Words of a !Kung Woman. *In "Memories of a !Kung Girlhood," we hear the remembrances of Nisa, recalling her childhood and marriage. This book became a surprise best-seller.*

After her death in 1996, the Marjorie Shostak Scholarship Fund was established at the University of Texas at Austin to aid students in Namibia and Botswana.

Located in South-Central Africa, Botswana became independent from British rule in 1966. Because of its landlocked location, Botswana continues to be economically dependent on South Africa and Zimbabwe, which controls railroad routes through Botswana. Religious practices are equally divided between Christianity and traditional tribal beliefs. The current president (as of 1998) of this democratic republic is Festus Mogae.

Before You Read

As you read, notice the stages that mark Nisa's evolution from an immature girl to someone who accepts her role as an adult woman in !Kung society.

———————◆———————

1   I remember when my mother was pregnant with Kumsa. I was still small (about four years old) and I asked, "Mommy, that baby inside you . . . when that baby is born, will it come out from your bellybut-

ton?" She said, "No, it won't come out from there. When you give birth, a baby comes from here." And she pointed to her genitals.

2   When she gave birth to Kumsa, I wanted the milk she had in her breasts, and when she nursed him, my eyes watched as the milk spilled out. I cried all night . . . cried and cried.

3   Once when my mother was with him and they were lying down asleep, I took him away from her and put him down on the other side of the hut. Then I lay down beside her. While she slept I squeezed some milk and started to nurse, and nursed and nursed and nursed. Maybe she thought it was him. When she woke and saw me she cried, "Where . . . tell me . . . what did you do with Kumsa? Where is he?"

4   I told her he was lying down inside the hut. She grabbed me and pushed me hard away from her. I lay there and cried. She took Kumsa, put him down beside her, and insulted me by cursing my genitals.

5   "Are you crazy? Nisa-Big Genitals, what's the matter with you? What craziness grabbed you that you took a baby, dropped him somewhere else, and then lay down beside me and nursed? I thought it was Kumsa."

6   When my father came home, she told him, "Do you see what kind of mind your daughter has? Hit her! She almost killed Kumsa. This little baby, this little thing here, she took from my side and dropped him somewhere else. I was lying here holding him and fell asleep. She came and took him away, left him by himself, then lay down where he had been and nursed. Now, hit her!"

7   I said, "You're lying! Me . . . Daddy, I didn't nurse. Really I didn't. I don't even want her milk anymore."

8   He said, "If I ever hear of this again, I'll hit you. Now, don't ever do that again!"

9   I said, "Yes, he's my little brother, isn't he? My little baby brother and I *love* him. I won't do that again. He can nurse all by himself. Daddy, even if you're not here, I won't try to steal Mommy's breasts. They belong to my brother."

10   We lived and lived, and as I kept growing, I started to carry Kumsa around on my shoulders. My heart was happy and I started to love him. I carried him everywhere. I would play with him for a while, and whenever he started to cry, I'd take him over to mother to nurse. Then I'd take him back with me and we'd play together again.

11   That was when Kumsa was still little. But once he was older and started to talk and then to run around, that's when we were mean to each other all the time. Sometimes we hit each other. Other times I grabbed him and bit him and said, "Ooooh . . . what is this thing that has such a horrible face and no brains and is so mean? Why is it so mean to me when I'm not doing anything to it?" Then he said, "I'm going to *hit* you!" And I said, "You're just a *baby!* I, *I* am the one who's

ABOUT THE !KUNG

Nisa is a 50-year-old !Kung woman, one of an estimated 13,000 !Kung San living on the northern fringe of the Kalahari Desert in southern Africa. Much of her life—as daughter, sister, wife, mother, and lover—has been spent in the semi-nomadic pursuit of food and water in the arid savanna.

Like many !Kung, Nisa is a practiced storyteller. The !Kung have no written language with which to record their experiences, and people sit around their fires for hours recounting recent events and those long past. Voices rise and fall, hands move in dramatic gestures, and bird and animal sounds are imitated as stories are told and retold, usually with much exaggeration.

I collected stories of Nisa's life as part of my anthropological effort to record the lives of !Kung women in their own words. Nisa enjoyed working with the machine that "grabs your voice" and the interviews with her produced 25 hours of tape and 425 pages of transcription. The excerpts included here are faithful to her narrative except where awkward or discontinuous passages have been modified or deleted, and where long passages have been shortened.

Although most of Nisa's memories are typical of !Kung life, her early memories, like those of most people, are probably idiosyncratic mixtures of fact and fantasy. Her memories of being hit for taking food are probably not accurate. The !Kung tend to be lenient and indulgent with their children, and researchers have rarely observed any physical punishment or the withholding of food.

Strong feelings of sibling rivalry, like those Nisa describes, are common. !Kung women wean their children as soon as they find they are pregnant again because they believe the milk belongs to the fetus. Children are not usually weaned until they are three or four years old, which tends to make them resent their younger siblings. Nisa's complaints about being given too little food probably stem from her jealousy of her little brother.

Despite the lack of privacy, !Kung parents are generally discreet in their sexual activity. As children become aware of it, they engage each other in sexual play. Parents say they do not approve of this play but do little to stop it.

Many !Kung girls first marry in their early teens, but these relationships are not consummated until the girls begin menstruating around the age of 16. Early marriages are relatively unstable. Nisa was betrothed twice before marrying Tashay.

The exclamation point at the beginning of !Kung represents one of the many click sounds in the !Kung language. Clicks are made by the tongue breaking air pockets in different parts of the mouth; but the notation for clicks has been eliminated in all cases except for the name of the !Kung people. Nisa, for instance, should be written as N≠isa.

Marjorie Shostak

going to hit *you*. Why are you so miserable to me?" I insulted him and he insulted me and then I insulted him back. We just stayed together and played like that.

12   Once, when our father came back carrying meat, we both called out, "Ho, ho. Daddy! Ho, ho, Daddy!" But when I heard him say, "Daddy, Daddy," I yelled, "Why are you greeting my father? He's *my* father, isn't he? You can only say, 'Oh, hello Father.'" But he called out, "Ho, ho . . . Daddy!" I said, "Be quiet! Only *I* will greet him. Is he your father? I'm going to hit you!"

13   We fought and argued until Mother finally stopped us. Then we just sat around while she cooked the meat.

14   This was also when I used to take food. It happened over all kinds of food—sweet *nin* berries or *klaru* bulbs . . . other times it was mongongo nuts. Sometimes before my mother left to go gathering, she'd leave food inside a leather pouch and hang it high on one of the branches inside the hut.

15   But as soon as she was gone, I'd take some of whatever food was left in the bag. If it was *klaru*, I'd find the biggest bulbs and take them. I'd hang the bag back on the branch and go sit somewhere to eat them.

16   One time I sat down in the shade of a tree while my parents gathered food nearby. As soon as they had moved away from me, I climbed the tree where they had left a pouch hanging, full of *klaru*, and took the bulbs.

17   I had my own little pouch, the one my father had made me, and I took the bulbs and put them in the pouch. Then I climbed down and sat waiting for my parents to return.

18   They came back. "Nisa, you ate the *klaru*! What do you have to say for yourself?" I said, "Uhn uh, I didn't eat them."

19   I started to cry. Mother hit me and yelled, "Don't take things. You can't seem to understand! I tell you but you don't listen. Don't your ears hear when I talk to you?"

20   I said, "Uhn uh. Mommy's been making me feel bad for too long now. She keeps saying I steal things and hits me so that my skin hurts. I'm going to stay with Grandma!"

21   But when I went to my grandmother, she said, "No, I can't take care of you now. If I try you will be hungry. I am old and just go gathering one day at a time. In the morning I just rest. We would sit together and hunger would kill you. Now go back and sit beside your mother and father."

22   I said, "No, Daddy will hit me. Mommy will hit me. I want to stay with you."

23   So I stayed with her. Then one day she said, "I'm going to bring you back to your mother and father." She took me to them, saying, "Today I'm giving Nisa back to you. But isn't there someone here who will take good care of her? You don't just hit a child like this one. She likes food and likes to eat. All of you are lazy and you've just left her

so she hasn't grown well. You've killed this child with hunger. Look at her now, how small she still is."

24   Oh, but my heart was happy! Grandmother was scolding Mother! I had so much happiness in my heart that I laughed and laughed. But then, when Grandmother went home and left me there, I cried and cried.

25   My father started to yell at me. He didn't hit me. His anger usually came out only from his mouth. "You're so senseless! Don't you realize that after you left, everything felt less important? We wanted you to be with us. Yes, even your mother wanted you and missed you. Today, everything will be all right when you stay with us. Your mother will take you where she goes; the two of you will do things together and go gathering together."

26   Then when my father dug *klaru* bulbs, I ate them, and when he dug *chon* bulbs, I ate them. I ate everything they gave me, and I wasn't yelled at any more.

27   Mother and I often went to the bush together. The two of us would walk until we arrived at a place where she collected food. She'd set me down in the shade of a tree and dig roots or gather nuts nearby.

28   Once I left the tree and went to play in the shade of another tree. I saw a tiny steenbok, one that had just been born, hidden in the grass and among the leaves. It was lying there, it's little eyes just looking out at me.

29   I thought, "What should I do?" I shouted, *"Mommy!"* I just stood there and it just lay there looking at me.

30   Suddenly I knew what to do—I ran at it, trying to grab it. But it jumped up and ran away and I started to chase it. It was running and I was running and it was crying as it ran. Finally, I got very close and put my foot in its way, and it fell down. I grabbed its legs and started to carry it back. It was crying, "Ehn . . . ehn . . . ehn. . . ."

31   Its mother had been close by and when she heard it call, she came running. As soon as I saw her, I started to run again. I wouldn't give it back to its mother!

32   I called out, "Mommy! Come! Help me with this steenbok! Mommy! The steenbok's mother is coming for me! Run! Come! Take this steenbok from me."

33   But soon the mother steenbok was no longer following, so I took the baby, held its feet together, and banged it hard against the sand until I killed it. It was no longer crying; it was dead. I felt wonderfully happy. My mother came running and I gave it to her to carry.

34   The two of us spent the rest of the day walking in the bush. While my mother was gathering, I sat in the shade of a tree, waiting and playing with the dead steenbok. I pick it up. I tried to make it sit up, to open its eyes. I looked at them. After mother had dug enough *sha* roots, we left and returned home.

35   My father had been out hunting that day and had shot a large steenbok with his arrows. He had skinned it and brought it back hanging on a branch.

36   "Ho, ho. Daddy killed a steenbok!" I said, "Mommy! Daddy! I'm not going to let anyone have any of *my* steenbok. Now *don't* give it to anyone else. After you cook it, just my little brother and I will eat it, just the two of us."

37   I remember another time when we were traveling from one place to another and the sun was burning. It was the hot, dry season and there was no water anywhere. The sun was burning! Kumsa had already been born and I was still small.

38   After we had been walking a long time, my older brother Dau spotted a beehive. We stopped while he and my father chopped open the tree. All of us helped take out the honey. I filled my own little container until it was completely full.

39   We stayed there, eating the honey, and I found myself getting very thirsty. Then we left and continued to walk, I carrying my honey and my digging stick. Soon the heat began killing us and we were all dying of thirst. I started to cry because I wanted water so badly.

40   After a while, we stopped and sat down in the shade of a baobab tree. There was still no water anywhere. We just sat in the shade like that.

41   Finally my father said, "Dau, the rest of the family will stay here under this baobab. But you, take the water containers and get us some water. There's a well not too far away."

42   Dau collected the empty ostrich eggshell containers and the large clay pot and left. I lay there, already dead from thirst and thought, "If I stay with Mommy and Daddy, I'll surely die of thirst. Why don't I follow my big brother and go drink water with him?"

43   With that I jumped up and ran after him, crying out, calling to him, following his tracks. But he didn't hear me. I kept running . . . crying and calling out.

44   Finally, he heard something and turned to see. There I was, "Oh no!" he said. "Nisa's followed me. What can I do with her now that she's here?" He just stood there and waited for me to catch up. He picked me up and carried me high up on his shoulder, and along we went. He really liked me!

45   The two of us went on together. We walked and walked and walked and walked. Finally, we reached the well. I ran to the water and drank, and soon my heart was happy again. We filled the water containers, put them in a twine mesh sack, and my brother carried it on his back. Then he took me and put me on his shoulder again.

46   We walked the long way back until we arrived at the baobab where out parents were sitting. They drank the water. Then they said, "How well our children have done, bringing us this water! We are alive once again!"

47   We just stayed in the shade of the baobab. Later we left and traveled to another water hole where we settled for a while. My heart was happy . . . eating honey and just living.

48   We lived there, and after some time passed, we saw the first rain clouds. One came near but just hung in the sky. More rain clouds came over and they too just stood there. Then the rain started to spill itself and it came pouring down.

49   The rainy season had finally come. The sun rose and set, and the rain spilled itself and fell and kept falling. It fell without ceasing. Soon the water pans were full. And my heart! My heart within me was happy and we lived and ate meat and mongongo nuts. There was more meat and it was all delicious.

50   And there were caterpillars to eat, those little things that crawl along going "mmm . . . mmmmm . . . mmmmm. . . ." People dug roots and collected nuts and berries and brought home more and more food. There was plenty to eat, and people kept bringing meat back on sticks and hanging it in the trees.

51   My heart was bursting. I ate lots of food, and my tail was wagging, always wagging about like a little dog. I'd laugh with my little tail, laugh with a little donkey's laugh, a tiny thing that is. I'd throw my tail one way and the other, shouting, "Today I'm going to eat caterpillars . . . *cat-er-pillars!*" Some people gave me meat broth to drink, and others prepared the skins of caterpillars and roasted them for me to eat, and I ate and ate and ate. Then I went to sleep.

52   But that night, after everyone was dead asleep, I peed right in my sleeping place. In the morning, when everyone got up, I just lay there. The sun rose and had set itself high in the sky, and I was still lying there. I was afraid of people shaming me. Mother said, "Why is Nisa acting like this and refusing to leave her blankets when the sun is sitting up in the sky? Oh . . . she has probably wet herself!"

53   When I did get up, my heart felt miserable. I thought, "I've peed on myself and now everyone's going to laugh at me." I asked one of my friends, "How come, after I ate all those caterpillars, when I went to sleep I peed in my bed?" Then I thought, "Tonight, when this day is over, I'm going to lie down separate from the others. If I pee in my bed again, won't mother and father hit me?"

54   When a child sleeps beside her mother, in front, and her father sleeps behind and makes love to her mother, the child watches. Her parents don't fear her, a small child, because even if the child sees, even if she hears, she is unaware of what it is her parents are doing. She is still young and without sense. Perhaps this is the way the child learns. The child is still senseless, without intelligence, and just watches.

55   If the child is a little boy, when he plays with other children, he plays sex with them and teaches it to himself, just like a baby rooster teaches itself. The little girls also learn it by themselves.

56 Little boys are the first ones to know its sweetness. Yes, a young girl, while she is still a child, her thoughts don't know it. A boy has a penis, and maybe, while he is still inside his mother's belly, he already knows about sex.

57 When you are a child you play at nothing things. You build little huts and play. Then you come back to the village and continue to play. If people bother you, you get up and play somewhere else.

58 Once we left a pool of rain water where we had been playing and went to the little huts we had made. We stayed there and played at being hunters. We went out tracking animals, and when we saw one, we struck it with our make-believe arrows. We took some leaves and hung them over a stick and pretended it was meat. Then we carried it back to our village. When we got back, we stayed there and ate the meat and then the meat was gone. We went out again, found another animal, and killed it.

59 Sometimes the boys asked if we wanted to play a game with our genitals and the girls said no. We said we didn't want to play that game, but would like to play other games. The boys told us that playing sex was what playing was all about. That's the way we grew up.

60 When adults talked to me I listened. Once they told me that when a young woman grows up, she takes a husband. When they first talked to me about it, I said: "What? What kind of thing am I that I should take a husband? Me, when I grow up, I won't marry. I'll just lie by myself. If I married a man, what would I think I would be doing it for?"

61 My father said: "Nisa, I am old. I am your father and I am old; your mother's old, too. When you get married, you will gather food and give it to your husband to eat. He also will do things for you and give you things you can wear. But if you refuse to take a husband, who will give you food to eat? Who will give you things to have? Who will give you things to wear?"

62 I said to my father and mother, "No. There's no question in my mind—I refuse a husband. I won't take one. Why should I? As I am now, I am still a child and won't marry."

63 Then I said to Mother, "Why don't you marry the man you want for me and sit him down beside Father? Then you'll have two husbands."

64 Mother said: "Stop talking nonsense. I'm not going to marry him; you'll marry him. A husband is what I want to give you. Yet you say I should marry him. Why are you playing with me with this talk?"

65 We just continued to live after that, kept on living and more time passed. One time we went to the village where Old Kantla and his son Tashay were living. My friend Nhuka and I had gone to the water well to get water, and Tashay and his family were there, having just come back from the bush. When Tashay saw me, he decided he wanted to marry me. He called Nhuka over and said, "Nhuka, that young woman, that beautiful young woman . . . what is her name?"

66   Nhuka told him my name was Nisa, and he said, "That young woman . . . I'm going to tell Mother and Father about her. I'm going to ask them if I can marry her."

67   The next evening there was a dance at our village, and Tashay and his parents came. We sang and danced into the night. Later his father said, "We have come here, and now that the dancing is finished, I want to speak to you. Give me your child, the child you gave birth to. Give her to me, and I will give her to my son. Yesterday, while we were at the well, he saw your child. When he returned he told me in the name of what he felt that I should come and ask for her today so I could giver her to him."

68   My mother said, "Yes . . . but I didn't give birth to a woman, I bore a child. She doesn't think about marriage, she just doesn't think about the inside of her marriage hut."

69   Then my father said, "Yes, I also conceived that child, and it is true: She just doesn't think about marriage. When she marries a man, she leaves him and marries another man and leaves him and gets up and marries another man and leaves him. She refuses men completely. There are two men whom she has already refused. So when I look at Nisa today, I say she is not a woman."

70   Then Tashay's father said, "Yes, I have listened to what you have said. That, of course, is the way of a child; it is a child's custom to do that. She gets married many times until one day she likes one man. Then they stay together. That is a child's way."

71   They talked about the marriage and agreed to it. In the morning Tashay's parents went back to their camp, and we went to sleep. When the morning was late in the sky, his relatives came back. They stayed around and his parents told my aunt and my mother that they should all start building the marriage hut. They began building it together, and everyone was talking and talking. There were a lot of people there. Then all the young men went and brought Tashay to the hut. They stayed around together near the fire. I was at Mother's hut. They told two of my friends to get me. But I said to myself, "Ooooh . . . I'll just run away."

72   When they came, they couldn't find me. I was already out in the bush, and I just sat there by the base of a tree. Soon I heard Nhuka call out, "Nisa . . . Nisa . . . my friend . . . there are things there that will bite and kill you. Now leave there and come back here."

73   They came and brought me back. Then they laid me down inside the hut. I cried and cried, and people told me: "A man is not something that kills you; he is someone who marries you, and becomes like your father or your older brother. He kills animals and gives you things to eat. Even tomorrow he would do that. But because you are crying, when he kills an animal, he will eat it himself and won't give you any. Beads, too. He will get some beads, and he won't give them to you. Why are you afraid of your husband and why are you crying?"

74   I listened and was quiet. Later Tashay lay down by the mouth of the hut, near the fire, and I was inside. He come in only after he thought I was asleep. Then he lay down and slept. I woke while it was still dark and thought, "How am I going to jump over him? How can I get out and go to Mother's hut?" Then I thought, "This person has married me . . . yes." And, I just lay there. Soon the rain came and beat down and it fell until dawn broke.

75   In the morning, he got up first and sat by the fire. I was frightened. I was so afraid of him, I just lay there and waited for him to go away before I got up.

76   We lived together a long time and began to learn to like one another before he slept with me. The first time I didn't refuse. I agreed just a little and he lay with me. But the next morning my insides hurt. I took some leaves and wound them around my waist, but it continued to hurt. Later that day I went with the women to gather mongongo nuts. The whole time I thought "Ooooh . . . what has he done to my insides that they feel this way."

77   That evening we lay down again. But this time I took a leather strap, held my skin apron tightly against me, tied up my genitals with it, and then tied the strap to the hut's frame. I didn't want him to take me again. The two of us lay there and after a while he started to touch me. When he reached my stomach, he felt the leather strap. He felt around to see what it was. He said, "What is this woman doing? Yesterday she lay with me so nicely when I came to her. Why has she tied up her genitals this way?"

78   He sat me up and said, "Nisa . . . Nisa . . . what happened? Why are you doing this?" I didn't answer him.

79   "What are you so afraid of that you tied your genitals?"

80   I said, "I'm not afraid of anything."

81   He said, "No, now tell me what you are afraid of. In the name of what you did, I am asking you."

82   I said, "I refuse because yesterday when you touched me my insides hurt."

83   He said, "Do you see me as someone who kills people? Am I going to eat you? I am not going to kill you. I have married you and I want to make love to you. Have you seen any man who has married a woman and who just lives with her and doesn't have sex with her?"

84   I said, "No, I still refuse it! I refuse sex. Yesterday my insides hurt, that's why."

85   He said, "Mmm. Today you will lie there by yourself. But tomorrow I will take you."

86   The next day I said to him, "Today I'm going to lie here, and if you take me by force, you will have me. You will have me because today I'm just going to lie here. You are obviously looking for some 'food,' but I don't know if the food I have is food at all, because even if you have some, you won't be full."

87   I just lay there and he did his work.

88   We lived and lived, and soon I started to like him. After that I was a grown person and said to myself, "Yes, without doubt, a man sleeps with you. I thought maybe he didn't."

89   We lived on, and then I loved him and he loved me, and I kept on loving him. When he wanted me I didn't refuse and he just slept with me. I thought, "Why have I been so concerned about my genitals? They are after all, not so important. So why was I refusing them?"

90   I thought that and gave myself to him and gave and gave. We lay with one another, and my breasts had grown very large. I had become a woman.

FOR FURTHER INFORMATION

Lee, Richard B., and Irven De Vore, eds. *Kalahari Hunter–Gatherers: Studies of the !Kung San and Their Neighbors.* Harvard University Press, 1976.
Lee, Richard B., and Irven De Vore, eds. *Man the Hunter.* Aldine, 1968.
Marshall, Lorna. *The !Kung of Nyae Nyae.* Harvard University Press, 1976.
Shostak, Marjorie. "Life before Horticulture: An African Gathering and Hunting Society." *Horticulture,* Vol. 55, No. 2, 1977.

✧ *Evaluating the Text*

1. How would you characterize Nisa's relationships with family members? How does she interact with her mother, father, older brother, baby brother, and grandmother? What explains the changes in her attitude toward her baby brother as she grows up?

2. What does the episode in which she describes killing the baby steenbok reveal about her inner conflict about becoming an adult?

3. Describe the circumstances that lead to Nisa's marriage to Tashay. What change in attitude must she undergo before the marriage takes place? What can you infer about the kinds of problems she faces in adapting to the role of a married woman in !Kung society? Keep in mind that she has left several prospective husbands before Tashay.

✧ *Exploring Different Perspectives*

1. Discuss how both Shostak's account and Douchan Gersi's narrative (see "Initiated into an Iban Tribe of Headhunters") point out interesting paradoxes between societies where initiation rituals play a central role.

2. Compare the cultural values and expectations connected with marriage among the !Kung with those of traditional Chinese culture mentioned by Sucheng Chan in "You're Short, Besides!"

✧ Extending Viewpoints through Writing

1. What unexpected similarities can you discover between the !Kung and contemporary American society in terms of disciplining children, the role played by grandparents (including their concern that their grandchildren are too thin), sibling rivalry, bed-wetting, playing sexual games, and finding husbands for daughters who are fussy?

2. Nisa's narrative was originally elicited as answers to questions she was asked over a period of time by Shostak. How do recurring motifs in this account suggest the kinds of questions Shostak asked Nisa? What conclusions might you draw about the relationship between Nisa and Shostak from the answers that Nisa gave?

Hanan al-Shaykh

The Persian Carpet

◆

Hanan al-Shaykh was born in 1945 in Lebanon and was raised in a tradi-
tional Shiite Moslem family. She began her studies at the American College
for Girls in Cairo in 1963 and four years later returned to Beirut where she
worked as a journalist and began writing short stories and novels. Origi-
nally written in Arabic, al-Shaykh's works have been published in Lebanon
and have been acclaimed for her capacity to realistically create situations in
which her protagonists, often women, gain a new perspective despite the
cultural pressures forced upon them. Two of her novels, The Story of
Zahra *(1986) and* Women of Sand and Myrrh *(1989), have been trans-*
lated into English. "The Persian Carpet," translated by Denys Johnson-
Davies (1983) from Arabic Short Stories, *closely observes the behavior*
and emotions of a girl who is forced to realize that the circumstances lead-
ing to her parents getting divorced were very different from what she had
believed as a child. Her latest work is a novel, Only in London *(2001).*

Located on the Mediterranean Sea, Lebanon is a republic in the Mid-
dle East bordered to the north and east by Syria and to the south by Israel.
The site of the ancient maritime city-state Phoenicia, the region fell to suc-
cessive Middle Eastern powers. Christianity was introduced under the
Roman Empire in the first century and persisted even after the coming of
Islam with the Arab conquest in the seventh century. Since independence
in 1945, Lebanon has been plagued by civil strife between the Palestine
Liberation Organization (PLO), Syrian, and Israeli forces, as well as in-
digenous Christian and Muslim factions. However, under a peace accord
reached in 1990, militias representing these different factions withdrew
from the capital, Beirut, and the Lebanese Army established control. With
the fifteen-year civil war behind them, the Lebanese have begun the process
of rebuilding the country's infrastructure. In July 1997, the United States
lifted a ten-year ban on travel to Lebanon by U.S. citizens.

Before You Read

As you read, evaluate whether you would consider the narrator/protag-
onist to be reliable or unreliable. In what way do the mother's actions
transgress the cultural values of this Muslim society?

◆

1   When Maryam had finished plaiting my hair into two pigtails, she
put her finger to her mouth and licked it, then passed it over my eye-

brows, moaning: "Ah, what eyebrows you have—they're all over the place!" She turned quickly to my sister and said: "Go and see if your father's still praying." Before I knew it my sister had returned and was whispering "He's still at it," and she stretched out her hands and raised them skywards in imitation of him. I didn't laugh as usual, nor did Maryam; instead, she took up the scarf from the chair, put it over her hair and tied it hurriedly at the neck. Then, opening the wardrobe carefully, she took out her handbag, placed it under her arm and stretched out her hands to us. I grasped one and my sister the other. We understood that we should, like her, proceed on tiptoe, holding our breath as we made our way out through the open front door. As we went down the steps, we turned back towards the door, then towards the window. Reaching the last step, we began to run, only stopping when the lane had disappeared out of sight and we had crossed the road and Maryam had stopped a taxi.

2   Our behaviour was induced by fear, for today we would be seeing my mother for the first time since her separation by divorce from my father. He had sworn he would not let her see us, for, only hours after the divorce, the news had spread that she was going to marry a man she had been in love with before her family had forced her into marrying my father.

3   My heart was pounding. This was not from fear or from running but was due to anxiety and a feeling of embarrassment about the meeting that lay ahead. Though in control of myself and my shyness, I knew that I would be incapable—however much I tried—of showing my emotions, even to my mother; I would be unable to throw myself into her arms and smother her with kisses and clasp her head as my sister would do with such spontaneity. I had thought long and hard about this ever since Maryam had whispered in my ear—and in my sister's—that my mother had come from the south and that we were to visit her secretly the following day. I began to imagine that I would make myself act exactly as my sister did, that I would stand behind her and imitate her blindly. Yet I know myself: I have committed myself to myself by heart. However much I tried to force myself, however much I thought in advance about what I should and shouldn't do, once I was actually faced by the situation and was standing looking down at the floor, my forehead puckered into an even deeper frown, I would find I had forgotten what I had to resolved to do. Even then, though I would not give up hope but would implore my mouth to break into a smile; it would none the less be to no avail.

4   When the taxi came to a stop at the entrance to a house, where two lions stood on columns of red sandstone, I was filled with delight and immediately forgot my apprehension. I was overcome with happiness at the thought that my mother was living in a house where two lions stood at the entrance. I heard my sister imitate the roar of a lion and I turned to her in envy. I saw her stretching up her hands in an attempt

to clutch the lions. I thought to myself: She's always uncomplicated and jolly, her gaiety never leaves her, even at the most critical moments—and here she was, not a bit worried about this meeting.

5   But when my mother opened the door and I saw her, I found myself unable to wait and rushed forward in front of my sister and threw myself into her arms. I had closed my eyes and all the joints of my body had grown numb after having been unable to be at rest for so long. I took in the unchanged smell of her hair, and I discovered for the first time how much I had missed her and wished that she would come back and live with us, despite the tender care shown to us by my father and Maryam. I couldn't rid my mind of that smile of hers when my father agreed to divorce her, after the religious sheikh had intervened following her threats to pour kerosene over her body and set fire to herself if my father wouldn't divorce her. All my senses were numbed by that smell of her, so well perserved in my memory. I realized how much I had missed her, despite the fact that after she'd hurried off behind her brother to get into the car, having kissed us and started to cry, we had continued with the games we were playing in the lane outside our house. As night came, and for the first time in a long while we did not hear her squabbling with my father, peace and quiet descended upon the house—except that is for the weeping of Maryam, who was related to my father and had been living with us in the house ever since I was born.

6   Smiling, my mother moved me away from her so that she could hug and kiss my sister, and hug Maryam again, who had begun to cry. I heard my mother, who was in tears, say to her "Thank you," and she wiped her tears with her sleeve and looked me and my sister up and down, saying: "God keep them safe, how they've sprung up!" She put both arms round me, while my sister buried her head in my mother's waist, and we all began to laugh when we found that it was difficult for us to walk like that. Reaching the inner room, I was convinced her new husband was inside because my mother said, sniffing: "Mahmoud loves you very much and he would like it if your father would give you to me so that you can live with us and become his children too." My sister laughed and answered: "Like that we'd have two fathers." I was still in a benumbed state, my hand placed over my mother's arm, proud at the way I was behaving, at having been able without any effort to be liberated from myself, from my shackled hands, from the prison of my shyness, as I recalled to mind the picture of my meeting with my mother, how I had spontaneously thrown myself at her, something I had thought wholly impossible, and my kissing her so hard I had closed my eyes.

7   Her husband was not there. As I stared down at the floor I froze. In confusion I looked at the Persian carpet spread out on the floor, then gave my mother a long look. Not understanding the significance of my look, she turned and opened a cupboard from which she threw me

an embroidered blouse, and moving across to a drawer in the dressing-table, she took out an ivory comb with red hearts painted on it and gave it to my sister. I stared down at the Persian carpet, trembling with burning rage. Again I looked at my mother and she interpreted my gaze as being one of tender longing, so she put her arms round me, saying: "You must come every other day, you must spend the whole of Friday at my place." I remained motionless, wishing that I could re-move her arms from around me and sink my teeth into that white fore-arm. I wished that the moment of meeting could be undone and re-enacted, that she could again open the door and I could stand there—as I should have done—with my eyes staring down at the floor and my forehead in a frown.

8   The lines and colours of the Persian carpet were imprinted on my memory. I used to lie on it as I did my lessons; I'd be so close to it that I'd gaze at its pattern and find it looking like slices of red water-melon repeated over and over again. But when I sat down on the couch, I would see that each slice of melon had changed into a comb with thin teeth. The cluster of flowers surrounding its four sides were purple-coloured. At the beginning of summer my mother would put moth-balls on it and on the other ordinary carpets and would roll them up and place them on top of the cupboard. The room would look stark and depressing until autumn came, when she would take them up to the roof and spread them out. She would gather up the mothballs, most of which had dissolved from the summer's heat and humidity, then, having brushed them with a small broom, she'd leave them there. In the evening she'd bring them down and lay them out where they be-longed. I would be filled with happiness as their bright colours once again brought the room back to life. This particular carpet, though, had disappeared several months before my mother was divorced. It had been spread out on the roof in the sun and in the afternoon my mother had gone up to get it and hadn't found it. She had called my father and for the first time I had seen his face flushed with anger. When they came down from the roof, my mother was in a state of fury and bewil-derment. She got in touch with the neighbors, all of whom swore they hadn't seen it. Suddenly my mother exclaimed: "Ilya!" Everyone stood speechless: not a word from my father or from my sister or from our neighbours Umm Fouad and Abu Salman. I found myself crying out: "Ilya? Don't say such a thing, it's not possible."

9   Ilya was an almost blind man who used to go round the houses of the quarter repairing cane chairs. When it came to our turn, I would see him, on my arrival back from school, seated on the stone bench outside the house with piles of straw in front of him and his red hair glinting in the sunlight. He would deftly take up the strands of straw and, like fishes, they'd slip through the mesh. I would watch him as he coiled them round with great dexterity, then bring them out again until

he had formed a circle of straw for the seat of the chair, just like the one that had been there before. Everything was so even and precise: it was as though his hands were a machine and I would be amazed at the speed and nimbleness of his fingers. Sitting as he did with his head lowered, it looked as though he were using his eyes. I once doubted that he could see more than vague shapes in front of him, so I squatted down and looked into his rosy-red face and was able to see his half-closed eyes behind his glasses. They had in them a white line that pricked at my heart and sent me hurrying off to the kitchen, where I found a bag of dates on the table, and I heaped some on a plate and gave them to Ilya.

10   I continued to stare at the carpet as the picture of Ilya, red of face and hair, appeared to me. I was made aware of his hand as he walked up the stairs on his own; of him sitting on his chair, of his bargaining over the price for his work, of how he ate and knew that he had finished everything on the plate, of his drinking from the pitcher, with the water flowing easily down his throat. Once at midday, having been taught by my father that before entering a Muslim house he should say "Allah" before knocking at the door and entering, as a warning to my mother in case she were unveiled, my mother rushed at him and asked him about the carpet. He made no reply, merely making a sort of sobbing noise. As he walked off, he almost bumped into the table and, for the first time, tripped. I went up to him and took him by the hand. He knew me by the touch of my hand, because he said to me in a half-whisper: "Never mind, child." Then he turned round to leave. As he bent over to put on his shoes, I thought I saw tears on his cheeks. My father didn't let him leave before saying to him: "Ilya, God will forgive you if you tell him the truth." But Ilya walked off, steadying himself against the railings. He took an unusually long time as he felt his way down the stairs. Then he disappeared from sight and we never saw him again.

✧ Evaluating the Text

1. What circumstances have made it necessary for the protagonist and her sister to visit their mother in secret?

2. What details suggest how much it means to her to see her mother again? Why is her reaction on first seeing her mother especially poignant and ironic in view of what she discovers subsequently?

3. Why does seeing the Persian carpet cause the young girl to experience such a dramatic change in attitude toward the mother? How does seeing what Ilya, the blind man, meant to her enable the reader to understand her feelings of anger?

✧ *Exploring Different Perspectives*

1. Contrast the relationship Christy Brown has with his mother in "The Letter ' A'" with the one the young girl has with hers in "The Persian Carpet."

2. Discuss the consequences of the betrayal of trust that the young girls experience in "The Persian Carpet" and in Nawal El Saadawi's "Circumcision of Girls."

✧ *Extending Viewpoints through Writing*

1. Did you ever experience a moment of disillusionment with an adult member of your family that represented a turning point in your relationship? Describe your experience.

2. Write about one of your grandparents or parents through an object you connect with him or her. Under what circumstances did you first come across this object? What associations connect this object with your parent or grandparent?

3. Discuss a belief you once held that you no longer hold. What evidence led you to hold that original belief? Was it something you were told, read, or personally experienced? What new experiences raised doubts about this belief? How did you change your attitude in response to these new experiences? What actions have you taken which you would not have taken previously that reflect this changed attitude or revised belief?

Wakako Yamauchi

And the Soul Shall Dance

Wakako Yamauchi was born in Westmoreland, California, in 1924, to parents who had immigrated from Japan. During World War II the family was sent to an internment camp in Arizona where Yamauchi worked on the camp newspaper, the Poston Chronicle. *After the war, she took courses in design, drawing, and painting in Los Angeles, and from 1960 to 1974 submitted short stories and drawings to the* Los Angeles Rafu Shimpo, *a Japanese-American daily publication. The following short story was first published in 1974 and in 1976 she expanded it into a play that was nominated by the Los Angeles Drama Critics Circle as outstanding new play of the year. "And the Soul Shall Dance" reveals the intergenerational conflicts and tensions in an immigrant family and paints a complex and subtle portrait of a second wife and teenage stepdaughter struggling to survive in a new country.*

Before You Read
Imagine what it would be like to grow up in a very isolated environment where friends were few and far between.

1   It's all right to talk about it now. Most of the principals are dead, except, of course, me and my younger brother, and possibly Kiyoko Oka, who might be near forty-five now, because, yes, I'm sure of it, she was fourteen then. I was nine, and my brother about four, so he hardly counts at all. Kiyoko's mother is dead, my father is dead, my mother is dead, and her father could not have lasted all these years with his tremendous appetite for alcohol and pickled chilies—those little yellow ones, so hot they could make your mouth hurt; he'd eat them like peanuts and tears would surge from his bulging thyroid eyes in great waves and stream down the dark coarse terrain of his face.

2   My father farmed then in the desert basin resolutely named Imperial Valley, in the township called Westmoreland; twenty acres of tomatoes, ten of summer squash, or vice versa, and the Okas lived maybe a mile, mile and a half, across an alkaline road, a stretch of greasewood, tumbleweed and white sand, to the south of us. We didn't hobnob much with them, because you see, they were a childless couple and we were a family: father, mother, daughter, and son, and we went to the Buddhist church on Sundays where my mother taught Japanese, and

the Okas kept pretty much to themselves. I don't mean they were un-friendly; Mr. Oka would sometimes walk over (he rarely drove) on rainy days, all dripping wet, short and squat under a soggy newspaper, pretending to need a plow-blade or a file, and he would spend the af-ternoon in our kitchen drinking sake and eating chilies with my father. As he got progressively drunker, his large mouth would draw down and with the stream of tears, he looked like a kindly weeping bullfrog.

3   Not only were they childless, impractical in an area where large families were looked upon as labor potentials, but there was a certain strangeness about them. I became aware of it the summer our bath-house burned down, and my father didn't get right down to building another, and a Japanese without a bathhouse . . . well, Mr. Oka offered us the use of his. So every night that summer we drove to the Okas for our bath, and we came in frequent contact with Mrs. Oka, and this is where I found the strangeness.

4   Mrs. Oka was small and spare. Her clothes hung on her like loose skin and when she walked, the skirt about her legs gave her a sort of webbed look. She was pretty in spite of the boniness and the dull cal-ico and the barren look; I know now that she couldn't have been over thirty. Her eyes were large and a little vacant, although once I saw them fill with tears; the time I insisted we take the old Victrola over and we played our Japanese records for her. Some of the songs were sad, and I imagined the nostalgia she felt, but my mother said the tears were probably from yawning or from the smoke of her cigarettes. I thought my mother resented her for not being more hospitable; in-deed, never a cup of tea appeared before us, and between them the conversation of women was totally absent: the rise and fall of gentle voices, the arched eyebrows, the croon of polite surprise. But more than this, Mrs. Oka was *different*.

5   Obviously she was shy, but some nights she disappeared alto-gether. She would see us drive into her yard and then lurch from sight. She was gone all evening. Where could she have hidden in that two-roomed house—where in that silent desert? Some nights she would wait out our visit with enormous forbearance, quietly pushing wisps of stray hair behind her ears and waving gnats away from her great moist eyes, and some nights she moved about with nervous agitation, her khaki canvas shoes slapping loudly as she walked. And sometimes there appeared to be welts and bruises on her usually smooth brown face, and she would sit solemnly, hands on lap, eyes large and intent on us. My mother hurried us home then: "Hurry, Masako, no need to wash well; hurry."

6   You see, being so poky, I was always last to bathe. I think the Okas bathed after we left because my mother often reminded me to keep the water clean. The routine was to lather outside the tub (there were buckets and pans and a small wooden stool), rinse off the soil and

soap, and then soak in the tub of hot hot water and contemplate. Rivulets of perspiration would run down the scalp.

7   When my mother pushed me like this, I dispensed with ritual, rushed a bar of soap around me and splashed about a pan of water. So hastily toweled, my wet skin strapped the clothes to me, impeding my already clumsy progress. Outside, my mother would be murmuring her many apologies and my father, I knew, would be carrying my brother whose feet were already sandy. We would hurry home.

8   I thought Mrs. Oka might be insane and I asked my mother about it, but she shook her head and smiled with her mouth drawn down and said that Mrs. Oka loved her sake. This was unusual, yes, but there were other unusual women we knew. Mrs. Nagai was brought by her husband from a geisha house; Mrs. Tani was a militant Christian Scientist; Mrs. Abe, the midwife, was occult. My mother's statement explained much: sometimes Mrs. Oka was drunk and sometimes not. Her taste for liquor and cigarettes was a step in the realm of men; unusual for a Japanese wife, but at that time, in that place, and to me, Mrs. Oka loved her sake in the way my father loved his, in the way of Mr. Oka, and the way I loved my candy. That her psychology may have demanded this anesthetic, that she lived with something unendurable, did not occur to me. Nor did I perceive the violence of emotions that the purple welts indicated—or the masochism that permitted her to display these wounds to us.

9   In spite of her masculine habits, Mrs. Oka was never less than a woman. She was no lady in the area of social amenities; but the feminine in her was innate and never left her. Even in her disgrace, she was a small broken sparrow, slightly floppy, too slowly enunciating her few words, too carefully rolling her Bull Durham, cocking her small head and moistening the ocher tissue. Her aberration was a protest of the life assigned her; it was obstinate, but unobserved, alas, unheeded. "Strange" was the only concession we granted her.

10   Toward the end of summer, my mother said we couldn't continue bathing at the Okas'; when winter set in we'd all catch our death from the commuting and she'd always felt dreadful about our imposition on Mrs. Oka. So my father took the corrugated tin sheets he'd found on the highway and had been saving for some other use and built up our bathhouse again. Mr. Oka came to help.

11   While they raised the quivering tin walls, Mr. Oka began to talk. His voice was sharp and clear above the low thunder of the metal sheets.

12   He told my father he had been married in Japan previously to the present Mrs. Oka's older sister. He had a child by the marriage, Kiyoko, a girl. He had left the two to come to America intending to send for them soon, but shortly after his departure, his wife passed away from an obscure stomach ailment. At the time, the present Mrs. Oka was young and had foolishly become involved with a man of poor

reputation. The family was anxious to part the lovers and conveniently arranged a marriage by proxy and sent him his dead wife's sister. Well that was all right, after all, they were kin, and it would be good for the child when she came to join them. But things didn't work out that way, year after year he postponed calling for his daughter, couldn't get the price of fare together, and the wife—ahhh, the wife, Mr. Oka's groan was lost in the rumble of his hammering.

13   He cleared his throat. The girl was now fourteen, he said, and begged to come to America to be with her own real family. Those relatives had forgotten the favor he'd done in accepting a slightly used bride, and now tormented his daughter for being forsaken. True, he'd not sent much money, but if they knew, if they only knew how it was here.

14   "Well," he sighed, "who could be blamed? It's only right she be with me anyway."

15   "That's right," my father said.

16   "Well, I sold the horse and some other things and managed to buy a third-class ticket on the Taiyo-Maru. Kiyoko will get here the first week of September." Mr. Oka glanced toward my father, but my father was peering into a bag of nails. "I'd be much obliged to you if your wife and little girl," he rolled his eyes toward me, "would take kindly to her. She'll be lonely."

17   Kiyoko-san came in September. I was surprised to see so very nearly a woman; short, robust, buxom: the female counterpart of her father; thyroid eyes and protruding teeth, straight black hair banded impudently into two bristly shucks, Cuban heels and white socks. Mr. Oka brought her proudly to us.

18   "Little Masako here," for the first time to my recollection, he touched me; he put his rough fat hand on the top of my head, "is very smart in school. She will help you with your school work, Kiyoko," he said.

19   I had so looked forward to Kiyoko-san's arrival. She would be my soul mate; in my mind I had conjured a girl of my own proportion: thin and tall, but with the refinement and beauty I didn't yet possess that would surely someday come to the fore. My disappointment was keen and apparent. Kiyoko-san stepped forward shyly, then retreated with a short bow and small giggle, her fingers pressed to her mouth.

20   My mother took her away. They talked for a long time—about Japan, about enrollment in American school, the clothes Kiyoko-san would need, and where to look for the best values. As I watched them, it occurred to me that I had been deceived: this was not a child, this was a woman. The smile pressed behind her fingers, the way of her nod, so brief, like my mother when father scolded her: the face was inscrutable, but something—maybe spirit—shrank visibly, like a piece of silk in water. I was disappointed; Kiyoko-san's soul was barricaded in her unenchanting appearance and the smile she fenced behind her fingers.

21   She started school from third grade, one below me, and as it turned out, she quickly passed me by. There wasn't much I could help her with except to drill her on pronunciation—the "L" and "R" sounds. Every morning walking to our rural school: land, leg, library, loan, lot; every afternoon returning home: ran, rabbit, rim, rinse, roll. That was the extent of our communication; friendly but uninteresting.

22   One particularly cold November night—the wind outside was icy; I was sitting on my bed, my brother's and mine, oiling the cracks in my chapped hands by lamplight—someone rapped urgently at our door. It was Kiyoko-san; she was hysterical, she wore no wrap, her teeth were chattering, and except for the thin straw zori, her feet were bare. My mother led her to the kitchen, started a pot of tea, and gestured to my brother and me to retire. I lay very still but because of my brother's restless tossing and my father's snoring, was unable to hear much. I was aware, though, that drunken and savage brawling had brought Kiyoko-san to us. Presently they came to the bedroom. I feigned sleep. My mother gave Kiyoko-san a gown and pushed me over to make room for her. My mother spoke firmly: "Tomorrow you will return to them; you must not leave them again. They are your people." I could almost feel Kiyoko-san's short nod.

23   All night long I lay cramped and still, afraid to intrude into her hulking back. Two or three times her icy feet jabbed into mine and quickly retreated. In the morning I found my mother's gown neatly folded on the spare pillow. Kiyoko-san's place in bed was cold.

24   She never came to weep at our house again but I know she cried: her eyes were often swollen and red. She stopped much of her giggling and routinely pressed her fingers to her mouth. Our daily pronunciation drill petered off from lack of interest. She walked silently with her shoulders hunched, grasping her books with both arms, and when I spoke to her in my halting Japanese, she absently corrected my prepositions.

25   Spring comes early in the Valley; in February the skies are clear though the air is still cold. By March, winds are vigorous and warm and wild flowers dot the desert floor, cockleburs are green and not yet tenacious, the sand is crusty underfoot, everywhere there is a smell of things growing and the first tomatoes are showing green and bald.

26   As the weather changed, Kiyoko-san became noticeably more cheerful. Mr. Oka, who hated so to drive, could often been seen steering his dusty old Ford over the road that passes our house, and Kiyoko-san sitting in front would sometimes wave gaily to us. Mrs. Oka was never with them. I thought of these trips as the westernizing of Kiyoko-san: with a permanent wave, her straight black hair became tangles of tiny frantic curls; between her textbooks she carried copies of *Modern Screen* and *Photoplay*, her clothes were gay with print and piping, and she bought a pair of brown suede shoes with alligator trim.

I can see her now picking her way gingerly over the deceptive white peaks of alkaline crust.

27   At first my mother watched their coming and going with vicarious pleasure. "Probably off to a picture show; the stores are all closed at this hour," she might say. Later her eyes would get distant and she would muse, "They've left her home again; Mrs. Oka is alone again, poor woman."

28   Now when Kiyoko-san passed by or came in with me on her way home, my mother would ask about Mrs. Oka—how is she, how does she occupy herself these rainy days, or these windy or warm or cool days. Often the answers were polite: "Thank you, we are fine," but sometimes Kiyoko-san's upper lip would pull over her teeth and her voice would become very soft and she would say, "Drink, always drinking and fighting." And those times my mother would invariably say, "Endure, soon you will be marrying and going away."

29   Once a young truck driver delivered crates at the Oka farm and he dropped back to our place to tell my father that Mrs. Oka had lurched behind his truck while he was backing up, and very nearly let him kill her. Only the daughter pulling her away saved her, he said. Thoroughly unnerved, he stopped by to rest himself and talk about it. Never, never, he said in wide-eyed wonder, had he seen a drunken Japanese woman. My father nodded gravely, "Yes, it's unusual," he said and drummed his knee with his fingers.

30   Evenings were longer now, and when my mother's migraines drove me from the house in unbearable self-pity, I would take walks in the desert. One night with the warm wind against me, the dune primrose and yellow poppies closed and fluttering, the greasewood swaying in languid orbit, I lay on the white sand beneath a shrub and tried to disappear.

31   A voice sweet and clear cut through the half-dark of the evening:

> Red lips press against a glass
> Drink the purple wine
>   And the soul shall dance.

32   Mrs. Oka appeared to be gathering flowers. Bending, plucking, standing, searching, she added to a small bouquet she clasped. She held them away; looked at them slyly, lids lowered, demure, then in a sudden and sinuous movement, she broke into a stately dance. She stopped, gathered more flowers, and breathed deeply into them. Tossing her head, she laughed—softly, beautifully, from her dark throat. The picture of her imagined grandeur was lost to me, but the delusion that transformed the bouquet of tattered petals and sandy leaves, and the aloneness of a desert twilight into a fantasy that brought such joy and abandon made me stir with discomfort. The sound broke Mrs. Oka's dance. Her eyes grew large and her neck tense—like a cat on the

prowl. She spied me in the bushes. A peculiar chill ran through me. Then abruptly and with childlike delight, she scattered the flowers around her and walked away singing:

Falling, falling, petals on a wind . . .

33   That was the list time I saw Mrs. Oka. She died before the spring harvest. It was pneumonia. I didn't attend the funeral, but my mother said it was sad. Mr. Oka looked peaceful and the minister expressed the irony of the long separation of Mother and Child and the short-lived re-union; hardly a year together, she said. We went to help Kiyoko-san address and stamp those black-bordered acknowledgments.

34   When harvest was over, Mr. Oka and Kiyoko-san moved out of the Valley. We never heard from them or saw them again and I suppose in a large city, Mr. Oka found some sort of work, perhaps as a janitor or a dishwasher and Kiyoko-san grew up and found someone to marry.

✧ Evaluating the Text

1. Under what circumstances did Mrs. Oka come to marry her husband and how might these explain her actions?

2. How do the images used to describe Mrs. Oka's dance symbolize all that her life could have been? How does the setting help the reader to understand Mrs. Oka's despair?

3. In what ways does the narrator change as a result of knowing Mr. Oka's daughter, Kiyoko-san? How does the narrator's interpretation of Mrs. Oka's predicament differ from that of her mother?

✧ Exploring Different Perspectives

1. How do both Sucheng Chan's account and this story offer insight into the ways in which women are viewed in traditional Asian cultures?

2. Compare what the narrators learn about the private lives of adults and how this information changes them in this story and in Hanan al-Shaykh's "The Persian Carpet."

✧ Extending Viewpoints through Writing

1. In your opinion, who is more of a victim, Kiyoko-san or her step-mother, Mrs. Oka? Explain your answer.

2. In a few paragraphs, explain how knowing the Okas, and especially Kiyoko-san, has fundamentally changed the way the narrator sees herself as a Japanese American.

Connecting Cultures

———◆———

Christy Brown, "The Letter 'A'"

Compare and contrast the attitudes of the parents toward their children in Christy Brown's account and in Mahdokht Kashkuli's story "The Button" in Chapter 5.

Sucheng Chan, "You're Short, Besides!"

What contrasting attitudes toward disabilities emerge from Sucheng Chan's account and Lennard J. Davis's analysis (see "Visualizing the Disabled Body," Chapter 3)?

Nawal El Saadawi, "The Circumcision of Girls"

After reading Susan Bordo's "Never Just Pictures" (Chapter 3), write an essay exploring how cultural pressures created by manipulating body images of women in contemporary America are as damaging psychologically as female circumcision is in the Middle East.

Douchan Gersi, "Initiated into an Iban Tribe of Headhunters"

The initiation ritual to which Gersi is subjected is similar in some respects to that of the near-death rituals practiced in Haiti by the voudon priests, albeit for very different objectives. Compare and contrast Douchan Gersi's account and Gino Del Guercio's analysis in "The Secrets of Haiti's Living Dead," Chapter 8.

Tepilit Ole Saitoti, "The Initiation of a Maasai Warrior"

Discuss facing danger in order to gain peer acceptance as a theme in both Saitoti's account and in Alonso Salazar's "The Lords of Creation" (Chapter 5).

Marjorie Shostak, "Memories of a !Kung Girlhood"

Compare the cultural values and expectations that precede marriage among the !Kung with those described by Serena Nanda in "Arranging a Marriage in India" (Chapter 3).

Hanan al-Shaykh, "The Persian Carpet"

In what sense do both Hanan al-Shaykh's and Tayeb Salih's stories (see "A Handful of Dates," Chapter 1) hinge on the disillusionment of the narrators?

Wakako Yamauchi, "And the Soul Shall Dance"

Discuss the problems that face young Japanese Americans who have to adapt to different cultures in this story and in Kazuo Ishiguro's "A Family Supper" (Chapter 1).

3

How Culture Shapes Gender Roles

$\blacklozenge$

Culture plays an enormous part in shaping our expectations attached to sex roles. This process, sometimes called *socialization,* determines how each of us assimilates our culture's ideas of what it means to act as a male or female. We tend to acquire a sense of our own sexual identity in conjunction with societal expectations. Yet, these expectations differ strikingly from culture to culture. For example, in male-dominated Islamic Middle Eastern societies, the gender roles and relationships between men and women are very different from those in modern industrial societies.

The characteristics that define gender roles have varied widely throughout history in cultures as diverse as those in Europe, the Orient, the Mideast, and the Americas. The responsibilities and obligations that collectively define what it means to be a woman or a man in different societies have changed dramatically in those societies that have themselves changed in recent times. The movement toward equality between the sexes—a transformation that has been only partially realized—has allowed women to assume positions of leadership and perform tasks in the workplace, in the professions, and in society that were traditionally reserved for men. The works in this chapter address the changing cultural expectations attached to being a man or a woman as well as the psychological and social stresses produced by these changes in redrawing the boundaries of gender roles, marriage, and parenthood.

How you see yourself is determined in large part by the social meanings attached to specific behavior for men and women in your culture—beginning with the fairy tales told to children, extending through the conceptions of masculinity and femininity promulgated by the media, and including opportunities available in the workplace.

The authors in this chapter provide insight into the way in which we acquire specific sexual identities, because of the cultural expectations,

161

pressures, and values that shape the choices we make. How we feel about ourselves and our life experiences reveals the powerful role gender stereotypes play in shaping our personal development. Some writers in this chapter speak out against the constricting effects of these rigid cultural expectations that enforce inflexible images of masculine and feminine behavior. These restrictive stereotypes legitimize and perpetuate gender inequality.

Ann Louise Bardach investigates the way *machismo* complicates the attitude toward AIDS in the Latino community in Miami, in "The Stealth Virus: AIDS and Latinos." Susan Bordo, in "Never Just Pictures," perceptively analyzes the cultural pressures that compel women to starve themselves to be thin. Judith Ortiz Cofer, in "The Myth of the Latin Woman," describes how different cultural expectations in her native Puerto Rico and the United States led her to be stereotyped as a "hot-blooded Latina." In "Visualizing the Disabled Body," Lennard J. Davis looks at the paradoxical double standard applied to physical imperfection in works of art and in human beings who are disabled. Elizabeth W. Fernea and Robert A. Fernea, in "A Look Behind the Veil," investigate the practice of *purdah* and its role in preserving Islamic values in a patriarchal culture. Serena Nanda, in "Arranging a Marriage in India," describes her participation in the lengthy process of getting her friend's son married. Ann M. Simmons, in "Where Fat Is a Mark of Beauty," describes how some Nigerian girls gain weight in a special "fattening room" in a culture where to be called a "slim princess" is an insult.

A timeless story, "Désirée's Baby," by Kate Chopin, offers a complex and thoughtful exploration of the consequences of endemic sexism and racism in turn-of-the-century Louisiana. Mahasweta Devi in her thought-provoking story, "Giribala," describes the social forces in Bengal, India, that permit a father to sell his daughters into prostitution.

Ann Louise Bardach

The Stealth Virus: AIDS and Latinos

◆

Ann Louise Bardach, recipient of the PEN West Award for Journalism and a contributing editor to Talk *magazine, examines contemporary issues for* Vanity Fair, The New Republic, *and other publications. She has also written* Troubled Waters: The Miami–Havana Showdown *(2001) and an article, "Elian: The Untold Story," for* George *magazine (May 2000), and* Cuba Confidential: Love and Vengeance in Miami and Havana *(2002). This essay on the effects of AIDS on the Latino community first appeared in* The New Republic *(June 1995).*

Before You Read

To help you follow Bardach's line of thought, underline passages that present research findings, expert opinions, and the results of surveys. Observe how Bardach uses these as evidence to support her thesis that AIDS has become prevalent in Miami's Latino community because of the mixed messages that *machismo* sends.

◆

1 Freddie Rodriguez is discouraged. He has just come from his afternoon's activity of trying to stop men from having unprotected sex in Miami's Alice Wainwright Park, a popular gay cruising spot. Rodriguez, 29, is a slim, handsome Cuban-American with a pale, worried face who works for Health Crisis Network. "I take a bag of condoms to the park with me and I try talking to people before they duck in the bushes and have sex," he explains. "I tell them how dangerous it is. Sometimes I beg them to use a condom. Sometimes they listen to me. Today, no one was interested." Most of the men, he says, are Latinos and range in age from 16 to 60. Many are married and would never describe themselves as gay. "Discrimination is not really the issue here. Most Latinos do not identify themselves as gay, so they're not discriminated against," he says, his voice drifting off. "Ours is a culture of denial."

2 To understand why the second wave of AIDS is hitting Latinos particularly hard, one would do well to start in Miami. Once a mecca for retirees, South Beach today is a frenzy of dance and sex clubs, for hetero- and homosexual alike. "We have the highest rate of heterosexual transmission in the country, the second-highest number of babies born with

AIDS and we are number one nationwide for teen HIV cases," says Randi Jenson, reeling off a litany that clearly exhausts him. Jenson supervises the Miami Beach HIV/AIDS Project and sits on the board of the Gay, Lesbian and Bisexual Community Center. "And we have the highest rate of bisexuality in the country." When I ask how he knows this, he says, "Trust me on this one, *we know* . . . The numbers to watch for in the future will be Hispanic women—the wives and girlfriends."

3   Already, AIDS is the leading cause of death in Miami and Fort Lauderdale for women ages 25 to 44, four times greater than the national average. According to the Centers for Disease Control and Prevention (CDC), AIDS cases among Hispanics have been steadily rising. But any foray into the Latino subculture shows that the numbers do not tell the whole story, and may not even tell half. CDC literature notes that "it is believed that AIDS-related cases and deaths for Latinos are understated by at least 30 percent. Many Hispanics do not and cannot access HIV testing and health care." Abetted by widespread shame about homosexuality, a fear of governmental and medical institutions (particularly among undocumented immigrants) and cultural denial as deep as Havana Harbor, AIDS is moving silently and insistently through Hispanic America. It is the stealth virus.

4   "No one knows how many Latino HIV cases are out there," Damian Pardo, an affable Cuban-American, who is president of the board of Health Crisis Network, tells me over lunch in Coral Gables. "All we know is that the numbers are not accurate—that the actual cases are far higher. Everyone in the community lies about HIV." Everyone, according to Pardo, means the families, the lovers, the priests, the doctors and the patients. "The Hispanic community in South Florida is far more affluent than blacks. More often than not, people see their own family doctor who simply signs a falsified death certificate. It's a conspiracy of silence and everyone is complicitous."

5   Freddie Rodriguez—smart, affluent, urbane—didn't learn that Luis, his Nicaraguan lover, was HIV-positive until it was too late to do anything about it. "He was my first boyfriend. He would get sick at times but he refused to take a blood test. He said that it was impossible for him to be HIV-positive. I believed him. One day, he disappeared. Didn't come home, didn't go to work—just disappeared." Frantic, Rodriguez called the police and started phoning hospitals. Finally, Luis turned up at Jackson Memorial Hospital. He had been discovered unconscious and rushed to intensive care. When Rodriguez arrived at the hospital, he learned that his lover was in the AIDS wing. Even then, Luis insisted it was a mistake. Two weeks later, he was dead. "I had to tell Luis's family that he was gay," Rodriguez says, "that I was his boyfriend and that he had died of AIDS. They knew nothing. He lived a completely secret life."

6   Although Rodriguez was enraged by his lover's cowardice, he understood his dilemma all too well. He remembered how hard it was to tell his own family. "When I was 22, I finally told my parents that I was gay. My mother screamed and ran out of the room. My father raised his hands in front of his eyes and told me, 'Freddie do you see what's in front of me? It's a big, white cloud. I do not hear anything, see anything and I cannot remember anything because it is all in this big white cloud.' And then he left the room." One of Rodriguez's later boyfriends, this one Peruvian, was also HIV-positive, but far more duplicitous. "He flat out lied to me when I asked him. He knew, but he only told me after we broke up, *after* we had unsafe sex," says Rodriguez, who remains HIV-negative. "Part of the *machismo* ethic," Rodriguez explains, "is not wearing a condom."

7   Miami's Body Positive, which provides psychological and nonclinical services to AIDS patients, is housed in a pink concrete bubble off Miami's Biscayne Boulevard. The building and much of its funding are provided by founder Doris Feinberg, who lost both her sons to AIDS during the late 1980s. The gay Cuban-American star of MTV's "The Real World," Pedro Zamora, worked here for the last five years of his life and started its P.O.P. program—Peer Outreach for Persons Who Are Positive. Ernie Lopez, a 26-year-old Nicaraguan who has been Body Positive's director for the last five years, estimates that 40 percent of the center's clients are Latino, in a Miami population that is 70 percent Hispanic. On the day I visit, I see mostly black men at the facility. Lopez warns me not to be fooled. "The Latino numbers are as high as the blacks, but they are not registered," he says. "Latinos want anonymity. They come in very late—when they are desperate and their disease is very progressed. Often it's too late to help them."

8   "*Soy completo,*" is what they often say in Cuba, meaning, "I'm a total human being." It is the preferred euphemism for bisexuality and in the *machista* politics of Latino culture, bisexuality is a huge step up from being gay. It is this cultural construct that prevents many Latin men from acknowledging that they could be vulnerable to HIV, because it is this cultural construct that tells them they are not gay. Why worry about AIDS if only gay men get AIDS? "To be bisexual is a code," says Ernesto Pujol, a pioneer in Latino AIDS education. "It means, 'I sleep with men but I still have power.' I think there is a legitimate group of bisexuals, but for many bisexuality is a codified and covered homosexuality." Self-definitions can get even more complex. "I'm not gay," a well-known intellectual told me in Havana last year. "How could I be gay? My boyfriend is married and has a family."

9   Without putting too fine a point on it, what defines a gay man in some segments of the Latino world is whether he's on the top or the bottom during intercourse. "The salient property of the *maricon*," my

Cuban friend adds, "is his passivity. If you're a 'top,'—*el bugaron*—you're not a faggot." Moreover, there are also many heterosexual Latino men who do not regard sex with another man as a homosexual act. "A lot of heterosexual Latinos—say, after a few drinks—will fuck a transvestite as a surrogate woman," says Pujol, "and that is culturally acceptable—absolutely acceptable." Hence the potential for HIV transmission is far greater than in the mainstream Anglo world.

10   According to Pujol, "only Latinos in the States are interested in other gay men. They have borrowed the American liberated gay model. In Latin America, the hunt is for 'straight' men. Look at the transvestites on Cristina's (the Spanish-language equivalent of "Oprah") talk show. Their boyfriends are always some macho hunk from the *bodega*." Chino, a Cuban gay now living in Montreal, typifies the cultural divide. "I don't understand it here," he says scornfully. "It's like girls going out with girls."

11   "If you come out," says Jorge B., a Cuban artist in Miami Beach, "you lose your sex appeal to 'straight' men" (straight in this context meaning married men who have sex with other men). The Hispanic preference for "straight men" is so popular that bathhouses such as Club Bodycenter in Coral Gables are said to cater to a clientele of older married men who often pick up young lovers after work before joining their families for dinner. Some men will not risk going to a gay bar, says Freddie Rodriguez. "They go to public restrooms where they can't be identified." While many gay Hispanics do eventually "come out," they do so at a huge price—a shattering loss of esteem within their family and community. "The priest who did Mass at my grandfather's funeral denied communion to me and my brother," recalls Pardo. "He knew from my mother's confession that we were gay."

12   Latino attitudes here are, of course, largely imported, their cultural fingerprints lifted straight out of Havana, Lima or Guatemala City. Consider Chiapas, Mexico, where gay men were routinely arrested throughout the 1980s; many of their bodies were later found dumped in a mass grave. Or Ecuador, where it is against the law to be a homosexual, and effeminate behavior or dress can be grounds for arrest. Or Peru, where the Shining Path has targeted gays for assassination. Or Colombia, where death squads do the same, characteristically mutilating their victims' genitals.

13   While Latino hostility to homosexuals in the United States tends to be less dramatic, it can also be virulent, particularly when cradled in reactionary politics. In Miami, right-wing Spanish-language stations daily blast their enemies as "communists, traitors and Castro puppets." But the epithet reserved for the most despised is "homosexual" or *"maricon."* When Nelson Mandela visited Miami in 1990, he was denounced daily as a *"marijuanero maricon"*—a pot-smoking faggot—for having supported Fidel Castro.

✧ *Evaluating the Text*

1. Bardach characterizes AIDS as a "stealth virus" whose spread is fostered by "a culture of denial" and a "conspiracy of silence." What does she mean?

2. According to Bardach, in what respects are the values of Spanish culture in relationship to homosexuality and bisexuality at the root of the problem?

✧ *Exploring Different Perspectives*

1. Compare the significance of *machismo* and stereotyping of sexual roles in Latino culture in the analyses of Bardach and Judith Ortiz Cofer.

2. Discuss the issues of gender and race as expressed in Bardach's essay and in Kate Chopin's story, "Désirée's Baby."

✧ *Extending Viewpoints through Writing*

1. Questions of *machismo* are at the heart of Bardach's analysis. How would you define this concept? What values does it entail?

2. How do films such as *The Band Played On* (1993), *Philadelphia* (1994), or *Indian Summer* (1996) portray those with AIDS? What insights do these or other films offer into why society stigmatizes some diseases but not others?

Susan Bordo

Never Just Pictures

Susan Bordo is a professor of English and women's studies at the University of Kentucky and was awarded the Singletary Chair of Humanities. Bordo's book Unbearable Weight: Feminism, Western Culture and the Body *(1993) examines the myths, ideologies, and pathologies of the modern female body. She is also the author of* The Male Body: A New Look at Men in Public and Private *(1999). "Never Just Pictures" first appeared in* Twilight Zones: The Hidden Life of Cultural Images from Plato to O.J. *(1997).*

Before You Read

Before you read Bordo's essay, which raises questions about the images of women presented in advertising, think about some current ads for women's products. Do the ads encourage women to be dissatisfied with the way they look? Whether you are male or female, what part, if any, do the media play in your concept of how you should look?

Bodies and Fantasies

1   When Alicia Silverstone, the svelte nineteen-year-old star of *Clueless*, appeared at the Academy Awards just a smidge more substantial than she had been in the movie, the tabloids ribbed her cruelly, calling her "fatgirl" and "buttgirl" (her next movie role is Batgirl) and "more *Babe* than babe."[1] Our idolatry of the trim, tight body shows no signs of relinquishing its grip on our conceptions of beauty and normality. Since I began exploring this obsession it seems to have gathered momentum, like a spreading mass hysteria. Fat is the devil, and we are continually beating him—"eliminating" our stomachs, "busting" our thighs, "taming" our tummies—pummeling and purging our bodies, attempting to make them into something other than flesh. On television, infomercials hawking miracle diet pills and videos promising to turn our body parts into steel have become as commonplace as aspirin ads. There hasn't been a tabloid cover in the past few years that didn't boast of an inside scoop on some star's diet regime, a "fabulous" success story of weight loss, or a tragic relapse. (When they can't come up with a current one, they scrounge up an old one; a few weeks ago the *National Inquirer* ran a story on Joan Lunden's fifty-pound weight loss fifteen years ago!) Children in this culture grow up knowing that you

can never be thin enough and that being fat is one of the worst things one can be. One study asked ten- and eleven-year-old boys and girls to rank drawings of children with various physical handicaps; drawings of fat children elicited the greatest disapproval and discomfort, over pictures of kids with facial disfigurements and missing hands.

2   Psychologists commonly believe that girls with eating disorders suffer from "body image disturbance syndrome": they are unable to see themselves as anything but fat, no matter how thin they become. If this is a disorder, it is one that has become a norm of cultural perception. Our ideas about what constitutes a body in need of a diet have become more and more pathologically trained on the slightest hint of excess. This ideal of the body beautiful has largely come from fashion designers and models. (Movie stars, who often used to embody a more voluptuous ideal, are now modeling themselves after the models.) They have taught us "to love a woman's pelvis, her hipbones jutting out through a bias-cut gown . . . the clavicle in its role as a coat hanger from which clothes are suspended."[2] (An old fashion industry justification for skinniness in models was that clothes just don't "hang right" on heftier types.) The fashion industry has taught us to regard a perfect healthy, nonobese body [. . .] as an unsightly "before" ("Before CitraLean, no wonder they wore swimsuits like that"). In fact, those in the business have admitted that models have been getting thinner since 1993, when Kate Moss first repopularized the waif look. British models Trish Goff and Annie Morton make Moss look well fed by comparison,[3] and recent ad campaigns for Jil Sander go way beyond the thin-body-as-coat-hanger paradigm to a blatant glamorization of the cadaverous, starved look itself. [. . .] More and more ads featuring anorexic-looking young men are appearing too.

3   The main challenge to such images is a muscular aesthetic that *looks* more life-affirming but is no less punishing and compulsion-inducing in its demands on ordinary bodies. During the 1996 Summer Olympics— which were reported with unprecedented focus and hype on the fat-free beauty of muscular bodies—commentators celebrated the "health" of this aesthetic over anorexic glamour. But there is growing evidence of rampant eating disorders among female athletes, and it's hard to imagine that those taut and tiny Olympic gymnasts—the idols of preadolescents across the country—are having regular menstrual cycles. Their skimpy level of body fat just won't support it. During the Olympics I heard a commentator gushing about how great it was that the 1996 team was composed of eighteen- and nineteen-year-old women rather than little girls. To me it is far more disturbing that these nineteen-year-olds still *look* (and talk) like little girls. As I watched them vault and leap, my admiration for their tremendous skill and spirit was shadowed by thoughts of what was going on *inside* their body—the hormones unreleased because of insufficient body fat, the organ development delayed, perhaps halted.

4   Is it any wonder that despite media attention to the dangers of starvation dieting and habitual vomiting, eating disorders have spread throughout the culture?[4] In 1993 in *Unbearable Weight* I argued that the old clinical generalizations positing distinctive class, race, family, and "personality" profiles for the women most likely to develop an eating disorder were being blasted apart by the normalizing power of mass imagery. Some feminists complained that I had not sufficiently attended to racial and ethnic "difference" and was assuming the white, middle-class experience as the norm. Since then it has been widely acknowledged among medical professionals that the incidence of eating and body-image problems among African American, Hispanic, and Native American women has been grossly underestimated and is on the increase.[5] Even the gender gap is being narrowed, as more and more men are developing eating disorders and exercise compulsions too. (In the mid-eighties the men in my classes used to yawn and pass notes when we discussed the pressure to diet; in 1996 they are more apt to protest if the women in the class talk as though it's their problem alone.)

5   The spread of eating disorders, of course, is not just about images. The emergence of eating disorders is a complex, multilayered cultural "symptom," reflecting problems that are historical as well as contemporary, arising in our time because of the confluence of a number of factors.[6] Eating disorders are overdetermined in this culture. They have to do not only with new social expectations of women and ambivalence toward their bodies but also with more general anxieties about the body as the source of hungers, needs, and physical vulnerabilities not within our control. These anxieties are deep and long-standing in Western philosophy and religion, and they are especially acute in our own time. Eating disorders are also linked to the contradictions of consumer culture, which is continually encouraging us to binge on our desires at the same time as it glamorizes self-discipline and scorns fat as a symbol of laziness and lack of willpower. And these disorders reflect, too, our increasing fascination with the possibilities of reshaping our bodies and selves in radical ways, creating new bodies according to our mind's design.

6   The relationship between problems such as these and cultural images is complex. On the one hand, the idealization of certain kinds of bodies foments and perpetuates our anxieties and insecurities, that's clear. Glamorous images of hyperthin models certainly don't encourage a more relaxed or accepting attitude toward the body, particularly among those whose own bodies are far from that ideal. But, on the other hand, such images carry fantasized solutions *to* our anxieties and insecurities, and that's part of the reason why they are powerful. They speak to us not just about how to be beautiful or desirable but about how to get control of our lives, get safe, be cool, avoid hurt. When I look at the picture of a skeletal and seemingly barely breathing young woman [. . .], for example, I do not see a vacuous fashion ideal. I see a visual embodiment of what novelist and ex-anorexic Stephanie Grant

means when she says in her autobiographical novel, *The Passion of Alice*, "If I had to say my anorexia was about any single thing, I would have said it was about living without desire. Without longing of any kind."[7]

7 Now, this may not seem like a particularly attractive philosophy of life (or a particularly attractive body, for that matter). Why would anyone want to look like death, you might be asking. Why would anyone want to live without desire? But recent articles in both the *New Yorker* and the *New York Times* have noted a new aesthetic in contemporary ads, in which the models appear dislocated and withdrawn, with chipped black nail polish and greasy hair, staring out at the viewer in a deathlike trance, seeming to be "barely a person." Some have called this wasted look "heroin chic": ex-model Zoe Fleischauer recalls that "they wanted models that looked like junkies. The more skinny and fucked-up you look, the more everybody thinks you're fabulous."[8]

8 Hilton Als, in the *New Yorker*, interprets this trend as making the statement that fashion is dead and beauty is "trivial in relation to depression."[9] I read these ads very differently. Although the photographers may see themselves as ironically "deconstructing" fashion, the reality is that no fashion advertisement can declare fashion to be dead—it's virtually a grammatical impossibility. Put that frame around the image, whatever the content, and we are instructed to find it glamorous. These ads are not telling us that beauty is trivial in relation to depression, they are telling us that depression is beautiful, that being wasted is *cool* [. . .]. The question then becomes not "Is fashion dead?" but "Why has death become glamorous?"

9 Freud tells us that in the psyche death represents not the destruction of the self but its return to a state prior to need, thus freedom from unfulfilled longing, from anxiety over not having one's needs met. Following Freud, I would argue that ghostly pallor and bodily disrepair, in "heroin chic" images, are about the allure, the safety, of being beyond needing, beyond caring, beyond desire. Should we be surprised at the appeal of being without desire in a culture that has invested our needs with anxiety, stress, and danger, that has made us craving and hungering machines, creatures of desire, and then repaid us with addictions, AIDS, shallow and unstable relationships, and cutthroat competition for jobs and mates? To have given up the quest for fulfillment, to be unconcerned with the body or its needs—or its vulnerability—is much wiser than to care.

10 So, yes, the causes of eating disorders are "deeper" than just obedience to images. But cultural images themselves *are* deep. And the way they become imbued and animated with such power is hardly mysterious. Far from being the purely aesthetic inventions that designers and photographers would like to have us believe they are—"It's just fashion, darling, nothing to get all politically steamed up about"— they reflect the designers' cultural savvy, their ability to sense and give form to flutters and quakes in the cultural psyche. These folks have a

strong and simple motivation to hone their skills as cultural Geiger counters. It's called the profit motive. They want their images and the products associated with them to sell.

11   The profit motive can sometimes produce seemingly "transgressive" wrinkles in current norms. Recently designers such as Calvin Klein and Jil Sander have begun to use rather plain, ordinary-looking, unmadeup faces in their ad campaigns. Unlike the models in "heroin chic" ads, these men and women do not appear wasted so much as unadorned, unpolished, stripped of the glamorous veneer we have come to expect of fashion spreads. While many of them have interesting faces, few of them qualify as beautiful by any prevailing standards. They have rampant freckles, moles in unbeautiful places, oddly proportioned heads. Noticing these ads, I at first wondered whether we really were shifting into a new gear, more genuinely accepting of diversity and "flaws" in appearance. Then it suddenly hit me that these imperfect faces were showing up in clothing and perfume ads only and the *bodies* in these ads were as relentlessly normalizing as ever—not one plump body to complement the facial "diversity."

12   I now believe that what we are witnessing here is a commercial war. Clothing manufacturers, realizing that many people—particularly young people, at whom most of these ads are aimed—have limited resources and that encouraging them to spend all their money fixing up their faces rather than buying clothes is not in their best interests, are reasserting the importance of body over face as the "site" of our fantasies. In the new codes of these ads a too madeup look signifies a lack of cool, too much investment in how one looks. "Just Be," Calvin Klein tells us in a recent CK One ad. But looks—a lean body—still matter enormously in these ads, and we are still being told *how* to be—in the mode which best serves Calvin Klein. And all the while, of course, makeup and hair products continue to promote their own self-serving aesthetics of facial perfection.

NOTES

1. I give great credit to Alicia Silverstone for her response to these taunts. In *Vanity Fair* she says, "I do my best. But it's much more important to me that my brain be working in the morning than getting up early and doing exercise. . . . The most important thing for me is that I eat and that I sleep and that I get the work done, but unfortunately . . . it's the perception that women in film should look a certain way" ("Hollywood Princess," September 1996, pp. 292–294). One wonders how long she will manage to retain such a sane attitude!

2. Holly Brubach, "The Athletic Aesthetic," *The New York Times Magazine*, June 23, 1996, p. 51.

3. In early 1996 the Swiss watch manufacturer Omega threatened to stop advertising in British *Vogue* because of *Vogue's* use of such hyperthin models, but it later reversed this decision. The furor was reminiscent of boycotts that were threatened in 1994 when Calvin Klein and Coca-Cola first began to use photos of Kate Moss in their ads. In neither case has the fashion industry acknowledged any validity to the charge that their imagery encourages eating disorders. Instead, they have responded with defensive "rebuttals."

4. Despite media attention to eating disorders, an air of scornful impatience with "victim feminism" has infected attitudes toward women's body issues. Christina Hoff-Sommers charges Naomi Wolf (*The Beauty Myth*) with grossly inflating statistics on eating disorders and she poo-poos the notion that women are dying from dieting. Even if some particular set of statistics is inaccurate, why would Sommers want to deny the reality of the problem, which as a teacher she can surely see right before her eyes?

5. For the spread of eating disorders in minority groups, see, for example, "The Art of Integrating Diversity: Addressing Treatment Issues of Minority Women in the 90's," in *The Renfrew Perspective*, Winter 1994; see also Becky Thompson, *A Hunger So Wide and So Deep* (Minneapolis: University of Minnesota Press, 1994).

6. See my *Unbearable Weight* (Berkeley: University of California Press, 1993).

7. Stephanie Grant, *The Passion of Alice* (New York: Houghton Mifflin, 1995), 58.

8. Zoe Fleischauer quoted in "Rockers, Models, and the New Allure of Heroin," *Newsweek*, August 26, 1996.

9. Hilton Als, "Buying the Fantasy," *The New Yorker*, October 10, 1996, p. 70.

✦ Evaluating the Text

1. How do the pervasive eating disorders so common in U.S. culture suggest an underlying confusion in values associated with being fat?

2. What relationships between social classes, men and women, and ethnic minorities and mainstream society, underlie Bordo's thesis? What role do the media and advertising play in urging women to reshape their bodies to fit cultural stereotypes?

✦ Exploring Different Perspectives

1. How do Bordo and Lennard J. Davis (see "Visualizing the Disabled Body") address the issue of the stereotyping of the female body image in western cultures?

2. How do Bordo and Judith Ortiz Cofer (see "The Myth of the Latin Woman") deal with the psychological effects of stereotyping based on appearance?

✦ Extending Viewpoints through Writing

1. Our attitudes toward food are invariably connected with cultural messages about losing weight and being thin. Analyze the promotional claims for any weight loss program, diet, or exercise video, and in a short essay, discuss how cultural values are interwoven with the message.

2. You might rent the 2002 film, *Shallow Hal,* and in a few paragraphs, discuss what the movie says about American values regarding weight and appearance. To what extent has your own self-image been determined by prevailing cultural expectations of the kind described by Bordo? What parts of your body or aspects of your appearance would you change and why?

Judith Ortiz Cofer

The Myth of the Latin Woman

———————◆———————

Judith Ortiz Cofer, a poet and novelist, was born in 1952 in Hormigueros, Puerto Rico. After her father, a career navy officer, retired, the family set-tled in Georgia where Cofer attended Augusta College. During college she married and, with her husband and daughter, moved to Florida where she finished a master's degree in English at Florida Atlantic University. A fel-lowship allowed her to pursue graduate work at Oxford University, after which she returned to Florida and began teaching English and writing poetry. Her first volume of poetry, Peregrina *(1985), won the Riverstone International Poetry Competition and was followed by two more poetry collections,* Reaching for the Mainland *(1987) and* Terms of Survival *(1988). Her first novel,* The Line of the Sun *(1989), was listed as one of 1989's "twenty-five books to remember" by the New York City Public Li-brary System. Her recent works include a collection of short stories,* An Island Like You: Stories of the Barrio *(1995), and* The Year of Our Revolution *(1998). Cofer is a Professor of English and Creative Writing at the University of Georgia. In the following essay, drawn from her col-lection* The Latin Deli: Prose and Poetry *(1993), Cofer explores the de-structive effects of the Latina stereotype. Most recently, she has written* Women in Front of the Sun: On Becoming a Writer *(2000).*

Before You Read

As you read, notice how Cofer's desire to succeed as a writer is a reac-tion to the repeated instances in which she is misperceived because of her ethnicity.

———————◆———————

1   On a bus trip to London from Oxford University where I was earn-ing some graduate credits one summer, a young man, obviously fresh from a pub, spotted me and as if struck by inspiration went down on his knees in the aisle. With both hands over his heart he broke into an Irish tenor's rendition of "Maria" from *West Side Story*. My politely amused fellow passengers gave his lovely voice the round of gentle ap-plause it deserved. Though I was not quite as amused, I managed my version of an English smile: no show of teeth, no extreme contortions of the facial muscles—I was at this time of my life practicing reserve and cool. Oh, that British control, how I coveted it. But "Maria" had followed me to London, reminding me of a prime fact of my life: you

can leave the island, master the English language, and travel as far as you can, but if you are a Latina, especially one like me who so obviously belongs to Rita Moreno's gene pool, the island travels with you.

2   This is sometimes a very good thing—it may win you that extra minute of someone's attention. But with some people, the same things can make *you* an island—not a tropical paradise but an Alcatraz, a place nobody wants to visit. As a Puerto Rican girl living in the United States and wanting like most children to "belong," I resented the stereotype that my Hispanic appearance called forth from many people I met.

3   Growing up in a large urban center in New Jersey during the 1960s, I suffered from what I think of as "cultural schizophrenia." Our life was designed by my parents as a microcosm of their *casas* on the island. We spoke in Spanish, ate Puerto Rican food bought at the *bodega*, and practiced strict Catholicism at a church that allotted us a one-hour slot each week for mass, performed in Spanish by a Chinese priest trained as a missionary for Latin America.

4   As a girl I was kept under strict surveillance by my parents, since my virtue and modesty were, by their cultural equation, the same as their honor. As a teenager I was lectured constantly on how to behave as a proper *senorita*. But it was a conflicting message I received, since the Puerto Rican mothers also encouraged their daughters to look and act like women and to dress in clothes our Anglo friends and their mothers found too "mature" and flashy. The difference was, and is, cultural; yet I often felt humiliated when I appeared at an American friend's party wearing a dress more suitable to a semi-formal than to a playroom birthday celebration. At Puerto Rican festivities, neither the music nor the colors we wore could be too loud.

5   I remember Career Day in our high school, when teachers told us to come dressed as if for a job interview. It quickly became obvious that to the Puerto Rican girls "dressing up" meant wearing their mothers' ornate jewelry and clothing, more appropriate (by mainstream standards) for the company Christmas party than as daily office attire. That morning I had agonized in front of my closet, trying to figure out what a "career girl" would wear. I knew how to dress for school (at the Catholic school I attended, we all wore uniforms), I knew how to dress for Sunday mass, and I knew what dresses to wear for parties at my relatives' homes. Though I do not recall the precise details of my Career Day outfit, it must have been a composite of these choices. But I remember a comment my friend (an Italian American) made in later years that coalesced my impressions of that day. She said that at the business school she was attending, the Puerto Rican girls always stood out for wearing "everything at once." She meant, of course, too much jewelry, too many accessories. On that day at school we were simply made the negative models by the nuns, who

were themselves not credible fashion experts to any of us. But it was painfully obvious to me that to the others, in their tailored skirts and silk blouses, we must have seemed "hopeless" and "vulgar." Though I now know that most adolescents feel out of step much of the time, I also know that for the Puerto Rican girls of my generation that sense was intensified. The way our teachers and classmates looked at us that day in school was just a taste of the cultural clash that awaited us in the real world, where prospective employers and men on the street would often misinterpret our tight skirts and jingling bracelets as a "come-on."

6   Mixed cultural signals have perpetuated certain stereotypes—for example, that of the Hispanic woman as the "hot tamale" or sexual firebrand. It is a one-dimensional view that the media have found easy to promote. In their special vocabulary, advertisers have designated "sizzling" and "smoldering" as the adjectives of choice for describing not only the foods but also the women of Latin America. From conversations in my house I recall hearing about the harassment that Puerto Rican women endured in factories where the "boss-men" talked to them as if sexual innuendo was all they understood, and worse, often gave them the choice of submitting to their advances or being fired.

7   It is custom, however, not chromosomes, that leads us to choose scarlet over pale pink. As young girls, it was our mothers who influenced our decisions about clothes and colors—mothers who had grown up on a tropical island where the natural environment was a riot of primary colors, where showing your skin was one way to keep cool as well as to look sexy. Most important of all, on the island, women perhaps felt freer to dress and move more provocatively since, in most cases, they were protected by the traditions, mores, and laws of a Spanish/Catholic system of morality and machismo whose main rule was: *You may look at my sister, but if you touch her I will kill you.* The extended family and church structure could provide a young woman with a circle of safety in her small pueblo on the island; if a man "wronged" a girl, everyone would close in to save her family honor.

8   My mother has told me about dressing in her best party clothes on Saturday nights and going to the town's plaza to promenade with her girlfriends in front of the boys they liked. The males were thus given an opportunity to admire the women and to express their admiration in the form of *piropos:* erotically charged street poems they composed on the spot. (I have myself been subjected to a few *piropos* while visiting the island, and they can be outrageous, although custom dictates that they must never cross into obscenity.) This ritual, as I understand it, also entails a show of studied indifference on the woman's part; if she is "decent," she must not acknowledge the man's impassioned words. So I do understand how things can be lost in translation. When a Puerto Rican girl dressed in her idea of what is attractive meets a

man from the mainstream culture who has been trained to react to certain types of clothing as a sexual signal, a clash is likely to take place. I remember the boy who took me to my first formal dance leaning over to plant a sloppy, over-eager kiss painfully on my mouth; when I didn't respond with sufficient passion, he remarked resentfully: "I thought you Latin girls were supposed to mature early," as if I were expected to *ripen* like a fruit or vegetable, not just grow into womanhood like other girls.

9   It is surprising to my professional friends that even today some people, including those who should know better, still put others "in their place." It happened to me most recently during a stay at a classy metropolitan hotel favored by young professional couples for weddings. Late one evening after the theater, as I walked toward my room with a colleague (a woman with whom I was coordinating an arts program), a middle-aged man in a tuxedo, with a young girl in satin and lace on his arm, stepped directly into our path. With his champagne glass extended toward me, he exclaimed "Evita!"[1]

10   Our way blocked, my companion and I listened as the man half-recited, half-bellowed "Don't Cry for Me, Argentina." When he finished, the young girl said: "How about a round of applause for my daddy?" We complied, hoping this would bring the silly spectacle to a close. I was becoming aware that our little group was attracting the attention of the other guests. "Daddy" must have perceived this too, and he once more barred the way as we tried to walk past him. He began to shout-sing a ditty to the tune of "La Bamba"—except the lyrics were about a girl named Maria whose exploits rhymed with her name and gonorrhea. The girl kept saying "Oh, Daddy" and looking at me with pleading eyes. She wanted me to laugh along with the others. My companion and I stood silently waiting for the man to end his offensive song. When he finished, I looked not at him but at his daughter. I advised her calmly never to ask her father what he had done in the army. Then I walked between them and to my room. My friend complimented me on my cool handling of the situation, but I confessed that I had really wanted to push the jerk into the swimming pool. This same man—probably a corporate executive, well-educated, even worldly by most standards—would not have been likely to regale an Anglo woman with a dirty song in public. He might have checked his impulse by assuming that she could be somebody's wife or mother, or at least *somebody* who might take offense. But, to him, I was just an Evita or a Maria: merely a character in his cartoon-populated universe.

11   Another facet of the myth of the Latin woman in the United States is the menial, the domestic—Maria the housemaid or countergirl. It's true that work as domestics, as waitresses, and in factories is all that's

[1]A musical about Eva Duarte de Peron, the former first lady of Argentina.

available to women with little English and few skills. But the myth of the Hispanic menial—the funny maid, mispronouncing words and cooking up a spicy storm in a shiny California kitchen—has been perpetuated by the media in the same way that "Mammy" from *Gone with the Wind* became America's idea of the black woman for generations. Since I do not wear my diplomas around my neck for all to see, I have on occasion been sent to that "kitchen" where some think I obviously belong.

12   One incident has stayed with me, though I recognize it as a minor offense. My first public poetry reading took place in Miami, at a restaurant where a luncheon was being held before the event. I was nervous and excited as I walked in with notebook in hand. An older woman motioned me to her table, and thinking (foolish me) that she wanted me to autograph a copy of my newly published slender volume of verse, I went over. She ordered a cup of coffee from me, assuming that I was the waitress. (Easy enough to mistake my poems for menus, I suppose.) I know it wasn't an intentional act of cruelty. Yet of all the good things that happened later, I remember that scene most clearly, because it reminded me of what I had to overcome before anyone would take me seriously. In retrospect I understand that my anger gave my reading fire. In fact, I have almost always taken any doubt in my abilities as a challenge, the result most often being the satisfaction of winning a convert, of seeing the cold, appraising eyes warm to my words, the body language change, the smile that indicates I have opened some avenue for communication. So that day as I read, I looked directly at that woman. Her lowered eyes told me she was embarrassed at her faux pas, and when I willed her to look up at me, she graciously allowed me to punish her with my full attention. We shook hands at the end of the reading and I never saw her again. She has probably forgotten the entire incident, but maybe not.

13   Yet I am one of the lucky ones. There are thousands of Latinas without the privilege of an education or the entrees into society that I have. For them life is a constant struggle against the misconceptions perpetuated by the myth of the Latina. My goal is to try to replace the old stereotypes with a much more interesting set of realities. Every time I give a reading, I hope the stories I tell, the dreams and fears I examine in my work, can achieve some universal truth that will get my audience past the particulars of my skin color, my accent, or my clothes.

14   I once wrote a poem in which I called all Latinas "God's brown daughters." This poem is really a prayer of sorts, offered upward, but also, through the human-to-human channel of art, outward. It is a prayer for communication and for respect. In it, Latin women pray "in Spanish to an Anglo God/ with a Jewish heritage," and they are "fervently hoping/ that if not omnipotent,/ at least He be bilingual."

✧ Evaluating the Text

1. What characteristics define, from Cofer's perspective, the "Maria" stereotype in terms of style, clothes, and behavior? How has this stereotype been a source of harassment for Cofer?

2. How has the desire to destroy this stereotype and its underlying attitudes motivated Cofer to write the kinds of works she has?

3. How does Cofer use her personal experiences as a springboard to understanding sexual stereotyping of Latinas?

✧ Exploring Different Perspectives

1. How do both Judith Ortiz Cofer and Ann Louise Bardach (see "The Stealth Virus: AIDS and Latinos") seek to replace sexual stereotypes with realistic portraits?

2. In what way do conflicting societal expectations determine how a woman's appearance signifies how she is perceived, as analyzed by Judith Ortiz Cofer and by Lennard J. Davis (see "Visualizing the Disabled Body")?

✧ Extending Viewpoints through Writing

1. Have you ever been in a situation where someone who is unaware of your ethnic, racial, or religious background disparaged the group to which you belong? What did you do?

2. Create a character sketch of a male chauvinist.

Lennard J. Davis

Visualizing the Disabled Body

Lennard J. Davis is chair of the English department and a professor in the Department of Disability and Human Development at the University of Illinos at Chicago. He has written on disability for the Nation. *His previous books include* Factual Fictions: The Origins of the English Novel *(1983),* Resisting Novels: Etiology and Fiction *(1987), and* The Disabilities Study Reader *(1997). Although not hearing impaired himself, Davis was born to deaf parents and uttered his first word in sign language. Upon his father's death, Davis discovered the letters his parents wrote to each other during their courtship. He edited* Shall I Say a Kiss?: The Courtship Letters of a Deaf Couple, 1936–1938 *(1999), a unique window into the lives of a working-class, Jewish, British deaf couple prior to World War II. "Visualizing the Disabled Body" is drawn from* Enforcing Normalcy: Disability, Deafness, and the Body *(1995). Most recently, he has written* The Sonnets: A Novel *(2001).*

Before You Read

To what extent have the mass media shaped your concept of beauty and ugliness? What does the shift of descriptive terms from "handicapped" to "disabled" to "differently abled" suggest about changes in social attitudes?

> *A human being who is first of all an invalid is* all *body, therein lies his inhumanity and his debasement. In most cases he is little better than a carcass—.*
>> —Thomas Mann, *The Magic Mountain*

> *. . . the female is as it were a deformed male.*
>> —Aristotle, *Generation of Animals*

> *When I begin to wish I were crippled—even though I am perfectly healthy—or rather that I would have been better off crippled, that is the first step towards* butoh.
>> —Tatsumi Hijikata, co-founder of the Japanese
>> performance art/dance form *butoh*

1   She has no arms or hands, although the stump of her upper right arm extends just to her breast. Her left foot has been severed, and her face is badly scarred, with her nose torn at the tip, and her lower lip gouged out. Fortunately, her facial mutilations have been treated and are barely visible, except for minor scarring visible only up close. The big toe of her right foot has been cut off, and her torso is covered with scars, including a particularly large one between her shoulder blades, one that covers her shoulder, and one covering the tip of her breast where her left nipple was torn out.

2   Yet she is considered one of the most beautiful female figures in the world. When the romantic poet Heinrich Heine saw her he called her "Notre-Dame de la Beauté."

3   He was referring to the Venus de Milo.

4   Consider too Pam Herbert, a quadriplegic with muscular dystrophy, writing her memoir by pressing her tongue on a computer keyboard, who describes herself at twenty-eight years old:

> I weigh about 130 pounds; I'm about four feet tall. It's pretty hard to get an accurate measurement on me because both of my knees are permanently bent and my spine is curved, so 4' is an estimate. I wear size two tennis shoes and strong glasses; my hair is dishwater blonde and shoulder length. (S. E. Browne et al., eds, 1985. *With the Power of Each Breath: A Disabled Woman's Anthology.* Pittsburgh: Cleis Press, p. 147.)

5   In this memoir, she describes her wedding night:

> We got to the room and Mark laid me down on the bed because I was so tired from sitting all day. Anyway, I hadn't gone to the bathroom all day so Mark had to catheterize me. I had been having trouble going to the bathroom for many years, so it was nothing new to Mark, he had done it lots of times before.
>
> It was time for the biggest moment of my life, making love. Of course, I was a little nervous and scared. Mark was very gentle with me. He started undressing me and kissing me. We tried making love in the normal fashion with Mark on top and me on the bottom. Well, that position didn't work at all, so then we tried laying on our sides coming in from behind. That was a little better. Anyway, we went to sleep that night a little discouraged because we didn't have a very good lovemaking session. You would have thought that it would be great, but sometimes things don't always go the way we want them to. We didn't get the hang of making love for about two months. It hurt for a long time. (ibid., 155)

6   I take the liberty of bringing these two women's bodies together. Both have disabilities. The statue is considered the ideal of Western beauty and eroticism, although it is armless and disfigured. The living woman might be considered by many "normal" people to be physically repulsive, and certainly without erotic allure. The question I wish to ask is why does the impairment of the Venus de Milo in no way prevent "normal" people from considering her beauty, while Pam Herbert's disability becomes the focal point for horror and pity?

7   In asking this question, I am really raising a complex issue. On a social level, the question has to do with how people with disabilities are seen and why, by and large, they are de-eroticized. If, as I mentioned earlier, disability is a cultural phenomenon rooted in the senses, one needs to inquire how a disability occupies a field of vision, of touch, of hearing; and how that disruption or distress in the sensory field translates into psycho-dynamic representations. This is more a question about the nature of the subject than about the qualities of the object, more about the observer than the observed. The "problem" of the disabled has been put at the feet of people with disabilities for too long.

8   Normalcy, rather than being a degree zero of existence, is more accurately a location of bio-power, as Foucault would use the term. The "normal" person (clinging to that title) has a network of traditional ableist assumptions and social supports that empowers the gaze and interaction. The person with disabilities, until fairly recently, had only his or her own individual force or will. Classically, the encounter has been, and remains, an uneven one. Anne Finger describes it in strikingly visual terms by relating an imagined meeting between Rosa Luxemburg and Antonio Gramsci, each of whom was a person with disabilities, although Rosa is given the temporary power of the abled gaze:

> We can measure Rosa's startled reaction as she glimpses him the misshapen dwarf limping towards her in a second-hand black suit so worn that the cuffs are frayed and the fabric is turning green with age, her eye immediately drawn to this disruption in the visual field; the unconscious flinch; the realization that she is staring at him, and the too-rapid turning away of the head. And then, the moment after, the consciousness that the quick aversion of the gaze was as much of an insult as the stare, so she turns her head back but tries to make her focus general, not a sharp gape. Comrade Rosa, would you have felt a slight flicker of embarrassment? shame? revulsion? dread? of a feeling that can have no name?

In this encounter what is suppressed, at least in this moment, is the fact that Rosa Luxemburg herself is physically impaired (she walked with a limp for her whole life). The emphasis then shifts from the cultural norm to the deviation; Luxemburg, now the gazing subject, places herself in the empowered position of the norm, even if that position is not warranted.

9   Disability, in this and other encounters, is a disruption in the visual, auditory, or perceptual field as it relates to the power of the gaze. As such, the disruption, the rebellion of the visual, must be regulated, rationalized, contained. Why the modern binary—normal/abnormal—must be maintained is a complex question. But we can begin by accounting for the desire to split bodies into two immutable categories: whole and incomplete, abled and disabled, normal and abnormal, functional and dysfunctional.

10   In the most general sense, cultures perform an act of splitting (*Spaltung,* to use Freud's term). These violent cleavages of consciousness are as primitive as our thought processes can be. The young infant splits the good parent from the bad parent—although the parent is the same entity. When the child is satisfied by the parent, the parent is the good parent; when the child is not satisfied, the parent is bad. As a child grows out of the earliest phases of infancy, she learns to combine those split images into a single parent who is sometimes good and sometimes not. The residue of *Spaltung* remains in our inner life, personal and collective, to produce monsters and evil stepmothers as well as noble princes and fairy godmothers.

11   In this same primitive vein, culture tends to split bodies into good and bad parts. Some cultural norms are considered good and others bad. Everyone is familiar with the "bad body": too short or tall, too fat or thin, not masculine or feminine enough, not enough or too much hair on the head or other parts of the body, penis or breasts too small or (excepting the penis) too big. Furthermore, each individual assigns good and bad labels to body parts—good: hair, face, lips, eyes, hands; bad: sexual organs, excretory organs, underarms.

12   The psychological explanation may provide a reason why it is imperative for society at large to engage in *Spaltung.* The divisions whole/incomplete, able/disabled neatly cover up the frightening writing on the wall that reminds the hallucinated whole being that its wholeness is in fact a hallucination, a developmental fiction. *Spaltung* creates the absolute categories of abled and disabled, with concomitant defenses against the repressed fragmented body.

13   But a psychological explanation alone is finally insufficient. Historical specificity makes us understand that disability is a social process with an origin. So, why certain disabilities are labeled negatively while others have a less negative connotation is a question tied to complex social forces. It is fair to say, in general, that disabilities would be most dysfunctional in postindustrial countries, where the ability to perambulate or manipulate is so concretely tied to productivity, which in itself is tied to production. The body of the average worker, as we have seen,

becomes the new measure of man and woman. Michael Oliver, citing Ryan and Thomas (1980), notes:

> With the rise of the factory . . . [during industrialization] many more disabled people were excluded from the production process for "The speed of factory work, the enforced discipline, the time-keeping and production norms—all these were a highly un-favourable change from the slower, more self-determined and flexible methods of work into which many handicapped people had been integrated." (1990, 27)

Both industrial production and the concomitant standardization of the human body have had a profound impact on how we split up bodies.

14   We tend to group impairments into the categories either of "disabling" (bad) or just "limiting" (good). For example, wearing a hearing aid is seen as much more disabling than wearing glasses, although both serve to amplify a deficient sense. But loss of hearing is associated with aging in a way that nearsightedness is not. Breast removal is seen as an impairment of femininity and sexuality, whereas the removal of a foreskin is not seen as a diminution of masculinity. The coding of body parts and the importance attached to their selective function or dysfunction is part of a much larger system of signs and meanings in society, and is constructed as such.

15   "Splitting" may help us to understand one way in which disability is seen as part of a system in which value is attributed to body parts. The disabling of the body part or function is then part of a removal of value. The gradations of value are socially determined, but what is striking is the way that rather than being incremental or graduated, the assignment of the term "disabled," and the consequent devaluation are total. That is, the concept of disabled seems to be an absolute rather than a gradient one. One is either disabled or not. Value is tied to the ability to earn money. If one's body is productive, it is not disabled. People with disabilities continue to earn less than "normal" people and, even after the passage of the Americans with Disabilities Act, 69 percent of Americans with disabilities were unemployed (*New York Times*, 27 October 1994, A:22). Women and men with disabilites are seen as less attractive, less able to marry and be involved in domestic production.

16   The ideology of the assigning of value to the body goes back to preindustrial times. Myths of beauty and ugliness have laid the foundations for normalcy. In particular, the Venus myth is one that is dialectically linked to another. This embodiment of beauty and desire is tied to the story of the embodiment of ugliness and repulsion. So the appropriate mythological character to compare the armless Venus with is Medusa. Medusa was once a beautiful sea goddess who, because she had sexual intercourse with Poseidon at one of Athene's temples, was

turned by Athene into a winged monster with glaring eyes, huge teeth, protruding tongue, brazen claws, and writhing snakes for hair. Her hideous appearance has the power to turn people into stone, and Athene eventually completes her revenge by having Perseus kill Medusa. He finds Medusa by stealing the one eye and one tooth shared by the Graiae until they agree to help him. Perseus then kills Medusa by decapitating her while looking into his brightly polished shield, which neutralizes the power of her appearance; he then puts her head into a magic wallet that shields onlookers from its effects. When Athene receives the booty, she uses Medusa's head and skin to fashion her own shield.

17   In the Venus tradition, Medusa is a poignant double. She is the necessary counter in the dialectic of beauty and ugliness, desire and repulsion, wholeness and fragmentation. Medusa is the disabled woman to Venus's perfect body. The story is a kind of allegory of a "normal" person's intersection with the disabled body. This intersection is marked by the power of the visual. The "normal" person sees the disabled person and is turned to stone, in some sense, by the visual interaction. In this moment, the normal person suddenly feels self-conscious, rigid, unable to look but equally drawn to look. The visual field becomes problematic, dangerous, treacherous. The disability becomes a power derived from its otherness, its monstrosity, in the eyes of the "normal" person. The disability must be decapitated and then contained in a variety of magic wallets. Rationality, for which Athene stands, is one of the devices for containing, controlling, and reforming the disabled body so that it no longer has the power to terrorize. And the issue of mutilation comes up as well because the disabled body is always the reminder of the whole body about to come apart at the seams. It provides a vision of, a caution about, the body as a construct held together willfully, always threatening to become its individual parts—cells, organs, limbs, perceptions—like the fragmented, shared eye and tooth that Perseus ransoms back to the Graiae.

18   I have been concentrating on the physical body, but it is worth considering for a moment the issue of madness. While mental illness is by definition not related to the intactness of the body, nevertheless, it shows up as a disruption in the visual field. We "see" that someone is insane by her physical behavior, communication, and so on. Yet the fear is that the mind is fragmenting, breaking up, falling apart, losing itself—all terms we associate with becoming mad. With the considerable information we have about the biological roots of mental illness, we begin to see the disease again as a breaking up of "normal" body chemistry: amino acid production gone awry, depleted levels of certain polypeptide chains or hormones. Language production can become fragmentary, broken, in schizophrenic speech production. David Rothman points out that in eighteenth- and nineteenth-century America, insanity was seen as being caused by the fragmented nature of "modern"

life—particularly the pressures brought to bear on people by a society in which economic boundaries were disappearing. This fragmenting of society produced a fragmentation of the individual person. So the asylums that sprung up during this period recommended a cure that involved a removal from the urban, alienated, fragmented environment to rural hospitals in which order and precision could be restored. "A precise schedule and regular work became the two characteristics of the best private and public institutions. . . . The structure of the mental hospital would counteract the debilitating influences of the community" (Rothman 1971, 144). As Rothman notes, "Precision, certainty, regularity, order" were the words that were seen as embodying the essence of cure (ibid., 145). The mind would be restored to "wholeness" by restoring the body through manual labor. However, needless to add, one had to have a whole body to have a whole mind. The general metaphor here continues to be a notion of wholeness, order, clean boundaries, as opposed to fragmentations, disordered bodies, messy boundaries.

19   If people with disabilities are considered anything, they are or have been considered creatures of disorder—monsters, monstrous. Leslie Fieldler has taken some pains to show this in his book *Freaks*. If we look at Mary Shelley's *Frankenstein*, we find some of the themes we have been discussing emerge in novelistic form. First, we might want to note that we have no name for the creation of Dr Frankenstein other than "monster." (This linguistic lapsus is usually made up for in popular culture by referring to the creature itself as "Frankenstein," a terminology that confuses the creator with the created.) In reading the novel, or speaking about it, we can only call the creature "the monster." This linguistic limitation is worth noting because it encourages the reader to consider the creature a monster rather than a person with disabilities.

20   We do not often think of the monster in Mary Shelley's work as disabled, but what else is he? The characteristic of his disability is a difference in appearance. He is more than anything a disruption in the visual field. There is nothing else different about him—he can see, hear, talk, think, ambulate, and so on. It is worth noting that in popular culture, largely through the early film versions of the novel, the monster is inarticulate, somewhat mentally slow, and walks with a kind of physical impairment. In addition, the film versions add Ygor, the hunchbacked criminal who echoes the monster's disability in his own. Even in the recent film version by Kenneth Branagh, the creature walks with a limp and speaks with an impediment. One cannot dismiss this filtering of the creature through the lens of multiple disability. In order for the audience to fear and loathe the creature, he must be made to transcend the pathos of a single disability. Of course, it would be unseemly for a village to chase and torment a paraplegic or a person with acromegaly. Disabled people are to be pitied and ostracized; monsters are to be destroyed; audiences must not confuse the two.

21   In the novel, it is clear that Dr Frankenstein cannot abide his creation for only one reason—its hideous appearance. Indeed, the creature's only positive human contact is with the blind old man De Lacey, who cannot see the unsightly features. When De Lacey's family catches a glimpse of the creature, the women faint or run, and the men beat and pursue him. His body is a zone of repulsion; the reaction he evokes is fear and loathing. The question one wants to ask is why does a physical difference produce such a profound response?

22   The answer, I believe, is twofold. First, what is really hideous about the creature is not so much his physiognomy as what that appearance suggests. The *corps morcelé* makes its appearance immediately in the construction of the monster. Ironically, Dr Frankenstein adapts Zeuxis's notion of taking ideal parts from individuals to create the ideal whole body. As he says, "I collected bones from charnel houses. . . . The dissecting room and the slaughter-house furnished many of my materials" (Shelley 1990, 54–5). From these fragments, seen as loathsome and disgusting, Frankenstein assembles what he wishes to create—a perfect human. It is instructive in this regard to distinguish the Boris Karloff incarnation of the creature—with the bolt through his neck—or Branagh's grotesquely sewn creature, from the image that Mary Shelley would have us imagine. Dr Frankenstein tells us:

> His limbs were in proportion, and I had selected his features as beautiful. Beautiful!—Great God! His yellow skin scarcely covered the work of muscles and arteries beneath; his hair was of a lustrous black and flowing; his teeth of a pearly whiteness; but these luxuriances only formed a more horrid contrast with his watery eyes, that seemed almost of the same colour as the dun white sockets in which they were set, his shrivelled complexion and straight black lips. (ibid., 57)

23   What then constitutes the horror? If we add up the details, what we see is a well-proportioned man with long black hair, pearly white teeth, whose skin is somewhat deformed—resulting in jaundice and perhaps a tightness or thinness of the skin, a lack of circulation perhaps causing shriveling, watery eyes and darkened lips. This hardly seems to constitute horror rather than, say, pathos.

24   What is found to be truly horrifying about Frankenstein's creature is its composite quality, which is too evocative of the fragmented body. Frankenstein's reaction to this living *corps morcelé* is repulsion: "the beauty of the dream vanished, and breathless horror and disgust filled my heart" (ibid., 57). Frankenstein attempted to create a unified nude, an object of beauty and harmony—a Venus, in effect. He ended up with a Medusa whose existence reveals the inhering and enduring nature of the archaic endlessly fragmented body, endlessly repressed but endlessly reappearing.

❖ *Evaluating the Text*

1. How does the contrast between the Venus de Milo and Pam Herbert draw attention to the paradox governing cultural perceptions of people with disabilities?

2. How does the phenomenon known as "splitting" help explain the stereotyped perception of people with disabilities?

3. What broadening effect does Davis's discussion have by including Mary Shelley's *Frankenstein* and issues of mythology and madness?

4. How does each of the examples tie in with Davis's theory that "disability is a cultural phenomenon rooted in the senses"?

❖ *Exploring Different Perspectives*

1. How are Lennard J. Davis's and Judith Ortiz Cofer's analyses based on messages communicated through the perception of physical appearance?

2. Compare the effects of the tyranny of absolute categories of what is normal and abnormal in the analyses by Davis and Susan Bordo (see "Never Just Pictures").

❖ *Extending Viewpoints through Writing*

1. Recently, the terms "differently abled" or "person with disabilities" have been preferred to the term "disabled person." Earlier, the term "disabled" was used to replace "handicapped." To what extent did Davis's analysis make you realize how the category of disability is a relative rather than an absolute term? For example, what if one were to include dyslexia, myopia, learning impairments, arthritis, or obesity? Discuss how attempts to control these terms reflect a desire to control public perceptions of these states.

2. Select a film you have seen in recent years and discuss the treatment of the central character in terms of the filmmaker's depiction of the "disabled." For example, Disney's 1996 release of *The Hunchback of Notre Dame, Forrest Gump, Rain Man, Mask, Nell, Immortal Beloved,* or *Lorenzo's Oil.* In your opinion, why are films depicting the disabled so popular?

Elizabeth W. Fernea and Robert A. Fernea

A Look behind the Veil

◆

One of the most interesting examples of how clothes reflect cultural beliefs can be seen in the Middle Eastern custom of veiling women. Elizabeth W. Fernea and Robert A. Fernea have done extensive research in Iraq, Morocco, Egypt, and Afghanistan and are the authors of a number of books, including the award-winning The Arab World: Personal Encounters *(1987) and its sequel,* The Arab World: Forty Years of Change *(1997). Elizabeth W. Fernea has also written* In Search of Islamic Feminism: One Woman's Global Journey *(1998) and is currently professor of Middle Eastern studies at the University of Texas at Austin.*

Before You Read

As you read, consider the ways in which *purdah* defines how a woman must present herself in Middle Eastern cultures.

◆

1   What objects do we notice in societies other than our own? Ishi, the last of a "lost" tribe of North American Indians who stumbled into 20th Century California in 1911, is reported to have said that the truly interesting objects in the white man's culture were pockets and matches. Rifa'ah Tahtawi, one of the first young Egyptians to be sent to Europe to study in 1826, wrote an account of French society in which he noted that Parisians used many unusual articles of dress, among them something called a belt. Women wore belts, he said, apparently to keep their bosoms erect, and to show off the slimness of their waists and the fullness of their hips. Europeans are still fascinated by the Stetson hats worn by American cowboys; an elderly Dutch lady of our acquaintance recently carried six enormous Stetsons back to The Hague as presents for the male members of her family.

2   Many objects signify values in society and become charged with meaning, a meaning that may be different for members of the society and for observers of that society. The veil is one object used in Middle Eastern societies that stirs strong emotions in the West. "The feminine veil has become a symbol: that of the slavery of one portion of humanity," wrote French ethnologist Germaine Tillion in 1966. A hundred years earlier, Sir Richard Burton, British traveler, explorer, and translator of the *Arabian Nights*, recorded a different view. "Europeans inveigh against

this article [the face veil] . . . for its hideousness and jealous concealment of charms made to be admired," he wrote in 1855. "It is, on the contrary, the most coquettish article of woman's attire . . . it conceals coarse skins, fleshy noses, wide mouths and vanishing chins, whilst it sets off to best advantage what in these lands is most lustrous and liquid—the eye. Who has not remarked this at a masquerade ball?"

3   In the present generation, the veil and purdah, or seclusion, have become a focus of attention for Western writers, both popular and academic, who take a measure of Burton's irony and Tillion's anger to equate modernization of the Middle East with the discarding of the veil. "Iranian women return to veil in a resurgence of spirituality," headlines one newspaper; another writes, "Iran's 16 million women have come a long way since their floor-length cotton veil officially was abolished in 1935." The thousands of words written about the appearance and disappearance of the veil and of purdah do little to help us understand the Middle East or the cultures that grew out of the same Judeo-Christian roots as our own. The veil and the all-enveloping garments that inevitably accompany it (the *milayah* in Egypt, the *abbayah* in Iraq, the *chadoor* in Iran, the *yashmak* in Turkey, the *burga* in Afghanistan, and the *djellabah* and the *haik* in North Africa) are only the outward manifestations of a cultural pattern and idea that is rooted deep in Mediterranean society.

4   "Purdah" is a Persian word meaning curtain or barrier. The Arabic word for veiling and secluding comes from the root *hajaba*. A *hijab* is an amulet worn to keep away the evil eye; it also means a diaphragm used to prevent conception. The gatekeeper or doorkeeper who guards the entrance to a government minister's office is a *hijab*, and in casual conversation a person might say, "I want to be more informal with my friend so-and-so, but she always puts a *hijab* (barrier) between us."

5   In Islam, the Koranic verse that sanctions the barrier between men and women is called the Sura of the *hijab* (curtain): "Prophet, enjoin your wives, your daughters and the wives of true believers to draw their veils close round them. That is more proper, so that they may be recognized and not molested. Allah is forgiving and merciful."

6   Certainly seclusion and some forms of veiling had been practiced before the time of Muhammad, at least among the upper classes, but it was his followers who apparently felt that his women should be placed in a special category. According to history, the *hijab* was established after a number of occasions on which Muhammad's wives were insulted by people who were coming to the mosque in search of the prophet. When chided for their behavior, they said they had mistaken Muhammad's wives for slaves. The *hijab* was established, and in the words of the historian Nabia Abbott, "Muhammad's women found themselves, on the one hand, deprived of personal liberty, and on the other hand, raised to a position of honor and dignity."

7   The veil bears many messages and tells us many things about men and women in Middle East society; but as an object in and of itself it is far less important to members of the society than the values it represents. Nouha al Hejailan, wife of the Saudi Arabian ambassador to London, told Sally Quinn of *The Washington Post*, "If I wanted to take it all off (her *abbayah* and veil), I would have long ago. It wouldn't mean as much to me as it does to you." Early Middle Eastern feminists felt differently. Huda Sh'arawi, an early Egyptian activist who formed the first Women's Union, made a dramatic gesture of removing her veil in public to demonstrate her dislike of society's attitudes toward women and her defiance of the system. But Basima Bezirgan, a contemporary Iraqui feminist, says, "Compared to the real issues that are involved between men and women in the Middle East today, the veil is unimportant." A Moroccan linguist who buys her clothes in Paris laughs when asked about the veil. "My mother wears a *djellabah* and a veil. I have never worn them. But so what? I still cannot get divorced as easily as a man, and I am still a member of my family group and responsible to them for everything I do. What is the veil? A piece of cloth."

8   "The seclusion of women has many purposes," states Egyptian anthropologist Nadia Abu Zahra. "It expresses men's status, power, wealth, and manliness. It also helps preserve men's image of virility and masculinity, but men do not admit this; on the contrary they claim that one of the purposes of the veil is to guard women's honor." The veil and purdah are symbols of restriction, to men as well as to women. A respectable woman wearing a veil on a public street is signaling, "Hands off. Don't touch me or you'll be sorry." Cowboy Jim Sayre of Deadwood, South Dakota, says, "If you deform a cowboy's hat, he'll likely deform you." In the same way, a man who approaches a veiled woman is asking for trouble; not only the woman but also her family is shamed, and serious problems may result. "It is clear," says Egyptian anthropologist Ahmed Abou Zeid, "that honor and shame which are usually attributed to a certain individual or a certain kinship group have in fact a bearing on the total social structure, since most acts involving honor or shame are likely to affect the existing social equilibrium."

9   Veiling and seclusion almost always can be related to the maintenance of social status. Historically, only the very rich could afford to seclude their women, and the extreme example of this practice was found among the sultans of prerevolutionary Turkey. Stories of these secluded women, kept in harems and guarded by eunuchs, formed the basis for much of the Western folklore concerning the nature of male-female relationships in Middle East society. The stereotype is of course contradictory; Western writers have never found it necessary to reconcile the erotic fantasies of the seraglio with the sexual puritanism attributed to the same society.

10   Poor men could not always afford to seclude or veil their women, because the women were needed as productive members of the family

economic unit, to work in the fields and in cottage industries. Delta village women in Egypt have never been veiled, nor have the Berber women of North Africa. But this lack of veiling placed poor women in ambiguous situations in relation to strange men.

11   "In the village, no one veils, because everyone is considered a member of the same large family," explained Aisha bint Mohammed, a working-class wife of Marrakech. "But in the city, veiling is *sunnah*, required by our religion." Veiling is generally found in towns and cities, among all classes, where families feel that it is necessary to distinguish themselves from other strangers in the city.

12   Veiling and purdah not only indicate status and wealth, they also have some religious sanction and protect women from the world outside the home. Purdah delineates private space, distinguishes between the public and private sectors of society, as does the traditional architecture of the area. Older Middle Eastern houses do not have picture windows facing the street, nor walks leading invitingly to front doors. Family life is hidden from strangers; behind blank walls may lie courtyards and gardens, refuges from the heat, the cold, the bustle of the outside world, the world of non-kin that is not to be trusted. Outsiders are pointedly excluded.

13   Even within the household, among her close relatives, a traditional Muslim woman veils before those kinsmen whom she could legally marry. If her maternal or paternal male cousins, her brothers-in-law, or sons-in-law come to call, she covers her head, or perhaps her whole face. To do otherwise would be shameless.

14   The veil does more than protect its wearers from known and unknown intruders; it can also be used to conceal identity. Behind the anonymity of the veil, women can go about a city unrecognized and uncriticized. Nadia Abu Zahra reports anecdotes of men donning women's veils in order to visit their lovers undetected; women may do the same. The veil is such an effective disguise that Nouri Al-Said, the late prime minister of Iraq, attempted to escape death by wearing the *abbayah* and veil of a woman; only his shoes gave him away.

15   Political dissidents in many countries have used the veil for their own ends. The women who marched, veiled, through Cairo during the Nationalist demonstrations against the British after World War I were counting on the strength of Western respect for the veil to protect them against British gunfire. At first they were right. Algerian women also used the protection of the veil to carry bombs through French army checkpoints during the Algerian revolution. But when the French discovered the ruse, Algerian women discarded the veil and dressed like Europeans to move about freely.

16   The multiple meanings and uses of purdah and the veil do not explain how the pattern came to be so deeply embedded in Mediterranean society. Its origins lie somewhere in the basic Muslim attitudes about men's roles and women's roles. Women, according to Fatima

Mernissi, a Moroccan sociologist, are seen by men in Islamic societies as in need of protection because they are unable to control their sexuality, are tempting to men, and hence are a danger to the social order. In order words, they need to be restrained and controlled so that society may function in an orderly way.

17   The notion that women present a danger to the social order is scarcely limited to Muslim society. Anthropologist Julian Pitt-Rivers has pointed out that the supervision and seclusion of women is also to be found in Christian Europe, even though veiling was not usually practiced there. "The idea that women not subjected to male authority are a danger is a fundamental one in the writings of the moralists from the Archpriest of Talavera to Padre Haro, and it is echoed in the modern Andalusian *pueblo*. It is bound up with the fear of ungoverned female sexuality which had been an integral element of European folklore ever since prudent Odysseus lashed himself to the mast to escape the sirens."

18   Pitt-Rivers is writing about Mediterranean society, which, like all Middle Eastern societies, is greatly concerned with honor and shame rather than with individual guilt. The honor of the Middle Eastern extended family, its ancestors and its descendants, is the highest social value. The misdeeds of the grandparents are indeed visited on the children. Men and women always remain members of their natal families. Marriage is a legal contract but a fragile one that is often broken; the ties between brother and sister, mother and child, father and child are lifelong and enduring. The larger family is the group to which the individual belongs and to which the individual owes responsibility in exchange for the social and economic security that the family group provides. It is the group, not the individual, that is socially shamed or socially honored.

19   Male honor and female honor are both involved in the honor of the family, but each is expressed differently. The honor of a man, *sharaf*, is a public matter, involving bravery, hospitality, piety. It may be lost, but it may also be regained. The honor of a woman, *'ard*, is a private matter involving only one thing, her sexual chastity. Once lost, it cannot be regained. If the loss of female honor remains only privately known, a rebuke—and perhaps a reveiling—may be all that takes place. But if the loss of female honor becomes public knowledge, the other members of the family may feel bound to cleanse the family name. In extreme cases, the cleansing may require the death of the offending female member. Although such killings are now criminal offenses in the Middle East, suspended sentences are often given, and the newspapers in Cairo and Baghdad frequently carry sad stories of runaway sisters "gone bad" in the city and revenge taken upon them in the name of family honor by their brothers or cousins.

20   This emphasis on female chastity, many say, originated in the patrilineal society's concern with the paternity of the child and the inher-

itance that follows the male line. How does a man know that the child in his wife's womb is his own, and not that of another man? Obviously he cannot know unless his wife is a virgin at marriage. From this consideration may have developed the protective institutions called variously purdah, seclusion, or veiling.

21   Middle Eastern women also look upon seclusion as practical protection. In the Iraqi village where we lived from 1956 to 1958, one of us (Elizabeth) wore the *abbayah* and found that it provided a great sense of protection from prying eyes, dust, heat, flies. Parisian ladies visiting Istanbul in the 16th Century were so impressed by the ability of the all-enveloping garment to keep dresses clean of mud and manure and to keep women from being attacked by importuning men that they tried to introduce it into French fashion.

22   Perhaps of greater importance for many women reared in traditional cultures is the degree to which their sense of personal identity is tied to the use of the veil. Many women have told us that they felt self-conscious, vulnerable, and even naked when they first walked on a public street without the veil and *abbayah*—as if they were making a display of themselves.

23   The resurgence of the veil in countries like Morocco, Libya, and Algeria, which have recently established their independence from colonial dominance, is seen by some Middle Eastern and Western scholars as an attempt by men to reassert their Muslim identity and to reestablish their roles as heads of families. The presence of the veil is a sign that the males of the household are once more able to assume the responsibilities that were disturbed or usurped by foreign colonial powers.

24   But a veiled woman is seldom seen in Egypt or in many parts of Lebanon, Syria, Iran, Tunisia, Turkey, or the Sudan. And as respectable housewives have abandoned the veil, in some of these Middle Eastern countries prostitutes have put it on. They indicate their availability by manipulating the veil in flirtatious ways, but as Burton pointed out more than a century ago, prostitutes are not the first to discover the veil's seductiveness. Like women's garments in the West, the veil can be sturdy, utilitarian, and forbidding—or it can be filmy and decorative, hinting at the charms beneath it.

25   The veil is the outward sign of a complex reality. Observers are often deceived by the absence of that sign, and fail to see that in most Middle Eastern societies (and in many parts of Europe) basic attitudes are unchanged. Women who have taken off the veil continue to play the old roles within the family, and their chastity remains crucial. A woman's behavior is still the key to the honor and the reputation of her family.

26   In Middle Eastern societies, feminine and masculine continue to be strong polarities of identification. This is marked contrast to Western society, where for more than a generation social critics have been striv-

ing to blur distinctions in dress, in status, and in type of labor. Almost all Middle Eastern reformers (most of whom are middle and upper class) are still arguing from the assumption of a fundamental difference between men and women. They do not demand an end to the veil (which is passing out of use anyway) but an end to the old principles, which the veil symbolizes, that govern patrilineal society. Middle Eastern reformers are calling for equal access to divorce, child custody, and inheritance; equal opportunities for education and employment; abolition of female circumcision and "crimes of honor"; and a law regulating the age of marriage.

27   An English woman film director, after several months in Morocco, said in an interview, "This business about the veil is nonsense. We all have our veils, between ourselves and other people. That's not what the Middle East is about. The question is what veils are used for, and by whom." The veil triggers Western reactions simply because it is the dramatic, visible sign of vexing questions, questions that are still being debated, problems that have still not been solved, in the Middle East or in Western societies.

28   Given the biological differences between men and women, how are the sexes to be treated equitably? Men and women are supposed to share the labor of society and yet provide for the reproduction and nurture of the next generation. If male fear and awe of women's sexuality provokes them to control and seclude women, can they be assuaged? Rebecca West said long ago that "the difference between men and women is the rock on which civilization will split before it can reach any goal that could justify its expenditure of effort." Until human beings come to terms with this basic issue, purdah and the veil, in some form, will continue to exist in both the East and the West.

REFERENCES

Abou-Zeid, Ahmed, "Honor and Shame among the Bedouins of Egypt," *Honor and Shame: The Values of Mediterranean Society*, ed. by J. G. Peristiany, University of Chicago Press, 1966.

Fernea, Elizabeth Warnock, *Guests of the Sheik: An Ethnology of an Iraqi Village*, Doubleday/Anchor, 1969.

Fernea, Elizabeth Warnock, and Basima Qattan Bezirgan, eds., *Middle Eastern Muslim Women Speak*, University of Texas Press, 1977.

Levy, Reuben, *The Social Structure of Islam*, Cambridge University Press, 1965.

Mernissi, Fatima, *Beyond the Veil: Male-Female Dynamics in a Modern Muslim Society*, Schenkman Publishing Company, 1975.

Pitt-Rivers, Julian, *The Fate of Schechem: or The Politics of Sex*, Cambridge University Press, 1977.

✧ Evaluating the Text

1. Why, according to the authors, is the practice of veiling women in Middle Eastern countries most frequently encountered in affluent,

male-dominated extended families? What attitudes toward female sexuality help explain the veiling of women and the practice of *purdah*?

2. The authors use interviews and the testimony of experts to support their analysis as to why veiling and *purdah* continue to exist in Middle Eastern societies. Do you detect a bias on the authors' part either for or against this practice? Explain your answer.

3. How is the practice of veiling tied in with other important cultural values and institutions in Middle Eastern societies?

✦ Exploring Different Perspectives

1. How does the practice of veiling as depicted by Fernea and Fernea contrast with Ann M. Simmons's analysis of what makes a woman desirable in Nigerian culture (see "Where Fat Is a Mark of Beauty")?

2. What constraints operate within Puerto Rican culture, as described by Judith Ortiz Cofer, to guard the modesty of women, despite very different attitudes toward display, than in Middle Eastern societies that practice *purdah*?

✦ Extending Viewpoints through Writing

1. Select one of the following, and write an essay in response. Create a dialogue between someone who is in favor of the practice of veiling and someone who is very much against it. If you were a woman living in a society where wearing the chador was a matter of personal choice, would you choose to do so or not? Explain your answer. If you were a man in that society, would you prefer to see women completely veiled? Why or why not?

2. What current views on the question of *hijab* can you discover by consulting the following Web site: The Muslim Women's Home Page <http://www.jannah.org/sisters/?> To what extent have traditional cultural values changed since theFerneas did their groundbreaking study in 1979?

Serena Nanda

Arranging a Marriage in India

◆

Serena Nanda is professor of anthropology at John Jay College of Criminal Justice, City University of New York. Her fields of interest are visual anthropology, gender, and culture and law. She has carried out field studies in India, in tribal development, and on the social lives of women in urban India. Her published works include Cultural Anthropology, *third edition (1987),* American Cultural Pluralism and Law *(1990), and* Neither Man nor Woman: The Hijras of India *(1990), which won the Ruth Benedict Prize. In the following selection, which first appeared in* The Naked Anthropologist: Tales from Around the World, *edited by Philip R. DeVita (1992), Nanda looks at the cultural forces that have resulted in the practice of arranged marriages in Indian society.*

Before You Read

Note the kinds of considerations that are important in arranging a marriage in India and how these reflect important cultural values.

◆

Sister and doctor brother-in-law invite correspondence from North Indian professionals only, for a beautiful, talented, sophisticated, intelligent sister, 5'3", slim, M.A. in textile design, father a senior civil officer. Would prefer immigrant doctors, between 26–29 years. Reply with full details and returnable photo.

A well-settled uncle invites matrimonial correspondence from slim, fair, educated South Indian girl, for his nephew, 25 years, smart, M.B.A., green card holder, 5'6". Full particulars with returnable photo appreciated.
                    —Matrimonial Advertisements, *India Abroad*

1   In India, almost all marriages are arranged. Even among the educated middle classes in modern, urban India, marriage is as much a concern of the families as it is of the individuals. So customary is the practice of arranged marriage that there is a special name for a marriage which is not arranged: It is called a "love match."

2   On my first field trip to India, I met many young men and women whose parents were in the process of "getting them married." In many

197

cases, the bride and groom would not meet each other before the marriage. At most they might meet for a brief conversation, and this meeting would take place only after their parents had decided that the match was suitable. Parents do not compel their children to marry a person who either marriage partner finds objectionable. But only after one match is refused will another be sought.

3   As a young American woman in India for the first time, I found this custom of arranged marriage oppressive. How could any intelligent young person agree to such a marriage without great reluctance? It was contrary to everything I believed about the importance of romantic love as the only basis of a happy marriage. It also clashed with my strongly held notions that the choice of such an intimate and permanent relationship could be made only by the individuals involved. Had anyone tried to arrange my marriage, I would have been defiant and rebellious!

4   At the first opportunity, I began, with more curiosity than tact, to question the young people I met on how they felt about this practice. Sita, one of my young informants, was a college graduate with a degree in political science. She had been waiting for over a year while her parents were arranging a match for her. I found it difficult to accept the docile manner in which this well-educated young woman awaited the outcome of a process that would result in her spending the rest of her life with a man she hardly knew, a virtual stranger, picked out by her parents.

5   "How can you go along with this?" I asked her, in frustration and distress. "Don't you care who you marry?"

6   "Of course I care," she answered. "This is why I must let my parents choose a boy for me. My marriage is too important to be arranged by such an inexperienced person as myself. In such matters, it is better to have my parents' guidance."

7   I had learned that young men and women in India do not date and have very little social life involving members of the opposite sex. Although I could not disagree with Sita's reasoning, I continued to pursue the subject.

8   "But how can you marry the first man you have ever met? Not only have you missed the fun of meeting a lot of different people, but you have not given yourself the chance to know who is the right man for you."

9   "Meeting with a lot of different people doesn't sound like any fun at all," Sita answered. "One hears that in America the girls are spending more time worrying about whether they will meet a man and get married. Here we have the chance to enjoy our life and let our parents do this work and worrying for us."

10   She had me there. The high anxiety of the competition to "be popular" with the opposite sex certainly was the most prominent feature of life as an American teenager in the late fifties. The endless worrying

about the rules that governed our behavior and about our popularity ratings sapped both our self-esteem and our enjoyment of adolescence. I reflected that absence of this competition in India most certainly may have contributed to the self-confidence and natural charm of so many of the young women I met.

11   And yet, the idea of marrying a perfect stranger, whom one did not know and did not "love," so offended my American ideas of individualism and romanticism, that I persisted with my objections.

12   "I still can't imagine it," I said. "How can you agree to marry a man you hardly know?"

13   "But of course he will be known. My parents would never arrange a marriage for me without knowing all about the boy's family background. Naturally we will not rely only on what the family tells us. We will check the particulars out ourselves. No one will want their daughter to marry into a family that is not good. All these things we will know beforehand."

14   Impatiently, I responded, "Sita, I don't mean know the family, I mean, know the man. How can you marry someone you don't know personally and don't love? How can you think of spending your life with someone you may not even like?"

15   "If he is a good man, why should I not like him?" she said. "With you people, you know the boy so well before you marry, where will be the fun to get married? There will be no mystery and no romance. Here we have the whole of our married life to get to know and love our husband. This way is better, is it not?"

16   Her response made further sense, and I began to have second thoughts on the matter. Indeed, during months of meeting many intelligent young Indian people, both male and female, who had the same ideas as Sita, I saw arranged marriages in a different light. I also saw the importance of the family in Indian life and realized that a couple who took their marriage into their own hands was taking a big risk, particularly if their families were irreconcilably opposed to the match. In a country where every important resource in life—a job, a house, a social circle—is gained through family connections, it seemed foolhardy to cut oneself off from a supportive social network and depend solely on one person for happiness and success.

17   Six years later I returned to India to again do fieldwork, this time among the middle class in Bombay, a modern, sophisticated city. From the experience of my earlier visit, I decided to include a study of arranged marriages in my project. By this time I had met many Indian couples whose marriages had been arranged and who seemed very happy. Particularly in contrast to the fate of many of my married friends in the United States who were already in the process of divorce, the positive aspects of arranged marriages appeared to me to outweigh

the negatives. In fact, I thought I might even participate in arranging a marriage myself. I had been fairly successful in the United States in "fixing up" many of my friends, and I was confident that my match-making skills could be easily applied to this new situation, once I learned the basic rules. "After all," I thought, "how complicated can it be? People want pretty much the same things in a marriage whether it is in India or America."

18   An opportunity presented itself almost immediately. A friend from my previous Indian trip was in the process of arranging for the marriage of her eldest son. In India there is a perceived shortage of "good boys," and since my friend's family was eminently respectable and the boy himself personable, well educated, and nice looking, I was sure that by the end of my year's fieldwork, we would have found a match.

19   The basic rule seems to be that a family's reputation is most important. It is understood that matches would be arranged only within the same caste and general social class, although some crossing of sub-castes is permissible if the class positions of the bride's and groom's families are similar. Although dowry is now prohibited by law in India, extensive gift exchanges took place with every marriage. Even when the boy's family do not "make demands," every girl's family nevertheless feels the obligation to give the traditional gifts, to the girl, to the boy, and to the boy's family. Particularly when the couple would be living in the joint family—that is, with the boy's parents and his married brothers and their families, as well as with unmarried siblings—which is still very common even among the urban, upper-middle class in India, the girl's parents are anxious to establish smooth relations between their family and that of the boy. Offering the proper gifts, even when not called "dowry," is often an important factor in influencing the relationship between the bride's and groom's families and perhaps, also, the treatment of the bride in her new home.

20   In a society where divorce is still a scandal and where, in fact, the divorce rate is exceedingly low, an arranged marriage is the beginning of a lifetime relationship not just between the bride and groom but between their families as well. Thus, while a girl's looks are important, her character is even more so, for she is being judged as a prospective daughter-in-law as much as a prospective bride. Where she would be living in a joint family, as was the case with my friend, the girl's ability to get along harmoniously in a family is perhaps the single most important quality in assessing her suitability.

21   My friend is a highly esteemed wife, mother, and daughter-in-law. She is religious, soft-spoken, modest, and deferential. She rarely gossips and never quarrels, two qualities highly desirable in a woman. A family that has the reputation for gossip and conflict among its womenfolk will not find it easy to get good wives for their sons. Parents will not want to send their daughter to a house in which there is conflict.

22   My friend's family were originally from North India. They had lived in Bombay, where her husband owned a business, for forty years. The family had delayed in seeking a match for their eldest son because he had been an Air Force pilot for several years, stationed in such remote places that it had seemed fruitless to try to find a girl who would be willing to accompany him. In their social class, a military career, despite its economic security, has little prestige and is considered a drawback in finding a suitable bride. Many families would not allow their daughters to marry a man in an occupation so potentially dangerous and which requires so much moving around.

23   The son had recently left the military and joined his father's business. Since he was a college graduate, modern, and well traveled, from such a good family, and, I thought, quite handsome, it seemed to me that he, or rather his family, was in a position to pick and choose. I said as much to my friend.

24   While she agreed that there were many advantages on their side, she also said, "We must keep in mind that my son is both short and dark; these are drawbacks in finding the right match." While the boy's height had not escaped my notice, "dark" seemed to me inaccurate; I would have called him "wheat" colored perhaps, and in any case, I did not realize that color would be a consideration. I discovered, however, that while a boy's skin color is a less important consideration than a girl's, it is still a factor.

25   An important source of contacts in trying to arrange her son's marriage was my friend's social club in Bombay. Many of the women had daughters of the right age, and some had already expressed an interest in my friend's son. I was most enthusiastic about the possibilities of one particular family who had five daughters, all of whom were pretty, demure, and well educated. Their mother had told my friend, "You can have your pick for your son, whichever one of my daughters appeals to you most."

26   I saw a match in sight. "Surely," I said to my friend, "we will find one there. Let's go visit and make our choice." But my friend held back; she did not seem to share my enthusiasm, for reasons I could not then fathom.

27   When I kept pressing for an explanation of her reluctance, she admitted, "See, Serena, here is the problem. The family has so many daughters, how will they be able to provide nicely for any of them? We are not making any demands, but still, with so many daughters to marry off, one wonders whether she will even be able to make a proper wedding. Since this is our eldest son, it's best if we marry him to a girl who is the only daughter, then the wedding will truly be a gala affair." I argued that surely the quality of the girls themselves made up for any deficiency in the elaborateness of the wedding. My friend admitted this point but still seemed reluctant to proceed.

28   "Is there something else," I asked her, "some factor I have missed?" "Well," she finally said, "there is one other thing. They have one daughter already married and living in Bombay. The mother is always complaining to me that the girl's in-laws don't let her visit her own family often enough. So it makes me wonder, will she be that kind of mother who always wants her daughter at her own home? This will prevent the girl from adjusting to our house. It is not a good thing." And so, this family of five daughters was dropped as a possibility.

29   Somewhat disappointed, I nevertheless respected my friend's reasoning and geared up for the next prospect. This was also the daughter of a woman in my friend's social club. There was clear interest in this family and I could see why. The family's reputation was excellent; in fact, they came from a subcaste slightly higher than my friend's own. The girl, who was an only daughter, was pretty and well educated and had a brother studying in the United States. Yet, after expressing an interest to me in this family, all talk of them suddenly died down and the search began elsewhere.

30   "What happened to that girl as a prospect?" I asked one day. "You never mention her any more. She is so pretty and so educated, what did you find wrong?"

31   "She is too educated. We've decided against it. My husband's father saw the girl on the bus the other day and thought her forward. A girl who 'roams about' the city by herself is not the girl for our family." My disappointment this time was even greater, as I thought the son would have liked the girl very much. But then I thought, my friend is right, a girl who is going to live in a joint family cannot be too independent or she will make life miserable for everyone. I also learned that if the family of the girl has even a slightly higher social status than the family of the boy, the bride may think herself too good for them, and this too will cause problems. Later my friend admitted to me that this had been an important factor in her decision not to pursue the match.

32   The next candidate was the daughter of a client of my friend's husband. When the client learned that the family was looking for a match for their son, he said, "Look no further, we have a daughter." This man then invited my friends to dinner to see the girl. He had already seen their son at the office and decided that "he liked the boy." We all went together for tea, rather than dinner—it was less of a commitment—and while we were there, the girl's mother showed us around the house. The girl was studying for her exams and was briefly introduced to us.

33   After we left, I was anxious to hear my friend's opinion. While her husband liked the family very much and was impressed with his client's business accomplishments and reputation, the wife didn't like the girl's looks. "She is short, no doubt, which is an important plus point, but she is also fat and wears glasses." My friend obviously thought she could do better for her son and asked her husband to make

his excuses to his client by saying that they had decided to postpone the boy's marriage indefinitely.

34   By this time almost six months had passed and I was becoming impatient. What I had thought would be an easy matter to arrange was turning out to be quite complicated. I began to believe that between my friend's desire for a girl who was modest enough to fit into her joint family, yet attractive and educated enough to be an acceptable partner for her son, she would not find anyone suitable. My friend laughed at my impatience: "Don't be so much in a hurry," she said. "You Americans want everything done so quickly. You get married quickly and then just as quickly get divorced. Here we take marriage more seriously. We must take all the factors into account. It is not enough for us to learn by our mistakes. This is too serious a business. If a mistake is made we have not only ruined the life of our son or daughter, but we have spoiled the reputation of our family as well. And that will make it much harder for their brothers and sisters to get married. So we must be very careful."

35   What she said was true and I promised myself to be more patient, though it was not easy. I had really hoped and expected that the match would be made before my year in India was up. But it was not to be. When I left India my friend seemed no further along in finding a suitable match for her son than when I had arrived.

36   Two years later, I returned to India and still my friend had not found a girl for her son. By this time, he was close to thirty, and I think she was a little worried. Since she knew I had friends all over India, and I was going to be there for a year, she asked me to "help her in this work" and keep an eye out for someone suitable. I was flattered that my judgment was respected, but knowing now how complicated the process was, I had lost my earlier confidence as a matchmaker. Nevertheless, I promised that I would try.

37   It was almost at the end of my year's stay in India that I met a family with a marriageable daughter whom I felt might be a good possibility for my friend's son. The girl's father was related to a good friend of mine and by coincidence came from the same village as my friend's husband. This new family had a successful business in a medium-sized city in central India and were from the same subcaste as my friend. The daughter was pretty and chic; in fact, she had studied fashion design in college. Her parents would not allow her to go off by herself to any of the major cities in India where she could make a career, but they had compromised with her wish to work by allowing her to run a small dressmaking boutique from their home. In spite of her desire to have a career, the daughter was both modest and home-loving and had had a traditional, sheltered upbringing. She had only one other sister, already married, and a brother who was in his father's business.

38   I mentioned the possibility of a match with my friend's son. The girl's parents were most interested. Although their daughter was not eager to marry just yet, the idea of living in Bombay—a sophisticated, extremely fashion-conscious city where she could continue her education in clothing design—was a great inducement. I gave the girl's father my friend's address and suggested that when they went to Bombay on some business or whatever, they look up the boy's family.

39   Returning to Bombay on my way to New York, I told my friend of this newly discovered possibility. She seemed to feel there was potential but, in spite of my urging, would not make any moves herself. She rather preferred to wait for the girl's family to call upon them. I hoped something would come of this introduction, though by now I had learned to rein in my optimism.

40   A year later I received a letter from my friend. The family had indeed come to visit Bombay, and their daughter and my friend's daughter, who were near in age, had become very good friends. During that year, the two girls had frequently visited each other. I thought things looked promising.

41   Last week I received an invitation to a wedding: My friend's son and the girl were getting married. Since I had found the match, my presence was particularly requested at the wedding. I was thrilled. Success at last! As I prepared to leave for India, I began thinking, "Now, my friend's younger son, who do I know who has a nice girl for him . . . ?"

EPILOGUE

This essay was written from the point of view of a family seeking a daughter-in-law. Arranged marriage looks somewhat different from the point of view of the bride and her family. Arranged marriage continues to be preferred, even among the more educated, westernized sections of the Indian population. Many young women from these families still go along, more or less willingly, with the practice and also with the specific choices of their families. Young women do get excited about the prospects of their marriage, but there is also ambivalence and increasing uncertainty as the bride contemplates leaving the comfort and familiarity of her own home where, as a "temporary guest," she had often been indulged, to live among strangers. Even in the best situation she will now come under the close scrutiny of her husband's family. How she dresses, how she behaves, how she gets along with others, where she goes, how she spends her time, her domestic abilities—all this and much more—will be observed and commented on by a whole new set of relations. Her interaction with her family of birth will be monitored and curtailed considerably. Not only will she leave their home, but with increasing geographic mobility she may also live very far from them, perhaps even on another continent. Too much expression of her fondness for her own family or her desire to visit them may be interpreted as an inability to adjust to her new family and may become a source of conflict. In an arranged marriage the burden of adjustment is clearly heavier for a woman than for a man. And this is in the best of situations.

In less happy circumstances, the bride may be a target of resentment and hostility from her husband's family, particularly her mother-in-law or her husband's unmarried sisters, for whom she is now a source of competition for the affection, loyalty, and economic resources of their son or brother. If she is psychologically or even physically abused, her options are limited, because returning to her parents' home or divorce is still very stigmatized. For most Indians, marriage and motherhood are still considered the only suitable roles for a woman, even for those who have careers, and few women can comfortably contemplate remaining unmarried. Most families still consider "marrying off" their daughter as a compelling religious duty and social necessity. This increases a bride's sense of obligation to make the marriage a success, at whatever cost to her own personal happiness.

The vulnerability of a new bride may also be intensified by the issue of dowry, which, although illegal, has become a more pressing issue in the consumer-conscious society of contemporary urban India. In many cases, if a groom's family is not satisfied with the amount of dowry that a bride brings to her marriage, the young bride will be constantly harassed to get her parents to give more. In extreme cases, the bride may even be murdered, and the murder disguised as an accident or suicide. This also offers the husband's family an opportunity to arrange another match for him, thus bringing in another dowry. This phenomenon, called dowry death, calls attention not just to the evils of dowry, but also to larger issues of the powerlessness of women.

✦ Evaluating the Text

1. From an Indian perspective, what are the advantages of an arranged marriage?

2. What considerations are taken into account in arranging a marriage in India?

3. What role does Nanda play in helping to find a suitable bride for her friend's son? How would you characterize Nanda's attitude toward arranged marriage and in what way does it change over the course of events?

✦ Exploring Different Perspectives

1. Contrast the effects of social class and caste on arranged marriages in India in Nanda's account and in Mahasweta Devi's story, "Giribala."

2. Compare the expectations regarding the role of women by their families in India according to Nanda and in Nigerian culture as described by Ann M. Simmons in "Where Fat Is a Mark of Beauty."

✧ Extending Viewpoints through Writing

1. Would you ever consider allowing your parents to arrange a marriage for you? If so, why would this be more advantageous or disadvantageous than finding someone for yourself?

2. What circumstances led your parents to get married? What considerations, in your opinion, played the most important role?

3. What did this essay add to your understanding of the pressures couples experience when getting married in India? To what extent are these pressures similar to or different from those experienced by couples in the United States?

Ann M. Simmons

Where Fat Is a Mark of Beauty

◆

Ann M. Simmons is a staff writer for The Los Angeles Times *where this article first appeared on September 30, 1998.*

Nigeria is a nation in western Africa on the Gulf of Guinea bordered by Niger to the north, Chad and Cameroon to the east and Benin (which was a center of commerce and culture from the fourteenth to the seventeenth centuries) to the west. Its capital and largest city is Lagos. Nigeria has been independent from Britain since 1960. It is Africa's most populous country and the most prosperous nation due to its oil wealth. Its recent political history has been marred by a series of coups and counter coups between various ethnic and religious groups, and its poor human rights record has led many countries to suspend development programs.

Before You Read

Consider how the message to young Nigerian girls is different from those of our society and what the reasons might be for these differences.

◆

1   Margaret Bassey Ene currently has one mission in life: gaining weight.

2   The Nigerian teenager has spent every day since early June in a "fattening room" specially set aside in her father's mud-and-thatch house. Most of her waking hours are spent eating bowl after bowl of rice, yams, plantains, beans and gari, a porridge-like mixture of dried cassava and water.

3   After three more months of starchy diet and forced inactivity, Margaret will be ready to reenter society bearing the traditional mark of female beauty among her Efik people: fat.

4   In contrast to many Western cultures where thin is in, many culture-conscious people in the Efik and other communities in Nigeria's southeastern Cross River state hail a woman's rotundity as a sign of good health, prosperity and allure. The fattening room is at the center of a centuries-old rite of passage from maidenhood to womanhood. The months spent in pursuit of poundage are supplemented by daily visits from elderly matrons who impart tips on how to be a successful wife and mother. Nowadays, though, girls who are not yet marriage-bound do a tour in the rooms purely as a coming-of-age ceremony.

And sometimes, nursing mothers return to the rooms to put on more weight.

5   "The fattening room is like a kind of school where the girl is taught about motherhood," said Sylvester Odey, director of the Cultural Center Board in Calabar, capital of Cross River state. "Your daily routine is to sleep, eat and grow fat."

6   Like many traditional African customs, the fattening room is facing relentless pressure from Western influences. Health campaigns linking excess fat to heart disease and other illnesses are changing the eating habits of many Nigerians, and urban dwellers are opting out of the time-consuming process.

7   Effiong Okon Etim, an Efik village chief in the district of Akpabuyo, said some families cannot afford to constantly feed a daughter for more than a few months. That compares with a stay of up to two years, as was common earlier this century, he said.

8   But the practice continues partly because "people might laugh at you because you didn't have money to allow your child to pass through the rite of passage," Etim said. What's more, many believe an unfattened girl will be sickly or unable to bear children.

9   Etim, 65, put his two daughters in a fattening room together when they were 12 and 15 years old, but some girls undergo the process as early as age 7, after undergoing the controversial practice of genital excision.

Bigger Is Better, According to Custom

10   As for how fat is fat enough, there is no set standard. But the unwritten rule is the bigger the better, said Mkoyo Edet, Etim's sister.

11   "Beauty is in the weight," said Edet, a woman in her 50s who spent three months in a fattening room when she was 7. "To be called a 'slim princess' is an abuse. The girl is fed constantly whether she likes it or not."

12   In Margaret's family, there was never any question that she would enter the fattening room.

13   "We inherited it from our forefathers; it is one of the heritages we must continue," said Edet Essien Okon, 25, Margaret's stepfather and a language and linguistics graduate of the University of Calabar. "It's a good thing to do; it's an initiation rite."

14   His wife, Nkoyo Effiong, 27, agreed: "As a woman, I feel it is proper for me to put my daughter in there, so she can be educated."

15   Effiong, a mother of five, spent four months in a fattening room at the age of 10.

16   Margaret, an attractive girl with a cheerful smile and hair plaited in fluffy bumps, needs only six months in the fattening room because she was already naturally plump, her stepfather said.

17   During the process, she is treated as a goddess, but the days are monotonous. To amuse herself, Margaret has only an instrument made out of a soda bottle with a hole in it, which she taps on her hand to play traditional tunes.

18   Still, the 16-year-old says she is enjoying the highly ritualized fattening practice.

19   "I'm very happy about this," she said, her belly already distended over the waist of her loincloth. "I enjoy the food, except for gari."

20   Day in, day out, Margaret must sit cross-legged on a special stool inside the secluded fattening room. When it is time to eat, she sits on the floor on a large, dried plantain leaf, which also serves as her bed. She washes down the mounds of food with huge pots of water and takes traditional medicine made from leaves and herbs to ensure proper digestion.

21   As part of the rite, Margaret's face is decorated with a white, clay-like chalk.

22   "You have to prepare the child so that if a man sees her, she will be attractive," Chief Etim said.

23   Tufts of palm leaf fiber, braided and dyed red, are hung around Margaret's neck and tied like bangles around her wrists and ankles. They are adjusted as she grows.

24   Typically, Margaret would receive body massages using the white chalk powder mixed with heavy red palm oil. But the teen said her parents believe the skin-softening, blood-stimulating massages might cause her to expand further than necessary.

25   Margaret is barred from doing her usual chores or any other strenuous physical activities. And she is forbidden to receive visitors, save for the half a dozen matrons who school Margaret in the etiquette of the Efik clan.

26   They teach her such basics as how to sit, walk and talk in front of her husband. And they impart wisdom about cleaning, sewing, child care and cooking—Efik women are known throughout Nigeria for their chicken pepper soup, pounded yams and other culinary creations.

27   "They advise me to keep calm and quiet, to eat the gari, and not to have many boyfriends so that I avoid unwanted pregnancy," Margaret said of her matron teachers. "They say that unless you have passed through this, you will not be a full-grown woman."

28   What little exercise Margaret gets comes in dance lessons. The matrons teach her the traditional ekombi, which she will be expected to perform before an audience on the day she emerges from seclusion—usually on the girl's wedding day, Etim said.

29   But Okon said his aim is to prepare his stepdaughter for the future, not to marry her off immediately. Efik girls receive more education than girls in most parts of Nigeria, and Okon hopes Margaret will return to school and embark on a career as a seamstress before getting married.

Weddings Also Steeped in Tradition

30   Once she does wed, Margaret will probably honor southeastern Nigeria's rich marriage tradition. It begins with a letter from the family of the groom to the family of the bride, explaining that "our son has seen a flower, a jewel, or something beautiful in your family, that we are interested in," said Josephine Effah-Chukwuma, program officer for women and children at the Constitutional Rights Project, a law-oriented nongovernmental organization based in the Nigerian commercial capital of Lagos.

31   If the girl and her family consent, a meeting is arranged. The groom and his relatives arrive with alcoholic beverages, soft drinks and native brews, and the bride's parents provide the food. The would-be bride's name is never uttered, and the couple are not allowed to speak, but if all goes well, a date is set for handing over the dowry. On that occasion, the bride's parents receive about $30 as a token of appreciation for their care of the young woman. "If you make the groom pay too much, it is like selling your daughter," Effah-Chukwuma said. Then, more drinks are served, and the engagement is official.

32   On the day of the wedding, the bride sits on a specially built wooden throne, covered by an extravagantly decorated canopy. Maidens surround her as relatives bestow gifts such as pots, pans, brooms, plates, glasses, table covers—everything she will need to start her new home. During the festivities, the bride changes clothes three times.

33   The high point is the performance of the ekombi, in which the bride twists and twirls, shielded by maidens and resisting the advances of her husband. It is his task to break through the ring and claim his bride.

34   Traditionalists are glad that some wedding customs are thriving despite the onslaught of modernity.

35   Traditional weddings are much more prevalent in southeastern Nigeria than so-called white weddings, introduced by colonialists and conducted in a church or registry office.

36   "In order to be considered married, you have to be married in the traditional way," said Maureen Okon, a woman of the Qua ethnic group who wed seven years ago but skipped the fattening room because she did not want to sacrifice the time. "Tradition identifies a people. It is important to keep up a culture. There is quite a bit of beauty in Efik and Qua marriages."

✧ *Evaluating the Text*

1. What culturally based assumptions guide Nigerian girls during their confinement in a "fattening room" before marriage?

2. What qualities do Nigerian men value in their wives, according to Simmons, and how does the preparation of the would-be bride meet these qualifications?

✧ Exploring Different Perspectives

1. Compare and contrast the concept of female beauty and the extent to which American and Nigerian culture shape the expectations for girls in each society in Simmons's article and in Susan Bordo's "Never Just Pictures."

2. How do the selections by Simmons and Lennard J. Davis (see "Visualizing the Disabled Body") reveal that female beauty is determined by cultural expectations?

✧ Extending Viewpoints through Writing

1. Discuss in a short essay which society's concept of beauty, Western or Nigerian, appeals to you and why?

2. To what extent is this rite of passage, as described in Simmons's article, designed to preserve traditional values in the face of the pressure of modern European values, brought in through colonial occupation?

Kate Chopin

Désirée's Baby

Kate Chopin (1851–1904) was born Katherine O'Flaherty, the daughter of a successful St. Louis businessman and his French Creole wife. After her father died in 1855, Kate was raised by her mother and great-grandmother. When she was nineteen, she married Oscar Chopin and accompanied him to New Orleans where he established himself as a cotton broker. After his business failed, they moved to his family plantation in Louisiana where he opened a general store. After his sudden death in 1883, Chopin managed the plantation for a year, but then decided to return to St. Louis with her six children. She began to submit stories patterned on the realistic fiction of Guy de Maupassant to local papers and national magazines, including the Saturday Evening Post *and* Atlantic Monthly. *Her stories of Creole life were widely praised for their realistic delineation of Creole manners and customs and were later collected in* Bayou Folk *(1894) and* A Night in Acadie *(1897). Her novel* The Awakening *(1899), although widely praised as a masterpiece for its frank depiction of its heroine's sexual awakening and need for self-fulfillment, created a public controversy. Chopin's uncompromising delineation of the pressures of class and race in Louisiana at the time are clearly seen in the poignant story "Désirée's Baby" (1899).*

Before You Read

Consider the extent to which the character of Désirée serves as a vehicle for the expression of Chopin's views on race and class.

1   As the day was pleasant, Madame Valmondé drove over to L'Abri to see Désirée and the baby.

2   It made her laugh to think of Désirée with a baby. Why, it seems but yesterday that Désirée was little more than a baby herself; when Monsieur in riding through the gateway of Valmondé had found her lying asleep in the shadow of the big stone pillar.

3   The little one awoke in his arms and began to cry for "Dada." That was as much as she could do or say. Some people thought she might have strayed there of her own accord, for she was of the toddling age. The prevailing belief was that she had been purposely left by a party of Texans, whose canvas-covered wagons, late in the day, had crossed the ferry that Coton Maïs kept, just below the plantation. In time Madame

Valmondé abandoned every speculation but the one that Désirée had been sent to her by a beneficent Providence to be the child of her affection, seeing that she was without child of the flesh. For the girl grew to be beautiful and gentle, affectionate and sincere—the idol of Valmondé.

4   It was no wonder, when she stood one day against the stone pillar in whose shadow she had lain asleep, eighteen years before, that Armand Aubigny riding by and seeing her there, had fallen in love with her. That was the way all the Aubignys fell in love, as if struck by a pistol shot. The wonder was that he had not loved her before; for he had known her since his father brought him home from Paris, a boy of eight, after his mother died there. The passion that awoke in him that day, when he saw her at the gate, swept along like an avalanche, or like a prairie fire, or like anything that drives headlong over all obstacles.

5   Madame Valmondé bent her portly figure over Désirée and kissed her, holding her an instant tenderly in her arms. Then she turned to the child.

6   "This is not the baby!" she exclaimed, in startled tones. French was the language spoken at Valmondé in those days.

7   "I knew you would be astonished," laughed Désirée, "at the way he has grown. The little *cochon de lait!*[1] Look at his legs, mamma, and his hands and fingernails,—real fingernails. Zandrine had to cut them this morning. Isn't it true, Zandrine?"

8   The woman bowed her turbaned head majestically, "Mais si, Madame."

9   "And the way he cries," went on Désirée, "is deafening. Armand heard him the other day as far away as La Blanche's cabin."

10   Madame Valmondé had never removed her eyes from the child. She lifted it and walked with it over to the window that was lightest. She scanned the baby narrowly, then looked as searchingly at Zandrine, whose face was turned to gaze across the fields.

11   "Yes, the child has grown, has changed," said Madame Valmondé, slowly, as she replaced it beside its mother. "What does Armand say?"

12   Désirée's face became suffused with a glow that was happiness itself.

13   "Oh, Armand is the proudest father in the parish, I believe, chiefly because it is a boy, to bear his name; though he says not—that he would have loved a girl as well. But I know it isn't true. I know he says that to please me. And mamma," she added, drawing Madame Valmondé's head down to her, and speaking in a whisper, "he hasn't punished one of them—not one of them—since baby is born. Even Négrillon, who pretended to have burnt his leg that he might rest from work—he only laughed, and said Négrillon was a great scamp. Oh, mama, I'm so happy; it frightens me."

[1]*cochon de lait:* Literally "pig of milk"—a big feeder.

14   What Désirée said was true. Marriage, and later the birth of his son, had softened Armand Aubigny's imperious and exacting nature greatly. This was what made the gentle Désirée so happy, for she loved him desperately. When he frowned she trembled, but loved him. When he smiled, she asked no greater blessing of God. But Armand's dark, handsome face had not often been disfigured by frowns since the day he fell in love with her.

15   When the baby was about three months old, Désirée awoke one day to the conviction that there was something in the air menacing her peace. It was at first too subtle to grasp. It had only been a disquieting suggestion; an air of mystery among the blacks; unexpected visits from far-off neighbors who could hardly account for their coming. Then a strange, an awful change in her husband's manner, which she dared not ask him to explain. When he spoke to her, it was with averted eyes, from which the old love light seemed to have gone out. He absented himself from home; and when there, avoided her presence and that of her child, without excuse. And the very spirit of Satan seemed suddenly to take hold of him in his dealings with the slaves. Désirée was miserable enough to die.

16   She sat in her room, one hot afternoon, in her *peignoir*, listlessly drawing through her fingers the strands of her long, silky brown hair that hung about her shoulders. The baby, half naked, lay asleep upon her own great mahogany bed, that was like a sumptuous throne, with its satin-lined half canopy. One of La Blanche's little quadroon boys—half naked too—stood fanning the child slowly with a fan of peacock feathers. Désirée's eyes had been fixed absently and sadly upon the baby, while she was striving to penetrate the threatening mist that she felt closing about her. She looked from her child to the boy who stood beside him; and back again, over and over. "Ah!" It was a cry that she could not help, which she was not conscious of having uttered. The blood turned like ice in her veins, and a clammy moisture gathered upon her face.

17   She tried to speak to the little quadroon boy; but no sound would come, at first. When he heard his name uttered, he looked up, and his mistress was pointing to the door. He laid aside the great, soft fan, and obediently stole away, over the polished floor, on his bare tiptoes.

18   She stayed motionless, with gaze riveted upon her child, and her face the picture of fright.

19   Presently her husband entered the room, and without noticing her, went to a table and began to search among some papers which covered it.

20   "Armand," she called to him, in a voice which must have stabbed him, if he was human. But he did not notice. "Armand," she said again. Then she rose and tottered towards him. "Armand," she panted once more, clutching his arm, "look at our child. What does it mean? Tell me."

21   He coldly but gently loosened her fingers from about his arm and thrust the hand away from him. "Tell me what it means!" she cried despairingly.

22   "It means," he answered lightly, "that the child is not white; it means that you are not white."

23   A quick conception of all that this accusation meant for her nerved her with unwonted courage to deny it. "It is a lie; it is not true, I am white! Look at my hair, it is brown; and my eyes are gray, Armand, you know they are gray. And my skin is fair," seizing his wrist. "Look at my hand, whiter than yours, Armand," she laughed hysterically.

24   "As white as La Blanche's," he returned cruelly, and went away leaving her alone with their child.

25   When she could hold a pen in her hand, she sent a despairing letter to Madame Valmondé.

26   "My mother, they tell me I am not white. Armand has told me I am not white. For God's sake tell them it is not true. You must know it is not true. I shall die. I must die. I cannot be so unhappy, and live."

27   The answer that came was as brief:

28   "My own Désirée: Come home to Valmondé; back to your mother who loves you. Come with your child."

29   When the letter reached Désirée she went with it to her husband's study, and laid it open upon the desk before which he sat. She was like a stone image: silent, white, motionless after she placed it there.

30   In silence he ran his cold eyes over the written words. He said nothing. "Shall I go, Armand?" she asked in tones sharp with agonized suspense.

31   "Yes, go."

32   "Do you want me to go?"

33   "Yes, I want you to go."

34   He thought Almighty God had dealt cruelly and unjustly with him; and felt, somehow, that he was paying Him back in kind when he stabbed thus into his wife's soul. Moreover he no longer loved her, because of the unconscious injury she had brought upon his home and his name.

35   She turned away like one stunned by a blow, and walked slowly towards the door, hoping he would call her back.

36   "Good-by, Armand," she moaned.

37   He did not answer her. That was his last blow at fate.

38   Désirée went in search of her child. Zandrine was pacing the sombre gallery with it. She took the little one from the nurse's arms with no word of explanation, and descending the steps, walked away, under the live-oak branches.

39   It was an October afternoon; the sun was just sinking. Out in the still fields the Negroes were picking cotton.

40   Désirée had not changed the thin white garment nor the slippers which she wore. Her hair was uncovered and the sun's rays brought a golden gleam from its brown meshes. She did not take the broad, beaten road which led to the far-off plantation of Valmondé. She walked across a deserted field, where the stubble bruised her tender feet, so delicately shod, and tore her thin gown to shreds.

41   She disappeared among the reeds and willows that grew thick along the banks of the deep, sluggish bayou; and she did not come back again.

42   Some weeks later there was a curious scene enacted at L'Abri. In the centre of the smoothly swept back yard was a great bonfire. Armand Aubigny sat in the wide hallway that commanded a view of the spectacle; and it was he who dealt out to a half dozen negroes the material which kept this fire ablaze.

43   A graceful cradle of willow, with all its dainty furbishings, was laid upon the pyre, which had already been fed with the richness of a priceless *layette*. Then there were silk gowns, and velvet and satin ones added to these; laces, too, and embroideries; bonnets and gloves; for the *corbeille*[2] had been of rare quality.

44   The last thing to go was a tiny bundle of letters; innocent little scribblings that Désirée had sent to him during the days of their espousal. There was the remnant of one back in the drawer from which he took them. But it was not Désirée's; it was part of an old letter from his mother to his father. He read it. She was thanking God for the blessing of her husband's love:

45   "But, above all," she wrote, "night and day, I thank the good God for having so arranged our lives that our dear Armand will never know that his mother, who adores him, belongs to the race that is cursed with the brand of slavery."

✧ Evaluating the Text

1. What can you infer about Armand's character and his past behavior from the fact that he has not punished one slave since his baby was born? How does his behavior toward Désirée change after the baby is three months old? What causes this change in his behavior?

2. What did you assume Désirée would do when she realizes Armand values his social standing more than he does her? In retrospect, what clues would have pointed you toward the truth disclosed at the end of the story?

[2]*Corbeille:* a basket of linens, clothing, and accessories collected in anticipation of a baby's birth.

✦ Exploring Different Perspectives

1. How do the underlying cultural assumptions regarding gender, race, and class explain the reactions of the characters in the stories by Chopin and Mahasweta Devi (see "Giribala")?

2. Contrast Judith Ortiz Cofer's (see "The Myth of the Latin Woman") reactions to sexual and racial stereotyping in today's world with Chopin's depiction of Désirée and discuss the differences between these two worlds in America.

✦ Extending Viewpoints through Writing

1. In a short essay, discuss the picture you formed of the society in which Chopin's story took place (late 1800s in Louisiana) and the extent to which race and class determined people's behavior.

2. At the end of the story, we discover that Armand is of mixed racial parentage and assume that Désirée is white. How would the impact of the story change if we also knew that Désirée was of a mixed racial background as well as Armand?

Mahasweta Devi

Giribala

◆

*Mahasweta Devi was born in East Bengal in 1926, moved to West Bengal
as an adolescent, and studied at Visva-Bharati and Calcutta universities
where she received a master's degree in English. From a family with widespread literary and political influence, Devi joined the Gananatya, a group
of highly accomplished, keenly political actors and writers who took the revolutionary step of bringing theater, on themes of burning interest in rural
Bengal, to villages. Subsequently, she became a writer and journalist while
holding a job as a college teacher in Calcutta. Over a period of years she has
studied and lived among the tribal and outcast communities in southwest
Bengal and southeast Bihar. Her stories, collected in* Agnigarbha *(Womb
of Fire) (1978) and in* Imaginary Maps *(1994), focus on the semilandless
tribals and untouchables who are effectively denied rights guaranteed by
the constitution, including a legal minimum wage. Her unique style of narrative realism reflects this emphasis on observations drawn from actual situations, persons, dialects, and idioms. "Giribala," translated into English
from Bengali by Bardhan Kalpana, was first published in the magazine*
Prasad *(Autumn 1982), a journal Devi created as a kind of people's magazine, which she still edits. Like her other stories, "Giribala" reflects carefully researched information Devi gathered directly from the lives of the
rural underclass. This story tells the shocking tale of a woman whose husband sells their young daughters into prostitution.*

*In 1997, Devi won the Magsaysay award, considered to be the Asian
equivalent of the Nobel prize, and donated the cash prize of $50,000 to a
tribal welfare society.*

Before You Read
Imagine what life would be like in a culture where the caste, or social class
into which you were born determined every aspect of your life.

◆

1   Giribala[1] was born in a village called Talsana, in the Kandi subdi-
vision of Murshidabad district.[2] Nobody ever imagined that she could
think on her own, let alone act on her own thought. This Giribala, like

---

[1]Literally, "mountain girl."
[2]In the United Province, near New Delhi.

so many others, was neither beautiful nor ugly, just an average-looking girl. But she had lovely eyes, eyes that somehow made her appearance striking.

2   In their caste, it was still customary to pay a bride-price. Aulchand gave Giri's father eighty rupees[3] and a heifer before he married her. Giri's father, in turn, gave his daughter four tolas[4] of silver, pots and pans, sleeping mats, and a cartload of mature bamboo that came from the bamboo clumps that formed the main wealth of Giri's father. Aulchand had told him that only because his hut had burned down did he need the bamboo to rebuild it. This was also the reason he gave for having to leave her with them for a few days—so that he could go to build a home for them.

3   Aulchand thus married Giri, and left. He did not come back soon.

4   Shortly after the marriage, Bangshi Dhamali,[5] who worked at the sub-post office in Nishinda, happened to visit the village. Bangshi enjoyed much prestige in the seven villages in the Nishinda area, largely due to his side business of procuring patients for the private practice of the doctor who was posted at the only hospital in the area. That way, the doctor supplemented his hospital salary by getting paid by the patients thus diverted from the hospital, and Bangshi supplemented his salary of 145 rupees from the sub-post office with the commission he got for procuring those patients. Bangshi's prestige went up further after he started using the medical terms he had picked up from being around the doctor.

5   For some reason that nobody quite recalled, Bangshi addressed Giri's father as uncle. When Bangshi showed up on one of his patient-procuring trips, he looked up Giri's father and remarked disapprovingly about what he had just learned from his trip to another village, that he had given his only daughter in marriage to Aulchand, of all people.

6   "Yes. The proposal came along, and I thought he was all right."

7   "Obviously, you thought so. How much did he pay?"

8   "Four times twenty and one."

9   "I hope you're ready to face the consequences of what you've done."

10   "What consequences?"

11   "What can I say? You know that I'm a government servant myself and the right-hand man of the government doctor. Don't you think you should have consulted me first? I'm not saying that he's a bad sort, and I will not deny there was a time when I smoked *ganja*[6] with him. But I know what you don't know—the money he gave you as bride-price

---

[3]Approximately $20.
[4]One tola = .40 ounce.
[5]Literally, mischievous.
[6]Marijuana cigarettes, also known as "pip."

was not his. It's Channan's. You see, Channan's marriage had been arranged in Kalhat village. And Aulchand, as Channan's uncle, was trusted with the money to deliver as bride-price on behalf of Channan. He didn't deliver it there."

12   "What?"

13   "Channan's mother sat crying when she learned that Aulchand, who had been living under their roof for so long, could cheat them like that. Finally, Channan managed to get married by borrowing from several acquaintances who were moved by his plight."

14   "He has no place of his own? No land for a home to stand on?"

15   "Nothing of the sort."

16   "But he took a cartload of my bamboo to rebuild the hut on his land!"

17   "I was going to tell you about that too. He sold that bamboo to Channan's aunt for a hundred rupees and hurried off to the Banpur fair."

18   Giri's father was stunned. He sat with his head buried in his hands. Bangshi went on telling him about other similar tricks Aulchand had been pulling. Before taking leave, he finally said, perhaps out of mercy for the overwhelmed man, "He's not a bad one really. Just doesn't have any land, any place to live. Keeps traveling from one fair to another, with some singing party or other. That's all. Otherwise, he's not a bad sort."

19   Giri's father wondered aloud, "But Mohan never told me any of these things! He's the one who brought the proposal to me!"

20   "How could he, when he's Aulchand's right hand in these matters?"

21   When Giri's mother heard all this from Giri's father, she was livid. She vowed to have her daughter married again and never to send her to live with the cheat, the thief.

22   But when after almost a year Aulchand came back, he came prepared to stop their mouths from saying what they wanted to say. He brought a large taro root, a new sari for his bride, a squat stool of jackfruit wood for his mother-in-law, and four new jute sacks for his father-in-law. Giri's mother still managed to tell him the things they had found out from Bangshi. Aulchand calmly smiled a generous, forgiving smile, saying, "One couldn't get through life if one believed everything that Bangshi-*dada* said.[7] Your daughter is now going to live in a brick house, not a mere mud hut. That's true, not false."

23   So, Giri's mother started to dress her only daughter to go to live with her husband. She took time to comb her hair into a nice bun,

---

[7]*Dada,* meaning elder brother, is also used to refer politely to or to address a friend or acquaintance older than oneself, but not older enough to be referred to or addressed as uncle. [Author's note.]

while weeping and lamenting, partly to herself and partly to her daughter, "This man is like a hundred-rooted weed in the yard. Bound to come back every time it's been pulled out. What he just told us are all lies, I know that. But with what smooth confidence he said those lies!"

24   Giri listened silently. She knew that although the groom had to pay a bride-price in their community, still a girl was only a girl. She had heard so many times the old saying: "A daughter born, To husband or death, She's already gone." She realized that her life in her own home and village was over, and her life of suffering was going to begin. Silently she wept for a while, as her mother tended to grooming her. Then she blew her nose, wiped her eyes, and asked her mother to remember to bring her home at the time of Durga puja[8] and to feed the red-brown cow that was her charge, adding that she had chopped some hay for the cow, and to water her young *jaba* tree that was going to flower someday.

25   Giribala, at the age of fourteen, then started off to make her home with her husband. Her mother put into a bundle the pots and pans that she would be needing. Watching her doing that, Aulchand remarked, "Put in some rice and lentils too. I've got a job at the house of the *babu*. Must report to work the moment I get back. There'll be no time to buy provisions until after a few days."

26   Giribala picked up the bundle of rice, lentils, and cooking oil and left her village, walking a few steps behind him. He walked ahead, and from time to time asked her to walk faster, as the afternoon was starting to fade. He took her to another village in Nishinda, to a large brick house with a large garden of fruit trees of all kinds. In the far corner of the garden was a crumbling hovel meant for the watchman. He took her to it. There was no door in the door opening. As if answering her thought, Aulchand said, "I'll fix the door soon. But you must admit the room is nice. And the pond is quite near. Now go on, pick up some twigs and start the rice."

27   "It's dark out there! Do you have a kerosene lamp?"

28   "Don't ask me for a kerosene lamp, or this and that. Just do what you can."

29   A maid from the babu's household turned up and saved Giri. She brought a kerosene lamp from the house and showed Giri to the pond, complaining about Aulchand and cautioning her about him. "What kind of heartless parents would give a tender young girl to a no-good ganja addict? How can he feed you? He has nothing. Gets a pittance taking care of the babu's cattle and doing odd jobs. Who knows how he manages to feed himself, doing whatever else he does! If you've

---

[8]Rituals designed to worship a household goddess of good fortune.

been brought up on rice, my dear, you'd be wise enough to go back home tomorrow to leave behind the bits of silver that you have got on you."

30   But Giri did not go back home the next day for safekeeping her silver ornaments. Instead, in the morning she was found busy plastering with mud paste the exposed, uneven bricks of the wall of the crumbling room. Aulchand managed to get an old sheet of tin from the babu and nailed it to a few pieces of wood to make it stand; then he propped it up as a door for the room. Giri promptly got herself employed in the babu household for meals as her wage. After a few months, Aulchand remarked about how she had managed to domesticate a vagabond like him, who grew up without parents, never stayed home, and always floated around.

31   Giri replied, "Go, beg the babus for a bit of the land. Build your own home."

32   "Why will they give me land?"

33   "They will if you plead for the new life that's on its way. Ask them if a baby doesn't deserve to be born under a roof of its own. Even beggars and roving street singers have some kind of home."

34   "You're right. I too feel sad about not having a home of my own. Never felt that way before, though."

35   The only dream they shared was a home of their own.

36   However, their firstborn, a daughter they named Belarani,[9] was born in the crumbling hovel with the tin door. Before the baby was even a month old, Giri returned to her work in the babu household, and, as if to make up for her short absence from work, she took the heavy sheets, the flatweave rugs, and the mosquito nets to the pond to wash them clean. The lady of the house remarked on how she put her heart into the work and how clean her work was!

37   Feeling very magnanimous, the lady then gave Giri some of her children's old clothes, and once in a while she asked Giri to take a few minutes' break from work to feed the baby.

38   Belarani was followed by another daughter, Poribala, and a son, Rajib, all born in the watchman's hovel at the interval of a year and a half to two years. After the birth of her fourth child, a daughter she named Maruni,[10] she asked the doctor at the hospital, where she went for this birth, to sterilize her.

39   By then Aulchand had finally managed to get the babu's permission to use a little area of his estate to build a home for his family. He

[9]Literally, "pretty queen."

[10]Literally meaning a girl likely to die; the name is perhaps intended to repel death, following the belief that death takes first the lives people want to cling to most. [Author's note.]

had even raised a makeshift shack on it. Now he was periodically going away for other kinds of work assigned to him.

40   He was furious to learn that Giri had herself sterilized, so furious that he beat her up for the first time. "Why did you do it? Tell me, why?"

41   Giri kept silent and took the beating. Aulchand grabbed her by the hair and punched her a good many times. Silently she took it all. After he had stopped beating because he was tired and his anger temporarily spent, she calmly informed him that the Panchayat[11] was going to hire people for the road building and pay the wages in wheat.

42   "Why don't you see your father and get some bamboo instead?"

43   "What for?"

44   "Because you're the one who has been wanting a home. I could build a good one with some bamboo from your father."

45   "We'll both work on the Panchayat road and have our home. We'll save some money by working harder."

46   "If only we could mortgage or sell your silver trinkets, . . . "

47   Giribala did not say anything to his sly remark; she just stared at him. Aulchand had to lower his eyes before her silent stare. Giri had put her silver jewelry inside the hollow of a piece of bamboo, stuffed it up and kept it in the custody of the lady of the house she worked for. Belarani too started working there, when she was seven years old, doing a thousand odd errands to earn her meals. Bela was now ten, and growing like a weed in the rainy season. Giri would need the silver to get her married someday soon. All she had for that purpose was the bit of silver from her parents and the twenty-two rupees she managed to save from her years of hard work, secretly deposited with the mistress of the house, away from Aulchand's reach.

48   "I'm not going to sell my silver for a home. My father gave all he could for that, a whole cartload of bamboo, one hundred and sixty-two full stems, worth a thousand rupees at that time even in the markets of Nishinda."

49   "The same old story comes up again!" Aulchand was exasperated.

50   "Don't you want to see your own daughter married someday?"

51   "Having a daughter only means having to raise a slave for others. Mohan had read my palm and predicted a son in the fifth pregnancy. But, no, you had to make yourself sterile, so you could turn into a whore."

52   Giri grabbed the curved kitchen knife and hissed at him, "If ever I hear you say those evil things about me, I'll cut off the heads of the children and then my own head with this."

---

[11]Governing body of the local village, usually mde up of five officials ("pancha" means "five").

53   Aulchand quickly stopped himself, "Forget I said it. I won't, ever again."

54   For a few days after that he seemed to behave himself. He was sort of timid, chastised. But soon, probably in some way connected with the grudge of being chastised by her, the vile worm inside his brain started to stir again; once again Mohan, his trick master, was his prompter.

55   Mohan had turned up in the midst of the busy days they were spending in the construction of a bus road that was going to connect Nishinda with Krishnachawk.[12] Giri and Aulchand were both working there and getting as wages the wheat for their daily meals. Mohan too joined them to work there, and he sold his wheat to buy some rice, a pumpkin, and occasionally some fish to go with the wheat bread. He had remained the same vagabond that he always was, only his talking had become more sophisticated with a bohemian style picked up from his wanderings to cities and distant villages. He slept in the little porch facing the room occupied by Giri and her family.

56   Sitting there in the evenings, he expressed pity for Aulchand, "Tch! Tch! You seem to have got your boat stuck in the mud, my friend. Have you forgotten all about the life we used to have?"

57   Giri snapped at him, "You can't sit here doing your smart talking, which can only bring us ruin."

58   "My friend had such a good singing voice!"

59   "Perhaps he had that. Maybe there was money in it too. But that money would never have reached his home and fed his children."

60   Mohan started another topic one evening. He said that there was a great shortage of marriage-age girls in Bihar,[13] so that the Biharis with money were coming down for Bengali brides and paying a bundle for that! He mentioned that Sahadeb Bauri, a fellow he knew, a low-caste fellow like themselves, received five hundred rupees for having his daughter married to one of those bride-searching Biharis.

61   "Where is that place?" Aulchand's curiosity was roused.

62   "You wouldn't know, my friend, even if I explained where it is. Let me just say that it's very far and the people there don't speak Bengali."

63   "They paid him five hundred rupees?" Aulchand was hooked in.

64   "Yes, they did."

65   The topic was interrupted at that point by the noise that rose when people suddenly noticed that the cowshed of Kali-babu,[14] the Panchayat big shot, was on fire. Everybody ran in that direction to throw bucketfuls of water at it.

[12]A major junction.

[13]A state near Bengal.

[14]Kali means dark complexion; literally, "black."

66   Giri forgot about the topic thus interrupted. But Aulchand did not.

67   Something must have blocked Giri's usual astuteness because she suspected nothing from the subsequent changes in her husband's tone.

68   For example, one day he said, "Who wants your silver? I'll get my daughter married and also my shack replaced with bricks and tin. My daughter looks lovelier every day from the meals in the babu home!"

69   Giri's mind sensed nothing at all to be alerted to. She only asked, "Are you looking for a groom for her?"

70   "I don't have to look. My daughter's marriage will just happen."

71   Giri did not give much thought to this strange answer either. She merely remarked that the sagging roof needed to be propped up soon.

72   Perhaps too preoccupied with the thought of how to get the roof propped up, Giri decided to seek her father's help and also to see her parents for just a couple of days. Holding Maruni to her chest and Rajib and Pori by the hand, she took leave of Belarani, who cried and cried because she was not being taken along to visit her grandparents. Giri, also crying, gave her eight annas to buy sweets to eat, telling her that she could go another time because both of them could not take off at the same time from their work at the babu's place, even if for only four days, including the two days in walking to and from there.

73   She had no idea that she was never to see Bela again. If she had, she would not only have taken her along, but she would also have held her tied to her bosom, she would not have let her out of her sight for a minute. She was Giri's beloved firstborn, even though Giri had to put her to work at the babu household ever since she was only seven; that was the only way she could have her fed and clothed. Giri had no idea when she started for her parents' village, leaving Bela with a kiss on her forehead.

74   "A daughter born, To husband or death, She's already gone." That must be why seeing the daughter makes the mother's heart sing! Her father had been very busy trying to sell his bamboo and acquiring two *bighas*[15] of land meanwhile. He was apologetic about not being able in all this time to bring her over for a visit, and he asked her to stay on a few more days once she had made the effort to come on her own. Her mother started making puffed rice and digging up the taro root she had been saving for just such a special occasion. While her hands worked making things for them to eat, she lamented about what the marriage had done to her daughter, how it had tarnished her bright complexion, ruined her abundant hair, and made her collarbones stick out. She kept asking her to stay a few more days, resting and eating to

---

[15]One *bigha* is roughly one-third of an acre. [Author's note.]

repair the years of damage. Giri's little brother begged her to stay for a month.

75   For a few days, after many years, Giri found rest and care and heaping servings of food. Her father readily agreed to give her the bamboo, saying how much he wanted his daughter to live well, in a manner he could be proud of. Giri could easily have used a few tears and got some other things from her father. Her mother asked her to weep and get a maund[16] of rice too while he was in the giving mood. But Giri did not do that. Giri was not going to ask for anything from her loved ones unless she absolutely had to. She walked over to the corner of the yard, to look at the hibiscus she had planted when she was a child. She watched with admiration its crimson flowers and the clean mud-plastered yard and the new tiles on the roof. She also wondered if her son Rajib could stay there and go to the school her brother went to. But she mentioned nothing to her parents about this sudden idea that felt like a dream.

76   She just took her children to the pond, and, with the bar of soap she had bought on the way, she scrubbed them and herself clean. She washed her hair too. Then she went to visit the neighbors. She was feeling lighthearted, as if she were in heaven, without the worries of her life. Her mother sent her brother to catch a fish from the canal, the new irrigation canal that had changed the face of the area since she last saw it. It helped to raise crops and catch fish throughout the year. Giri felt an unfamiliar wind of fulfillment and pleasure blowing in her mind. There was not the slightest hint of foreboding.

77   Bangshi Dhamali happened to be in the village that day, and he too remarked on how Giri's health and appearance had deteriorated since she went to live with that no-good husband of hers. He said that if only Aulchand were a responsible father and could look after the older kids, she could have gone to work in the house of the doctor who was now living in Bahrampur town, and after some time she could take all the children over there and have them all working for food and clothing.

78   Giri regarded his suggestion with a smile, and asked him instead, "Tell me, dad, how is it that when so many destitute people are getting little plots of land from the government, Rajib's father can't?"

79   "Has he ever come to see me about it? Ever sought my advice on anything? I'm in government service myself, and the right-hand man of the hospital doctor as well. I could easily have gotten him a plot of land."

80   "I'm going to send him to you as soon as I get back."

81   It felt like a pleasant dream to Giri, that they could have a piece of land of their own for a home of their own. She knew that her husband

[16]Equal to approximately 85 pounds.

was a pathetic vagabond. Still, she felt a rush of compassion for him. A man without his own home, his own land. How could such a man help being diffident and demoralized?

82   "Are you sure, Bangshi-dada? Shall I send him to you then?"

83   "Look at your own father. See how well he's managed things. He's now almost a part of the Panchayat. I don't know what's the matter with uncle, though. He could have seen to it that Aulchand got a bit of the land being distributed. I once told him as much, and he insulted me in the marketplace, snapped at me that Aulchand should be learning to use his own initiative."

84   Giri decided to ignore the tendentious remark and keep on pressing Bangshi instead, "Please, Bangshi-dada, you tell me what to do. You know how impractical that man is. The room he's put up in all these years doesn't even have a good thatch roof. The moon shines into it all night and the sun all day. I'm hoping to get Bela married someday soon. Where am I going to seat the groom's party? And, dada, would you look for a good boy for my daughter?"

85   "There is a good boy available. Obviously, you don't know that. He's the son of my own cousin. Just started a grocery store of his own."

86   Giri was excited to learn that, and even Rajib's face lit up as he said that he could then go to work as a helper in his brother-in-law's shop and could bring home salt and oil on credit. Giri scolded him for taking after his father, wanting to live on credit rather than by work.

87   Giri ended up staying six days with her parents instead of two. She was about to take leave, wearing a sari without holes that her mother gave her, a bundle of rice on her head, and cheap new shirts and pants on her children. Just then, like the straw suddenly blown in, indicating the still unseen storm, Bangshi Dhamali came in a rush to see her father.

88   "I don't want to say if it is bad news or good news, uncle, but what I just heard is incredible. Aulchand had told Bela that he was going to take her to see her grandparents. Then with the help of Mohan, he took her to Kandi town, and there he got the scared twelve-year-old, the timid girl who had known only her mother, married to some strange man from Bihar. There were five girls like Bela taken there to be married to five unknown blokes. The addresses they left are all false. This kind of business is on the rise. Aulchand got four hundred rupees in cash. The last thing he was seen doing was, back from drinking with Mohan, crying and slobbering, 'Bela! Bela!' while Kali-babu of the village Panchayat was shouting at him."

89   The sky seemed to come crashing down on Giribala's head. She howled with pain and terror. Her father got some people together and went along with her, vowing to get the girl back, to break the hands of the girl's father, making him a cripple, and to finish Mohan for good.

90   They could not find Mohan. Just Aulchand. On seeing them, he kept doing several things in quick succession. He vigorously twisted his own ears and nose to show repentance, he wept, perhaps with real grief, and from time to time he sat up straight, asserting that because Bela was his daughter it was nobody else's business how he got her married off.

91   They searched the surrounding villages as far as they could. Giri took out the silver she had deposited with the mistress of the house and went to the master, crying and begging him to inform the police and get a paid announcement made over the radio about the lost girl. She also accused them, as mildly as she could in her state of mind, for letting the girl go with her father, knowing as they did the lout that he was.

92   The master of the house persuaded Giri's father not to seek police help because that would only mean a lot of trouble and expense. The terrible thing had happened after all; Bela had become one more victim of this new business of procuring girls on the pretext of marriage. The police were not going to do much for this single case; they would most probably say that the father did it after all. Poor Bela had this written on her forehead!

93   Finally, that was the line everybody used to console Giri. The master of the house in which she and Bela worked day and night, the neighbors gathered there, even Giri's father ended up saying that— about the writing on the forehead that nobody could change. If the daughter was to remain hers, that would have been nice, they said in consolation, but she was only a daughter, not a son. And they repeated the age-old saying: "A daughter born, To husband or death, She's already gone."

94   Her father sighed and said with philosophical resignation, "It's as if the girl sacrificed her life to provide her father with money for a house."

95   Giri, crazed with grief, still brought herself to respond in the implied context of trivial bickering, "Don't send him any bamboo, father. Let the demon do whatever he can on his own."

96   "It's useless going to the police in such matters," everybody said.

97   Giri sat silently with her eyes closed, leaning against the wall. Even in her bitter grief, the realization flashed through her mind that nobody was willing to worry about a girl child for very long. Perhaps she should not either. She too was a small girl once, and her father too gave her away to a subhuman husband without making sufficient inquiries.

98   Aulchand sensed that the temperature in the environment was dropping. He started talking defiantly and defending himself to her father by blaming Giri and answering her remark about him. "Don't overlook your daughter's fault. How promptly she brought out her silver chain to get her daughter back! If she had brought it out earlier, then there would have been a home for us and no need to sell my

daughter. Besides, embarrassed as I am to tell you this, she had the operation to get cleaned out, saying, 'What good was it having more children when we can't feed the ones we've got?' Well, I've shown what good it can be, even if we got more daughters. So much money for a daughter!"

99   At this, Giri started hitting her own head against the wall so violently that she seemed to have suddenly gone insane with grief and anger. They had to grapple with her to restrain her from breaking her head.

100   Slowly the agitation died down. The babu's aunt gave Giri a choice nugget of her wisdom to comfort her. "A daughter, until she is married, is her father's property. It's useless for a mother to think she has any say."

101   Giri did not cry any more after that night.

102   Grimly, she took Pori to the babu's house, to stay there and work in place of Bela, and told her that she would kill her if she ever went anywhere with her father. In grim silence, she went through her days of work and even more work. When Aulchand tried to say anything to her, she did not answer; she just stared at him. It scared Aulchand. The only time she spoke to him was to ask, "Did you really do it only because you wanted to build your home?"

103   "Yes. Believe me."

104   "Ask Mohan to find out where they give the children they buy full meals to eat. Then go and sell the other three there. You can have a brick and concrete house. Mohan must know it."

105   "How can you say such a dreadful thing, you merciless woman? Asking me to sell the children. Is that why you got sterilized? And why didn't you take the bamboo that your father offered?"

106   Giri left the room and lay down in the porch to spend the night there. Aulchand whined and complained for a while. Soon he fell asleep.

107   Time did the ultimate, imperceptible talking! Slowly Giri seemed to accept it. Aulchand bought some panels of woven split-bamboo for the walls. The roof still remained covered with leaves. Rajib took the work of tending the babu's cattle. Maruni, the baby, grew into a child, playing by herself in the yard. The hardest thing for Giri now was to look at Pori because she looked so much like Bela, with Bela's smile, Bela's way of watching things with her head tilted to one side. The mistress of the house was full of similar praise for her work and her gentle manners.

108   Little Pori poured her heart into the work at the babu household, as if it were far more than a means to the meals her parents couldn't provide, as if it were her vocation, her escape. Perhaps the work was the disguise for her silent engagement in constant, troubling thoughts. Why else would she sweep all the rooms and corridors ten times a day, when nobody had asked her to? Why did she carry those jute sacks for paddy

storage to the pond to wash them diligently? Why else would she spend endless hours coating the huge unpaved yard with a rag dipped in mud-dung paste until it looked absolutely smooth from end to end?

109   When Pori came home in the evening, worn out from the day's constant work, Giri, herself drained from daylong work, would feed her some puffed rice or chickpea flour that she might happen to have at home. Then she would go and spend most of the evening roaming alone through the huge garden of the babus, absently picking up dry twigs and leaves for the stove and listening to the rustle of leaves, the scurrying of squirrels in the dark. The night wind soothed her raging despair, as it blew her matted hair, uncombed for how long she did not remember.

110   The gentle face of her firstborn would then appear before her eyes, and she would hear the sound of her small voice, making some little plea on some little occasion. "Ma, let me stay home today and watch you make the puffed rice. If they send for me, you can tell them that Bela would do all the work tomorrow, but she can't go today. Would you, Ma, please?"

111   Even when grown up, with three younger ones after her, she loved to sleep nestled next to her mother. Once her foot was badly cut and bruised. The squat stool that the babu's aunt sat on for her oil massage had slipped and hit her foot. She bore the pain for days, until applying the warm oil from a lamp healed it. Whenever Giri had a fever, Bela somehow found some time in between her endless chores at the babu household to come to cook the rice and run back to work.

> Bela, Belarani, Beli—
> Her I won't abandon.
> Yet my daughter named Beli,
> To husband or death she's gone!

112   Where could she be now? How far from here? In which strange land? Giri roamed the nights through the trees, and she muttered absently, "Wherever you are, my daughter, stay alive! Don't be dead! If only I knew where you were, I'd go there somehow, even if I had to learn to fly like birds or insects. But I don't know where you were taken. I wrote you a letter, with the babu's help, to the address they left. You couldn't have got it, daughter, because it's a false address."

113   Absently Giri would come back with the twigs, cook the rice, feed Maruni, eat herself, and lie down with her children, leaving Aulchand's rice in the pot.

114   The days without work she stayed home, just sitting in the porch. The days she found work, she went far—by the bus that now plied along the road they had worked on a few years ago, the bus that now took only an hour and a half to reach Kandi town. There, daily-wage work was going on, digging feeder channels from the main canal. The

babu's son was a labor contractor there. He also had the permit for running a bus. Giri took that bus to work.

115   There, one day she came across Bangshi Dhamali. He was sincere when he said that he had difficulty recognizing her. "You've ruined your health and appearance. Must be the grief for that daughter. But what good is grieving going to do after all?"

116   "Not just that. I'm now worried about Pori. She's almost ten."

117   "Really! She was born only the other day, the year the doctor built his house, and electricity came to Nishinda. Pori was born in that year."

118   "Yes! If only I had listened to what you said to me about going to work at the doctor's house and taken the children to town! My son now tends the babu's cattle. If I had gone then, they could all be in school now!"

119   "Don't know about your children being able to go to school. But I do know that the town is now flooded with jobs. You could put all your children to work at least for daily meals."

120   Giri was aware that her thinking of sending her children to school annoyed Bangshi. She yielded, "Anyway, Bangshi-dada. What good is it being able to read a few pages if they've to live on manual labor anyway? What I was really going to ask you is to look for a boy for my Pori."

121   "I'll tell Aulchand when I come to know of one."

122   "No. No. Make sure that you tell me."

123   "Why are you still so angry with him? He certainly made a mistake. Can't it be forgiven? Negotiating a daughter's wedding can't be done with the mother. It makes the groom's side think there's something wrong in the family. When it comes to your son's wedding, the bride's side would talk to you. It's different with the daughter."

124   "At least let me know about it all, before making a commitment."

125   "I'll see what I can do. I happen to know a rickshaw plier in Krishnachawk. Not very young, though. About twenty-five, I think."

126   "That's all right. After what happened to Bela, the groom's age is not my main concern."

127   "Your girl will be able to live in Krishnachawk. But the boy has no land, he lives by plying a rented rickshaw, which leaves him with barely five rupees a day. Makes a little extra by rolling bidis[17] at night. Doesn't have a home yet. He wants to get married because there's nobody to cook for him and look after him at the end of the day."

128   "You try for him. If it works out, I'd have her wedding this winter."

129   The total despondency in her mind since losing Bela suddenly moved a little to let in a glimmer of hope for Pori. She went on hopefully, saying, "I'll give her everything I've got. After that, I'll have just Maruni to worry about. But she's still a baby. I'll have time to think. Let

---

[17]Tobacco cigarettes rolled with leaves.

me tell you Bangshi-dada, and I'm saying this not because she's my daughter, my Pori looks so lovely at ten. Perhaps the meals at the babu house did it. Come dada, have some tea inside the shop."

130   Bangshi sipped the tea Giri bought him and informed her that her father was doing very well for himself, adding to his land and his stores of paddy, and remarked what a pity it was that he didn't help her much!

131   "It may not sound nice, sister. But the truth is that blood relation is no longer the main thing these days. Uncle now mixes with his equals, those who are getting ahead like himself, not with those gone to the dogs, like your man, even if you happen to be his daughter."

132   Giri just sighed, and quietly paid for the tea with most of the few coins tied in one end of the sari and tucked in her waist. Before taking leave, she earnestly reminded Bangshi about her request for finding a good husband for Pori.

133   Bangshi did remember. When he happened to see Aulchand shortly after that, he mentioned the rickshaw plier. Aulchand perked up, saying that he too was after a boy who plied a rickshaw, though his did it in Bahrampur, a bit further away but a much bigger place than Krishnachawk. The boy had a fancy beard, mustache, and hair, and he talked so smart and looked so impressive in some dead Englishman's pants and jacket he had bought for himself at the second-hand market. Aulchand asked Bangshi not to bother himself anymore about the rickshaw plier he had in mind.

134   Next time Giri saw Bangshi, she asked him if he had made contact with the rickshaw plier in Krishnachawk. He said that he had talked with Aulchand about it meanwhile and that she need not worry about it.

135   Aulchand then went looking for Mohan, his guide in worldly matters. And why not? There was not a place Mohan hadn't been to, all the nearby small towns in West Bengal that Aulchand had only heard of: Lalbagh, Dhulian, Jangipur, Jiaganj, Farakka. In fact, Aulchand didn't even know that Mohan was now in a business flung much further, procuring girls for whorehouses in the big cities, where the newly rich businessmen and contractors went to satisfy their new-found appetite for the childlike, underdeveloped bodies of Bengali pubescent girls. Fed well for a few months, they bloomed so deliciously that they yielded back within a couple of years the price paid to procure them.

136   But it was very important to put up a show of marriage to procure them. It was no longer possible to get away with just paying some money for the girl. Any such straight procurer was now sure to get a mass beating from the Bengali villagers. Hence, the need for stories about a shortage of marriage-age girls in Bihar and now the need for something even more clever. The weddings now had to look real, with

a priest and all that. Then there would have to be some talk about the rituals that must be performed at the groom's place according to their local customs to complete the marriage, and so with the family's permission they must get back right away.

137   The "grooms from Bihar looking for brides in Bengal" story had circulated long enough. Newer tactics became necessary. The local matchmakers, who got a cut in each deal, were no longer informed enough about what was going on, but they sensed that it held some kind of trouble for their occupation. They decided not to worry too much about exactly how the cheating was done. They just took the position that they were doing what the girl's parents asked them to do—to make contact with potential grooms. They played down their traditional role as the source of information about the groom's family and background.

138   The girls' families too decided to go ahead despite the nonperformance of their usual source of information. Their reason for not talking and investigating enough was that the high bride-price they were offered and the little dowry they were asked to pay might then be revealed, and, because there was no dearth of envious people, someone might undo the arrangement. In some cases, they thought that they had no choice but an out-of-state groom because even in their low-caste communities, in which bride-price was customary, the Bengali grooms wanted several thousands of rupees in watches, radios, bicycles, and so on.

139   Since the incident of Bela, Kali-babu of the Panchayat refused to hire Aulchand on the road project or any other construction under the Panchayat. Aulchand found himself a bit out of touch, but, with plenty of free time, he went away for a few days trying to locate Mohan.

140   Mohan, meanwhile, was doing exceedingly well considering that he never got past the fourth grade in school. He had set up another business like a net around the block development office of Nishinda, to catch the peasants who came there for subsidized fertilizers and loans, part of which they somehow managed to lose to Mohan before they could get back to their village. Mohan was an extremely busy man these days.

141   He firmly shook his head at Aulchand's request, saying, "Count me out. Mohan Mandal has done enough of helping others. To help a father get his daughter married is supposed to be a virtue. You got the money. What did I get? The other side at least paid me forty rupees in broker's fee. And you? You used your money all on bamboo wallpanels. Besides, I'm afraid of your wife."

142   "She's the one who wants a rickshaw plier in a nearby town."

143   "Really?"

144   "Yes. But listen. You stay out of the thing and just put me in touch with a rickshaw plier boy in a big town like Bahrampur. My daughter

will be able to live there; we'll go there to visit them. I'd like nothing better. Bela's mother too might be pleased with me."

145   "You want to make up with your wife this way, right?"

146   "I'd like to. The woman doesn't think of me as a human being. I want to show her that I can get my daughter married well without anyone's help. Only you can supply me that invisible help."

147   Mohan laughed and said, "All right. But I'll not get involved. I'll just make the contact, that's all. What if the big-town son-in-law has a long list of demands?"

148   "I'll have to borrow."

149   "I see. Go home now. I'll see what I can do."

150   Mohan gave it some thought. He must be more careful this time. He must keep the "groom from Bihar" setup hidden one step away and have a rickshaw plier boy in front, the one who will do the marrying and then pass her on. Aulchand's plea thus gave birth to a new idea in Mohan's head, but first he had to find a rickshaw plier boy. Who could play the part? He must go to town and check with some of his contacts.

151   Talking about Pori's marriage did reduce the distance between Giribala and Aulchand. Finally, one day Mohan informed Aulchand that he had the right match. "How much does he want?" Aulchand asked.

152   "He's already got a watch and a radio. He plies a cycle-rickshaw, so he wants no bicycle. Just the clothes for bride and groom, bed, shoes, umbrella, stuff like that. Quite a bargain, really."

153   "How much will he pay in bride-price?"

154   "One hundred rupees."

155   "Does he have a home for my daughter to live in?"

156   "He has a rented room. But he owns the cycle-rickshaw."

157   Aulchand and Giri were happy. When the future groom came to see the bride, Giri peeked from behind the door, studying him intently. Big, well-built body, well-developed beard and mustache. He said that his name was Manohar Dhamali. In Bahrampur, there was indeed a rickshaw plier named Manohar Dhamali. But this man's real name was Panu. He had just been acquitted from a robbery charge, due to insufficient evidence. Aulchand didn't know about this part. After getting out of jail, Panu had just married a girl like Poribala in Jalangi, another in Farakka, and delivered them to the "groom from Bihar" gang. He was commissioned to do five for five-hundred rupees. Not much for his efforts, he thought, but not bad with his options at the moment. Panu had plans to move further away, to Shiliguri, to try new pastures as soon as this batch was over and he had some money in hand.

158   At the time of Bela's marriage, no relative was there, not even Giribala. This time, Giri's parents came. Women blew conch shells and ululated happily to solemnize each ritual. Giri, her face shining with sweat and excited oil glands, cooked rice and meat curry for the guests. She brought her silver ornaments from the housemistress and

put them on Pori, who was dressed in a new sari that Giri's mother had brought. Her father had brought a sackful of rice for the feast. The babu family contributed fifty rupees. The groom came by bus in the company of five others. Pori looked even more like Bela. She was so lovely in the glow on her skin left from the turmeric rub and in the red *alta* [18] edging her small feet.

159   Next day, with the groom she took the bus and left for the town.

160   That was the last time Giri saw Pori's face. The day after, Aulchand went to the town with Rajib and Giri's young brother to visit the newly married couple, as the custom required. The night advanced, but they did not return. Very, very late in the night, Giri heard the sound of footsteps of people coming in, but silently. Giri knew at once. She opened the door, and saw Bangshi Dhamali holding Rajib's hand. Rajib cried out, "Ma!" Giri knew the terrible thing had happened again. Silently she looked on them. Giri's brother told her. There wasn't much to tell. They did find a Manohar Dhamali in the town, but he was a middle-aged man. They asked the people around and were told that it must be another of Panu's acts. He was going around doing a lot of marrying. He seemed to be linked with some kind of gang.

161   Giri interrupted to ask Bangshi, "And Mohan is not behind this?"

162   "He's the mastermind behind this new play."

163   "And where's Rajib's father? Why isn't he with you?"

164   "He ran to catch Mohan when he heard that Mohan got five to seven hundred rupees from it. He left shouting incoherently, 'I want my daughter. I want my money.'"

165   Giri's little porch was again crowded with sympathetic, agitated people, some of them suggesting that they find Mohan and beat him up, others wanting to go to the police station, but all of them doing just a lot of talking. "Are we living in a lawless land?" Lots of words, lots of noise.

166   Close to dawn, Aulchand came home. Overwhelmed by the events, he had finally gone to get drunk and he was talking and bragging, "I found out where he got the money from. Mohan can't escape Aulchand-sardar.[19] I twisted his neck until he coughed up my share of the money. Why shouldn't I get the money? The daughter is mine, and he'll be the one to take the money from putting her in a phony marriage? Where's Pori's mother? Foolish woman, you shouldn't have done that operation. The more daughters we have, the more money we can have. Now I'm going to have that home of ours done. Oh-ho-ho, my little Pori!"

167   Aulchand cried and wept and very soon he fell asleep on the porch. Giribala called up all her strength to quietly ask the crowd to go home. After they left, Giri sat by herself for a long time, trying to think what she should do now. She wanted to be dead. Should she jump into the

---

[18]Colored design traditionally worn before a marriage.

[19]Literally, "chief"; in the context, a form of self-praise.

canal? Last night, she heard some people talking, correctly perhaps, that the same fate may be waiting for Maruni too.

168   "Making business out of people's need to see their daughters married. Giri, this time you must take it to the police with the help of the babu. Don't let them get away with it. Go to the police, go to court."

169   Giri had looked on, placing her strikingly large eyes on their faces, then shaking her head. She would try nothing! Aulchand got his money at his daughter's expense. Let him try. Giri firmly shook her head.

170   Bangshi had remarked before leaving, "God must have willed that the walls come from one daughter and the roof from the other."

171   Giri had silently gazed at his face too with her striking eyes.

172   After some time, Aulchand was crying and doing the straw roof at the same time. The more tears he shed, the more dry-eyed Giri became.

173   The babu's elderly aunt tried to console her with her philosophy of clichés, "Not easy to be a daughter's mother. They say that a daughter born is already gone, either to husband or to death. That's what happened to you. Don't I know why you aren't crying? They say that one cries from a little loss, but turns into stone with too much loss. Start working again. One gets used to everything except hunger."

174   Giri silently gazed at her too, as she heard the familiar words coming out of her mouth. Then she requested her to go and tell the babu's wife that Giri wanted to withdraw her deposited money immediately. She went to collect the money. She put it in a knot in her sari and tucked the knot in her waist.

175   She came back and stood by the porch, looking at the home Aulchand was building. Nice room. The split-bamboo woven panels of the wall were neatly plastered with mud and were now being topped with a new straw roof. She had always dreamed of a room like this. Perhaps that was wanting too much. That was why Beli and Pori had to become prostitutes—yes, prostitutes. No matter what euphemism is used, nobody ever sets up home for a girl bought with money.

176   Nice room. Giri thought she caught a flitting glimpse of Aulchand eyeing little Maruni while tying up the ends of the straw he had laid on the roof. Giri silently held those striking eyes of hers steadily on Aulchand's face for some time, longer than she had ever done before. And Aulchand thought that no matter how great her grief was, she must be impressed with the way their home was turning out after all.

177   The next morning brought the biggest surprise to all. Before sunrise, Giribala had left home, with Maruni on her hip and Rajib's hand held in hers. She had walked down to the big road and caught the early morning bus to the town. Later on, it also became known that at the Nishinda stop she had left a message for Pori's father with Bangshi Dhamali. The message was that Giri wanted Aulchand to live in his

new room happily forever. But Giri was going away from his home to work in other people's homes in order to feed and raise her remaining children. And if he ever came to the town looking for her, she would put her neck on the rail line before a speeding train.

178   People were so amazed, even stunned by this that they were left speechless. What happened to Bela and Pori was happening to many others these days. But leaving one's husband was quite another matter. What kind of woman would leave her husband of many years just like that? Now, they all felt certain that the really bad one was not Aulchand, but Giribala. And arriving at this conclusion seemed to produce some kind of relief for their troubled minds.

179   And Giribala? Walking down the unfamiliar roads and holding Maruni on her hip and Rajib by the hand, Giribala only regretted that she had not done this before. If she had left earlier, then Beli would not have been lost, then Pori would not have been lost. If only she had had this courage earlier, her two daughters might have been saved.

180   As this thought grew insistent and hammered inside her brain, hot tears flooded her face and blurred her vision. But she did not stop even to wipe her tears. She just kept walking.

✧ Evaluating the Text

1. Under what circumstances did Aulchand marry Giribala? How does the reality of Giribala's married life contrast with the promises Aulchand made to her and her parents? In what respects has he deceived them?

2. How would you characterize the relationship between Aulchand and his right-hand man, Mohan? Who, in your opinion, is more to blame for what happens? Explain your reasons.

3. What measures does Giribala take to prevent Pori, their other young daughter, from suffering the same fate as Bela? Why do her efforts come to naught?

✧ Exploring Different Perspectives

1. Compare the set of circumstances that lead to arranged marriages in Devi's story and in Marjorie Shostak's account, "Memories of a !Kung Girlhood."

2. Compare and contrast the very different kinds of negotiations for arranging marriages in India, according to social class, in this story and in Serena Nanda's account, "Arranging a Marriage in India."

✧ Extending Viewpoints through Writing

1. What insights does the story provide into how the caste system and cultural traditions, such as the bride-price, function in the social context of Bengali culture?

2. To what extent is the effectiveness of Devi's story a result of the matter of fact, objective tone she employs in describing such shocking events? Devi is active in promoting social reform for women in Bengal and her works are written in part to bring about these reforms. How might "Giribala" have this effect?

Connecting Cultures

◆

Ann Louise Bardach, "The Stealth Virus: AIDS and Latinos"

Compare the perspectives on homosexuality in Bardach's account and that of Luis Sepulveda in "Daisy" in Chapter 6.

Susan Bordo, "Never Just Pictures"

Discuss the cultural pressures on personal appearance as described by Susan Bordo and Slavenka Drakulić in "On Bad Teeth" in Chapter 8.

Judith Ortiz Cofer, "The Myth of the Latin Woman"

Compare and contrast the male and female stereotyping of Hispanics in Judith Ortiz Cofer's narrative and Victor Villaseñor's account in "Rain of Gold" in Chapter 4.

Lennard J. Davis, "Visualizing the Disabled Body"

What differing attitudes toward disabilities emerge from Lennard J. Davis's analysis and Sucheng Chan's account (see "You're Short, Besides!" in Chapter 2)?

Elizabeth W. Fernea and Robert A. Fernea, "Looking Behind the Veil"

How does *purdah* and veiling, discussed by Fernea and Fernea, play a role in enhancing the mystery of the Bedouin girl in Nabil Gorgy's story, "Cairo Is a Small City," in Chapter 8?

Serena Nanda, "Arranging a Marriage in India"

Compare the cultural values and expectations that precede marriage among the !Kung in Marjorie Shostak's "Memories of a !Kung Girlhood" in Chapter 2 with those described by Serena Nanda.

Ann M. Simmons, "Where Fat Is a Mark of Beauty"

How does the manipulation of the female body image reflect dominant cultural values in modern Nigeria as described by Simmons and in traditional China as discussed by Valerie Steele and John S. Major (see "China Chic: East Meets West" in Chapter 8)?

Kate Chopin, "Désirée's Baby"

How does race in Chopin's story serve the same function as caste does in modern India (see Viramma's "A Pariah's Life" in Chapter 5)?

Mahasweta Devi, "Giribala"

How have cultural prejudices against girls resulted in their economic exploitation and their being treated as second-class citizens in China (see Daniela Deane's "The Little Emperors" in Chapter 1) and in Bengal as depicted by Devi?

4

How Work Creates Identity

◆————————

The way we identify ourselves in terms of the work we do is far-reaching. Frequently, the first question we ask when we meet someone is, "What do you do?" Through work we define ourselves and others; yet, cultural values also play a part in influencing how we feel about the work we do.

In addition to providing a means to live, work has an important psychological meaning in our culture. Some societies value work more than leisure; in other cultures, the reverse is true and work is viewed as something you do just to provide the necessities of life. In the United States, the work you perform is intertwined with a sense of identity and self-esteem.

Work in most societies involves the exchange of goods and services. In tribal cultures, as distinct from highly industrialized cultures, there is little job specialization, although age and gender determine what tasks one performs. Economics may range from the barter system where goods are traded to more complex market economies based on the reciprocal exchange of goods and services for money.

The attitude people have toward the work they do varies within and among cultures. For example, think of the momentous change in attitude toward the work that women do in terms of equal opportunity and equal pay.

Barbara Ehrenreich went "undercover" in order to discover the reality of the lives of unskilled workers and reports her results in "Nickel-and-Dimed." In Japan, Tomoyuki Iwashita, in "Why I Quit the Company," explains how the seeming security of lifetime employment does not offset sacrificing one's life for the corporation. An American teacher in China, Mark Salzman, describes (in "Lessons") the unusual bargain he struck with the renowned master, Pan Quingfu, to exchange English lessons for instruction in Chinese martial arts. Few working conditions are as harrowing as those firefighters and police officers confronted following the September 11, 2001 catastrophe, as described by Dennis Smith in "Report from Ground Zero." Victor Villaseñor, in "Rain of Gold," re-creates the moment when his father had to prove himself as a Mexican worker on his first day blasting rocks in a mine.

From Brazil, Machado de Assis spins a thought-provoking tale, "A Canary's Ideas," about the consequences when one's avocation becomes an obsession. In "The Stolen Party," Liliana Heker dramatizes the anguish of a young girl in Argentina who learns her mother's job as a maid has more influence on her life than she would have expected.

Barbara Ehrenreich

Nickel-and-Dimed

On (Not) Getting by in America

◆

Barbara Ehrenreich is an investigative reporter who went undercover to discover the realities of the low-wage service worker. She was researching the consequences of the changes in the welfare system passed in 1995 that limited the length of time that single women with dependent children could receive benefits. The question she tried to answer was whether unskilled workers could generate an income they could live on without help from the government. As her following report reveals, the answer is no. This piece was originally published in Harper's *magazine, 1999, and later was included in her book* Nickel-and-Dimed: On (Not) Getting by in America *(2001).*

Before You Read

Notice how Ehrenreich draws on her own experiences to raise the larger issue of how difficult it is for unskilled workers to survive on a minimum wage. To help you understand her rather complicated analysis, underline and annotate those parts of the selection in which she explores the economic day-to-day consequences of being a worker on the margins of our society.

◆

1   At the beginning of June 1998 I leave behind everything that normally soothes the ego and sustains the body—home, career, companion, reputation, ATM card—for a plunge into the low-wage workforce. There, I become another, occupationally much diminished "Barbara Ehrenreich"—depicted on job-application forms as a divorced homemaker whose sole work experience consists of housekeeping in a few private homes. I am terrified, at the beginning, of being unmasked for what I am: a middle-class journalist setting out to explore the world that welfare mothers are entering, at the rate of approximately 50,000 a month, as welfare reform kicks in. Happily, though, my fears turn out to be entirely unwarranted: during a month of poverty and toil, my name goes unnoticed and for the most part unuttered. In this parallel universe where my father never got out of the mines and I never got through college, I am "baby," "honey," "blondie," and, most commonly, "girl."

2   My first task is to find a place to live. I figure that if I can earn $7 an hour—which, from the want ads, seems doable—I can afford to spent $500 on rent, or maybe, with severe economies, $600. In the Key West area, where I live, this pretty much confines me to flophouses and trailer homes—like the one, a pleasing fifteen-minute drive from town, that has no air-conditioning, no screens, no fans, no television, and, by way of diversion, only the challenge of evading the land-lord's Doberman pinscher. The big problem with this place, though, is the rent, which at $675 a month is well beyond my reach. All right, Key West is expensive. But so is New York City, or the Bay Area, or Jackson Hole, or Telluride, or Boston, or any other place where tourists and the wealthy compete for living space with the people who clean their toilets and fry their hash browns.[1] Still, it is a shock to realize that "trailer trash" has become, for me, a demographic cat-egory to aspire to.

3   So I decide to make the common trade-off between affordability and convenience, and go for a $500-a-month efficiency thirty miles up a two-lane highway from the employment opportunities of Key West, meaning forty-five minutes if there's no road construction and I don't get caught behind some sun-dazed Canadian tourists. I hate the drive, along a roadside studded with white crosses commemorating the more effective head-on collisions, but it's a sweet little place—a cabin, more or less, set in the swampy back yard of the converted mobile home where my landlord, an affable TV repairman, lives with his bartender girlfriend. Anthropologically speaking, a bustling trailer park would be preferable, but here I have a gleaming white floor and a firm mat-tress, and the few resident bugs are easily vanquished.

4   Besides, I am not doing this for the anthropology. My aim is noth-ing so mistily subjective as to "experience poverty" or find out how it "really feels" to be a long-term low-wage worker. I've had enough un-chosen encounters with poverty and the world of low-wage work to know it's not a place you want to visit for touristic purposes; it just smells too much like fear. And with all my real-life assets—bank ac-count, IRA, health insurance, multiroom home—waiting indulgently in the background, I am, of course, thoroughly insulated from the ter-rors that afflict the genuinely poor.

---

[1]According to the Department of Housing and Urban Development, the "fair-market rent" for an efficiency is $551 here in Monroe County, Florida. A compara-ble rent in the five boroughs of New York City is $704; in San Francisco, $713; and in the heart of Silicon Valley, $808. The fair-market rent for an area is defined as the amount that would be needed to pay rent plus utilities for "privately owned, de-cent, safe, and sanitary rental housing of a modest (non-luxury) nature with suit-able amenities." [Author's note]

5   No, this is a purely objective, scientific sort of mission. The human-itarian rationale for welfare reform—as opposed to the more punitive and stingy impulses that may actually have motivated it—is that work will lift poor women out of poverty while simultaneously inflating their self-esteem and hence their future value in the labor market. Thus, whatever the hassles involved in finding child care, transporta-tion, etc., the transition from welfare to work will end happily, in greater prosperity for all. Now there are many problems with this com-forting prediction, such as the fact that the economy will inevitably un-dergo a downturn, eliminating many jobs. Even without a downturn, the influx of a million former welfare recipients into the low-wage la-bor market could depress wages by as much as 11.9 percent, according to the Economic Policy Institute (EPI) in Washington, D.C.

6   But is it really possible to make a living on the kinds of jobs cur-rently available to unskilled people? Mathematically, the answer is no, as can be shown by taking $6 to $7 an hour, perhaps subtracting a dol-lar or two an hour for child care, multiplying by 160 hours a month, and comparing the result to the prevailing rents. According to the National Coalition for the Homeless, for example, in 1998 it took, on average na-tionwide, an hourly wage of $8.89 to afford a one-bedroom apartment, and the Preamble Center for Public Policy estimates that the odds against a typical welfare recipient's landing a job at such a "living wage" are about 97 to 1. If these numbers are right, low-wage work is not a solution to poverty and possibly not even to homelessness.

7   It may seem excessive to put this proposition to an experimental test. As certain family members keep unhelpfully reminding me, the viability of low-wage work could be tested, after a fashion, without ever leaving my study. I could just pay myself $7 an hour for eight hours a day, charge myself for room and board, and total up the num-bers after a month. Why leave the people and work that I love? But I am an experimental scientist by training. In that business, you don't just sit at a desk and theorize; you plunge into the everyday chaos of nature, where surprises lurk in the most mundane measurements. Maybe, when I got into it, I would discover some hidden economies in the world of the low-wage worker. After all, if 30 percent of the work-force toils for less than $8 an hour, according to the EPI, they may have found some tricks as yet unknown to me. Maybe—who knows?—I would even to able to detect in myself the bracing psychological effects of getting out of the house, as promised by the welfare wonks at places like the Heritage Foundation. Or, on the other hand, maybe there would be unexpected costs—physical, mental, or financial—to throw off all my calculations. Ideally, I should do this with two small children in tow, that being the welfare average, but mine are grown and no one is willing to lend me theirs for a month-long vacation in penury. So this

is not the perfect experiment, just a test of the best possible case: an un-encumbered woman, smart and even strong, attempting to live more or less off the land.

8 On the morning of my first full day of job searching, I take a red pen to the want ads, which are auspiciously numerous. Everyone in Key West's booming "hospitality industry" seems to be looking for someone like me—trainable, flexible, and with suitably humble expec-tations as to pay. I know I possess certain traits that might be advanta-geous—I'm white and, I like to think, well-spoken and poised—but I decide on two rules: One, I cannot use any skills derived from my edu-cation or usual work—not that there are a lot of want ads for satirical essayists anyway. Two, I have to take the best-paid job that is offered me and of course do my best to hold it; no Marxist rants or sneaking off to read novels in the ladies' room. In addition, I rule out various oc-cupations for one reason or another. Hotel front-desk clerk, for exam-ple, which to my surprise is regarded as unskilled and pays around $7 an hour, gets eliminated because it involves standing in one spot for eight hours a day. Waitressing is similarly something I'd like to avoid, because I remember it leaving me bone tired when I was eighteen, and I'm decades of varicosities and back pain beyond that now. Telemar-keting, one of the first refuges of the suddenly indigent, can be dis-missed on grounds of personality. This leaves certain supermarket jobs, such as deli clerk, or housekeeping in Key West's thousands of hotel and guest rooms. Housekeeping is especially appealing, for rea-sons both atavistic and practical: it's what my mother did before I came along, and it can't be too different from what I've been doing part-time, in my own home, all my life.

9 So I put on what I take to be a respectful-looking outfit of ironed Bermuda shorts and scooped-neck T-shirt and set out for a tour of the local hotels and supermarkets. Best Western, Econo Lodge, and HoJo's all let me fill out application forms, and these are, to my relief, inter-ested in little more than whether I am a legal resident of the United States and have committed any felonies. My next step is Winn-Dixie, the supermarket, which turns out to have a particularly onerous appli-cation process, featuring a fifteen-minute "interview" by computer since, apparently, no human on the premises is deemed capable of rep-resenting the corporate point of view. I am conducted to a large room decorated with posters illustrating how to look "professional" (it helps to be white and, if female, permed) and warning of the slick promises that union organizers might try to tempt me with. The interview is multiple choice: Do I have anything, such as child-care problems, that might make it hard for me to get to work on time? Do I think safety on the job is the responsibility of management? Then, popping up cun-ningly out of the blue: How many dollars' worth of stolen goods have

I purchased in the last year? Would I turn in a fellow employee if I caught him stealing? Finally, "Are you an honest person?"

10 Apparently, I ace the interview, because I am told that all I have to do is show up in some doctor's office tomorrow for a urine test. This seems to be a fairly general rule: if you want to stack Cheerio boxes or vacuum hotel rooms in chemically fascist America, you have to be willing to squat down and pee in front of some health worker (who has no doubt had to do the same thing herself). The wages Winn-Dixie is offering—$6 and a couple of dimes to start with—are not enough, I decide, to compensate for this indignity.[2]

11 I lunch at Wendy's, where $4.99 gets you unlimited refills at the Mexican part of the Superbar, a comforting surfeit of refried beans and "cheese sauce." A teenage employee, seeing me studying the want ads, kindly offers me an application form, which I fill out, though here, too, the pay is just $6 and change an hour. Then it's off for a round of the locally owned inns and guest-houses. At "The Palms," let's call it, a bouncy manager actually takes me around to see the rooms and meet the existing housekeepers, who, I note with satisfaction, look pretty much like me—faded ex-hippie types in shorts with long hair pulled back in braids. Mostly, though, no one speaks to me or even looks at me except to proffer an application form. At my last stop, a palatial B&B, I wait twenty minutes to meet "Max," only to be told that there are no jobs now but there should be one soon, since "nobody lasts more than a couple weeks." (Because none of the people I talked to knew I was a reporter, I have changed their names to protect their privacy and, in some cases perhaps, their jobs.)

12 Three days go by like this, and, to my chagrin, no one out of the approximately twenty places I've applied calls me for an interview. I had been vain enough to worry about coming across as too educated for the jobs I sought, but no one even seems interested in finding out how overqualified I am. Only later will I realize that the want ads are not a reliable measure of the actual jobs available at any particular time. They are, as I should have guessed from Max's comment, the employers' insurance policy against the relentless turnover of the low-wage workforce.

[2]According to the *Monthly Labor Review* (November 1996), 28 percent of work sites surveyed in the service industry conduct drug tests (corporate workplaces have much higher rates), and the incidence of testing has risen markedly since the Eighties. The rate of testing is highest in the South (56 percent of work sites polled), with the Midwest in second place (50 percent). The drug most likely to be detected— marijuana, which can be detected in urine for weeks—is also the most innocuous, while heroin and cocaine are generally undetectable three days after use. Prospective employees sometimes try to cheat the tests by consuming excessive amounts of liquids and taking diuretics and even masking substances available through the Internet. [Author's note]

Most of the big hotels run ads almost continually, just to build a supply of applicants to replace the current workers as they drift away or are fired, so finding a job is just a matter of being at the right place at the right time and flexible enough to take whatever is being offered that day. This finally happens to me at one of the big discount hotel chains, where I go, as usual, for housekeeping and am sent, instead, to try out as a waitress at the attached "family restaurant," a dismal spot with a counter and about thirty tables that looks out on a parking garage and features such tempting fare as "Pollish [sic] sausage and BBQ sauce" on 95-degree days. Phillip, the dapper young West Indian who introduces himself as the manager, interviews me with about as much enthusiasm as if he were a clerk processing me for Medicare, the principal questions being what shifts can I work and when can I start. I mutter something about being woefully out of practice as a waitress, but he's already on to the uniform: I'm to show up tomorrow wearing black slacks and black shoes; he'll provide the rust-colored polo shirt with HEARTHSIDE embroidered on it, though I might want to wear my own shirt to get to work, ha ha. At the word "tomorrow," something between fear and indignation rises in my chest. I want to say, "Thank you for your time, sir, but this is just an experiment, you know, not my actual life."

13   So begins my career at the Hearthside, I shall call it, one small profit center within a global discount hotel chain, where for two weeks I work from 2:00 till 10:00 P.M. for $2.43 an hour plus tips.[3] In some futile bid for gentility, the management has barred employees from using the front door, so my first day I enter through the kitchen, where a red-faced man with shoulder-length blond hair is throwing frozen steaks against the wall and yelling, "Fuck this shit!" "That's just Jack," explains Gail, the wiry middle-aged waitress who is assigned to train me. "He's on the rag again"—a condition occasioned, in this instance, by the fact that the cook on the morning shift had forgotten to thaw out the steaks. For the next eight hours, I run after the agile Gail, absorbing bits of instruction along with fragments of personal tragedy. All food must be trayed, and the reason she's so tired today is that she woke up in a cold sweat thinking of her boyfriend, who killed himself recently in an upstate prison. No refills on lemonade. And the reason he was in prison is that a few DUIs caught up with him, that's all, could have happened to anyone. Carry the creamers to the table in a monkey

---

[3]According to the Fair Labor Standards Act, employers are not required to pay "tipped employees," such as restaurant servers, more than $2.13 an hour in direct wages. However, if the sum of tips plus $2.13 an hour falls below the minimum wage, or $5.15 an hour, the employer is required to make up the difference. This fact was not mentioned by managers or otherwise publicized at either of the restaurants where I worked. [Author's note]

bowl, never in your hand. And after he was gone she spent several months living in her truck, peeing in a plastic pee bottle and reading by candlelight at night, but you can't live in a truck in the summer, since you need to have the windows down, which means anything can get in, from mosquitoes on up.

14   At least Gail puts to rest any fears I had of appearing overqualified. From the first day on, I find that of all the things I have left behind, such as home and identity, what I miss the most is competence. Not that I have ever felt utterly competent in the writing business, in which one day's success augurs nothing at all for the next. But in my writing life, I at least have some notion of procedure: do the research, make the outline, rough out a draft, etc. As a server, though, I am beset by requests like bees: more iced tea here, ketchup over there, a to-go box for table fourteen, and where are the high chairs, anyway? Of the twenty-seven tables, up to six are usually mine at any time, though on slow afternoons or if Gail is off, I sometimes have the whole place to myself. There is the touch-screen computer-ordering system to master, which is, I suppose, meant to minimize server-cook contact, but in practice requires constant verbal fine-tuning: "That's gravy on the mashed, okay? None on the meatloaf," and so forth—while the cook scowls as if I were inventing these refinements just to torment him. Plus, something I had forgotten in the years since I was eighteen: about a third of a server's job is "side work" that's invisible to customers—sweeping, scrubbing, slicing, refilling, and restocking. If it isn't all done, every little bit of it, you're going to face the 6:00 P.M. dinner rush defenseless and probably go down in flames. I screw up dozens of times at the beginning, sustained in my shame entirely by Gail's support—"It's okay, baby, everyone does that sometime"—because, to my total surprise and despite the scientific detachment I am doing my best to maintain, I care.

15   The whole thing would be a lot easier if I could just skate through it as Lily Tomlin in one of her waitress skits, but I was raised by the absurd Booker T. Washingtonian precept that says: If you're going to do something, do it well. In fact, "well" isn't good enough by half. Do it better than anyone has ever done it before. Or so said my father, who must have known what he was talking about because he managed to pull himself, and us with him, up from the mile-deep copper mines of Butte to the leafy suburbs of the Northeast, ascending from boilermakers to martinis before booze beat out ambition. As in most endeavors I have encountered in my life, doing it "better than anyone" is not a reasonable goal. Still, when I wake up at 4:00 A.M. in my own cold sweat, I am not thinking about the writing deadlines I'm neglecting; I'm thinking about the table whose order I screwed up so that one of the boys didn't get his kiddie meal until the rest of the family had moved on to their Key Lime pies. That's the other powerful

motivation I hadn't expected—the customers, or "patients," as I can't help thinking of them on account of the mysterious vulnerability that seems to have left them temporarily unable to feed themselves. After a few days at the Hearthside, I feel the service ethic kick in like a shot of oxytocin, the nurturance hormone. The plurality of my customers are hard-working locals—truck drivers, construction workers, even housekeepers from the attached hotel—and I want them to have the closest to a "fine dining" experience that the grubby circumstances will allow. No "you guys" for me; everyone over twelve is "sir" or "ma'am." I ply them with iced tea and coffee refills; I return, mid-meal, to inquire how everything is; I doll up their salads with chopped raw mushrooms, summer squash slices, or whatever bits of produce I can find that have survived their sojourn in the cold-storage room mold-free.

16   There is Benny, for example, a short, tight-muscled sewer repairman, who cannot even think of eating until he has absorbed a half hour of air-conditioning and ice water. We chat about hyperthermia and electrolytes until he is ready to order some finicky combination like soup of the day, garden salad, and a side of grits. There are the German tourists who are so touched by my pidgin "Willkommen" and "Ist alles gut?" that they actually tip. (Europeans, spoiled by their trade-union-ridden, high-wage welfare states, generally do not know that they are supposed to tip. Some restaurants, the Hearthside included, allow servers to "grat" their foreign customers, or add a tip to the bill. Since this amount is added before the customers have a chance to tip or not tip, the practice amounts to an automatic penalty for imperfect English.) There are the two dirt-smudged lesbians, just off their construction shift, who are impressed enough by my suave handling of the fly in the piña colada that they take the time to praise me to Stu, the assistant manager. There's Sam, the kindly retired cop, who has to plug up his tracheotomy hole with one finger in order to force the cigarette smoke into his lungs.

17   Sometimes I play with the fantasy that I am a princess who, in penance for some tiny transgression, has undertaken to feed each of her subjects by hand. But the non-princesses working with me are just as indulgent, even when this means flouting management rules—concerning, for example, the number of croutons that can go on a salad (six). "Put on all you want," Gail whispers, "as long as Stu isn't looking." She dips into her own tip money to buy biscuits and gravy for an out-of-work mechanic who's used up all his money on dental surgery, inspiring me to pick up the tab for his milk and pie. Maybe the same high levels of agape can be found throughout the "hospitality industry." I remember the poster decorating one of the apartments I looked at, which said "If you seek happiness for yourself you will never find it. Only when you seek happiness for others will it come to you," or

words to that effect—an odd sentiment, it seemed to me at the time, to find in the dank one-room basement apartment of a bellhop at the Best Western. At the Hearthside, we utilize whatever bits of autonomy we have to ply our customers with the illicit calories that signal our love. It is our job as servers to assemble the salads and desserts, pouring the dressings and squirting the whipped cream. We also control the number of butter patties our customers get and the amount of sour cream on their baked potatoes. So if you wonder why Americans are so obese, consider the fact that waitresses both express their humanity and earn their tips through the covert distribution of fats.

18   Ten days into it, this is beginning to look like a livable lifestyle. I like Gail, who is "looking at fifty" but moves so fast she can alight in one place and then another without apparently being anywhere between them. I clown around with Lionel, the teenage Haitian busboy, and catch a few fragments of conversation with Joan, the svelte forty-ish hostess and militant feminist who is the only one of us who dares to tell Jack to shut the fuck up. I even warm up to Jack when, on a slow night and to make up for a particularly unwarranted attack on my abilities, or so I imagine, he tells me about his glory days as a young man at "coronary school"—or do you say "culinary"?—in Brooklyn, where he dated a knock-out Puerto Rican chick and learned everything there is to know about food. I finish up at 10:00 or 10:30, depending on how much side work I've been able to get done during the shift, and cruise home to the tapes I snatched up at random when I left my real home—Marianne Faithfull, Tracy Chapman, Enigma, King Sunny Ade, the Violent Femmes—just drained enough for the music to set my cranium resonating but hardly dead. Midnight snack is Wheat Thins and Monterey Jack, accompanied by cheap white wine on ice and whatever AMC has to offer. To bed by 1:30 or 2:00, up at 9:00 or 10:00, read for an hour while my uniform whirls around in the landlord's washing machine, and then it's another eight hours spent following Mao's central instruction, as laid out in the Little Red Book, which was: Serve the people.

19   I could drift along like this, in some dreamy proletarian idyll, except for two things. One is management. If I have kept this subject on the margins thus far it is because I still flinch to think that I spent all those weeks under the surveillance of men (and later women) whose job it was to monitor my behavior for signs of sloth, theft, drug abuse, or worse. Not that managers and especially "assistant managers" in low-wage settings like this are exactly the class enemy. In the restaurant business, they are mostly former cooks or servers, still capable of pinch-hitting in the kitchen or on the floor, just as in hotels they are likely to be former clerks, and paid a salary of only about $400 a week. But everyone knows they have crossed over to the other side, which is,

crudely put, corporate as opposed to human. Cooks want to prepare tasty meals; servers want to serve them graciously; but managers are there for only one reason—to make sure that money is made for some theoretical entity that exists far away in Chicago or New York, if a corporation can be said to have a physical existence at all. Reflecting on her career, Gail tells me ruefully that she had sworn, years ago, never to work for a corporation again. "They don't cut you no slack. You give and you give, and they take."

20   Managers can sit—for hours at a time if they want—but it's their job to see that no one else ever does, even when there's nothing to do, and this is why, for servers, slow times can be as exhausting as rushes. You start dragging out each little chore, because if the manager on duty catches you in an idle moment, he will give you something far nastier to do. So I wipe, I clean, I consolidate ketchup bottles and recheck the cheesecake supply, even tour the tables to make sure the customer evaluation forms are all standing perkily in their places— wondering all the time how many calories I burn in these strictly theatrical exercises. When, on a particularly dead afternoon, Stu finds me glancing at a *USA Today* a customer has left behind, he assigns me to vacuum the entire floor with the broken vacuum cleaner that has a handle only two feet long, and the only way to do that without incurring orthopedic damage is to proceed from spot to spot on your knees.

21   On my first Friday at the Hearthside there is a "mandatory meeting for all restaurant employees," which I attend, eager for insight into our overall marketing strategy and the niche (your basic Ohio cuisine with a tropical twist?) we aim to inhabit. But there is no "we" at this meeting. Phillip, our top manager except for an occasional "consultant" sent out by corporate headquarters, opens it with a sneer: "The break room—it's disgusting. Butts in the ashtrays, newspapers lying around, crumbs." This windowless little room, which also houses the time clock for the entire hotel, is where we stash our bags and civilian clothes and take our half-hour meal breaks. But a break room is not a right, he tells us. It can be taken away. We should also know that the lockers in the break room and whatever is in them can be searched at any time. Then comes gossip; there has been gossip; gossip (which seems to mean employees talking among themselves) must stop. Off-duty employees are henceforth barred from eating at the restaurant, because "other servers gather around them and gossip." When Phillip has exhausted his agenda of rebukes, Joan complains about the condition of the ladies' room and I throw in my two bits about the vacuum cleaner. But I don't see any backup coming from my fellow servers, each of whom has subsided into her own personal funk; Gail, my role model, stares sorrowfully at a point six inches from her nose. The meeting ends when Andy, one of the cooks, gets up, muttering about breaking up his day off for this almighty bullshit.

22   Just four days later we are suddenly summoned into the kitchen at 3:30 P.M., even though there are live tables on the floor. We all—about ten of us—stand around Phillip, who announces grimly that there has been a report of some "drug activity" on the night shift and that, as a result, we are now to be a "drug-free" workplace, meaning that all new hires will be tested, as will possibly current employees on a random basis. I am glad that this part of the kitchen is so dark, because I find myself blushing as hard as if I had been caught toking up in the ladies' room myself: I haven't been treated this way—lined up in the corridor, threatened with locker searches, peppered with carelessly aimed accusations—since junior high school. Back on the floor, Joan cracks, "Next they'll be telling us we can't have sex on the job." When I ask Stu what happened to inspire the crackdown, he just mutters about "management decisions" and takes the opportunity to upbraid Gail and me for being too generous with the rolls. From now on there's to be only one per customer, and it goes out with the dinner, not with the salad. He's also been riding the cooks, prompting Andy to come out of the kitchen and observe—with the serenity of a man whose customary implement is a butcher knife—that "Stu has a death wish today."

23   Later in the evening, the gossip crystallizes around the theory that Stu is himself the drug culprit, that he uses the restaurant phone to order up marijuana and sends one of the late servers out to fetch it for him. The server was caught, and she may have ratted Stu out or at least said enough to cast some suspicion on him, thus accounting for his pissy behavior. Who knows? Lionel, the busboy, entertains us for the rest of the shift by standing just behind Stu's back and sucking deliriously on an imaginary joint.

24   The other problem, in addition to the less-than-nurturing management style, is that this job shows no sign of being financially viable. You might imagine, from a comfortable distance, that people who live, year in and year out, on $6 to $10 an hour have discovered some survival stratagems unknown to the middle class. But no. It's not hard to get my co-workers to talk about their living situations, because housing, in almost every case, is the principal source of disruption in their lives, the first thing they fill you in on when they arrive for their shifts. After a week, I have compiled the following survey:

- Gail is sharing a room in a well-known downtown flophouse for which she and a roommate pay about $250 a week. Her roommate, a male friend, has begun hitting on her, driving her nuts, but the rent would be impossible alone.

- Claude, the Haitian cook, is desperate to get out of the two-room apartment he shares with his girlfriend and two other, unrelated, people. As far as I can determine, the other Haitian men (most of whom only speak Creole) live in similarly crowded situations.

- Annette, a twenty-year-old server who is six months pregnant and has been abandoned by her boyfriend, lives with her mother, a postal clerk.

- Marianne and her boyfriend are paying $170 a week for a one-person trailer.

- Jack, who is, at $10 an hour, the wealthiest of us, lives in a trailer he owns, paying only the $400-a-month lot fee.

- The other white cook, Andy, lives on his dry-docked boat, which, as far as I can tell from his loving descriptions, can't be more than twenty feet long. He offers to take me out on it, once it's repaired, but the offer comes with inquiries as to my marital status, so I do not follow up on it.

- Tina and her husband are paying $60 a night for a double room in a Days Inn. This is because they have no car and the Days Inn is within walking distance of the Hearthside. When Marianne, one of the breakfast servers, is tossed out of her trailer for subletting (which is against the trailer-park rules), she leaves her boyfriend and moves in with Tina and her husband.

- Joan, who had fooled me with her numerous and tasteful outfits (hostesses wear their own clothes), lives in a van she parks behind a shopping center at night and showers in Tina's motel room. The clothes are from thrift shops.[4]

25   It strikes me, in my middle-class solipsism, that there is gross improvidence in some of these arrangements. When Gail and I are wrapping silverware in napkins—the only task for which we are permitted to sit—she tells me she is thinking of escaping from her roommate by moving into the Days Inn herself. I am astounded: How can she even think of paying between $40 and $60 a day? But if I was afraid of sounding like a social worker, I come out just sounding like a fool. She squints at me in disbelief, "And where am I supposed to get a month's rent and a month's deposit for an apartment?" I'd been feeling pretty smug about my $500 efficiency, but of course it was made possible only by the $1,300 I had allotted myself for start-up costs when I began my low-wage life: $1,000 for the first month's rent and deposit, $100 for initial groceries and cash in my pocket, $200 stuffed away for emergencies. In poverty, as in certain propositions in physics, starting conditions are everything.

---

[4]I could find no statistics on the number of employed people living in cars or vans, but according to the National Coalition for the Homeless's 1997 report, "Myths and Facts About Homelessness," nearly one in five homeless people (in twenty-nine cities across the nation) is employed in a full- or part-time job. [Author's note]

26   There are no secret economies that nourish the poor; on the contrary, there are a host of special costs. If you can't put up the two months' rent you need to secure an apartment, you end up paying through the nose for a room by the week. If you have only a room, with a hot plate at best, you can't save by cooking up huge lentil stews that can be frozen for the week ahead. You eat fast food, or the hot dogs and styrofoam cups of soup that can be microwaved in a convenience store. If you have no money for health insurance—and the Hearthside's niggardly plan kicks in only after three months—you go without routine care or prescription drugs and end up paying the price. Gail, for example, was fine until she ran out of money for estrogen pills. She is supposed to be on the company plan by now, but they claim to have lost her application form and need to begin the paperwork all over again. So she spends $9 per migraine pill to control the headaches she wouldn't have, she insists, if her estrogen supplements were covered. Similarly, Marianne's boyfriend lost his job as a roofer because he missed so much time after getting a cut on his foot for which he couldn't afford the prescribed antibiotic.

27   My own situation, when I sit down to assess it after two weeks of work, would not be much better if this were my actual life. The seductive thing about waitressing is that you don't have to wait for payday to feel a few bills in your pocket, and my tips usually cover meals and gas, plus something left over to stuff into the kitchen drawer I use as a bank. But as the tourist business slows in the summer heat, I sometimes leave work with only $20 in tips (the gross is higher, but servers share about 15 percent of their tips with the bus-boys and bartenders). With wages included, this amounts to about the minimum wage of $5.15 an hour. Although the sum in the drawer is piling up, at the present rate of accumulation it will be more than a hundred dollars short of my rent when the end of the month comes around. Nor can I see any expenses to cut. True, I haven't gone the lentil-stew route yet, but that's because I don't have a large cooking pot, pot holders, or a ladle to stir with (which cost about $30 at Kmart, less at thrift stores), not to mention onions, carrots, and the indispensable bay leaf. I do make my lunch almost every day—usually some slow-burning, high-protein combo like frozen chicken patties with melted cheese on top and canned pinto beans on the side. Dinner is at the Hearthside, which offers its employees a choice of BLT, fish sandwich, or hamburger for only $2. The burger lasts longest, especially if it's heaped with gut-puckering jalapeños, but by midnight my stomach is growling again.

28   So unless I want to start using my car as a residence, I have to find a second, or alternative, job. I call all the hotels where I filled out housekeeping applications weeks ago—the Hyatt, Holiday Inn, Econo Lodge, Hojo's, Best Western, plus a half dozen or so locally run guesthouses. Nothing. Then I start making the rounds again, wasting whole

mornings waiting for some assistant manager to show up, even dipping into places so creepy that the front-desk clerk greets you from behind bulletproof glass and sells pints of liquor over the counter. But either someone has exposed my real-life housekeeping habits—which are, shall we say, mellow—or I am at the wrong end of some infallible ethnic equation: most, but by no means all, of the working housekeepers I see on my job searches are African Americans, Spanish-speaking, or immigrants from the Central European post-Communist world, whereas servers are almost invariably white and monolingually English-speaking. When I finally get a positive response, I have been identified once again as server material. Jerry's, which is part of a well-known national family restaurant chain and physically attached here to another budget hotel chain, is ready to use me at once. The prospect is both exciting and terrifying, because, with about the same number of tables and counter seats, Jerry's attracts three or four times the volume of customers as the gloomy old Hearthside.

29   I start out with the beautiful, heroic idea of handling the two jobs at once, and for two days I almost do it: the breakfast/lunch shift at Jerry's, which goes till 2:00, arriving at the Hearthside at 2:10, and attempting to hold out until 10:00. In the ten minutes between jobs, I pick up a spicy chicken sandwich at the Wendy's drive-through window, gobble it down in the car, and change from khaki slacks to black, from Hawaiian to rust polo. There is a problem, though. When during the 3:00 to 4:00 P.M. dead time I finally sit down to wrap silver, my flesh seems to bond to the seat. I try to refuel with a purloined cup of soup, as I've seen Gail and Joan do dozens of times, but a manager catches me and hisses "No eating!" though there's not a customer around to be offended by the sight of food making contact with a server's lips. So I tell Gail I'm going to quit, and she hugs me and says she might just follow me to Jerry's herself.

30   But the chances of this are miniscule. She has left the flophouse and her annoying roommate and is back to living in her beat-up old truck. But guess what? she reports to me excitedly later that evening: Phillip has given her permission to park overnight in the hotel parking lot, as long as she keeps out of sight, and the parking lot should be totally safe, since it's patrolled by a hotel security guard! With the Hearthside offering benefits like that, how could anyone think of leaving?

31   True, I take occasional breaks from this life, going home now and then to catch up on e-mail and for conjugal visits (though I am careful to "pay" for anything I eat there), seeing *The Truman Show* with friends and letting them buy my ticket. And I still have those what-am-I-doing-here moments at work, when I get so homesick for the printed word that I obsessively reread the six-page menu. But as the days go by, my old life is beginning to look exceedingly strange. The e-mails

and phone messages addressed to my former self come from a distant race of people with exotic concerns and far too much time on their hands. The neighborly market I used to cruise for produce now looks forbiddingly like a Manhattan yuppie emporium. And when I sit down one morning in my real home to pay bills from my past life, I am dazzled at the two- and three-figure sums owed to outfits like Club BodyTech and Amazon.com.

32   Management at Jerry's is generally calmer and more "professional" than at the Hearthside, with two exceptions. One is Joy, a plump, blowsy woman in her early thirties, who once kindly devoted several minutes to instructing me in the correct one-handed method of carrying trays but whose moods change disconcertingly from shift to shift and even within one. Then there's B.J., a.k.a. B.J.-the-bitch, whose contribution is to stand by the kitchen counter and yell, "Nita, your order's up, move it!" or, "Barbara, didn't you see you've got another table out there? Come on, girl!" Among other things, she is hated for having replaced the whipped-cream squirt cans with big plastic whipped-cream-filled baggies that have to be squeezed with both hands—because, reportedly, she saw or thought she saw employees trying to inhale the propellant gas from the squirt cans, in the hope that it might be nitrous oxide. On my third night, she pulls me aside abruptly and brings her face so close that it looks as if she's planning to butt me with her forehead. But instead of saying, "You're fired," she says, "You're doing fine." The only trouble is I'm spending time chatting with customers: "That's how they're getting you." Furthermore I am letting them "run me," which means harassment by sequential demands: you bring the ketchup and they decide they want extra Thousand Island; you bring that and they announce they now need a side of fries; and so on into distraction. Finally she tells me not to take her wrong. She tries to say things in a nice way, but you get into a mode, you know, because everything has to move so fast.[5]

33   I mumble thanks for the advice, feeling like I've just been stripped naked by the crazed enforcer of some ancient sumptuary law: No chatting for you, girl. No fancy service ethic allowed for the serfs. Chatting with customers is for the beautiful young college-educated servers in the downtown carpaccio joints, the kids who can make $70 to $100 a night. What had I been thinking? My job is to move orders from tables

---

[5]In *Workers in a Lean World: Unions in the International Economy* (Verso, 1997), Kim Moody cites studies finding an increase in stress-related workplace injuries and illness between the mid-1980s and the early 1990s. He argues that rising stress levels reflect a new system of "management by stress," in which workers in a variety of industries are being squeezed to extract maximum productivity, to the detriment of their health. [Author's note]

to kitchen and then trays from kitchen to tables. Customers are, in fact, the major obstacle to the smooth transformation of information into food and food into money—they are, in short, the enemy. And the painful thing is that I'm beginning to see it this way myself. There are the traditional asshole types—frat boys who down multiple Buds and then make a fuss because the steaks are so emaciated and the fries so sparse—as well as the variously impaired—due to age, diabetes, or literacy issues—who require patient nutritional counseling.

34   I make friends, over time, with the other "girls" who work my shift: Nita, the tattooed twenty-something who taunts us by going around saying brightly, "Have we started making money yet?" Ellen, whose teenage son cooks on the graveyard shift and who once managed a restaurant in Massachusetts but won't try out for management here because she prefers being a "common worker" and not "ordering people around." Easy-going fiftyish Lucy, with the raucous laugh, who limps toward the end of the shift because of something that has gone wrong with her leg, the exact nature of which cannot be determined without health insurance. We talk about the usual girl things—men, children, and the sinister allure of Jerry's chocolate peanut-butter cream pie—though no one, I notice, ever brings up anything potentially expensive, like shopping or movies. As at the Hearthside, the only recreation ever referred to is partying, which requires little more than some beer, a joint, and a few close friends. Still, no one here is homeless, or cops to it anyway, thanks usually to a working husband or boyfriend. All in all, we form a reliable mutual-support group: If one of us is feeling sick or overwhelmed, another one will "bev" a table or even carry trays for her. If one of us is off sneaking a cigarette or a pee,[6] the others will do their best to conceal her absence from the enforcers of corporate rationality.

35   But my saving human connection—my oxytocin receptor, as it were—George, the nineteen-year-old, fresh-off-the-boat Czech dishwasher. We get to talking when he asks me, tortuously, how much cigarettes cost at Jerry's. I do my best to explain that they cost over a

---

[6]Until April 1998, there was no federally mandated right to bathroom breaks. According to Marc Linder and Ingrid Nygaard, authors of *Void Where Prohibited: Rest Breaks and the Right to Urinate on Company Time* (Cornell University Press, 1997), "The right to rest and void at work is not high on the list of social or political causes supported by professional or executive employees, who enjoy personal workplace liberties that millions of factory workers can only daydream about. . . . While we were dismayed to discover that workers lacked an acknowledged legal right to void at work, (the workers) were amazed by outsiders' naïve belief that their employers would permit them to perform this basic bodily function when necessary. . . . A factory worker, not allowed a break for six-hour stretches, voided into pads worn inside her uniform; and a kindergarten teacher in a school without aides had to take all twenty children with her to the bathroom and line them up outside the stall door when she voided." [Author's note]

dollar more here than at a regular store and suggest that he just take one from the half-filled packs that are always lying around on the break table. But that would be unthinkable. Except for the one tiny earring signaling his allegiance to some vaguely alternative point of view, George is a perfect straight arrow—crew-cut, hardworking, and hungry for eye contact. "Czech Republic," I ask, "or Slovakia?" and he seems delighted that I know the difference. "Václav Havel," I try. "Velvet Revolution, Frank Zappa?" "Yes, yes, 1989," he says, and I realize we are talking about history.

36   My project is to teach George English. "How are you today, George?" I say at the start of each shift. "I am good, and how are you today, Barbara?" I learn that he is not paid by Jerry's but by the "agent" who shipped him over—$5 an hour, with the agent getting the dollar or so difference between that and what Jerry's pays dishwashers. I learn also that he shares an apartment with a crowd of other Czech "dishers," as he calls them, and that he cannot sleep until one of them goes off for his shift, leaving a vacant bed. We are having one of our ESL sessions late one afternoon when B.J. catches us at it and orders "Joseph" to take up the rubber mats on the floor near the dishwashing sinks and mop underneath. "I thought your name was George," I say loud enough for B.J. to hear as she strides off back to the counter. Is she embarrassed? Maybe a little, because she greets me back at the counter with "George, Joseph—there are so many of them!" I say nothing, neither nodding nor smiling, and for this I am punished later when I think I am ready to go and she announces that I need to roll fifty more sets of silverware and isn't it time I mixed up a fresh four-gallon batch of blue-cheese dressing? May you grow old in this place, B.J., is the curse I beam out at her when I am finally permitted to leave. May the syrup spills glue your feet to the floor.

37   I make the decision to move closer to Key West. First, because of the drive. Second and third, also because of the drive: gas is eating up $4 to $5 a day, and although Jerry's is as high-volume as you can get, the tips average only 10 percent, and not just for a newbie like me. Between the base pay of $2.15 an hour and the obligation to share tips with the busboys and dishwashers, we're averaging only about $7.50 an hour. Then there is the $30 I had to spend on the regulation tan slacks worn by Jerry's servers—a setback it could take weeks to absorb. (I had combed the town's two downscale department stores hoping for something cheaper but decided in the end that these marked-down Dockers, originally $49, were more likely to survive a daily washing.) Of my fellow servers, everyone who lacks a working husband or boyfriend seems to have a second job: Nita does something at a computer eight hours a day; another welds. Without the forty-five-minute commute, I can picture myself working two jobs and having the time to shower between them.

38   So I take the $500 deposit I have coming from my landlord, the $400 I have earned toward the next month's rent, plus the $200 reserved for emergencies, and use the $1,100 to pay the rent and deposit on trailer number 46 in the Overseas Trailer Park, a mile from the cluster of budget hotels that constitute Key West's version of an industrial park. Number 46 is about eight feet in width and shaped like a barbell inside, with a narrow region—because of the sink and the stove—separating the bedroom from what might optimistically be called the "living" area, with its two-person table and half-sized couch. The bathroom is so small my knees rub against the shower stall when I sit on the toilet, and you can't just leap out of the bed, you have to climb down to the foot of it in order to find a patch of floor space to stand on. Outside, I am within a few yards of a liquor store, a bar that advertises "free beer tomorrow," a convenience store, and a Burger King—but no supermarket or, alas, laundromat. By reputation, the Overseas park is a nest of crime and crack, and I am hoping at least for some vibrant, multicultural street life. But desolation rules night and day, except for a thin stream of pedestrian traffic heading for their jobs at the Sheraton or 7-Eleven. There are not exactly people here but what amounts to canned labor, being preserved from the heat between shifts.

39   In line with my reduced living conditions, a new form of ugliness arises at Jerry's. First we are confronted—via an announcement on the computers through which we input orders—with the new rule that the hotel bar is henceforth off-limits to restaurant employees. The culprit, I learn through the grapevine, is the ultra-efficient gal who trained me—another trailer-home dweller and a mother of three. Something had set her off one morning, so she slipped out for a nip and returned to the floor impaired. This mostly hurts Ellen, whose habit it is to free her hair from its rubber band and drop by the bar for a couple of Zins before heading home at the end of the shift, but all of us feel the chill. Then the next day, when I go for straws, for the first time I find the dry-storage room locked. Ted, the portly assistant manager who opens it for me, explains that he caught one of the dishwashers attempting to steal something, and, unfortunately, the miscreant will be with us until a replacement can be found—hence the locked door. I neglect to ask what he had been trying to steal, but Ted tells me who he is—the kid with the buzz cut and the earring. You know, he's back there right now.

40   I wish I could say I rushed back and confronted George to get his side of the story. I wish I could say I stood up to Ted and insisted that George be given a translator and allowed to defend himself, or announced that I'd find a lawyer who'd handle the case pro bono. The mystery to me is that there's not much worth stealing in the dry-storage room, at least not in any fenceable quantity: "Is Gyorgi here, and am having 200—maybe 250—ketchup packets. What do you say?"

My guess is that he had taken—if he had taken anything at all—some Saltines or a can of cherry-pie mix, and that the motive for taking it was hunger.

41   So why didn't I intervene? Certainly not because I was held back by the kind of moral paralysis that can pass as journalistic objectivity. On the contrary, something new—something loathsome and servile— had infected me, along with the kitchen odors that I could still sniff on my bra when I finally undressed at night. In real life I am moderately brave, but plenty of brave people shed their courage in concentration camps, and maybe something similar goes on in the infinitely more congenial milieu of the low-wage American workplace. Maybe, in a month or two more at Jerry's, I might have regained my crusading spirit. Then again, in a month or two I might have turned into a differ- ent person altogether—say, the kind of person who would have turned George in. But this is not something I am slated to find out.

42   I can do this two-job thing, is my theory, if I can drink enough caffeine and avoid getting distracted by George's ever more obvious suffering.[7] The first few days after being caught he seemed not to un- derstand the trouble he was in, and our chirpy little conversations had continued. But the last couple of shifts he's been listless and unshaven, and tonight he looks like the ghost we all know him to be, with dark half-moons hanging from his eyes. At one point, when I am briefly im- mobilized by the task of filling little paper cups with sour cream for baked potatoes, he comes over and looks as if he'd like to explore the limits of our shared vocabulary, but I am called to the floor for a table. I resolve to give him all my tips that night and to hell with the experi- ment in low-wage money management. At eight, Ellen and I grab a snack together standing at the mephitic end of the kitchen counter, but I can only manage two or three mozzarella sticks and lunch had been a mere handful of McNuggets. I am not tired at all, I assure myself, though it may be that there is simply no more "I" left to do the tiredness monitoring. What I would see, if I were more alert to the situation, is that the forces of destruction are already massing against me. There is only one cook on duty, a young man names Jesus ("Hay-Sue," that is) and he is new to the job. And there is Joy, who shows up to take over in the mid- dle of the shift, wearing high heels and a long, clingy white dress and fuming as if she'd just been stood up in some cocktail bar.

[7]In 1996, the number of persons holding two or more jobs averaged 7.8 million, or 6.2 percent of the workforce. It was about the same rate for men and for women (6.1 versus 6.2), though the kinds of jobs differ by gender. About two thirds of multiple jobholders work one job full-time and the other part-time. Only a heroic minority— 4 percent of men and 2 percent of women—work two full-time jobs simultaneously. (From John F. Stinson Jr., "New Data on Multiple Jobholding Available from the CPS," in the *Monthly Labor Review,* March 1997.) [Author's note]

43   Then it comes, the perfect storm. Four of my tables fill up at once. Four tables is nothing for me now, but only so long as they are obligingly staggered. As I bev table 27, tables 25, 28, and 24 are watching enviously. As I bev 25, 24 glowers because their bevs haven't even been ordered. Twenty-eight is four yuppyish types, meaning everything on the side and agonizing instructions as to the chicken Caesars. Twenty-five is a middle-aged black couple, who complain, with some justice, that the iced tea isn't fresh and the tabletop is sticky. But table 24 is the meteorological event of the century: ten British tourists who seem to have made the decision to absorb the American experience entirely by mouth. Here everyone has at least two drinks—iced tea and milk shake, Michelob and water (with lemon slice, please)—and a huge promiscuous orgy of breakfast specials, mozz sticks, chicken strips, quesadillas; burgers with cheese and without, sides of hash browns with cheddar, with onions, with gravy, seasoned fries, plain fries, banana splits. Poor Jesus! Poor me! Because when I arrive with their first tray of food—after three prior trips just to refill bevs— Princess Di refuses to eat her chicken strips with her pancake-and-sausage special, since, as she now reveals, the strips were meant to be an appetizer. Maybe the others would have accepted their meals, but Di, who is deep into her third Michelob, insists that everything else go back while they work on their "starters." Meanwhile, the yuppies are waving me down for more decaf and the black couple looks ready to summon the NAACP.

44   Much of what happened next is lost in the fog of war. Jesus starts going under. The little printer on the counter in front of him is spewing out orders faster than he can rip them off, much less produce the meals. Even the invincible Ellen is ashen from stress. I bring table 24 their reheated main courses, which they immediately reject as either too cold or fossilized by the microwave. When I return to the kitchen with their trays (three trays in three trips), Joy confronts me with arms akimbo: "What is this?" She means the food—the plates of rejected pancakes, hash browns in assorted flavors, toasts, burgers, sausages, eggs. "Uh, scrambled with cheddar," I try, "and that's . . ." "NO," she screams in my face. "Is it a traditional, a super-scramble, an eye-opener?" I pretend to study my check for a clue, but entropy has been up to its tricks, not only on the plates but in my head, and I have to admit that the original order is beyond reconstruction. "You don't know an eye-opener from a traditional?" she demands in outrage. All I know, in fact, is that my legs have lost interest in the current venture and have announced their intention to fold. I am saved by a yuppie (mercifully not one of mine) who chooses this moment to charge into the kitchen to bellow that his food is twenty-five minutes late. Joy screams at him to get the hell out of her kitchen, please, and then turns on Jesus in a fury, hurling an empty tray across the room for emphasis.

45   I leave. I don't walk out, I just leave. I don't finish my side work or pick up my credit-card tips, if any, at the cash register or, of course, ask Joy's permission to go. And the surprising thing is that you *can* walk out without permission, that the door opens, that the thick tropical night air parts to let me pass, that my car is still parked where I left it. There is no vindication in this exit, no fuck-you surge of relief, just an overwhelming, dank sense of failure pressing down on me and the entire parking lot. I had gone into this venture in the spirit of science, to test a mathematical proposition, but somewhere along the line, in the tunnel vision imposed by long shifts and relentless concentration, it became a test of myself, and clearly I have failed. Not only had I flamed out as a housekeeper/server, I had even forgotten to give George my tips, and, for reasons perhaps best known to hardworking, generous people like Gail and Ellen, this hurts. I don't cry, but I am in a position to realize, for the first time in many years, that the tear ducts are still there, and still capable of doing their job.

46   When I moved out of the trailer park, I gave the key to number 46 to Gail and arranged for my deposit to be transferred to her. She told me that Joan is still living in her van and that Stu had been fired from the Hearthside. I never found out what happened to George.

47   In one month, I had earned approximately $1,040 and spent $517 on food, gas, toiletries, laundry, phone, and utilities. If I had remained in my $500 efficiency, I would have been able to pay the rent and have $22 left over (which is $78 less than the cash I had in my pocket at the start of the month). During this time I bought no clothing except for the required slacks and no prescription drugs or medical care (I did finally buy some vitamin B to compensate for the lack of vegetables in my diet). Perhaps I could have saved a little on food if I had gotten to a supermarket more often, instead of convenience stores, but it should be noted that I lost almost four pounds in four weeks, on a diet weighted heavily toward burgers and fries.

48   How former welfare recipients and single mothers will (and do) survive in the low-wage workforce, I cannot imagine. Maybe they will figure out how to condense their lives—including child-raising, laundry, romance, and meals—into the couple of hours between full-time jobs. Maybe they will take up residence in their vehicles, if they have one. All I know is that I couldn't hold two jobs and I couldn't make enough money to live on with one. And I had advantages unthinkable to many of the long-term poor—health, stamina, a working car, and no children to care for and support. Certainly nothing in my experience contradicts the conclusion of Kathryn Edin and Laura Lein, in their recent book *Making Ends Meet: How Single Mothers Survive Welfare and Low-Wage Work,* that low-wage work actually involves more hardship and deprivation than life at the mercy of the welfare state. In the coming months

and years, economic conditions for the working poor are bound to worsen, even without the almost inevitable recession. As mentioned earlier, the influx of former welfare recipients into the low-skilled workforce will have a depressing effect on both wages and the number of jobs available. A general economic downturn will only enhance these effects, and the working poor will of course be facing it without the slight, but nonetheless often saving, protection of welfare as a backup.

49   The thinking behind welfare reform was that even the humblest jobs are morally uplifting and psychologically buoying. In reality they are likely to be fraught with insult and stress. But I did discover one redeeming feature of the most abject low-wage work—the camaraderie of people who are, in almost all cases, far too smart and funny and caring for the work they do and the wages they're paid. The hope, of course, is that someday these people will come to know what they're worth, and take appropriate action.

✧ Evaluating the Text

1. What kinds of hard choices does Ehrenreich have to make and what trade-offs is she constantly forced to consider in her no-win situation as an unskilled worker?

2. What insight does Ehrenreich's experience offer into the lives and conditions of the working poor? Which of her encounters did you find particularly surprising?

✧ Exploring Different Perspectives

1. Compare the circumstances Ehrenreich has put herself in with those of Rosaura's mother in Liliana Heker's story.

2. Compare Ehrenreich's experiences with those of Victor Villaseñor in "Rain of Gold" in her efforts to earn a day's wages.

✧ Extending Viewpoints through Writing

1. Among the many issues that Ehrenreich touches upon such as homelessness, drug testing in the workplace, and workers who need to hold two jobs in order to support themselves, which did you find the most interesting? Explore this topic in a short essay and support your observation with evidence drawn from the text and from library and Internet research.

2. How did reading this article change any preconceptions you may have had about the working poor in our society? Explain your answer.

Tomoyuki Iwashita

Why I Quit the Company

◆

Tomoyuki Iwashita signed on to work for a prominent Japanese corporation just after graduating from college. The life of the typical "salaryman" did not appeal to him for reasons he explains in "Why I Quit the Company," which originally appeared in The New Internationalist, *May 1992. He is currently a journalist based in Tokyo.*

Before You Read

Consider the insights this piece offers into corporate life in Japan and why a well-paid worker would drop out.

◆

1   When I tell people that I quit working for the company after only a year, most of them think I'm crazy. They can't understand why I would want to give up a prestigious and secure job. But I think I'd have been crazy to stay, and I'll try to explain why.

2   I started working for the company immediately after graduating from university. It's a big, well-known trading company with about 6,000 employees all over the world. There's a lot of competition to get into this and other similar companies, which promise young people a wealthy and successful future. I was set on course to be a Japanese "yuppie."

3   I'd been used to living independently as a student, looking after myself and organizing my own schedule. As soon as I started working all that changed. I was given a room in the company dormitory, which is like a fancy hotel, with a twenty-four-hour hot bath service and all meals laid on. Most single company employees live in a dormitory like this, and many married employees live in company apartments. The dorm system is actually a great help because living in Tokyo costs more than young people earn—but I found it stifling.

4   My life rapidly became reduced to a shuttle between the dorm and the office. The working day is officially eight hours, but you can never leave the office on time. I used to work from nine in the morning until eight or nine at night, and often until midnight. Drinking with colleagues after work is part of the job; you can't say no. The company building contained cafeterias, shops, a bank, a post office, a doctor's office, a barber's. . . . I never needed to leave the building. Working, drinking, sleeping, and standing on a horribly crowded commuter

265

train for an hour and a half each way: This was my life. I spent all my time with the same colleagues; when I wasn't involved in entertaining clients on the weekend, I was expected to play golf with my colleagues. I soon lost sight of the world outside the company.

5   This isolation is part of the brainwashing process. A personnel manager said: "We want excellent students who are active, clever, and tough. Three months is enough to train them to be devoted businessmen." I would hear my colleagues saying: "I'm not making any profit for the company, so I'm not contributing." Very few employees claim all the overtime pay due to them. Keeping an employee costs the company 50 million yen ($400,000) a year, or so the company claims. Many employees put the company's profits before their own mental and physical well-being.

6   Overtiredness and overwork leave you little energy to analyze or criticize your situation. There are shops full of "health drinks," cocktails of caffeine and other drugs, which will keep you going even when you're exhausted. *Karoshi* (death from overwork) is increasingly common and is always being discussed in the newspapers. I myself collapsed from working too hard. My boss told me: "You should control your health; it's your own fault if you get sick." There is no paid sick leave; I used up half of my fourteen days' annual leave because of sickness.

7   We had a labor union, but it seemed to have an odd relationship with the management. A couple of times a year I was told to go home at five o'clock. The union representatives were coming around to investigate working hours; everyone knew in advance. If it was "discovered" that we were all working overtime in excess of fifty hours a month our boss might have had some problem being promoted; and our prospects would have been affected. So we all pretended to work normal hours that day.

8   The company also controls its employees' private lives. Many company employees under thirty are single. They are expected to devote all their time to the company and become good workers; they don't have time to find a girlfriend. The company offers scholarships to the most promising young employees to enable them to study abroad for a year or two. But unmarried people who are on these courses are not allowed to get married until they have completed the course! Married employees who are sent to train abroad have to leave their families in Japan for the first year.

9   In fact, the quality of married life is often determined by the husband's work. Men who have just gotten married try to go home early for a while, but soon have to revert to the norm of late-night work. They have little time to spend with their wives and even on the weekend are expected to play golf with colleagues. Fathers cannot find time to communicate with their children and child rearing is largely left to

mothers. Married men posted abroad will often leave their family behind in Japan; they fear that their children will fall behind in the
fiercely competitive Japanese education system.

10   Why do people put up with this? They believe this to be a normal
working life or just cannot see an alternative. Many think that such
personal sacrifices are necessary to keep Japan economically successful. Perhaps, saddest of all, Japan's education and socialization
processes do not equip people with the intellectual and spiritual resources to question and challenge the status quo. They stamp out even
the desire for a different kind of life.

11   However, there are some signs that things are changing. Although
many new employees in my company were quickly brainwashed,
many others, like myself, complained about life in the company and seriously considered leaving. But most of them were already in fetters—
of debt. Pleased with themselves for getting into the company and anticipating a life of executive luxury, these new employees throw their
money around. Every night they are out drinking. They buy smart
clothes and take a taxi back to the dormitory after the last train has
gone. They start borrowing money from the bank and soon they have a
debt growing like a snowball rolling down a slope. The banks demand
no security for loans; it's enough to be working for a well-known company. Some borrow as much as a year's salary in the first few months.
They can't leave the company while they have such debts to pay off.

12   I was one of the few people in my intake of employees who didn't
get into debt. I left the company dormitory after three months to share
an apartment with a friend. I left the company exactly one year after I
entered it. It took me a while to find a new job, but I'm working as a
journalist now. My life is still busy, but it's a lot better than it was. I'm
lucky because nearly all big Japanese companies are like the one I
worked for, and conditions in many small companies are even worse.

13   It's not easy to opt out of a life-style that is generally considered to
be prestigious and desirable, but more and more young people in
Japan are thinking about doing it. You have to give up a lot of superfi-
cially attractive material benefits in order to preserve the quality of
your life and your sanity. I don't think I was crazy to leave the company. I think I would have gone crazy if I'd stayed.

✧ Evaluating the Text

1. What features of Iwashita's account address the crucial issue of his
   company's attempt to totally control the lives of employees?

2. What psychological effects led him to actually quit his secure job?

3. In what important respects do Japanese corporate employees differ
   from their American counterparts? In what ways are they similar?

❖ Exploring Different Perspectives

1. Compare the very different perspectives of Iwashita and Barbara Ehrenreich (see "Nickel-and-Dimed"). Describe any underlying commonalities that you can find in these very different accounts of Japanese life.

2. How does the issue of exploitation occur in Iwashita's article and in Liliana Heker's story, "The Stolen Party"?

❖ Extending Viewpoints through Writing

1. Drawing on work experiences you have had, discuss any similarities and differences you found on the question of conformity and subservience to the company. Analyze the different motivations that drive Japanese and American workers.

2. If you were in Iwashita's situation, would you have made the same decision he did? Why or why not?

Mark Salzman

Lessons

◆

Mark Salzman graduated Phi Beta Kappa, summa cum laude from Yale in 1982 with a degree in Chinese language and literature. From 1982 to 1984, he lived in Chang-sha, Hunan, in the People's Republic of China, where he taught English at Hunan Medical College. There he studied under Pan Qingfu, one of China's greatest traditional boxers and martial arts masters. In October 1985, he was invited back to China to participate in the National Martial Arts Competition and Conference in Tianjin. Iron and Silk *(1986) recounts his adventures and provides a fascinating behind-the-scenes glimpse into the workings of Chinese society. His experiences also formed the basis for a 1991 film of the same name starring the author. He has written four novels:* Eclipse *(1991),* The Laughing Sutra *(1992),* The Soloist *(1994), and* Lying Awake *(2000). He is also the author of a memoir,* Lost in Place: Growing Up Absurd in Suburbia *(1995).*

"Lessons," from Iron and Silk, *describes the extraordinary opportunity that studying martial arts with Pan Qingfu offered, along with the comic misunderstandings produced by their being from such different cultures.*

The People's Republic of China is ruled by a government established in 1949 after the victory of Mao Zedong (Tse-tung) and his communist forces against the Nationalist forces of Chiang Kai-Chek, who fled to Taiwan and set up a government in exile. Under Mao's leadership, industry was nationalized and a land reform program, based on collectivization, was introduced. China entered the Korean War against United Nations forces between 1950 and the Armistice of 1953. China's modern history has been characterized by cycles of liberalization followed by violent oppression. In 1957, reaction against the so-called "let a hundred flowers bloom" period led to a crackdown against intellectuals. In 1966, Mao launched the Cultural Revolution to purge the government and society of liberal elements. After Mao's death in 1976, a backlash led to the imprisoning of Mao's wife, Jiang Qing, and three colleagues (the "Gang of Four"). A period of liberalization once again followed, as Deng Xiaoping came to power in 1977 and adopted more conciliatory economic, social, and political policies. The United States recognized the People's Republic of China as a valid government on January 1, 1979. The pattern reemerged in June 1989, when government troops were sent into Tiananmen

Square to crush the prodemocracy movement. Zhao Ziyang, who had shown sympathy toward the students, was ousted and replaced by hardliner Jing Zemin. The June events, in which thousands are reported to have died, led to a crackdown and execution of sympathizers throughout China, despite widespread international condemnation. A behind-the-scenes power struggle in 1992 by Deng Xiaoping has led to some economic market style reforms although political liberalization still is not allowed.

The period when Salzman was in China coincided with liberal developments within the society, under the leadership of Zhan Ziyang as prime minister, and a more conciliatory relationship with the United States. President Reagan visited China in April 1984 and signed an agreement on nuclear cooperation in nonmilitary areas. In September 1984, China and Britain signed accords designed to facilitate the return of Hong Kong (a British crown colony leased in 1898 for ninety-nine years) to Chinese control in 1997.

Before You Read

As you read, evaluate the attitudes toward success and failure that Salzman discovers to be characteristic of the Chinese.

————————◆————————

1   I was to meet Pan at the training hall four nights a week, to receive private instruction after the athletes finished their evening workout. Waving and wishing me good night, they politely filed out and closed the wooden doors, leaving Pan and me alone in the room. First he explained that I must start from scratch. He meant it, too, for beginning that night, and for many nights thereafter, I learned how to stand at attention. He stood inches away from me and screamed, "Stand straight!" then bored into me with his terrifying gaze. He insisted that I maintain eye contact for as long as he stood in front of me, and that I meet his gaze with one of equal intensity. After as long as a minute of this silent torture, he would shout "At ease!" and I could relax a bit, but not smile or take my eyes away from his. We repeated this exercise countless times, and I was expected to practice it four to six hours a day. At the time, I wondered what those staring contests had to do with wushu, but I came to realize that everything he was to teach me later was really contained in those first few weeks when we stared at each other. His art drew strength from his eyes; this was his way of passing it on.

2   After several weeks I came to enjoy staring at him. I would break into a sweat and feel a kind of heat rushing up through the floor into my legs and up into my brain. He told me that when standing like that, I must at all times be prepared to duel, that at any moment he might attack, and I should be ready to defend myself. It exhilarated me to face off with him, to feel his power and taste the fear and anticipation of the blow. Days and weeks passed, but the blow did not come.

3   One night he broke the lesson off early, telling me that tonight was special. I followed him out of the training hall, and we bicycled a short distance to his apartment. He lived with his wife and two sons on the fifth floor of a large, anonymous cement building. Like all the urban housing going up in China today, the building was indistinguishable from its neighbors, mercilessly practical and depressing in appearance. Pan's apartment had three rooms and a small kitchen. A private bathroom and painted, as opposed to raw, cement walls in all the rooms identified it as the home of an important family. The only decoration in the apartment consisted of some silk banners, awards and photographs from Pan's years as the national wushu champion and from the set of *Shaolin Temple*. Pan's wife, a doctor, greeted me with all sorts of homemade snacks and sat me down at a table set for two. Pan sat across from me and poured two glasses of baijiu. He called to his sons, both in their teens, and they appeared from the bedroom instantly. They stood in complete silence until Pan asked them to greet me, which they did, very politely, but so softly I could barely hear them. They were handsome boys, and the elder, at about fourteen, was taller than me and had a moustache. I tried asking them questions to put them at ease, but they answered only by nodding. They apparently had no idea how to behave toward something like me and did not want to make any mistakes in front of their father. Pan told them to say good night, and they, along with his wife, disappeared into the bedroom. Pan raised his glass and proposed that the evening begin.

4   He told me stories that made my hair stand on end, with such gusto that I thought the building would shake apart. When he came to the parts where he vanquished his enemies, he brought his terrible hand down on the table or against the wall with a crash, sending our snacks jumping out of their serving bowls. His imitations of cowards and bullies were so funny I could hardly breathe for laughing. He had me spellbound for three solid hours; then his wife came in to see if we needed any more food or baijiu. I took the opportunity to ask her if she had ever been afraid for her husband's safety when, for example, he went off alone to bust up a gang of hoodlums in Shenyang. She laughed and touched his right hand. "Sometimes I figured he'd be late for dinner." A look of tremendous satisfaction came over Pan's face, and he got up to use the bathroom. She sat down in his chair and looked at me. "Every day he receives tens of letters from all over China, all from people asking to become his student. Since he made the movie, it's been almost impossible for him to go out during the day." She refilled our cups, then looked at me again. "He has trained professionals for more than twenty-five years now, but in all that time he has accepted only one private student." After a long pause, she gestured at me with her chin. "You." Just then Pan came back into the room, returned to his seat and started a new story. This one was about a spear:

5   While still a young man training for the national wushu competition, Pan overheard a debate among some of his fellow athletes about
the credibility of an old story. The story described a famous warrior as
being able to execute a thousand spear-thrusts without stopping to
rest. Some of the athletes felt this to be impossible: after fifty, one's
shoulders ache, and by one hundred the skin on the left hand, which
guides the spear as the right hands thrusts, twists and returns it, begins to blister. Pan had argued that surely this particular warrior
would not have been intimidated by aching shoulders and blisters,
and soon a challenge was raised. The next day Pan went out into a
field with a spear, and as the other athletes watched, executed one
thousand and seven thrusts without stopping to rest. Certain details
of the story as Pan told it—that the bones of his left hand were exposed, and so forth—might be called into question, but the number of
thrusts I am sure is accurate, and the scar tissue on his left palm indicates that it was not easy for him.

6   One evening later in the year, when I felt discouraged with my
progress in a form of Northern Shaolin boxing called "Changquan," or
"Long Fist," I asked Pan if he thought I should discontinue the training. He frowned, the only time he ever seemed genuinely angry with
me, and said quietly, "When I say I will do something, I do it, exactly
as I said I would. In my whole life I have never started something
without finishing it. I said that in the time we have, I would make your
wushu better than you could imagine, and I will. Your only responsibility to me is to practice and to learn. My responsibility to you is much
greater! Every time you think your task is great, think how much
greater mine is. Just keep this in mind: if you fail"—here he paused to
make sure I understood—"I will lose face."

7   Though my responsibility to him was merely to practice and to
learn, he had one request that he vigorously encouraged me to fulfill—
to teach him English. I felt relieved to have something to offer him, so I
quickly prepared some beginning materials and rode over to his house
for the first lesson. When I got there, he had a tape recorder set up on a
small table, along with a pile of oversized paper and a few felt-tip pens
from a coloring set. He showed no interest at all in my books, but sat
me down next to the recorder and pointed at the pile of paper. On each
sheet he had written out in Chinese dozens of phrases, such as "We'll
need a spotlight over there," "These mats aren't springy enough," and
"Don't worry—it's just a shoulder dislocation." He asked me to write
down the English translation next to each phrase, which took a little
over two and a half hours. When I was finished, I asked him if he could
read my handwriting, and he smiled, saying that he was sure my
handwriting was fine. After a series of delicate questions, I determined
that he was as yet unfamiliar with the alphabet, so I encouraged him
to have a look at my beginning materials. "That's too slow for me," he

said. He asked me to repeat each of the phrases I'd written down five times into the recorder, leaving enough time after each repetition for him to say it aloud after me. "The first time should be very slow—one word at a time, with a pause after each word so I can repeat it. The second time should be the same. The third time you should pause after every other word. The fourth time read it through slowly. The fifth time you can read it fast." I looked at the pile of phrase sheets, calculated how much time this would take, and asked if we could do half today and half tomorrow, as dinner was only three hours away. "Don't worry!" he said, beaming. "I've prepared some food for you here. Just tell me when you get hungry." He sat next to me, turned on the machine, then turned it off again. "How do you say, 'And now, Mark will teach me English'?" I told him how and he repeated it, at first slowly, then more quickly, twenty or twenty-one times. He turned the machine on. "And now, Mark will teach me English." I read the first phrase, five times as he had requested, and he pushed a little note across the table. "Better read it six times," it read, "and a little slower."

8   After several weeks during which we nearly exhausted the phrasal possibilities of our two languages, Pan announced that the time had come to do something new. "Now I want to learn routines." I didn't understand. "Routines?" "Yes. Everything, including language, is like wushu. First you learn the basic moves, or words, then you string them together into routines." He produced from his bedroom a huge sheet of paper made up of smaller pieces taped together. He wanted me to write a story on it. The story he had in mind was a famous Chinese folk tale, "How Yu Gong Moved the Mountain." The story tells of an old man who realized that, if he only had fields where a mountain stood instead, he would have enough arable land to support his family comfortably. So he went out to the mountain with a shovel and a bucket and started to take the mountain down. All his neighbors made fun of him, calling it an impossible task, but Yu Gong disagreed: it would just take a long time, and after several tens of generations had passed, the mountain would at last become a field and his family would live comfortably. Pan had me write this story in big letters, so that he could paste it up on his bedroom wall, listen to the tape I was to make and read along as he lay in bed.

9   Not only did I repeat this story into the tape recorder several dozen times—at first one word at a time, and so on—but Pan invited Bill, Bob and Marcy over for dinner one night and had them read it a few times for variety. After they had finished, Pan said that he would like to recite a few phrases for them to evaluate and correct. He chose some of his favorite sentences and repeated each seven or eight times without a pause. He belted them out with such fierce concentration we were all afraid to move lest it disturb him. At last he finished and looked at me, asking quietly if it was all right. I nodded and he seemed

overcome with relief. He smiled, pointed at me and said to my friends, "I was very nervous just then. I didn't want him to lose face."

10   While Pan struggled to recite English routines from memory, he began teaching me how to use traditional weapons. He would teach me a single move, then have me practice it in front of him until I could do it ten times in a row without a mistake. He always stood about five feet away from me, with his arms folded, grinding his teeth, and the only time he took his eyes off me was to blink. One night in the late spring I was having a particularly hard time learning a move with the staff. I was sweating heavily and my right hand was bleeding, so the staff had become slippery and hard to control. Several of the athletes stayed on after their workout to watch and to enjoy the breeze that sometimes passed through the training hall. Pan stopped me and indicated that I wasn't working hard enough. "Imagine," he said, "that you are participating in the national competition, and those athletes are your competitors. Look as if you know what you are doing! Frighten them with your strength and confidence." I mustered all the confidence I could, under the circumstances, and flung myself into the move. I lost control of the staff, and it whirled straight into my forehead. As if in a dream, the floor raised up several feet to support my behind, and I sat staring up at Pan while blood ran down across my nose and a fleshy knob grew between my eyebrows. The athletes sprang forward to help me up. They seemed nervous, never having had a foreigner knock himself out in their training hall before, but Pan, after asking if I felt all right, seemed positively inspired. "Sweating and bleeding. Good."

11   Every once in a while, Pan felt it necessary to give his students something to think about, to spur them on to greater efforts. During one morning workout two women practiced a combat routine, one armed with a spear, the other with a *dadao*, or halberd. The dadao stands about six feet high and consists of a broadsword attached to a thick wooden pole, with an angry-looking spike at the far end. It is heavy and difficult to wield even for a strong man, so it surprised me to see this young woman, who could not weigh more than one hundred pounds, using it so effectively. At one point in their battle the woman with the dadao swept it toward the other woman's feet, as if to cut them off, but the other woman jumped up in time to avoid the blow. The first woman, without letting the blade of the dadao stop, brought it around in another sweep, as if to cut the other woman in half at the waist. The other woman, without an instant to spare, bent straight from the hips so that the dadao slashed over her back and head, barely an inch away. This combination was to be repeated three times in rapid succession before moving on to the next exchange. The

women practiced this move several times, none of which satisfied Pan. "Too slow, and the weapon is too far away from her. It should graze her back as it goes by." They tried again, but still Pan growled angrily. Suddenly he got up and took the dadao from the first woman. The entire training hall went silent and still. Without warming up at all, Pan ordered the woman with the spear to get ready, and to move fast when the time came. His body looked as though electricity had suddenly passed through it, and the huge blade flashed toward her. Once, twice the dadao flew beneath her feet, then swung around in a terrible arc and rode her back with flawless precision. The third time he added a little twist at the end, so that the blade grazed up her neck and sent a little decoration stuck in her pigtails flying across the room.

12   I had to sit down for a moment to ponder the difficulty of sending an object roughly the shape of an oversized shovel, only heavier, across a girl's back and through her pigtails, without guide ropes or even a safety helmet. Not long before, I had spoken with a former troupe member who, when practicing with this instrument, had suddenly found himself on his knees. The blade, unsharpened, had twirled a bit too close to him and passed through his Achilles' tendon without a sound. Pan handed the dadao back to the woman and walked over to me. "What if you had made a mistake?" I asked. "I never make mistakes," he said, without looking at me.

✧ Evaluating the Text

1. What is the relevance of the Chinese folk tale "How Yu Gong Moved the Mountain" to Salzman's apprenticeship?

2. What evidence can you cite to show that Pan applies the same standard (based on fear of "losing face") to Mark as he does to himself? What part does the concept of "losing face" play in Chinese culture, and what values are expressed through this term?

3. What similarities can you discover between Pan's approach to learning English and his methods of teaching Chinese martial arts?

4. What factors do you believe might explain why Pan chooses Mark to be the only private student he has ever had?

5. What conclusions can you draw about the standard of living in China from the way in which Pan and his family live? Keep in mind that being a champion in martial arts is comparable to being an outstanding baseball, football, or basketball player and that Pan's wife is a physician.

✧ *Exploring Different Perspectives*

1. Compare and contrast the impression that you get of Victor Villa-señor's father in "Rain of Gold" with that of Pan in Salzman's account. What common features do both men have?

2. To what extent does the Asian concept of shame, or "losing face," play an important part in the accounts by Salzman and by To-moyuki Iwashita?

✧ *Extending Viewpoints through Writing*

1. Describe an experience, including martial arts instruction, that you have had that gave you insight into Salzman's experiences.

2. If you could master anything you wished, what would it be, and who would you want to be your teacher? Would you want to learn from someone like Pan?

3. To what extent does the concept of shame, or "losing face," play an important role in Chinese culture? What part does this idea play in Mark Salzman's account?

Dennis Smith

Report from Ground Zero

◆

Dennis Smith began his career as a firefighter in the New York Fire Department. In 1972, he published his first book, the New York Times *bestseller,* Report from Engine Co. 82. *He is the author of nine other books, including his memoir,* A Song for Mary: An Irish-American Memory *(1999). Immediately after two hijacked jets struck the twin towers of the World Trade Center on the morning of September 11, 2001, Smith reported to Manhattan's Ladder Co. 16 to volunteer in the rescue effort.* Report from Ground Zero *(2002) is a dramatic narrative of this three-month period, a time that has permanently altered the landscape and character of America. In the following excerpt from the book, we hear the testimony of a battalion chief, Joe Pfeifer.*

Before You Read

Consider how Smith places this personal account in the context of a momentous historical event.

◆

Chief Joe Pfeifer

Battalion 1

1   Joe Pfeifer has been a battalion chief for five years, and has been working the downtown area with the 1st Battalion. He is a thin, athletic man, with a studious air. If you saw him in a suit, you might take him for a lawyer, or a financial expert. If you mention his name in a group of firefighters, they invariably say, "Chief Pfeifer? The best."

2   On this pleasant morning he is standing in his shirtsleeves at the intersection of Church Street and Lispenard Street. It is 8:48 A.M. and the day is already summer clear. He has been sent to this location with the men of Engine 7 and Ladder 1 to investigate a report of a gas leak. Ladder 8 pulls up as Chief Pfeifer takes a gas meter from his van, a small device with a long thin neck, at the end of which is a sensor. The chief circles a grating in the street with the meter until it buzzes, indicating a slight presence of gas. Sewer gas, maybe?

3   Suddenly a shadow falls over the street corner, and a firefighter, Steven Olsen of Ladder 1, looks up. It is accompanied by a heavy, roaring sound that is abnormal and surprising. *You never hear planes roaring*

over Manhattan, Chief Pfeifer thinks. It is also much lower than it should be. All the firefighters are now staring upward, as is a film crew that is shooting a documentary about firefighters. It is a plane. Chief Pfeifer's gaze follows the path of the plane, and he has a clear view as it crashes into the north tower of the World Trade Center, near the top, somewhere around the ninetieth floor. There is no discussion among the fire companies as they rush into their trucks and speed fourteen blocks south.

4   In the chief's van, Chief Pfeifer hears the Manhattan dispatcher announce that a plan has gone into tower 1 of the World Trade Center. The chief reaches for the telephone.

5   "Battalion 1 to Manhattan."

6   "Okay," the dispatcher answers. It is John Lightsey who is working the microphone this shift.

7   "We have another report of a fire," Chief Pfeifer says, calmly and resolutely. He knows these are public airwaves. "It looks like a plane has steamed into the building. Transmit a third alarm. We'll have a staging area at Vesey and West streets. Have the third-alarm assignment go into that area, the second-alarm assignment go to the building."

8   "Ten-four," Lightsey answers.

9   He next hears on the radio. "Division 1 is on the air."

10   "Ten-four, Division 1. You have a full third-alarm assignment." Chief Pfeifer now knows that Chief Hayden is on his way. He and Chief Hayden have been colleagues for a long time, and he is glad this is the deputy on assignment today.

11   When he reaches the staging area and steps into the street, he sees a large amount of fire and white smoke lifting from the top of the building to the sky. Behind him, Jules Naudet follows with his video camera. Chief Pfeifer pulls his heavy bunker pants over his trousers, and steps into his boots. He puts his helmet on, a leather helmet painted over with white enamel, which has been the traditional style of the FDNY for more than a hundred years. His own has a large front piece that reads, in large antiqued lettering: BATTALION CHIEF. There is a shower of debris falling, and he runs through it into the building, straight through to the elevator control bank, where he sets up a command post. He notices that all the twenty-five-foot-high windows that surround the lobby, at least in this northwest section of the building, have been blown out, and people are walking through the frames. They undoubtedly were broken upon the impact of the plane, which means the building must have shook violently.

12   A maintenance worker runs to him, saying, "We have a report of people trapped in a stairwell on 78.'"

13   "Okay, 78," he answers. People have begun staggering through the lobby, badly burned, while others are running. The firefighters of Ladder 10 appear, as does an officer who reports to the chief.

14   "I want you to go to 78," Chief Pfeifer says.

15   "What floor, Chief?" the officer asks. It is almost as if he does not want to register the floor number, anticipating the length of the climb, the weight of the equipment he has to carry, and the smoke and fire that will confront him there.

16   "Seventy-eight."

17   Just then Chief Hayden arrives. The unspoken transfer of command is passed from Chief Pfeifer, even as they realize they are all in this together. The elevator control bank stands behind a five-foot marble wall, and Chief Hayden and Chief Pfeifer station themselves behind it. As firefighters report in, they speak to the chiefs as customers do over a high counter in a meat market. Civilians are running past the firefighters, leaving the lobby as the firefighters are entering it. The firefighters move more deliberately, carrying equipment and hose, for they know they have to conserve their energy to ascend the highest building in the city.

18   Chief Hayden and Chief Pfeifer are very focused and exacting. Not a voice is raised in any discussion between firefighters and fire chiefs. Chief Bill McGovern of Battalion 2 joins them. About thirty firefighters have gathered, patiently awaiting assignment, hose and tools at their feet. As their orders are issued they disappear into the building, and other firefighters appear, among them the men of Engine 10. In front of the elevator bank counter, the field communications unit begins to set up a portable command station consisting of a large suitcaselike piece of equipment on four legs, with a magnetic board where the list of entering fire companies can be logged. Just behind them, firefighters are dressing the windows, breaking off the dangerously hanging shards of glass.

19   Lieutenant Kevin Pfeifer and the men of Engine 33 arrive and report to Chief Pfeifer. The chief seems surprised to see his brother now in front of him, for he knew that Kevin had put in for a couple of weeks off, combining vacation days and mutual trading of working tours with another officer, just to study for the upcoming captain's test.

20   "The fire is reported," Chief Pfeifer says, "on 78 or 80." There is none of the normal joking between them. Kevin nods, needing no further information, and then the two brothers lock their eyes together for a few moments of shared and worried concern before Kevin leads his men to the stairs. Their names can be read on their bunker coats as they depart: PFEIFER, BOYLE, ARCE, MAYNARD, KING, EVANS.

21   Rescue 1 arrives with Captain Hatton carrying an extra bottle of air, followed by Tom Schoales and the men of Engine 4. The affiliation of firefighters is designated by the front piece of their helmets, on which is their company and badge number. A group of police officers passes through the lobby and disappears into the stairwell, all with masks, air tanks, and blue hard hats. They are carrying large nylon satchels filled with their tools and ropes. These are members of the elite emergency service unit of the NYPD.

22   Chief of Safety Turi has also arrived and speaks with Chief Hayden. Assistant Chief of Department Callan steps into the lobby and takes command, almost automatically. He speaks into his handy-talkie, "Battalion 7 . . . Battalion 7 . . ."

23   Captain Jonas and the men of Ladder 6 enter and speak momentarily with Chief Hayden and then to Chief Pfeifer. Just as they take their orders there is a loud crashing sound outdoors. Debris, some large and burning, showers down from the crash floors, hitting the ground with such force that pieces shoot into the lobby like shrapnel. Someone says, "I just saw a plane go into the other building."

24   Tom Von Essen, the fire commissioner, appears, but no one goes to greet him. He is on the civilian side of the department, and his counsel will not be sought by the fire chiefs.

25   It is 9:03 A.M. All of the chiefs have radios to their ears, and they do not seem surprised by the news of *a second plane*. Maybe it is responsible for all the burning debris outside.

26   The fire commissioner walks over to the huddled chiefs and listens for a few moments, then moves away. A firefighter from Rescue 1 is standing before the command post waiting for someone to tell him the location of his company so that he can catch up with them. Another firefighter passes with a length of folded hose on his shoulder, ninety feet long and forty pounds.

27   The field com firefighter says, holding a phone, "I have Battalion 2 here."

28   Chief Pfeifer takes the line to speak to Chief McGovern, who has now gone up into the building. Chief Hayden says to an officer, "I have a report of trapped people in this tower up on 71."

29   The deputy fire commissioners are now on the scene and are standing off to the side with the fire commissioner. The firefighters of Ladder 1 move to the command post, receive their orders, and then quickly advance into the building. Chief Hayden is talking in the middle of the group of fire chiefs when he is suddenly interrupted by a loud report, as if a very large shotgun has been fired. Startled, he turns toward the sound and realizes it has come from the impact of a falling body, the first person to jump on this side of the building.

30   An African American firefighter nearby looks profoundly pensive as he moves to a wall and scans the lobby.

31   Deputy Commissioner Bill Feehan stops to assist a group of people in the lobby. One says, "Please take me out of here." Bill Feehan was once the chief of department, the highest uniformed rank, but today he knows that he is also on the civilian side. He directs them to proceed in the direction they are going, to keep moving, and reassures them. It is Commissioner Feehan's way, to keep everyone reassured.

32   The fire companies keep stepping up to the command post, as orderly as in a parade. They stop briefly as their company officer speaks to one of the chiefs to receive instruction.

33   Few firefighters are in the lobby at one time now, for they are all quickly and methodically dispatched to their work, going up, up, as high as the sixtieth floor. All the while there is an incessant whistling from the firefighters' Air Paks, the crashing of debris outside, and the frightful *bang, bang, bang* as the bodies begin to fall one after another.

34   Chief Hayden is in a discussion with the chief of safety.

35   "But," he is saying, "we have to get those people out!" He doesn't gesture, he doesn't flail his arms, but the tension in his voice is noticeable. All the chiefs are by now beginning to appreciate the extent of the terrible scene above them, getting worse by the second.

36   Engine 16 comes into the lobby as more emergency police officers and EMTs move in and out of the building. A probationary firefighter, his orange front piece denoting the short period of time he has served in the department, stands alone, waiting for his officer, looking ambivalent, as if he is trying to gauge the dangers that surround him. None of the firefighters remaining on the floor are talking among themselves. As they wait for their orders, every one of them exudes an undeniable apprehension, as if they suspect, each of them, that an almost certain doom faces this group. But for now, all they really know is that this is the toughest job they have ever faced.

37   A voice is heard, a chief's command, "All units down to the lobby."

38   There is another sudden crash and breaking glass, as bodies continue to fall from the very top floors, ninety floors up, traveling at 120 miles per hour. The sound has become a part of the environment, and hardly anyone reacts to it.

39   A field com firefighter stands before the opened suitcase of the command unit. There is a telephone connected to it and lined boxes with titles written across the open lid: STAGING AREA, ADDRESS, ALARMS, R&R, CONTROL. In the boxes are white tags for the fire companies in both buildings.

40   Father Mychal Judge appears, in his turnout jacket and white helmet. He stands off to the side, his hands on his hips, careful to stay out of the way of the huddles. The loud whistling in the background is now coming in series of fours, *scheeeeee, scheeeeee, scheeeeee.* It is from the alarm packs of firefighters that are going off, what they call the personal alert alarm, designed to locate them when they are down.

41   Yelling is the preferred form of communication between men who are not sharing radio waves. Police officers in shirtsleeves and men from the mayor's Office of Emergency Management are all about, mostly on cell phones and handy-talkies. On a balcony above them a crowd of men and women moves forward in an orderly way. Where have they come from, a stairwell or an elevator? These are survivors. The *bangs* of the falling bodies in the plaza are now regular, and almost syncopated.

42   Father Judge's lips move in silent prayer as four firefighters pass him carrying a Stokes basket. The Franciscan is so focused in his

meditation, so completely one with his inner voice as it is connecting with his God, that it appears he is straining himself and that the power of his prayer is outpacing the ability of his heart to keep up. Chief Pfeifer notices that the priest seems to be carrying a great burden in the midst of this disaster, and he is struck by his aloneness, praying so feverishly, like Christ in the Garden of Gethsemene. Finally, a man goes over to Father Judge and shakes his hand. "I'm Michael Angelini," he says. Father Judge is pleased to see him, for Michael's father, Joe, is a member of Rescue 1 and also the president of the department's Catholic fraternal association. "Ahh," Father Judge says. "Your mother and father were recently at my jubilee celebration. I will pray for your family, Michael." Father Judge taps him on the shoulder as well. It is the human thing. A handshake is not quite sufficient. Michael leaves the priest's side, and Father Judge is again left alone with his prayers. He has no one to counsel, no one to console, no one to shepherd. It is only him and God now, together, trying to work the greatest emergency New York has ever seen. It is obvious that Father Judge is trying to make some agreement about the safety of his firefighters.

43   A Port Authority police officer in white shirtsleeves has the attention, momentarily, of the chiefs. Chief Pfeifer tells a firefighter to write TOWER 1 across the panel top where they are standing, the elevator control bank. Then Chief Pfeifer begins to call in his radio for 44, when a loud noise is heard, a new and odd noise, a rumble. No, it is a roar.

44   It is 9:59 A.M.

45   Chief Pfeifer looks up to the ceiling as if to concentrate his hearing. Suddenly, he turns and runs toward the escalators behind him. Four fire patrolmen in their red helmets, from the insurance-industry-supported fire patrol, are just ahead, and Chief Callan and Chief Hayden are following closely behind.

46   And in the midst of the roar, a great cloud chases them, and then envelops them, until, almost immediately, all is black. It is black as midnight. The roar has lasted only sixteen seconds, a great rumble wave, flinging a tidal wave of ash against the building. And now, just as suddenly, all is quiet. It is a profound quiet, in a profound darkness. Within this stillness the men are one with their thoughts, and asking themselves, *Am I alive?*

47   After a few minutes pass there is a faint rustling. People begin to call out and flashlight beams shine vaguely through the whirling dust. It is reassuring to realize they are a sign that men in the lobby have survived. It seems as if it is snowing, thick clouds of pulverized concrete mixed with pulverized marble, and computers and office chairs, and teapots, and . . .

48   A voice asks, "Is everybody all right?"

49   "Yeah, I'm okay," someone answers.

50   "Hey guys, we need a hand here."

51   "Right. We got four guys."

52   "Top of the escalator."

53   "Yeah. Go."

54   "Joe?"

55   "Pete, where are you, Pete?"

56   "Where are the stairs?"

57   "Everybody join hands. Keep together."

58   "We gotta get out of here."

59   Chief Pfeifer radios: "All units, tower 1, evacuate the building."

60   "Here are the stairs."

61   Chief Pfeifer takes the lead when the group sees Father Judge on the ground, and they all rush to him. Chief Pfeifer loosens the priest's collar, but he isn't breathing. The prayers have consumed all his energy, and he wasn't able to survive the shock of this catastrophe, this enveloping cloud. They work on him now, mouth to mouth, but the environment is dangerous. They can't just stay here, and they look for something to place Father Judge in, a stretcher, a Stokes basket. Michael Angelini finds a wooden board, and they carefully lay the priest's body on it, and they lift him up and out.

62   The powder begins to lift as the sound of crashing continues. Chief Pfeifer reaches a mezzanine and heads down a corridor, completely gray with ash.

63   A firefighter who is following close behind asks, "Where are we headed?"

64   Another *bang*.

65   It is a long wide corridor, the pedestrian walkway over West Street, two stories above ground.

66   Chief Pfeifer is thinking, *The whole building came down and we have to get everyone safely out.*

67   Mayday, Mayday, Mayday.

68   He notices the blue tape strung between the columns of the corridor, as if someone had prognosticated an emergency scene.

69   "Battalion 1 to Division 1."

70   "You okay?"

71   He has raised the division and learns that they have evacuated safely through a window on the east side of West Street. He turns and walks the long corridor for the third time until he comes to a set of stairs that take him down to the street.

72   On West Street the rigs are parked up and down the road, the apparatus of Rescue 1, High-rise Unit 3, pumpers and ladder trucks from Manhattan and Brooklyn.

73   The chief hears someone say, "I can't believe this can happen."

74   There is an eerie, otherworldly nature to the surface of the street. It is like the soft earth beneath the boardwalk at Coney Island. But here

the ground is strewn with millions of pieces of paper. It is quiet, a heavy quiet like the quiet beneath the boardwalk at night.

75   Just a sliver of the Vista Hotel is standing. Could it be? Tower 2, the south tower, has come down, and the entire tract across West Street that had once been the tallest building in the world is now a field of rubble and raging fire, and . . .

76   And people. How many people were in that building? How many cops? How many firefighters?

77   *And Kevin*, Chief Pfeifer thinks. At least Kevin is in the north tower. He lifts his radio transmitter to his mouth.

78   "Battalion 1 to Engine 33," he asks searchingly. "Battalion 1 to Engine 33. Lieutenant Pfeifer?"

79   But there is no answer.

80   The air above the pile that was tower 2 is a haze and now an impenetrable cloud and gold with fire.

81   Chief Pfeifer is standing beneath the overpass on the Vesey Street side, the overpass that crosses West Street and connects the Financial Center to the World Trade Center. He surveys the site before him, and he is planning strategy.

82   Two trees are lying in the street, still green, but a gray green.

83   He walks to Vesey Street and meets with Chief Cassano and Chief Hayden, still uncertain about exactly what has happened, for smoke obscures everything. The south tower has collapsed. But all of it, half of it?

84   It is 10:28 A.M. when the sound, that terrible roar erupts again, as people scream, "Run, run!"

85   Everyone is rushing in a different direction; Chief Pfeifer heads toward the river, still accompanied by the cameraman who is following him around. He doesn't see that just behind him a policewoman has been hit by a piece of flying glass and has been thrown to the ground. Someone stops to help her as Chief Pfeifer darts between a car and a truck. The cameraman hits the ground and the chief, in his bunker gear, falls on top of him, covering him from the debris crashing all around them.

86   As it had before, the cloud changes from a brown haze to one of complete blackness. There is just one thought in Joe Pfeifer's mind now: *Oh, God, I want to see my family again*. He closes his eyes and waits for something to crush him.

87   But the din stops, and the smoke begins to lift a little, lightening in color back to dirty brown. Then, suddenly, loud gunshots ring out, just down the street at Vesey and West. For one fleeting moment the thought of an invading army crosses his mind. *Now they are shooting at me*. His eyes are crusted, and he can barely see, but he makes his way back to the corner of West and Vesey.

88   It is almost as if snow had fallen, for the gray dust mutes all ambient sound. But, eerily, there is no sound, no screaming, not even crackling from his two radios.

89   He has no idea how many people are lost, or where they are, or where his brother might be. *I am out here*, he thinks, *I am more visible. My brother will come looking for me. He'll find me easily enough.* He sees the rig of Engine 33 on Vesey Street and goes to check the riding list. He knows Kevin is on the list, but, still, just to make certain, he will check everything.

90   Each chief has stepped out from the place he has sought for cover and heads for a different area of the devastation. They seem to develop a sectoring plan without articulating or drawing it, without the formal convention. They consult with one another by radio, remaining in their separate locations, directing work, any work that advances the idea of rescue. Get the men out. Get the people out. There is no actual command structure.

91   Chief Pfeifer receives a communication that several firefighters are trapped in the north tower, Chief Picciotto with Captain Jonas and Ladder 6, between the second and fifth floors. But where could what used to be these floors even be? That operation lasts for several hours, and it is reassuring when the men are rescued along with a civilian man and woman.

92   The chief tries again and again to place a phone call to his wife, but every line he gets goes dead. He repeatedly circles the entire site looking for his brother. He doesn't see Kevin, or anyone from Engine 33. He tries to ignore the pain that is pressing at the center of his stomach, the feeling of everything sinking away.

93   It is 11:00 P.M.

94   He can't walk anymore and looks for a car, a bus, anything to take him back to the firehouse. But there is nothing, so he sets off on foot. On Duane Street, the firehouse is dark. He doesn't stop to change clothes but gets in his car and drives home to Middle Village. Because all the bridges, highways, and tunnels are closed, he has to keep presenting identification.

95   It is near midnight when he arrives home, covered, head to toe, with garbage and soot. He goes upstairs where his wife, Ginny, rushes out, hugging him and crying, followed by his two children. The four of them stand in the hall, locked in their embrace.

96   He is exhausted and can barely keep his injured, beaten eyes open. He thinks of his brother, his last thought of the day. *We will find him tomorrow*, he thinks. *We will find Kevin tomorrow.*

✧ *Evaluating the Text*

    1. This account from the perspective of Chief Pfeifer is a harrowing portrayal of the challenges that faced the rescuers. Which details did you find particularly compelling in re-creating the experiences that confronted the NYFD (New York Fire Department) on September 11, 2001?

2. How did the personal encounters that Smith reports enhance the drama of what Chief Pfeifer and his men went through on that day?

✦ Exploring Different Perspectives

1. Compare what motivates Victor Villaseñor in "Rain of Gold" and the firefighters that Smith describes in this essay in terms of the physical and psychological challenges they confront.

2. How do the accounts of Smith and Tomoyuki Iwashita offer complementary perspectives on the everyday lives of office workers until the extraordinary event Smith describes endangers them and transforms them into tragic victims along with their rescuers?

✦ Extending Viewpoints through Writing

1. In a short essay, discuss the impact of the events of September 11, 2001 on any aspect of American society.

2. How did the events of September 11, 2001 alter the public perception of firefighters, the police, and EMS workers in terms of the work they do every day?

Victor Villaseñor

Rain of Gold

—————◆—————

Victor Villaseñor was born in 1940 in the barrio of Carlsbad, California, to immigrant parents. He attended the University of San Diego and Santa Clara University. Villaseñor was a construction worker in California from 1965 to 1970 and has attained recognition as an authentic voice of the Chicano community. Although he flunked English in college (because of his fifth-grade reading ability), later trips to Mexico and introduction to art, history, and works of literature by Homer, F. Scott Fitzgerald, and James Joyce crystallized his decision to become a writer. Completely self-taught, Villaseñor wrote for ten years, completing nine novels and sixty-five short stories, and he received more than 260 rejections before he sold his first book Macho! *in 1973. He since has written an acclaimed work of nonfiction,* Rain of Gold *(1992), from which the following excerpt is drawn, and its sequel,* Wild Steps of Heaven *(1995), which is a saga of the Villaseñor family. More recently, he has written a historical narrative,* Authentic Family-Style Mexican Cooking *(1997).*

Mexico was inhabited as far back as 20,000 B.C. Before the arrival of the Spanish in the early sixteenth century, great Indian civilizations, such as the Aztecs and Mayas, flourished. A wave of Spanish explorers, including Hernán Cortés, arrived in the 1500s, overthrew the Aztec empire, and turned Mexico into a colony of Spain, until Mexico achieved its independence in 1821. Although recently Mexico's economy has been on the rebound, previous cycles of economic instability and the earthquake that devastated Mexico City (one of the largest cities in the world with a population of nearly 17 million) in 1985, have led many to cross the border into the United States in hope of finding work.

In 1988, Carlos Salinas de Gortari was elected president, promising to bring democratic reforms. Legislative elections in 1991 endorsed Gortari's efforts. Mexico, along with Canada and the United States, negotiated the North American Free Trade Agreement (NAFTA), which is intended to reduce tariffs and increase trade between these countries. A new government was formed in 1994 under the leadership of Ernesto Zedillo of the Institutional Revolutionary Party (PRI). Following the devaluation of the peso in December 1994, an emergency economic plan was introduced to reduce inflation and stimulate investment, and it appears to have been successful. Vincente Fox was elected president in 2000.

Before You Read

Notice how Villaseñor structures this account to build up to the ultimate confrontation while at the same time giving an accurate picture of racial attitudes in the early twentieth century.

1   The weeks passed and Doña Margarita prayed to God, asking him to heal her son's wounds. God heard her prayers and the bandages came off. Juan could see in the broken bathroom mirror that he had a long, swollen scar, thick as a worm, across his chin and all the way to his left ear. Turning his head side to side, he discovered that if he lowered his chin and kept his head slightly turned to the left, the scar wasn't quite as noticeable.

2   He decided to grow a beard and keep it until the red ridge of swollen flesh went down. In some ways he'd been very lucky. It had been such a clean, razor-sharp knife, the wound would eventually disappear.

3   A couple of days later, Juan went to town to look for work. He was broke. The two bastards had stolen all of his money. He had to get some tortillas on the table before he went searching for those two sons-of- bitches to kill them.

4   In town, Juan found out that they were hiring at a local rock quarry, so he walked out to the quarry while the sun was still low. Getting there, Juan could see that there were at least fifty other Mexicans waiting to be hired ahead of him. The tall, lanky Anglo who was doing the hiring dropped the clipboard to his side. "Well, that's it for today," he said. "But you guys just all come on out tomorrow and maybe you'll get lucky."

5   Hearing the word, "lucky," Juan became suspicious. As a professional gambler, he never liked to leave anything to chance. He glanced around at his fellow countrymen, wondering what they were going to do about this. But he could see that they weren't going to do anything.

6   Juan took up ground. "Excuse me," he said. "But I'm new in town, so I'd like to know how you do your hiring. Should I give you my name for tomorrow, or do you only hire the same men every day?"

7   The tall Anglo smiled at him as if he'd said something ridiculous. "What's your name?" asked the Anglo.

8   "Juan Villa*señor*," said Juan, pronouncing the double "l's" of his name like a "y" and giving his name a dignified, natural sound.

9   "Well, Juan Vilee-senoreee," said the foreman, twisting his name into something ugly, "you just come on out here tomorrow if you want a job. That's all you gotta do. You ain't got to know no more. Catch my lingo, *amigo?*" And saying this, the man rocked back and forth on his feet and spit on the ground. Juan could see that the man was so mad that his jaw was twitching. But Juan said nothing. He simply lowered

his eyes and turned to go. His heart was pounding. Why, this bastard had twisted his name into a piece of dog shit.

10   The other workmen moved aside, letting Juan pass by. Juan could feel the foreman's eyes burning into his back. But he already knew that he was never going to return. This bastard could take his job and stick it up his ass, as far as Juan was concerned.

11   But Juan had gone no more than a few yards when another Anglo came out of the office. "Doug!" he yelled at the man with the clipboard. "We need another powder man! Ask them if any of 'em has a license!"

12   "Hell, Jim, they ain't nothing but Mexicans," he said.

13   "Ask 'em," repeated the big, beefy man named Jim.

14   "¡Oye! ¡Espérense!" called Doug in perfectly good Spanish. "Do any of you have a powder license?"

15   Juan had a license to handle dynamite from the Copper Queen in Montana, but he glanced around to see if anyone had priority over him. No one raised his hand.

16   "I got one," said Juan.

17   "Where'd you get your license?" asked Doug.

18   "From the Copper Queen Mining Company," said Juan.

19   "Oh, in Arizona," said Jim.

20   "No, from Montana," said Juan.

21   The two Anglos glanced at each other. They were a long way from Montana.

22   "Let's see your license," said Doug.

23   Calmly, deliberately, Juan walked back to the two Anglos. They both towered over him. But Juan's mammoth neck and thick shoulders were wider than either of theirs.

24   He brought out his wallet and carefully took the paper out of his billfold that said he was licensed to do dynamite work. He handed it to Doug, who unfolded it, glanced it over, then handed it to Jim.

25   Reading it, Jim said, "Looks good to me," and he handed the paper back to Doug. "Hire him."

26   "All right, Juan Villaseñor-eee," said Doug, pronouncing Juan's last name with less of a mean twist this time, "you got a job for the day. But just one little screw-up and you're out! Now go over to that shed and ask for Kenny. Show him your license and he'll fix you up."

27   "Sure," said Juan, taking back his license and going across the yard.

28   Everywhere were Mexicans bent over shovels and picks. It was a huge rock quarry. They looked like ants crawling about the great slab of rock that had been cut away from the mountain. Teams of horses and mules were moving the loads of rock, and the Mexicans drove these teams, too.

29   At the toolshed, Juan asked for Kenny. An old Anglo came up. He was chewing tobacco. He was short and thick and his eyes sparkled

with humor. Juan liked him immediately. He didn't have that dried-out, sour-mean look of Doug's. He handed him his license.

30   "So how long you been a powder man, eh?" asked Kenny, looking over the license.

31   "Oh, three or four years," said Juan.

32   "All in Montana?" asked Kenny, walking over to the sledge hammers and bars.

33   Juan froze, but only for a moment. He'd originally learned his trade in prison at Turkey Flat, but he saw no reason for this man to know that. So he lied. "Yes," he said, "all in Montana."

34   "I see," said Kenny, coming forward with a sledge and a fistful of bars. He looked into Juan's eyes, but Juan didn't shy away. "Well," said the old man, handing Juan the tools, "where or how a man learned his trade ain't my concern." He spat a long stream of brown juice. "What interests me is the result," he added.

35   Walking around the shed, they headed for the cliff of cut rock in the distance. Climbing halfway up the face of the cliff, Kenny showed Juan where he wanted him to drill his holes to set the charges. Juan set his tools down and slipped off his jacket. The other dynamite men were already hard at work, drilling their holes. They were all Anglos.

36   Juan glanced up at the sun and saw that it was already beginning to get hot. He slipped his shirt out of his pants so it would hang loose and the sweat could drip off him freely. He'd learned this trick from an old Greek when he'd worked in Montana. A big, loose shirt could work like an air conditioner. Once the sweat started coming fast, the garment would hold it and let the sun evaporate the sweat like a cooling unit.

37   Juan could feel the other powder men watching him. A couple of them had already stripped down to their waists and they were bare-chested to the sun. They were all huge, well-muscled men and towered over Juan. But Juan felt no need to hurry or show off. He'd worked with the best of them up in Montana before he'd gone to work for Duel. He knew his trade.

38   Spitting into the palms of his thick hands, Juan set his feet and picked up his short bar with his left hand and his sledge hammer with his right. He centered the point of the bar on the rock in front of him and he raised the sledge over his head, coming down real soft and easy on the head of the bar. He did this again and again, turning the bar each time with his left hand. He knew that Kenny and the other powder men were watching him, but he never let on. He just kept up a soft, steady, easy pace. He wasn't about to push the sledge. He would let the weight of the big hammer do the work for him all day long. Only a stupid, young fool pushed the iron. An experienced man let the iron do the work for him.

39   Kenny brought out his chew, cut off a piece, put it in his mouth and continued watching, but Juan still felt no nervousness. He'd worked at his trade for three months at Turkey Flat, and in Montana he'd done it

for nearly three years, so he knew that he was good at his job. He wasn't one of these men who rushed in the morning to show off to the boss and then had nothing left to give in the afternoon. No, he could work all day long, from sunup until sundown, without ever slowing down. In fact, he was so steady and sure at his job that he'd won many a bet in Montana by placing a dime on the head of the bar and hitting it so smoothly that the dime wouldn't fall off, even after a hundred hits. An old Greek had also taught him this trick. Why, he could make the sledge and the bar sing, once he got going.

40   It was noon, and the sunlight was blinding hot on the great slab of rock. Juan had gone past all the Anglo powder men except one. This Anglo was huge. His name was Jack, and he wasn't just big, he was extremely well-muscled. But Juan wasn't impressed by this. He'd seen many big, strong men collapse under the hot, noon sun. And Jack had been one of the first to strip to the waist to show off his muscles, so he was now sweating fast and Juan knew that he wouldn't be able to keep up his pace all afternoon.

41   Juan decided to slow down and not push the man. He'd already proven himself. All he had to do now was give an honest day's work.

42   Then the horn blew, and it was time to eat lunch. The powder men all took their tools and put them in the shade so they wouldn't get too hot to handle when they came back to work.

43   Jack, the big man, came walking up close to Juan. It looked like he was going to say hello to him and shake his hand; but he didn't. He just laughed and turned away, joking with the other powder men. Juan didn't take offense, figuring that he was just having fun. He walked alongside Jack, hoping that maybe he and the big man could quit the competition that had started up between them and they could become friends. After all, he'd become friends with many Greeks and Anglos in Montana. But walking across the yard, the powder men acted as if Juan didn't exist.

44   Then, when they got in line to wash up before they ate, and it was Juan's turn to wash, the man in front of Juan didn't hand him the tin cup. No, he dropped it, instead. At first, Juan thought it was an accident, but then, when he bent over to pick up the cup, the man kicked it away.

45   Juan stood up and saw that all the powder men were sneering at him, especially Jack, who was grinning ear-to-ear. Quickly, Juan lowered his eyes so none of them would see what he was thinking. And he turned and walked away, tall and slow and with all the dignity he could muster. These smart-ass *gringos* had just made up his mind for him. This afternoon they were going to see a Greek-trained drilling machine.

46   He never once turned to glance back at them. No, he just kept going across the yard as slowly and proudly as he could. Getting to the Mexicans under the shade of a tree, he was given a cup when it was his turn to drink and wash up. But he had no lunch to eat, so he just sat down to rest.

47   Oh, it was a good thing that he hadn't brought his gun to work, or he would have been tempted to kill Jack and the seven other powder men. No one ridiculed him. Not even in prison when he'd been a child and they'd tried to rape him. He was his father's son when it came to having a terrible temper. He was truly of the crazy Villa*señors*. Why, he'd once seen his father grab a mule's leg that had kicked him and yank it up to bite it, dislocating the mule's hip. Then his father had beaten the mule to death with his bare fists.

48   Juan was sitting there, seething with rage, when a thick-necked Mexican named Julio called him over.

49   "*Amigo*," he said, "come and eat with us."

50   Julio and several other Mexican men were sitting under a tree, heating their tacos on a shovel that they'd washed.

51   "No, *gracias*," said Juan, "you go ahead and eat . . . to your health, my blessings." And saying this, Juan moved his hand, palm up, welcoming the man to fulfill himself. It was a very Mexican gesture, one especially common in the mountainous area of Jalisco.

52   "So you're from Jalisco, eh?" said Julio, turning over the bean tacos with a stick on the shovel.

53   "Why, yes, how did you know?" asked Juan.

54   Julio laughed. "Oh, I'm just a visionary from Guanajuato," he said, "who's seen that gesture of the hand too many times not to know a *tapatío*." A *tapatío* was what the people from Jalisco were called.

55   "Come on, don't be so proud," said another Mexican named Rodolfo. "You got nothing to eat and you got to be strong for this afternoon." Rodolfo was tall and slender and had pockmarks all over his face, but he wasn't hard to look at. His eyes had a twinkle of mischief, and he had that confident air of a man who'd seen many battles. "We all saw that little movement of the cup across the yard. Those powder men, they're all *cabrones!*"[1]

56   "You saw it, eh?" said Juan, glancing across the yard to the powder men who were all sitting together and eating.

57   "Of course," said Rodolfo, "and we knew it was coming the moment we learned that one of our people had gotten a job so elevated."

58   "Go ahead," said Julio to Juan, taking the shovel off the little fire, "take a taco before this son-of-a-bitch schoolteacher from Monterrey eats all our lunches again." Saying this, Julio picked up one of the tacos with his fingertips from the hot shovel and tossed it to Juan, who reflexively caught it. "Eat, *hombre*," he said to Juan good-naturedly, "so you can fart like a burro and screw those *gringo* sons-of-bitches this afternoon!"

59   "Which leads us to a very important question," said Rodolfo, the tall schoolteacher from Monterrey, "just how'd you ever get up there, anyway?"

---

[1]*Cabrones* is a derogatory term that slanders masculinity

60   "I have a powder license," said Juan, starting to eat.

61   "Oh, and how did you manage that miracle?" asked Rodolfo. "Hell, we got men here who know how to drill and set dynamite with the best of them, but none of them has been able to get a license." He ate his taco in two huge bites, working his big, lean jaws like a wolf.

62   "In Montana," said Juan, eating in small, courteous bites to show that he wasn't starving—but he was. "The Greeks up there, they'd never seen a Mexican, and so they'd thought I was Chinese and they made me a driller, thinking all Chinese know powder."

63   The Mexicans burst out laughing. But Rodolfo laughed the hardest of all.

64   "So that's how it's done, eh?" said Rodolfo. "We *Mejicanos* got to be Chinese!"

65   "It worked for me," said Juan, laughing, too.

66   "I'll be damned," said the teacher, reaching for another taco. "Next you'll tell me that we'd be better off if we were Negroes, too."

67   "Shit, yes!" said Julio, who was very dark-skinned. "The blacker the better!"

68   They all laughed and ate together and Juan felt good to be back among his people. The jokes, the gestures, and the way they laughed with their heads thrown back and their mouths open, it was all so familiar.

69   Then the horn blew, and it was time to get back to work. The pock-faced man came close to Juan. "Be careful, my friend," he said. "That scar you wear may only be a small token compared to what awaits you this afternoon."

70   Juan nodded, having thought that no one could see his scar with his five-day-old beard. "*Gracias*," he said, "but I haven't gotten this far in life without being as wary as the chick with the coyote."

71   The tall man laughed, offering Juan his hand. "Rodolfo Rochin."

72   Juan took the schoolteacher's hand. "Juan Villa*señor*," he said.

73   "He's right," said Julio, coming up. "They're going to try and kill you. Hell, if they don't, soon we'll have all their jobs."

74   Juan nodded. "I'll be careful," he said.

75   "Good," said the thick man. "Julio Sanchez."

76   "Juan Villa*señor*," said Juan once again.

77   Then Juan turned and started across the open yard, and all the Mexicans watched after him. Not one of their people had ever worked up on the cliff before.

78   Picking up his tools, Juan walked by the powder men and climbed up the cliff. Jack came up and took his place alongside Juan, grinning at him. But Juan paid him no attention and went to work, iron singing at a good, steady pace.

79   Jack picked up his sledge and tore at the rock. He was still half a hole ahead of Juan and wanted to keep it like that. The big man pounded at the rock, arms pumping, iron pounding, and he tried to

pull farther ahead of Juan. But Juan only smiled, glancing up at the hot sun, his ally.

80   The sun was going down, and it was the last hour of the day when Juan came up even with Jack. The other powder men stopped their work and watched. Jack grinned, still feeling confident, and began his new hole. He was huge and rippling with muscle, but Juan could see that he was all used up because he just didn't have the rhythm of the hammer down to a steady song.

81   Juan grinned back at Jack, spat into his hands, and began his new hole, too. But at a much slower pace. And the big man pulled ahead of him and the other powder men laughed, truly enjoying it. But Rodolfo and Julio and the other Mexicans down below knew what was coming. So they stopped their work and looked up at the two men pounding the iron up on the tall cliff.

82   The muscles were standing on the big man's back, and his forearms were corded up into huge ropes. But still, Juan kept going at a slow, steady, easy pace, fully realizing that the boiling white sun was on his side and the *gringo* wouldn't be able to keep up his reckless pace for long.

83   Kenny saw what was going on, and he started for the cliff to bring the senseless competition to a stop when Doug came up behind him.

84   "Don't, Shorty," he said to Kenny. "Let that little bastard kill himself, trying to keep up with Big Jack."

85   Kenny never even smiled. Juan was his own size, so he just spat out a stream of tobacco, already knowing who was going to win. "Whatever you say, Doug," he said.

86   And Kenny and Doug took up watch, too.

87   Jack was pounding on, tearing into his bar with his big sledge, but he could see that Juan was keeping up with him at a much slower rhythm. It seemed like magic. Juan was going so easy and, yet, his iron was still drilling into the stone at a good pace.

88   Jack began to tire but he was tough, so he just forced his body to go harder. His lungs screamed for air, his huge muscles began to cramp, but he'd die before he gave up and let a Mexican beat him.

89   But then here came Juan, coming in for the kill, and he now picked up the pace, too. Juan was catching up to Jack, closing fast, and then going past him with good, steady power when, suddenly, a bunch of bars came sliding down the face of the cliff from above them.

90   "Watch out!" yelled Kenny.

91   Juan just managed to leap out of the way before the bars struck him.

92   Kenny turned to Doug and saw that he was grinning ear-to-ear. "All right!" barked Kenny. "No more of this horseshit! Now all of you, get back to work! You got thirty minutes to quitting time, damn it!"

93   Turning in their tools that afternoon, Kenny took Juan aside. "*Amigo*," he said, "you and me, we're short, so we don't got to always go around being the big man. Jack, he's not so bad, believe me. I know

him. It's just that a lot is expected of him." He cut a new chew with his pocket knife, offering Juan some, but Juan refused. "I like your work," he added, putting the new cut in his mouth, "you ease off *mañana* and I promise you that you got a job here as long as I'm powder foreman."

94 Juan looked into the old man's bright, blue eyes, blue like his own father's. "You got a deal," he said.

95 "Good," said Kenny, and he put his knife away and stuck out his hand and Juan took it.

96 This was the first time that Juan had ever met a man who had even bigger, thicker hands than his own. Why, Kenny's hands were monstrous, just like his own father's.

97 That day, Juan Salvador was paid two dollars, twice as much as the regular laborers. Walking back to town that afternoon with his people, Juan was a hero. He was the Mexican who screwed the *cabrón gringo!*

✦ Evaluating the Text

1. How do the initial reactions to Juan's request for work reveal the racial prejudice against Mexicans that existed in his father's time?

2. How does the encounter between Juan and Jack dramatize the separation of Anglos from Mexicans and the antagonism between them that was quite typical in the work gangs?

3. What means does Villaseñor use to structure the account in a suspenseful way?

✦ Exploring Different Perspectives

1. How do the accounts by Villaseñor and Dennis Smith (see "Report from Ground Zero") involve proving oneself in dangerous situations?

2. Discuss the respective struggle against the ongoing stereotypes based on gender or ethnicity in the accounts by Villaseñor and Barbara Ehrenreich (see "Nickel-and-Dimed").

✦ Extending Viewpoints through Writing

1. Did you ever have to prove yourself against prevailing stereotypes? What were they? Describe what happened?

2. In several places in Villaseñor's account, he makes a point of commenting on the more efficient way of working that his father had developed, which enabled him to outperform seemingly more powerful men. What techniques have you developed to make your work, including study habits, more efficient? Describe them and tell how you developed them.

Machado de Assis

A Canary's Ideas

♦

Joaquim María Machado de Assis (1839–1908) was born in Rio de Janiero where he lived most of his life. He is considered Brazil's greatest writer and is best known for his keen psychological insight and pessimistic vision revealed in his subtly ironic novels. His father, a house painter, was a mulatto Brazilian, the son of former slaves; his mother was a white Portuguese immigrant from the Azores. Machado attended only five years of elementary school. Beyond that, he educated himself and became fluent in several languages, including French, Spanish, and English. He began supporting himself at age fifteen, working at a variety of jobs, including typesetting, proofreading, and editing. In 1874 he entered the civil service in the Ministry of Agriculture and for the last thirty-four years of his life led the quiet, unturbulent life of a happily married, but childless, government bureaucrat. He used the financial security of his civil service position to carry on an astonishingly prolific career as a writer. Machado's early love was the theater, and by the time he was thirty he had written nineteen plays and opera librettos, most of them produced by theater companies in the city. He was also a skilled poet and regular newspaper columnist. After 1870, he turned his attention primarily to short stories and novels. His first great success was Epitaph of a Small Winner *(1881), written from a startlingly original point of view, namely the posthumous memoirs of the narrator, Braz Cubas—a tongue-in-cheek account of his life.*

Machado's second novel, Philosopher or Dog? *(1891), and his acknowledged masterpiece,* Dom Casmurro *(1900), both feature protagonists who are reflective skeptics tinged with madness. These unreliable narrators are a feature of his work. His close attention to the protagonist's stream of consciousness, his cool irony, unexpected juxtaposition of times, characters, and value systems conveyed in a forceful, unique style anticipate many features of the twentieth-century novel. He is now acknowledged by critics to be a master of the early modern novel, equal to Gustave Flaubert and Henry James. His complete works fill thirty-one volumes, and he is the author of over 100 short stories, of which "A Canary's Ideas," translated by Jack Schmitt and Lorie Ishimatsu (1976), is typical. In this story, an egocentric, reasoning canary forms his impression of the universe by what surrounds him at the moment.*

The largest South American country, Brazil occupies almost half of the continent and is the only country in South America whose culture,

*history, and language were shaped by Portugal, whose first permanent
settlement in what is present-day São Paulo occurred in 1532. Since the
Europeans landed in 1500, the population of native tribes has been reduced from an estimated 6 million to 200,000 today. Brazil's population
is an amalgam of Indian, black, and European strains. In 2002, Brazil
won its fifth World Cup in soccer.*

Before You Read

Consider whether the narrator's egotism is symbolized by the canary.

✦

1   A man by the name of Macedo, who had a fancy for ornithology,
related to some friends an incident so extraordinary that no one took
him seriously. Some came to believe he had lost his mind. Here is a
summary of his narration.

2   At the beginning of last month, as I was walking down the street, a
carriage darted past me and nearly knocked me to the ground. I escaped by quickly side-stepping into a secondhand shop. Neither the
racket of the horse and carriage nor my entrance stirred the proprietor,
dozing in a folding chair at the back of the shop. He was a man of
shabby appearance: his beard was the color of dirty straw, and his
head was covered by a tattered cap which probably had not found a
buyer. One could not guess that there was any story behind him, as
there could have been behind some of the objects he sold, nor could
one sense in him that austere, disillusioned sadness inherent in the objects which were remnants of past lives.

3   The shop was dark and crowded with the sort of old, bent, broken,
tarnished, rusted articles ordinarily found in secondhand shops, and
everything was in that state of semidisorder befitting such an establishment. This assortment of articles, though banal, was interesting.
Pots without lids, lids without pots, buttons, shoes, locks, a black shirt,
straw hats, fur hats, picture frames, binoculars, dress coats, a fencing
foil, a stuffed dog, a pair of slippers, gloves, nondescript vases,
epaulets, a velvet satchel, two hatracks, a slingshot, a thermometer,
chairs, a lithographed portrait by the late Sisson, a backgammon
board, two wire masks for some future Carnival—all this and more,
which I either did not see or do not remember, filled the shop in the
area around the door, propped up, hung, or displayed in glass cases as
old as the objects inside them. Further inside the shop were many objects of similar appearance. Predominant were the large objects—
chests of drawers, chairs, and beds—some of which were stacked on
top of others which were lost in the darkness.

4   I was about to leave, when I saw a cage hanging in the doorway. It
was as old as everything else in the shop, and I expected it to be empty

so it would fit in with the general appearance of desolation. However, it wasn't empty. Inside, a canary was hopping about. The bird's color, liveliness, and charm added a note of life and youth to that heap of wreckage. It was the last passenger of some wrecked ship, who had arrived in the shop as complete and happy as it had originally been. As soon as I looked at the bird, it began to hop up and down, from perch to perch, as if it meant to tell me that a ray of sunshine was frolicking in the midst of that cemetery. I'm using this image to describe the canary only because I'm speaking to rhetorical people, but the truth is that the canary thought about neither cemetery nor sun, according to what it told me later. Along with the pleasure the sight of the bird brought me, I felt indignation regarding its destiny and softly murmured these bitter words:

5   "What detestable owner had the nerve to rid himself of this bird for a few cents? Or what indifferent soul, not wishing to keep his late master's pet, gave it away to some child, who sold it so he could make a bet on a soccer game?"

6   The canary, sitting on top of its perch, trilled this reply:

7   "Whoever you may be, you're certainly not in your right mind. I had no detestable owner, nor was I given to any child to sell. Those are the delusions of a sick person. Go and get yourself cured, my friend. . . ."

8   "What?" I interrupted, not having had time to become astonished. "So your master didn't sell you to this shop? It wasn't misery or laziness that brought you, like a ray of sunshine, to this cemetery?"

9   "I don't know what you mean by 'sunshine' or 'cemetery.' If the canaries you've seen use the first of those names, so much the better, because it sounds pretty, but really, I'm sure you're confused."

10   "Excuse me, but you couldn't have come here by chance, all alone. Has your master always been that man sitting over there?"

11   "What master? That man over there is my servant. He gives me food and water every day, so regularly that if I were to pay him for his services, it would be no small sum, but canaries don't pay their servants. In fact, since the world belongs to canaries, it would be extravagant for them to pay for what is already in the world."

12   Astonished by these answers, I didn't know what to marvel at more—the language or the ideas. The language, even though it entered my ears as human speech, was uttered by the bird in the form of charming trills. I looked all around me so I could determine if I were awake and saw that the street was the same, and the shop was the same dark, sad, musty place. The canary, moving from side to side, was waiting for me to speak. I then asked if it were lonely for the infinite blue space. . . .

13   "But, my dear man," trilled the canary, "what does 'infinite blue space' mean?"

14   "But, pardon me, what do you think of this world? What is the world to you?"

15   "The world," retorted the canary, with a certain professorial air, "is a secondhand shop with a small rectangular bamboo cage hanging from a nail. The canary is lord of the cage it lives in and the shop that surrounds it. Beyond that, everything is illusion and deception."

16   With this, the old man woke up and approached me, dragging his feet. He asked me if I wanted to buy the canary. I asked if he had acquired it in the same way he had acquired the rest of the objects he sold and learned that he had bought it from a barber, along with a set of razors.

17   "The razors are in very good condition," he said.

18   "I only want the canary."

19   I paid for it, ordered a huge, circular cage of wood and wire, and had it placed on the veranda of my house so the bird could see the garden, the fountain, and a bit of blue sky.

20   It was my intention to do a lengthy study of this phenomenon, without saying anything to anyone until I could astound the world with my extraordinary discovery. I began by alphabetizing the canary's language in order to study its structure, its relation to music, the bird's appreciation of aesthetics, its ideas and recollections. When this philological and psychological analysis was done, I entered specifically into the study of canaries: their origin, their early history, the geology and flora of the Canary Islands, the bird's knowledge of navigation, and so forth. We conversed for hours while I took notes, and it waited, hopped about, and trilled.

21   As I have no family other than two servants, I ordered them not to interrupt me, even to deliver a letter or an urgent telegram or to inform me of an important visitor. Since they both knew about my scientific pursuits, they found my orders perfectly natural and did not suspect that the canary and I understood each other.

22   Needless to say, I slept little, woke up two or three times each night, wandered about aimlessly, and felt feverish. Finally, I returned to my work in order to reread, add, and emend. I corrected more than one observation, either because I had misunderstood something or because the bird had not expressed it clearly. The definition of the world was one of these. Three weeks after the canary's entrance into my home, I asked it to repeat to me its definition of the world.

23   "The world," it answered, "is a sufficiently broad garden with a fountain in the middle, flowers, shrubbery, some grass, clear air, and a bit of blue up above. The canary, lord of the world, lives in a spacious cage, white and circular, from which it looks out on the rest of the world. Everything else is illusion and deception."

24   The language of my treatise also suffered some modifications, and I saw that certain conclusions which had seemed simple were actually presumptuous. I still could not write the paper I was to send to the National Museum, the Historical Institute, and the German universities,

not due to a lack of material but because I first had to put together all my observations and test their validity. During the last few days, I neither left the house, answered letters, nor wanted to hear from friends or relatives. The canary was everything to me. One of the servants had the job of cleaning the bird's cage and giving it food and water every morning. The bird said nothing to him, as if it knew the man was completely lacking in scientific background. Besides, the service was no more than cursory, as the servant was not a bird lover.

25   One Saturday I awoke ill, my head and back aching. The doctor ordered complete rest. I was suffering from an excess of studying and was not to read or even think, nor was I even to know what was going on in the city or the rest of the outside world. I remained in this condition for five days. On the sixth day I got up, and only then did I find out that the canary, while under the servant's care, had flown out of its cage. My first impulse was to strangle the servant—I was choking with indignation and collapsed into my chair, speechless and bewildered. The guilty man defended himself, swearing he had been careful, but the wily bird had nevertheless managed to escape.

26   "But didn't you search for it?"

27   "Yes, I did, sir. First it flew up to the roof, and I followed it. It flew to a tree, and then who knows where it hid itself? I've been asking around since yesterday. I asked the neighbors and the local farmers, but no one has seen the bird."

28   I suffered immensely. Fortunately, the fatigue left me within a few hours, and I was soon able to go out to the veranda and the garden. There was no sign of the canary. I ran everywhere, making inquiries and posting announcements, all to no avail. I had already gathered my notes together to write my paper, even though it would be disjointed and incomplete, when I happened to visit a friend who had one of the largest and most beautiful estates on the outskirts of town. We were taking a stroll before dinner when this question was trilled to me:

29   "Greetings, Senhor Macedo, where have you been since you disappeared?"

30   It was the canary, perched on the branch of a tree. You can imagine how I reacted and what I said to the bird. My friend presumed I was mad, but the opinions of friends are of no importance to me. I spoke tenderly to the canary and asked it to come home and continue our conversations in that world of ours, composed of a garden, a fountain, a veranda, and a white circular cage.

31   "What garden? What fountain?"

32   "The world, my dear bird."

33   "What world? I see you haven't lost any of your annoying professorial habits. The world," it solemnly concluded, "is an infinite blue space, with the sun up above."

34   Indignant, I replied that if I were to believe what it said, the world could be anything—it had even been a secondhand shop. . . .

35   "A secondhand shop?" it trilled to its heart's content. "But is there really such a thing as a secondhand shop?"

✧ Evaluating the Text

1. How is the narrator characterized? In what way is he defined by his zealous amateur interest in ornithology?

2. In what different circumstances does the narrator encounter the canary? How does the canary redefine its conception of the world to suit each new environment in which it finds itself?

3. In what ways are the canary and the narrator similar to each other? Keep in mind the circumstances in which the canary is first encountered and what the narrator hopes to achieve through his research.

✧ Exploring Different Perspectives

1. Compare the psychological profiles of the narrator in "A Canary's Ideas" with that of Tomoyuki Iwashita in "Why I Quit the Company."

2. Compare the energy and effort involved in what Barbara Ehrenreich does as a researcher studying her subject with the obsessed ornithologist in Assis's story who devotes his life to his "talking" canary.

✧ Extending Viewpoints through Writing

1. Marlon Brando once defined an actor as "a guy who, if you ain't talking about him, ain't listening." Describe the most egocentric person you have ever known or someone whose hobby or work took over his or her life.

2. How do pet's often reflect submerged aspects of their owners' personalities? What actions did a pet of yours ever take that led you to believe it possessed intelligence and was able to communicate its feelings and intentions to you?

Liliana Heker

The Stolen Party

◆

The Argentine writer Liliana Heker was born in Buenos Aires in 1943. As editor-in-chief of two literary magazines, the Escarahajo de Oro, *and the* Ornitorrinco *("The Platypus"), Heker provided an invaluable forum for writers and critics for over twenty-five years. This period coincided with Argentina's descent into chaos under military dictatorships. Her influential published works include* Those That Saw the Bramble *(1966),* Zona de Clivage *(1988),* The Edges of the Real Thing *(1991), and* The Aim of History *(1996). Heker's short story, "The Stolen Party," translated by Alberto Manguel for his anthology* Other Fires *(1985), is a work of great social insight and literary power. It has since become the title story of Heker's collection of short stories in English (1994).*

Argentina, the second largest nation in South America after Brazil, won independence from Spain in 1819 and quickly became a favored destination for European immigrants, who today make up a sizeable majority of the population. Repeated coups and military dictatorships have marked Argentina's history in the twentieth century. General Juan Perón came to power in 1944, established a dictatorship and ruled with the aid of his wife Eva Perón ("Evita") until he was overthrown by a military coup in 1955. He returned to power in 1973, died in 1974, and was succeeded by his third wife, Isabel, who was overthrown by a military coup in March 1976. The junta made up of commanders of the military was led by General Jorge Videla. Under his rule, tens of thousands of political opponents who had supported Perón were seized, often never to be seen again. In 1982, Argentina's unsuccessful war against Great Britain over the Falkland Islands (Islas Malvinas) *led to the fall of General Leopoldo Galtieri, who had replaced Videla the year before, and to democratic elections in 1983, which returned the country to civilian rule. In 1989, a Peronist, Carlos Raúl Menem, was elected president as Argentina faced devastating inflation and a deteriorating economy. Peronists lost their majority in the 1997 legislative elections and in 1999, Menem was succeeded by Fernando de la Rua.*

BeforeYou Read

As you read Heker's story, consider the extent to which children are sensitive or oblivious to the status of different occupations.

◆

1   As soon as she arrived she went straight to the kitchen to see if the monkey was there. It was: What a relief! She wouldn't have liked to admit that her mother had been right. *Monkeys at a birthday?* her mother had sneered. *Get away with you, believing any nonsense you're told!* She was cross, but not because of the monkey, the girl thought; it's just because of the party.

2   "I don't like you going," she told her. "It's a rich people's party."

3   "Rich people go to Heaven too," said the girl, who studied religion at school.

4   "Get away with Heaven," said the mother. "The problem with you, young lady, is that you like to fart higher than your ass."

5   The girl didn't approve of the way her mother spoke. She was barely nine, and one of the best in her class.

6   "I'm going because I've been invited," she said. "And I've been invited because Luciana is my friend. So there."

7   "Ah yes, your friend," her mother grumbled. She paused. "Listen, Rosaura," she said at last. "That one's not your friend. You know what you are to them? The maid's daughter, that's what."

8   Rosaura blinked hard: She wasn't going to cry. Then she yelled: "Shut up! You know nothing about being friends!"

9   Every afternoon she used to go to Luciana's house and they would both finish their homework while Rosaura's mother did the cleaning. They had their tea in the kitchen and they told each other secrets. Rosaura loved everything in the big house, and she also loved the people who lived there.

10   "I'm going because it will be the most lovely party in the whole world, Luciana told me it would. There will be a magician, and he will bring a monkey and everything."

11   The mother swung around to take a good look at her child, and pompously put her hands on her hips.

12   "Monkeys at a birthday?" she said. "Get away with you, believing any nonsense you're told!"

13   Rosaura was deeply offended. She thought it unfair of her mother to accuse other people of being liars simply because they were rich. Rosaura too wanted to be rich, of course. If one day she managed to live in a beautiful palace, would her mother stop loving her? She felt very sad. She wanted to go to that party more than anything else in the world.

14   "I'll die if I don't go," she whispered, almost without moving her lips.

15   And she wasn't sure whether she had been heard, but on the morning of the party she discovered that her mother had starched her Christmas dress. And in the afternoon, after washing her hair, her mother rinsed it in apple vinegar so that it would be all nice and shiny. Before going out, Rosaura admired herself in the mirror, with her white dress and glossy hair, and thought she looked terribly pretty.

16   Señora Ines also seemed to notice. As soon as she saw her, she said:

17   "How lovely you look today, Rosaura."

18   Rosaura gave her starched skirt a slight toss with her hands and walked into the party with a firm step. She said hello to Luciana and asked about the monkey. Luciana put on a secretive look and whispered into Rosaura's ear: "He's in the kitchen. But don't tell anyone, because it's a surprise."

19   Rosaura wanted to make sure. Carefully she entered the kitchen and there she saw it: deep in thought, inside its cage. It looked so funny that the girl stood there for a while, watching it, and later, every so often, she would slip out of the party unseen and go and admire it. Rosaura was the only one allowed into the kitchen. Señora Ines had said: "You yes, but not the others, they're much too boisterous, they might break something." Rosaura had never broken anything. She even managed the jug of orange juice, carrying it from the kitchen into the dining room. She held it carefully and didn't spill a single drop. And Señora Ines had said: "Are you sure you can manage a jug as big as that?" Of course she could manage. She wasn't a butterfingers, like the others. Like that blonde girl with the bow in her hair. As soon as she saw Rosaura, the girl with the bow had said:

20   "And you? Who are you?"

21   "I'm a friend of Luciana," said Rosaura.

22   "No," said the girl with the bow, "you are not a friend of Luciana because I'm her cousin and I know all her friends. And I don't know you."

23   "So what," said Rosaura. "I come here every afternoon with my mother and we do our homework together."

24   "You and your mother do your homework together?" asked the girl, laughing.

25   "I and Luciana do our homework together," said Rosaura, very seriously.

26   The girl with the bow shrugged her shoulders.

27   "That's not being friends," she said. "Do you go to school together?"

28   "No."

29   "So where do you know her from?" said the girl, getting impatient.

30   Rosaura remembered her mother's words perfectly. She took a deep breath.

31   "I'm the daughter of the employee," she said.

32   Her mother had said very clearly: "If someone asks, you say you're the daughter of the employee; that's all." She also told her to add: "And proud of it." But Rosaura thought that never in her life would she dare say something of the sort.

33   "What employee?" said the girl with the bow. "Employee in a shop?"

34   "No," said Rosaura angrily. "My mother doesn't sell anything in any shop, so there."

35   "So how come she's an employee?" said the girl with the bow.

36   Just then Señora Ines arrived saying *shh shh,* and asked Rosaura if she wouldn't mind helping serve out the hotdogs, as she knew the house so much better than the others.

37   "See?" said Rosaura to the girl with the bow, and when no one was looking she kicked her in the shin.

38   Apart from the girl with the bow, all the others were delightful. The one she liked best was Luciana, with her golden birthday crown; and then the boys. Rosaura won the sack race, and nobody managed to catch her when they played tag. When they split into two teams to play charades, all the boys wanted her for their side. Rosaura felt she had never been so happy in all her life.

39   But the best was still to come. The best came after Luciana blew out the candles. First the cake. Señora Ines had asked her to help pass the cake around, and Rosaura had enjoyed the task immensely, because everyone called out to her, shouting "Me, me!" Rosaura remembered a story in which there was a queen who had the power of life or death over her subjects. She had always loved that, having the power of life or death. To Luciana and the boys she gave the largest pieces, and to the girl with the bow she gave a slice so thin one could see through it.

40   After the cake came the magician, tall and bony, with a fine red cape. A true magician: He could untie handkerchiefs by blowing on them and make a chain with links that had no openings. He could guess what cards were pulled out from a pack, and the monkey was his assistant. He called the monkey "partner." "Let's see here, partner," he would say, "turn over a card." And, "Don't run away, partner: Time to work now."

41   The final trick was wonderful. One of the children had to hold the monkey in his arms and the magician said he would make him disappear.

42   "What, the boy?" they all shouted.

43   "No, the monkey!" shouted back the magician.

44   Rosaura thought that this was truly the most amusing party in the whole world.

45   The magician asked a small fat boy to come and help, but the small fat boy got frightened almost at once and dropped the monkey on the floor. The magician picked him up carefully, whispered something in his ear, and the monkey nodded almost as if he understood.

46   "You mustn't be so unmanly, my friend," the magician said to the fat boy.

47   "What's unmanly?" said the fat boy.

48   The magician turned around as if to look for spies.

49   "A sissy," said the magician. "Go sit down."

50   Then he stared at all the faces, one by one. Rosaura felt her heart tremble.

51   "You, with the Spanish eyes," said the magician. And everyone saw that he was pointing at her.

52   She wasn't afraid. Neither holding the monkey, nor when the magician made him vanish; not even when, at the end, the magician flung his red cape over Rosaura's head and uttered a few magic words . . . and the monkey reappeared, chattering happily, in her arms. The children clapped furiously. And before Rosaura returned to her seat, the magician said:

53   "Thank you very much, my little countess."

54   She was so pleased with the compliment that a while later, when her mother came to fetch her, that was the first thing she told her.

55   "I helped the magician and he said to me, 'Thank you very much, my little countess.'"

56   It was strange because up to then Rosaura had thought that she was angry with her mother. All along Rosaura had imagined that she would say to her: "See that the monkey wasn't a lie?" But instead she was so thrilled that she told her mother all about the wonderful magician.

57   Her mother tapped her on the head and said: "So now we're a countess!"

58   But one could see that she was beaming.

59   And now they both stood in the entrance, because a moment ago Señora Ines, smiling, had said: "Please wait here a second."

60   Her mother suddenly seemed worried.

61   "What is it?" she asked Rosaura.

62   "What is what?" said Rosaura. "It's nothing; she just wants to get the presents for those who are leaving, see?"

63   She pointed at the fat boy and at a girl with pigtails who were also waiting there, next to their mothers. And she explained about the presents. She knew, because she had been watching those who left before her. When one of the girls was about to leave, Señora Ines would give her a bracelet. When a boy left, Señora Ines gave him a yo-yo. Rosaura preferred the yo-yo because it sparkled, but she didn't mention that to her mother. Her mother might have said: "So why don't you ask for one, you blockhead?" That's what her mother was like. Rosaura didn't feel like explaining that she'd be horribly ashamed to be the odd one out. Instead she said:

64   "I was the best-behaved at the party."

65   And she said no more because Señora Ines came out into the hall with two bags, one pink and one blue.

66   First she went up to the fat boy, gave him a yo-yo out of the blue bag, and the fat boy left with his mother. Then she went up to the girl and gave her a bracelet out of the pink bag, and the girl with the pigtails left as well.

67   Finally she came up to Rosaura and her mother. She had a big smile on her face and Rosaura liked that. Señora Ines looked down at

her, then looked up at her mother, and then said something that made Rosaura proud:

68   "What a marvelous daughter you have, Herminia."

69   For an instant, Rosaura thought that she'd give her two presents: the bracelet and the yo-yo. Señora Ines bent down as if about to look for something. Rosaura also leaned forward, stretching out her arm. But she never completed the movement.

70   Señora Ines didn't look in the pink bag. Nor did she look in the blue bag. Instead she rummaged in her purse. In her hand appeared two bills.

71   "You really and truly earned this," she said handing them over. "Thank you for all your help, my pet."

72   Rosaura felt her arms stiffen, stick close to her body, and then she noticed her mother's hand on her shoulder. Instinctively she pressed herself against her mother's body. That was all. Except her eyes. Rosaura's eyes had a cold, clear look that fixed itself on Señora Ines's face.

73   Señora Ines, motionless, stood there with her hand outstretched. As if she didn't dare draw it back. As if the slightest change might shatter an infinitely delicate balance.

✦ Evaluating the Text

1. How do all the events at the party coupled with Rosaura's expectations lead her to believe that she was an invited guest?

2. Implicit in the title is the concept that the party has been "stolen." There are many different ways to interpret this title. For example, Rosaura behaves as if she is a guest when in fact she is not. How do you understand the title?

3. Examine carefully Rosaura's responses to her mother, her feelings when she is chosen to distribute the birthday cake, and is allowed to hold the monkey, and how she understands Señora Ines's comment that she is "a marvelous daughter." Collectively, do these suggest she is repressing her real position as a social inferior and is simply not "getting it"? Why or why not?

✦ Exploring Different Perspectives

1. Compare the overlapping perspectives on being an unskilled low-wage employee in Liliana Heker's story with Barbara Ehrenreich's experiences in "Nickel-and-Dimed."

2. Compare the rebellion or lack of it toward the limits that one's job creates in Liliana Heker's story and in Villaseñor's account, "Rain of Gold."

✧ Extending Viewpoints through Writing

1. Rosaura suffers when she discovers her real social position is not what she had believed. Have you ever felt that a sense of belonging was stolen from you because of class limitations? Describe your experience.

2. The display of wealth is an important feature of Heker's story. Have you ever attended a party where the purpose was to impress others with an extravagant display? Describe in detail the setting and events at this party and the extent to which your view of yourself changed in this environment.

Connecting Cultures

Barbara Ehrenreich, "Nickel-and-Dimed"

Discuss the contrast between the working class as portrayed on television according to Anita Gates (in "America Has a Class System. See 'Frasier'" in Chapter 5) and the reality that Ehrenreich describes.

Tomoyuki Iwashita, "Why I Quit the Company"

What distinctive Japanese values underlie Iwashita's account and Kazuo Ishiguro's story, "Family Supper," in Chapter 1?

Mark Salzman, "Lessons"

Compare Salzman's narrative with that of David R. Counts (see "Too Many Bananas" in Chapter 8) in terms of the lessons learned from the cultures in which they lived.

Dennis Smith, "Report from Ground Zero"

Discuss the characteristics that constitute an icon, whether embodied in the NYFD described by Smith, or the popular Latina singer, described by Ilan Stavans in "Santa Selena" in Chapter 8.

Victor Villaseñor, "Rain of Gold"

Discuss the theme of powerlessness versus overcoming odds in Victor Villaseñor's narrative and Gloria Anzaldúa's story, "Cervicide" in Chapter 7.

Machado de Assis, "A Canary's Ideas"

Compare the role of delusion and obsession in the stories by Assis and Catherine Lim (see "Paper" in Chapter 5).

Liliana Heker, "The Stolen Party"

Compare the mother–daughter relationship in Heker's story with that of Mary Crow Dog and her mother in "Civilize Them with a Stick" in Chapter 5.

5

Class and Caste

———————◆———————

Every society can be characterized in terms of social class. Although the principles by which class is identified vary widely from culture to culture, from the amount of money you earn in the United States to what kind of accent you speak with in England to what religious caste you are born into in India, class serves to set boundaries around individuals in terms of opportunities and possibilities. The concept of class in its present form has been in force for only a few hundred years in Western cultures. In prior times, for example, in medieval Europe, your position and chances in life were determined at birth by the *estate* into which you were born, whether that of peasant, clergy, or noble.

Conflicts based on inequalities of social class are often intertwined with those of race, because minorities usually receive the least education, have the least political clout, earn the least income, and find work in occupations considered menial without the possibility of advancement. In some societies, such as in India, for example, an oppressive caste system based on tradition has, until recently, been responsible for burdening the "untouchables" with the most onerous tasks.

Class conditions our entire lives by setting limitations that determine, more than we might like to admit, who we can be friends with, what our goals are, and even who we can marry. Class reflects the access one has to important resources, social privileges, choices, and a sense of control over one's life. Although caste in India is something one cannot change, social stratification in the United States is less rigid and upward mobility is possible through a variety of means such as work, financial success, marriage, and education. More frequently, however, a *de facto* class system can be said to exist in terms of health care, salaries, housing, and opportunities for education that varies greatly for the rich and the poor.

The writers in this chapter explore many of the less obvious connections between social class and the control people exercise over their lives. Raymonde Carroll, in "Sex, Money, and Success," investigates why money for Americans or sex for the French is used by each culture as a vehicle for establishing social status. Mary Crow Dog and Richard

310

Erdoes, in "Civilize Them with a Stick," recount the racism experienced by Native Americans attending a government-run boarding school. Anita Gates, in "America Has a Class System. See 'Frasier,'" studies the comedic possibilities of class differences and what they reveal about American society in her analysis of the popular sitcom. Alonso Salazar, in "The Lords of Creation," provides a firsthand account of a teenage contract killer's life in the underworld of Colombia's drug capital, Medellín. Although officially outlawed, those of the caste known as "untouchables" lead lives similar to that described by Viramma in her autobiographical account, "A Pariah's Life."

Mahdokht Kashkuli, in "The Button," describes the circumstances of a family in modern-day Iran that force them to place one of their children in an orphanage. From Singapore, Catherine Lim, in "Paper," explores the tragic consequences of greed in this tale of a middle-class couple's entanglement with the Singapore Stock Exchange.

Raymonde Carroll

Sex, Money, and Success

——————◆——————

Why is bragging about sexual conquests as much a status symbol for the French as boasting about business success is for Americans? Raymonde Carroll has investigated this question and provides some surprising answers. Born in Tunisia, Carroll was educated in France and the United States. She was trained as an anthropologist and studied the culture of Micronesia while living for three years on the Pacific atoll Nukuoro. She presently teaches in the Department of Romance Languages at Oberlin College. This selection is drawn from her book, Cultural Misunderstandings: The French-American Experience *(translated by Carol Volk, 1988).*

Traditionally an ally of the United States, France was a world power and cultural center in Europe during the reign of Louis XIV (1653–1715). The French absolute monarchy was brought to an end during the French Revolution, a tumultuous period that set the stage for Napoleon's rise to power during the late eighteenth century. France emerged from the Napoleonic Wars as a modern bureaucratic state dominated by the bourgeoisie (middle class), a social structure that endures to the present. In the twentieth century, France has endured two world wars fought on its territory and has been involved in colonial wars in Indochina and Algeria. The difficulty of governing a people so exasperating and stimulating was perhaps best stated by Charles de Gaulle (president from 1959 to 1969), who returned France to a position of prestige in world affairs: "How can you be expected to govern a country that has 246 kinds of cheese?" In 1981 François Mitterrand, a socialist, was elected president of the republic and served in that capacity until his death in 1995. After his death, Jacques Chirac became the president of the republic and brought in a conservative government headed by Edouard Balladur as prime minister. In 2002, Chirac survived a challenge from the right wing candidate, Le Pen, and was re-elected.

Before You Read

Notice how Carroll integrates the speaking voices of both the French and the Americans into her analysis. Consider why sexual conquests and money are two time-honored indicators by which people measure personal success.

——————◆——————

1 Money. For a French person, the face of an American could easily be replaced by a dollar sign. A sign of "incurable materialism," of arrogance, of power, of "vulgar," unrefined pleasure . . . the list goes on. I have never read a book about Americans, including those written with sympathy, which did not speak of the "almighty dollar"; I have never had or heard a conversation about Americans which did not mention money.

2 Foreigners often discover with "horror" or "repulsion" that "everything in the United States is a matter of money." Indeed, one need only read the newspapers to find constant references to the price of things. Thus, a fire is not a news item but an entity (natural or criminal), the dimensions of which are calculated by what it has destroyed—for example, ". . . a house worth two hundred *thousand* dollars . . ." In fact, if it is at all possible to attach a price to something, as approximate as it may be, that price will surely be mentioned. Thus, a French woman became indignant toward her American brother-in-law: "He showed us the engagement ring he had just bought, and he just had to give us all the details about the deal he got in buying the diamond. . . . Talk about romantic!" I cannot even count the number of informants who had similar stories to tell ("I was admiring the magnificent antique pieces in his living room, and do you know what he did? He gave me the price of each piece, with all kinds of details I hadn't asked for. I felt truly uncomfortable . . . really . . ."). Many French informants claimed to be shocked by the "constant showing off," the "lack of taste typical of nouveaux riches" and added, some not in so many words, "As for me, you know, I am truly repulsed by money."

3 On the other side, many Americans expressed surprise at the frequency with which French people spoke about money, only to say that "they weren't interested in it" ("so why talk about it?"), or at the frequency with which they say "it's too expensive" about all types of things. Some find the French to be "cheap" ("They always let you pay") or "hypocritical" ("Why, then, do the French sell arms to just anyone?"), too respectful of money to trifle with it, or too petty to take risks. The list of adjectives hurled from either side on this topic seems particularly long.

4 Yet a brief examination of certain ethnographic details left me puzzled. For instance, what is the American article, about the forest fire that destroyed the row of two-hundred-thousand-dollar homes in California, really saying? Living in the United States, I know that a house worth two hundred thousand dollars in California is far from a palace; on the contrary. Thus, if I took the price quoted literally, I would misinterpret the article as meaning that the fire had destroyed a row of quite ordinary houses—in which case the mention of the "price" is uninformative, uninteresting, and useless. Therefore, what

this article conveys, by talking about hundreds of thousands of dollars, is the fact that the fire destroyed very valuable homes. This meaning is also conveyed by the use of the word "homes," which connotes individuality and uniqueness, rather than "houses," which suggests plain buildings. The mention of the price, therefore, carries meaning of a different nature: I think that this "price" serves only as a common point of reference; it does not represent the true monetary values but a symbolic value which can be grasped immediately by anyone reading this article. A French equivalent would be a reference to the period ("from the seventeenth century") with no mention of the state of the building.

5   Similarly, it is difficult to take the example of the engagement ring literally ("I'm a tightwad"; "I'm not romantic"); it is more comprehensible if we interpret it as a message with a different meaning. For the American in question, having obtained a discount in no way altered the true value of the diamond or the symbolic value of the gesture; this "feat" probably made the gesture even more significant because of the time and attention devoted to it (the worst gift is the one that demands no effort) and probably earned him the admiration and appreciation of his fiancée.

6   The study of cases in which money is mentioned would require an entire book. . . . I will content myself merely with raising the question here and will indicate the general orientation of my interpretation.

7   The striking thing is that money is charged with a multiplicity of meanings in American culture, that it has attained a level of abstraction difficult to imagine elsewhere. Money represents both good and bad, dependence and independence, idealism and materialism, and the list of opposites can go on indefinitely, depending on whom one speaks to. It is power, it is weakness, seduction, oppression, liberation, a pure gamble, a high-risk sport; a sign of intelligence, a sign of love, a sign of scorn; able to be tamed, more dangerous than fire; it brings people together, it separates them, it is constructive, it is destructive; it is reassuring, it is anxiety-producing; it is enchanting, dazzling, frightening; it accumulates slowly or comes in a windfall; it is displayed, it is invisible; it is solid, it evaporates. It is everything and nothing, it is sheer magic, it exists and does not exist at the same time; it is a mystery. The subject provokes hatred, scorn, or impassioned defense from Americans themselves, who are constantly questioning themselves on the topic.

8   I believe that one association remains incontestable, no matter how much resentment it provokes. Money symbolizes success. It is not enough to have money to be admired, but quite the contrary; there is no excuse for the playboy who squanders an inherited fortune. To earn money, a lot of money, and to spend it, is to give the most concrete, the

most visible sign that one has been able to realize one's potential, that one has not wasted the "opportunities" offered by one's parents or by society, and that one always seeks to move on, not to stagnate, to take up the challenge presented in the premises shaping the education of children. . . .

9   As a result, money has become a common denominator. It is supposed to be accessible to all, independent of one's origins. And if it creates classes, it also allows free access to those classes to whoever wants to enter. (Let's not forget that we are talking here about "local verities," about cultural premises, and not about social realities.) Money is therefore the great equalizer, in the sense that the highest social class is, in principle, open to everyone, and that while those who are born into this social class have definite advantages, they must nonetheless deserve to remain there, must "prove themselves." And the newspapers are filled with enough stories of poor people turned millionaires to reinforce this conviction.

10   From this perspective, it is understandable that one does not hide one's success but displays it, shows it off. By making my humble origins known, by displaying my success, I am not trying to humiliate others (although it is possible that I, personally, am a real "stinker"), but I am showing others that it is possible, I am encouraging emulation through example, I am reaffirming a cultural truth: "if I can do it, you can do it." Hence the constant copresence of dreams and success, that is to say, the constant reaffirmation that the impossible is possible, and that attaining the dream depends solely on me. The logical, and ironic, conclusion to all this is the essentially idealistic significance of money in American culture, which does not exclude its "materialistic" utilization.

11   I do not believe that the misunderstanding between the French and Americans concerning money can be resolved by performing a parallel analysis of the meaning of money in French culture, not because money is not a concern for the French, but because I believe that what Americans express through money is expressed by the French in another domain.

12   From this brief analysis, I will reiterate three points. The first is that money in America serves as a common point of reference, a shortcut for communication, a means of defining a context that is recognizable by all and comprehensible no matter what one's financial situation may be. The second is that it is not in bad taste to recount one's triumphs, one's success in this domain, whether it is a matter of having obtained a half-price diamond or of having accumulated a veritable fortune, insofar as this in no way implies that I wish to put down others, that I am conceited, and so on, characteristics which depend not on money but on my personality. And the third is that money is accessible to all, makes possible upward mobility, that is to say, access to any class.

13   To the extent that these three points I just made are not "true" for
French culture—and that they might in fact provoke "real repulsion"—
one must look in a realm other than that of money for what carries the
same message. . . .

14   The repulsion with which many French people react to the "bad
taste" of Americans who "brag about their wealth," "show off their
money," and so on closely resembles the disgust with which many
Americans speak of the "bad taste," the "vulgarity" of French people
who "brag about their sexual exploits," "are proud of their sexual successes," which is a subject reserved by Americans for the "uncivilized"
world of locker rooms, for the special and forced intimacy of these
dressing rooms for athletes. (Although the expression "locker-room
talk" traditionally evokes male conversation, it is just as applicable today to female locker-room talk.) The repugnance on the part of "tasteful" Americans to speak in public about their successes with men or
women or their sexual "conquests" is interpreted, among the French,
as additional proof of American "puritanism," whereas the French
"modesty" concerning public conversations about money would tend
to be interpreted by Americans as a type of French "puritanism."

15   This reciprocal accusation of "bad taste" led me to wonder if what
was true for financial successes and conquests in American culture was
not true for seduction, for amorous conquests, for sexual successes in
French culture.

16   While it is not looked on favorably, in France, to show off one's
money or titles, one may speak of one's amorous conquests without
shocking anyone (unless one does it to belittle others with one's superiority, to insult them, etc., in which case it is not the subject that is important but the manner in which a particular person makes use of it).
We have, in France, a great deal of indulgence and admiration for the
"irresistible" man or woman, for "charmers" large and small of both
cases. Seduction is an art which is learned and perfected.

17   Like money for Americans, amorous seduction is charged with a
multiplicity of contradictory meanings for the French, depending on
the person to whom one is speaking and the moment one raises the
topic. Nonetheless, if a (French) newspaper article defines a particular
person as *séduisante*, the term does not refer to indisputable characteristics but to a category recognizable by all, to a common point of reference, to a comprehensible descriptive shortcut. (It is interesting to note
that the American translation of *séduisante* would be "attractive," a
word which, as opposed to the French, evokes identifiable and predictable characteristics. The word *seductive*—not an adequate translation—evokes manipulation and the negative connotations attached to
taking advantage of naiveté.)

18   Seduction, as I have said, is an art for the French. It is not enough
to be handsome or beautiful to seduce; a certain intelligence and exper-

tise are necessary, which can only be acquired through a long apprenticeship, even if this apprenticeship begins in the most tender infancy. (Thus, an ad for baby clothing, a double spread in the French version of the magazine *Parents*, shows the perfect outfit for the "heartbreak girl" and for the "playboy"; this is an indication of the extent to which this quality is desirable, since I assume the ad is geared toward the parents who provide for and teach these babies, and not toward the babies themselves.) It is therefore "normal" for me to be proud of my successes, for me to continually take up the challenge of new conquests, for me never to rest on my laurels, for me not to waste my talent. It is therefore not in "bad taste" to talk about it (bad taste and seduction are, in a sense, mutually exclusive in French). What is more, I can "freely" share my secrets and my "reflections" on the subject of men or women—a topic I have thoroughly mastered.

19　Like money for Americans, seduction for the French may be the only true class equalizer. In fact, one of the greatest powers of amorous seduction is precisely the fact that it permits the transgression of class divisions. The French myths of the "kept woman," of the attractiveness of the *midinette* (a big-city shopgirl or office clerk, who is supposed to be very sentimental), of the seductive powers of "P'tit Louis" (a "hunk," a good dancer, from the working class), and the innumerable seducers of both sexes in French novels, songs, and films are sufficient proof.

20　The interest of a parallel such as the one I have just established is that it shows how astonishingly similar meanings can be expressed in areas which seem to be completely unrelated. Yet the greatest attraction of cultural analysis, for me, is the possibility of replacing a dull exchange of invectives with an exploration that is, at the very least, fascinating—a true feast to which I hereby invite you.

✦ Evaluating the Text

1. What culturally based misunderstandings do the French and Americans have about each other in terms of money and sex?

2. How is the approach Carroll takes that of an anthropologist who is interested in why success is measured in such different ways in France and the United States?

3. The playboy (womanizer) in France is regarded very differently from his American counterpart. What differences in cultural values between the two countries explain this perception?

✦ Exploring Different Perspectives

1. Although Carroll depicts Americans as money obsessed, how does Catherine Lim's story, "Paper," show it to be more universal?

2. Discuss the different forms that social mobility takes in Carroll's account and in Anita Gates's report, "America Has a Class System. See 'Frasier.'"

✧ *Extending Viewpoints through Writing*

1. Write a short essay in which you support or challenge Carroll's claim by exploring the way in which the subjects of money and sex are treated in a range of magazines. In what ways do magazines devoted to money (such as *Money* and *Forbes*) focus on business success in the same way that magazines devoted to sex (such as *Playboy*) commodify seduction?

2. Carroll asserts that seduction in France and money in America signify social mobility. Write a short rebuttal to Carroll's argument in which you give equal importance to race and ethnicity as indicators of social class.

Mary Crow Dog and Richard Erdoes

Civilize Them with a Stick

———————◆———————

Mary Crow Dog (who later took the name Mary Brave Bird) was born in 1956 and grew up on a South Dakota reservation in a one-room cabin without running water or electricity. She joined the new movement of tribal pride sweeping Native-American communities in the 1960s and 1970s and was at the siege of Wounded Knee, South Dakota, in 1973. She married the American Indian Movement (AIM) leader Leonard Crow Dog, the movement's chief medicine man. Her powerful autobiography Lakota Woman, *written with Richard Erdoes, one of America's leading writers on Native-American affairs and the author of eleven books, became a national best-seller and won the American Book Award for 1991. In it she describes what it was like to grow up a Sioux in a white-dominated society. Her second book,* Ohitka Woman *(1993), also written with Richard Erdoes, continues the story of a woman whose struggle for a sense of self and freedom is a testament to her will and spirit. In "Civilize Them with a Stick," from* Lakota Woman, *the author recounts her personal struggle as a young student at a boarding school run by the Bureau of Indian Affairs.*

> . . . Gathered from the cabin, the wickiup, and the tepee,
> partly by cajolery and partly by threats;
> partly by bribery and partly by force,
> they are induced to leave their kindred
> to enter these schools and take upon themselves
> the outward appearance of civilized life.
> —Annual report of the Department of Interior, 1901

Before You Read

Notice how the quote from the Department of Interior (1901) that precedes Mary Crow Dog's essay provides an ironic contrast to the conditions she describes.

———————◆———————

1   It is almost impossible to explain to a sympathetic white person what a typical old Indian boarding school was like; how it affected the Indian child suddenly dumped into it like a small creature from another world, helpless, defenseless, bewildered, trying desperately and

instinctively to survive and sometimes not surviving at all. I think such children were like the victims of Nazi concentration camps trying to tell average, middle-class Americans what their experience had been like. Even now, when these schools are much improved, when the buildings are new, all gleaming steel and glass, the food tolerable, the teachers well trained and well intentioned, even trained in child psychology—unfortunately the psychology of white children, which is different from ours—the shock to the child upon arrival is still tremendous. Some just seem to shrivel up, don't speak for days on end, and have an empty look in their eyes. I know of an eleven-year-old on another reservation who hanged herself, and in our school, while I was there, a girl jumped out of the window, trying to kill herself to escape an unbearable situation. That first shock is always there. . . .

2   The mission school at St. Francis was a curse for our family for generations. My grandmother went there, then my mother, then my sisters and I. At one time or other every one of us tried to run away. Grandma told me once about the bad times she had experienced at St. Francis. In those days they let students go home only for one week every year. Two days were used up for transportation, which meant spending just five days out of three hundred and sixty-five with her family. And that was an improvement. Before grandma's time, on many reservations they did not let the students go home at all until they had finished school. Anybody who disobeyed the nuns was severely punished. The building in which my grandmother stayed had three floors, for girls only. Way up in the attic were little cells, about five by five by ten feet. One time she was in church and instead of praying she was playing jacks. As punishment they took her to one of those little cubicles where she stayed in darkness because the windows had been boarded up. They left her there for a whole week with only bread and water for nourishment. After she came out she promptly ran away, together with three other girls. They were found and brought back. The nuns stripped them naked and whipped them. They used a horse buggy whip on my grandmother. Then she was put back into the attic—for two weeks.

3   My mother had much the same experiences but never wanted to talk about them, and then there I was, in the same place. The school is now run by the BIA—the Bureau of Indian Affairs—but only since about fifteen years ago. When I was there, during the 1960s, it was still run by the Church. The Jesuit fathers ran the boys' wing and the Sisters of the Sacred Heart ran us—with the help of the strap. Nothing had changed since my grandmother's days. I have been told recently that even in the '70s they were still beating children at that school. All I got out of school was being taught how to pray. I learned quickly that I would be beaten if I failed in my devotions or, God forbid, prayed the wrong way, especially prayed in Indian to Wakan Tanka, the Indian Creator.

4   The girls' wing was built like an F and was run like a penal institution. Every morning at five o'clock the sisters would come into our
large dormitory to wake us up, and immediately we had to kneel
down at the sides of our beds and recite the prayers. At six o'clock we
were herded into the church for more of the same. I did not take kindly
to the discipline and to marching by the clock, left-right, left-right. I
was never one to like being forced to do something. I do something because I feel like doing it. I felt this way always, as far as I can remember, and my sister Barbara felt the same way. An old medicine man
once told me: "Us Lakotas are not like dogs who can be trained, who
can be beaten and keep on wagging their tails, licking the hand that
whipped them. We are like cats, little cats, big cats, wildcats, bobcats,
mountain lions. It doesn't matter what kind, but cats who can't be
tamed, who scratch if you step on their tails." But I was only a kitten
and my claws were still small.

5   Barbara was still in the school when I arrived and during my first
year or two she could still protect me a little bit. When Barb was a
seventh-grader she ran away together with five other girls, early in
the morning before sunrise. They brought them back in the evening.
The girls had to wait for two hours in front of the mother superior's
office. They were hungry and cold, frozen through. It was wintertime
and they had been running the whole day without food, trying to
make good their escape. The mother superior asked each girl, "Would
you do this again?" She told them that as punishment they would not
be allowed to visit home for a month and that she'd keep them busy on
work details until the skin on their knees and elbows had worn off. At
the end of her speech she told each girl, "Get up from this chair and
lean over it." She then lifted the girls' skirts and pulled down their underpants. Not little girls either, but teenagers. She had a leather strap
about a foot long and four inches wide fastened to a stick, and beat the
girls, one after another, until they cried. Barb did not give her that satisfaction but just clenched her teeth. There was one girl, Barb told me,
the nun kept on beating and beating until her arm got tired.

6   I did not escape my share of the strap. Once, when I was thirteen
years old, I refused to go to Mass. I did not want to go to church because I did not feel well. A nun grabbed me by the hair, dragged me
upstairs, made me stoop over, pulled my dress up (we were not allowed at the time to wear jeans), pulled my panties down, and gave
me what they called "swats"—twenty-five swats with a board around
which Scotch tape had been wound. She hurt me badly.

7   My classroom was right next to the principal's office and almost
every day I could hear him swatting the boys. Beating was the common punishment for not doing one's homework, or for being late to
school. It had such a bad effect upon me that I hated and mistrusted
every white person on sight, because I met only one kind. It was not

until much later that I met sincere white people I could relate to and be friends with. Racism breeds racism in reverse.

8   The routine at St. Francis was dreary. Six A.M., kneeling in church for an hour or so; seven o'clock, breakfast; eight o'clock, scrub the floor, peel spuds, make classes. We had to mop the dining room twice every day and scrub the tables. If you were caught taking a rest, doodling on the bench with a fingernail or knife, or just rapping, the nun would come up with a dish towel and just slap it across your face, saying, "You're not supposed to be talking, you're supposed to be working!" Monday mornings we had cornmeal mush, Tuesday oatmeal, Wednesday rice and raisins, Thursday cornflakes, and Friday all the leftovers mixed together or sometimes fish. Frequently the food had bugs or rocks in it. We were eating hot dogs that were weeks old, while the nuns were dining on ham, whipped potatoes, sweet peas, and cranberry sauce. In winter our dorm was icy cold while the nuns' rooms were always warm.

9   I have seen little girls arrive at the school, first-graders, just fresh from home and totally unprepared for what awaited them, little girls with pretty braids, and the first thing the nuns did was chop their hair off and tie up what was left behind their ears. Next they would dump the children into tubs of alcohol, a sort of rubbing alcohol, "to get the germs off." Many of the nuns were German immigrants, some from Bavaria, so that we sometimes speculated whether Bavaria was some sort of Dracula country inhabited by monsters. For the sake of objectivity I ought to mention that two of the German fathers were great linguists and that the only Lakota–English dictionaries and grammars which are worth anything were put together by them.

10   At night some of the girls would huddle in bed together for comfort and reassurance. Then the nun in charge of the dorm would come in and say, "What are the two of you doing in bed together? I smell evil in this room. You girls are evil incarnate. You are sinning. You are going to hell and burn forever. You can act that way in the devil's frying pan." She would get them out of bed in the middle of the night, making them kneel and pray until morning. We had not the slightest idea what it was all about. At home we slept two and three in a bed for animal warmth and a feeling of security.

11   The nuns and the girls in the two top grades were constantly battling it out physically with fists, nails, and hair-pulling. I myself was growing from a kitten into an undersized cat. My claws were getting bigger and were itching for action. About 1969 or 1970 a strange young white girl appeared on the reservation. She looked about eighteen or twenty years old. She was pretty and had long, blond hair down to her waist, patched jeans, boots, and a backpack. She was different from any other white person we had met before. I think her name was Wise. I do not know how she managed to overcome our reluctance and dis-

trust, getting us into a corner, making us listen to her, asking us how we were treated. She told us that she was from New York. She was the first real hippie or Yippie we had come across. She told us of people called the Black Panthers, Young Lords, and Weathermen. She said, "Black people are getting it on. Indians are getting it on in St. Paul and California. How about you?" She also said, "Why don't you put out an underground paper, mimeograph it. It's easy. Tell it like it is. Let it all hang out." She spoke a strange lingo but we caught on fast.

12   Charlene Left Hand Bull and Gina One Star were two full-blood girls I used to hang out with. We did everything together. They were willing to join me in a Sioux uprising. We put together a newspaper which we called the *Red Panther*. In it we wrote how bad the school was, what kind of slop we had to eat—slimy, rotten, blackened potatoes for two weeks—the way we were beaten. I think I was the one who wrote the worst article about our principal of the moment, Father Keeler. I put all my anger and venom into it. I called him a goddam wasičun son of a bitch. I wrote that he knew nothing about Indians and should go back to where he came from, teaching white children whom he could relate to. I wrote that we knew which priests slept with which nuns and that all they ever could think about was filling their bellies and buying a new car. It was the kind of writing which foamed at the mouth, but which also lifted a great deal of weight from one's soul.

13   On Saint Patrick's Day, when everybody was at the big powwow, we distributed our newspapers. We put them on windshields and bulletin boards, in desks and pews, in dorms and toilets. But someone saw us and snitched on us. The shit hit the fan. The three of us were taken before a board meeting. Our parents, in my case my mother, had to come. They were told that ours was a most serious matter, the worst thing that had ever happened in the school's long history. One of the nuns told my mother, "Your daughter really needs to be talked to." "What's wrong with my daughter?" my mother asked. She was given one of our *Red Panther* newspapers. The nun pointed out its name to her and then my piece, waiting for mom's reaction. After a while she asked, "Well, what have you got to say to this? What do you think?"

14   My mother said, "Well, when I went to school here, some years back, I was treated a lot worse than these kids are. I really can't see how they can have any complaints, because we was treated a lot stricter. We could not even wear skirts halfway up our knees. These girls have it made. But you should forgive them because they are young. And it's supposed to be a free country, free speech and all that. I don't believe what they done is wrong." So all I got out of it was scrubbing six flights of stairs on my hands and knees, every day. And no boy-side privileges.

15   The boys and girls were still pretty much separated. The only time one could meet a member of the opposite sex was during free time,

between four and five-thirty, in the study hall or on benches or the volleyball court outside, and that was strictly supervised. One day Charlene and I went over to the boys' side. We were on the ball team and they had to let us practice. We played three extra minutes, only three minutes more than we were supposed to. Here was the nuns' opportunity for revenge. We got twenty-five swats. I told Charlene, "We are getting too old to have our bare asses whipped that way. We are old enough to have babies. Enough of this shit. Next time we fight back." Charlene only said, "Hoka-hay!"

16   We had to take showers every evening. One little girl did not want to take her panties off and one of the nuns told her, "You take those underpants off—or else!" But the child was ashamed to do it. The nun was getting her swat to threaten the girl. I went up to the sister, pushed her veil off, and knocked her down. I told her that if she wanted to hit a little girl she should pick on me, pick one her own size. She got herself transferred out of the dorm a week later.

17   In a school like this there is always a lot of favoritism. At St. Francis it was strongly tinged with racism. Girls who were near-white, who came from what the nuns called "nice families," got preferential treatment. They waited on the faculty and got to eat ham or eggs and bacon in the morning. They got the easy jobs while the skins, who did not have the right kind of background—myself among them—always wound up in the laundry room sorting out ten bushel baskets of dirty boys' socks every day. Or we wound up scrubbing the floors and doing all the dishes. The school therefore fostered fights and antagonism between whites and breeds, and between breeds and skins. At one time Charlene and I had to iron all the robes and vestments the priests wore when saying Mass. We had to fold them up and put them into a chest in the back of the church. In a corner, looking over our shoulders, was a statue of the crucified Savior, all bloody and beaten up. Charlene looked up and said, "Look at that poor Indian. The pigs sure worked him over." That was the closest I ever came to seeing Jesus.

18   I was held up as a bad example and didn't mind. I was old enough to have a boyfriend and promptly got one. At the school we had an hour and a half for ourselves. Between the boys' and the girls' wings were some benches where one could sit. My boyfriend and I used to go there just to hold hands and talk. The nuns were very uptight about any boy-girl stuff. They had an exaggerated fear of anything having even the faintest connection with sex. One day in religion class, an all-girl class, Sister Bernard singled me out for some remarks, pointing me out as a bad example, an example that should be shown. She said that I was too free with my body. That I was holding hands which meant that I was not a good example to follow. She also said that I wore unchaste dresses, skirts which were too short, too suggestive, shorter than regulations permitted, and for that I would be punished. She

dressed me down before the whole class, carrying on and on about my unchastity.

19   I stood up and told her, "You shouldn't say any of those things, miss. You people are a lot worse than us Indians. I know all about you, because my grandmother and my aunt told me about you. Maybe twelve, thirteen years ago you had a water stoppage here in St. Francis. No water could get through the pipes. There are water lines right under the mission, underground tunnels and passages where in my grandmother's time only the nuns and priests could go, which were off-limits to everybody else. When the water backed up they had to go through all the water lines and clean them out. And in those huge pipes they found the bodies of newborn babies. And they were white babies. They weren't Indian babies. At least when our girls have babies, they don't do away with them that way, like flushing them down the toilet, almost.

20   "And that priest they sent here from Holy Rosary in Pine Ridge because he molested a little girl. You couldn't think of anything better than dump him on us. All he does is watch young women and girls with that funny smile on his face. Why don't you point him out for an example?"

21   Charlene and I worked on the school newspaper. After all we had some practice. Every day we went down to Publications. One of the priests acted as the photographer, doing the enlarging and developing. He smelled of chemicals which had stained his hands yellow. One day he invited Charlene into the darkroom. He was going to teach her developing. She was developed already. She was a big girl compared to him, taller too. Charlene was nicely built, not fat, just rounded. No sharp edges anywhere. All of a sudden she rushed out of the darkroom, yelling to me, "Let's get out of here! He's trying to feel me up. That priest is nasty." So there was this too to contend with—sexual harassment. We complained to the student body. The nuns said we just had a dirty mind.

22   We got a new priest in English. During one of his first classes he asked one of the boys a certain question. The boy was shy. He spoke poor English, but he had the right answer. The priest told him, "You did not say it right. Correct yourself. Say it over again." The boy got flustered and stammered. He could hardly get out a word. But the priest kept after him: "Didn't you hear? I told you to do the whole thing over. Get it right this time." He kept on and on.

23   I stood up and said, "Father, don't be doing that. If you go into an Indian's home and try to talk Indian, they might laugh at you and say, 'Do it over correctly. Get it right this time!'"

24   He shouted at me, "Mary, you stay after class. Sit down right now!"

25   I stayed after class, until after the bell. He told me, "Get over here!"

26   He grabbed me by the arm, pushing me against the blackboard, shouting, "Why are you always mocking us? You have no reason to do this."

27   I said, "Sure I do. You were making fun of him. You embarrassed him. He needs strengthening, not weakening. You hurt him. I did not hurt you."

28   He twisted my arm and pushed real hard. I turned around and hit him in the face, giving him a bloody nose. After that I ran out of the room, slamming the door behind me. He and I went to Sister Bernard's office. I told her, "Today I quit school. I'm not taking any more of this, none of this shit anymore. None of this treatment. Better give me my diploma. I can't waste any more time on you people."

29   Sister Bernard looked at me for a long, long time. She said, "All right, Mary Ellen, go home today. Come back in a few days and get your diploma." And that was that. Oddly enough, that priest turned out okay. He taught a class in grammar, orthography, composition, things like that. I think he wanted more respect in class. He was still young and unsure of himself. But I was in there too long. I didn't feel like hearing it. Later he became a good friend of the Indians, a personal friend of myself and my husband. He stood up for us during Wounded Knee and after. He stood up to his superiors, stuck his neck way out, became a real people's priest. He even learned our language. He died prematurely of cancer. It is not only the good Indians who die young, but the good whites, too. It is the timid ones who know how to take care of themselves who grow old. I am still grateful to that priest for what he did for us later and for the quarrel he picked with me—or did I pick it with him?—because it ended a situation which had become unendurable for me. The day of my fight with him was my last day in school.

✧ Evaluating the Text

1. What aspects of life at the government boarding school most clearly illustrate the government's desire to transform Native Americans? How did Mary Crow Dog react to the experiences to which she was subjected at the government-run school?

2. What historical insight did the experiences of Mary Crow Dog's mother and grandmother provide into those of Mary Crow Dog herself?

3. Why was the incident of the underground newspaper a crucial one for Mary Crow Dog?

✧ Exploring Different Perspectives

1. How do both Mary Crow Dog's account and Mahdokht Kashkuli's story "The Button" dramatize the effects of being raised by the state?

2. In what sense are Native Americans the untouchables or outcasts in the United States in ways that are comparable to Viramma as recounted in "A Pariah's Life"? What explains the very different reactions both have in their respective situations?

✧ Extending Viewpoints through Writing

1. What experiences have you had that made you aware of institutionalized racism?

2. How did this essay give you insight into the vast difference between the traditional culture of Native Americans and their lives in the present?

Anita Gates

America Has a Class System.
See "Frasier"

◆

Anita Gates is a staff writer for The New York Times *and in this 1998 article, she examines the representation of social class in the popular sitcom, "Frasier," for what it reveals about American society. (This show has won 30 Emmys.) In her view, the enduring appeal of this show is due, in no small part, to its humorous treatment of social-class foibles and the conflicts between upper-class and working-class lifestyles.*

Before You Read

Consider the many ways differences in social class are depicted in the television sitcom "Frasier" to see if you agree with Gates's analysis.

◆

1   Dr. Frasier Crane's apartment says a lot about him. The tan suede sofa is a copy of one Coco Chanel had in her Paris atelier. The view is the Seattle skyline. There are Lichtensteins on the wall, a baby grand in the alcove and a finely ground Kenya blend in the coffeemaker.

2   All Frasier (Kelsey Grammer) really wants is to be Cary Grant, but he can never quite pull it off. Even when he, his ex-wife and his brother find themselves in bathrobes (but let's call them dressing gowns) in a great Art Deco hotel room discussing irony, superegos, eggs Florentine and—oh, by the way—a tiny sexual infidelity, as he did in a recent episode, Frasier can't help summing it all up with "Well, isn't this peachy?"

3   And if Frasier's own failings weren't enough to sabotage his efforts at urban sophistication, there's his father, Martin Crane (John Mahoney), retired cop, beer drinker, television watcher, plain speaker, whose sense of style is symbolized by the dreadful striped easy chair with duct-tape accents that he has plunked down in the middle of his son's elegant minimalism.

4   The dangers of class mobility in America have never been more eloquently addressed. And class is a subject long overdue for discussion, now that three or four people have admitted that they would have liked Paula Jones better if she'd gone to all the right schools.

5   There may be a hundred reasons that "Frasier" has been a hit sitcom since NBC introduced it in 1993 or why it has won the best-comedy

Emmy Award every year it has been on the air, but for many viewers the heart of the series is the Cranes' intrafamily culture clash, the kind that's bound to occur when blue-collar Americans send their children to Harvard.

6   American television has never dealt much with the class system, possibly because of the lingering belief that we don't have one. Most series have picked a socioeconomic level and stuck with it: struggling working class from "The Life of Riley" to "Roseanne," solidly, comfortably middle class from "Father Knows Best" to "Home Improvement," or filthy rich on "Dallas" and "Dynasty."

7   One of the few conspicuously rich households on the 1998 schedule belongs to Maxwell Sheffield on "The Nanny," a sitcom about a Broadway producer with a British accent who hires and learns to love a loud young woman with a Queens accent and very short skirts. The class gap on "The Nanny" is exaggerated for broad laughs, just as a larger gap was on "The Beverly Hillbillies" 30 years ago. Even "Fresh Prince of Bel Air," Will Smith's sitcom about an inner-city teenager relocated to his wealthy relatives' home in a posh part of Los Angeles, tended to rely on stereotypes about the stuffy rich.

8   The closest thing to a serious portrayal of class mobility must have been "The Millionaire," the 1950's series about a billionaire who liked to amuse himself by giving $1 million (tax free, that was the great part) to some deserving stranger. The half-hour was devoted to the story of how the lucky man or woman handled that new-found wealth—usually badly.

9   But on innumerable shows, especially rags-to-riches mini-series, that sort of transition is a snap. Maybe that's because television has usually treated class differences as if they were strictly about net worth. Lucy and Ricky Ricardo often had more money than Fred and Ethel Mertz, because Ricky was a successful band leader (and eventually a movie actor), but they never seemed to have different tastes in fashion, food or art. At least not to the degree found among the Cranes.

10   Viewers quickly learned who they were dealing with during the first season of "Frasier" when, over latte at Cafe Nervosa, Frasier's dapper brother, Niles, described a trick he had played on someone at his wine club: switching labels between a Château Petrus and a Foureas-Dupré. "What scamps you are!" said Frasier. "His face must have turned redder than a Pichon-Longueville." The difference between the brothers is that Frasier knows they're being pretentious; Niles honestly doesn't.

11   David Hyde Pierce, who plays Niles, has said that his character was originally explained to him as "what Frasier would be if he had never gone to Boston and never been exposed to the people at Cheers."

12   Frasier's character was created in 1984 for "Cheers," then NBC's highest-rated sitcom, as a love interest for Diane Chambers (Shelley Long). A psychiatrist with elbow patches and pear-shaped vowels, he was an educated and sophisticated contrast to the jovially working-class gang that hung out at the show's namesake Boston bar. Diane left Frasier at the altar, but he kept his seat at the bar, looking down his nose at the others' failings for eight more seasons. Luckily for Frasier, Martin never flew into town to reveal his son's humble origins. "Cheers," in the tradition of a class-free America, acknowledged taste and economic differences, but in script after script it insisted that the postal worker and the professor might really socialize.

13   Back in Seattle, Frasier has given that sort of thing up, possibly because he gets enough blue-collar atmosphere at home.

14   Maybe, the Crane boys sometimes wonder, there was a switched-at-birth mistake at the hospital. "Frasier, is he our real father?" Niles once asked. Frasier answered tolerantly: "Now don't start that again. We've been having this discussion since we were children."

15   At times the brothers think they might be able to sophisticate Martin by exposing him to the finer things. Frasier recalls that even their own tastes were not always beyond reproach. "Remember," he tells Niles, "when you used to think the *1812 Overture* was a great piece of classical music?" Niles smiles wistfully. "Was I ever that young?" he says.

16   But that strategy doesn't work, and neither does Frasier's attempt to buy his father an Armani suit. Martin insists on stopping at a discount store, where he finds a wrinkle-resistant sharkskin ensemble instead. Offered any restaurant in town for his birthday celebration, Dad wants to go to Hoppy's Old Heidelberg. Which may be better than the steak place he once dragged his sons to, where patrons choose their meal from "the steak trolley" and anyone wearing a necktie has it cut off—even it it's Hugo Boss.

17   Although Frasier earns his living in broadcasting (giving psychiatric advice on a radio call-in show), he makes fun of his father's unfortunate television habit. When he buys Martin a telescope, he says, "Just think of it as having 100 more channels to watch."

18   But Martin won't let his sons undermine his confidence in his common-man tastes and often gives as good as he gets. He refers to Frasier's breakfast of a bran muffin and a touch of yogurt as "girlie food" and corrects Niles when he describes the cuisine at a certain restaurant as "to die for." "Niles, your country and your family are to die for," Martin reminds him. "Food is to eat." Martin isn't oblivious to changing standards around him; he just thinks they're insane. "A dollar fifty for coffee?" he says in one show. "What kind of world are we living in?"

19   One of Martin's finest moments comes when Frasier, planning an old-fashioned live radio play, explains to Niles, "People of Dad's generation would sit around at night listening to the radio, absolutely mesmerized." Before Niles has a chance to say that yes, he's well aware of that, Martin gives his older son a look and says, "We were a simple people."

20   One reason "Frasier" works is that both classes are made up of good people with values, which happen to be expressed in different ways. The show gives both coastal yuppies and Middle America a good name.

21   Kelsey Grammer once described his character, at a Museum of Television and Radio seminar, as "flawed and silly and pompous and full of himself" but "genuinely kind" and "totally vulnerable."

22   And then there's Niles. Niles, who is so out of touch with the mainstream that he explains creative visualization by suggesting that a radio listener might have "a dog-eared copy of 'Middlemarch'" nearby. That he tries to order a Stoli gibson with three pearl onions at a theme restaurant. (Niles who, by the way, mentions his $400 Bruno Maglis months before O.J. Simpson mentions his.) Niles of the cute smirk and boyish blond good looks (Leonardo DiCaprio in 15 years, if he takes care of himself) and tart tongue. Lilith, Frasier's formidable ex-wife, is in town? "Ah," says Niles, "that explains why blood was pouring from all my faucets this morning."

23   But also Niles who, despite his elegance, can't dance ("Start with your left foot," suggests his instructor. "Which one?" Niles asks, all too honestly). And who has a painful case of unspoken, unrequited love for Daphne Moon (Jane Leeves), his father's young English (working-class) live-in physical therapist.

24   Which could begin a list of things the "Frasier" writers are doing right: unrequited love as an opportunity for bawdy double-entendre (Daphne to Niles: "I'm beginning to think I should spend an hour or two on the couch with you"), the lovable dog whom the lead character hates, Niles's never-seen monster of an estranged wife and occasional excursions into farce.

25   The writers throw in literary and theatrical references—without explanation, God bless them—to the likes of Dorothy Parker ("What fresh hell is this?"), "A Chorus Line" ("I'm a dancer. A dancer dances.") and "Hamlet," sort of ("We're a hit. A palpable hit.").

26   While most sitcoms change scenes with a shot of the exterior of a building and some perky music, "Frasier" does it with subtitles, like "A Coupla White Guys Sittin' 'Round Talkin'" and "Could Guy's Last Name Be Feydeau?"

27   The show is just plain smart. But America might not forgive the Crane brothers their sophistication, their culinary pretensions and their decorating budgets if they didn't have Martin around to remind them where they came from.

❖ *Evaluating the Text*

    1. What role do the symbols of upper-class and working-class life play in the storylines of "Frasier"? How do markers of social class define the main characters?

    2. According to Gates, how does the television sitcom "Frasier" exploit the comedic possibilities of class differences in American society?

❖ *Exploring Different Perspectives*

    1. To what extent do the characters on "Frasier" reflect the themes discussed by Raymonde Carroll in "Sex, Money and Success"?

    2. How do the characters in Catherine Lim's story take all too seriously the icons of success that are the subject of comedy on "Frasier"?

❖ *Extending Viewpoints through Writing*

    1. If you have ever seen "Frasier" do you agree with Gates's assessment of the show? Why or why not? What other sitcoms have you seen that could be analyzed in the same way?

    2. Analyze the function that sitcoms play in American culture and analyze your favorite sitcom in terms of the themes that Gates discusses.

Alonso Salazar

The Lords of Creation

———————◆———————

Alonso Salazar is a leading Colombian journalist and social scientist. Salazar journeyed into the jails, hospitals, and shantytowns of Medellín, Colombia's second largest city and drug capital, to interview teenage contract killers, their families, priests, and self-defense vigilantes. His book, Born to Die in Medellín *(1990), provides a graphic exploration of one of the most violent societies in the world. "The Lords of Creation," translated by Nick Caistor, taken from this book, provides riveting insight into the world of Medellín's youth gangs.*

The only South American country with both Pacific and Caribbean coastlines, the republic of Colombia is bordered by Panama to the northwest, Venezuela to the northeast, Ecuador and Peru to the south, and Brazil to the southeast. After being conquered by the Spanish in the 1530s, Colombia's struggle for independence from Spain began in 1810, lasted nine years, and ended with the victory of Simón Bolívar in 1819. From its inception, the republic of New Granada, as it was then called (which originally included Venezuela, Ecuador, and Panama) was torn by the opposition between federalist liberals and centralist conservatives. As many as 100,000 people were killed in a civil war that raged from 1899 to 1903. Civil war again erupted in 1948, and orderly government was restored as a result of compromise between liberals and conservatives in 1958. Widespread poverty and a political climate destabilized by guerilla warfare in urban areas led to a precarious economy ostensibly dependent on coffee, its major legal crop, but even more dependent on the illegal growth and trafficking in marijuana and cocaine. After several rounds of elections, Ernesto Samper was elected president in August 1994 for a four-year term. In 1998, the Conservative Party challenger, Andres Pastrana, won a run-off election. In 2000, the government's initiative to end the narcotics trade met with fierce opposition and produced even more drug-related violence.

Before You Read

Consider the social pressures that lead to gang membership in Medellín, Colombia, and the horrific day-to-day lives of these teenagers and how they are similar to and different from gangs in the United States.

———————◆———————

1   Silhouetted against the full moon, the shape of a headless cat strung up by its paws. Its blood has been collected in a bowl on the

floor. Only a few drops continue to fall. As each one hits the bowl it makes tiny ripples, which grow until the whole surface seems full of tossing waves. Waves that shake to the noise of heavy rock being played at full blast. The cat's head is in the corner, its luminous green eyes staring sightlessly. Fifteen people are taking part in the silent ritual. The city is spread below them.

2   Warm blood is mixed with wine in a glass. The blood of a cat that climbs walls, leaps nonchalantly from fence to fence, walks on the silent pads of its paws across rooftops, vanishes effortlessly into the shadows of night. Cat's blood, full of the urge to pounce unerringly on its prey. Blood that conjures up strange energies, that speeds the brain.

3   Antonio recalls in a jumble of images the moment of his own initiation into one of the teenage gangs in a neighbourhood on the hills of north-east Medellín. In his feverish dreams as he fights for life, he sees himself on the streets again. Strange shapes appear in the sea of city lights. They raise the cup to seal their pact. There is no need for words, they all know what they are committing themselves to, what the laws are, the rewards and the punishment. From now on they will be all for one and one for all, they will be as one. They'll be the lords of creation.

4   But now Antonio is in the San Rafael Ward of the Saint Vincent de Paul hospital. A military ward, full of the wounded and the dying, the victims of an unequal war waged day and night along undefined fronts on the streets of Medellín. One Tuesday, three months earlier, Antonio was blasted with a shotgun as he boarded a bus in his neighbourhood. The shot perforated his stomach, leaving him hovering between life and death. Although only twenty, Antonio has often faced death, but has never felt it so close to him. He knows, even though he won't admit it, that he's not going to make it. He has a skinny body, a face drained of colour, dark eyes sunk in huge sockets. He begins to tell me his life story in a calm voice, searching inside himself, as if taking stock for reasons of his own.

Antonio

5   When I was a kid I used to get a bit of money using a home-made pistol. Then Lunar and Papucho—they're both dead now—let me have proper guns, so I started to steal and kill for real. You get violent because there are a lot of guys who want to tell you what to do, to take you over, just because you're a kid. You've got to keep your wits about you, to spread your own wings. That's what I did, and off I flew; anybody who got in my way paid for it.

6   I learned that lesson from my family. From the old woman, who's tough as nails. She's with me whatever I do. She might not look much, but she's always on my side. The only regret I have in quitting this

earth is leaving her on her own. To know she might be all alone in her old age. She's fought hard all her life, and she doesn't deserve that.

7   My old man died about 14 years ago. He was a hard case too, and taught me a lot, but he was always at the bottle, and left us in the lurch. That was why I had to fend for myself, to help my ma and my brothers and sisters. That's how I started in a gang—but also because it was something inside me, I was born with this violent streak.

8   Lunar, the leader of the gang, was only a teenager but he was tough all right. He'd been in the business for years already. He lived in Bello for a while and knew the people from Los Monjes. He learned a lot from them, so when he came to live here he started up his own gang. He had a birthmark or *lunar* on his cheek, that's how he got the nickname. It was thanks to him and Papucho, the other leader, that I learned how to do things properly.

9   I'll never forget the first time I had to kill someone. I had already shot a few people, but I'd never seen death close up. It was in Copacabana, a small place near Medellín. We were breaking into a farmhouse one morning when the watchman suddenly appeared out of nowhere. I was behind a wall, he ran in front of me, I looked up and was so startled I emptied my revolver into him. He was stone dead. That was tough, I won't lie, it was tough for me to take. For two weeks I couldn't eat a thing because I saw his face even in my food . . . but after that it got easy. You learn to kill without it disturbing your sleep.

10   Now it's me who's the gang leader. Papucho was killed by the guys up on the hill there. They set a trap for him and he fell for it. They asked him to do a job for them, then shot him to pieces. A friend of his was behind it, who'd sold out. Lunar made me second-in-command because we understood each other almost without speaking—we didn't need words.

11   Lunar didn't last much longer; he was never one to back down from a fight, never a chicken. He really enjoyed life; he always said we were all playing extra time anyway. And he was enjoying himself when he died: he was at a dance about three blocks down the hill when they shot him three times in the back. He was on his own because he reckoned there were no skunks down there. The kid who shot him died almost before he could blink. We tracked him down that same night, and sent him on his trip to the stars.

12   After Lunar's death another wise guy thought he'd take over the gang. I had to get tough and show him who was boss. For being such a smart ass now he's pushing up the dirt as well. It's me who gives the orders round here, I say what we do and don't do. There were about fifty of us to begin with, but a lot of them have been killed or put inside, and others have grassed. There's only twenty of us real hard cases left. They're all teenagers, between 15 and 18. I'm the oldest. A lot get killed or caught, but more always want to join, to get some action.

13 Whenever anyone wants to join I ask around: "Who is this kid? Can I trust him?" Then I decide if he can join or not. They're all kids who see things as they are; they know they won't get anywhere by working or studying, but if they join us they'll have ready money. They join because they want to, not because we force them. We don't tell anybody they have to. Not all of them are really poor, some do it for their families, others because they want to live in style.

14 Before we finally choose someone we give him a test: to take something somewhere, to carry guns and to keep them hidden. Then finally we give them a job to do. If the kid shows he can do it, then he's one of us. But if he ever grasses on us, if he shoots his mouth off, if he gets out of line, then he's dead meat. Everyone understands that. Then again, we support each other all we can; "If you haven't got something and I have, take it, friend—as a gift, not a loan." We also help if someone's in trouble. We look after each other, but nobody can double-cross us.

15 We take good care of our guns, because they're hard to come by. The last kid I shot died because of that.

16 "Antonio, help me out will you brother? Lend me a gun for a job I have to do," he said to me.

17 "I'll let you have this .38, but be sure you give it back tomorrow; you know the rules."

18 I lent it to him because the kid had always been straight with us, but this time he wasn't. So I went to talk to him, and he came up with a really strange excuse. He said the law had taken it from him. I gave him another two days, and when he didn't show up I passed the death sentence. He knew he was a marked man, so he didn't make any attempt to hide. It was easy for me.

19 The thing is, it's hard to find guns. You either have to shoot a guy to get his, or buy them, and a good weapon costs. We nearly always buy them from the police, and they sell us the ammo too. I've also bought grenades from a retired army guy. We've had T-55s, 32-shot mini-Uzis, 9mm Ingrands, but we usually use sawn-off shotguns, pistols and revolvers. We're all good shots.

20 We practise late at night, two, three in the morning, in some woods over at Rionegro. We set up a line of bottles and fire at them. I smash the lot. You have to keep a steady hand when you're on a job, you only have one chance to kill someone, you can't afford to miss. You only have a few seconds so you have to know what you're doing: if the dummy doesn't die, you could. You have to know how to handle your weapon, to shoot straight, and how to make your get-away. We learn a lot from films. We get videos of people like Chuck Norris, Black Cobra, Commando, or Stallone, and watch how they handle their weapons, how they cover each other, how they get away. We watch the films and discuss tactics.

21   We learn to ride motor bikes on the hills round here. They're all souped up, really quick. Most of them are stolen; we buy papers for them for 20,000 pesos[1] down at the traffic police. Our territory is from the bus terminal down to the school. People who don't mess with us have no problems, but anyone who tries to muscle in either gets out or dies. We help the people in our neighbourhood, they come to us and say: "we've got nothing to eat," so we help them and keep them happy. And when we've done a job that pays well, we make sure they get some. We look after them so that they're on our side. Whenever someone tries to move in on our territory, I personally go and kneecap them as a warning they should never come back.

22   Lots of kids in the neighbourhood want to be in a gang. All I tell them is if that's what they want to do they have to be serious about it, but I don't force them to join. Most of them start by stealing cars, then they save up to buy a shotgun, which is the cheapest weapon around. We give them cartridges so they can get started.

23   I reckon I've killed 13 people. That's 13 I've killed personally, I don't count those we've shot when we're out as a gang. If I die now, I'll die happy. Killing is our business really, we do other jobs, but mostly we're hired to kill people.

24   People from all sorts of places contract us: from Bellavista jail, from El Poblado, from Itagüí. People who don't want to show their faces, and take you on to get rid of their problem for them. I try to work out whether our client means business, if he can pay us. We charge according to who we have to hit: if he's important, we charge more. We're putting our lives, our freedom, our guns on the line. If we have to leave the city to deal with some big shot, our price is anything up to three million. Here in Medellín the lowest we go is half a million.

25   We don't care who we have to give it to, we know it has to be done, that's all there is to it. Whoever it may be: I have no allegiances. I'll drive the bike and gun anyone down myself, no problem. Sometimes we don't even know who it is we have to kill. You hear later who the hit was, from the news on the radio. It's all the same to us, we've done our job, that's all.

26   Whenever I have to kill someone, all I think is: too bad for him he crossed my path. If their back is towards me, I call out, so I can make sure I've got the right guy, and when he turns round, I give it to him. I don't worry about it, I don't worry about running into the law, or that things will go wrong, nothing like that. I only hope I don't kill a woman or a child in a shoot-out. If I'm going to kill, there has to be a reason for it.

[1]£1 = 545 pesos (1990).

27   Once we went out to a small town to deal with a local councillor. We don't usually know who is giving us the contract, but in this case it was more or less direct contact, and we realised that the guy who wanted him dead was the leader of a political party. We kept well away from him after that, because you can be the ones who end up paying. They can easily have you rubbed out as well to get rid of witnesses. We made a million on that job.

28   The week before, we went to the town to see the lie of the land. We were shown the client, we took a look at where the police were, worked out how to get out afterwards. On the Saturday, I went back with a girlfriend. She was carrying the weapon—a submachine gun—in her bag. We took a room in the best hotel, pretending we were a honeymoon couple. We took our time checking out the town, making sure nothing could go wrong.

29   On the Sunday, two of the gang stole a car in Medellín, and kept the owner in a room in Guayaquil until the job was done. One of them drove to the town and parked where we'd agreed, right on time. The councillor always liked to have a coffee in a corner bar after his meetings. My girlfriend showed up with the gun around two in the afternoon. I took it and waited for the action. Waiting like that really gets you down. You get real nervous. I've found a trick which always helps me: I get a bullet, take out the lead, and pour the gunpowder into a hot black coffee. I drink the lot, and that steadies my nerves.

30   At ten to six I left the hotel and sat waiting in the bar. It was a hot evening, and there were a lot of people on the street. I saw our car arrive and park a few metres away. The target came in a couple of minutes later. On the dot as promised.

31   It was beginning to get dark, which is always useful. I took another good look round to make sure there was nothing unusual going on, then paid for my drink. When the waiter was giving me my change, I pulled out the submachine gun and started firing. Everybody hit the floor. When something like that happens in a small town, they all stay well out of it, no one is expecting it. I went over and put a final bullet in him, because some of these guys are really tough and you have to make sure of your money. It was all over in seconds. While I had been firing, they had started the car, so I walked to it as calm as could be, and got in. We made sure we didn't drive too fast out of town. We made as if we were going out on the main highway, but then headed off down a side road. We drove for about a quarter of an hour, then left the car by the roadside. We walked for an hour, until we came to a safe house on a farm owned by a friend of the politician who had hired us. We caught a bus back to Medellín about five o'clock the next morning. They sent the gun back to us a few days later. Everything had been well planned and worked like clockwork.

32   That night we had a huge party. We'd already had the pay-off, so as the saying goes: "the dead to their graves, the living to the dance." It was like Christmas. We bought a pig, crates of beer and liquor, set up a sound system in the street, and gave it all we'd got 'til morning.

33   The bus struggles up the hill, along narrow twisting streets full of people and shops. From this main road you have to walk another two blocks up a narrow alley-way, then climb a gully before you reach the Montoya family's house. The roof is made of corrugated iron and cardboard; the walls are not plastered, just painted with a blue wash. Red geraniums flower outside. The house is three tiny rooms. Posters of movie stars and rock musicians cover the walls. Lost in one corner under a layer of cobwebs is a small picture of the Virgin of El Carmen. A horseshoe and a piece of aloe vera hang over the front door to bring good luck.

34   Doña Azucena, Antonio's mother, is a small, thin woman. Her face shows the marks of all she has been through in her life. Two children, aged four and six, whom she had by her second husband, cling to her legs. She works in a cafe in the centre of Medellín. A few years ago, when she still had legs worth showing off, she worked in the Porteño bar in Guayaquil. The kind of bar where men go to drink liquor and pick up women. Doña Azucena takes some photos out of an old album which show her in high heels, a mini skirt, and wearing bright scarlet lipstick. She would never dream of showing them to her children. It was in that bar, to the sound of music from Olimpo Cárdenas and Julio Jaramillo, that her second husband fell in love with her. A much older man, she lived with him for four years until one weekend, she never knew why, he walked out and didn't come back. She didn't miss him, because her older children had never got on with him, and because she herself had lost all her affection for him.

Doña Azucena

35   In the bar there's a big picture of a man hanging from a branch. A tiger is trying to climb the tree, there's a rattlesnake in the tree-top, and under the branch is a pool full of crocodiles. I used to look at that picture and think my life was exactly like that. Wherever I've been, I've lost out.

36   I can remember it like it was yesterday. I was at a rural school in Liborina, a beautiful part of the country. It was May, the month of the Holy Virgin, and we were preparing to celebrate. Our teacher, who was called Petronilla, asked me to pick some roses for the altar, and said I should make sure to cut all the thorns off. I went down a path below the school where there were some lovely rose bushes. I picked them and sat

down to snip the thorns off. Then I went back to the school and gave them to the teacher. She took them, but a splinter got caught in her finger, so suddenly she drew back her hand and slapped me across the face. Without even thinking about it, I slashed at her with the knife, the one I'd used to cut the roses. She was badly wounded, but they managed to save her life. That was the end of school for me.

37   I've always had a quick temper, I've never let anyone put anything over on me. That's how my family was, that's how my children are. I was born in Urrao, but we had to leave there when I was still little because of the political violence. My father, whose name was Antonio too, was a die-hard Liberal, every weekend he'd go into town, get drunk, and start shouting "Up with the Liberals!" for everyone to hear. As soon as the violence started, we began to get death threats.

38   Once my father and his brothers had to take on a bunch of Conservative thugs who were terrorising the area. We knew they'd come up after us. So the men borrowed some shotguns and took up their positions on a bit of a hill just below the house. When they saw the Conservatives arrive, they fired at them and they ran off.

39   That same evening Don Aquileo, a neighbour who was a Conservative too, but who got on well with us, came up to see us. He told us that down in town everyone was saying they'd get together and come up and finish us off. There'd already been other tremendous massacres in the countryside, so we decided to get out that same night and go to Liborina, where we had family. Later some Liberal guerrillas got organised in Urrao, led by Captain Franco. But that was after we left. We had a dreadful time there, I can remember passing lots of mutilated bodies by the roadsides, those are things you never forget.

40   A few years later, I was a teenager by then, we moved on to Chigorodó, in Urabá, because they said the land was fertile there. We began to clear a farm in the jungle, about two hours from the nearest town. That was where my mother María died. The climate killed her. The weather was impossible. Up there the heat is hellish, and it can rain the whole day long. It was a struggle to clear the jungle, but eventually we were able to plant bananas and maize.

41   The good times didn't last long. We'd just begun to harvest our crops, when the violence began there too. Not between Conservatives and Liberals, but just between people for no reason at all. There was a store where we all used to go at weekends to talk and drink. But soon people began to fight with machetes. The men got drunk and killed each other without ever knowing why, or rather, at the slightest excuse.

42   My brothers have always been difficult, they've fought with almost everyone. But above all they got into trouble with a family called García, who came from Dabeiba. There were about ten of them, all dangerous men. It was when they started threatening us that we decided to sell up and come to Medellín.

43   We settled in the Barrio Popular. We built a place up on this hill, just when people had started moving in. Soon everywhere was full of shacks. People who had lost their land in the country because of the violence, and had come to the city to escape.

44   I can remember the day when Don Polo was out laying the floor for his place. He'd come from Andes with his family. The police on horseback turned up, and wanted to take him away. We all used to help each other, to protect ourselves, so I went out and started to shout at them.

45   "You can't take him if you haven't got an arrest warrant."

46   "You're not the law, you bitch, we are, and we know what we're doing," one of them shouted back, pointing his rifle at me.

47   I was really angry by then, and I thought well, if I'm going to die then so be it, may God forgive me all my sins but this injustice shouldn't be allowed to happen. Other people began pouring out of their houses. Then a police car arrived. We were still arguing, and one of the police hit me with the butt of his rifle.

48   "Come on, it's you we're going to arrest for causing an obstruction," he said, pushing me into the car.

49   I began to kick out, and my neighbours all closed round the car, saying: "You've no right to take Doña Azucena."

50   "Drive off," the captain told his driver.

51   "Which way? D'you want me to kill all these people?"

52   They all crowded closer and closer round the car, and finally pulled me out. The other policemen on horseback were shouting insults all the time. Then a young fellow hit one of them with a stick, and they all fired at him. The rest of us ran off. They picked up his body and left. They took him to the hospital, but he died. Things like that happened all the time, the police would come up to destroy our houses, but we'd all stand firm. A lot of lives were lost. That's why we've never liked the law, it seems they're always out to get the poor.

53   It was around that time that I married Diego Montoya. He was a young man who had just moved to Medellín from Puerto Berrío. I went with him against my family's wishes; they didn't like him because he was black. We went to live with one of his sisters over in Santa Cruz. For a few years it was good, he looked after me and remembered all the little details—everything was fine. We had five children, almost one after the other: Claudia, Diego, Antonio, Orlando, and Nelly.

54   But gradually Diego went downhill. He became a tremendous drinker and would give me almost nothing for the kids, so I had to go and find work, first of all in houses over in Laureles, then in a bar in Guayaquil. One day when I came back from work I found my eldest daughter Claudia with her leg all bloody. Diego's sister's eldest son had sliced her with a saw because she had picked up something he was working with. I took my belt off, went to find the boy, and gave him a good thrashing. His mother tried to defend him, so I started on

her too. When Diego came back later that night, I told him what had happened. His sister went whining to him, and told him he should teach me a lesson.

55   "He's not going to teach me any lesson, you do it if you want to," I told her.

56   "But he's your husband," she replied.

57   "That he may be, but if I have to show him what's what, I will."

58   Diego got really angry and left. By the time he returned I was in bed, reading a magazine by candlelight.

59   "I'm leaving, thanks for everything. All your things are on the table," I told him.

60   I'd put his revolver and some money he'd given me on the table by the bed. He didn't say a word, but got into bed. At about five in the morning, he got up again. He stood there for a minute staring at me, then went over to our daughter's bed, stroked her hair, gave her a kiss, and began to cry.

61   "Wake up sweetheart, wake up so we can talk about it," he said to me, shaking me gently by the shoulder.

62   "There's nothing for us to talk about. I've already given you back all your things, what more do I owe you?"

63   "Can't you wait 'til Saturday so I can sort things out?"

64   "When did you ever sort things out? All you do is make one promise after another, then spend every cent you earn on whores and booze."

65   "Just wait, in the next few days I'm expecting a big note, I promise I'll hand it over to you," he begged, and my heart softened.

66   "OK, let's see; if you love your children and want to stay with them, then buy us somewhere to live, that's the only condition. I'll give you all day today to think about it, if you don't come up with something by tonight, I'm off."

67   He didn't come back to sleep that night, but the next day, Saturday, he arrived very early. He took me and the children to look at a plot of land in the Barrio Popular. We did the deal there and then, and the following week had already built a place. We've been living in this gully ever since.

68   This is where I brought up my children. Diego died 14 years ago, a few months after he had an accident that crippled him. While he was at home sick he told people's fortunes for them. He knew a lot. Just by looking at the palm of someone's hand he could tell what was wrong, what their illness was, if they had been smoking too much dope, if a woman had the evil eye on them. Then he'd give them a cure or take the spell off them. He learned from his father, who practised these things down in Puerto Berrío. I asked him to teach me, but he always said: "You're too black-hearted, if you learned this, you'd use it to harm people."

69   It's true that in some ways I can be hard. I wouldn't harm a soul, but if anyone crosses me, they're in for it. That's what I've always taught my children, that they've got to make people respect them. They've got it in their blood, they were born as rebellious as me. My eldest worked for a while in the building trade, but then he fell in with some friends and began to go wrong. At first they dealt in marijuana, then they started with robberies. At the moment he's doing three years in Acacías, Meta, for assault.

70   Ever since he was little, Antonio's been the wildest of the lot. The same thing happened to him at school as me, although I've never told them my story. In his third year at primary school they had a teacher who used to punish them terribly, so one day Antonio and a friend waited for him outside the school and stabbed him with a knife. Since then, Antonio's been on the streets.

71   It was Diego, his older brother, who got him started in crime. Antonio was only eleven when he was sent to a remand home, in Floresta. He'd had a fight with a neighbour's boy, Doña Blanca's son, a kid's quarrel. But then Alberto, her older son, threatened to give him a hiding. I spoke to them and said that if anyone was going to give him a hiding it would be me. In return they insulted me, and that drove my kids wild. Without my knowing it, Diego gave Antonio a gun.

72   "If you let that Alberto lay a finger on you, I'll give you another hiding myself. You have to show you're a Montoya," Diego told him.

73   One day soon after, I was making lunch when I heard some shots and a terrific row outside. I ran out and saw Alberto lying on the pavement. Antonio had shot him five times. Fortunately he didn't die, but since then it's been war between our two families. Two of them have died, and my sons have been wounded several times.

74   After Antonio got out of the remand home he studied plumbing and electrics at the San José school. But that didn't last long, he was soon back on the streets. A few days later I saw him with a couple of boys who were a good bit older than him, Papucho and Lunar, both of them dead now. They were the ones who sealed his fate. People began to be afraid of them, grassed on them to the police, and they came looking for them.

75   All I can say is that he's been a good son to me. I've had to work in bars all these years to earn enough to keep my family. It's hard for a woman on her own. Antonio is the one who's helped me the most. He's never drunk a lot, and whenever he's done a job he always brings something back for the house.

76   I've been with him through thick and thin. Whenever he's inside I always go and visit him. I've often had to struggle with the police, but I've made sure they respect me as a woman. I've made a vow to the Fallen Christ of Girardota to make sure my boy gets well quickly. That's what I want, I want him to get well and go and find the coward

who shot him, things can't stay like this. None of my family is going to feel safe with that fellow around.

77   Antonio knew they wanted to kill him, that's why he left home. That Tuesday, he came up here in the morning and was chatting with the girls, playing with the dog. I went down to the main street to buy things for lunch. As I was coming back I saw two of the Capucho gang on the corner. That scared me, but I walked past them calmly, as if I hadn't even seen them.

78   "Antonio, get away from here, they're out to get you," I told him when I reached home.

79   "Don't worry, ma, the day I die I'll have my bags packed and ready, but today isn't the day," he said laughing, lying back on the bed.

80   In the afternoon he went round to his girlfriend Claudia's house next door. He was still joking about, listening to music as if nothing was wrong. At six I saw the others again, they were at the bottom of the gully. They had their hands in their pockets, and were staring up our way. The worst of it was that Antonio didn't have any protection. I went and found him and told him what was going on.

81   "It looks bad out there, I think you should find some way to get away."

82   "Cool it, ma, I'll be off in a minute. Go round to Gitano's place and tell him to bring a couple of guns up here, that there's going to be some action."

83   I sneaked out the back way and went to find Gitano.

84   "Doña Azucena, he's not back from town, and anyway he hasn't got any guns either," they told me.

85   When I told Antonio that Gitano wasn't around, he looked worried, but pretended everything was all right.

86   "I'm going over the wall at the back here," he said. "You two go out the front and act normal, while I get away."

87   We went out and sat on the front porch to chat. The Capucho boys were still down at the bottom of the gully, so I relaxed a bit. But then 15 minutes later I got a call from the hospital.

88   "We have your boy Antonio Montoya here, he's in a bad way."

89   In the three months since then I've been down there every afternoon between two and five, when you can visit them. Every week the hospital is full of wounded kids, they come and go, new ones take the place of those who get better, but Antonio is still there. I don't know how all this is going to end.

90   The priest went to give him confession yesterday, I've no idea what Antonio told him about his life. When the priest came out he greeted me very formally. "Don't worry, he has repented and is at peace with God," he told me. And that did bring me peace of mind. Even though I'm not much of a believer it's always better to know you're at peace with God.

Antonio

91   I'd like to be out on the streets of my neighbourhood again, that's my territory. I love walking down them. I've always got my wits about me of course, my eyes wide open and my gun in my pocket, because I've got as many enemies as friends. You never know where you might get shot from. A lot of people are after me, I've got a lot of admirers in other gangs. The law is also on my tail. If I get out of here, I'm going to be real careful.

92   There've always been gangs in our neighbourhood: the Nachos, the Montañeros, Loco Uribe's gang, the Calvos . . . and as the song says: "this bed ain't big enough for everyone." You have to be on the lookout, if you're not careful one of the other gangs muscles in and people start leaving you. You have to make sure of your territory, that's the main thing. The biggest war we ever had was with the Nachos, who were hired killers like us. When they first showed up we did nothing, but then they started throwing their weight around, upsetting people. Until one day Martín, one of our gang, told them where to get off, and they shot him. That same night we went up to their place and taught them a lesson. Six of us went up there in groups of two: we met up on the street corner where they hung out, and took them completely by surprise. We shot two of them. They thought they were such tough guys they never even imagined anyone would come for them.

93   A few days later they came for us. We were waiting for them. I put a handkerchief over my face, put on a baseball cap, and went out with my submachine gun. Others from the gang were covering me, watching what would happen.

94   "We want peace, not war," one of the Nachos shouted.

95   "We don't want peace, what we want is war," Lunar shouted back, and fired off a volley into the air.

96   Of course they didn't really want peace, what they were trying to do was to see all our faces so they could pick us off. In the end they retreated back up the gully. "Get them to start making your coffins," they shouted from up top.

97   From then on it was war. They would come down into the gully, we'd go and raid them, both sides would try to ambush each other . . . it was a real shootin' war that left a lot of people dead.

98   The Nachos went to pieces after the police got their leader in a raid. Even I have to admit that the guy was a real man: he and this other guy were fighting it out with the pigs for hours. They say that when Nacho had only one bullet left he shut himself in the bathroom of the house they were holed up in and shot himself in the head. After that his gang was nothing, they had no stomach for a fight. A few days later the law arrested about twenty of them, and now they're all in Bellavista for a good long while.

99   The gang wars have been tough: whole families have been wiped out in vendettas. What happens is if one of the gang or one of your relatives gets killed, you go out and get the bastard who did it, or one of his family; but we never touch women. If you don't react, they walk all over you.

100   We also fight police, but it's easier with them. They're shit scared when they come up here, and we know our own territory. Of course they've caught me twice, and I ended up in Bellavista as well.

101   The first time was the hardest. I'd been holed up in a house in a nearby neighbourhood. About midnight I woke up to hear them knocking the door down.

102   "Open up, this is the police," they shouted.

103   I tried to escape out the back, but the place was surrounded. Before I could do a thing, the police were everywhere. They put me into the patrol car without even letting me get dressed, and took me off to the F-2 headquarters. All they found in the house were three guns we had stashed there.

104   At the station they put me in a tub with water up to my neck. They left me there all night freezing my balls off, and ran electric current through me too. They kept asking me about the others in the gang, who the leaders were, but I didn't say a word.

105   "Think you're a real tough guy, don't you, you fairy," they shouted, kicking me as hard as they could in the stomach.

106   I didn't think I was tough at all, but to grass on people is the lowest you can go. They asked me about enemies of mine, but I didn't even give them away, although I knew where they hung out. It's like Cruz Medina sings in the tango: "Don't anyone ask who wounded me so, you're wasting your time, you'll never know. Let me die here in peace, and don't be surprised at that, when a man is a man, he won't squeal like a rat."

107   I was sent to Bellavista prison for illegal possession of firearms. I didn't have a record, and they couldn't get anything out of me, so they got mad. They even tried to get people from the neighbourhood to testify against me, but nobody would. There may be people who hate your guts, but they know that if they start blabbing, they're signing their own death warrants. Either you get them once you're out, or one of the gang does it for you.

108   I was three months in the slammer. That was only about long enough to get over the beating the pigs had given me. I met several of the gang in the jail. I was lucky that the boss man on our block was an old guy I'd done a job for, who liked me. If you end up in Bellavista with no one to look after you, you're done for. You get kicked from block to block until you end up in the worst hole, where they steal everything you've got, even your sex.

109   That's why I was lucky, because I had someone to look out for me. Of course I met up with a few of my old enemies too, some of the Na-

chos and others. But the worst was a guy called Pepe, whose brother I had shot. I told the boss man about him, and he said: "Tell him to get out of here, and if he cuts up rough about it, send him to the funeral parlour."

110   I sent the message to Pepe, and a few days later he changed blocks. Whatever the boss man says goes. Nobody in there can do anything without his permission.

111   Once I got into a fight. I had some air-cushion Nike running shoes, the ones that cost 20,000 pesos. Two guys came up to me: "Listen, sweetheart, get those shoes off, they've been sold," one of them said, a switchblade in his hand.

112   "You listen. Tell whoever bought them to come and take them off, I'm too tired," I said, pulling out a metal bar I had hidden in my jacket.

113   Three of my gang appeared out of nowhere, and we set on them. I ended up stabbing one right in the heart. He died on the way to the infirmary. The other one got away. One of us was wounded too, but nothing serious. In Bellavista they don't even bother to make any enquiries, they know no one will say a word. Anyone who's been hit gets his own back if he can, if not, he chokes on it.

114   I paid my way out of Bellavista. There are people who act as go-betweens with the judges. My case was easy, because it wasn't a serious charge and nobody came forward to accuse me of anything else. I paid around 250,000 pesos. Or rather, some associates of the gang who'd just done a job paid it for me.

115   After that I went back to my patch, to my normal life. Half the time I'm happy, the other half I'm worked up. When I haven't got anything to do, I get up late, it's almost dark by the time I hit the streets. I hang around the street corners listening to rock music with the gang or I go to a bar with my girl to listen to love songs or country music.

116   My girl is called Claudia. I know I can trust her, she knows what I do, and backs me up, but she doesn't want to get involved at all. She works in a dress factory and comes home early every day. She's got expensive tastes: she likes new clothes, jewels, all the fancy stuff, and I give her everything she wants. At the weekend either we go out to bars in Bello, or dance salsa, or go down into Manrique to listen to some smoochy music. She's a good-looker, but what I most like about her is that she's serious. Because there's a lot of girls who make your eyes pop, but most of them are just good for a quick lay, a one night stand. Sometimes we like to party at the houses we hide up in, and we get girls in. Fabulous women, but they're only out for what they can get from you. The only real girlfriend I've had is Claudia.

117   Things have got very difficult. This gang's appeared called the Capuchos, they're killing people all over the place. It was them who shot me. I knew they were after me, that's why I split from home. But then I got it into my head to go up and say hello to the old woman and

Claudia. I thought everything was quiet because the police were snooping around the neighbourhood a lot at the time. I didn't want any trouble, so I went up there without a weapon. Ma soon told me that they were out looking for me. I wasn't worried, I knew they wouldn't dare come up to the house. It's in a narrow gully, so long as you're under cover you can take on anyone.

118   I was waiting for some of the gang to arrive with the guns so we could get rid of those guys. By the time night fell and they hadn't arrived, I realised things were getting serious. So I climbed out of the back of the house and made for the road up top. I walked about a block, and saw a bus coming down, so I waved it to stop. Just as I was getting on, I saw a kid about two metres from me with a shotgun. Then I felt this heat spreading all through my body, and that was the last I knew. I was out for four days before I came round. What got me most was that a lot of people in the neighbourhood knew what was going on but didn't warn me. The Capuchos had every exit staked. I guess it's everyone's turn sometime, and that day it was mine.

119   What I wish is that they had killed me there and then, without time for me to let out a sigh or feel any pain, or even to say "they've got me." I'd have preferred that to this feeling that my body and my mind are being torn apart. Having to stare death in the face all day long, grinning and beckoning at me, but not daring to come any closer. Better to die straight off, so you don't get to see how all your so-called friends abandon you. In here you realise that people are only with you in the good times. As Don Olimpo sings: "When you're on top of the world, you can have friends galore, but when fate trips you up, you'll see it's all lies, they won't want you any more." I don't care about dying, we were all born to die. But I want to die quickly, without all this pain and loneliness.

120   Last night Antonio had his final dream. He dreamt he was up again on the flat roof of the house in the gully where he'd been happiest, blowing his mind with all his gang to the music of drums and electric guitars.

121   The city at night is fabulous, it's all light and darkness. I feel just like one of those dots, lost in a sea of light. That's what we are, a tiny light, or maybe a patch of darkness. In the end, we're all or nothing. We can do great things, but we're all mortal. Look closely at the yellow lights, and they turn into all colours, they spread upwards until they make a rainbow in the night. Then they're like a huge cascade of white water that is falling and falling into a deep, invisible well. Then the water gushes out again, this time like a giant flame, making a great bonfire that devours everything. Afterwards there are only red embers and ashes, which are blown everywhere. Now everything is a desert, noth-

ing grows, nothing blooms. The city at night is a screen, a lot of images that flash in front of your eyes. Take a good look at the buildings in the centre. They're pointed-headed monsters. You can see their long arms stretching out, trying to catch something. It's us they're trying to grab. But we're as high and as far away as a cloud. We're on the heights where we can look down on everything, where nothing can touch us. We're the lords of all creation.

✦ Evaluating the Text

1. What picture do you get of Antonio, his relationship with other gang members, and the reasons for his life of violence? What insight does this interview give you into the values of being a member of a gang?

2. Describe the circumstances that surround recruitment, weapons used, training, role models, and the nature of the jobs performed.

3. What insight do you get from learning about Antonio's mother, Doña Azucena, that sheds light on the direction his life has taken?

✦ Exploring Different Perspectives

1. How do the different cultural factors explain the reactions of Antonio's mother in this account and the reactions of the mother in Viramma's "A Pariah's Life"?

2. What insight do the accounts by Salazar and Mary Crow Dog (see "Civilize Them with a Stick") provide into rebellion against mainstream society?

✦ Extending Viewpoints through Writing

1. Have you ever belonged to a gang or club? Describe your experiences, emphasizing the advantages and disadvantages you found in being a member.

2. Describe the role popular music and films play in Antonio's life. Are there songs or movies that you have seen that have had as strong an effect in shaping your outlook as those mentioned by Antonio?

Viramma

A Pariah's Life

◆

Viramma is an agricultural worker and midwife in Karani, a village in southeast India. She is a member of the caste known as untouchable. She has told her life story over a period of ten years to Josiane and Jean-Luc Racine. She communicates an impression of great strength and fatalism (of her twelve children, only three survive) and her account, translated by Will Hobson, which first appeared in GRANTA, Spring 1997, is a vivid portrait of one at the margin of society.

Before You Read

Consider the unusual superstitions and rituals by which Viramma lives her life and her status as an untouchable in Indian society.

◆

1   I am the midwife here. I was born in the village of Velpakkam in Tamil Nadu, and when I married, I came to Karani, my husband's village. I was still a child then. I am a farm worker and, like all my family, I am a serf, bonded to Karani's richest landowner. We are Pariahs. We live apart from the other castes; we eat beef, we play the drums at funerals and weddings because only we can touch cow hide; we work the land. My son Anbin corrects me when I say "Pariah"; he says we should use the word "Harijan."[1] Every day people from the political parties come to the village and tell us to demand higher wages, to fight the caste system. And they mean well. But how would we survive? We have no land, not even a field.

2   We midwives help women during labour and are paid twenty rupees a month by the state. When a woman goes into labour, her relatives come and find me: "Eldest sister-in-law! The woman's in pain at home!" So I drop everything; I go and see her, examine her, turn her round one way, then the other; I pester her a bit and then tell her more or less when the child is going to be born. And it always turns out as I said it would. When the child is born, I cut the cord with a knife and tell one of the other women attending to find a hoe and a crowbar and to dig a hole in the channel near the house. I wait for the placenta to

---

[1]*Harijan* means "loved ones of God." The name change was suggested by Mahatma Gandhi.

come out and go and bury it immediately. Then I take care of the mother. I stretch her out on a mat, propped up with pillows, wash the baby with soap and hot water and lay it down next to its mother. Then I put a sickle and some margosa leaves at the head of the mat, so spirits don't come near them—those rogue spirits love to prowl around the lanes in the evening or at night, eating any food left lying on the ground and trying to possess people.

3   It's well known that they follow us everywhere we go, when we're hoeing or planting out; when we're changing our sanitary towels; when we're washing our hair. They sense that we're going to visit a woman in labour and then they possess us. That's why we put down the sickle and the margosa leaves. After the birth I'll visit the mother quite often, to make sure everything's going all right. If impurities have stayed in the womb, I'll cook the leaves of the "cow's itch" plant, extract the juice and make the mother drink it three times.

4   That's how a birth happens here. We Pariahs prefer to have babies at home. I tell the nurse if the newborns are boys or girls, and she goes and enters them in the registers at Pondicherry hospital. In the past, we'd take women to hospital only in emergencies. We went there in an ox-cart or a rickshaw, and often the woman died on the way. Nowadays doctors visit the villages and give medicines and tonics to women when they become pregnant. In the sixth or seventh month they're meant to go to the dispensary for a check-up. A nurse also comes to the village. Yes, everything has changed now.

5   I had my twelve children alone; I didn't let anyone near me. "Leave me in peace," I always said to the nurses. "It will come out on its own! Why do you want to rummage around in there?" I always give birth very gently—like stroking a rose. It never lasts long: I'm not one of those women whose labours drag on all night, for days even.

6   When I'm giving birth I first make a point of preparing a tray for Ettiyan—the god of death's assistant—and his huge men, with their thick moustaches and muscly shoulders. On the tray I put green mangoes, coconuts and other fruit as well as some tools: a hoe, a crowbar, a basket, so that they can set to work as soon as the child comes out of the sack in our womb. Yes! I've seen enough to know what I'm talking about. I've had a full bushel of children! Everything we eat goes into that sack: that's how the child grows. Just think what a mystery it is. With the blood he collects over ten months, Isvaran [the god Siva] moulds a baby in our womb. Only he can do that. Otherwise how could a sperm become a child?

7   I've always had plenty of milk. It used to flow so much that the front of my sari was all stiff. It's well known that we breastfeed our children for a long time. That prevents us from having another child immediately. If we were always pregnant, how could we work and eat? Rich

women can stretch their legs and take a rest. But to get my rice, I have to work: planting out, hoeing, grazing the cows, collecting wood. When we've got a little one in our arms, it's the same: we take it everywhere, and we worry, because while we're working we don't really know what it's doing, where it is. That's why we try to wait at least three years, until the child grows up, walks and can say, "Dad," "Mum," "That's our cow." That's what we take as a sign. Then we can start "talking" again, "doing it." If we time it like this, the child will be strong and chubby.

8   But Isvaran has given me a baby a year. Luckily my blood has stayed the same; it hasn't turned, and my children have never been really emaciated. Of course that also depends on the way you look after them. For me, that used to be my great worry! I managed to feed them well. As soon as I had a little money, I'd buy them sweets. I'd make them rice whenever I could, some *dosai*, some *idli*. I'd put a little sugar in cow's milk. . . . That's how I took care of them. There are some women who just let their children be without giving them regular meals. Human beings can only live if you put at least a little milk in their mouths when they're hungry! It happens with us that some women skip their children's mealtimes when they're working. But how do you expect them to grow that way?

9   Isvaran has done his work well; he's put plenty of children in my womb: beautiful children, born in perfect health. It's only afterwards that some have died. One of diarrhoea, another of apoplexy. All of them have walked! Two of my children even came to the peanut harvest. I pierced their noses to put a jewel in. I plaited their hair and put flowers in it and pretty *potteu* on their foreheads, made with paste. I took good care of my little ones. I never neglected them. I dressed them neatly. If high-caste people saw them running in the street, they'd talk to them kindly, thinking that they were high-caste children.

10   How many children have I had? Wait . . . I've had twelve. The first was a girl, Muttamma. Then a boy, Ganesan. After that, a girl, Arayi. *Ayo!* After that I don't remember any more. But I've definitely had twelve: we registered them at the registry office. Yes, when there's a birth, you have to go there and declare it. "Here Sir, I've had a boy or a girl and I name it Manivelu, Nataraja or Perambata." Down there they enter all that into a big ledger. *Ayo!* If we went to that office, perhaps they could tell us how many children I've had and their names as well. *Ayo!* Look at that, I don't remember any more. They're born; they die. I've haven't got all my children's names in my head: all I have left are Miniyamma, my fourth child; Anbin, my eighth; and Sundari, my eleventh.

11   A pregnant woman is prey to everything that roams around her: ghosts, ghouls, demons, the evil spirits of people who have committed suicide or died violent deaths. She has to be very careful, especially if she is a Pariah. We Pariah women have to go all over the place, graz-

ing the cattle, collecting wood. We're outside the whole time, even when the sun's at its height. Those spirits take advantage of this: they grab us and possess us so we fall ill, or have miscarriages. Something like that happened to me when I was pregnant with my second child.

12   One of my nephews died suddenly, the day after his engagement. One night when I was asleep I saw him sitting on me—I felt him! My husband told me that I had squeezed him very tight in my arms, that I'd been delirious and mumbling something. The following day we decided that the boy needed something, and that's why he'd come. My husband went to get bottles of arrack and palm wine. I arranged the offerings in the middle of the house: betel, areca nuts, lime, a big banana leaf with a mountain of rice, some salt fish, some toast, a cigar, bottles of alcohol, a jar of water and a beautiful oil lamp. In the meantime my husband went to find the priest from the temple of Perumal [Vishnu]—he's the one responsible for funerals. The priest asked us to spread river sand next to the offerings. He called on Yama, the god of death, and drew the sign of Yama in the sand. We ate that evening as usual and went to sleep in a corner. You must never sleep opposite the door, because a spirit might slap you when it comes in if it finds you in its way. You have to be brave when a spirit arrives! In fact you won't see it; you only hear its footsteps, like the sound of little bells, *djang, djang,* when an ox-cart goes by. It goes *han! han! han!* as if it's craving something. It always comes with its messengers, all tied to each other with big ropes. You hear them walking with rhythmic, heavy steps: *ahum! ahum! ahum!*

13   We were very afraid. As soon as the spirit came in, the lamp went out in a flash, even though it was full of oil. We heard it walking about and eating its fill and then suddenly it fled. We heard it running away very fast. When day broke soon after it had gone, we rushed to see what had happened. The rice was scattered, everywhere. On the sand we found a cat's paw-print, and part of Yama's sign had been rubbed out. The spirit had come in the form of a cat! While we were waiting for the priest to come, we collected the offerings in a big wicker basket. The priest himself was very satisfied and said that the spirit wouldn't come back. But I fell ill soon after and had a miscarriage.

14   There are worse spirits, though: the *katteri,* for example, who spy on women when they are pregnant. You have to be very careful with them. There are several sorts of *katteri*: Rana Katteri, who has bleeding wounds and drinks blood; or Irsi Katteri, the foetus eater—she's the one who causes miscarriages. As soon as she catches the smell of a foetus in a woman's womb, she's there, spying, waiting for her chance. We can tell immediately that it's that bitch at work if there are black clots when a baby aborts: she sucks up the good blood and leaves only the bad.

15   My first three children were born at my mother's house. Their births went well, and they died in good shape. It was the spirit living in that house who devoured them. My grandfather knew about sorcery.

People came to see him; they used to say that he called up the spirit, talked to it and asked it to go along with him when he went out. It lived with him, basically. When my grandfather died, we tried to drive it away but it was no use; it used to come back in the form of my grandfather; it joined in conversations, calling my grandmother by her name like her dead husband used to. And my grandmother used to answer back, "Ah! The only answer I'll give you is with my broom, you dog! I recognize you! I know who you are! Get out of here!" It would just throw tamarind seeds at her face. When a sorcerer came from Ossur to try and get rid of it, it turned vicious. The sorcerer told us he couldn't do anything against it. The spirit had taken root in that ground. It was old and cunning: we were the ones who had to go. It destroyed everything! Everything! A garlic clove couldn't even grow! My father had to sell his paddy field. I gave birth three times there: none of those children survived. The spirit ate them as and when they were born. Nothing prospered. That's how it is with the spirits.

16   All my children have been buried where they died: the first ones at Velpakkam, the others at Karani. My mother insisted we burn the first-born and throw her ashes in the river so a sorcerer didn't come and get them. The ashes or bones of first-borns are coveted by magicians. A tiny bit of ash or hair is enough for them. You see them with a hoe on their shoulder prowling around where a first-born has been burnt or buried. We made sure that everything disappeared. We have a saying that if you dissolve the ashes completely in water, you'll immediately have another child.

17   Until they grow up, we mothers always have a fire in our belly for our children: we must feed them, keep them from sickness, raise them to become men or women who can work. One of my three sisters died of a kind of tuberculosis. She had been married and she left a son. I brought him up after her death, but like his mother, he was often ill. Before she died, my sister had prayed that he would become strong, so I took up her prayers. I went into three houses and in each one I asked for a cubit of fabric. I put the three bits of fabric on the ground and laid the child on them. Then I went into three other houses and exchanged the child for three measures of barley, saying, "The child is yours; the barley is mine." Of course afterwards I would get the child back. Then I went to three other houses to collect handfuls of dirt. I mixed the three handfuls, spread them out and rolled the baby in them, saying, "Your name will be Kuppa! You are Kuppa! You have been born of dirt!" Then I pierced his nostril with a silver thread which I twisted into a ring. That worked very well for him! He's still alive and he still wears that ring in his nose today.

18   What is more important for us women than children? If we don't draw anything out of our womb, what's the use of being a woman? A

woman who has no son to put a handful of rice in her mouth, no daughter to close her eyes, is an unhappy woman. She or her parents must have failed in their dharma. I been blessed in that way: Isvaran has filled my womb. Ah, if all my children were alive, they'd do all the trades in the world! One would be a labourer, another a carpenter. I would have made one of them study. We could have given two daughters away in marriage and enjoyed our grandchildren. I would be able to go and rest for a month with each of my sons. Yes, we would have been proud of our children.

✦ *Evaluating the Text*

1. In what specific ways does the caste into which Viramma was born determine every aspect of her life?

2. Folk beliefs and superstitions play a very important role in Viramma's world. What are some of these and how does her belief in them provide an explanation for the things that have happened to her?

3. From a Western perspective, Viramma's attitude toward childbearing is unusual. However, she earns her living as a midwife and has become reconciled to the death of most of her own children. What cultural values unique to India does she embody?

✦ *Exploring Different Perspectives*

1. Compare and contrast the everyday life, and attitude as social outcasts, of Viramma and Mary Crow Dog (see "Civilize Them with a Stick").

2. In your opinion, would Viramma, despite great poverty, have ever considered placing one of her children in an orphanage as the parents did in Kashkuli's story "The Button"? Why or why not?

✦ *Extending Viewpoints through Writing*

1. Have you ever known anyone whose explanation for events was rooted in superstition? What were the events and what were the superstitions that explained them?

2. What is your own attitude toward having large families? Do you think people should have as many children as they want? Why or why not? As a research project, you might investigate the one-child policy in China.

Mahdokht Kashkuli

The Button

———————◆———————

Mahdokht Kashkuli was born in 1950 in Teheran, Iran. She was married at age fourteen and, unlike similar marriages, hers did not prevent her from pursuing an education. She succeeded in obtaining her bachelor of arts in performing literature from Teheran University. By 1982 she had completed two master's degrees, one in library science and one in linguistics, and a doctorate in the language, culture, and religion of ancient Iran from the same university. She started her career first as a researcher for Iranian Educational Television from 1975 to 1985 and then as a professor of performing literature at Teheran University. Her short stories, including "The Fable of Rain in Iran," "The Fable of Creation in Iran," "Our Customs, Our Share," "The Pearl and the Moon," and "Tears and Water," have won her national recognition. She is presently working on a novel. "The Button," translated by Soraya Sullivan, was first published in the summer of 1978 in the periodical Arash. *This short story explores the heartbreaking consequences of a family's poverty in contemporary Iran.*

Iran, known as Persia until 1935, is an Islamic republic south of Russia and northeast of Saudi Arabia. Shiite Islam has been the state religion since the 1500s. Iran has the largest population of Shiite Moslems in the world. The Qur'an (Koran), the scripture of the Moslems, is made up of revelations delivered to Mohammed by the Angel Gabriel and also includes revelations to other prophets (Adam, Noah, Abraham, Isaac, Jacob, Joseph, Moses, and Jesus). The discovery of oil in Iran in the early 1900s made the country the object of British and Russian attempts at domination. Between 1925 and 1979, Iran was ruled by the Shahs (father and son), whose regime was supported by the United States, until Muhammad Reza Shah Pahlevi was ousted by popular opposition and replaced by the aged Moslem leader Ayatollah Ruhollah Khomeini. Since this time, the clergy (Mullahs) have carried out a conservative and fundamentalist interpretation of Islam. In 1979, Iranian militants seized the U.S. embassy in Teheran and held the occupants hostage until a negotiated agreement freed them in 1981. Concurrently, a full-scale border war with Iraq began in 1980 and ended eight years later, with casualties estimated at 1 million. In June 1989, Khomeini died, four months after exhorting the Moslem world to assassinate British author Salman Rushdie for writing The Satanic Verses *(1988), a novel perceived as blasphemous to Islam. Hashemi Rafsanjani first came to power as president in 1989 and, despite*

opposition from fundamentalist clerics, was re-elected in June 1993. In
May 1997, a moderate cleric, Mohammad Khatami, won Iran's first free
presidential election and called for establishing better relations with the
West. Pro-Khatami reform candidates won 73 percent of the parliamen-
tary seats in February 2000.

Before You Read

Observe the clues as to the harsh economic circumstances of this poverty-
stricken family in Iran and the extent to which Kashkuli is critical of religious fatalism.

———————◆———————

1   My sister was perched in the doorway, sobbing bitterly; her curly,
russet hair was stuck to her sweaty forehead. My mother was doing
her wash by the pond, paying no attention to my sister's sobs or my father's shouts, "Hurry up Reza! Move it!" I was holding on to the edge
of the mantle shelf tightly, wishing that my hand would remain glued
there permanently. It was only a few nights ago that I had heard, with
my own ears, my father's voice whispering to my mother, "Woman,
stop grumbling! God knows that my heart is aching too, but we don't
have a choice. I can't even provide them with bread. What else can I
do? This way, we'll have one less mouth to feed." I had cocked my ears
to hear who that "one less mouth to feed" was. I remained frozen,
holding my breath for a few minutes; then I heard my father say, "Reza
is the naughtiest of all; the most restless. Akbar and Asghar are more
tame, and we can't send the girls away. It's not wise." Suddenly a dry
cough erupted from my mouth. My father called out, "Reza! Reza! Are
you awake?" I did not answer him. He fell silent, and then my
mother's snorts followed the awkward silence. My father went on,
"Woman, who said the orphanage is a bad place? They teach the kids,
they feed them, they clothe them. At least this one will have a chance
to live a good life." My mother's snorts stopped. She groaned, "I don't
know. I don't know anything. Just do what you think is best." And
then there was silence.

2   Why are they going to make me the "one less mouth to feed"?
What is an orphanage? I wish I hadn't nibbled the bread on my way
home from the bakery; I wish I hadn't quarreled with Asghar; I wish I
hadn't messed around with my mother's yarn, as if it were a ball; I
wish I hadn't pulled the bottle out of Kobra's mouth, and drunk her
milk; I wish I could stay still, like the mannequin in the clothing store
at the corner. Then they wouldn't make me the "one less mouth to
feed." My pillow was soaked with tears.

3   I ran outside with puffy eyes the next morning. Ahmad was standing at the other end of the alley, keeping watch for Husain so he could
pick a fight with him. I yelled, "Ahmad, Ahmad! What's an orphanage?"

Keeping his eyes still on the door to Husain's house, Ahmad said, "It's a place where they put up poor people's children." "Have you been there?" I asked. He shouted indignantly, "Listen to this goddamn wretch! You can't be nice to anyone these days!" I ran back to the house, scared. If Ahmad hadn't been waiting for Husain, he surely would have beaten me up.

4   My father's screams shot up again, "Are you deaf? Hurry up, it's late!" I released my grip on the shelf and went down the stairs. The saltiness of my tears burned my face. My father said, "What's wrong? Why are you crying? Come, my boy! Come wash your face!" Then he took my hand and led me to the pond and splashed a handful of the murky water on my face. He wiped my face with his coat lining. I became uneasy. My father seldom showed signs of affection; I suspected that he was being affectionate because he had decided to make me the "one less mouth to feed." We walked towards the door. He pulled aside the old cotton rug hanging before the door with his bony hands. Then he said, in a tone as if he were talking to himself, "One thousand . . . God knows, I had to pull a thousand strings before they agreed to admit you."

5   I asked, while I kept my head down, "Why?" My father screamed angrily, "He asks why again! Because!" I lowered my head. My eyes met his shoes. They were strangely crooked and worn out; maybe he had them on wrong. . . . The lower part of his long underwear showed from beneath his pants. He was wearing a belt to hold his loose pants up, and they creased like my mother's skirt. "I'm telling you, Reza, a thousand strings," he repeated. "You must behave when you get there." I didn't look at him but said grudgingly, "I don't want to behave!"

6   He threw a darting glance at me and raved, his hand rising to cuff me on the back of the neck but he changed his mind and said instead, "They'll teach you how to behave yourself." Indignantly I said, "I don't want to go to an orphanage, and if you take me there, I'll run away." I pulled my hand out of his quickly and ran ahead, knowing that he'd hit me this time. But he didn't. He only said, "You think they admit everyone? I've been running around for a year, resorting to everyone I know." I said, "Dad, I don't want to go to the orphanage. They keep poor children there." "What do you think you are, rich?" my father said. "Listen to him use words bigger than his mouth!" And he broke out laughing. When he laughed I saw his gold teeth. There were two of them. I thought to myself, "What does it take to be rich? My father has gold teeth, my mother has gold teeth, and my brother has a fountain pen." I looked at his face. He wasn't laughing anymore; his face had turned gray. I said spontaneously, "Dad, is the landlord rich?" He didn't hear me, or it seemed he didn't, and said absentmindedly, "What?" I said, "Nothing."

7   I thought about the landlord. He sends his oldest son or his young daughter to collect the rent two weeks before the rent is due. His oldest son enters my father's shop and stands in the front of the mirror, scrutinizing himself, resting one hand on his waist. My father rushes to him and says, "Do you want a haircut?" The landlord's son responds, "No. You just gave me one on Thursday." My father says politely, "What can I do for you, then?" The landlord's son says, "Is the rent ready?" My father answers, "Give me a few more days. Tell Haji Agha I'll pay before the due date." And the next day his young daughter shows up in the shop. She is so small that she can hardly see herself in the mirror. She holds her veil tightly under her chin with those tiny, delicate hands, and says, "Hello!" My father smiles and says, "Hello, cutie pie! What can I do for you?" The girl laughs cheerfully and says, "My father sent me after the rent. If it's ready, give it to me." My father picks a sugar cube out of the sugar bowl, puts it gently in her palm, and says, "Tell Haji Agha, fine!"

8   We reached the intersection. My father held my hand in his tightly and stopped to look around. We then crossed the street. He was mumbling to himself, "The damn thing is so far away. . . ."

9   I felt sick. I said, "Wait a minute!" He eyed me curiously and said, "Why, what's wrong?" I said, "I'm tired; I don't want to go to the orphanage." He mimicked me, pursing his lips, and said, "You don't understand! You were always dumb, dense!"

10   I remembered that my father was always unhappy with me, although I swept the shop every day and watered the China roses he had planted in front of the shop. I would take my shirt off on hot summer afternoons and jump in the brook with my underpants. The elastic of my pants was always loose and I always tried to tie it into a knot, never succeeding to make it tight enough to stay. In the brook, I held my pants with one hand while I watered the China roses with a small bowl. It felt nice and cool there. Flies would gather around my shoulders and arms. Grandmother used to say, "God made flies out of wax." But I didn't understand why they didn't melt in the hot sun; they flew off my body and landed on the China rose flowers and I shook the branches with my bowl to disperse them. The flowers were my father's and no fly was allowed to sit on them. In spite of all my efforts, my father was always unhappy with me; he was unhappy with my mother, with my sisters and brothers, with the landlord, and with the neighbors. But he was happy with one person: God. He would sigh, tap himself hard on the forehead, and say, "Thank God!"

11   I said to him one day, "Why are you thanking God, Dad?" Suddenly, he hit me in the mouth with the back of his hand. My upper lip swelled and my mouth tasted bloody. I was used to the taste of blood

because whenever I bled in the nose, I tasted blood in my mouth. I covered my mouth, walked to the garden and spat in the dirt. I looked at the bubbles on my spittle, tapped myself on the forehead and said, "Thank God!" Then I picked up a piece of watermelon skin lying on the brook and smacked it on the head of a yellow dog that always used to nap by the electric post. The yellow dog only opened its eyes, looked at me indifferently, and shut its eyes again, thanking God, perhaps.

12   We passed another street before we got to the bus station. A few people were waiting in line; one of them was sitting at the edge of the brook. My father took my hand and led me to the front of the bus line. Someone said, "This is not the end of the line, old man!" I only looked at my father.

13   He said to me, "Ignore him. Just stay right here!" The bus came and my father pushed me towards it. I tore my feet off the ground and jumped on the coach-stop, feeling as if I were floating in the air. Someone said, "Old man, the end of the line is on the other side! Look how people give you a headache on a Monday morning!" My father didn't hear him; he pushed me forward. I was stuck between a seat and the handle bar. . . . So, today is Monday. . . . Every week on Monday my mother does her wash. The clothesline spread around the entire yard. I liked the smell of damp clothes. In spite of my mother's curses, I liked cupping my hands underneath the dripping clothes so that the water that dripped could tickle my palms. Every Monday we had yogurt soup for lunch. My brother and I would take a bowl to the neighborhood dairy store to buy yogurt. On the way back, we took turns licking the surface of the yogurt. When we handed the bowl to my mother, she would scream at us and beat the first one of us she could get her hands on. . . . I felt depressed. I wished I could jump out the window.

14   The bus stopped at a station and we got off. My father walked ahead of me while I dragged my feet along behind him.

15   He waited for me to catch up, then he said, "Move it! He walks like a corpse. Hurry up, it's late!" I stopped momentarily and said, "Dad, I don't want to go. I don't want to go to the orphanage." My father froze in his spot. He said incredulously, "What did you say? You think you know what's good for you? Don't you want to become a decent human being some day? They have rooms, there. They have food, and they'll teach you everything you need to learn to get a decent job." I sobbed, "To hell with anyone who has a decent job. To hell with decent jobs. I don't want one! I like staying home. I like playing with Asghar and Akbar. I want to sell roasted corn with the kids from the neighborhood in the summer. I want to help you out in the shop. I don't want to go."

My father sprang towards me, but suddenly retreated and became affectionate. He said, "Let's go, good boy! We're almost there." I felt sorry for him because every time he was kind he looked miserable. My father was walking ahead of me and I was following him, dragging my feet on the street like that yellow dog. On the next street, we stopped in front of a big metal door. A chair was placed inside the door to keep it ajar. A man was sitting on the chair, playing with a ring of prayer beads. He had on a navy blue coat with metal buttons. His eyes were half-closed and his mouth was open. His cheeks were puffy, as if he had a toothache. My father greeted him and said, "Mr. Guard!" The man opened his eyes. Strands of blood ran through the white of his eyes. He said with a gloomy voice, "What is it, what do you want?" My father thrust his hand in both his pockets, took out an envelope and extended it toward the guard with both hands. The man looked at my father, then threw a threatening glance at me. He yawned, stared at the envelope for a while (I didn't believe he could read), shook his head, coughed, and said, "They won't leave you alone; one leaves, another comes!" Then he pushed the door with the tip of his shoes. The door opened just enough to let me in.

After my father walked through the doorway behind me, the guard gave him the envelope and said, "The first door!" My father was walking fast, and when he opened the hallway door, my heart started beating violently and I started to cry. He said, "My boy, my sweet Reza, this is a nice place. The people here are nice, the kids are all your own age. . . ."

He didn't finish his sentence. He pushed on the door. The door opened and I saw a woman inside the room. I wished she were my mother, but she was heavier than my mother, with a deep vertical wrinkle between her eyebrows. She wore a blue uniform and her hair was a bleached blonde.

My father pushed me further in and said, "Greet her, Reza! Greet her!" I didn't feel like greeting anyone.

My father handed the woman the envelope. She opened it, pulled the letter out halfway, and started reading it. Then she turned to my father and said, "Go to the office so they can complete his file."

My father leaped and ran out the door. Then, as though he had remembered something, he returned and stood in front of the door, rubbing his hand on the wood frame of the door. He raised one hand to tap on his forehead and say, "Thank God," but stopped, rubbed his forehead gently and sighed. His eyes were as moist and shiny as the eyes of the yellow dog hanging around his shop. Her head still lowered on the letter, the woman said, "Go, old man! What are you waiting for? Go to the office!" Father took a few steps backwards, then tore himself from the door and disappeared into the corridor.

22   The woman looked at me, then turned her gaze toward the window and fixed it there. While she had her back to me, she said, "Don't cry, boy! Please don't, I'm not in the mood!" Then she turned around and put her hands on my shoulders. Her hands were as heavy as my mother's but not as warm. She took my hand and walked me toward the door. We passed one corridor, and entered another. Then we entered a room, then another corridor and another room. There were a few people in the room. One was sitting in the doorway, whistling; one was leaning against the desk; one was sitting in a chair writing something. Although the room was furnished with chairs and desks, it was not warm. The woman said, "Say hello to these people!" I looked at her but didn't say anything. I didn't feel like talking to them. I didn't hear what they said to each other, either. I only wanted to sit still and look at them. We left that room and went into another. There was another woman there. I wished she were my mother. She was wearing a blue uniform and had a red scarf around her neck. I think she had a cold because she sniffled constantly. As soon as she saw me, she checked me out thoroughly and spoke with a nasal voice, "Is he new here? I don't know where we're going to put him." She then opened a closet, took out a uniform and said to me, "Take your jacket off and wear this!" Then she continued, "Take your shirt off, too. How long has it been since your last shower?" I didn't answer. Her words hit my ears and bounced right off. She went toward the closet again and asked, "Are you done?" I looked around and then looked at myself, my eyes becoming fixed on my jacket. It had only one button. The button had belonged to my mother's jacket before she used it to replace my missing button. The woman's voice went on, "Quit stalling, boy! Hurry up, I have tons of work to do!"

23   I put my hand on the button and pulled it out, then hid it in my palm. The woman said, "Are you done?" I said, "Yes!"

24   I thrust the button in my uniform pocket and wiped my tears with the back of my hand.

✧ *Evaluating the Text*

1. Of what imagined crimes does the narrator accuse himself that might explain why he is the one to be sent to an orphanage instead of one of his three siblings?

2. How would you characterize the boy's relationship with his father? In your view, what has caused the father to choose him to be the one out of his four children to be sent to an orphanage?

3. How does Reza's attitude toward the button reveal his feelings and emotions?

✧ *Exploring Different Perspectives*

1. How do both Kashkuli and Catherine Lim (in "Paper") use common everyday items to symbolize the experiences of their protagonists?

2. How do both Kashkuli's "The Button" and Mary Crow Dog's "Civilize Them with a Stick" deal with the issue of what happens to children who are raised by the state?

✧ *Extending Viewpoints through Writing*

1. What insight does this story provide into the prevailing economic and social conditions in modern Iranian society?

2. Write about one of your grandparents or parents through an object you connect with him or her. Under what circumstances did you first come across this object? What associations connect this object with your parent or grandparent?

Catherine Lim

Paper

$\blacklozenge$

Catherine Lim is one of Singapore's foremost writers. She currently works for the Curriculum Development Institute of Singapore, writing English-language instructional materials for use in the primary schools. Her widely praised collections of short stories include Little Ironies— Stories of Singapore *(1978), from which "Paper" is taken,* Or Else, The Lightning God and Other Stories *(1980), and* The Shadow of a Shadow of a Dream—Love Stories of Singapore *(1981). She is also the author of three novels,* They Do Return *(1982),* The Serpent's Tooth *(1983), and* The Teardrop Story Woman *(1998). Her short stories have been compared to those of Guy de Maupassant for their accuracy of observation, clarity in presentation of character, and precise detail. Lim's stories reveal a wealth of information about the forces, customs, and pressures that shape the lives of the Chinese community in Singapore, a densely populated metropolis in which Chinese, Malay, and Indian cultures coexist and thrive. "Paper" is set against the turbulent background of the Singapore Stock Exchange, a volatile financial market reflecting the seemingly limitless possibilities of one of the world's most productive financial, industrial, and commercial centers. This story dramatically explores how the lure of easy money leads a man and his wife to tragic consequences.*

The city of Singapore (in Malay, "City of Lions") and about sixty islets make up the Republic of Singapore, at the southern tip of the Malay peninsula. The British East India Company purchased it in 1819 through the efforts of Sir T. S. Raffles. After occupation by the Japanese in World War II, Singapore became a British colony in 1946 and an independent self-governing state in 1959. Although it is the smallest country in Southeast Asia, Singapore has the second highest standard of living in eastern Asia, second only to Japan. The People's Action Party has governed continuously since 1965 and its leader Lee Kuan Yew was prime minister until 1990 when he was succeeded by Goh Chok Tung.

Before You Read

Notice the way in which the main characters fall victim to the intoxicating speculation of the Singapore Stock Exchange in ways not unlike those who were caught in the dot-com bubble.

1   He wanted it, he dreamed of it, he hankered after it, as an addict after his opiate. Once the notion of a big beautiful house had lodged itself in his imagination, Tay Soon nurtured it until it became the consuming passion of his life. A house. A dream house such as he had seen on his drives with his wife and children along the roads bordering the prestigious housing estates on the island, and in the glossy pages of *Homes* and *Modern Living*. Or rather, it was a house which was an amalgam of the best, the most beautiful aspects of the houses he had seen. He knew every detail of his dream house already, from the aluminum sliding doors to the actual shade of the dining room carpet to the shape of the swimming pool. Kidney. He rather liked that shape. He was not ashamed of the enthusiasm with which he spoke of the dream house, an enthusiasm that belonged to women only, he was told. Indeed, his enthusiasm was so great that it had infected his wife and even his children, small though they were. Soon his wife Yee Lian was describing to her sister Yee Yeng, the dream house in all its perfection of shape and decor, and the children were telling their cousins and friends, "My daddy says that when our house is ready . . . "

2   They talked of the dream house endlessly. It had become a reality stronger than the reality of the small terrace house which they were sharing with Tay Soon's mother, to whom it belonged. Tay Soon's mother, whose little business of selling bottled curries and vegetable preserves which she made herself, left her little time for dreams, clucked her tongue and shook her head and made sarcastic remarks about the ambitiousness of young people nowadays.

3   "What's wrong with this house we're staying in?" she asked petulantly. "Aren't we all comfortable in it?"

4   Not as long as you have your horrid ancestral altars all over the place, and your grotesque sense of colour—imagine painting the kitchen wall bright pink. But Yee Lian was tactful enough to keep the remarks to herself, or to make them only to her sister Yee Yeng, otherwise they were sure to reach the old lady, and there would be no end to her sharp tongue.

5   The house—the dream house—it would be a far cry from the little terrace house in which they were all staying now, and Tay Soon and Yee Lian talked endlessly about it, and it grew magnificently in their imaginations, this dream house of theirs with its timbered ceiling and panelled walls and sunken circular sitting room which was to be carpeted in rich amber. It was no empty dream, for there was much money in the bank already. Forty thousand dollars had been saved. The house would cost many times that, but Tay Soon and Yee Lian with their good salaries would be able to manage very well. Once they took care of the down payment, they would be able to pay back monthly over a period of ten years—fifteen, twenty—what did it matter how long it took as long as the dream house was theirs? It had become the symbol of the

peak of earthly achievement, and all of Tay Soon's energies and devotion were directed towards its realisation. His mother said, "You're a show-off; what's so grand about marble flooring and a swimming pool? Why don't you put your money to better use?" But the forty thousand grew steadily, and after Tay Soon and Yee Lian had put in every cent of their annual bonuses, it grew to forty eight thousand, and husband and wife smiled at the smooth way their plans were going.

6   It was a time of growing interest in the stock market. The quotations for stocks and shares were climbing the charts, and the crowds in the rooms of the broking houses were growing perceptibly. Might we not do something about this? Yee Lian said to her husband. Do you know that Dr. Soo bought Rustan Banking for four dollars and today the shares are worth seven dollars each? The temptation was great. The rewards were almost immediate. Thirty thousand dollars' worth of NBE became fifty-five thousand almost overnight. Tay Soon and Yee Lian whooped. They put their remaining eighteen thousand in Far East Mart. Three days later the shares were worth twice that much. It was not to be imagined that things could stop here. Tay Soon secured a loan from his bank and put twenty thousand in OHTE. This was a particularly lucky share; it shot up to four times its value in three days.

7   "Oh, this is too much, too much," cried Yee Lian in her ecstasy, and she sat down with pencil and paper, and found after a few minutes' calculation that they had made a cool one hundred thousand in a matter of days.

8   And now there was to be no stopping. The newspapers were full of it, everybody was talking about it, it was in the very air. There was plenty of money to be made in the stock exchange by those who had guts—money to be made by the hour, by the minute, for the prices of stocks and shares were rising faster than anyone could keep track of them! Dr. Soo was said—he laughingly dismissed it as a silly rumour— Dr. Soo was said to have made two million dollars already. If he sold all his shares now, he would be a millionaire twice over. And Yee Yeng, Yee Lian's sister, who had been urged with sisterly goodwill to come join the others make money, laughed happily to find that the shares she had bought for four twenty on Tuesday had risen to seven ninety-five on Friday—she laughed and thanked Yee Lian who advised her not to sell yet, it was going further, it would hit the ten-dollar mark by next week. And Tay Soon both laughed and cursed—cursed that he had failed to buy a share at nine dollars which a few days later had hit seventeen dollars! Yee Lian said reproachfully, "I thought I told you to buy it, darling," and Tay Soon had beaten his forehead in despair and said, "I know, I know, why didn't I! Big fool that I am!" And he had another reason to curse himself—he sold five thousand West Parkes at sixteen twenty-three per share, and saw, to his horror, West Parkes climb to eighteen ninety the very next day!

9   "I'll never sell now," he vowed. "I'll hold on. I won't be so foolish." And the frenzy continued. Husband and wife couldn't talk or think of anything else. They thought fondly of their shares—going to be worth a million altogether soon. A million! In the peak of good humour, Yee Lian went to her mother-in-law, forgetting the past insults, and advised her to join the others by buying some shares; she would get her broker to buy them immediately for her, there was sure money in it. The old lady refused curtly, and to her son later, she showed great annoyance, scolding him for being so foolish as to put all his money in those worthless shares. "Worthless!" exploded Tay Soon. "Do you know, Mother, if I sold all my shares today, I would have the money to buy fifty terrace houses like the one you have?"

10   His wife said, "Oh, we'll just leave her alone. I was kind enough to offer to help her make money. But since she's so nasty and ungrateful, we'll leave her alone." The comforting, triumphant thought was that soon, very soon, they would be able to purchase their dream house; it would be even more magnificent than the one they had dreamt of, since they had made almost a—Yee Lian preferred not to say the sum. There was the old superstitious fear of losing something when it is too often or too directly referred to, and Yee Lian had cautioned her husband not to make mention of their gains.

11   "Not to worry, not to worry," he said jovially, not superstitious like his wife. "After all, it's just paper gains so far."

12   The downward slide, or the bursting of the bubble as the newspapers dramatically called it, did not initially cause much alarm. For the speculators all expected the shares to bounce back to their original strength and thence continue the phenomenal growth, but that did not happen. The slide continued.

13   Tay Soon said nervously, "Shall we sell? Do you think we should sell?" but Yee Lian said stoutly, "There is talk that this decline is a technical thing only—it will be over soon, and then the rise will continue. After all, see what is happening in Hong Kong and London and New York. Things are as good as ever."

14   "We're still making, so not to worry," said Yee Lian after a few days. Their gains were pared by half. A few days later, their gains were pared to marginal.

15   There is talk of a recovery, insisted Yee Lian. Do you know, Tay Soon, Dr. Soo's wife is buying up some OHTE and West Parkes now? She says these two are sure to rise. She has some inside information that these two are going to climb past the forty-dollar mark—

16   Tay Soon sold all his shares and put the money in OHTE and West Parkes. OHTE and West Parkes crashed shortly afterwards. Some began to say the shares were not worth the paper of the certificates.

17   "Oh, I can't believe, I can't believe it," gasped Yee Lian, pale and sick. Tay Soon looked in mute horror at her.

18   "All our money was in OHTE and West Parkes," he said, his lips dry.

19   "That stupid Soo woman!" shrieked Yee Lian. "I think she deliberately led me astray with her advice! She's always been jealous of me—ever since she knew we were going to build a house grander than hers!"

20   "How are we going to get our house now?" asked Tay Soon in deep distress, and for the first time he wept. He wept like a child, for the loss of all his money, for the loss of the dream house that he had never stopped loving and worshipping.

21   The pain bit into his very mind and soul, so that he was like a madman, unable to go to his office to work, unable to do anything but haunt the broking houses, watching with frenzied anxiety for the OHTE and West Parkes to show him hope. But there was no hope. The decline continued with gleeful rapidity. His broker advised him to sell, before it was too late, but he shrieked angrily, "What! Sell at a fraction at which I bought them! How can this be tolerated!"

22   And he went on hoping against hope.

23   He began to have wild dreams in which he sometimes laughed and sometimes screamed. His wife Yee Lian was afraid and she ran sobbing to her sister who never failed to remind her curtly that all her savings were gone, simply because when she wanted to sell, Yee Lian had advised her not to.

24   "But what is your sorrow compared to mine," wept Yee Lian, "see what's happening to my husband. He's cracking up! He talks to himself, he doesn't eat, he has nightmares, he beats the children. Oh, he's finished!"

25   Her mother-in-law took charge of the situation, while Yee Lian, wide-eyed in mute horror at the terrible change that had come over her husband, shrank away and looked to her two small children for comfort. Tight-lipped and grim, the elderly woman made herbal medicines for Tay Soon, brewing and straining for hours, and got a Chinese medicine man to come have a look at him.

26   "There is a devil in him," said the medicine man, and he proceeded to make him a drink which he mixed with the ashes of a piece of prayer paper. But Tay Soon grew worse. He lay in bed, white, haggard and delirious, seeming to be beyond the touch of healing. In the end, Yee Lian, on the advice of her sister and friends, put him in hospital.

27   "I have money left for the funeral," whimpered the frightened Yee Lian only a week later, but her mother-in-law sharply retorted, "You leave everything to me! I have the money for his funeral, and I shall give him the best! He wanted a beautiful house all his life; I shall give him a beautiful house now!"

28   She went to the man who was well-known on the island for his beautiful houses, and she ordered the best. It would come to nearly a thousand dollars, said the man, a thin, wizened fellow whose funereal gauntness and pallor seemed to be a concession to his calling.

29   That doesn't matter, she said, I want the best. The house is to be made of superior paper, she instructed, and he was to make it to her specifications. She recollected that he, Tay Soon, had often spoken of marble flooring, a timbered ceiling and a kidney-shaped swimming pool. Could he simulate all these in paper?

30   The thin, wizened man said, "I've never done anything like that before. All my paper houses for the dead have been the usual kind—I can put in paper furniture and paper cars, paper utensils for the kitchen and paper servants, all that the dead will need in the other world. But I shall try to put in what you've asked for. Only it will cost more."

31   The house when it was ready, was most beautiful to see. It stood seven feet tall, a delicate framework of wire and thin bamboo strips covered with finely worked paper of a myriad colours. Little silver flowers, scattered liberally throughout the entire structure, gave a carnival atmosphere. There was a paper swimming pool (round, as the man had not understood "kidney") which had to be fitted inside the house itself, as there was no provision for a garden or surrounding grounds. Inside the house were paper figures; there were at least four servants to attend to the needs of the master who was posed beside two cars, one distinctly a Chevrolet and the other a Mercedes.

32   At the appointed time, the paper house was brought to Tay Soon's grave and set on fire there. It burned brilliantly, and in three minutes was a heap of ashes on the grave.

✦ Evaluating the Text

1. To what extent are Tay Soon and his wife and children caught up in the idea of buying a magnificent dream house? How does the elaborate nature of the house Tay Soon wishes to own symbolize the peak of achievement?

2. How does Lim establish that Tay Soon's mother (with whom Tay Soon and his wife live) is indifferent to and even critical of their dream house? How would you characterize the difference in values of Tay Soon and his wife as compared with those of his mother?

3. What is Lim's attitude toward the events she describes in her story? How do you think she feels toward her characters—Tay Soon, Yee Lian, and Tay Soon's mother?

4. Why doesn't Tay Soon sell his shares and capitalize on his first remarkable gains instead of staying in the market in hopes of being able to build an even more magnificent house? What in Tay Soon's nature makes him his own worst enemy?

5. What role does Tay Soon's wife, Yee Lian, play in contributing to the entire disaster? You might examine her actions both at the beginning

of the story and later when the disastrous outcome might still have been averted.

6. How does the recurrent mention of the word *paper* (paper profits, certificates of paper, prayer paper, a paper house, and shares not worth the paper they are printed on) focus the reader's attention on one of the story's central themes?

7. Analyze the structure of the story, and follow its development through the four separate scenes of ever-rising tension and final resolution. How would you describe the action in each of these scenes?

8. How does the miniature paper house that Tay Soon's mother has constructed for him after his death contrast ironically to the magnificent dream house Tay Soon had envisioned? How does the contrast of these two houses (the miniature paper version of his dream house) dramatize the story's central theme?

✦ Exploring Different Perspectives

1. How does the contrast between the predicaments of Tay Soon and his wife and Mahdokht Kashkuli's characters in "The Button" illustrate the difference between genuine needs and illusory desires?

2. Compare Lim's story with Anita Gates's analysis as they illustrate class striving in Singapore and in America.

✦ Extending Viewpoints through Writing

1. If you have ever been involved in a gambling venture in which the psychological dynamics of greed and fear were operating, describe the experiences.

2. What is your attitude toward deferring material gratification? Did you find yourself valuing the fantasies you had about a vacation, car, clothes, jewelry, or whatever, in ways comparable to the feelings of Tay Soon?

3. To discover what you really value, consider the following hypothetical situation: a raging fire has started where you live. You can save only one item other than another person or a pet. What item would you save? How does the value of this item (material, sentimental, or both) imply what is really important to you? Discuss your reactions.

Connecting Cultures

◆

Raymonde Carroll, "Sex, Money, and Success"

What overlapping insights do Carroll and Poranee Natadecha-Sponsel in "Individualism as an American Cultural Value" (Chapter 7) offer into American society?

Mary Crow Dog, "Civilize Them with a Stick"

How does the phenomenon of diminished self-esteem as a result of propaganda by those in power enter into the accounts by Mary Crow Dog and Ngũgĩ wa Thiong'o (see "Decolonising the Mind," Chapter 6)?

Anita Gates, "America Has a Class System. See 'Frasier'"

How do both Gates and Itabari Njeri (in "What's in a Name?" Chapter 7) explore the comic possibilities of social class and race (in Njeri's case)?

Alonso Salazar, "The Lords of Creation"

What personal and cultural differences explain the reactions of the protagonists in Salazar's account and in Victor Villaseñor's "Rain of God" (Chapter 4)?

Viramma, "A Pariah's Life"

Compare and contrast the superstitions and cultural beliefs in Viramma's account with those in Bessie Head's story, "Looking for a Rain God" (Chapter 8).

Mahdokht Kashkuli, "The Button"

How does the button, and the Persian carpet in Hanan al-Shaykh's story (see "The Persian Carpet" in Chapter 2), symbolize the respective emotional states of the protagonists?

Catherine Lim, "Paper"

Discuss the different attitudes toward money and possessions in Lim's story and in Octavio Paz's analysis "Fiesta" (Chapter 8).

6

The Individual
in Society

---◆---

No conflicts between different points of view are more dramatic than those between individual citizens and the nation-states to which they relinquish a certain degree of freedom in exchange for the benefits that can be achieved only through collective political and social institutions, such as the military and the legal, health care, and educational systems. The allegiance that individuals owe their governments and the protection of individual rights that citizens expect in return have been the subject of intense analysis through the ages by such figures as Socrates in Plato's *Apology* and *Crito,* Henry David Thoreau in *Civil Disobedience*, and Martin Luther King, Jr., in "A Letter from Birmingham Jail." The readings that follow continue this debate by providing accounts drawn from many different societies and revealing assumptions and expectations very different, in many cases, from those that characterize our own democratic form of government.

The concept of the state includes those political processes and organizations that serve as the means through which individuals and groups obtain and employ power. Political organization in different cultures may take a variety of forms, whether that of a chieftain in a tribal culture or more complex distributions of power and authority in societies like that of the United States, with two parties, an electoral college, judges, courts, prisons, armed forces, a state department, and other institutions designed to maintain and regulate order.

In theory, the legal processes of a society exist to enforce that society's concept of justice and its accompanying norms, laws, and customs. In practice, however, penalties and fines, imprisonment, torture, ostracism, and even death are meted out in many cultures in far more arbitrary ways.

In the former Yugoslavia, for example, the use of the phrase *ethnic cleansing* has served to conceal a genocidal policy in which state power was employed to destroy entire groups of people on grounds of presumed ethnicity.

A politicized environment within a state has an intensely corrosive effect on personal relationships when individual loyalties clash with officially decreed allegiances. Authors in many countries and cultures describe the seductive and persuasive powers the state can mobilize through propaganda and the threat of force to manipulate its citizens. Regimes also remain in power by channeling the frustrations of one group against another. Many of the following selections explore the predicaments of ordinary citizens trying to survive oppression.

Stephen Chapman in "The Prisoner's Dilemma" examines how practices of punishment in Eastern cultures differ from those in the West. Lawrence Metzger's interviews of university students in Beijing in "Irony Square" reveal a search for values in China under communism. The Chilean author, Luis Sepulveda, in "Daisy" displays an unusual ironic detachment in his account of coping with the literary pretensions of his prison guard. Speaking from a postcolonial perspective in Kenya, Ngũgĩ wa Thiong'o, in "Decolonising the Mind," analyzes the damaging psychological consequences of having been forbidden by the British rulers to write or speak his native language while in school. With unusual honesty, Rae Yang in "At the Center of the Storm" tells how she and the other Red Guards tyrannized school teachers and others who had been authority figures before Mao Tse Tung's Cultural Revolution. Based on a true incident in Cyprus, Panos Ioannides's story, "Gregory," explores the question of conscience during wartime. A story, "The Wedgwood Tea Set," whose form may remind you of an allegory or parable, by the Serbian writer, Milorad Pavić, probes the deceptive nature of geopolitical realities.

Stephen Chapman

The Prisoner's Dilemma

---◆---

Stephen Chapman (b. 1954) has served as the associate editor of the New Republic *and is currently a columnist and editorial writer with the* Chicago Tribune. *He is a native of Texas who attended Harvard. In "The Prisoner's Dilemma" (which first appeared in the* New Republic *of March 8, 1980), Chapman calls into question the widely held assumption that the system of imprisonment as punishment employed in the West is more humane and less barbaric than the methods of punishment (including flogging, stoning, and amputation) practiced in Eastern Islamic nations.*

With India's independence in 1947, the nation of Pakistan was established as a separate Muslim state comprising two regions on either side of India separated by a thousand miles with East Pakistan sharing a border with Burma. The creation of the Indo-Pakistani border was followed by an exodus of seven million Hindus to India and an equal number of Muslims to Pakistan. In 1971, East Pakistan declared its independence and took the name Bangladesh. Pakistan's precarious economic conditions worsened in the 1980s, when millions of refugees fleeing the Soviet invasion of Afghanistan poured into Pakistan. In 1988 Benazir Bhutto became the first woman to govern a Muslim country, a position she held for two years, until she was ousted by a no-confidence vote in the National Assembly because of accusations of nepotism and corruption. She was replaced by Nawaz Sharif in 1990. In 1999, General Pervaiz Musharraf came to power in a military coup, and subsequently has supported the United States in the war against terrorism. The regional dispute with India over Kashmir brought both nations to the brink of war in 2002.

Before You Read
As you read, notice the very different objectives punishment serves in Eastern and Western cultures.

---◆---

> *If the punitive laws of Islam were applied for only one year,*
> *all the devastating injustices would be uprooted. Misdeeds*
> *must be punished by the law of retaliation; cut off the hands*
> *of the thief; kill the murderers; flog the adulterous woman*
> *or man. Your concerns, your "humanitarian" scruples are*
> *more childish than reasonable. Under the terms of Koranic*
> *law, any judge fulfilling the seven requirements (that he*

have reached puberty, be a believer, know the Koranic laws
perfectly, be just, and not be affected by amnesia, or be a
bastard, or be of the female sex) is qualified to be a judge in
any type of case. He can thus judge and dispose of twenty
trials in a single day, whereas the Occidental justice may
take years to argue them out.
 —from Sayings of the Ayatollah Khomeni (Bantam Books)

1   One of the amusements of life in the modern West is the opportunity to observe the barbaric rituals of countries that are attached to the customs of the dark ages. Take Pakistan, for example, our newest ally and client state in Asia. Last October President Zia, in harmony with the Islamic fervor that is sweeping his part of the world, revived the traditional Moslem practice of flogging lawbreakers in public. In Pakistan, this qualified as mass entertainment, and no fewer than 10,000 law-abiding Pakistanis turned out to see justice done to 26 convicts. To Western sensibilities the spectacle seemed barbaric—both in the sense of cruel and in the sense of pre-civilized. In keeping with Islamic custom each of the unfortunates—who had been caught in prostitution raids the previous night and summarily convicted and sentenced— was stripped down to a pair of white shorts, which were painted with a red stripe across the buttocks (the target). Then he was shackled against an easel, with pads thoughtfully placed over the kidneys to prevent injury. The floggers were muscular, fierce-looking sorts—convicted murderers, as it happens—who paraded around the flogging platform in colorful loincloths. When the time for the ceremony began, one of the floggers took a running start and brought a five-foot stave down across the first victim's buttocks, eliciting screams from the convict and murmurs from the audience. Each of the 26 received from five to 15 lashes. One had to be carried from the stage unconscious.

2   Flogging is one of the punishments stipulated by Koranic law, which has made it a popular penological device in several Moslem countries, including Pakistan, Saudi Arabia, and, most recently, the ayatollah's Iran. Flogging, or *Tá zir*, is the general punishment prescribed for offenses that don't carry an explicit Koranic penalty. Some crimes carry automatic *hadd* punishments—stoning or scourging (a severe whipping) for illicit sex, scourging for drinking alcoholic beverages, amputation of the hands for theft. Other crimes—as varied as murder and abandoning Islam—carry the death penalty (usually carried out in public). Colorful practices like these have given the Islamic world an image in the West, as described by historian G. H. Jansen, "of blood dripping from the stumps of amputated hands and from the striped backs of malefactors, and piles of stones barely concealing the battered bodies of adulterous couples." Jansen, whose book *Militant Islam* is generally effusive in its praise of Islamic practices, grows squeamish

when considering devices like flogging, amputation, and stoning. But they are given enthusiastic endorsement by the Koran itself.

3   Such traditions, we all must agree, are no sign of an advanced civilization. In the West, we have replaced these various punishments (including the death penalty in most cases) with a single device. Our custom is to confine criminals in prison for varying lengths of time. In Illinois, a reasonably typical state, grand theft carries a punishment of three to five years; armed robbery can get you from six to 30. The lowest form of felony theft is punishable by one to three years in prison. Most states impose longer sentences on habitual offenders. In Kentucky, for example, habitual offenders can be sentenced to life in prison. Other states are less brazen, preferring the more genteel sounding "indeterminate sentence," which allows parole boards to keep inmates locked up for as long as life. It was under an indeterminate sentence of one to 14 years that George Jackson served 12 years in California prisons for committing a $70 armed robbery. Under a Texas law imposing an automatic life sentence for a third felony conviction, a man was sent to jail for life last year because of three thefts adding up to less than $300 in property value. Texas also is famous for occasionally imposing extravagantly long sentences, often running into hundreds or thousands of years. This gives Texas a leg up on Maryland, which used to sentence some criminals to life plus a day—a distinctive if superfluous flourish.

4   The punishment *intended* by Westen societies in sending their criminals to prison is the loss of freedom. But, as everyone knows, the actual punishment in most American prisons is of a wholly different order. The February 2 riot at New Mexico's state prison in Santa Fe, one of several bloody prison riots in the nine years since the Attica bloodbath, once again dramatized the conditions of life in an American prison. Four hundred prisoners seized control of the prison before dawn. By sunset the next day 33 inmates had died at the hands of other convicts and another 40 people (including five guards) had been seriously hurt. Macabre stories came out of prisoners being hanged, murdered with blowtorches, decapitated, tortured, and mutilated in a variety of gruesome ways by drug-crazed rioters.

5   The Santa Fe penitentiary was typical of most maximum-security facilities, with prisoners subject to overcrowding, filthy conditions, and routine violence. It also housed first-time, non-violent offenders, like check forgers and drug dealers, with murderers serving life sentences. In a recent lawsuit, the American Civil Liberties Union called the prison "totally unfit for human habitation." But the ACLU says New Mexico's penitentiary is far from the nation's worst.

6   That American prisons are a disgrace is taken for granted by experts of every ideological stripe. Conservative James Q. Wilson has criticized our "crowded, antiquated prisons that require men and women to live

in fear of one another and to suffer not only deprivation of liberty but a brutalizing regimen." Leftist Jessica Mitford has called our prisons "the ultimate expression of injustice and inhumanity." In 1973 a national commission concluded that "the American correctional system today appears to offer minimum protection to the public and maximum harm to the offender." Federal courts have ruled that confinement in prisons in 16 different states violates the constitutional ban on "cruel and unusual punishment."

7   What are the advantages of being a convicted criminal in an advanced culture? First there is the overcrowding in prisons. One Tennessee prison, for example, has a capacity of 806, according to accepted space standards, but it houses 2300 inmates. One Louisiana facility has confined four and five prisoners in a single six-foot-by-six-foot cell. Then there is the disease caused by overcrowding, unsanitary conditions, and poor or inadequate medical care. A federal appeals court noted that the Tennessee prison had suffered frequent outbreaks of infectious diseases like hepatitis and tuberculosis. But the most distinctive element of American prison life is its constant violence. In his book *Criminal Violence, Criminal Justice,* Charles Silberman noted that in one Louisiana prison, there were 211 stabbings in only three years, 11 of them fatal. There were 15 slayings in a prison in Massachusetts between 1972 and 1975. According to a federal court, in Alabama's penitentiaries (as in many others), "robbery, rape, extortion, theft and assault are everyday occurrences."

8   At least in regard to cruelty, it's not at all clear that the system of punishment that has evolved in the West is less barbaric than the grotesque practices of Islam. Skeptical? Ask yourself: would you rather be subjected to a few minutes of intense pain and considerable public humiliation, or to be locked away for two or three years in a prison cell crowded with ill-tempered sociopaths? Would you rather lose a hand or spend 10 years or more in a typical state prison? I have taken my own survey on this matter. I have found no one who does not find the Islamic system hideous. And I have found no one who, given the choices mentioned above, would not prefer its penalties to our own.

9   The great divergence between Western and Islamic fashions in punishment is relatively recent. Until roughly the end of the 18th century, criminals in Western countries rarely were sent to prison. Instead they were subjected to an ingenious assortment of penalties. Many perpetrators of a variety of crimes simply were executed, usually by some imaginative and extremely unpleasant method involving prolonged torture, such as breaking on the wheel, burning at the stake, or drawing and quartering. Michel Foucault's book *Discipline and Punishment: The Birth of the Prison* notes one form of capital punishment in which the condemned man's "belly was opened up, his entrails quickly ripped out, so that he had time to see them, with his own eyes, being thrown on the fire; in which he was finally decapitated and his body quartered." Some

criminals were forced to serve on slave galleys. But in most cases various corporal measures such as pillorying, flogging, and branding sufficed.

10   In time, however, public sentiment recoiled against these measures. They were replaced by imprisonment, which was thought to have two advantages. First, it was considered to be more humane. Second, and more important, prison was supposed to hold out the possibility of rehabilitation—purging the criminal of his criminality—something that less civilized punishments did not even aspire to. An 1854 report by inspectors of the Pennsylvania prison system illustrates the hopes nurtured by humanitarian reformers:

> Depraved tendencies, characteristic of the convict, have been restrained by the absence of vicious association, and in the mild teaching of Christianity, the unhappy criminal finds a solace for an involuntary exile from the comforts of social life. If hungry, he is fed; if naked, he is clothed; if destitute of the first rudiments of education, he is taught to read and write; and if he has never been blessed with a means of livelihood, he is schooled in a mechanical art, which in after life may be to him the source of profit and respectability. Employment is not his toil nor labor, weariness. He embraces them with alacrity, as contributing to his moral and mental elevation.

11   Imprisonment is now the universal method of punishing criminals in the United States. It is thought to perform five functions, each of which has been given a label by criminologists. First, there is simple *retribution:* punishing the lawbreaker to serve society's sense of justice and to satisfy the victims' desire for revenge. Second, there is *specific deterrence:* discouraging the offender from misbehaving in the future. Third, *general deterrence:* using the offender as an example to discourage others from turning to crime. Fourth, *prevention:* at least during the time he is kept off the streets, the criminal cannot victimize other members of society. Finally, and most important, there is *rehabilitation:* reforming the criminal so that when he returns to society he will be inclined to obey the laws and able to make an honest living.

12   How satisfactorily do American prisons perform by these criteria? Well, of course, they do punish. But on the other scores they don't do so well. Their effect in discouraging future criminality by the prisoner or others is the subject of much debate, but the soaring rates of the last 20 years suggest that prisons are not a dramatically effective deterrent to criminal behavior. Prisons do isolate convicted criminals, but only to divert crime from ordinary citizens to prison guards and fellow inmates. Almost no one contends anymore that prisons rehabilitate their inmates. If anything, they probably impede rehabilitation by forcing inmates into prolonged and almost exclusive association with other criminals. And prisons cost a lot of money. Housing a typical prisoner in a typical prison costs far more than a stint at a top university. This cost would be justi-

fied if prisons did the job they were intended for. But it is clear to all that prisons fail on the very grounds—humanity and hope of rehabilitation—that caused them to replace earlier, cheaper forms of punishment.

13   The universal acknowledgment that prisons do not rehabilitate criminals has produced two responses. The first is to retain the hope of rehabilitation but do away with imprisonment as much as possible and replace it with various forms of "alternative treatment," such as psychotherapy, supervised probation, and vocational training. Psychiatrist Karl Menninger, one of the principal critics of American penology, has suggested even more unconventional approaches, such as "a new job opportunity or a vacation trip, a course of reducing exercises, a cosmetic surgical operation or a herniotomy, some night school courses, a wedding in the family (even one for the patient!), an inspiring sermon." The starry-eyed approach naturally has produced a backlash from critics on the right, who think that it's time to abandon the goal of rehabilitation. They argue that prisons perform an important service just by keeping criminals off the streets, and thus should be used with that purpose in mind.

14   So the debate continues to rage in all the same old ruts. No one, of course, would think of copying the medieval practices of Islamic nations and experimenting with punishments such as flogging and amputation. But let us consider them anyway. How do they compare with our American prison system in achieving the ostensible objectives of punishment? First, do they punish? Obviously they do, and in a uniquely painful and memorable way. Of course any sensible person, given the choice, would prefer suffering these punishments to years of incarceration in a typical American prison. But presumably no Western penologist would criticize Islamic punishments on the grounds that they are not barbaric enough. Do they deter crime? Yes, and probably more effectively than sending convicts off to prison. Now we read about a prison sentence in the newspaper, then think no more about the criminal's payment for his crimes until, perhaps, years later we read a small item reporting his release. By contrast, one can easily imagine the vivid impression it would leave to be wandering through a local shopping center and to stumble onto the scene of some poor wretch being lustily flogged. And the occasional sight of an habitual offender walking around with a bloody stump at the end of his arm no doubt also would serve as a forceful reminder that crime does not pay.

15   Do flogging and amputation discourage recidivism? No one knows whether the scars on his back would dissuade a criminal from risking another crime, but it is hard to imagine that corporal measures could stimulate a higher rate of recidivism than already exists. Islamic forms of punishment do not serve the favorite new right goal of simply isolating criminals from the rest of society, but they may achieve the same purpose of making further crimes impossible. In the movie *Bonnie and Clyde*, Warren Beatty successfully robs a bank with his arm in a

sling, but this must be dismissed as artistic license. It must be extraordinarily difficult, at the very least, to perform much violent crime with only one hand.

16   Do the medieval forms of punishment rehabilitate the criminal? Plainly not. But long prison terms do not rehabilitate either. And it is just as plain that typical Islamic punishments are no crueler to the convict than incarceration in the typical American state prison.

17   Of course there are other reasons besides its bizarre forms of punishment that the Islamic system of justice seems uncivilized to the Western mind. One is the absence of due process. Another is the long list of offenses—such as drinking, adultery, blasphemy, "profiteering," and so on—that can bring on conviction and punishment. A third is all the ritualistic mumbojumbo in pronouncements of Islamic law (like that talk about puberty and amnesia in the ayatollah's quotation at the beginning of this article). Even in these matters, however, a little cultural modesty is called for. The vast majority of American criminals are convicted and sentenced as a result of plea bargaining, in which due process plays almost no role. It has been only half a century since a wave of religious fundamentalism stirred this country to outlaw the consumption of alcoholic beverages. Most states also still have laws imposing austere constraints on sexual conduct. Only two weeks ago the *Washington Post* reported that the FBI had spent two and a half years and untold amounts of money to break up a nationwide pornography ring. Flogging the clients of prostitutes, as the Pakistanis did, does seem silly. But only a few months ago Mayor Koch of New York was proposing that clients caught in his own city have their names broadcast by radio stations. We are not so far advanced on such matters as we often like to think. Finally, my lawyer friends assure me that the rules of jurisdiction for American courts contain plenty of petty requirements and bizarre distinctions that would sound silly enough to foreign ears.

18   Perhaps it sounds barbaric to talk of flogging and amputation, and perhaps it is. But our system of punishment also is barbaric, and probably more so. Only cultural smugness about their system and willful ignorance about our own make it easy to regard the one as cruel and the other as civilized. We inflict our cruelties away from public view, while nations like Pakistan stage them in front of 10,000 onlookers. Their outrages are visible; ours are not. Most Americans can live their lives for years without having their peace of mind disturbed by the knowledge of what goes on in our prisons. To choose imprisonment over flogging and amputation is not to choose human kindness over cruelty, but merely to prefer that our cruelties be kept out of sight, and out of mind.

19   Public flogging and amputation may be more barbaric forms of punishment than imprisonment, even if they are not more cruel. Soci-

ety may pay a higher price for them, even if the particular criminal does not. Revulsion against officially sanctioned violence and infliction of pain derives from something deeply ingrained in Western conscience, and clearly it is something admirable. Grotesque displays of the sort that occur in Islamic countries probably breed a greater tolerance for physical cruelty, for example, which prisons do not do precisely because they conceal their cruelties. In fact it is our admirable intolerance for calculated violence that makes it necessary for us to conceal what we have not been able to do away with. In a way this is a good thing, since it holds out the hope that we may eventually find a way to do away with it. But in another way it is a bad thing, since it permits us to congratulate ourselves on our civilized humanitarianism while violating its norms in this one area of our national life.

✦ Evaluating the Text

1. What are the five objectives that imprisonment is supposed to achieve in Western culture? How satisfactorily do American prisons perform these functions?

2. How do the practices of punishment in Eastern cultures differ from those in Western societies? What is Chapman's attitude toward these practices in comparison with Western methods of punishment?

3. How does Chapman use comparison and contrast to more clearly illustrate the differences between them?

✦ Exploring Different Perspectives

1. Explore the differences between Luis Sepulveda's experiences in "Daisy" with the practices Chapman describes. How is being punished as a political prisoner different from being punished as a criminal?

2. Compare the differences in ethical assumptions during wartime (as in "Gregory") and those that operate in everyday life.

✦ Extending Viewpoints through Writing

1. Write a short essay that answers Chapman's question, "Would you rather be subjected to a few minutes of intense pain and considerable public humiliation, or be locked away for two or three years in a prison cell crowded with ill-tempered sociopaths?"

2. In your opinion, what is the significance of the fact that in the West punishment is private and follows secular guidelines whereas in Eastern cultures punishment is public and follows Islamic law?

Lawrence Metzger

Irony Square

Lawrence Metzger received a Ph.D. in psychology from Saybrook Institute, San Francisco, and has taught at the University of California at Berkeley and at universities in Korea. He is a psychologist and social worker who has traveled extensively and written widely on generational changes in China, South Korea, and Indonesia. He is the author of From Denial to Recovery *(1988). The following interviews with students at Beijing University illuminate significant changes in Chinese culture in the wake of the events in Tiananmen Square from 1989 to the present.*

Before You Read

Underline key points in Metzger's essay to better understand how his analysis offers insight into the conflict between traditional Chinese customs and modern communist values.

1   I was in Beijing for the first time in my life, stuck in a taxi in slow-moving traffic. The ride would be a long one, on dank and dusty streets, through the heart of the city, and north to Beijing University. Professor "Han" had assured me that students would be waiting to take part in my research, and I feared being late. At the side of Tiananmen Square we slowed to a crawl. The immense space, flat and featureless in the grey light, looked benign. Clusters of camera-snapping tourists ambled behind flag-toting guides who spouted data about emperors and armies whose deeds spanned a thousand years. Smiling vendors tagged after them, offering dragon-faced kites and hand-painted fans.

2   I had wandered in the square the day before, a few hours after arriving in China. I needed to be in Tiananmen, needed to feel the hardness of its reality under my feet. Unlike the tourists, whose thoughts may have been about how much walking they must do, or when the next Chinese banquet would occur, I came to Tiananmen with a heavy heart. I thought of bringing flowers, but didn't want to draw attention. My memory had been scorched by the fires of a decade earlier, when students who sought liberty found only bullets and bloodshed. I had watched the events unfold on television over a two-month period. At that time, the spring of 1989, I was taking part in research on Asian

studies at the Institute for the Study of Social Change at the University of California at Berkeley. I was finally indulging my interest in Asia after busy years of being a psychotherapist and teaching counseling skills on the Berkeley campus. At meetings and in classrooms, I was delighted to find students and professors from all over Asia. One of them, Cheng, was from Beijing. Often I spotted him in the lounge, sitting before the television set in the weeks leading up to the Tiananmen massacre. He seemed mesmerized by the pictures coming from Beijing. On the day when the students paraded their newly made statue, the Goddess of Democracy, Cheng worried aloud to the small group gathered at the TV.

3   "Look at them. They look so happy." He leaned toward the tube, intently scanning the faces in the picture. He was looking for his younger brother, a first year student at Beijing University. Cheng clutched his knees, his hands taut. "I never would do what they are doing. They go too far." He was old enough to remember the Cultural Revolution, when children were trained in school to venerate Mao Zedong as a god, and to memorize his prosaic messages as gifts from heaven. Perhaps he was one of the millions of children who paraded before Mao, crying with happiness as they raised his Little Red Book in a salute. I never got to ask. Cheng disappeared after the June 4th massacre. I heard that he had flown to China to be with his family. No one knew about his brother. And no one knew how many students had died in the square, perhaps hundreds, perhaps thousands.

4   I looked north toward the soaring roofs of the Forbidden City. Above the main portal where emperors once passed, Mao's huge portrait loomed over the square, his bald head beaming heaven's light. Ironic that this father of revolution gazed down on the killing ground of those like himself who sought change. But I reminded myself that despots send dissidents to prison or the grave, and Mao had done the latter by the millions.

5   The taxi lurched through a traffic light and away from the square, heading into the central part of the city. My thoughts and feelings were distracted by the images around me. We passed dreary rows of flat-faced buildings, untouched by imagination or even pride of ownership, all colorless in the grey polluted air. Lumbering trucks and buses puffed up a stew of noise and foul smells. Small cars competed for precious space, often cutting each other off by only inches. Had I reached out a hand, I would have lost it. Behind us, at every stop, a tailgating driver screeched on the brakes. There was nothing I could do but try to calm myself. I settled back in the seat and closed my eyes. I started to count my breaths in an attempt at meditation, but the stench of the traffic congested my lungs and mocked my efforts. How ironic: I was in the country where Buddhism had once calmed millions, but like

most Chinese customs during the half century of Communist rule, it had been expunged, sent packing, along with other great traditions.

6   The taxi slowed as we passed through the gates of Beijing University. Suddenly the grey sky parted and the sun came out, as if even the heavens gave special recognition to China's best and brightest. Young people walked along grassy paths, under the shade of gentle trees, carrying books to class. For me it was like coming home: a familiar world where knowledge was shared, ideas considered: the basis of change for the future. That at least was my hope. But China was an enigma. Perhaps if I fiddled at its locks I might open a few of its realities. The car came to a stop and the driver turned to me, smiling quiet words that I did not understand. He pointed to the building before us. I gathered my briefcase, paid him, and stepped into China's version of Harvard. Inside, I climbed the darkened stairs to the third floor. There was a musty odor to the place, as if too many feet had trod too much sameness, too much required conformity; but of course that was only my prejudice. I really didn't know what to expect, and needed to maintain objectivity.

7   In the corridor, widely spaced dim bulbs shadowed walls badly in need of paint. Open doors revealed classrooms where students crowded together at old desks. I located Professor Han in his small cluttered office. Books lined the walls and papers were sorted in piles on his desk. A couple of chairs for student conferences filled the space. Steam rose from an old kettle on a hot plate.

8   "Hello, hello," he said as I entered. He rose to greet me. He was about five foot seven, had an engaging smile in a reassuring face, and looked to be in his mid-thirties. He wore a bright polyester tie over a carefully creased white shirt. His dark suit coat hung on a metal hanger on the wall behind his desk.

9   "I hope you did not have trouble with transportation?"

10   "No," I assured him. "The taxi driver was helpful, and I left extra time to get here."

11   "You will have tea, yes?" As he poured it, he told me that the first student to be interviewed was waiting in a room nearby. Other students would come on the hour as I had requested. "They are very interested in meeting you, an American teacher from Berkeley."

12   That was a relief. I could look forward to a day of meeting students without fear. A few days earlier a professor at another university had cancelled my visit at the last minute—the government refused to grant permission, he said.

13   "Thanks very much for arranging the interviews, and for the tea." I raised the cup and sipped the hot, smoky liquid. My tension melted away.

14   After our brief conversation, the professor escorted me to another small room where "Lin" was waiting. She rose as we entered. Her gaze, behind plain plastic glasses, was direct but softened with cordiality. She

was dressed casually in jeans and a simple shirt. Her jet-black hair hung straight to the base of her neck and melded into her tawny complexion. She wore no makeup. I set down my notebook and tape recorder on the table. "I hope you have not waited long."

15   "No," she smiled. "Not long."

16   Professor Han turned toward the door. "I will come for you at noon for lunch," he said, and I thanked him.

17   As we sat down at the table, Lin handed me the Family History Questionnaire she had filled out. I had sent it in advance, and the professor had distributed it to the volunteers. I looked it over. Lin was 21 years old, a senior majoring in mathematics. Her family lived in a village a thousand kilometers from Beijing. Her father was a farmer with a ninth grade education, and her mother had graduated from high school and was a teacher. The family had lived on the same small farm for at least six generations.

18   I needed to put some structure under the interview to facilitate our talk. "Thanks for filling out the form. Let me tell you about the research: it's about changes in families over three generations in three developing countries: China, South Korea, and Indonesia. All those countries have lived through many changes since 1945 and I'm interested in hearing about the effect on families." That was my stated agenda. What I didn't say was that every developing country in Asia wanted to get rich but feared that it would lead to problems they saw on American TV: crime and violence, family breakdown, and aggressive individualism. The questionnaire would serve as a skeleton for the interview, a jumping off point into the lives of the students. Who were they? How did their lives differ from those of their parents and grandparents? What changes were occurring generationally about values? Was there a movement away from family and group identity toward individualism? If so, were there conflicts in the family as the result of changes? And in China particularly, were today's university students as rebellious as their 1989 cousins, or had they learned to keep quiet?

19   I looked back at the form. "You are very far from home."

20   "Yes, very far."

21   "How did your family feel about your move to Beijing?"

22   "My parents were very happy for me," she said, slowly mouthing the foreign words. "My mother especially because she was my teacher at home—she help me when I was child."

23   "And did your grandparents feel the same?"

24   She became thoughtful and looked toward the window, as if seeking the answers there. "My grandmother was afraid. She never go far from our village. But my grandfather argue with her. He told her I will be safe at university."

25   "It must have been a big change for you to come from a small village to the capital."

26   "Yes, very different." She lived in a dormitory, four girls in a small, crowded room, but she didn't complain about it. I had heard about the crowded conditions from Chinese students in Berkeley.

27   "The change is not easy, but I make friends here, so that is nice."

28   I looked back at the line on the form about education. "There was a big difference in education in your family, especially between your mother, who became a teacher, and her parents."

29   Lin nodded. "I think so. My grandparents had no school at all. And my grandmother, her feet were bound in the old way—old women in our village were like that. So when my mother was a child and liberation came, my grandmother was happy that girls can go to school and learn."

30   It was a typical family background in rural areas of China before the Communist government took over in 1949. One of the first changes was the establishment of basic education. A second priority was to give women equal status with men since, as Mao Zedong said, "they hold up half of heaven." This was an extraordinary reversal of male dominance after 2,000 years of Confucian insistence on patriarchy. Many women took advantage of education and often gained responsible positions. In recent years, however, there have been reports of women being pushed out of jobs and roles after age 40, especially among less educated women.

31   I asked about purchases her family had made in recent years, such as a house or apartment, or consumer goods.

32   Her face brightened, as if she had been waiting for me to ask. "My father build a house. It is two stories. There is a kitchen and bathroom."

33   "Is that a big change from the past?"

34   "Oh yes. In the past we have only two small rooms with dirt floor and no bathroom."

35   The family raised vegetables and sold them in the market of a nearby city. Many rural families had made great strides in recent years as they were permitted to act independently, rather than turn everything over to a farming collective as in the past.

36   In answer to a question about household purchases, Lin wrote that her parents had bought a TV, a wash machine, furniture, a pressure cooker, and a sewing machine. "Our family is more modern now. We have more comfort. They even can send me to university." She said it with simple pride. "Things are much improved."

37   I asked about her plans for the future. "I am major in mathematics. Maybe I will have job in government." Although she maintained eye contact with me when she said it, I thought I detected some doubt.

38   "Is that what you want to do, work for the government?"

39   She hesitated, and then added as if to herself: "Maybe I can work in business. I can make much money in business."

40   "Will you be able to do that?"

41   "Maybe. I am not sure."

42   Only a few years earlier the government had kept a stranglehold on citizens by controlling education, housing, employment, health care, and geographic location. Permission was needed to do almost anything. Opportunities could be sweetened by *guanzi* (connections) and payoffs. It was a major reason for the explosion of protest in Tiananmen Square in 1989. I wasn't sure whether those directives had expired completely.

43   "Are you able to work where you want, in government or private industry?"

44   "Yes, I think so." But she didn't sound too sure. I went back to the questionnaire.

45   "I see that both your parents and grandparents are in arranged marriages." I looked up. "Will you do the same? Will you let your parents find a husband for you?"

46   She giggled. "Of course not. Would they find a farmer for me in their little village? No. Probably I will meet someone here in Beijing or another city where I will work." Lin assured me that arranged marriages no longer happened in China, except perhaps among poor people in rural areas. But that constituted at least 70 percent of the people.

47   I was impressed by how far she had come from her background, and told her so.

48   She nodded in agreement. "There is more freedom for me than for my parents. I can decide about occupation, what kind of person I will be. I will choose my own husband." She glanced toward the window as if to seize another thought, and then declared simply: "I will do my best to let my parents agree with my choices, but if they do not accept them, I will insist." She smiled again. "It is very different now than for my parents."

49   It obviously was. And for me as well. The darkness of Tiananmen had begun to pass. I could feel myself shifting emotional gears, and looked forward to meeting more students.

50   "Zhu" walked into the room with the easy self assurance of an athlete. He was sturdily built and square jawed. I soon learned that he was very much a soldier's son: quiet, controlled, direct. His answers were polite but often limited. Although his English vocabulary was good, he had more difficulty constructing English sentences than other students.

51   "My father is colonel in army," he said in answer to a question, and then lapsed into silence. I scanned down the questionnaire. His father was the youngest of four children, and his mother the youngest of six. Both were the only ones in their families to attend and graduate from college. The mother has been a teacher in a middle school for many years. All four grandparents were listed as peasants with no education

at all. In the grandparents' time, getting enough food was a daily concern. In recent years, compared with relatives, Zhu's immediate family has been well off. His two older brothers are university graduates and have good jobs. But he recalled a childhood when there was only a small apartment for his family of five.

52　　Zhu is majoring in physics and will soon graduate. "What will you do after graduation?"

53　　He gave me a quizzical look. "I don't know. I don't think about it."

54　　That was startling. How could someone so close to graduation at a top university not think about his plans? I decided to try another way. "When you are 25, what do you think your life will be like?"

55　　"Maybe happy." Long pause before he added, "Maybe I will study for Ph.D." But he was uncertain how he would use the degree. "Maybe I will teach. Maybe I will work for government if I have a chance." His voice trailed off. "I don't think about it much."

56　　But if he was uncertain or indifferent about his career direction, he was definite about another possibility.

57　　"Would you like to be more independent than you are now?"

58　　His answer was quick and emphatic: "Yeah! I should get money and raise a family, and I can help my parents." He was elated by the prospect.

59　　"Would you like to be rich?"

60　　"Yeah! Very rich! I love money." He laughed at the declaration. It was the first moment of ease in the interview. He told me he had a girl friend in Beijing for the past year and they would probably marry when he was thirty.

61　　"Will she wait nine years?"

62　　"I think so."

63　　While the interview with Zhu was limited by his reserve and our joint language problems, the next student had no difficulty presenting important matters about her life.

64　　"Yan" had already traveled outside China—a rare experience for a young Chinese. Although she was dressed as informally as Lin in jeans and blouse, she seemed more poised and mature. Her light skin was set off dramatically by her lustrous hair, which she occasionally pulled back from her face. Her English was quick and sure, and the context of her thoughts clear, though tenses and articles might be incorrect.

65　　"Last summer I go to Indonesia. I have aunt and uncle in Jakarta and I stay with them. Also I go to Bali and Bandung."

66　　She apparently noted my startled reaction because she added, "My friends were surprised that my mother let me go to Indonesia, but she always encourage me to be independent. Even when I was twelve I travel alone for two days on train to Beijing." And then, unexpectedly, she added, "My mother is a traveler also. Last summer she go to Europe."

67   The travel was a surprise. The typical income in urban China is not much more than $100 per month, hardly enough to travel abroad.

68   Yan had listed the occupations of both parents as "government officials," which was likely to mean they received special privileges, such as a better than average apartment, more government services, and even freedom to travel abroad. But when I asked Yan about the work her parents did as government officials, her English failed her. "My mother works in a government department—something about family. And my father works in highways department." Questions about the jobs revealed nothing more specific, and I needed to move on.

69   I turned back to her written answers on the form. In response to a question about changes that had occurred in the family's economic status over three generations, she wrote, "When my grandparents were young they were fighting for the independence of the country. At that time, there were many children in the family and they were used to being hungry. In my parents' time things were better—there was more food—but many things common nowadays were luxuries then."

70   Yan's family history could serve as a microcosm of decades of change in China. Her grandparents' generation lived through the bitter and bloody Japanese invasion and occupation of China, which ended with World War II. After the war, the country was torn apart as Chinese Nationalist troops fought Chinese Communists. Finally, in 1949, the Nationalists fled from the mainland to Taiwan and Mao's Communist forces took control of China. It was important to be on the right side of the winners.

71   "My grandfather believed in the revolution. Even when he was in high school he was a leader. So he join Mao's army after high school and became a leader in army."

72   That badge of courage could merit special privileges from the new rulers. Those who helped them achieve power were given jobs or farm land and other benefits. But those who were considered supporters of the Nationalists were regarded as "tainted" and were often imprisoned or killed, and their possessions confiscated. Millions were considered tainted. Nor was the reward or punishment temporary: the situation of parents and grandparents endured into following generations, until Mao died in 1976. Then the new regime of Deng Xiaoping canceled many of the old edicts. Yan's family had apparently been on the right side. She repeated her quote about her grandparents "fighting for the revolution" three times; it appeared to be a family mantra that had protected them for decades. But even so, in the final twenty years of Mao's life the country was so mismanaged that almost no one avoided suffering. Yan's story about her parents when they were young is typical.

73   "My parents did not finish high school because they were sent to countryside to help peasants on farms in southern China. After some

years they were sent to the North, near Mongolia, to work with peasants there."

74   "Do you know when your parents were sent to the farms?"

75   "It was . . . I'm not very sure . . . maybe during 1960s."

76   "Could it be 1966?"

77   "Yes . . . somewhere in there."

78   "Did they want to go to college after high school?"

79   "Yes, but universities and schools were closed."

80   "How long were they working on farms?"

81   "Uh . . . working on the farms?" She looked away, considering it slowly.

82   "Did they ever tell you about that?"

83   "They didn't say that very clearly. Maybe four years, or more than that."

84   "Did they tell you why they were sent to Mongolia?"

85   "No, they never say about that."

86   The period of the Cultural Revolution in China, from 1966 to 1976, was one of the strangest anywhere in modern times. Silence about it did not surprise me. I learned in this and succeeding interviews that the decade seemed almost a forbidden subject, not only to be excluded when talking to foreigners, but apparently within Chinese families as well.

87   Most of the parents of the students I interviewed were born soon after World War II and were teenagers when the Cultural Revolution began. They had already been trained in their schools to venerate Mao Zedong as a god, and to spout quotes about him: "Chairman Mao is our great saving star." "We are all Chairman Mao's good little children." But by 1966 Mao had made so many blunders in managing the country that his own position was threatened.

88   It started in 1957 with the campaign to "Let A Hundred Flowers Bloom," an invitation to the country's intellectuals to offer suggestions about possible improvements. One Harvard-trained physician recommended that the Communist Party officials running his hospital, all of them uneducated peasants, be replaced with doctors. Within weeks the government turned on the physician and thousands of other critics, sending them off to camps to be reeducated as proper Communists while alternating their schooling with beatings and manual labor. The physician spent years breaking rocks in a quarry while his wife, also a doctor, was reduced to cleaning toilets in the same hospital where she had treated patients.

89   The government's opposition to the best and brightest minds succeeded in decapitating the country, leading to inevitable mismanagement. But it was ordinary people who suffered most. During "The Great Leap Forward" of 1958–60, 650 million Chinese were mobilized

in round-the-clock ant-like efforts to build roads, dams, factories, and cities. Crude backyard foundries were constructed to compete with modern steel mills in the West. To stoke the fires, workers denuded the landscape of trees. After the trees were gone, many farmers tossed their tools into the furnaces to keep up with the demands of local Party bosses. Meanwhile, those functionaries sent false reports of achievement to Beijing. Farmers were too busy working in government projects to harvest their much reduced crops, and famine settled over the country. As many as 30 million people died.

90   At the highest government levels, opposition to Mao's policies grew. To protect his position, he turned to the children who had been carefully trained to regard him as a savior of the country. Millions of teenagers donned the armband of the Red Guards and were ordered to attack the "Four Olds: old ideas, customs, habits, and cultures." Teenagers were delighted to have an excuse to punish their teachers, destroy ancient buildings, and break into private homes seeking books, art, and anything else they decided was alien to Mao's revolution. A recording of Mozart was sufficient to brand its owner as an enemy of the state who deserved a beating and years of imprisonment. As the kids reveled in their new power, they expelled officials from their posts, sometimes taking over their jobs. Bands of teenagers competed and fought with each other to prove their loyalty to Mao. Once they obtained guns and urban streets became battle zones, Mao's hurried solution was to send the children off to farms to assist peasants.

91   Did Yan know anything about these events? Did her history books mention them at all? Had her parents protected her by not revealing the information? Of course, even if she did know, it was doubtful that any student would discuss such knowledge with a foreigner. The questions intrigued me, but they could not be answered in the interviews. I looked back to the questionnaire.

92   "Yan, I see that both your parents graduated from universities. Do you know when that was?"

93   "It was after they return from North. The system of the university open maybe in 1976, or 1978, I don't know. After I was born. They were praying to go to university. It was first time youngsters, the whole country, could go to university again. At first only father go to university. I was baby. When I was older, mother go to university also."

94   "Do you remember that period?"

95   "I remember my mother with her books. She help me with my studies too."

96   Yan's parents were among the lucky ones. Most of their contemporaries never returned to the educational system. College entrance examinations resumed after a ten-year lapse. Of the millions who took the tests, only five percent gained entrance to universities. Many in

the generation of the Red Guards who had begun life as urban youth and were meant to follow their parents as managers, teachers and civil servants were instead sent to factories or farms and never found their way back. Today, they are often referred to as China's Lost Generation. In contrast, Yan's parents became government officials, an elite segment of the society.

97   "It was fortunate that your parents could complete their education after years of working on farms."

98   Yan passed her hand over the books she had carried to the meeting, as if they were family talismans. "Always my parents tell me how important is education. They want me to do my best."

99   During the three and a half years that Yan has been away from home her parents have visited whenever they can, and Yan is especially close to her mother. "She is very interesting person. We talk about many things. We are two women now, not mother and child. Always she tells me that I must be sure that I don't do something to please someone—that I do it for myself. My parents teach me this. They want me to have my own dream and fight for it."

100   I was impressed by Yan's balancing act. She was obviously close to her parents but seemed also to be independent. I had read about the specialness of the single child in modern China. Often they were said to be like spoiled princes. But Yan was no spoiled child waiting for people to do things for her, nor were other students I interviewed. It appeared that her parents had done all the right things. Only later did I have time to ponder whether she, and the other equally impressive young people I met, had been trained to be independent by parents who had sacrificed that quality in their devotion to Mao when they were young. Perhaps they knew too well the dangers of blind obedience, and needed to help their children avoid the problems they had lived through.

101   I would have enjoyed hearing more about the family, but was concerned about the time. Professor Han would arrive to take me to lunch soon, and I needed to wrap up the interview.

102   "Yan, you are 22 now. What do you think your life will be like when you are 27 or 28?"

103   Her expression changed from confidence to uncertainty, but in a moment turned back again. "As you know, I want to travel. Also I want to make my parents more comfortable, help them do whatever they want to do, especially after they stop work."

104   I waited for her to say more, but the pause lengthened, providing its own answer.

105   "I haven't thought much about my life at 27 or 28."

106   That was surprising in someone so sure of herself.

107   "What about marriage?"

108   "Marriage?" The question startled her.

109   "Is that part of your dreams for the future?"

110   "It is not really a dream. It is not very important in my dreams." And then, offhand, as if to assure herself and me: "I have a boyfriend from high school. He likes to travel also. Maybe we can go to Europe together."

111   Her response was so different from what it would have been in America that I wanted to pursue the subject, but we were interrupted when Professor Han poked his head in the door and asked if I were ready to go to lunch. I clicked off the recorder and assured the professor that we were finished. I turned to Yan.

112   "Thanks so much for the interview. I enjoyed talking with you very much." And then a fleeting thought: "Your parents sound so interesting that I'm sorry I did not get a chance to meet them."

113   She smiled broadly and looked very pretty—a young woman whose future might be rich. She thanked me for my comment, picked up her books and was gone. For an instant I stared at the door, thinking about the love her parents had poured into her, and because of it, how lucky she was to go into the world with so much confidence.

114   I gathered my things. As we walked down the corridor Professor Han asked me how the interviews were going. I assured him I was very pleased about the information I was gathering, but I was also puzzled about a couple of issues. "I'm surprised the students haven't thought much about their future beyond the university. And marriage also seems not very important."

115   As we approached the staircase, the professor considered the issues. "Well, I think it's because so many changes are taking place in China that students think only about what they must do today. Tomorrow is for tomorrow."

116   We had reached the bottom of the stairs. I pushed the door open and waited for the professor to pass through in front of me. He hesitated momentarily—perhaps there was still a shadow of old Confucian respect for my age—and then bowed slightly and moved ahead. As we walked among students in the shade of young trees, I looked forward to the coming interviews.

✧ *Evaluating the Text*

1. What kinds of discoveries did Metzger make as to the ways in which the lives of students had changed in the years following the demonstrations at Tiananmen Square in 1989?

2. How did the students and faculty Metzger interviewed illustrate a broad spectrum of typical experiences?

✧ Exploring Different Perspectives

1. Compare the experiences of the students Metzger interviewed with those reported by Rae Yang in "The Center of the Storm" and evaluate the changes in Chinese culture.

2. To what extent do the students Metzger interviews still fear the government monitoring their lives in ways dramatized in Ngũgĩ wa Thiong'o's account?

✧ Extending Viewpoints through Writing

1. If you were interviewed by someone visiting your campus from another country, how would your responses differ from those whom Metzger interviewed?

2. Do some research on the Internet on the state of education at Beijing University and write a short report that updates Metzger's findings.

Luis Sepulveda

Daisy

——————◆——————

The Chilean expatriot novelist Luis Sepulveda takes us inside the prison where he was confined and reveals, with surprising good humor, one of his experiences. This chapter, translated by Chris Andrews and drawn from Full Circle: A South American Journey, *reveals Sepulveda's ironic sensibility as he tries to evade torture and remain an honest critic of his jailer's literary efforts. His works include his acclaimed detective novel* The Old Man Who Read Love Stories *(1992) and* The Name of the Bullfighter *(1996). He is also the author of a novel, and the screenplay for the film,* Zorba and Lucky *(1998).*

Chile, whose name comes from an Indian word Tchil *meaning "the deepest point of the earth," is located on the west coast of South America, bordered by Peru, Bolivia, Argentina, and the Pacific Ocean. It stretches like a ribbon 2,800 miles from north to south and is only 265 miles at its widest point. It is composed of three distinct climatic and geographic regions. The range of Andes mountains reaching more than 22,000 feet above sea level separate it from Argentina. Spain conquered northern Chile from the native Incas in the mid 1500s, but met continued resistance from the tribal Indians who lived in the south. The struggle for independence from Spanish rule was achieved in 1818. Chile was democratic until the overthrow of President Salvador Allende in 1973 under a U.S.-supported military coup. A repressive military junta headed by General Augusto Pinochet gained control until 1990, when he stepped down. His elected successors have gained a measure of confidence with the population over the last decade. Probably due to the free and compulsory system of education, Chile has one of the highest literacy rates in Latin America. Presidential elections in 2000 were won by the socialist candidate, Ricardo Lagos.*

Before You Read

Consider the unusual importance that literature takes on in this most unlikely environment.

——————◆——————

1   The military had rather inflated ideas of our destructive capacity. They questioned us about plans to assassinate all the officers in American military history, to blow up bridges and seal off tunnels, and to

prepare for the landing of a terrible foreign enemy whom they could not identify.

2   Temuco is a sad, grey, rainy city. No-one would call it a tourist attraction, and yet the barracks of the Tucapel regiment came to house a sort of permanent international convention of sadists. The Chileans, who were the hosts, after all, were assisted in the interrogations by primates from Brazilian military intelligence—they were the worst—North Americans from the State Department, Argentinian paramilitary personnel, Italian neo-fascists and even some agents of Mossad.

3   I remember Rudi Weismann, a Chilean with a passion for the South and sailing, who was tortured and interrogated in the gentle language of the synagogues. This infamy was too much for Rudi, who had thrown in his lot with Israel: he had worked on a kibbutz, but in the end his nostalgia for Tierra del Fuego had brought him back to Chile. He simply could not understand how Israel could support such a gang of criminals, and though till then he had always been a model of good humour, he dried up like a neglected plant. One morning we found him dead in his sleeping bag. No need for an autopsy, his face made it clear: Rudi Weismann had died of sadness.

4   The commander of the Tucapel regiment—a basic respect for paper prevents me from writing his name—was a fanatical admirer of Field Marshal Rommel. When he found a prisoner he liked, he would invite him to recover from the interrogations in his office. After assuring the prisoner that everything that happened in the barracks was in the best interests of our great nation, the commander would offer him a glass of Korn—somebody used to send him this insipid, wheat-based liquor from Germany—and make him sit through a lecture on the Afrika Korps. The guy's parents or grandparents were German, but he couldn't have looked more Chilean: chubby, short-legged, dark untidy hair. You could have mistaken him for a truck driver or a fruit vendor, but when he talked about Rommel he became the caricature of a Nazi guard.

5   At the end of the lecture he would dramatise Rommel's suicide, clicking his heels, raising his right hand to his forehead to salute an invisible flag, muttering "Adieu geliebtes Vaterland," and pretending to shoot himself in the mouth. We all hoped that one day he would do it for real.

6   There was another curious officer in the regiment: a lieutenant struggling to contain a homosexuality that kept popping out all over the place. The soldiers had nicknamed him Daisy, and he knew it.

7   We could all tell that it was a torment for Daisy not to be able to adorn his body with truly beautiful objects, and the poor guy had to make do with the regulation paraphernalia. He wore a .45 pistol, two cartridge clips, a commando's curved dagger, two hand grenades, a torch, a walkie-talkie, the insignia of his rank and the silver wings of

the parachute corps. The prisoners and the soldiers thought he looked like a Christmas tree.

8   This individual sometimes surprised us with generous and apparently disinterested acts—we didn't know that the Stockholm syndrome could be a military perversion. For example, after the interrogations he would suddenly fill our pockets with cigarettes or the highly prized aspirin tablets with vitamin C. One afternoon he invited me to his room.

9   "So you're a man of letters," he said, offering me a can of Coca-Cola.

10   "I've written a couple of stories. That's all," I replied.

11   "You're not here for an interrogation. I'm very sorry about what's happening, but that's what war is like. I want us to talk as one writer to another. Are you surprised? The army has produced some great men of letters. Think of Don Alonso de Ercilla y Zúñiga, for example."

12   "Or Cervantes," I added.

13   Daisy included himself among the greats. That was his problem. If he wanted adulation, he could have it. I drank the Coca-Cola and thought about Garcés, or rather, about his chicken, because, incredible as it seems, the cook had a chicken called Dulcinea, the name of Don Quixote's mistress.

14   One morning it jumped the wall which separated the common-law prisoners from the POWs, and it must have been a chicken with deep political convictions, because it decided to stay with us. Garcés caressed it and sighed, saying: "If I had a pinch of pepper and a pinch of cumin, I'd make you a chicken marinade like you've never tasted."

15   "I want you to read my poems and give me your opinion, your honest opinion," said Daisy, handing me a notebook.

16   I left that room with my pockets full of cigarettes, caramel sweets, tea bags and a tin of US Army marmalade. That afternoon I started to believe in the brotherhood of writers.

17   They transported us from the prison to the barracks and back in a cattle truck. The soldiers made sure there was plenty of cow shit on the floor of the truck before ordering us to lie face down with our hands behind our necks. We were guarded by four of them, with North American machine guns, one in each corner of the truck. They were almost all young guys brought down from northern garrisons, and the harsh climate of the South kept them flu-ridden and in a perpetually filthy mood. They had orders to fire on the bundles—us—at the slightest suspect movement, or on any civilian who tried to approach the truck. But as time wore on, the discipline gradually relaxed and they turned a blind eye to the packet of cigarettes or piece of fruit thrown from a window, or the pretty and daring girl who ran beside the truck blowing us kisses and shouting: "Don't give up, comrades! We'll win!"

18   Back in prison, as always, we were met by the welcoming committee organised by Doctor "Skinny" Pragnan, now an eminent psychiatrist

in Belgium. First he examined those who couldn't walk and those who had heart problems, then those who had come back with a dislocation or with ribs out of place. Pragnan was expert at estimating how much electricity had been put into us on the grill, and patiently determined who would be able to absorb liquids in the next few hours. Then finally it was time to take communion: we were given the aspirin with vitamin C and an anticoagulant to prevent internal haematomas.

19   "Dulcinea's days are numbered," I said to Garcés, and looked for a corner in which to read Daisy's notebook.

20   The elegantly inscribed pages were redolent of love, honey, sublime suffering and forgotten flowers. By the third page I knew that Daisy hadn't even gone to the trouble of reusing the ideas of the Mexican poet Amado Nervo—he'd simply copied out his poems word for word.

21   I called out to Peyuco Gálvez, a Spanish teacher, and read him a couple of lines.

22   "What do you think, Peyuco?"

23   "Amado Nervo. The book is called *The Interior Gardens.*"

24   I had got myself into a real jam. If Daisy found out that I knew the work of this sugary poet Nervo, then it wasn't Garcés's chicken whose days were numbered, but mine. It was a serious problem, so that night I presented it to the Council of Elders.

25   "Now, Daisy, would he be the passive or the active type?" enquired Iriarte.

26   "Stop it, will you. My skin's at risk here," I replied.

27   "I'm serious. Maybe our friend wants to have an affair with you, and giving you the notebook was like dropping a silk handkerchief. And like a fool you picked it up. Perhaps he copied out the poems for you to find a message in them. I've known queens who seduced boys by lending them *Demian* by Hermann Hesse. If Daisy is the passive type, this business with Amado Nervo means he wants to test your nerve, so to speak. And if he's the active type, well, it would have to hurt less than a kick in the balls."

28   "Message my arse. He gave you the poems as his own, and you should say you liked them a lot. If he was trying to send a message, he should have given the notebook to Garcés; he's the only one who has an interior garden. Or maybe Daisy doesn't know about the pot plant," remarked Andrés Müller.

29   "Let's be serious about this. You have to say something to him, and Daisy mustn't even suspect that you know Nervo's poems," declared Pragnan.

30   "Tell him you liked the poems, but that the adjectives strike you as a bit excessive. Quote Huidobro: when an adjective doesn't give life, it kills. That way you'll show him that you read his poems carefully and that you are criticising his work as a colleague," suggested Gálvez.

31   The Council of Elders approved of Gálvez's idea, but I spent two weeks on tenterhooks. I couldn't sleep. I wished they would come and take me to be kicked and electrocuted so I could give the damned notebook back. In those two weeks I came to hate good old Garcés:

32   "Listen, mate, if everything goes well, and you get a little jar of capers as well as the cumin and the pepper, we'll have such a feast with that chicken."

33   After a fortnight, I found myself at last stretched out face down on the mattress of cowpats with my hands behind my neck. I thought I was going mad: I was happy to be heading towards a session of the activity known as torture.

34   Tucapel barracks. Service Corps. In the background, the perpetual green of Cerro Ñielol, sacred to the Mapuche Indians. There was a waiting room outside the interrogation cell, like at the doctor's. There they made us sit on a bench with our hands tied behind our backs and black hoods over our heads. I never understood what the hoods were for, because once we got inside they took them off, and we could see the interrogators—the toy soldiers who, with panic-stricken faces, turned the handle of the generator, and the health officers who attached the electrodes to our anuses, testicles, gums and tongue, and then listened with stethoscopes to see who was faking and who had really passed out on the grill.

35   Lagos, a deacon of the Emmaus International ragmen, was the first to be interrogated that day. For a year they had been working him over to find out how the organisation had come by a couple of dozen old military uniforms which had been found in their warehouses. A trader who sold army surplus gear had donated them. Lagos screamed in pain and repeated over and over what the soldiers wanted to hear: the uniforms belonged to an invading army which was preparing to land on the Chilean coast.

36   I was waiting for my turn when someone took off the hood. It was Lieutenant Daisy.

37   "Follow me," he ordered.

38   We went into an office. On the desk I saw a tin of cocoa and a carton of cigarettes which were obviously there to reward my comments on his literary work.

39   "Did you read my poesy?" he asked, offering me a seat.

40   Poesy. Daisy said poesy, not poetry. A man covered with pistols and grenades can't say "poesy" without sounding ridiculous and effete. At that moment he revolted me, and I decided that even if it meant pissing blood, hissing when I spoke and being able to charge batteries just by touching them, I wasn't going to lower myself to flattering a plagiarising faggot in uniform.

41   "You have pretty handwriting, Lieutenant. But you know these poems aren't yours," I said, giving him back the notebook.

42   I saw him begin to shake. He was carrying enough arms to kill me several times over, and if he didn't want to stain his uniform, he could order someone else to do it. Trembling with anger he stood up, threw what was on the desk onto the floor and shouted:

43   "Three weeks in the cube. But first, you're going to visit the chiropodist, you piece of subversive shit!"

44   The chiropodist was a civilian, a landholder who had lost several thousand hectares in the land reform, and who was getting his revenge by participating in the interrogations as a volunteer. His speciality was peeling back toenails, which led to terrible infections.

45   I knew the cube. I had spent my first six months of prison there in solitary confinement: it was an underground cell, one and a half metres wide by one and a half metres long by one and a half metres high. In the old days there had been a tannery in the Temuco jail, and the cube was used to store fat. The walls still stank of fat, but after a week your excrement fixed that, making the cube very much a place of your own.

46   You could only stretch out across the diagonal, but the low temperatures of southern Chile, the rainwater and the soldiers' urine made you want to curl up hugging your legs and stay like that wishing yourself smaller and smaller, so that eventually you could live on one of the islands of floating shit, which conjured up images of dream holidays. I was there for three weeks, running through Laurel and Hardy films, remembering the books of Salgari, Stevenson and London word by word, playing long games of chess, licking my toes to protect them from infection. In the cube I swore over and over again never to become a literary critic.

✦ Evaluating the Text

1. To what paradoxical aspects of prison life does Sepulveda have to adapt in order to survive?

2. What unusual mixture of character traits and aspirations does Daisy display, given his role as prison guard and torturer? What kind of relationship does Sepulveda have with Daisy?

3. In what ways is Sepulveda's style unusual, given his predicament? In what sense might his style itself be a way of coping with the dangerous circumstances with which he was confronted?

✦ Exploring Different Perspectives

1. Compare Luis Sepulveda's narrative with Panos Ioannides's story "Gregory" in terms of the moral dilemmas involved and the authors' use of irony.

2. To what extent do the accounts by Luis Sepulveda and Ngũgĩ wa Thiong'o ("Decolonising the Mind") reveal the psychological value placed on authenticity in language and literature as a strategy of rebellion?

✧ Extending Viewpoints through Writing

1. If you had been in the same situation as Sepulveda, would you have been as honest as he was? Why or why not?

2. Plagiarism is a moral problem with which students are often confronted. What experiences have you had either directly or indirectly? Tell what happened.

Ngũgĩ wa Thiong'o

Decolonising the Mind

◆───────────◆

Ngũgĩ wa Thiong'o is regarded as one of the most important contempo-
rary writers on the African continent. He wrote his first novels, Weep
Not, Child *(1964) and* The River Between *(1965), in English, and*
Caitaani Mũtharava-Ini *(translated as* Devil on the Cross, *1982) in*
his native language, Gĩkũyũ. He was chairman of the department of liter-
ature at the University of Nairobi until his detention without trial by the
Kenyan authorities in 1977, an account of which appeared under the title
Detained: A Writer's Prison Diary *(1981). The international outcry*
over his imprisonment eventually produced his release. This selection
comes from Decolonising the Mind: The Politics of Language in
African Literature *(1986), a work that constitutes, says Ngũgĩ, "my*
farewell to English as a vehicle for any of my writings." Subsequently, he
has written novels and plays in Gĩkũyũ.

    Kenya is a republic in East Africa. Discoveries by anthropologists
and archaeologists in the Great Rift Valley in Kenya have unearthed re-
mains of what may be the earliest known humans, believed to be some
two million years old. German missionaries were the first Europeans to
make their way into Kenya in 1844, making contact with the then-
ruling Maasai (for more background on the Maasai, see p. 122) and
Kĩkũyũ tribes. The Imperial British East Africa Company wrested po-
litical control from Germany, and Kenya became a British protectorate
in 1890 and a Crown Colony in 1920. Increasingly violent confronta-
tions between European settlers and the Kĩkũyũs reached a crisis in the
1950s during the terror campaign of the Mau Mau rebellion. In re-
sponse, the British declared a state of emergency, which was not lifted
until 1960.

    Originally a leader of the Mau Mau uprising, Jomo Kenyatta be-
came Kenya's first president in 1964, on the first anniversary of
Kenya's independence, and served until his death in 1978. Continuing
opposition and unrest prompted Kenyatta's government to imprison po-
litical dissidents, including Ngũgĩ wa Thiong'o. Kenyatta's successor,
Daniel T. arap Moi, has yielded to pressure to open the country to an
open-party democracy. National elections were held in December 1992,
which returned Moi to power amid tensions threatening the democrati-
zation process. Moi was reelected as president on January 5, 1998. Moi
was succeeded by Mwai Kibaki in 2002.

Black Africans of forty different ethnic groups make up 97 percent of the population. The official languages are Swahili and English. The situation described by Thiong'o has changed to the extent that children are now taught in their native languages for the first three years of school, after which instruction is exclusively in English.

Before You Read

Underline the key points in Thiong'o's analysis and the supporting examples that clarify his thesis.

━━━━━━━━━━━━━━━ ✦ ━━━━━━━━━━━━━━━

1   I was born into a large peasant family: father, four wives and about twenty-eight children. I also belonged, as we all did in those days, to a wider extended family and to the community as a whole.

2   We spoke Gĩkũyũ as we worked in the fields. We spoke Gĩkũyũ in and outside the home. I can vividly recall those evenings of story-telling around the fireside. It was mostly the grown-ups telling the children but everybody was interested and involved. We children would re-tell the stories the following day to other children who worked in the fields picking the pyrethrum flowers, tea-leaves or coffee beans of our European and African landlords.

3   The stories, with mostly animals as the main characters, were all told in Gĩkũyũ. Hare, being small, weak but full of innovative wit and cunning, was our hero. We identified with him as he struggled against the brutes of prey like lion, leopard, hyena. His victories were our victories and we learnt that the apparently weak can outwit the strong. We followed the animals in their struggle against hostile nature— drought, rain, sun, wind—a confrontation often forcing them to search for forms of co-operation. But we were also interested in their struggles amongst themselves, and particularly between the beasts and the victims of prey. These twin struggles, against nature and other animals, reflected real-life struggles in the human world.

4   Not that we neglected stories with human beings as the main characters. There were two types of characters in such human-centred narratives: the species of truly human beings with qualities of courage, kindness, mercy, hatred of evil, concern for others; and a man-eat-man two-mouthed species with qualities of greed, selfishness, individualism and hatred of what was good for the larger co-operative community. Co-operation as the ultimate good in a community was a constant theme. It could unite human beings with animals against ogres and beasts of prey, as in the story of how dove, after being fed with castor-oil seeds, was sent to fetch a smith working far away from home and whose pregnant wife was being threatened by these man-eating two-mouthed ogres.

5   There were good and bad story-tellers. A good one could tell the same story over and over again, and it would always be fresh to us, the listeners. He or she could tell a story told by someone else and make it more alive and dramatic. The differences really were in the use of words and images and the inflexion of voices to effect different tones.

6   We therefore learnt to value words for their meaning and nuances. Language was not a mere string of words. It had a suggestive power well beyond the immediate and lexical meaning. Our appreciation of the suggestive magical power of language was reinforced by the games we played with words through riddles, proverbs, transpositions of syllables, or through nonsensical but musically arranged words.[1] So we learnt the music of our language on top of the content. The language, through images and symbols, gave us a view of the world, but it had a beauty of its own. The home and the field were then our pre-primary school but what is important, for this discussion, is that the language of our evening teach-ins, and the language of our immediate and wider community, and the language of our work in the fields were one.

7   And then I went to school, a colonial school, and this harmony was broken. The language of my education was no longer the language of my culture. I first went to Kamaandura, missionary run, and then to another called Maanguuũ run by nationalists grouped around the Gĩkũyũ Independent and Karinga Schools Association. Our language of education was still Gĩkũyũ. The very first time I was ever given an ovation for my writing was over a composition in Gĩkũyũ. So for my first four years there was still harmony between the language of my formal education and that of the Limuru peasant community.

8   It was after the declaration of a state of emergency over Kenya in 1952 that all the schools run by patriotic nationalists were taken over by the colonial regime and were placed under District Education Boards chaired by Englishmen. English became the language of my formal education. In Kenya, English became more than a language: it was *the* language, and all the others had to bow before it in deference.

9   Thus one of the most humiliating experiences was to be caught speaking Gĩkũyũ in the vicinity of the school. The culprit was given

---

[1]Example from a tongue twister: "Kaana ka Nikoora koona koora: na ko koora koona kaana ka Nikoora koora koora." I'm indebted to Wangui wa Goro for this example. 'Nichola's child saw a baby frog and ran away: and when the baby frog saw Nichola's child it also ran away.' A Gĩkũyũ-speaking child has to get the correct tone and length of vowel and pauses to get it right. Otherwise it becomes a jumble of *k*'s and *r*'s and *na*'s [Author's note].

corporal punishment—three to five strokes of the cane on bare but-tocks—or was made to carry a metal plate around the neck with in-scriptions such as I AM STUPID or I AM A DONKEY. Sometimes the culprits were fined money they could hardly afford. And how did the teachers catch the culprits? A button was initially given to one pupil who was supposed to hand it over to whoever was caught speaking his mother tongue. Whoever had the button at the end of the day would sing who had given it to him and the ensuing process would bring out all the culprits of the day. Thus children were turned into witch-hunters and in the process were being taught the lucrative value of being a traitor to one's immediate community.

10　　　The attitude to English was the exact opposite: any achievement in spoken or written English was highly rewarded; prizes, prestige, ap-plause; the ticket to higher realms. English became the measure of in-telligence and ability in the arts, the sciences, and all the other branches of learning. English became *the* main determinant of a child's progress up the ladder of formal education.

11　　　As you may know, the colonial system of education in addition to its apartheid racial demarcation had the structure of a pyramid: a broad primary base, a narrowing secondary middle, and an even nar-rower university apex. Selections from primary into secondary were through an examination, in my time called Kenya African Preliminary Examination, in which one had to pass six subjects ranging from Maths to Nature Study and Kiswahili. All the papers were written in English. Nobody could pass the exam who failed the English language paper no matter how brilliantly he had done in the other subjects. I remem-ber one boy in my class of 1954 who had distinctions in all subjects ex-cept English, which he had failed. He was made to fail the entire exam. He went on to become a turn boy in a bus company. I who had only passes but a credit in English got a place at the Alliance High School, one of the most elitist institutions for Africans in colonial Kenya. The requirements for a place at the University, Makerere University Col-lege, were broadly the same: nobody could go on to wear the under-graduate red gown, no matter how brilliantly they had performed in all the other subjects unless they had a credit—not even a simple pass!—in English. Thus the most coveted place in the pyramid and in the system was only available to the holder of an English language credit card. English was the official vehicle and the magic formula to colonial elitedom.

12　　　Literary education was now determined by the dominant lan-guage while also reinforcing that dominance. Orature (oral literature) in Kenyan languages stopped. In primary school I now read simplified Dickens and Stevenson alongside Rider Haggard. Jim Hawkins, Oliver Twist, Tom Brown—not Hare, Leopard, and Lion—were now my daily companions in the world of imagination. In secondary school, Scott and G. B. Shaw vied with more Rider Haggard, John Buchan, Alan Paton, Captain W. E. Johns. At Makerere I read English: from Chaucer to T. S. Eliot with a touch of Graham Greene.

13   Thus language and literature were taking us further and further from ourselves to other selves, from our world to other worlds.

14   What was the colonial system doing to us Kenyan children? What were the consequences of, on the one hand, this systematic suppression of our languages and the literature they carried, and on the other the elevation of English and the literature it carried? To answer those questions, let me first examine the relationship of language to human experience, human culture, and the human perception of reality.

15   Language, any language, has a dual character: it is both a means of communication and a carrier of culture. Take English. It is spoken in Britain and in Sweden and Denmark. But for Swedish and Danish people English is only a means of communication with non-Scandinavians. It is not a carrier of their culture. For the British, and particularly the English, it is additionally, and inseparably from its use as a tool of communication, a carrier of their culture and history. Or take Swahili in East and Central Africa. It is widely used as a means of communication across many nationalities. But it is not the carrier of a culture and history of many of those nationalities. However in parts of Kenya and Tanzania, and particularly in Zanzibar, Swahili is inseparably both a means of communication and a carrier of the culture of those people to whom it is a mother-tongue.

16   Culture transmits or imparts those images of the world and reality through the spoken and the written language, that is through a specific language. In other words, the capacity to speak, the capacity to order sounds in a manner that makes for mutual comprehension between human beings is universal. This is the universality of language, a quality specific to human beings. It corresponds to the universality of the struggle against nature and that between human beings. But the particularity of the sounds, the words, the word order into phrases and sentences, and the specific manner, or laws, of their ordering is what distinguishes one language from another. Thus a specific culture is not transmitted through language in its universality but in its particularity as the language of a specific community with a specific history. Written literature and orature are the main means by which a particular language transmits the images of the world contained in the culture it carries.

17   Language as communication and as culture are then products of each other. Communication creates culture: culture is a means of com-

munication. Language carries culture, and culture carries, particularly through orature and literature, the entire body of values by which we come to perceive ourselves and our place in the world. How people perceive themselves affects how they look at their culture, at their politics and at the social production of wealth, at their entire relationship to nature and to other beings. Language is thus inseparable from ourselves as a community of human beings with a specific form and character, a specific history, a specific relationship to the world.

18   So what was the colonialist imposition of a foreign language doing to us children?

19   The real aim of colonialism was to control the people's wealth: what they produced, how they produced it, and how it was distributed; to control, in other words, the entire realm of the language of real life. Colonialism imposed its control of the social production of wealth through military conquest and subsequent political dictatorship. But its most important area of domination was the mental universe of the colonised, the control, through culture, of how people perceived themselves and their relationship to the world. Economic and political control can never be complete or effective without mental control. To control a people's culture is to control their tools of self-definition in relationship to others.

20   For colonialism this involved two aspects of the same process: the destruction or the deliberate undervaluing of a people's culture, their art, dances, religions, history, geography, education, orature and literature, and the conscious elevation of the language of the coloniser. The domination of a people's language by the languages of the colonising nations was crucial to the domination of the mental universe of the colonised.

21   Take language as communication. Imposing a foreign language, and suppressing the native languages as spoken and written, were already breaking the harmony previously existing between the African child and the three aspects of language. Since the new language as a means of communication was a product of and was reflecting the 'real language of life' elsewhere, it could never as spoken or written properly reflect or imitate the real life of that community. This may in part explain why technology always appears to us as slightly external, *their* product and not *ours*. The word "missile" used to hold an alien faraway sound until I recently learnt its equivalent in Gĩkũyũ, *ngurukuhĩ*, and it made me apprehend it differently. Learning, for a colonial child, became a cerebral activity and not an emotionally felt experience.

22   But since the new, imposed languages could never completely break the native languages as spoken, their most effective area of domination was the third aspect of language as communication, the written. The language of an African child's formal education was foreign. The language

of the books he read was foreign. The language of his conceptualisation was foreign. Thought, in him, took the visible form of a foreign language. So the written language of a child's upbringing in the school (even his spoken language within the school compound) became divorced from his spoken language at home. There was often not the slightest relationship between the child's written world, which was also the language of his schooling, and the world of his immediate environment in the family and the community. For a colonial child, the harmony existing between the three aspects of language as communication was irrevocably broken. This resulted in the disassociation of the sensibility of that child from his natural and social environment, what we might call colonial alienation. The alienation became reinforced in the teaching of history, geography, music, where bourgeois Europe was always the centre of the universe.

23   This disassociation, divorce, or alienation from the immediate environment becomes clearer when you look at colonial language as a carrier of culture.

24   Since culture is a product of the history of a people which it in turn reflects, the child was now being exposed exclusively to a culture that was a product of a world external to himself. He was being made to stand outside himself to look at himself. *Catching Them Young* is the title of a book on racism, class, sex, and politics in children's literature by Bob Dixon. "Catching them young" as an aim was even more true of a colonial child. The images of this world and his place in it implanted in a child take years to eradicate, if they ever can be.

25   Since culture does not just reflect the world in images but actually, through those very images, conditions a child to see that world in a certain way, the colonial child was made to see the world and where he stands in it as seen and defined by or reflected in the culture of the language of imposition.

26   And since those images are mostly passed on through orature and literature it meant the child would now only see the world as seen in the literature of his language of adoption. From the point of view of alienation, that is of seeing oneself from outside oneself as if one was another self, it does not matter that the imported literature carried the great humanist tradition of the best in Shakespeare, Goethe, Balzac, Tolstoy, Gorky, Brecht, Sholokhov, Dickens. The location of this great mirror of imagination was necessarily Europe and its history and culture and the rest of the universe was seen from the centre.

27   But obviously it was worse when the colonial child was exposed to images of his world as mirrored in the written languages of his coloniser. Where his own native languages were associated in his impressionable mind with low status, humiliation, corporal punishment, slow-footed intelligence and ability or downright stupidity, non-intelligibility and

barbarism, this was reinforced by the world he met in the works of such geniuses of racism as a Rider Haggard or a Nicholas Monsarrat; not to mention the pronouncement of some of the giants of western intellectual and political establishment, such as Hume (". . . the negro is naturally inferior to the whites . . . "),[2] Thomas Jefferson (". . . the blacks . . . are inferior to the whites on the endowments of both body and mind . . . "),[3] or Hegel with his Africa comparable to a land of childhood still enveloped in the dark mantle of the night as far as the development of self-conscious history was concerned. Hegel's statement that there was nothing harmonious with humanity to be found in the African character is representative of the racist images of Africans and Africa such a colonial child was bound to encounter in the literature of the colonial languages.[4] The results could be disastrous.

28   In her paper read to the conference on the teaching of African literature in schools held in Nairobi in 1973,[5] entitled "Written Literature and Black Images," the Kenyan writer and scholar Professor Mīcere Mūgo related how a reading of the description of Gagool as an old African woman in Rider Haggard's *King Solomon's Mines* had for a long time made her feel mortal terror whenever she encountered old African women. In his autobiography *This Life,* Sydney Poitier describes how, as a result of the literature he had read, he had come to associate Africa with snakes. So on arrival in Africa and being put up in a modern hotel in a modern city, he could not sleep because he kept on looking for snakes everywhere, even under the bed. These two have been able to pinpoint the origins of their fears. But for most others the negative image becomes internalised and it affects their cultural and even political choices in ordinary living.

[2]Quoted in Eric Williams, *A History of the People of Trinidad and Tobago,* London 1964, p. 32 [Author's note].

[3]Ibid, p. 31 [Author's note].

[4]In references to Africa in the introduction to his lectures in *The Philosophy of History,* Hegel gives historical, philosophical, rational expression and legitimacy to every conceivable European racist myth about Africa. Africa is even denied her own geography where it does not correspond to myth. Thus Egypt is not part of Africa; and North Africa is part of Europe. Africa proper is the especial home of ravenous beasts, snakes of all kinds. The African is not part of humanity. Only slavery to Europe can raise him, possibly, to the lower ranks of humanity. Slavery is good for the African. "Slavery is in and for itself *injustice,* for the essence of humanity is *freedom;* but for this man must be matured. The gradual abolition of slavery is therefore wiser and more equitable than its sudden removal." (Hegel, *The Philosophy of History,* Dover edition, New York: 1956, pp. 91–9.) Hegel clearly reveals himself as the nineteenth-century Hitler of the intellect [Author's note].

[5]The paper is now in Akivaga and Gachukiah's *The Teaching of African Literature in Schools,* published by Kenya Literature Bureau [Author's note].

✧ *Evaluating the Text*

1. In what way would stories involving animals as heroes be especially important to the children to whom they were told? How might the nature of the conflicts in the animal stories better prepare children to deal with conflicts in real life? To what extent do these stories transmit cultural values by stressing the importance of resourcefulness, self-esteem, a connection to the past, and a pride in one's culture?

2. In addition to transmitting cultural values, how did hearing these stories, along with riddles and proverbs, imbue children with a love of the language of Gĩkũyũ and enhance their responsiveness to and skill with features of narrative, imagery, inflection, and tone? How did hearing different people tell the same stories contribute to their development of critical abilities in distinguishing whether a given story was told well or poorly?

3. Describe the disruption Thiong'o experienced when he first attended a colonial school, where he was forbidden to speak the language of the community from which he came. How do the kinds of punishments meted out for speaking Gĩkũyũ give you some insight into how psychologically damaging such an experience could be for a child? Which of the examples Thiong'o gives, in your opinion, most clearly reveals the extent to which speaking English was rewarded? In what way was the knowledge of English the single most important determinant of advancement?

4. Explain how the British as colonizers of Kenya sought to achieve dominance by (1) devaluing native speech, dance, art, and traditions and (2) promoting the worth of everything British, including the speaking of English. How does changing the language a people are allowed to speak change the way they perceive themselves and their relationship to those around them? Why did the British try to make it impossible for Kenyans to draw on the cultural values and traditions embodied in their language, Gĩkũyũ? Why was it also in the British interest to encourage and even compel Kenyans to look at themselves only through a British perspective? How was this view reinforced by teaching Kenyans British literature?

✧ *Exploring Different Perspectives*

1. Compare the accounts by Thiong'o and Rae Yang (see "At the Center of the Storm") in terms of reprogramming citizens to accept a "correct" ideology, whether that of British colonialism or Mao Tse Tung's Cultural Revolution.

2. Compare perspectives on education in Kenya, according to Thiong'o, and in China, according to Lawrence Metzger's findings in terms of government intervention.

✧ Extending Viewpoints through Writing

1. For a research project, you might compare Thiong'o's discussion of the stories he heard as a child with Bruno Bettleheim's study *The Uses of Enchantment: The Meaning and Importance of Fairy Tales* (1976). Bettleheim suggests that these traditional forms of story-telling help children build inner strength by acknowledging that real evil exists while offering hope that those who are resourceful can overcome the evil.

2. Discuss the extent to which Thiong'o's argument expresses a rationale similar to that advanced by proponents of bilingualism. You might also wish to consider the similarities and differences in political terms between the situation Thiong'o describes and that of a Hispanic or Chinese child in the United States. If you come from a culture where English was not your first language, to what extent did your experiences match Thiong'o's when you entered a school where English was the required language?

Rae Yang

At the Center of the Storm

◆

Rae Yang, who teaches East Asian Studies at Dickinson College, offers an unusual perspective of one who grew up in China and, at the age of fifteen, joined the Red Guards in Beijing. Her account of her life working on a pig farm and the political and moral crises that she experienced as a result of the Cultural Revolution offers a unique portrait of someone who was a committed, and even fanatic, revolutionary, who only later had misgivings about what the Red Guards had done. The following chapter is drawn from Spider Eaters *(1997).*

China's modern history has been characterized by cycles of liberalization followed by violent oppression. In 1957, reaction against the so-called "let a hundred flowers bloom" period led to a crackdown against intellectuals. In 1966, Mao launched the Cultural Revolution to purge the government and society of liberal elements. Revolutionary Red Guards composed of ideologically motivated young men and women acted with the army to attack so-called bourgeois elements in the government and in the culture at large. After Mao's death in 1976, a backlash led to the imprisoning of Mao's wife, Jiang Qing, and three colleagues (the "Gang of Four").

Before You Read

As you read consider the insight you gain as to why Mao Tse Tung chose young people to spearhead his Cultural Revolution.

◆

1   From May to December 1966, the first seven months of the Cultural Revolution left me with experiences I will never forget. Yet I forgot things almost overnight in that period. So many things were happening around me. The situation was changing so fast. I was too excited, too jubilant, too busy, too exhausted, too confused, too uncomfortable. . . . The forgotten things, however, did not all go away. Later some of them sneaked back into my memory, causing me unspeakable pain and shame. So I would say that those seven months were the most terrible in my life. Yet they were also the most wonderful! I had never felt so good about myself before, nor have I ever since.

2   In the beginning, the Cultural Revolution exhilarated me because suddenly I felt that I was allowed to think with my own head and say

what was on my mind. In the past, the teachers at 101 had worked hard to make us intelligent, using the most difficult questions in mathematics, geometry, chemistry, and physics to challenge us. But the mental abilities we gained, we were not supposed to apply elsewhere. For instance, we were not allowed to question the teachers' conclusions. Students who did so would be criticized as "disrespectful and conceited," even if their opinions made perfect sense. Worse still was to disagree with the leaders. Leaders at various levels represented the Communist Party. Disagreeing with them could be interpreted as being against the Party, a crime punishable by labor reform, imprisonment, even death.

3   Thus the teachers created a contradiction. On the one hand, they wanted us to be smart, rational, and analytical. On the other hand, they forced us to be stupid, to be "the teachers' little lambs" and "the Party's obedient tools." By so doing, I think, they planted a sick tree; the bitter fruit would soon fall into their own mouths.

4   When the Cultural Revolution broke out in late May 1966, I felt like the legendary monkey Sun Wukong, freed from the dungeon that had held him under a huge mountain for five hundred years. It was Chairman Mao who set us free by allowing us to rebel against authorities. As a student, the first authority I wanted to rebel against was Teacher Lin, our homeroom teacher—in Chinese, *banzhuren*. As *banzhuren*, she was in charge of our class. A big part of her duty was to make sure that we behaved and thought correctly.

5   Other students in my class might have thought that I was Teacher Lin's favorite. As our Chinese teacher, she read my papers in front of the class once in a while. That was true. (Only she and I knew that the grades I got for those papers rarely went above 85. I could only imagine what miserable grades she gave to others in our class.) She also chose me to be the class representative for Chinese, which meant if others had difficulties with the subject, I was to help them. In spite of all these, I did not like Teacher Lin! She had done me a great wrong in the past. I would never forget it.

6   In my opinion, Lin was exactly the kind of teacher who, in Chairman Mao's words, "treated the students as their enemies." In 1965, we went to Capital Steel and Iron Company in the far suburb of Beijing to do physical labor. One night there was an earthquake warning. We were made to stay outdoors to wait for it. By midnight, no earthquake had come. Two o'clock, still all quiet. Three o'clock, four o'clock, five. . . . The night was endless. Sitting on the cold concrete pavement for so many hours, I was sleepy. I was exhausted. My only wish at the moment was to be allowed to go into the shack and literally "hit the hay." Without thinking I grumbled: "Ai! How come there is still no earthquake?"

7   Who should have thought that this remark was overheard by Teacher Lin? All of a sudden she started criticizing me in a loud voice.

8   "The workers and the poor and lower-middle peasants would never say such a thing! Think of all the property that will be damaged by an earthquake. Think of all the lives that may be lost! Now you are looking forward to an earthquake! Only class enemies look forward to earthquakes! Where did your class feelings go? Do you have any proletarian feelings at all? . . . "

9   She went on and on. Her shrill voice woke up everybody, my classmates as well as students in the other five parallel classes. All were sitting outside at the moment. Everybody turned to watch us. Three hundred pairs of eyes! It was such a shame! I felt my cheeks burning. I wanted to defend myself. I wanted to tell Teacher Lin that although there might be some truth in what she said, I had never been in an earthquake. I was merely tired and wished the whole thing over. Besides, I was only half awake when I said that. I was not looking forward to an earthquake!

10   In fact, what I really wanted to tell her was that I knew why she was making such a fuss about my remark, which if she had not seized would have drifted away and scattered in the morning breeze like a puff of vapor: she was using this as an opportunity to show off her political correctness in front of all these teachers and students. At my cost! Later she might be able to cash in on it, using it as her political capital. . . .

11   But of course I knew it would be crazy for me to talk back like that. Contradicting the teacher would only lead me into more trouble. So I swallowed the words that were rolling on the tip of my tongue and lowered my head. Hot tears assaulted my eyes. Tears of anger. Tears of shame. I bit my lips to force them back. *Let's wait and see, Teacher Lin. Someday I will have my revenge. On you!*

12   Now the time had come for the underdogs to speak up, to seek justice! Immediately I took up a brush pen, dipped it in black ink and wrote a long *dazibao* (criticism in big characters). Using some of the rhetorical devices Teacher Lin had taught us, I accused her of lacking proletarian feelings toward her students, of treating them as her enemies, of being high-handed, and suppressing different opinions. When I finished and showed it to my classmates, they supported me by signing their names to it. Next, we took the *dazibao* to Teacher Lin's home nearby and pasted it on the wall of her bedroom for her to read carefully day and night. This, of course, was not personal revenge. It was answering Chairman Mao's call to combat the revisionist educational line. If in the meantime it caused Teacher Lin a few sleepless nights, so be it! This revolution was meant to "touch the soul" of people, an unpopular teacher in particular.

13   Teacher Lin, although she was not a good teacher in my opinion, was not yet the worst. Teacher Qian was even worse. He was the polit-

ical teacher who had implemented the Exposing Third Layer of Thoughts campaign. In the past many students believed that he could read people's minds. Now a *dazibao* by a student gave us a clue as to how he acquired this eerie ability. Something I would not have guessed in a thousand years! He had been reading students' diaries in class breaks, while we were doing physical exercise on the sports ground. The student who wrote the *dazibao* felt sick one day and returned to his classroom earlier than expected. There he had actually seen Qian sneak a diary from a student's desk and read it. The student kept his silence until the Cultural Revolution, for Qian was his *banzhuren.*

14   So this was Qian's so-called "political and thought work"! What could it teach us but dishonesty and hypocrisy? Such a "glorious" example the school had set for us, and in the past we had revered him so much! Thinking of the nightmare he gave me, I was outraged. "Take up a pen, use it as a gun." I wrote another *dazibao* to denounce Teacher Qian.

15   Within a few days *dazibao* were popping up everywhere like bamboo shoots after a spring rain, written by students, teachers, administrators, workers, and librarians. Secrets dark and dirty were exposed. Everyday we made shocking discoveries. The sacred halo around the teachers' heads that dated back two thousand five hundred years to the time of Confucius disappeared. Now teachers must drop their pretentious airs and learn a few things from their students. Parents would be taught by their kids instead of vice versa, as Chairman Mao pointed out. Government officials would have to wash their ears to listen to the ordinary people. Heaven and earth were turned upside down. The rebellious monkey with enormous power had gotten out. A revolution was underway.

16   Looking back on it, I should say that I felt good about the Cultural Revolution when it started. It gave me a feeling of superiority and confidence that I had never experienced before. Yet amidst the new freedom and excitement, I ran into things that made me very uncomfortable.

17   I remember one day in July, I went to have lunch at the student dining hall. On the way I saw a crowd gathering around the fountain. I went over to take a look. The fountain had been a pleasant sight in the past. Sparkling water swaying in the wind among green willow twigs, making the air fresh and clean. In Beijing it was a luxury ordinary middle schools did not enjoy. When the Cultural Revolution broke out, the water was turned off. Now the bottom of the fountain was muddy, littered with wastepaper and broken glass.

18   On this day I saw a teacher in the fountain, a middle-aged man. His clothes were muddy. Blood was streaming down his head, as a number of students were throwing bricks at him. He tried to dodge the bricks. While he did so, without noticing it, he crawled in the fountain, round and round, like an animal in the zoo. Witnessing such a scene,

I suddenly felt sick to my stomach. I would have vomited, if I had not quickly turned round and walked away. Forget about lunch. My appetite was gone.

19   Sitting in an empty classroom, I wondered why this incident upset me so much: *This is the first time I've seen someone beaten. Moreover this person isn't a stranger. He's a teacher at 101. Do I pity him? Maybe a little? Maybe not. After all I don't know anything about him. He might be a counterrevolutionary or a bad element. He might have done something very bad; thus he deserved the punishment. Something else bothers me, then—not the teacher. What is it?*

20   Then it dawned on me that I was shocked by the ugliness of the scene. *Yes. That's it! In the past when I read about torture in revolutionary novels, saw it in movies, and daydreamed about it, it was always so heroic, so noble; therefore it was romantic and beautiful. But now, in real life, it happened in front of me. It's so sordid! I wish I'd seen none of it! I don't want the memory to destroy my hero's dream.*

21   This teacher survived; another was not so fortunate. Teacher Chen, our art teacher, was said to resemble a spy in the movies. He was a tall, thin man with sallow skin and long hair, which was a sign of decadence. Moreover, he seemed gloomy and he smoked a lot. "If a person weren't scheming or if he didn't feel very unhappy in the new society, why would he smoke like that?" a classmate asked me, expecting nothing but heartfelt consent from me. "Not to say that in the past he had asked students to draw naked female bodies in front of plaster statues to corrupt them!" For these "crimes," he was beaten to death by a group of senior students.

22   When I heard this, I felt very uncomfortable again. The whole thing seemed a bad joke to me. Yet it was real! Teacher Chen had taught us the year before and unlike Teacher Lin and Teacher Qian, he had never treated students as his enemies. He was polite and tolerant. If a student showed talent in painting, he would be delighted. On the other hand, he would not embarrass a student who "had no art cells." I had never heard complaints about him before. Yet somehow he became the first person I knew who was killed in the Cultural Revolution.

23   Living next door to Teacher Chen was Teacher Jiang, our geography teacher. While Teacher Chen was tall and lean, Teacher Jiang was short and stout. Both were old bachelors, who taught auxiliary courses. Before the Cultural Revolution Teacher Jiang was known for two things. One was his unkempt clothes. The other was the fact that he never brought anything but a piece of chalk to class. Yet many students said that he was the most learned teacher at 101. He had many maps and books stored in his funny big head.

24   If Teacher Jiang had been admired by students before, he became even more popular after the revolution started and Teacher Chen was killed. Since August 1966 Red Guards were allowed to travel free of

charge to places all over China. Before we set off, everybody wanted to get a few tips from him, and afterwards we'd love to tell him a few stories in return. It was our chance to show off what we had learned from the trips. Thus from August to December, Teacher Jiang had many visitors. Happy voices and laughter were heard from across the lotus pond in front of his dorm house. At night lights shone through his windows often into the small hours. Geography turned out a true blessing for Teacher Jiang, while art doomed Teacher Chen.

25   In contrast to the teachers who lost control over their lives in 1966, we students suddenly found power in our hands. Entrance examinations for senior middle school and college were canceled. Now it was entirely up to us to decide what we would do with our time. This was a big change. In the past, decisions had always been made for us by our parents, teachers, and leaders. At school, all courses were required and we took them according to a fixed schedule, six classes a day, six days a week. College was the same as middle schools. After college, the state would assign everybody a job, an iron rice bowl. Like it or not, it would be yours for life.

26   Now those who had made decisions for us—teachers, parents, administrators—were swept aside by the storm. We were in charge. We could do things on our own initiative. We made plans. We carried them out. So what did we do? Instead of routine classes, we organized meetings at which we shared our family history. (People who spoke up at such meetings were of course revolutionary cadres' children. Others could only listen.) I remember Wu, a girl from a high-ranking cadre's family, told a story that left a deep impression on me.

27   In 1942 Japanese troops raided the Communist base in the north. At this time Wu's older brother was only several months old. He was a beautiful baby boy, with a chubby face and the mother's large brown eyes. The mother gave him the name Precious. Day and night she longed for the father to come back from the front to meet his firstborn.

28   But before the father returned, the Japanese invaders came. Wu's mother took the baby and fled to the mountains. She and many others hid in a cavern. The enemy soldiers came near, searching for them. At this moment the baby woke up and was about to cry. Her mother had no choice but to cover his mouth with her own hand. Or else all would have been found and killed by the Japanese.

29   The baby was in agony. He struggled with all his might for his life. His lovely little face turned red and then blue. His tiny hands grabbed at his mother's, desperately trying to push it away so that he could breathe. His plump little feet kicked helplessly. The mother's heart was pierced by ten thousand arrows, but she did not dare loosen her grip. Finally the Japanese went away. By then the baby had turned cold in her arms.

30   Wu burst into tears and we all cried with her.

31   *Why does she cry like that? Yes. I understand. The brother! Because he died so tragically, he will always be loved most by the parents. The perfect child. The most "precious" one, the one they sacrificed for the revolution. Wu and her other siblings cannot rival him, no matter how good they are. . . .*

32   But of course that was not why she cried or why we cried with her on that day. We cried because we were deeply moved by the heroic struggle and tremendous sacrifice made by our parents and older brothers and sisters. The stories we told at such meetings convinced us that our lives were on the line: if we should allow the revolution to deteriorate, the evil imperialists and beastly Nationalists would come back. As a slogan of the thirties went, "Cut the grass and eliminate the roots"—if we did not act, they would kill our parents who were revolutionary cadres and make sure that none of us would survive to seek revenge on them.

33   Suddenly I felt that these classmates of mine were dearer to me than my own brothers and sisters. I loved them! They loved me! Today we shed tears in the same room. Tomorrow we would shed blood in the same ditch. I was willing to sacrifice my life for any of them, while before the Cultural Revolution I mistrusted them, seeing them as nothing but my rivals.

34   In fact, it was not fear for our lives but pride and a sense of responsibility that fired us up. Chairman Mao had said that we were the morning sun. We were the hope. The future of China and the fate of humankind depended on us. The Soviet Union and East European countries had changed colors. Only China and Albania remained true to Marxism and Leninism. By saving the revolution in China, we were making history. We must uproot bureaucracy and corruption in China, abolish privileges enjoyed by government officials and the intelligentsia, reform education, reform art and literature, reform government organizations. . . . In short, we must purify China and make it a shining example. Someday the whole world would follow us onto this new path.

35   Aside from sharing family history, we biked to universities and middle schools all over Beijing to read *dazibao* and attend mass rallies where Lin Biao, Zhou Enlai, and Mao's wife, Jiang Qing, showed up to give speeches. I first heard the term "Red Guard" in late June at Middle School attached to Qinghua University, two months before most Chinese would hear of it. It was an exciting idea. On our way back, my schoolmates and I were so preoccupied with the notion that our bikes stopped on a riverbank. Next thing I remember, we were tearing up our red scarves, which only a month before had been the sacred symbol of the Young Pioneers. Now they represented the revisionist educational line and to tear them up was a gesture of rebellion. We tied the strips of red cloth around our left arms in the style of workers' pickets

of the 1920s. When we rode away from the spot, we had turned ourselves into Red Guards.

36 People in the street noticed our new costume: faded army uniforms that had been worn by our parents, red armbands, wide canvas army belts, army caps, the peaks pulled down low by girls in the style of the boys. . . . Some people smiled at us. Some waved their hands. Their eyes showed surprise, curiosity, excitement, admiration. I don't think I saw fear. Not yet.

37 When people smiled at us, we smiled back, proud of ourselves. Our eyes were clear and bright. Our cheeks rosy and radiant. Red armbands fluttered in the wind. We pedaled hard. We pedaled fast. All of us had shiny new bikes, a luxury most Chinese could not afford at the time. (In my case, Father had bought me a new bike so as to show his support for the Cultural Revolution. Being a dreamer himself, he believed, or at least hoped, that the Cultural Revolution would purify the Communist Party and save the revolution.)

38 When we rang the bells, we rang them in unison, for a long time. It was not to warn people to get out of our way. It was to attract their attention. Or maybe we just wanted to listen to the sound. The sound flew up, crystal clear and full of joy, like a flock of white doves circling in the blue sky. At the time, little did I know that this was the first stir of a great storm that would soon engulf the entire country.

39 On August 18, 1966, I saw Chairman Mao for the first time. The night before, we set off from 101 on foot a little after midnight and arrived at Tian'anmen Square before daybreak. In the dark we waited anxiously. Will Chairman Mao come? was the question in everybody's mind. Under a starry sky, we sang.

40 "Lifting our heads we see the stars of Beidou [the Big Dipper], lowering our heads we are longing for Mao Zedong, longing for Mao Zedong. . . . "

41 We poured our emotions into the song. Chairman Mao who loved the people would surely hear it, for it came from the bottom of our hearts.

42 Perhaps he did. At five o'clock, before sunrise, like a miracle he walked out of Tian'anmen onto the square and shook hands with people around him. The square turned into a jubilant ocean. Everybody was shouting "Long live Chairman Mao!" Around me girls were crying; boys were crying too. With hot tears streaming down my face, I could not see Chairman Mao clearly. He had ascended the rostrum. He was too high, or rather, the stands for Red Guard representatives were too low.

43 Earnestly we chanted: "We-want-to-see-Chair-man-Mao!" He heard us! He walked over to the corner of Tian'anmen and waved at us. Now I could see him clearly. He was wearing a green army uniform

and a red armband, just like all of us. My blood was boiling inside me. I jumped and shouted and cried in unison with a million people in the square. At that moment, I forgot myself; all barriers that existed between me and others broke down. I felt like a drop of water that finally joined the mighty raging ocean. I would never be lonely again.

44   The night after, we celebrated the event at 101. Everybody joined the folk dance called *yangge* around bonfires. No one was shy. No one was self-conscious. By then, we had been up and awake for more than forty hours, but somehow I was still bursting with energy. Others seemed that way too. After dancing a couple of hours, I biked all the way home to share the happiness with my parents. By this time, they no longer minded that I woke them up at three o'clock in the morning. In fact, they had urged me to wake them up whenever I got home so that they could hear the latest news from me about the revolution.

45   Seeing Chairman Mao added new fuel to the flame of our revolutionary zeal. The next day, my fellow Red Guards and I held a meeting to discuss our next move. Obviously if we loved Chairman Mao, just shouting slogans was not enough. We must do something. But what could we do? By mid-August the teachers at 101 had been criticized and some were detained in "cow sheds." Even the old school principal, Wang Yizhi, had been "pulled down from the horse" because of her connection with Liu Shaoqi, the biggest capitalist-roader in the Party. On campus, little was left for us to rebel against. Therefore, many Red Guards had walked out of schools to break "four olds" (old ideas, old culture, old customs and old habits) in the city.

46   This was what we should do. Only first we had to pinpoint some "four olds." I suggested that we go to a nearby restaurant to get rid of some old practices. Everybody said: "Good! Let's do it!" So we jumped onto our bikes and rushed out like a gust of wind.

47   Seeing a group of Red Guards swarming in, everybody in the restaurant tensed up. In August, people began to fear Red Guards who summoned the wind, raised the storm, and spread terror all over China. Small talk ceased. All eyes were fastened on us.

48   I stepped forward and began ritualistically: "Our great leader Chairman Mao teaches us, 'Corruption and waste are very great crimes.'" After that, I improvised: "Comrades! In today's world there are still many people who live in poverty and have nothing to eat. So we should not waste food. Nor should we behave like bourgeois ladies and gentlemen who expect to be waited on by others in a restaurant. From now on, people who want to eat in this restaurant must follow new rules: One, go to the window to get your own food. Two, carry it to the table yourselves. Three, wash your own dishes. Four, you must finish the food you ordered. Otherwise you may not leave the restaurant!"

49   While I said this, I saw some people change color and sweat broke out on their foreheads. They had ordered too much food. Now they

had to finish it under the watchful eyes of a group of Red Guards. This was not an enviable situation. But nobody in the restaurant protested. Contradicting a Red Guard was asking for big trouble. It was like playing with thunderbolts and dynamite. So people just lowered their heads and swallowed the food as fast as they could. Some of them might develop indigestion afterwards, but I believed it was their own fault. By showing off their wealth at a restaurant, they wasted the blood and sweat of the peasants. Now they got caught and lost face. This should teach them a lesson!

50   While my comrades and I were breaking "four olds" at restaurants, other Red Guards were raiding people's homes all over the city. News of victory poured in: Red Guards discovered guns, bullets, old deeds, gold bars, foreign currency, yellow books and magazines (pornography). . . . Hearing this, people in my group became restless. But somehow I was not eager to raid homes, and I did not ask myself why. "We are busy making revolution at restaurants, aren't we?"

51   Then one day an old woman stopped us in the street and insisted that we go with her to break some "four olds" in the home of a big capitalist. None of us could say No to this request. So she led us to the home of a prominent overseas Chinese, where the "four olds" turned out to be flowers.

52   The courtyard we entered was spacious. A green oasis of cool shade, drifting fragrance, and delicate beauty: tree peonies and bamboo were planted next to Tai Lake rocks. Orchids and chrysanthemums grew along a winding path inlaid with cobblestones. A trellis of wisteria stood next to a corridor. Goldfish swam under water lilies in antique vats. . . .

53   *Strange! Why does this place look familiar? I am sure I've never been here before. Could it be I've seen it in a dream? . . .*

54   Suddenly the answer dawned on me: *this place looks just like Nainai's home. Nainai's home must have been raided. Maybe several times by now. Is she still there? Did they kick her out? Is she all right? And what happened to the beautiful flowers she and Third Aunt planted? . . . No use thinking about such things! I can't help her anyway. She is a capitalist. I am a Red Guard. I have nothing to do with her!*

55   *The question in front of me now is what to do with these flowers. Smash them! Uproot them! Trample them to the ground! Flowers, plants, goldfish, birds, these are all bourgeois stuff. The new world has no place for them. My fellow Red Guards have already started. I mustn't fall behind.*

56   So I lifted up a flowerpot and dropped it against a Tai Lake rock. Bang! The sound was startling. *Don't be afraid. The first step is always the most difficult.* Bang! Bang! *Actually it isn't so terrible. Now I've started, I can go on and on. To tell the truth, I even begin to enjoy breaking flowerpots! Who would have thought of that? . . .*

57   After a while, we were all out of breath. So we ordered the family to get rid of the remaining flowers in three days, pledging that we'd

come back to check on them. Then we left. Behind us was a world of broken pots, spilled soil, fallen petals, and bare roots. Another victory of Mao Zedong thought.

58   On my way home, surprise caught up with me. I was stopped by a group of Red Guards whom I did not know. They told me that my long braids were also bourgeois stuff. Hearing this, I looked around and saw Red Guards stand on both sides of the street with scissors in their hands. Anyone who had long or curly hair would be stopped by them, their hair cut off on the spot in front of jeering kids. Suddenly I felt my cheeks burning. To have my hair cut off in the street was to lose face. So I pleaded with them, vowing that I would cut my braids as soon as I got home. They let me go. For the time being, I coiled my braids on top of my head and covered them with my army cap.

59   Fearing that other surprises might be in store for me in the street, I went straight home. There I found Aunty in dismay. It turned out that she too had seen Red Guards cutting long hair in the street. So she did not dare leave home these couple of days and we were about to run out of groceries.

60   "What shall I do?" she asked me. "If I cut my hair, won't I look like an old devil, with short white hair sticking up all over my head?" Her troubled look reminded me that since her childhood, Aunty always had long hair. Before she was married, it was a thick, long braid. Then a bun, for a married woman, which looked so elegant on the back of her head. Even in Switzerland, she had never changed her hairstyle. But now neither she nor I had any choice. If we did not want to lose face in the street, we'd better do it ourselves at home.

61   While Aunty and I were cutting each other's hair, my parents were burning things in the bathroom. The idea was the same: to save face and avoid trouble, better destroy all the "four olds" we had before others found them out. So they picked out a number of Chinese books, burned them together with all the letters they had kept and some old photographs. The ash was flushed down the toilet. Repair the house before it rains. That was wise. No one could tell whose home would be raided next. Better be prepared for the worst.

62   Now suddenly it seemed everybody in my family had trouble, including Lian, who was eleven. His problem was our cat, Little Tiger. Lian found him three years ago playing hide and seek in a lumber yard. Then he was a newborn kitten. So little that he did not even know how to drink milk. Aunty taught us how to feed him. Put milk in a soupspoon. Tilt it to make the milk flow slowly through the depression in the middle of the handle. Put the tip of the handle into the kitten's tiny mouth. He tasted the milk. He liked it. He began to drink it. By and by the kitten grew into a big yellow cat with black stripes. On his forehead, three horizontal lines formed the Chinese character *wang*, which means king. We called him Little Tiger because in China the tiger is king of all animals.

63   Little Tiger's life was in danger now, for pets were considered bourgeois too. This morning Lian had received an ultimatum from kids who were our neighbors. It said we had to get rid of Little Tiger in three days or else they would come and take revolutionary action. This time we could not solve the problem by doing it ourselves. Little Tiger was a member of our family. We had to think of a way to save his life.

64   Aunty suggested that we hide him in a bag, take him out to a faraway place, and let him go. He would become a wild cat. Good idea. Only I did not want to do this. What would people say if they found that I, a Red Guard, was hiding a cat in my bag? So I told Lian to do it and went back to school. Since the Cultural Revolution started, I had a bed in the student dormitory and spent most of the nights there.

65   A few days later when I came back home, Aunty told me what had happened to Little Tiger. (Lian himself wouldn't talk about it.) When Lian took him out, he was spotted by the boys who had given him the ultimatum. Noticing something was moving in his bag, they guessed it was the cat. They grabbed the bag, swung it round, and hit it hard against a brick wall. "Miao!" Little Tiger mewed wildly. The boys laughed. It was fun. They continued to hit him against the wall. Lian started to cry and he begged them to stop. Nobody listened to him. Little Tiger's blood stained the canvas bag, leaving dark marks on the brick wall. But he was still alive. Only his mewing became weak and pitiable. Too bad a cat had nine lives! It only prolonged his suffering and gave the boys more pleasure. Bang! Bang! Little Tiger was silent. Dead at last. Lian ran back and cried in Aunty's arms for a long time.

66   A week after our cat was killed by the boys, a neighbor whom I called Guma killed herself. On that day, I happened to be home. I heard a commotion outside and looked. Many people were standing in front of our building. When I went out, I saw clearly that Guma was hanging from a pipe in the bathroom. Another gruesome sight I could not wipe from my memory.

67   Why did she kill herself? Nobody knew the answer. Before she died, she was a typist at the college. A quiet little woman. She had no enemies; no historical problems. Nobody had struggled against her. So people assumed that she killed herself for her husband's sake.

68   The love story between her and her husband must have been quite dramatic. Mother said a writer had interviewed them because he wanted to write a book about it. Guma's husband, whom I called Guzhang, was a professor in the French department. I used to like him a lot because of his refined, gentle manner and the many interesting books he owned. Recently, however, it became known that Guzhang had serious historical problems. In his youth he had studied in France and joined the Communist Party there. Later somehow he dropped out of the Party and turned away from politics. Because of this, he was accused of being a renegade. A renegade he seemed to me, like one who was a coward in revolutionary novels and movies. The following story would prove my point.

69   After Guma killed herself, Guzhang wanted to commit suicide too. He went to the nearby Summer Palace and jumped into the lake. But the place he jumped was too shallow. After a while he climbed out, saying the water was too cold. When people at the college heard this story, he became a laughingstock. Even Aunty remarked: "You may know people for a long time and still you don't know their hearts. Who should have thought that Guma, a woman so gentle and quiet, was so resolute, while Guzhang, a big man, did not have half her courage."

70   These words seemed sinister. To tell the truth, I was alarmed by them. Just a couple of days before a nanny had killed herself at the nearby University of Agriculture. The old woman was a proletarian pure and simple. So why did she kill herself?

71   Her death was caused by a new chapter in the breaking "four olds" campaign. The idea was actually similar to mine: in the past bourgeois ladies and gentlemen were waited on hand and foot by the working people. In the new society such practices should be abolished. The working people would no longer serve and be exploited by bourgeois ladies and gentlemen. Thus the new rule said those who were labeled bourgeois ladies and gentlemen were not allowed to use nannies. As for those who were not labeled bourgeois ladies and gentlemen, they were not allowed to use nannies either. Because if they used nannies, it was proof enough that they were bourgeois ladies and gentlemen, and bourgeois ladies and gentlemen were not allowed to use nannies. Thus according to the new rule, no family was allowed to use nannies.

72   As a result, the old woman killed herself, because she lost her job and had no children to support her. Though she had saved some money for her old age, another new rule had it all frozen in the bank.

73   Aunty was in exactly the same situation. When she first came to work for us, she was forty-six. Then her son died. Now she was sixty-two, an old woman by traditional standards. Right now all her savings were frozen in the bank. Whether someday she might get them back or not, and if yes when, was anybody's guess. Now the deadline set by the Red Guards of the college for all the nannies to leave was drawing near. Recently Aunty made me uneasy. I was frightened by her eyes. They were so remote, as if they were in a different world. I could not get in touch with them. Then she made that strange comment about being resolute. Could she mean. . . ?

74   On the evening before Aunty left (fortunately she had kept her old home in the city, to which now she could return), Father gathered our whole family together. Solemnly he made a pledge to her. He said that he would continue to support her financially for as long as she lived. Although for the time being she had to leave, she would always be a member of our family. She needn't worry about her old age.

75   That was, in my opinion, the exact right thing to say at the right moment. Even today when I look back on it, I am proud of Father for

what he said on that hot summer evening thirty years ago. By then tens of thousands of nannies were being driven out of their employers' homes in Beijing, and who knows how many in the whole country. But few people had the kindness and generosity to say what Father said.

76 Aunty said nothing in return. But she was moved. From then on, she took our family to be her own. Instead of a burden, she became a pillar for our family through one storm after another. She did not quit until all her strength was used up.

✧ Evaluating the Text

1. As a result of the Cultural Revolution, how did personal animosities, jealousies, and the desire for revenge become legitimized in the new political environment?

2. What principles motivated the Red Guards? What different areas of society were touched by them? Why were most of their activities involved with destruction of every kind—even including cutting off Yang's braids?

3. As her narrative proceeds, Yang has several experiences that lead her to question her initial zeal. What are some of these and how do they change her attitude?

✧ Exploring Different Perspectives

1. Compare Yang's account with Panos Ioannides's story, "Gregory," in terms of conscience or remorse for actions taken that turned out to be totally unnecessary.

2. Compare Rae Yang's narrative with Lawrence Metzger's account for complementary perspectives on tumultuous periods in China.

✧ Extending Viewpoints through Writing

1. Yang is completely honest in admitting the excesses in which she participated and about which she was very enthusiastic. Did you ever have a change of heart about something about which you were at one time zealous? Describe your experience. What caused you to change your attitude?

2. Yang presents a comprehensive picture of the topsy-turvy effect the Cultural Revolution had on Chinese society when it imbued the Red Guards with power over teachers, parents, administrators, and others who once had power over them. What scenario can you imagine would occur in American society if a comparable table-turning revolution took place?

Panos Ioannides

Gregory

♦

Panos Ioannides was born in Cyprus in 1935 and was educated in Cyprus, the United States, and Canada. He has been the head of TV programs at Cyprus Broadcasting Corporation. Ioannides is the author of many plays, which have been staged or telecast internationally, and has written novels, short stories, and radio scripts. "Gregory" was written in 1963 and first appeared in The Charioteer, a Review of Modern Greek Literature *(1965). The English translation is by Marion Byron and Catherine Raisiz. This compelling story is based on a true incident that took place during the Cypriot Liberation struggle against the British in the late 1950s. Ioannides takes the unusual approach of letting the reader experience the torments of a soldier ordered to shoot a prisoner, Gregory, who had saved his life and was his friend.*

Cyprus is an island republic with a population of nearly 700,000 situated in the eastern Mediterranean south of Turkey and west of Syria and has been inhabited since 6500 B.C. Seventy-seven percent of the people are of Greek origin, living mainly in the south, and the remaining population, situated in the north, is of Turkish descent. Cyprus came under British administration in 1878 and was annexed by Britain in 1914. The quest among Greek Cypriots for self-rule and union with Greece has been a source of continuous civil discord, erupting in 1955 into a civil war. The conflict was aggravated by Turkish support of Turkish Cypriot demands for partition of the island. A settlement was reached in 1959 including provisions for both union with Greece and partition. In 1960, Makarios III, leader of the Greek Cypriot Nationalists, was elected president, a development that did not prevent continued fighting. A United Nations peace-keeping force was sent to Cyprus in 1965. In 1974, in response to the overthrow by Greek Army officers of the Makarios regime, Turkey invaded Cyprus. Since then, Cyprus has remained a divided state, and little progress has been made toward reunification. The Greek sector is led by President Glafcos Ierides who was reelected in 1998. Cyprus has been invited to join the European Union (EU) in 2004.

Before You Read

Evaluate to what extent the story is more effective because it is told from the perspective of the narrator/executioner rather than Gregory.

1. My hand was sweating as I held the pistol. The curve of the trigger was biting against my finger.

2. Facing me, Gregory trembled.

3. His whole being was beseeching me, "Don't!"

4. Only his mouth did not make a sound. His lips were squeezed tight. If it had been me, I would have screamed, shouted, cursed.

5. The soldiers were watching. . . .

6. The day before, during a brief meeting, they had each given their opinions: "It's tough luck, but it has to be done. We've got no choice."

7. The order from Headquarters was clear: "As soon as Lieutenant Rafel's execution is announced, the hostage Gregory is to be shot and his body must be hanged from a telegraph pole in the main street as an exemplary punishment."

8. It was not the first time that I had to execute a hostage in this war. I had acquired experience, thanks to Headquarters which had kept entrusting me with these delicate assignments. Gregory's case was precisely the sixth.

9. The first time, I remember, I vomited. The second time I got sick and had a headache for days. The third time I drank a bottle of rum. The fourth, just two glasses of beer. The fifth time I joked about it, "This little guy, with the big pop-eyes, won't be much of a ghost!"

10. But why, dammit, when the day came did I have to start thinking that I'm not so tough, after all? The thought had come at exactly the wrong time and spoiled all my disposition to do my duty.

11. You see, this Gregory was such a miserable little creature, such a puny thing, such a nobody, damn him.

12. That very morning, although he had heard over the loudspeakers that Rafel had been executed, he believed that we would spare his life because we had been eating together so long.

13. "Those who eat from the same mess tins and drink from the same water canteen," he said, "remain good friends no matter what."

14. And a lot more of the same sort of nonsense.

15. He was a silly fool—we had smelled that out the very first day Headquarters gave him to us. The sentry guarding him had got dead drunk and had dozed off. The rest of us with exit permits had gone from the barracks. When we came back, there was Gregory sitting by the sleeping sentry and thumbing through a magazine.

16. "Why didn't you run away, Gregory?" we asked, laughing at him, several days later.

17. And he answered, "Where would I go in this freezing weather? I'm O.K. here."

18. So we started teasing him.

19. "You're dead right. The accommodations here are splendid. . . . "

20. "It's not so bad here," he replied. "The barracks where I used to be are like a sieve. The wind blows in from every side. . . . "

21   We asked him about his girl. He smiled.

22   "Maria is a wonderful person," he told us. "Before I met her she was engaged to a no-good fellow, a pig. He gave her up for another girl. Then nobody in the village wanted to marry Maria. I didn't miss my chance. So what if she is second-hand. Nonsense. Peasant ideas, my friend. She's beautiful and good-hearted. What more could I want? And didn't she load me with watermelons and cucumbers every time I passed by her vegetable garden? Well, one day I stole some cucumbers and melons and watermelons and I took them to her. 'Maria,' I said, 'from now on I'm going to take care of you.' She started crying and then me, too. But ever since that day she has given me lots of trouble—jealousy. She wouldn't let me go even to my mother's. Until the day I was recruited, she wouldn't let me go far from her apron strings. But that was just what I wanted. . . . "

23   He used to tell this story over and over, always with the same words, the same commonplace gestures. At the end he would have a good laugh and start gulping from his water jug.

24   His tongue was always wagging! When he started talking, nothing could stop him. We used to listen and nod our heads, not saying a word. But sometimes, as he was telling us about his mother and family problems, we couldn't help wondering, "Eh, well, these people have the same headaches in their country as we've got."

25   Strange, isn't it!

26   Except for his talking too much, Gregory wasn't a bad fellow. He was a marvelous cook. Once he made us some apple tarts, so delicious we licked the platter clean. And he could sew, too. He used to sew on all our buttons, patch our clothes, darn our socks, iron our ties, wash our clothes. . . .

27   How the devil could you kill such a friend?

28   Even though his name was Gregory and some people on his side had killed one of ours, even though we had left wives and children to go to war against him and his kind—but how can I explain? He was our friend. He actually liked us! A few days before, hadn't he killed with his own bare hands a scorpion that was climbing up my leg? He could have let it send me to hell!

29   "Thanks, Gregory!" I said then, "Thank God who made you. . . . "

30   When the order came, it was like a thunderbolt. Gregory was to be shot, it said, and hanged from a telegraph pole as an exemplary punishment.

31   We got together inside the barracks. We sent Gregory to wash some underwear for us.

32   "It ain't right."

33   "What is right?"

34   "Our duty!"

35   "Shit!"

36   "If you dare, don't do it! They'll drag you to court-martial and then bang-bang. . . . "

37   Well, of course. The right thing is to save your skin. That's only logical. It's either your skin or his. His, of course, even if it was Gregory, the fellow you've been sharing the same plate with, eating with your fingers, and who was washing your clothes that very minute.

38   What could I do? That's war. We had seen worse things.

39   So we set the hour.

40   We didn't tell him anything when he came back from the washing. He slept peacefully. He snored for the last time. In the morning, he heard the news over the loudspeaker and he saw that we looked gloomy and he began to suspect that something was up. He tried talking to us, but he got no answers and then he stopped talking.

41   He just stood there and looked at us, stunned and lost. . . .

Now, I'll squeeze the trigger. A tiny bullet will rip through his chest. Maybe I'll lose my sleep tonight but in the morning I'll wake up alive.

Gregory seems to guess my thoughts. He puts out his hand and asks, "You're kidding, friend! Aren't you kidding?"

What a jackass! Doesn't he deserve to be cut to pieces? What a thing to ask at such a time. Your heart is about to burst and he's asking if you're kidding. How can a body be kidding about such a thing? Idiot! This is no time for jokes. And you, if you're such a fine friend, why don't you make things easier for us? Help us kill you with fewer qualms? If you would get angry—curse our Virgin, our God—if you'd try to escape it would be much easier for us and for you.

So it is *now*.

Now, Mr. Gregory, you are going to pay for your stupidities wholesale. Because you didn't escape the day the sentry fell asleep; because you didn't escape yesterday when we sent you all alone to the laundry—we did it on purpose, you idiot! Why didn't you let me die from the sting of the scorpion?

So now don't complain. It's all your fault, nitwit.

Eh? What's happening to him now?

Gregory is crying. Tears flood his eyes and trickle down over his cleanshaven cheeks. He is turning his face and pressing his forehead against the wall. His back is shaking as he sobs. His hands cling, rigid and helpless, to the wall.

Now is my best chance, now that he knows there is no other solution and turns his face from us.

I squeeze the trigger.

Gregory jerks. His back stops shaking up and down.

I think I've finished him! How easy it is. . . . But suddenly he starts crying out loud, his hands claw at the wall and try to pull it down. He screams, "No, no. . . . "

I turn to the others. I expect them to nod, "That's enough."

They nod, "What are you waiting for?"

I squeeze the trigger again.

The bullet smashed into his neck. A thick spray of blood spurts out.

Gregory turns. His eyes are all red. He lunges at me and starts punching me with his fists.

"I hate you, hate you. . . ," he screams.

I emptied the barrel. He fell and grabbed my leg as if he wanted to hold on.

42   He died with a terrible spasm. His mouth was full of blood and so were my boots and socks.

43   We stood quietly, looking at him.

44   When we came to, we stooped and picked him up. His hands were frozen and wouldn't let my legs go.

45   I still have their imprints, red and deep, as if made by a hot knife.

46   "We will hang him tonight," the men said.

47   "Tonight or now?" they said.

48   I turned and looked at them one by one.

49   "Is that what you all want?" I asked.

50   They gave me no answer.

51   "Dig a grave," I said.

52   Headquarters did not ask for a report the next day or the day after. The top brass were sure that we had obeyed them and had left him swinging from a pole.

53   They didn't care to know what happened to that Gregory, alive or dead.

✧ Evaluating the Text

1. Much of the story's action takes place during the few seconds when the narrator must decide whether to pull the trigger. Why do you think Ioannides chooses to tell the story from the executioner's point of view rather than from Gregory's? What in the narrator's past leads his superiors (and the narrator himself) to conclude that he is the one best-suited to kill Gregory?

2. What details illustrate that Gregory has become a friend to the narrator and other soldiers? In what way does he embody the qualities

of humanity, decency, and domestic life that the soldiers were forced to leave behind? Why is his innocence a source of both admiration and irritation? How does Gregory's decision to marry Maria suggest the kind of person he is and answer the question as to why he doesn't try to escape when he is told he is going to be killed? What explains why he doesn't perceive the threat to his life even at the moment the narrator points a gun at his head?

3. Discuss the psychological process that allows the narrator to convert his anguish at having to shoot Gregory into a justification for doing so.

4. When the narrator fires the first shot, why does he hope the other soldiers will stop him from firing again? Why don't they stop him? At the end, how does the narrator's order not to hang Gregory's body reveal his distress after shooting Gregory? Why is it ironic that the higher-ups never inquire whether their orders have been carried out? What does this imply and why does it make the narrator feel even worse?

✦ Exploring Different Perspectives

1. Compare and contrast the moral dilemma that faces the narrator in "Gregory" with that faced by Rae Yang as a Red Guard in her memoir, "At the Center of the Storm."

2. How does the theme of public punishment as an object lesson by governments enter into Panos Ioannides's story and Stephen Chapman's discussion in "The Prisoner's Dilemma"?

✦ Extending Viewpoints through Writing

1. In your opinion, is Gregory a good person or just a fool who is stupid enough to get killed when he does not have to die?

2. If you were in the narrator's shoes, what would you have done? Do you think you would have made yourself hate Gregory, as the narrator did, in order to be able to kill him?

Milorad Pavić

The Wedgwood Tea Set

Milorad Pavić, one of the best known contemporary Serbian prose writers, was born in 1929 in Belgrade. He has been credited with the invention of a kind of fiction that gives the impression of an inexhaustible text through the blending of the fantastic into realistic narratives. This "hyperfiction," as it is known, is well illustrated by the following story, "The Wedgwood Tea Set," translated by Darka Topali, which originally appeared in The Prince of Fire: An Anthology of Contemporary Serbian Short Stories, *edited by Radmila J. Gorup and Madezda Obradovic (1998). Notable among Pavić's works are* Landscape Painted with Tea *(1988),* Dictionary of the Khazars *(1988), and* The Inner Side of the Wind *(1993).*

The Balkans (Balkan means "forested mountain" in Turkish) to which Milorad Pavić, who himself is Serbian, refers at the end of his story are the states that occupy the mountainous Balkan Peninsula of southeastern Europe, an area that was part of the Ottoman Empire. It is usually considered to include Albania, Bulgaria, Greece, Romania, European Turkey, and the states that were formerly part of Yugoslavia (Bosnia, Hercegovina, Croatia, Macedonia, and Slovenia) and present-day Yugoslavia (Serbia and Montenegro). The peninsula was at times part of ancient Greece and the Roman and Byzantine Empires and was ruled by Turks as part of the Ottoman Empire from the late fifteenth century to the end of the Balkan Wars in 1913. The term Balkanization *has entered common usage as referring to the disintegration of a geographic area into politically contentious groups. A war in 1999 between NATO forces and Serbia was followed by a period of enforced peace under NATO occupation. NATO's intervention came in response to Serbian aggression against ethnic Albanians (about 14 percent of the population of Serbia), most of whom were living in the province of Kosovo.*

Before You Read

Have you ever been part of a study group where you knew very little about the personal lives of your fellow students?

---

1   In the story you are about to read, the protagonists' names will be given at the end instead of the beginning.

2   At the capital's mathematics faculty, my younger brother, who was a student of philology and military science, introduced us to each other.

Since she was searching for a companion with whom to prepare for Mathematics I, we began studying together, and as she did not come from another town as I did, we studied in her parents' big house. Quite early each morning, I passed by the shining Layland-Buffalo car, which belonged to her. In front of the door I would stoop down and look for a stone, put it in my pocket, ring the doorbell, and go upstairs. I carried no books, notebooks, or instruments; everything stayed at her place and was always ready for work. We studied from seven to nine, then we were served breakfast and would continue till ten; from ten to eleven we would usually go over the material already covered. All that time, I would be holding the stone in my hand. In case I should doze off, it would fall on the floor and wake me up before anyone noticed. After eleven she would continue to study, but not I. So we prepared for the mathematics exam every day except Sunday, when she studied alone. She very quickly realized that I could not keep up with her and that my knowledge lagged more and more behind hers. She thought that I went home to catch up on the lessons I had missed, but she never said a thing. "Let everyone like an earthworm eat his own way through," she thought, aware that by teaching another she wasn't teaching herself.

3   When the September term came, we agreed to meet on the day of the examination and take the exam together. Excited as she was, she didn't have time to be especially surprised that I didn't show up and that I did not take the exam, either. Only after she had passed the exam did she ask herself what had happened to me. But I didn't appear till winter. "Why should every bee gather honey, anyway?" she concluded, but still asked herself sometimes, "What's he up to? He is probably one of those smile-carriers, who buys his merchandise in the East, and sells it in the West, or vice versa. . . . "

4   When Mathematics II was on the agenda, she suddenly met me one morning, noticing with interest the new patches on my elbows and the newly grown hair, which she had not seen before. It was again the same. Each morning I would come at a certain hour, and she would descend through the green and layered air, as if through water full of cool and warm currents, open the door for me, sleepy, but with that mirror-breaking look of hers. She would watch for one moment how I squeezed out my beard into the cap and how I took off my gloves. Bringing together the middle finger and the thumb, with a decisive gesture I would simultaneously turn them inside out, thus taking them both off with the same movement. When that was over, she would immediately go to work. She made up her mind to study with all her strength, which happened daily. With untiring will and regularity, she delved into all details of the subject, no matter if it was morning, when we started out fresh, after breakfast, or toward the end, when she worked a bit more slowly but not skipping a single thing. I would still quit at eleven, and she would soon notice again that I couldn't

concentrate on what I was doing, that my looks grew old in an hour, and that I was behind her again. She would look at my feet, one of which was always ready to step out, while the other was completely still. Then they would change positions.

5   When the January term arrived, she had the feeling that I could not pass the exam, but she was silent, feeling a trifle guilty herself. "Anyway," she concluded, "should I kiss his elbow to make him learn? If he cuts bread on his head, that's his own affair. . . . "

6   When I didn't show up then either, she was nevertheless surprised, and after finishing the exam looked for the list of candidates to check whether I was perhaps scheduled for the afternoon or some other day. To her great surprise, my name wasn't on the list for that day at all—or any other day, for that matter. It was quite obvious: I hadn't even signed up for that term.

7   When we saw each other again in May, she was preparing Concrete. When she asked me if I was studying for the exams I had not taken before, I told her that I, too, was preparing Concrete, and we continued to study together as in the old times, as if nothing had happened. We spent the whole spring studying, and when the June term came, she had already realized that I would not appear this time, either, and that she wouldn't be seeing me till fall. She watched me pensively with beautiful eyes so far apart that there was space between them for an entire mouth. And naturally, things were the same once again. She took and passed the Concrete exam, and I didn't even bother to come. Returning home satisfied with her success, but totally puzzled as far as my position was concerned, she noticed that, in the hurry of the previous day, I had forgotten my notebooks. Among them she caught sight of my student's booklet. She opened it and discovered with astonishment that I was not a student of mathematics at all, but of something else, and that I had been passing my exams regularly. She recalled the interminable hours of our joint study, which for me must have been a great strain without purpose, a big waste of time, and she asked the inevitable question: what for? Why did I spend all that time with her studying subjects that had nothing to do with my interests and the exams that I had to pass? She started thinking and came to one conclusion: one should always be aware of what is passed over in silence. The reason for all that was not the exam but she herself. Who would have thought that I would be so shy and unable to express my feelings for her? She immediately went to the rented room where I lived with a couple of people my age from Asia and Africa, was surprised by the poverty she saw, and received the information that I had gone home. When they also gave her the address of a small town near Salonica, she took her Buffalo without hesitation and started off toward the Aegean coast in search of me, having made up her mind to act as if she had discovered nothing unusual. So it was.

8   She arrived at sunset and found the house she had been told about wide open, with a great white bull tied to a nail, upon which fresh bread was impaled. Inside she noticed a bed, on the wall an icon, below the icon a red tassel, a pierced stone tied to a string, a top, a mirror, and an apple. A young naked person with long hair was lying on the bed, tanned by the sun, back turned to the window and resting on one elbow. The long ridge of the spine, which went all the way down the back and ended between the hips, curving slightly, vanished beneath a rough army blanket. She had the impression that the girl would turn any moment and that she would also see her breasts, deep, strong, and glowing in the warm evening. When that really took place, she saw that it was not a woman at all lying on the bed. Leaning on one arm I was chewing my moustache full of honey, which substituted for dinner. When she was noticed and brought into the house, she could still not help thinking of that first impression of finding a female person in my bed. But that impression, as well as the fatigue from a long drive, were soon forgotten. From a mirror-bottomed plate she received a double dinner: for herself and her soul in the mirror: some beans, a nut, and fish, and before the meal a small silver coin, which she held, as did I, under the tongue while eating. So one supper fed all four of us: the two of us and our two souls in the mirrors. After dinner she approached the icon and asked me what it represented.

9   "A television set," I told her. In other words, it is the window to another world which uses mathematics quite different from yours.

10   "How so?" she asked.

11   "Quite simple," I answered. "Machines, space crafts, and vehicles built on the basis of your quantitative mathematical evaluations are founded upon three elements, which are completely lacking in quantity. These are: singularity, the point, and the present moment. Only a sum of singularities constitutes a quantity; singularity itself is deprived of any quantitative measurement. As far as the point is concerned, since it doesn't have a single dimension, not width or height or length or depth, it can undergo neither measurement nor computation. The smallest components of time, however, always have one common denominator: that is the present moment, and it, too, is devoid of quantity and is immeasureable. Thus, the basic elements of your quantitative science represent something to whose very nature every quantitative approach is alien. How then should I believe in such a science? Why are machines made according to these quantitative misconceptions of such a short lifespan, three, four or more times shorter than the human ones? Look, I also have a white 'buffalo' like you. Only, he is made differently from yours, which was manufactured at Layland. Try him out and you will see that in a way he is better than the one you own."

12   "Is he tame?" she asked, smiling.

13   "Certainly," I answered. "Go ahead and try."

14   In front of the door she stroked the big white bull and slowly climbed onto his back. When I also mounted him, turning my back to the horns and facing her, I drove him by the sea, so that he had two feet in the water and the other two feet on the sand. She was surprised at first when I started to undress her. Piece by piece of her clothing fell into the water; then she started unbuttoning me. At one moment she stopped riding on the bull and started riding on me, feeling that I was growing heavier and heavier inside her. The bull beneath us did everything that we would otherwise have had to do ourselves, and she could tell no longer who was driving her pleasure, the bull or I. Sitting upon the double lover, she saw through the night how we passed by a forest of white cypresses, by people who were gathering dew and pierced stones on the seashore, by people who were building fires inside their own shadows and burning them up, by two women bleeding light, by a garden two hours long, where birds sang in the first hour and evening came in the second, where fruit bloomed in the first and there was a blizzard behind the winds. Then she felt that all the weight from me had passed into her and that the spurred bull had suddenly turned and taken her into the sea, leaving us finally to the waves that would separate us. . . .

15   However, she never told me a word about her discovery. In the fall, when she was getting ready to graduate and when I offered to study with her again, she was not the least bit surprised. As before, we studied every day from seven until breakfast and then until half past ten; only now she did not try to help me master the subject I was doing and also stayed after ten-thirty for half an hour, which separated us from the books. When she graduated in September, she wasn't surprised at all when I didn't take the examination with her.

16   She was really surprised when she did not see me any more after that. Not that day, nor the following days, weeks, or examination terms. Never again. Astonished, she came to the conclusion that her assessment of my feelings for her was obviously wrong. Confused at not being able to tell what it was all about, she sat one morning in the same room in which we had studied together for years; then she caught sight of the Wedgwood tea set, which had been on the table since breakfast. Then she realized. For months, day after day, with tremendous effort and an immeasurable loss of time and energy, I had worked with her only in order to get a warm breakfast every morning, the only meal I was able to eat during those years. Having realized that, she asked herself another thing. Was it possible that in fact I hated her?

17   At the end, there is one more obligation left: to name the protagonists of this story. If the reader has not thought of it already, here is the answer. My name is the Balkans. Hers, Europe.

✦ Evaluating the Text

1. How does the narrator in the story present himself? What unusual details suggest things may not be as they appear?

2. What course of events does the narrator's relationship follow with the girl with whom he is studying?

3. After discovering who the protagonists really are, what new perspective did you gain on the events in the story? Specifically, what does the title mean?

✦ Exploring Different Perspectives

1. What insight do both Milorad Pavić's story and Ngũgĩ wa Thiong'o's narrative, "Decolonising the Mind," offer into the methods and consequences of colonization?

2. Compare Pavić's story with Luis Sepulveda's account, "Daisy," as narratives of attempted accommodation with the ruling powers.

✦ Extending Viewpoints through Writing

1. Milorad Pavić uses the framework of students preparing for exams as a microcosm for larger issues of politics and power. How have your own experiences as a student made you more sensitive to disparities in the gap between those with power and the powerless?

2. Try to compose your own parable or allegory using individuals as countries, as Pavić does, to represent social conditions and power relationships.

Connecting Cultures

———◆———

Stephen Chapman, "The Prisoner's Dilemma"

Evaluate the choices facing the protagonist in Gloria Anzaldúa's story "Cervicide" (Chapter 7) with those facing the hypothetical prisoner in Chapman's essay.

Lawrence Metzger, "Irony Square"

To what extent do Metzger's interviews refute Daniela Deane's thesis in "The Little Emperors" (Chapter 1)?

Luis Sepulveda, "Daisy"

To what extent do the protagonists in "Daisy" and in Albert Camus's story "The Guest" (Chapter 7) find themselves in no-win situations?

Ngũgĩ wa Thiong'o, "Decolonising the Mind"

In what ways do both Ngũgĩ wa Thiong'o and Mary Crow Dog (see "Civilize Them with a Stick," Chapter 5) add to your understanding of what life is like for native people living under the domination of a different culture?

Rae Yang, "At the Center of the Storm"

Discuss the theme of revenge as it is presented in Rae Yang's narrative and in Nabil Gorgy's story, "Cairo Is a Small City" (Chapter 8).

Panos Ioannides, "Gregory"

In what sense are the protagonists in the stories by Panos Ioannides and Gloria Anzaldúa (see "Cervicide," Chapter 7) coerced into killing someone or something they care about because of political circumstances in which they find themselves?

Milorad Pavić, "The Wedgwood Tea Set"

Compare Pavić's story with David R. Counts's narrative, "Too Many Bananas" (Chapter 7), in terms of a network of social relationships that springs from something necessary and basic, that is, food.

7

Strangers in a Strange Land

———————◆———————

In some ways, our age—the age of the refugee, of the displaced person, and of mass immigration—is defined by the condition of exile. Being brought up in one world and then emigrating to a different culture inevitably produces feelings of alienation. Moving to another country involves living among people who dress differently, eat different foods, have different customs, and speak a different language. Understandably, forming relationships with people whose cultural frame of reference is often radically different from one's own invariably leads to "culture shock," to a greater or lesser degree. Without insight into the norms that govern behavior in a new environment, it is often difficult for immigrants to interpret the actions of others: to know what particular facial expressions and gestures might mean, what assumptions govern physical contact, how people express and resolve conflicts, or what topics of conversation are deemed appropriate.

The jarring, intense, and often painful emotional experience of having to redefine oneself in a strange land, of trying to reconcile conflicting cultural values, forces immigrants to surrender all ideas of safety, the comfort of familiar surroundings, and a common language. Ironically, the condition of *not* belonging, of being caught between two cultures, at home in neither, gives the exile the chance to develop a tolerance for conflicting messages and the ability to see things from outside the controlling frame of reference of a single culture.

The works in this chapter explore the need of those who have left home, whether as refugees, immigrants, or travelers, to make sense of their lives in a new place. These selections offer many perspectives on the experience of learning a new language and the void created by the failure to communicate, the intolerance of the dominant culture toward minorities, and the chance to create a new life for oneself.

George Carlin, in "A Place for Your Stuff," satirizes Americans' dependence on their "stuff," especially when traveling to a strange place.

439

In Napoleon A. Chagnon's, "Doing Fieldwork among the Yąnomamö," we can experience the meaning of "culture shock," as Chagnon became aware of the vast difference in values and attitudes that separated him from the people in this Brazilian tribe among whom he lived for forty-one months. David R. Counts, in "Too Many Bananas," reveals the many lessons about reciprocity he learned while doing fieldwork in New Guinea. Palden Gyatso, a Tibetan monk living in India, describes in "Autobiography of a Tibetan Monk," his happiness at meeting the Dalai Lama coupled with his sadness at seeing his fellow Tibetan exiles. For Vietnamese immigrants, says Jesse W. Nash, in his essay, "Confucius and the VCR," Asian films are the only real link to the culture they left behind. Poranee Natadecha-Sponsel in "Individualism as an American Cultural Value" describes the often perplexing cultural differences that she experienced after moving to the United States from Thailand. In "What's in a Name?" Itabari Njeri explains how adopting a name of African origin changed her life.

The Chicana writer Gloria Anzaldúa, in "Cervicide," tells a poignant story of a Mexican-American family living on the Texas border. Albert Camus's story, "The Guest," is a masterful dramatization of the inevitability of personal choice in the politicized environment of the Algerian conflict.

George Carlin

A Place for Your Stuff

George Carlin's social criticism, presented in the guise of stand-up comedy, has made him one of the most successful performers over the past forty years. He was awarded the Lifetime Achievement Award in 2001 at the 15th Annual American Comedy Awards. In this classic monologue, reprinted from Brain Droppings *(1997), Carlin looks at our love-hate relationship with our possessions. Carlin's hilarious monologue will strike many people as being right on target. His latest work is* Napalm and Silly Putty *(2001).*

Before You Read

Notice how Carlin uses irony and exaggeration to get his point across. Consider how many times you use the word *stuff* (or hear it) in the course of a day.

1   Hi! How are ya? You got your stuff with you? I'll bet you do. Guys have stuff in their pockets; women have stuff in their purses. Of course, some women have pockets, and some guys have purses. That's okay. There's all different ways of carryin' your stuff.

2   Then there's all the stuff you have in your car. You got stuff in the trunk. Lotta different stuff: spare tire, jack, tools, old blanket, extra pair of sneakers. Just in case you wind up barefoot on the highway some night.

3   And you've got other stuff in your car. In the glove box. Stuff you might need in a hurry: flashlight, map, sunglasses, automatic weapon. You know. Just in case you wind up barefoot on the highway some night.

4   So stuff is important. You gotta take care of your stuff. You gotta have a *place* for your stuff. Everybody's gotta have a place for their stuff. That's what life is all about, tryin' to find a place for your stuff! That's all your house is: a place to keep your stuff. If you didn't have so much stuff, you wouldn't *need* a house. You could just walk around all the time.

5   A house is just a pile of stuff with a cover on it. You can see that when you're taking off in an airplane. You look down and see all the little piles of stuff. Everybody's got his own little pile of stuff. And they lock it up! That's right! When you leave your house, you gotta lock it up.

441

Wouldn't want somebody to come by and *take* some of your stuff. 'Cause they always take the *good* stuff! They don't bother with that crap you're saving. Ain't nobody interested in your fourth-grade arithmetic papers. *National Geographics*, commemorative plates, your prize collection of Navajo underwear; they're not interested. They just want the good stuff; the shiny stuff; the electronic stuff.

6   So when you get right down to it, your house is nothing more than a place to keep your stuff . . . while you go out and get . . . *more stuff*. 'Cause that's what this country is all about. Tryin' to get more stuff. Stuff you don't want, stuff you don't need, stuff that's poorly made, stuff that's overpriced. Even stuff you can't afford! Gotta keep on gettin' more stuff. Otherwise someone else might wind up with more stuff. Can't let that happen. Gotta have the most stuff.

7   So you keep gettin' more and more stuff, and puttin' it in different places. In the closets, in the attic, in the basement, in the garage. And there might even be some stuff you left at your parents' house: baseball cards, comic books, photographs, souvenirs. Actually, your parents threw that stuff out long ago.

8   So now you got a houseful of stuff. And, even though you might like your house, you gotta move. Gotta get a bigger house. Why? Too much stuff! And that means you gotta move all your stuff. Or maybe, put some of your stuff in storage. Storage! Imagine that. There's a whole industry based on keepin' an eye on other people's stuff.

9   Or maybe you could sell some of your stuff. Have a yard sale, have a garage sale! Some people drive around all weekend just lookin' for garage sales. They don't have enough of their own stuff, they wanna buy other people's stuff.

10   Or you could take your stuff to the swap meet, the flea market, the rummage sale, or the auction. There's a lotta ways to get rid of stuff. You can even give your stuff away. The Salvation Army and Goodwill will actually come to your house and pick up your stuff and give it to people who don't have much stuff. It's part of what economists call the Redistribution of Stuff.

11   OK, enough about your stuff. Let's talk about other people's stuff. Have you ever noticed when you visit someone else's house, you never quite feel at home? You know why? No room for your stuff! Somebody *else's* stuff is all over the place. And what crummy stuff it is! "God! Where'd they get *this* stuff?"

12   And you know how sometimes when you're visiting someone, you unexpectedly have to stay overnight? It gets real late, and you decide to stay over? So they put you in a bedroom they don't use too often . . . because Grandma died in it eleven years ago! And they haven't moved any of her stuff? Not even the vaporizer?

13   Or whatever room they put you in, there's usually a dresser or a nightstand, and there's never any room on it for your stuff. Someone

else's shit is on the dresser! Have you noticed that their stuff is shit, and your shit is stuff? "Get this shit off of here, so I can put my stuff down!" Crap is also a form of stuff. Crap is the stuff that belongs to the person you just broke up with. "When are you comin' over here to pick up the rest of your crap?"

14   Now let's talk about traveling. Sometimes you go on vacation, and you gotta take some of your stuff. Mostly stuff to wear. But which stuff should you take? Can't take all your stuff. Just the stuff you really like; the stuff that fits you well that month. In effect, on vacation, you take a smaller, "second version" of your stuff.

15   Let's say you go to Honolulu for two weeks. You gotta take two big suitcases of stuff. Two weeks, two big suitcases. That's the stuff you check onto the plane. But you also got your carry-on stuff, plus the stuff you bought in the airport. So now you're all set to go. You got stuff in the overhead rack, stuff under the seat, stuff in the seat pocket, and stuff in your lap. And let's not forget the stuff you're gonna steal from the airline: silverware, soap, blanket, toilet paper, salt and pepper shakers. Too bad those headsets won't work at home.

16   And so you fly to Honolulu, and you claim your stuff—if the airline didn't drop it in the ocean—and you go to the hotel, and the first thing you do is put away your stuff. There's lots of places in a hotel to put your stuff.

17   "I'll put some stuff in here, you put some stuff in there. Hey, don't put your stuff in *there*! That's my stuff! Here's another place! Put some stuff in here. And there's another place! Hey, you know what? We've got more places than we've got stuff! We're gonna hafta go out and buy . . . *more stuff!!!*"

18   Finally you put away all your stuff, but you don't quite feel at ease, because you're a long way from home. Still, you sense that you must be OK, because you do have some of your stuff with you. And so you relax in Honolulu on that basis. That's when your friend from Maui calls and says, "Hey, why don't you come over to Maui for the weekend and spend a couple of nights over here?"

19   Oh no! Now whaddya bring? Can't bring all this stuff. You gotta bring an even *smaller* version of your stuff. Just enough stuff for a weekend on Maui. The "third version" of your stuff.

20   And, as you're flyin' over to Maui, you realize that you're really spread out now: You've got stuff all over the world!! Stuff at home, stuff in the garage, stuff at your parents' house (maybe), stuff in storage, stuff in Honolulu, and stuff on the plane. Supply lines are getting longer and harder to maintain!

21   Finally you get to your friends' place on Maui, and they give you a little room to sleep in, and there's a nightstand. Not much room on it for your stuff, but it's OK because you don't have much stuff now. You got your 8 x 10 autographed picture of Drew Carey, a large can of

gorgonzola-flavored Cheez Whiz, a small, unopened packet of brown confetti, a relief map of Corsica, and a family-size jar of peppermint-flavored, petrified egg whites. And you know that even though you're a long way from home, you must be OK because you do have a good supply of peppermint-flavored, petrified egg whites. And so you begin to relax in Maui on that basis. That's when your friend says, "Hey, I think tonight we'll go over to the other side of the island and visit my sister. Maybe spend the night over there."

22   Oh no! Now whaddya bring? Right! You gotta bring an even smaller version. The "fourth version" of your stuff. Just the stuff you *know* you're gonna need: Money, keys, comb, wallet, lighter, hankie, pen, cigarettes, contraceptives, Vaseline, whips, chains, whistles, dildos, and a book. Just the stuff you *hope* you're gonna need. Actually, your friend's sister probably has her own dildos.

23   By the way, if you go to the beach while you're visiting the sister, you're gonna have to bring—that's right—an even smaller version of your stuff: the "fifth version." Cigarettes and wallet. That's it. You can always borrow someone's suntan lotion. And then suppose, while you're there on the beach, you decide to walk over to the refreshment stand to get a hot dog? That's right, my friend! Number six! The most important version of your stuff: your wallet! Your wallet contains the only stuff you really can't do without.

24   Well, by the time you get home you're pretty fed up with your stuff and all the problems it creates. And so about a week later, you clean out the closet, the attic, the basement, the garage, the storage locker, and all the other places you keep your stuff, and you get things down to manageable proportions. Just the right amount of stuff to lead a simple and uncomplicated life. And that's when the phone rings. It's a lawyer. It seems your aunt has died . . . and left you all her stuff. Oh no! Now whaddya do? Right. You do the only thing you can do. The honorable thing. You tell the lawyer to stuff it.

✧ Evaluating the Text

1. According to Carlin, in what way is one's identity linked with the "stuff" one buys, and accumulates? What explains why people have very different views about their "stuff" than the "stuff" belonging to others?

2. How does Carlin's hypothetical example of deciding what to take to Maui illustrate his thesis that people become increasingly more uncomfortable when separated from their stuff?

3. In what way does Carlin's tone underscore the point he makes about American culture in particular and human nature in general?

✧ Exploring Different Perspectives

1. Compare and contrast how David R. Counts in New Guinea (see "Too Many Bananas") had to reprogram his cultural assumptions about money and what can substitute for it with Carlin's analysis of how Americans identify with their stuff.

2. How does Carlin's humorous, breezy, sarcastic tone make an important point in a lighthearted way in much the same way as does Itabari Njeri in "What's in a Name?"

✧ Extending Viewpoints through Writing

1. What would an archeologist of the future conclude about aspects of our culture from the items in your most cluttered drawer or closet? In a short essay, analyze these items as if they were artifacts.

2. What inanimate object would you save from a fire or flood and what does your choice reveal about what is important to you?

Napoleon A. Chagnon

Doing Fieldwork among the Yąnomamö

◆

Napoleon A. Chagnon is a renowned anthropologist whose research into the social aspects of tribal warfare among the Indians of South America are best represented by Yąnomamö: The Fierce People *(1968) and* Studying the Yąnomamö *(1974). In addition, he has written and produced more than twenty documentary films about the Yąnomamö, a tribe of roughly 10,000, living mostly in southern Venezuela and Brazil, for which he was awarded the Grand Prize of the Brussels' Film Festival in 1970.*

The largest South American country, Brazil occupies almost half of the continent and is the only country in South America whose culture, history, and language were shaped by Portugal, whose first permanent settlement in what is present-day São Paulo occurred in 1532. Since the Europeans landed in 1500, the population of native tribes has been reduced from an estimated 6 million to 200,000 today. Brazil's population is an amalgam of Indian, black, and European strains. Native Indians of several tribes (including the Yąnomamö studied by Chagnon) live along the Amazon River, which flows across northern Brazil to the Atlantic Ocean. The Yąnomamö have been subject to the steady encroachment of civilization as the Brazilian government, despite international pressure, has permitted wholesale destruction of the rain forest in the Amazon River basin. Despite being the world's largest coffee producer, in 1989 Brazil experienced the devastating combination of 600 percent inflation rates and the largest foreign debt of any developing nation. In 1990, President Collor instituted a program of price freezes, privatization of industry, higher utility rates, and devaluation of the currency (cruzado novo) *designed to revive the economy. These measures only crippled the economy further and along with suspicions of Collor's corruption led to his resignation in December 1992. In 2002, Luiz Inacio Lula da Silva was elected as the first leftist president.*

Before You Read

What does the term *culture shock* mean to you? Under what circumstances do you think you would experience it?

◆

1   The Yąnomamö[1] Indians live in southern Venezuela and the adjacent portions of northern Brazil. Some 125 widely scattered villages have populations ranging from 40 to 250 inhabitants, with 75 to 80 people the most usual number. In total numbers their population approaches 10,000 people, but this is merely a guess. Many of the villages have not yet been contacted by outsiders, and nobody knows for sure exactly how many uncontacted villages there are, or how many people live in them. By comparison to African or Melanesian tribes, the Yąnomamö population is small. Still, they are one of the largest unacculturated tribes left in all of South America.

2   But they have a significance apart from tribal size and cultural purity: the Yąnomamö are still actively conducting warfare. It is in the nature of man to fight, according to one of their myths, because the blood of "Moon" spilled on this layer of the cosmos, causing men to become fierce. I describe the Yąnomamö as "the fierce people" because that is the most accurate single phrase that describes them. That is how they conceive themselves to be, and that is how they would like others to think of them.

3   I spent nineteen months with the Yąnomamö,[2] during which time I acquired some proficiency in their language and, up to a point, submerged myself in their culture and way of life. The thing that impressed me most was the importance of aggression in their culture. I had the opportunity to witness a good many incidents that expressed individual vindictiveness on the one hand and collective bellicosity on the other. These ranged in seriousness from the ordinary incidents of wife beating and chest pounding to dueling and organized raiding by parties that set out with the intention of ambushing and killing men from enemy villages. One of the villages discussed in the chapters that

---

[1]The word Yąnomamö is nasalized through its entire length, indicated by the diacritical mark [ą]. When this mark appears on a word, the entire word is nasalized. The terminal vowel [-ö] represents a sound that does not occur in the English language. It corresponds to the phone [ɨ] of linguistic orthography. In normal conversation, Yąnomamö is pronounced like "Yah-no-mama," except that it is nasalized. Finally, the words having the [-ä] vowel are pronounced as that vowel with the "uh" sound of "duck." Thus the name Kąobawä would be pronounced "cow-ba-wuh," again nasalized. [Author's note]

[2]I spent a total of twenty-three months in South America of which nineteen were spent among the Yąnomamö on three separate field trips. The first trip, November 1964 through February 1966, was to Venezuela. During this time I spent thirteen months in direct contact with the Yąnomamö, using my periodic trips back to Caracas to visit my family and to collate the genealogical data I had collected up to that point. On my second trip, January through March 1967, I spent two months among Brazilian Yąnomamö and one more month with the Venezuelan Yąnomamö. Finally, I returned to Venezuela for three more months among the Yąnomamö, January through April 1968. [Author's note]

follow was raided approximately twenty-five times while I conducted the fieldwork, six times by the group I lived among.

4   The fact that the Yąnomamö live in a state of chronic warfare is reflected in their mythology, values, settlement pattern, political behavior, and marriage practices. Accordingly, I have organized this case study in such a way that students can appreciate the effects of warfare on Yąnomamö culture in general and on their social organization and politics in particular.

5   I collected the data under somewhat trying circumstances, some of which I will describe in order to give the student a rough idea of what is generally meant when anthropologists speak of "culture shock" and "fieldwork." It should be borne in mind, however, that each field situation is in many respects unique, so that the problems I encountered do not necessarily exhaust the range of possible problems other anthropologists have confronted in other areas. There are a few problems, however, that seem to be nearly universal among anthropological fieldworkers, particularly those having to do with eating, bathing, sleeping, lack of privacy and loneliness, or discovering that primitive man is not always as noble as you originally thought.

6   This is not to state that primitive man everywhere is unpleasant. By way of contrast, I have also done limited fieldwork among the Yąnomamö's northern neighbors, the Carib-speaking Makiritare Indians. This group was very pleasant and charming, all of them anxious to help me and honor bound to show any visitor the numerous courtesies of their system of etiquette. In short, they approached the image of primitive man that I had conjured up, and it was sheer pleasure to work with them. The recent work by Colin Turnbull (1966) brings out dramatically the contrast in personal characteristics of two African peoples he has studied.

7   Hence, what I say about some of my experiences is probably equally true of the experiences of many other fieldworkers. I write about my own experiences because there is a conspicuous lack of fieldwork descriptions available to potential fieldworkers. I think I could have profited by reading about the private misfortunes of my own teachers; at least I might have been able to avoid some of the more stupid errors I made. In this regard there are a number of recent contributions by fieldworkers describing some of the discomforts and misfortunes they themselves sustained.[3] Students planning to conduct fieldwork are urged to consult them.

[3]Maybury-Lewis 1967, "Introduction," and 1965b; Turnbull, 1966; L. Bohannan, 1964. Perhaps the most intimate account of the tribulations of a fieldworker is found in the posthumous diary of Bronislaw Malinowski (1967). Since the diary was not written for publication, it contains many intimate, very personal details about the writer's anxieties and hardships. [Author's note]

8 My first day in the field illustrated to me what my teachers meant when they spoke of "culture shock." I had traveled in a small, aluminum rowboat propelled by a large outboard motor for two and a half days. This took me from the Territorial capital, a small town on the Orinoco River, deep into Yąnomamö country. On the morning of the third day we reached a small mission settlement, the field "headquarters" of a group of Americans who were working in two Yąnomamö villages. The missionaries had come out of these villages to hold their annual conference on the progress of their mission work, and were conducting their meetings when I arrived. We picked up a passenger at the mission station, James P. Barker, the first non-Yanomamö to make a sustained, permanent contact with the tribe (in 1950). He had just returned from a year's furlough in the United States, where I had earlier visited him before leaving for Venezuela. He agreed to accompany me to the village I had selected for my base of operations to introduce me to the Indians. This village was also his own home base, but he had not been there for over a year and did not plan to join me for another three months. Mr. Barker had been living with this particular group about five years.

9 We arrived at the village, Bisaasi-teri, about 2:00 PM and docked the boat along the muddy bank at the terminus of the path used by the Indians to fetch their drinking water. It was hot and muggy, and my clothing was soaked with perspiration. It clung uncomfortably to my body, as it did thereafter for the remainder of the work. The small, biting gnats were out in astronomical numbers, for it was the beginning of the dry season. My face and hands were swollen from the venom of their numerous stings. In just a few moments I was to meet my first Yąnomamö, my first primitive man. What would it be like? I had visions of entering the village and seeing 125 social facts running about calling each other kinship terms and sharing food, each waiting and anxious to have me collect his genealogy. I would wear them out in turn. Would they like me? This was important to me; I wanted them to be so fond of me that they would adopt me into their kinship system and way of life, because I had heard that successful anthropologists always get adopted by their people. I had learned during my seven years of anthropological training at the University of Michigan that kinship was equivalent to society in primitive tribes and that it was a moral way of life, "moral" being something "good" and "desirable." I was determined to work my way into their moral system of kinship and become a member of their society.

10 My heart began to pound as we approached the village and heard the buzz of activity within the circular compound. Mr. Barker commented that he was anxious to see if any changes had taken place while he was away and wondered how many of them had died during his absence. I felt into my back pocket to make sure that my notebook

was still there and felt personally more secure when I touched it. Otherwise, I would not have known what to do with my hands.

11   The entrance to the village was covered over with brush and dry palm leaves. We pushed them aside to expose the low opening to the village. The excitement of meeting my first Indians was almost unbearable as I duck-waddled through the low passage into the village clearing.

12   I looked up and gasped when I saw a dozen burly, naked, filthy, hideous men staring at us down the shafts of their drawn arrows! Immense wads of green tobacco were stuck between their lower teeth and lips making them look even more hideous, and strands of dark-green slim dripped or hung from their noses. We arrived at the village while the men were blowing a hallucinogenic drug up their noses. One of the side effects of the drug is a runny nose. The mucus is always saturated with the green powder and the Indians usually let it run freely from their nostrils. My next discovery was that there were a dozen or so vicious, underfed dogs snapping at my legs, circling me as if I were going to be their next meal. I just stood there holding my notebook, helpless and pathetic. Then the stench of the decaying vegetation and filth struck me and I almost got sick. I was horrified. What sort of a welcome was this for the person who came here to live with you and learn your way of life, to become friends with you? They put their weapons down when they recognized Barker and returned to their chanting, keeping a nervous eye on the village entrances.

13   We had arrived just after a serious fight. Seven women had been abducted the day before by a neighboring group, and the local men and their guests had just that morning recovered five of them in a brutal club fight that nearly ended in a shooting war. The abductors, angry because they lost five of the seven captives, vowed to raid the Bisaasi-teri. When we arrived and entered the village unexpectedly, the Indians feared that we were the raiders. On several occasions during the next two hours the men in the village jumped to their feet, armed themselves, and waited nervously for the noise outside the village to be identified. My enthusiasm for collecting ethnographic curiosities diminished in proportion to the number of times such an alarm was raised. In fact, I was relieved when Mr. Barker suggested that we sleep across the river for the evening. It would be safer over there.

14   As we walked down the path to the boat, I pondered the wisdom of having decided to spend a year and a half with this tribe before I had even seen what they were like. I am not ashamed to admit, either, that had there been a diplomatic way out, I would have ended my fieldwork then and there. I did not look forward to the next day when I would be left alone with the Indians; I did not speak a word of their language, and they were decidedly different from what I had imagined them to be. The whole situation was depressing, and I wondered why I ever decided to switch from civil engineering to anthropology in the

first place. I had not eaten all day, I was soaking wet from perspiration, the gnats were biting me, and I was covered with red pigment, the result of a dozen or so complete examinations I had been given by as many burly Indians. These examinations capped an otherwise grim day. The Indians would blow their noses into their hands, flick as much of the mucus off that would separate in a snap of the wrist, wipe the residue into their hair, and then carefully examine my face, arms, legs, hair, and the contents of my pockets. I asked Mr. Barker how to say "Your hands are dirty"; my comments were met by the Indians in the following way: They would "clean" their hands by spitting a quantity of slimy tobacco juice into them, rub them together, and then proceed with the examination.

15   Mr. Barker and I crossed the river and slung our hammocks. When he pulled his hammock out of a rubber bag, a heavy, disagreeable odor of mildewed cotton came with it. "Even the missionaries are filthy," I thought to myself. Within two weeks, everything I owned smelled the same way, and I lived with that odor for the remainder of the fieldwork. My own habits of personal cleanliness reached such levels that I didn't even mind being examined by the Indians, as I was not much cleaner than they were after I had adjusted to the circumstances.

16   So much for my discovery that primitive man is not the picture of nobility and sanitation I had conceived him to be. I soon discovered that it was an enormously time-consuming task to maintain my own body in the manner to which it had grown accustomed in the relatively antiseptic environment of the northern United States. Either I could be relatively well fed and relatively comfortable in a fresh change of clothes and do very little fieldwork, or, I could do considerably more fieldwork and be less well fed and less comfortable.

17   It is appalling how complicated it can be to make oatmeal in the jungle. First, I had to make two trips to the river to haul the water. Next, I had to prime my kerosene stove with alcohol and get it burning, a tricky procedure when you are trying to mix powdered milk and fill a coffee pot at the same time: the alcohol prime always burned out before I could turn the kerosene on, and I would have to start all over. Or, I would turn the kerosene on, hoping that the element was still hot enough to vaporize the fuel, and start a small fire in my palm-thatched hut as the liquid kerosene squirted all over the table and walls and ignited. It was safer to start over with the alcohol. Then I had to boil the oatmeal and pick the bugs out of it. All my supplies, of course, were carefully stored in Indian-proof, rat-proof, moisture-proof, and insect-proof containers, not one of which ever served its purpose adequately. Just taking things out of the multiplicity of containers and repacking them afterward was a minor project in itself. By the time I had hauled the water to cook with, unpacked my food, prepared the oatmeal, milk, and coffee, heated water for dishes, washed and dried the dishes,

repacked the food in the containers, stored the containers in locked trunks and cleaned up my mess, the ceremony of preparing breakfast had brought me almost up to lunch time!

18   Eating three meals a day was out of the question. I solved the problem by eating a single meal that could be prepared in a single container, or, at most, in two containers, washed my dishes only when there were no clean ones left, using cold river water, and wore each change of clothing at least a week to cut down on my laundry problem, a courageous undertaking in the tropics. I was also less concerned about sharing my provisions with the rats, insects, Indians, and the elements, thereby eliminating the need for my complicated storage process. I was able to last most of the day on *café con leche*, heavily sugared espresso coffee diluted about five to one with hot milk. I would prepare this in the evening and store it in a thermos. Frequently, my single meal was no more complicated than a can of sardines and a package of crackers. But at least two or three times a week, I would do something sophisticated, like make oatmeal or boil rice and add a can of tuna fish or tomato paste to it. I even saved time by devising a water system that obviated the trips to the river. I had a few sheets of zinc roofing brought in and made a rain-water trap; I caught the water on the zinc surface, funneled it into an empty gasoline drum, and then ran a plastic hose from the drum to my hut. When the drum was exhausted in the dry season, I hired the Indians to fill it with water from the river.

19   I ate much less when I traveled with the Indians to visit other villages. Most of the time my travel diet consisted of roasted or boiled green plantains . . . that I obtained from the Indians, but I always carried a few cans of sardines with me in case I got lost or stayed away longer than I had planned. I found peanut butter and crackers a very nourishing food, and a simple one to prepare on trips. It was nutritious and portable, and only one tool was required to prepare a meal, a hunting knife that could be cleaned by wiping the blade on a leaf. More importantly, it was one of the few foods the Indians would let me eat in relative peace. It looked too much like animal feces to them to excite their appetites.

20   I once referred to the peanut butter as the dung of cattle. They found this quite repugnant. They did not know what "cattle" were, but were generally aware that I ate several canned products of such an animal. I perpetrated this myth, if for no other reason than to have some peace of mind while I ate. Fieldworkers develop strange defense mechanisms, and this was one of my own forms of adaptation. On another occasion I was eating a can of frankfurters and growing very weary of the demands of one of my guests for a share in my meal. When he asked me what I was eating, I replied: "Beef." He then asked, "What part of the animal are you eating?" to which I replied, "Guess!" He stopped asking for a share.

21   Meals were a problem in another way. Food sharing is important to the Yąnomamö in the context of displaying friendship. "I am hungry," is almost a form of greeting with them. I could not possibly have brought enough food with me to feed the entire village, yet they seemed not to understand this. All they could see was that I did not share my food with them at each and every meal. Nor could I enter into their system of reciprocities with respect to food; every time one of them gave me something "freely," he would dog me for months to pay him back, not with food, but with steel tools. Thus, if I accepted a plantain from someone in a different village while I was on a visit, he would most likely visit me in the future and demand a machete as payment for the time that he "fed" me. I usually reacted to these kinds of demands by giving a banana, the customary reciprocity in their culture—food for food—but this would be a disappointment for the individual who had visions of that single plantain growing into a machete over time.

22   Despite the fact that most of them knew I would not share my food with them at their request, some of them always showed up at my hut during mealtime. I gradually became accustomed to this and learned to ignore their persistent demands while I ate. Some of them would get angry because I failed to give in, but most of them accepted it as just a peculiarity of the subhuman foreigner. When I did give in, my hut quickly filled with Indians, each demanding a sample of the food that I had given one of them. If I did not give all a share, I was that much more despicable in their eyes.

23   A few of them went out of their way to make my meals unpleasant, to spite me for not sharing; for example, one man arrived and watched me eat a cracker with honey on it. He immediately recognized the honey, a particularly esteemed Yąnomamö food. He knew that I would not share my tiny bottle and that it would be futile to ask. Instead, he glared at me and queried icily, "Shaki![4] What kind of animal semen are you eating on that cracker?" His question had the desired effect, and my meal ended.

24   Finally, there was the problem of being lonely and separated from your own kind, especially your family. I tried to overcome this by seeking personal friendships among the Indians. This only complicated the matter because all my friends simply used my confidence to

---

[4]"Shaki," or, rather, "Shakiwä," is the name they gave me because they could not pronounce "Chagnon." They like to name people for some distinctive feature when possible. *Shaki* is the name of a species of noisome bee; they accumulate in large numbers around ripening bananas and make pests of themselves by eating into the fruit, showering the people below with the debris. They probably adopted this name for me because I was also a nuisance, continuously prying into their business, taking pictures of them, and, in general, being where they did not want me. [Author's note]

gain privileged access to my cache of steel tools and trade goods, and looted me. I would be bitterly disappointed that my "friend" thought no more of me than to finesse our relationship exclusively with the intention of getting at my locked up possessions, and my depression would hit new lows every time I discovered this. The loss of the possession bothered me much less than the shock that I was, as far as most of them were concerned, nothing more than a source of desirable items; no holds were barred in relieving me of these, since I was considered something subhuman, a non-Yąnomamö.

25   The thing that bothered me most was the incessant, passioned, and aggressive demands the Indians made. It would become so unbearable that I would have to lock myself in my mud hut every once in a while just to escape from it: Privacy is one of Western culture's greatest achievements. But I did not want privacy for its own sake; rather, I simply had to get away from the begging. Day and night for the entire time I lived with the Yąnomamö I was plagued by such demands as: "Give me a knife, I am poor!"; "If you don't take me with you on your next trip to Widokaiya-teri I'll chop a hole in your canoe!"; "Don't point your camera at me or I'll hit you!"; "Share your food with me!"; "Take me across the river in your canoe and be quick about it!"; "Give me a cooking pot!"; "Loan me your flashlight so I can go hunting tonight!"; "Give me medicine . . . I itch all over!"; "Take us on a week-long hunting trip with your shot-gun!"; and "Give me an axe or I'll break into your hut when you are away visiting and steal one!" And so I was bombarded by such demands day after day, months on end, until I could not bear to see an Indian.

26   It was not as difficult to become calloused to the incessant begging as it was to ignore the sense of urgency, the impassioned tone of voice, or the intimidation and aggression with which the demands were made. It was likewise difficult to adjust to the fact that the Yąnomamö refused to accept "no" for an answer until or unless it seethed with passion and intimidation—which it did after six months. Giving in to a demand always established a new threshold; the next demand would be for a bigger item or favor, and the anger of the Indians even greater if the demand was not met. I soon learned that I had to become very much like the Yąnomamö to be able to get along with them on their terms: sly, aggressive, and intimidating.

27   Had I failed to adjust in this fashion I would have lost six months of supplies to them in a single day or would have spent most of my time ferrying them around in my canoe or hunting for them. As it was, I did spend a considerable amount of time doing these things and did succumb to their outrageous demands for axes and machetes, at least at first. More importantly, had I failed to demonstrate that I could not be pushed around beyond a certain point, I would

have been the subject of far more ridicule, theft, and practical jokes than was the actual case. In short, I had to acquire a certain proficiency in their kind of interpersonal politics and to learn how to imply subtly that certain potentially undesirable consequences might follow if they did such and such to me. They do this to each other in order to establish precisely the point at which they cannot goad an individual any further without precipitating retaliation. As soon as I caught on to this and realized that much of their aggression was stimulated by their desire to discover my flash point, I got along much better with them and regained some lost ground. It was sort of like a political game that everyone played, but one in which each individual sooner or later had to display some sign that his bluffs and implied threats could be backed up. I suspect that the frequency of wife beating is a component of this syndrome, since men can display their ferocity and show others that they are capable of violence. Beating a wife with a club is considered to be an acceptable way of displaying ferocity and one that does not expose the male to much danger. The important thing is that the man has displayed his potential for violence and the implication is that other men better treat him with respect and caution.

28   After six months, the level of demand was tolerable in the village I used for my headquarters. The Indians and I adjusted to each other and knew what to expect with regard to demands on their part for goods, favors, and services. Had I confined my fieldwork to just that village alone, the field experience would have been far more enjoyable. But, as I was interested in the demographic pattern and social organization of a much larger area, I made regular trips to some dozen different villages in order to collect genealogies or to recheck those I already had. Hence, the intensity of begging and intimidation was fairly constant for the duration of the fieldwork. I had to establish my position in some sort of pecking order of ferocity at each and every village.

29   For the most part, my own "fierceness" took the form of shouting back at the Yąnomamö as loudly and as passionately as they shouted at me, especially at first, when I did not know much of heir language. As I became more proficient in their language and learned more about their political tactics, I became more sophisticated in the art of bluffing. For example, I paid one young man a machete to cut palm trees and make boards from the wood. I used these to fashion a platform in the bottom of my dugout canoe to keep my possessions dry when I traveled by river. That afternoon I was doing informant work in the village; the long-awaited mission supply boat arrived, and most of the Indians ran out of the village to beg goods from the crew. I continued to work in the village for another hour or so and went down to the

river to say "hello" to the men on the supply boat. I was angry when I discovered that the Indians had chopped up all my palm boards and used them to paddle their own canoes[5] across the river. I knew that if I overlooked this incident I would have invited them to take even greater liberties with my goods in the future. I crossed the river, docked amidst their dugouts, and shouted for the Indians to come out and see me. A few of the culprits appeared, mischievous grins on their faces. I gave a spirited lecture about how hard I had worked to put those boards in my canoe, how I had paid a machete for the wood, and how angry I was that they destroyed my work in their haste to cross the river. I then pulled out my hunting knife and, while their grins disappeared, cut each of their canoes loose, set it into the current, and let it float away. I left without further ado and without looking back.

30   They managed to borrow another canoe and, after some effort, recovered their dugouts. The headman of the village later told me with an approving chuckle that I had done the correct thing. Everyone in the village, except, of course, the culprits, supported and defended my action. This raised my status.

31   Whenever I took such action and defended my rights, I got along much better with the Yąnomamö. A good deal of their behavior toward me was directed with the forethought of establishing the point at which I would react defensively. Many of them later reminisced about the early days of my work when I was "timid" and a little afraid of them, and they could bully me into giving goods away.

32   Theft was the most persistent situation that required me to take some sort of defensive action. I simply could not keep everything I owned locked in trunks, and the Indians came into my hut and left at will. I developed a very effective means for recovering almost all the stolen items. I would simply ask a child who took the item and then take that person's hammock when he was not around, giving a spirited lecture to the others as I marched away in a faked rage with the thief's hammock. Nobody ever attempted to stop me from doing this, and almost all of them told me that my technique for recovering my possessions was admirable. By nightfall the thief would either appear with the stolen object or send it along with someone else to make an exchange. The others would heckle him for getting caught and being forced to return the item.

33   With respect to collecting the data I sought, there was a very frustrating problem. Primitive social organization is kinship organization, and to understand the Yąnomamö way of life I had to collect extensive genealogies. I could not have deliberately picked a more difficult group

---

[5]The canoes were obtained from missionaries, who, in turn, got them from a different tribe. [Author's note]

to work with in this regard: They have very stringent name taboos. They attempt to name people in such a way that when the person dies and they can no longer use his name, the loss of the word in the language is not inconvenient. Hence, they name people for specific and minute parts of things, such as "toenail of some rodent," thereby being able to retain the words "toenail" and "(specific) rodent," but not being able to refer directly to the toenail of that rodent. The taboo is maintained even for the living: One mark of prestige is the courtesy others show you by not using your name. The sanctions behind the taboo seem to be an unusual combination of fear and respect.

34   I tried to use kinship terms to collect genealogies at first, but the kinship terms were so ambiguous that I ultimately had to resort to names. They were quick to grasp that I was bound to learn everybody's name and reacted, without my knowing it, by inventing false names for everybody in the village. After having spent several months collecting names and learning them, this came as a disappointment to me: I could not cross-check genealogies with other informants from distant villages.

35   They enjoyed watching me learn these names. I assumed, wrongly, that I would get the truth to each question and that I would get the best information by working in public. This set the stage for converting a serious project into a farce. Each informant tried to outdo his peers by inventing a name ever more ridiculous than what I had been given earlier, or by asserting that the individual about whom I inquired was married to his mother or daughter, and the like. I would have the informant whisper the name of the individual in my ear, noting that he was the father of such and such a child. Everybody would then insist that I repeat the name aloud, roaring in hysterics as I clumsily pronounced the name. I assumed that the laughter was in response to the violation of the name taboo or to my pronunciation. This was a reasonable interpretation, since the individual whose name I said aloud invariably became angry. After I learned what some of the names meant, I began to understand what the laughter was all about. A few of the more colorful examples are: "hairy vagina," "long penis," "feces of the harpy eagle," and "dirty rectum." No wonder the victims were angry.

36   I was forced to do my genealogy work in private because of the horseplay and nonsense. Once I did so, my informants began to agree with each other and I managed to learn a few new names, real names. I could then test any new informant by collecting a genealogy from him that I knew to be accurate. I was able to weed out the more mischievous informants this way. Little by little I extended the genealogies and learned the real names. Still, I was unable to get the names of the dead and extend the genealogies back in time, and even my best informants continued to deceive me about their own close relatives. Most of them gave me the name of a living man as the father of some individual in order to avoid mentioning that the actual father was dead.

37   The quality of a genealogy depends in part on the number of generations it embraces, and the name taboo prevented me from getting
any substantial information about deceased ancestors. Without this information, I could not detect marriage patterns through time. I had to
rely on older informants for this information, but these were the most
reluctant of all. As I became more proficient in the language and more
skilled at detecting lies, my informants became better at lying. One of
them in particular was so cunning and persuasive that I was shocked
to discover that he had been inventing his information. He specialized
in making a ceremony out of telling me false names. He would look
around to make sure nobody was listening outside my hut, enjoin me
to never mention the name again, act very nervous and spooky, and
then grab me by the head to whisper the name very softly into my ear.
I was always elated after an informant session with him, because I had
several generations of dead ancestors for the living people. The others
refused to give me this information. To show my gratitude, I paid
him quadruple the rate I had given the others. When word got around
that I had increased the pay, volunteers began pouring in to give me
genealogies.

38   I discovered that the old man was lying quite by accident. A club
fight broke out in the village one day, the result of a dispute over the
possession of a woman. She had been promised to Rerebawä, a particularly aggressive young man who had married into the village. Rerebawä had already been given her older sister and was enraged when
the younger girl began having an affair with another man in the village, making no attempt to conceal it from him. He challenged the
young man to a club fight, but was so abusive in his challenge that the
opponent's father took offense and entered the village circle with his
son, wielding a long club. Rerebawä swaggered out to the duel and
hurled insults at both of them, trying to goad them into striking him
on the head with their clubs. This would have given him the opportunity to strike them on the head. His opponents refused to hit him, and
the fight ended. Rerebawä had won a moral victory because his opponents were afraid to hit him. Thereafter, he swaggered around and insulted the two men behind their backs. He was genuinely angry with
them, to the point of calling the older man by the name of his dead father. I quickly seized on this as an opportunity to collect an accurate
genealogy and pumped him about his adversary's ancestors. Rerebawä had been particularly nasty to me up to this point, but we became staunch allies: We were both outsiders in the local village. I then
asked about other dead ancestors and got immediate replies. He was
angry with the whole group and not afraid to tell me the names of the
dead. When I compared his version of the genealogies to that of the old
man, it was obvious that one of them was lying. I challenged his information and he explained that everybody knew that the old man was

deceiving me and bragging about it in the village. The names the old man had given me were the dead ancestors of the members of a village so far away that he thought I would never have occasion to inquire about them. As it turned out, Rerebawä knew most of the people in that village and recognized the names.

39   I then went over the complete genealogical records with Rerebawä, genealogies I had presumed to be in final form. I had to revise them all because of the numerous lies and falsifications they contained. Thus, after five months of almost constant work on the genealogies of just one group, I had to begin almost from scratch!

40   Discouraging as it was to start over, it was still the first real turning point in my fieldwork. Thereafter, I began taking advantage of local arguments and animosities in selecting my informants, and used more extensively individuals who had married into the group. I began traveling to other villages to check the genealogies, picking villages that were on strained terms with the people about whom I wanted information. I would then return to my base camp and check with local informants the accuracy of the new information. If the informants became angry when I mentioned the new names I acquired from the unfriendly group, I was almost certain that the information was accurate. For this kind of checking I had to use informants whose genealogies I knew rather well: they had to be distantly enough related to the dead person that they would not go into a rage when I mentioned the name, but not so remotely related that they would be uncertain of the accuracy of the information. Thus, I had to make a list of names that I dared not use in the presence of each and every informant. Despite the precautions, I occasionally hit a name that put the informant into a rage, such as that of a dead brother or sister that other informants had not reported. This always terminated the day's work with that informant, for he would be too touchy to continue any further, and I would be reluctant to take a chance on accidentally discovering another dead kinsman so soon after the first.

41   These were always unpleasant experiences, and occasionally dangerous ones, depending on the temperament of the informant. On one occasion I was planning to visit a village that had been raided about a week earlier. A woman whose name I had on my list had been killed by the raiders. I planned to check each individual on the list one by one to estimate ages, and I wanted to remove her name so that I would not say it aloud in the village. I knew that I would be in considerable difficulty if I said this name aloud so soon after her death. I called on my original informant and asked him to tell me the name of the woman who had been killed. He refused, explaining that she was a close relative of his. I then asked him if he would become angry if I read off all the names on the list. This way he did not have to say her name and could merely nod when I mentioned the right one. He was a fairly

good friend of mine, and I thought I could predict his reaction. He assured me that this would be a good way of doing it. We were alone in my hut so that nobody could overhear us. I read the names softly, continuing to the next when he gave a negative reply. When I finally spoke the name of the dead woman he flew out of his chair, raised his arm to strike me, and shouted: "You son-of-a-bitch! If you ever say that name again, I'll kill you!" He was shaking with rage, but left my hut quickly. I shudder to think what might have happened if I had said the name unknowingly in the woman's village. I had other, similar experiences in different villages, but luckily the dead person had been dead for some time and was not closely related to the individual into whose ear I whispered the name. I was merely cautioned to desist from saying any more names, lest I get people angry with me. . . .

✧ Evaluating the Text

1. What was Chagnon's purpose in going to study the Yąnomamö Indians of Brazil, the largest known culturally intact native tribe in the Americas?

2. What incidents reveal the major part that aggression plays in Yąnomamö culture? Does the way aggression is expressed toward Chagnon seem to differ from the way they express it toward each other?

3. What is the phenomenon known as *culture shock*, and what details does Chagnon give that most effectively illustrate it? Specifically, what contrasts can you discover between Chagnon's expectations and the experience of his first encounter with the Yąnomamö?

4. How do the Yąnomamö try to use reciprocal gift giving to extract Chagnon's prized possessions?

5. Discuss how the taboo involving revealing tribal names, of the living as well as the dead, presented an obstacle to Chagnon's research on the Yąnomamö's genealogy.

6. From Chagnon's account, what do you infer about the role of women in Yąnomamö society?

✧ Exploring Different Perspectives

1. In what respects is the methodology used by Chagnon, an anthropologist, similar to the methods used by David R. Counts in "Too Many Bananas"? How do both articles alert you to the kinds of research procedures and perspectives characteristic of anthropology?

2. Compare the respective cultural attitudes toward property in Yąnomamö society with those described by George Carlin in "A Place for Your Stuff."

✧ *Extending Viewpoints through Writing*

1. Have you ever experienced what might be called *culture shock*? Describe the circumstances and discuss what about the experience was so unsettling and challenged your expectations? What about this experience enables you to better understand Chagnon's reaction to the Yąnomamö?

2. To what extent does the psychology underlying reciprocal gift giving operate in contemporary American society among your family and friends? What are some of the similarities and differences from the way it operates in Yąnomamö culture?

3. Have you ever tried to construct a family tree? Describe your experiences. To what extent did you use the same methods of cross confirmation that Chagnon used?

David R. Counts

Too Many Bananas

David R. Counts teaches in the anthropology department at McMaster University in Ontario, Canada. Together with his wife, Dorothy A. Counts, he has edited a number of works, including Coping with the Final Tragedy: Dying and Grieving in Cross-Cultural Perspective *(1991) and* Aging and Its Transformations: Moving Toward Death in Pacific Societies *(1992). This selection is drawn from his book* The Humbled Anthropologist: Tales from the Pacific *(1990). The Counts are currently doing extensive research on the phenomena of the RV (recreation vehicle) community as a kind of "other" in American culture.*

New Guinea, the world's second-largest island after Greenland, is located in the Southwestern Pacific Ocean north of Australia. The western half of the island, known as Irian Jaya, is administered by Indonesia. Papua, which occupies the eastern half of New Guinea, was formerly a territory of Australia. It became the independent nation of Papua New Guinea in 1975. As one might gather from David R. Counts's article, the chief food crops are bananas, taro roots, and yams. The economy of New Guinea is one of the least developed of any area in the world. Most of the people farm land and grow their own food.

Before You Read

Counts's essay is divided into three sections. Take a moment after reading each section to write a brief summary of the new information in that part about the role of food in a barter society.

No Watermelon at All

1   The woman came all the way through the village, walking between the two rows of houses facing each other between the beach and the bush, to the very last house standing on a little spit of land at the mouth of the Kaini River. She was carrying a watermelon on her head, and the house she came to was the government "rest house," maintained by the villagers for the occasional use of visiting officials. Though my wife and I were graduate students, not officials, and had asked for permission to stay in the village for the coming year, we were living in the rest house while the debate went on about where a house would be built for us. When the woman offered to sell us the watermelon for two shillings,

we happily agreed, and the kids were delighted at the prospect of watermelon after yet another meal of rice and bully beef. The money changed hands and the seller left to return to her village, a couple of miles along the coast to the east.

2　　It seemed only seconds later that the woman was back, reluctantly accompanying Kolia, the man who had already made it clear to us that he was the leader of the village. Kolia had no English, and at that time, three or four days into our first stay in Kandoka Village on the island of New Britain in Papua New Guinea, we had very little Tok Pisin. Language difficulties notwithstanding, Kolia managed to make his message clear: The woman had been outrageously wrong to sell us the watermelon for two shillings and we were to return it to her and reclaim our money immediately. When we tried to explain that we thought the price to be fair and were happy with the bargain, Kolia explained again and finally made it clear that we had missed the point. The problem wasn't that we had paid too much; it was that we had paid at all. Here he was, a leader, responsible for us while we were living in his village, and we had shamed him. How would it look if he let guests in his village *buy* food? If we wanted watermelons, or bananas, or anything else, all that was necessary was to let him know. He told us that it would be all right for us to give little gifts to people who brought food to us (and they surely would), but *no one* was to sell food to us. If anyone were to try—like this woman from Lauvore—then we should refuse. There would be plenty of watermelons without us buying them.

3　　The woman left with her watermelon, disgruntled, and we were left with our two shillings. But we had learned the first lesson of many about living in Kandoka. We didn't pay money for food again that whole year, and we did get lots of food brought to us . . . but we never got another watermelon. That one was the last of the season.

LESSON 1: *In a society where food is shared or gifted as part of social life, you may not buy it with money.*

Too Many Bananas

4　　In the couple of months that followed the watermelon incident, we managed to become at least marginally competent in Tok Pisin, to negotiate the construction of a house on what we hoped was neutral ground, and to settle into the routine of our fieldwork. As our village leader had predicted, plenty of food was brought to us. Indeed, seldom did a day pass without something coming in—some sweet potatoes, a few taro, a papaya, the occasional pineapple, or some bananas—lots of bananas.

5　　We had learned our lesson about the money, though, so we never even offered to buy the things that were brought, but instead made gifts, usually of tobacco to the adults or chewing gum to the children. Nor were we so gauche as to haggle with a giver over how much of a return gift was appropriate, though the two of us sometimes conferred as to whether what had been brought was a "two-stick" or a "three-stick" stalk, bundle, or whatever. A "stick" of tobacco was a single large leaf, soaked in rum and then twisted into a ropelike form. This, wrapped in half a sheet of newsprint (torn for use as cigarette paper), sold in the local trade stores for a shilling. Nearly all of the adults in the village smoked a great deal, and they seldom had much cash, so our stocks of twist tobacco and stacks of the Sydney *Morning Herald* (all, unfortunately, the same day's issue) were seen as a real boon to those who preferred "stick" to the locally grown product.

6   We had established a pattern with respect to the gifts of food. When a donor appeared at our veranda we would offer our thanks and talk with them for a few minutes (usually about our children, who seemed to hold a real fascination for the villagers and for whom most of the gifts were intended) and then we would inquire whether they could use some tobacco. It was almost never refused, though occasionally a small bottle of kerosene, a box of matches, some laundry soap, a cup of rice, or a tin of meat would be requested instead of (or even in addition to) the tobacco. Everyone, even Kolia, seemed to think this arrangement had worked out well.

7   Now, what must be kept in mind is that while we were following their rules—or seemed to be—we were *really still buying food.* In fact we kept a running account of what came in and what we "paid" for it. Tobacco as currency got a little complicated, but since the exchange rate was one stick to one shilling, it was not too much trouble as long as everyone was happy, and meanwhile we could account for the expenditure of "informant fees" and "household expenses." Another thing to keep in mind is that not only did we continue to think in terms of our buying the food that was brought, we thought of them as *selling it.* While it was true they never quoted us a price, they also never asked us if we needed or wanted whatever they had brought. It seemed clear to us that when an adult needed a stick of tobacco, or a child wanted some chewing gum (we had enormous quantities of small packets of Wrigley's for just such eventualities) they would find something surplus to their own needs and bring it along to our "store" and get what they wanted.

8   By late November 1966, just before the rainy season set in, the bananas were coming into flush, and whereas earlier we had received banana gifts by the "hand" (six or eight bananas in a cluster cut from the stalk), donors now began to bring bananas, "for the children," by the *stalk!* The Kaliai among whom we were living are not exactly specialists in banana cultivation—they only recognize about thirty varieties, while some of their neighbors have more than twice that many—but the kinds they produce differ considerably from each other in size,

shape, and taste, so we were not dismayed when we had more than one stalk hanging on our veranda. The stalks ripen a bit at the time, and having some variety was nice. Still, by the time our accumulation had reached *four* complete stalks, the delights of variety had begun to pale a bit. The fruits were ripening progressively and it was clear that even if we and the kids ate nothing but bananas for the next week, some would still fall from the stalk onto the floor in a state of gross overripeness. This was the situation as, late one afternoon, a woman came bringing yet another stalk of bananas up the steps of the house.

9   Several factors determined our reaction to her approach: one was that there was literally no way we could possibly use the bananas. We hadn't quite reached the point of being crowded off our veranda by the stalks of fruit, but it was close. Another factor was that we were tired of playing the gift game. We had acquiesced in playing it—no one was permitted to sell us anything, and in turn we only gave things away, refusing under any circumstances to sell tobacco (or anything else) for money. But there had to be a limit. From our perspective what was at issue was that the woman wanted something and she had come to trade for it. Further, what she had brought to trade was something we neither wanted nor could use, and it should have been obvious to her. So we decided to bite the bullet.

10   The woman, Rogi, climbed the stairs to the veranda, took the stalk from where it was balanced on top of her head, and laid it on the floor with the words, "Here are some bananas for the children." Dorothy and I sat near her on the floor and thanked her for her thought but explained, "You know, we really have too many bananas—we can't use these; maybe you ought to give them to someone else. . . ." The woman looked mystified, then brightened and explained that she didn't want anything for them, she wasn't short of tobacco or anything. They were just a gift for the kids. Then she just sat there, and we sat there, and the bananas sat there, and we tried again. "Look," I said, pointing up to them and counting, "we've got four stalks already hanging here on the veranda—there are too many for us to eat now. Some are rotting already. Even if we eat only bananas, we can't keep up with what's here!"

11   Rogi's only response was to insist that these were a gift, and that she didn't want anything for them, so we tried yet another tack: "Don't *your* children like bananas?" When she admitted that they did, and that she had none at her house, we suggested that she should take them there. Finally, still puzzled, but convinced we weren't going to keep the bananas, she replaced them on her head, went down the stairs, and made her way back through the village toward her house.

12   As before, it seemed only moments before Kolia was making his way up the stairs, but this time he hadn't brought the woman in tow. "What was wrong with those bananas? Were they no good?" he demanded. We explained that there was nothing wrong with the bananas at all,

but that we simply couldn't use them and it seemed foolish to take them when we had so many and Rogi's own children had none. We obviously didn't make ourselves clear because Kolia then took up the same refrain that Rogi had—he insisted that we shouldn't be worried about taking the bananas, because they were a gift for the children and Rogi hadn't wanted anything for them. There was no reason, he added, to send her away with them—she would be ashamed. I'm afraid we must have seemed as if we were hard of hearing or thought he was, for our only response was to repeat our reasons. We went through it again—there they hung, one, two, three, *four* stalks of bananas, rapidly ripening and already far beyond our capacity to eat— we just weren't ready to accept any more and let them rot (and, we added to ourselves, pay for them with tobacco, to boot).

13   Kolia finally realized that we were neither hard of hearing nor intentionally offensive, but merely ignorant. He stared at us for a few minutes, thinking, and then asked: "Don't you frequently have visitors during the day and evening?" We nodded. Then he asked, "Don't you usually offer them cigarettes and coffee or milo?" Again, we nodded. "Did it ever occur to you to suppose," he said, "that your visitors might be hungry?" It was at this point in the conversation, as we recall, that we began to see the depth of the pit we had dug for ourselves. We nodded, hesitantly. His last words to us before he went down the stairs and stalked away were just what we were by that time afraid they might be. "When your guests are hungry, *feed them bananas!*"

LESSON 2: *Never refuse a gift, and never fail to return a gift. If you cannot use it, you can always give it away to someone else—there is no such thing as too much—there are never too many bananas.*

Not Enough Pineapples

14   During the fifteen years between that first visit in 1966 and our residence there in 1981 we had returned to live in Kandoka village twice during the 1970s, and though there were a great many changes in the village, and indeed for all of Papua New Guinea during that time, we continued to live according to the lessons of reciprocity learned during those first months in the field. We bought no food for money and refused no gifts, but shared our surplus. As our family grew, we continued to be accompanied by our younger children. Our place in the village came to be something like that of educated Kaliai who worked far away in New Guinea. Our friends expected us to come "home" when we had leave, but knew that our work kept us away for long periods of time. They also credited us with knowing much more about the rules of their way of life than was our due. And we sometimes shared the delusion that we understood life in the village, but even fif-

teen years was not long enough to relieve the need for lessons in learning to live within the rules of gift exchange.

15 In the last paragraph I used the word *friends* to describe the villagers intentionally, but of course they were not all our friends. Over the years some really had become friends, others were acquaintances, others remained consultants or informants to whom we turned when we needed information. Still others, unfortunately, we did not like at all. We tried never to make an issue of these distinctions, of course, and to be evenhanded and generous to all, as they were to us. Although we almost never actually refused requests that were made of us, over the long term our reciprocity in the village was balanced. More was given to those who helped us the most, while we gave assistance or donations of small items even to those who were not close or helpful.

16 One elderly woman in particular was a trial for us. Sara was the eldest of a group of siblings and her younger brother and sister were both generous, informative, and delightful persons. Her younger sister, Makila, was a particularly close friend and consultant, and in deference to that friendship we felt awkward in dealing with the elder sister.

17 Sara was neither a friend nor an informant, but she had been, since she returned to live in the village at the time of our second trip in 1971, a constant (if minor) drain on our resources. She never asked for much at a time. A bar of soap, a box of matches, a bottle of kerosene, a cup of rice, some onions, a stick or two of tobacco, or some other small item was usually all that was at issue, but whenever she came around it was always to ask for something—or to let us know that when we left, we should give her some of the furnishings from the house. Too, unlike almost everyone else in the village, when she came, she was always empty-handed. We ate no taro from her gardens, and the kids chewed none of her sugarcane. In short, she was, as far as we could tell, a really grasping, selfish old woman—and we were not the only victims of her greed.

18 Having long before learned the lesson of the bananas, one day we had a stalk that was ripening so fast we couldn't keep up with it, so I pulled a few for our own use (we only had one stalk at the time) and walked down through the village to Ben's house, where his five children were playing. I sat down on his steps to talk, telling him that I intended to give the fruit to his kids. They never got them. Sara saw us from across the open plaza of the village and came rushing over, shouting, "My bananas!" Then she grabbed the stalk and went off gorging herself with them. Ben and I just looked at each other.

19 Finally it got to the point where it seemed to us that we had to do something. Ten years of being used was long enough. So there came the afternoon when Sara showed up to get some tobacco—again. But this time, when we gave her the two sticks she had demanded, we confronted her.

20   First, we noted the many times she had come to get things. We didn't mind sharing things, we explained. After all, we had plenty of tobacco and soap and rice and such, and most of it was there so that we could help our friends as they helped us, with folktales, information, or even gifts of food. The problem was that she kept coming to get things, but never came to talk, or to tell stories, or to bring some little something that the kids might like. Sara didn't argue—she agreed. "Look," we suggested, "it doesn't have to be much, and we don't mind giving you things—but you can help us. The kids like pineapples, and we don't have any—the next time you need something, bring something—like maybe a pineapple." Obviously somewhat embarrassed, she took her tobacco and left, saying that she would bring something soon. We were really pleased with ourselves. It had been a very difficult thing to do, but it was done, and we were convinced that either she would start bringing things or not come. It was as if a burden had lifted from our shoulders.

21   It worked. Only a couple of days passed before Sara was back, bringing her bottle to get it filled with kerosene. But this time, she came carrying the biggest, most beautiful pineapple we had seen the entire time we had been there. We had a friendly talk, filled her kerosene container, and hung the pineapple up on the veranda to ripen just a little further. A few days later we cut and ate it, and whether the satisfaction it gave came from the fruit or from its source would be hard to say, but it was delicious. That, we assumed, was the end of that irritant.

22   We were wrong, of course. The next afternoon, Mary, one of our best friends for years (and no relation to Sara), dropped by for a visit. As we talked, her eyes scanned the veranda. Finally she asked whether we hadn't had a pineapple there yesterday. We said we had, but that we had already eaten it. She commented that it had been a really nice-looking one, and we told her that it had been the best we had eaten in months. Then, after a pause, she asked, "Who brought it to you?" We smiled as we said, "Sara!" because Mary would appreciate our coup— she had commented many times in the past on the fact that Sara only *got* from us and never gave. She was silent for a moment, and then she said, "Well, I'm glad you enjoyed it—my father was waiting until it was fully ripe to harvest it for you, but when it went missing I thought maybe it was the one you had here. I'm glad to see you got it. I thought maybe a thief had eaten it in the bush."

LESSON 3: *Where reciprocity is the rule and gifts are the idiom, you cannot demand a gift, just as you cannot refuse a request.*

23   It says a great deal about the kindness and patience of the Kaliai people that they have been willing to be our hosts for all these years despite our blunders and lack of good manners. They have taught us a lot, and these three lessons are certainly not the least important things we learned.

✧ *Evaluating the Text*

1. How does Counts's initial experience of offering money for watermelon teach him his first important lesson about the culture of New Guinea?

2. How does the idea of "too many bananas" sum up the important principle of reciprocity that Counts learns? In your own words, describe the principle involved.

3. How does the experience Counts has with Sara lead to his ironic realization of the third lesson about the culture of New Guinea?

✧ *Exploring Different Perspectives*

1. Compare Counts's essay with Poranee Natadecha-Sponsel's "Individualism as an American Cultural Value" as narratives of acculturation. What shifts in perspective are required of Counts and Natadecha-Sponsel?

2. In what ways do material goods take on symbolic importance in Counts's narrative and in Jesse W. Nash's "Confucius and the VCR"?

✧ *Extending Viewpoints through Writing*

1. What experiences have you had that involved the principle of reciprocity in your relationship with another? Discuss one incident and the lesson you learned.

2. If you were a "stranger in a strange land," would you feel more comfortable if you had many of your material possessions with you? Why or why not?

Palden Gyatso

Autobiography of a Tibetan Monk

◆——————

Palden Gyatso was born in 1933 into a well-off Tibetan family. He joined a rural Buddhist monastery at the age of ten. In 1960, he was arrested by the Chinese and spent the next thirty-two years in prison, where he was beaten and starved, but refused to cooperate with his torturers. Because he was skillful at Tibetan carpet weaving, his life was spared; but it was not until 1992 that he was released from prison, at which point he fled to India. Speaking as one of the many Tibetan Buddhist monks who suffered in Chinese prisons, Gyatso writes in this Prologue to Fire Under the Snow: The Autobiography of a Tibetan Monk *(1997) of his happiness at meeting the Dalai Lama.*

Since 1965, Tibet has been an autonomous region in southwest China, bordered by Myanmar, Nepal, India, Bhutan, and Pakistan. Tibet is a high, arid plateau surrounded by mountain ranges, including the renowned Himalayas in the south. The economy is primarily pastoral, based on raising livestock, particularly yaks, and barley. The harsh environment and its physical isolation kept Tibet independent for much of its history. Tibetans are of Mongolian descent and follow an indigenous form of Buddhism, the chief figure of which is the Dalai Lama, who is believed to be the reincarnation of the ancestor of all Tibetans. The events behind Palden Gyatso's narrative begin when the Chinese, in 1969, forcibly tried to assimilate the Tibetans. Religious worship was prohibited, and monasteries and religious sites were destroyed. Since then, the Chinese government has tolerated Tibetan Buddhism (except during the imposition of martial law in the capital city of Lhasa from 1989 to 1992). The Chinese have recently brought in great numbers of Han Chinese (now 14 percent of the population) in an effort to assert control over the Tibetans. The effort on the part of the Chinese government to eradicate the Tibetan identity has led many Tibetans to flee into exile in neighboring Nepal and India.

Before You Read

Consider how Gyatso provides insight into the political forces that have driven him into exile and what the meeting with the Dalai Lama means to him.

◆——————

1   It seemed that I had been preparing for this meeting all my life. After waiting outside a gate guarded by an Indian soldier in a khaki uniform, shivering in the monsoon wind and carrying an old Lee Enfield rifle at his side, I was body-searched by a young Tibetan in a blue suit. Then, a minute later, I was in the presence of the Dalai Lama. I had a strange feeling of both joy and sadness. I knew that had it not been for the tragedy that had befallen my country I could never have dreamed of such a meeting with the man we Tibetans call Kyabgon, the Saviour. The shabby guards, the simple bungalow shrouded in a murky mist, made the Dalai Lama's palace in exile a sad contrast to the vision of splendour that my country still conjures up in my mind.

2   Ever since leaving Lhasa, I had been thinking hard about what to tell the Dalai Lama. Should I begin with an account of my arrest? Should I tell him about all the people who had died from hunger, about the prisoners who had chosen to end their lives? Or should I tell him about the Tibetans who dutifully carried out the orders of the Chinese to curry favour and ensure a comfortable life? Perhaps I should tell him about the younger generation of Tibetans who now hold defiant demonstrations in prison, or about the Tibetan torturers who brutalise the bodies of their compatriots with blows and electric prods. After all, these torturers are Tibetans too, and were nourished by the same Land of Snows.

3   When I finally found myself in front of His Holiness, however, my mind became empty. At the sight of his maroon-robes and his friendly, grinning countenance I lowered my head, looking up only when he asked me a series of questions. "How did you escape? When were you first arrested? Which prison were you in?" he began. I should have realised that I was not the first prisoner to stand before him. For the last thirty-five years a steady stream of Tibetans have made their arduous escape across the Himalayas and found themselves standing before the Dalai Lama. They all do so in the hope of seeing him and whispering in his ear words they have rehearsed in their minds countless times. Every Tibetan who escapes over the mountains ends his or her journey with a short walk across the tarmac path to the audience room in Dharamsala and has the opportunity to utter the words that are carved on their hearts.

4   After I had been speaking for twenty minutes, the Dalai Lama stopped me. "You should write your story," he said. At the time I did not realise the significance of his advice. I decided I would write an account of my sufferings, including the names of all the people who had perished in the prison. The document would go to the Dalai Lama, so that these deaths should not go unrecorded. At the time, it never crossed my mind that I would write *a book*.

5   In Tibet we have a long tradition of writing biographies of great lamas and figures who attain a high degree of spirituality. These

books are known as *Namthar*. They are never merely good stories, but are intended to impart spiritual teachings and are read as guides to life. The power of these books is recognised by all. "When we read the *Namthar* of the great warrior King Gesar," the Tibetan saying goes, "even a beggar would be moved to pick up a sword; when we read the biography of the great hermit Milarepa, even a prince would wish to renounce the world."

6   When the suggestion was made that I should write my story, I was embarrassed and puzzled by people's interest. It was not that I had no desire to tell my story; on the contrary, one of the main reasons for my escape from Tibet was to be able to speak to the world. I had spent thirty years in prison and during that time I had experienced and witnessed unimaginable horrors. Every prisoner lives with the hope that somehow, once the world learns of their suffering, there will be a rush to help those who have fallen into the pit of hell.

7   In my prison, we used to sing, "one day the sun will shine through the dark clouds." The vision of the sun dispelling the dark clouds and our unbroken spirits kept us alive. It was not only prisoners who were resilient; so were ordinary men and women who lived their daily lives in the shadow of the Chinese Communist Party. Even today, young boys and girls who knew nothing of feudal Tibet and who are said to be the sons and daughters of the Party are crying out for freedom. Our collective will to resist what is unjust is like a fire that cannot be put out. Looking back, I can see that man's love of freedom is like a smouldering fire under snow.

8   Several days after my first visit to the Dalai Lama, I stood in the open yard of the new temple which faces His Holiness's palace. The Tibetans had named it Jokhang, after the holiest of all the temples in Lhasa. It had been rebuilt on a knoll and housed some of the religious images that had been rescued by devotees and smuggled across the Himalayas. In the Jokhang in Lhasa there is a bronze statue of the Buddha which was brought to Tibet in the seventh century A.D. as a gift from the Chinese princess who married the great Tibetan king, Srongsten Gampo. This historical event was regarded as of great significance by the Chinese. I remember being told the story again and again in prison, with the emphasis on how the betrothal of Princess Wenchen had brought culture to Tibet and unified the country with the motherland. In the beginning we used to ask, "Does this mean that Tibet also belongs to Nepal, because Srongsten Gampo was also married to a Nepalese princess?" Soon this sort of questioning came to be regarded as counterrevolutionary and was likely to earn you a term in prison.

9   The temple in Dharamsala was bursting with activity. Dozens of old people were circling the shrine and turning the prayer wheels, recreating that familiar music which in my childhood had mingled with

the mumbling voices of elderly pilgrims reciting the six-syllable mantra, *"Om mani pad me om."* The mist that shrouded the temple slowly dissolved and the plains of India appeared through the clouds. This incongruous sight of Tibetans in a foreign land finally convinced me that I should tell my story in writing, not to advertise my suffering but as a testimony to my country's torment. In this way I could show that while I might be free, my country was still occupied.

10   As I gazed towards the dusty plains of India, I was overwhelmed by sadness. I vividly recalled the routine of prison life, the regularity of study sessions, the confession meetings and the reward and punishment meetings, which had defined my life for the past thirty years. The scars of prison life remained painfully in my mind.

11   Dharamsala, with its lush green forests and rain, so different from Tibet, has become the resting place for so many of us. Every day, I meet fellow prisoners who have made the arduous journey to the foothills of the Himalayas. Their delight in being free is combined with a recognition of the past suffering of others. We congratulate each other on the sheer luck of surviving.

12   I am free in a foreign land, but lingering images of horror still haunt me. I am now living in a small hut nailed together from bits of tin and wood. The room is no bigger than the isolation unit in the prison. The torrents of monsoon rain beating on the tin roof keep me awake all night and the musty odour of damp clings to the walls and floor, although everyone says it will be better when the monsoon is over. In the next hut a group of youths who also made their way over the treacherous mountains listen to Lhasa Radio and cheerfully join in with the latest pop songs. It is strange how people still hanker for news of a place they have fled, and how they long to hear familiar sounds from home, as if to reassure themselves that they are alive.

13   Dharamsala is special not because it has become home for so many of us, but because it is the spiritual refuge of the Dalai Lama, the Buddha of Compassion. In prison we had uttered the name Dharamsala in hushed tones, developing a sense of reverence and awe for the place. Shortly after my arrival, I was given the task of interviewing other new arrivals to record their testimonies. I could not believe how many of us had the same story to tell. There was not a single individual without a story of horror and brutality, and I realised that all subjugated people share the common experience of bruised bodies, scattered lives and broken families.

14   Most of those who escape across the snowy peaks are young children. Some are sent away from home by their parents at the age of seven or eight in the hope that they will have a future in a foreign land. These are not the children of rich landlords or wealthy traders; they are the children of the same poor peasants whom the Communists claim to have liberated from servitude.

15   Dharamsala has a cosmopolitan character, with people from Japan, America, Israel and Europe mingling in the two narrow, muddy streets which form the main market of McLeod Ganj. I befriended many foreigners from countries I never knew existed, including a young English woman called Emily and a Dutch woman called Francisca, who regularly visited my hut to talk to me. It was during the course of those conversations that the story of my life began to unfold. I realised that because I had been lucky enough to survive, I was also duty bound to bear witness to the suffering of others.

16   Perhaps through the story of my life I can tell the story of my country and give expression to the pain felt by every Tibetan.

✧ Evaluating the Text

1. In light of his past experiences, what did Gyatso's meeting with the Dalai Lama represent to him? How did the advice he received change Gyatso's preconceptions about writing his autobiography?

2. Gyatso was clearly experiencing mixed emotions in his new home in Dharamsala, India. How would you characterize his conflict?

3. In what sense does Gyatso intend his memoir to be a voice for all those who wished to escape the oppressive Chinese Communist Party?

✧ Exploring Different Perspectives

1. How do Palden Gyatso's memoir and Albert Camus's story, "The Guest" treat the theme of exile from a religious and an existential perspective?

2. Compare the role played by radios and VCRs in permitting exiles to maintain a tenuous link with cultures left behind, as developed in Gyatso's memoir and Jesse W. Nash's account in "Confucius and the VCR."

✧ Extending Viewpoints through Writing

1. Is there a belief you hold so strongly that you would be willing to undergo imprisonment and possibly torture to defend it? What is it and why does it mean so much to you?

2. Tibet has always held a certain mystique for the West and has been the subject of a number of films (for example, *Shangri-La* [1953] and in *Seven Days in Tibet* [1997], starring Brad Pitt). Rent a video of such a film and discuss the values connected with Tibet. Present your opinion as to why it holds the allure it does.

Jesse W. Nash

Confucius and the VCR

◆————

Jesse W. Nash currently teaches religious studies at Loyola University, New Orleans. He is the author of Vietnamese Catholicism *(1992) and* Romance, Gender, and Religion in a Vietnamese-American Community *(1995). Nash has also studied the important role that videotaped films, imported from Taiwan and Hong Kong and dubbed into Vietnamese, play in the lives of Vietnamese immigrants in the United States. "Confucius and the VCR" originally appeared in* Natural History, *May 1988.*

Bordered by Cambodia and Laos to the west, China to the north, and the South China Sea to the east and south, Vietnam was first visited by European traders in the early sixteenth century. After the French captured Saigon in 1859, Vietnam was under the control of France until World War II, when the Viet Minh, a coalition of nationalists and communists, established a republic headed by Ho Chi Minh. France's attempts to reassert control resulted in the French Indochina War (1946–1954), in which the French were defeated. In the Geneva Conference of 1954, Vietnam was divided, pending nationwide free elections, into North Vietnam, controlled by communists, and South Vietnam, controlled by nationalists. Ngo Dinh Diem's refusal to hold these elections, out of fear of a communist victory, precipitated the Vietnam War of 1954–1975, in which South Vietnam, aided by the United States, fought communist insurgents, who were supported by North Vietnam. U.S. troops were withdrawn in 1973, after a cease-fire, and in 1975 the communists overran the south. The country was reunified as the Socialist Republic of Vietnam in 1976. In 1978, Vietnam invaded Cambodia, deposed the genocidal Pol Pot regime, and installed a government that remained until the Vietnamese withdrew in 1989. Since 1989, Vietnam has been committed to a policy of doi moi (renovation), which includes private enterprise and trade, an interest in tourism, and better relations with the United States. Some economic sanctions have been lifted since 1993 and the United States has opened a diplomatic office in Hanoi. Nash offers insight into the lives of great numbers of Vietnamese who fled the country during and after the war.

The unification of North and South Vietnam into the Socialist Republic of Vietnam took place formally in July 1976. Between 1975 and 1984, approximately 550,000 "boat people" found refuge abroad. By 1989, 57,000 in Hong Kong would be forcibly repatriated following agreements reached in 1992 between the Communist Party of Vietnam

and the United Kingdom. A new constitution was adopted in 1999 reaf-
firming the role of the Communist Party, but that also encouraged greater
economic freedoms for its citizens.

Before You Read

Underline and annotate the passages in which Nash develops his thesis
about the role Confucian values play in the films that are so popular with
Vietnamese immigrants. In what way do these films convey a different
sense of social order than American-made movies?

1   Vietnamese immigrants in the United States are intensely curious
about almost all movies or television shows, aptly referring to themselves as "movie addicts." The TV set and videocassette recorder have
become common features of their homes and are the focus of much
conversation concerning what it means to be an American and what it
means to be Vietnamese in the United States.

2   American television and movies worry many Vietnamese, especially parents and elders, who see them as glorifying the individual
and his or her war with the family, social institutions, the community,
and even the state. Reflecting the individualism of American culture,
conflict resolution typically occurs at the expense of the family or community (except in situation comedies usually panned as being "saccharine" or "unrealistic" by television critics). American movies and
television, many Vietnamese assert, are most effective in imagining
worlds of mistrust, promoting self-righteous rebellion, and legitimiz-
ing the desires of the individual.

3   The antiauthorianism of much of American television and movies
disturbs Vietnamese, but there are also offerings they commend, such
as "The Cosby Show," which explores and promotes values they themselves prize: familial loyalty, togetherness, and a resolution of conflicts
within the established social structures. Such shows, I've been told, remind the Vietnamese of their Confucian education and heritage.

4   Because the language of the immigrant community is still primarily Vietnamese, movies on videotapes imported from Taiwan and
Hong Kong and dubbed in Vietnamese form a significant portion of
the entertainment diet. The movies most favored are long, multitape
epics that run from five to more than twenty hours. These include
contemporary crime stories, soap operas, and romantic comedies, but
the clear favorites are the medieval-military-romance cum kung fu
extravaganzas.

5   There is a steady stream of customers at the various local shops
that rent imported videotapes. Neighbors, friends, and relatives compare notes on favorite films and stars. Posters and pocket photos of heroes and heroines are eagerly bought. Entire families will sit through

the night eating up the latest kung fu romance, their reddened eyes a testimony of devotion to the genre and quality of the film.

6   Atop nearly every TV set in the community rests a tape. While babysitting, grandmothers and aunts will place toddlers in front of the tube and play a Chinese film. (Depending on the time of day, little boys will cut in to watch "The Transformers," "Thundercats," or "G.I. Joe.") Young women confess that they would like to visit Hong Kong, where their favorite movies are made and their favorite stars live. Young men with a definite tendency to hesitancy and the doldrums are not so much reacting to a harsh social and familial atmosphere as modeling their behavior on the beloved melancholic hero of the Chinese movie. Older, more mature men are not immune to the wiles of the films either. I have observed formerly impassive faces creased with emotion and dampened by tears during the viewing of a particularly sad movie, the dialogue of which is punctuated by sniffling sounds and a periodic blowing of noses.

7   The plots of these films are complicated and try the patience of outside audiences to whom I have introduced these films. Their broad outline can best be described as a series of concentric circles of conflict. At the outer edge, there is a general global conflict, such as a war between the Chinese and the Mongols (the latter sure to bring heated boos from the audience). Moving toward the center, the scope of the conflict—but not its intensity—narrows to two families or two different kung fu schools. Judging either side is a difficult endeavor; the conflict is not merely a matter of an obvious good versus an obvious evil, as in American movies. Conflict is inherent in the human desire to form groups, whether the group is a family unit or a kung fu school. And beneath this umbrella of intergroup conflict, there is intragroup conflict. This kind of conflict is generally romantically induced when someone falls in love with a member of an opposing family or school.

8   While Western media are filled with conflict, they have nothing over the conflict-fraught Chinese film. Take, for example, *The Mighty Sword* (Than Chau Kiem Khach). Bac Phi, the hero, is a promising kung fu artist, whose master has high hopes of elevating him to take his own place upon retirement. To belong to a kung fu school is to belong to a family, with all that that entails in Oriental culture. The master is the father, and the other members are brothers and sisters. The school's members generally marry members of other schools to form alliances. As in any real family, there is considerable conflict and dissent, but the ideal of remaining faithful and obedient to the master is stressed.

9   Bac Phi's troubles begin when he helps a damsel, Lady Tuyet, who is being besieged by ruffians. She herself is an incredibly gifted kung fu fighter and, as fate would have it, perhaps the most beautiful woman in the world. They immediately fall in love—love at first sight being the rule in the world of Chinese film.

10   In the film one gets a feel for the Chinese and, by derivation, the Vietnamese way of romance. The hero and heroine do not touch; most certainly, they do not fondle or kiss. With a particularly sad melody in the background, they look into each other's eyes. The viewers all sigh and point; they know that the two are in love by "reading their eyes." Traditionally in Vietnam, lovers communicated with their eyes. Folklore, proverbs, and songs all depict a romance of the eyes: "Like a knife cutting the yellow betel leaf,/His eyes glance, her eyes dart back and forth." The stage is set for what appears to be a romance made in Heaven. Our two lovers vow to marry and to love each other forever.

11   After this moment, the meaning of the sad melody becomes apparent. The hero and heroine have pledged their love in ignorance of certain facts ruling the social reality around them. The lovers learn that their two schools are mortal enemies. Bac Phi's school and master are held to be responsible for the murder of Tuyet's father, and neither Bac Phi's master nor Tuyet's mother will countenance the marriage. The intragroup relationships of both lovers are strained. Tuyet and her mother are at odds and come to blows. Bac Phi's relationship with his best friend is strained, and he learns that his master is planning to have him marry another girl.

12   At this point in American television and movies, we would expect an easy solution to the problem. (To the dismay of the audience, I counseled "Elope!") The Chinese and Vietnamese solution is much more complicated. To decide between Tuyet and his school is not a simple matter, and characteristically for the Chinese hero, Bac Phi is paralyzed by the situation, torn between his lover and his quasi family, his desire and his duty. He becomes lovesick and pines away for Tuyet but never decides once and for all to choose her over his school.

13   To make matters worse, there are forces behind the scenes manipulating all involved as if they were puppets. Unseen powers are seeking to deepen the rift between Bac Phi's school and that of Tuyet. These powers attempt to undermine Bac Phi's love for and trust in Tuyet by posing one of their own as Tuyet and having him/her murder one of Bac Phi's schoolmates. An already impossible situation is raised to the nth degree. Bac Phi, because of his position in his school, must now avenge the death.

14   The conflict and its resolution are characteristic of the Vietnamese community. When I asked why the couple simply didn't run away and elope, the Vietnamese audience laughed. "That is the American way," I was told. "But we have a Confucian tradition." The Vietnamese were trained in Confucian values at school and at home. Confucianism, in a Vietnamese context, is a tradition of loyalty to one's family, superiors, and prior obligations. "We were always taught to love our parents more

than life itself," one woman observed. "Parents were more important than the man or woman you loved."

15   The conflict would not actually be resolved by Bac Phi and Tuyet eloping and abandoning the social units to which they belong. As the Vietnamese themselves ask, "Could Tuyet trust Bac Phi if he were to fudge on his obligations to his school?" If Bac Phi will sever the bonds of previously established relationships, such as those with friends and superiors, what guarantee does Tuyet have that, when she has lost her figure and taken on wrinkles, he won't abandon her and chase after a younger, more nubile woman? There is a logic of trust in the films and the community that forbids them to take advantage of a simplistic formula, namely, "If you want it, go for it." The Vietnamese, ever moralistic, will ask, "Is it right for you to want it?"

16   The conflict, in the case of *The Mighty Sword,* is eventually resolved by the defeat of the powers behind the scenes, by a change of heart and character on the part of Tuyet's mother and Bac Phi's master, and by the two lovers working to break the endless cycle of revenge and misunderstanding. The conflict is resolved within the social structures, not by their destruction. Despite the mazelike layers of deceit, fear, and manipulation, the movie ends affirming the ultimate worthwhileness of living in society, of being a social animal and not merely a lover.

17   Unlike most American television shows and movies, the Chinese hero does not always get the girl. A happy ending cannot be predicted. Although most Vietnamese I have talked to prefer a happy ending to their Chinese films, they appreciate and approve of the ethical message of a melancholic ending. "Love doesn't conquer all," one viewer told me, tears in his eyes. "Sometimes we have to pay for our mistakes. Sometimes we don't get what we want just because we want it." One woman recommended a particularly touching Chinese soap opera to me. "It has a very sad ending. It is very beautiful. It is very Confucian." She explained that the movie, which I later watched with a lump in my jaded throat, tried to teach that romance must be accompanied by ethics. One cannot simply be a lover. One also has to be a good son or daughter and citizen.

18   In America, where films and television shows tend to glorify the individual and romance, the Chinese films the Vietnamese adore reaffirm traditional values and help educate their children in the art of being Confucian. Traditional Vietnamese Confucianism has sneaked in through the back door, so to speak, through the VCR. American pluralism and technology have made this possible. They also may have let in a Trojan horse that promises to offer a venerable critique of certain American values. The Vietnamese may do American culture a favor by offering a countervision of what it means to be a social animal, and not merely an animal.

✧ Evaluating the Text

1. Beyond providing entertainment, what function do the foreign videos serve for the Vietnamese immigrant community?

2. Nash analyzes a Chinese film, *The Mighty Sword*, to illustrate the ways in which the values, mores, and expectations of these Chinese-made films differ from their American counterparts. What are some of these differences and what do they reveal about each culture?

3. How does the title suggest the distinctive contribution that Asian culture can offer to America?

✧ Exploring Different Perspectives

1. Compare the idealization of Chinese culture depicted by Nash with the reality of life in China from the perspective of a Tibetan exile (see Palden Gyatso, "Autobiography of a Tibetan Monk").

2. Discuss how important it is for the Vietnamese in America, according to Nash, and for African Americans, according to Itabari Njeri (see "What's in a Name?") to maintain an identity with their roots.

✧ Extending Viewpoints through Writing

1. Nash makes the point that some Chinese-made films offer "a countervision of what it means to be a social animal." Have you ever seen a movie that offered you a window into another culture? In what way was its perspective different from that presented in American films?

2. Nash observes that videos provide a portable means for preserving a cultural enclave for immigrants. When you watch movies in a foreign language, do you prefer them to be subtitled or dubbed into English? Explain your preference.

Poranee Natadecha-Sponsel

Individualism as an American Cultural Value

◆

Poranee Natadecha-Sponsel was born and raised in a multiethnic Thai and Malay region in the southern part of Thailand. She received her B.A. with honors in English and philosophy from Chulalongkorn University in Bangkok, Thailand, in 1969. She has lived in the United States for more than fifteen years, earning her M.A. in philosophy at Ohio University, in Athens, in 1973 and her Ed.D. in 1991 from the University of Hawaii at Manoa. She currently teaches interdisciplinary courses in women's studies and coordinates the mentoring program for new women faculty at the University of Hawaii at Manoa.

Before You Read

Consider the different cultural assumptions that govern what Thai people consider appropriate to ask strangers.

◆

1   "Hi, how are you?" "Fine, thank you, and you?" These are greetings that everybody in America hears and says every day—salutations that come ready-made and packaged just like a hamburger and fries. There is no real expectation for any special information in response to these greetings. Do not, under any circumstances, take up anyone's time by responding in depth to the programmed query. What or how you may feel at the moment is of little, if any, importance. Thai people would immediately perceive that our concerned American friends are truly interested in our welfare, and this concern would require polite reciprocation by spelling out the details of our current condition. We become very disappointed when we have had enough experience in the United States to learn that we have bored, amused, or even frightened many of our American acquaintances by taking the greeting "How are you?" so literally. We were reacting like Thai, but in the American context where salutations have a different meaning, our detailed reactions were inappropriate. In Thai society, a greeting among acquaintances usually requests specific information about the other person's condition, such as "Where are you going?" or "Have you eaten?"

2   One of the American contexts in which this greeting is most confusing and ambiguous is at the hospital or clinic. In these sterile and
ritualistic settings, I have always been uncertain exactly how to answer
when the doctor or nurse asks "How are you?" If I deliver a packaged
answer of "Fine," I wonder if I am telling a lie. After all, I am there in
the first place precisely because I am not so fine. Finally, after debating
for some time, I asked one nurse how she expected a patient to answer
the query "How are you?" But after asking this question, I then wondered if it was rude to do so. However, she looked relieved after I explained to her that people from different cultures have different ways
to greet other people and that for me to be asked how I am in the hospital results in awkwardness. Do I simply answer, "Fine, thank you,"
or do I reveal in accurate detail how I really feel at the moment? My
suspicion was verified when the nurse declared that "How are you?"
was really no more than a polite greeting and that she didn't expect
any answer more elaborate than simply "Fine." However, she told me
that some patients do answer her by describing every last ache and
pain from which they are suffering.

3   A significant question that comes to mind is whether the verbal
pattern of greetings reflects any social relationship in American culture. The apparently warm and sincere greeting may initially suggest
interest in the person, yet the intention and expectations are, to me,
quite superficial. For example, most often the person greets you
quickly and then walks by to attend to other business without even
waiting for your response! This type of greeting is just like a package
of American fast food! The person eats the food quickly without
enjoying the taste. The convenience is like many other American
accoutrements of living such as cars, household appliances, efficient
telephones, or simple, systematic, and predictable arrangements of
groceries in the supermarket. However, usually when this greeting is
delivered, it seems to lack a personal touch and genuine feeling. It is
little more than ritualized behavior.

4   I have noticed that most Americans keep to themselves even at social gatherings. Conversation may revolve around many topics, but little, if anything, is revealed about oneself. Without talking much about
oneself and not knowing much about others, social relations seem to
remain at an abbreviated superficial level. How could one know a person without knowing something about him or her? How much does
one need to know about a person to really know that person?

5   After living in this culture for more than a decade, I have learned
that there are many topics that should not be mentioned in conversations with American acquaintances or even close friends. One's personal life and one's income are considered to be very private and even
taboo topics. Unlike my Thai culture, Americans do not show interest

or curiosity by asking such personal questions, especially when one just meets the individual for the first time. Many times I have been embarrassed by my Thai acquaintances who recently arrived at the University of Hawaii and the East-West Center. For instance, one day I was walking on campus with an American friend when we met another Thai woman to whom I had been introduced a few days earlier. The Thai woman came to write her doctoral dissertation at the East-West Center where the American woman worked, so I introduced them to each other. The American woman greeted my Thai companion in Thai language, which so impressed her that she felt immediately at ease. At once, she asked the American woman numerous personal questions such as, How long did you live in Thailand? Why were you there? How long were you married to the Thai man? Why did you divorce him? How long have you been divorced? Are you going to marry a Thai again or an American? How long have you been working here? How much do you earn? The American was stunned. However, she was very patient and more or less answered all those questions as succinctly as she could. I was so uncomfortable that I had to interrupt whenever I could to get her out of the awkward situation in which she had been forced into talking about things she considered personal. For people in Thai society, such questions would be appropriate and not considered too personal let alone taboo.

6   The way Americans value their individual privacy continues to impress me. Americans seem to be open and yet there is a contradiction because they are also aloof and secretive. This is reflected in many of their behavior patterns. By Thai standards, the relationship between friends in American society seems to be somewhat superficial. Many Thai students, as well as other Asians, have felt that they could not find genuine friendship with Americans. For example, I met many American classmates who were very helpful and friendly while we were in the same class. We went out, exchanged phone calls, and did the same things as would good friends in Thailand. But those activities stopped suddenly when the semester ended.

7   Privacy as a component of the American cultural value of individualism is nurtured in the home as children grow up. From birth they are given their own individual, private space, a bedroom separate from that of their parents. American children are taught to become progressively independent, both emotionally and economically, from their family. They learn to help themselves at an early age. In comparison, in Thailand, when parents bring a new baby home from the hospital, it shares the parents' bedroom for two to three years and then shares another bedroom with older siblings of the same sex. Most Thai children do not have their own private room until they finish high school, and some do not have their own room until another sibling moves out,

usually when the sibling gets married. In Thailand, there are strong bonds within the extended family. Older siblings regularly help their parents to care for younger ones. In this and other ways, the Thai family emphasizes the interdependence of its members.

8   I was accustomed to helping Thai babies who fell down to stand up again. Thus, in America when I saw babies fall, it was natural for me to try to help them back on their feet. Once at a summer camp for East-West Center participants, one of the supervisors brought his wife and their ten-month-old son with them. The baby was so cute that many students were playing with him. At one point he was trying to walk and fell, so all the Asian students, males and females, rushed to help him up. Although the father and mother were nearby, they paid no attention to their fallen and crying baby. However, as the students were trying to help and comfort him, the parents told them to leave him alone; he would be all right on his own. The baby did get up and stopped crying without any assistance. Independence is yet another component of the American value of individualism.

9   Individualism is even reflected in the way Americans prepare, serve, and consume food. In a typical American meal, each person has a separate plate and is not supposed to share or taste food from other people's plates. My Thai friends and I are used to eating Thai style, in which you share food from a big serving dish in the middle of the table. Each person dishes a small amount from the serving dish onto his or her plate and finishes this portion before going on with the next portion of the same or a different serving dish. With the Thai pattern of eating, you regularly reach out to the serving dishes throughout the meal. But this way of eating is not considered appropriate in comparison to the common American practice where each person eats separately from his or her individual plate.

10   One time my American host, a divorcée who lives alone, invited a Thai girlfriend and myself to an American dinner at her home. When we were reaching out and eating a small portion of one thing at a time in Thai style, we were told to dish everything we wanted onto our plates at one time and that it was not considered polite to reach across the table. The proper American way was to have each kind of food piled up on your plate at once. If we were to eat in the same manner in Thailand, eyebrows would have been raised at the way we piled up food on our plates, and we would have been considered to be eating like pigs, greedy and inconsiderate of others who shared the meal at the table.

11   Individualism as a pivotal value in American culture is reflected in many other ways. Material wealth is not only a prime status marker in American society but also a guarantee and celebration of individualism—wealth allows the freedom to do almost anything, although

usually within the limits of law. The pursuit of material wealth through individual achievement is instilled in Americans from the youngest age. For example, I was surprised to see an affluent American couple, who own a large ranch house and two BMW cars, send their nine-year-old son to deliver newspapers. He has to get up very early each morning to deliver the papers, even on Sunday! During summer vacation, the boy earns additional money by helping in his parents' gift shop from 10 A.M. to 5 P.M. His thirteen-year-old sister often earns money by babysitting, even at night.

12   In Thailand, only children from poorer families work to earn money to help the household. Middle- and high-income parents do not encourage their children to work until after they have finished their education. They provide economic support in order to free their children to concentrate on and excel in their studies. Beyond the regular schooling, families who can afford it pay for special tutoring as well as training in music, dance, or sports. However, children in low- and middle-income families help their parents with household chores and the care of younger children.

13   Many American children have been encouraged to get paid for their help around the house. They rarely get any gifts free of obligations. They even have to be good to get Santa's gifts at Christmas! As they grow up, they are conditioned to earn things they want; they learn that "there is no such thing as a free lunch." From an early age, children are taught to become progressively independent economically from their parents. Also, most young people are encouraged to leave home at college age to be on their own. From my viewpoint as a Thai, it seems that American family ties and closeness are not as strong as in Asian families whose children depend on family financial support until joining the work force after college age. Thereafter, it is the children's turn to help support their parents financially.

14   Modern American society and economy emphasize individualism in other ways. The nuclear family is more common than the extended family, and newlyweds usually establish their own independent household rather than initially living with either the husband's or the wife's parents. Parents and children appear to be close only when the children are very young. Most American parents seem to "lose" their children by the teenage years. They don't seem to belong to each other as closely as do Thai families. Even though I have seen more explicit affectionate expression among American family members than among Asian ones, the close interpersonal spirit seems to be lacking. Grandparents have relatively little to do with the grandchildren on any regular basis, in contrast to the extended family, which is more common in Thailand. The family and society seem to be graded by age to the point that grandparents, parents, and children are separated by generational

subcultures that are evidently alienated from one another. Each group "does its own thing." Help and support are usually limited to whatever does not interfere with one's own life. In America, the locus of responsibility is more on the individual than on the family.

15   In one case I know of, a financially affluent grandmother with Alzheimer's disease is taken care of twenty-four hours a day by hired help in her own home. Her daughter visits and relieves the helper occasionally. The mature granddaughter, who has her own family, rarely visits. Yet they all live in the same neighborhood. However, each lives in a different house, and each is very independent. Although the mother worries about the grandmother, she cannot do much. Her husband also needs her, and she divides her time between him, her daughters and their children, and the grandmother. When the mother needs to go on a trip with her husband, a second hired attendant is required to care for the grandmother temporarily. When I asked why the granddaughter doesn't temporarily care for the grandmother, the reply was that she has her own life, and it would not be fair for the granddaughter to take care of the grandmother, even for a short period of time. Yet I wonder if it is fair for the grandmother to be left out. It seems to me that the value of individualism and its associated independence account for these apparent gaps in family ties and support.

16   In contrast to American society, in Thailand older parents with a long-term illness are asked to move in with their children and grandchildren if they are not already living with them. The children and grandchildren take turns attending to the grandparent, sometimes with help from live-in maids. Living together in the same house reinforces moral support among the generations within an extended family. The older generation is respected because of the previous economic, social, and moral support for their children and grandchildren. Family relations provide one of the most important contexts for being a "morally good person," which is traditionally the principal concern in the Buddhist society of Thailand.

17   In America, being young, rich, and/or famous allows one greater freedom and independence and thus promotes the American value of individualism. This is reflected in the mass appeal of major annual television events like the Super Bowl and the Academy Awards. The goal of superachievement is also seen in more mundane ways. For example, many parents encourage their children to take special courses and to work hard to excel in sports as a shortcut to becoming rich and famous. I know one mother who has taken her two sons to tennis classes and tournaments since the boys were six years old, hoping that at least one of them will be a future tennis star like Ivan Lendl. Other parents focus their children on acting, dancing, or musical talent. The children have to devote much time and hard work as well as sacrifice

the ordinary activities of youth in order to develop and perform their natural talents and skills in prestigious programs. But those who excel in the sports and entertainment industries can become rich and famous, even at an early age, as for example Madonna, Tom Cruise, and Michael Jackson. Television and other media publicize these celebrities and thereby reinforce the American value of individualism, including personal achievement and financial success.

18   Although the American cultural values of individualism and the aspiration to become rich and famous have had some influence in Thailand, there is also cultural and religious resistance to these values. Strong social bonds, particularly within the extended family, and the hierarchical structure of the kingdom run counter to individualism. Also, youth gain social recognition through their academic achievement. From the perspective of Theravada Buddhism, which strongly influences Thai culture, aspiring to be rich and famous would be an illustration of greed, and those who have achieved wealth and fame do not celebrate it publicly as much as in American society. Being a good, moral person is paramount, and ideally Buddhists emphasize restraint and moderation.

19   Beyond talent and skill in the sports and entertainment industries, there are many other ways that young Americans can pursue wealth. Investment is one route. One American friend who is only a sophomore in college has already invested heavily in the stock market to start accumulating wealth. She is just one example of the 1980s trend for youth to be more concerned with their individual finances than with social, political, and environmental issues. With less attention paid to public issues, the expression of individualism seems to be magnified through emphasis on lucrative careers, financial investment, and material consumption—the "Yuppie" phenomenon. This includes new trends in dress, eating, housing (condominiums), and cars (expensive European imports). Likewise, there appears to be less of a long-term commitment to marriage. More young couples are living together without either marriage or plans for future marriage. When such couples decide to get married, prenuptial agreements are made to protect their assets. Traditional values of marriage, family, and sharing appear to be on the decline.

20   Individualism as one of the dominant values in American culture is expressed in many ways. This value probably stems from the history of the society as a frontier colony of immigrants in search of a better life with independence, freedom, and the opportunity for advancement through personal achievement. However, in the beliefs and customs of any culture there are some disadvantages as well as advantages. Although Thais may admire the achievements and material wealth of American society, there are costs, especially in the value of individualism and associated social phenomena.

✧ Evaluating the Test

1. For the Thais, what are the kinds of private topics about which it would be rude to inquire? How do these differ from the topics that are taboo among Americans?

2. How do concepts of friendship and privacy differ in Natadecha-Sponsel's experience with the Thai and American cultures?

3. How do the examples involving the child who has fallen, the way food is served and eaten, and the newspaper route provide the author with significant insights into American cultural values? Do you agree with her interpretations?

✧ Exploring Different Perspectives

1. Compare the role that Buddhism plays for Thai immigrants in American culture, as described by Natadecha-Sponsel, with the role it plays for Palden Gyatso (see "Autobiography of a Tibetan Monk").

2. How do the accounts by Natadecha-Sponsel and Itabari Njeri (see "What's in a Name?") dramatize the relationship between language and identity for Thai immigrants and African Americans?

✧ Extending Viewpoints through Writing

1. How do concepts of the care of the elderly and Buddhist philosophy provide strikingly different models for behavior in Thailand and in the United States?

2. What incidents in your own experience illustrate the value placed on individualism in American culture, a value that those from other cultures might find strange?

Itabari Njeri

What's in a Name?

◆

Itabari Njeri is an arts critic, essayist, and reporter whose memoir Every Goodbye Ain't Gone *(1990), an eloquent testimony to the African-American experience, won the American Book Award. She is also a talented professional singer as well as writer, and was named "Best New Pop Vocalist" by MGM records. From 1986 to 1992, she was a staff writer for the* Los Angeles Times Magazine, *where the following essay first appeared. Her most recent book is* The Last Plantation *(1995).*

Before You Read

Consider to what extent Njeri's decision to change her name is due to a desire to be an individual as well as to disengage herself from objectionable racial associations.

◆

1   The decade was about to end when I started my first newspaper job. The seventies might have been the disco generation for some, but it was a continuation of the Black Power, post–civil rights era for me. Of course in some parts of America it was still the pre–civil rights era. And that was the part of America I wanted to explore. As a good reporter I needed a sense of the whole country, not just the provincial Northeast Corridor in which I was raised.

2   I headed for Greenville ("Pearl of the Piedmont"), South Carolina.

3   "*Wheeere*," some people snarled, their nostrils twitching, their mouths twisted so their top lips went slightly to the right, the bottom ones way down and to the left, "did you get *that* name from?"

4   Itabiddy, Etabeedy. Etabeeree. Eat a berry. Mata Hari. Theda Bara. And one secretary in the office of the Greenville Urban League told her employer: "It's Ms. Idi Amin."

5   Then, and now, there are a whole bunch of people who greet me with: "Hi, Ita." They think "Bari" is my last name. Even when they don't, they still want to call me "Ita." When I tell them my first name is Itabari, they say, "Well, what do people call you for short?"

6   "They don't call me anything for short," I say. "The name is Itabari."

7   Sophisticated white people, upon hearing my name, approach me as would a cultural anthropologist finding a piece of exotica right in his own living room. This happens a lot, still, at cocktail parties.

8   "Oh, what an unusual and beautiful name. Where are you from?"

9   "Brooklyn," I say. I can see the disappointment in their eyes. Just another home-grown Negro.

10   Then there are other white people, who, having heard my decidedly northeastern accent, will simply say, "What a lovely name," and smile knowingly, indicating that they saw Roots and understand.

11   Then there are others, black and white, who for different reasons take me through this number:

12   "What's your *real* name?"

13   "Itabari Njeri is my real, legal name," I explain.

14   "Okay, what's your *original* name?" they ask, often with eyes rolling, exasperation in their voices.

15   After Malcolm X, Muhammad Ali, Kareem Abdul-Jabbar, Ntozake Shange, and Kunta Kinte, who, I ask, should be exasperated by this question-and-answer game?

16   Nevertheless, I explain, "Because of slavery, black people in the Western world don't usually know their original names. What you really want to know is what my slave name was."

17   Now this is where things get tense. Four hundred years of bitter history, culture, and politics between blacks and whites in America is evoked by this one term, "slave name."

18   Some white people wince when they hear the phrase, pained and embarrassed by this reminder of their ancestors' inhumanity. Further, they quickly scrutinize me and conclude that mine was a post-Emancipation Proclamation birth. "You were never a slave."

19   I used to be reluctant to tell people my slave name unless I surmised that they wouldn't impose their cultural values on me and refuse to use my African name. I don't care anymore. When I changed my name, I changed my life, and I've been Itabari for more years now than I was Jill. Nonetheless, people will say: "Well, that's your *real* name, you were born in America and that's what I am going to call you." My mother tried a variation of this on me when I legalized my traditional African name. I respectfully made it clear to her that I would not tolerate it. Her behavior, and subsequently her attitude, changed.

20   But many black folks remain just as skeptical of my name as my mother was.

21   "You're one of those black people who changed their name, huh," they are likely to begin. "Well, I still got the old slave master's Irish name," said one man named O'Hare at a party. This man's defensive tone was a reaction to what I call the "blacker than thou" syndrome perpetrated by many black nationalists in the sixties and seventies. Those who reclaimed their African names made blacks who didn't do the same thing feel like Uncle Toms.

22   These so-called Uncle Toms couldn't figure out why they should use an African name when they didn't know a thing about Africa. Besides,

many of them were proud of their names, no matter how they had come by them. And it should be noted that after the Emancipation Proclamation in 1863, four million black people changed their names, adopting surnames such as Freeman, Freedman, and Liberty. They eagerly gave up names that slave masters had imposed upon them as a way of identifying their human chattel.

23 Besides names that indicated their newly won freedom, blacks chose common English names such as Jones, Scott, and Johnson. English was their language. America was their home, and they wanted names that would allow them to assimilate as easily as possible.

24 Of course, many of our European surnames belong to us by birthright. We are the legal as well as "illegitimate" heirs to the names Jefferson, Franklin, Washington, et al., and in my own family, Lord.

25 Still, I consider most of these names to be by-products of slavery, if not actual slave names. Had we not been enslaved, we would not have been cut off from our culture, lost our indigenous languages, and been compelled to use European names.

26 The loss our African culture is a tragic fact of history, and the conflict it poses is a profound one that has divided blacks many times since Emancipation: do we accept the loss and assimilate totally or do we try to reclaim our culture and synthesize it with our present reality?

27 A new generation of black people in America is reexamining the issues raised by the cultural nationalists and Pan-Africanists of the sixties and seventies: what are the cultural images that appropriately convey the "new" black aesthetic in literature and art?

28 The young Afro-American novelist Trey Ellis has asserted that the "New Black Aesthetic shamelessly borrows and reassembles across both race and class lines." It is not afraid to embrace the full implications of our hundreds of years in the New World. We are a new people who need not be tied to externally imposed or self-inflicted cultural parochialism. Had I understood that as a teenager, I might still be singing today.

29 Even the fundamental issue of identity and nomenclature, raised by Baraka and others twenty years ago, is back on the agenda: are we to call ourselves blacks or African-Americans?

30 In reality, it's an old debate. "Only with the founding of the American Colonization Society in 1816 did blacks recoil from using the term African in referring to themselves and their institutions," the noted historian and author Sterling Stuckey pointed out in an interview with me. They feared that using the term "African" would fuel white efforts to send them back to Africa. But they felt no white person had the right to send them back when they had slaved to build America.

31 Many black institutions retained their African identification, most notably the African Methodist Episcopal Church. Changes in black

self-identification in America have come in cycles, usually reflecting the larger dynamics of domestic and international politics.

32   The period after World War II, said Stuckey, "culminating in the Cold War years of Roy Wilkins's leadership of the NAACP," was a time of "frenzied integrationism." And there was "no respectable black leader on the scene evincing any sort of interest in Africa—neither the NAACP or the Urban League."

33   This, he said, "was an example of historical discontinuity, the likes of which we, as a people, had not seen before." Prior to that, for more than a century and a half, black leaders were Pan-Africanists, including Frederick Douglass. "He recognized," said Stuckey, "that Africa was important and that somehow one had to redeem the motherland in order to be genuinely respected in the New World."

34   The Reverend Jesse Jackson has, of course, placed on the national agenda the importance of blacks in America restoring their cultural, historical, and political links with Africa.

35   But what does it really mean to be called an African-American?

36   "Black" can be viewed as a more encompassing term, referring to all people of African descent. "Afro-American" and "African-American" refer to a specific ethnic group. I use the terms interchangeably, depending on the context and the point I want to emphasize.

37   But I wonder: as the twenty-first century breathes down our necks—prodding us to wake up to the expanding mélange of ethnic groups immigrating in record numbers to the United States, inevitably intermarrying, and to realize the eventual reshaping of the nation's political imperatives in a newly multicultural society—will the term "African-American" be as much of a racial and cultural obfuscation as the term "black"? In other words, will we be the only people, in a society moving toward cultural pluralism, viewed to have no history and no culture? Will we just be a color with a new name: African-American?

38   Or will the term be—as I think it should—an ethnic label describing people with a shared culture who descended from Africans, were transformed in (as well as transformed) America, and are genetically intertwined with myriad other groups in the United States?

39   Such a definition reflects the historical reality and distances us from the fallacious, unscientific concept of separate races when there is only one: *Homo sapiens.*

40   But to comprehend what should be an obvious definition requires knowledge and a willingness to accept history.

41   When James Baldwin wrote *Nobody Knows My Name*, the title was a metaphor—at the deepest level of the collective African-American psyche—for the blighting of black history and culture before the nadir of slavery and since.

42   The eradication or distortion of our place in world history and culture is most obvious in the popular media. Liz Taylor—and, for an

earlier generation, Claudette Colbert—still represent what Cleopatra—a woman of color in a multiethnic society, dominated at various times by blacks—looks like.

43   And in American homes, thanks to reruns and cable, a new generation of black kids grow up believing that a simpleton shouting "Dyno-mite!" is a genuine reflection of Afro-American culture, rather than a white Hollywood writer's stereotype.

44   More recently, *Coming to America*, starring Eddie Murphy as an African prince seeking a bride in the United States, depicted traditional African dancers in what amounted to a Las Vegas stage show, totally distorting the nature and beauty of real African dance. But with every burlesque-style pelvic thrust on the screen, I saw blacks in the audience burst into applause. They think that's African culture, too.

45   And what do Africans know of us, since blacks don't control the organs of communication that disseminate information about us?

46   "No!" screamed the mother of a Kenyan man when he announced his engagement to an African-American woman who was a friend of mine. The mother said marry a European, marry a white American. But please, not one of those low-down, ignorant, drug-dealing, murderous black people she had seen in American movies. Ultimately, the mother prevailed.

47   In Tanzania, the travel agent looked at me indignantly. "Njeri, that's Kikuyu. What are you doing with an African name?" he demanded.

48   I'd been in Dar es Salaam about a month and had learned that Africans assess in a glance the ethnic origins of the people they meet.

49   Without a greeting, strangers on the street in Tanzania's capital would comment, "Oh, you're an Afro-American or West Indian."

50   "Both."

51   "I knew it," they'd respond, sometimes politely, sometimes not.

52   Or, people I got to know while in Africa would mention, "I know another half-caste like you." Then they would call in the "mixed-race" person and say, "Please meet Itabari Njeri." The darker-complected African, presumably of unmixed ancestry, would then smile and stare at us like we were animals in the zoo.

53   Of course, this "half-caste" (which I suppose is a term preferable to "mulatto," which I hate, and which every person who understands its derogatory meaning—"mule"—should never use) was usually the product of a mixed marriage, not generations of ethnic intermingling. And it was clear from most "half-castes" I met that they did not like being compared to so mongrelized and stigmatized a group as Afro-Americans.

54   I had minored in African studies in college, worked for years with Africans in the United States, and had no romantic illusions as to how I would be received in the motherland. I wasn't going back to find my roots. The only thing that shocked me in Tanzania was being

called, with great disdain, a "white woman" by an African waiter. Even if the rest of the world didn't follow the practice, I then assumed everyone understood that any known or perceptible degree of African ancestry made one "black" in America by law and social custom.

55   But I was pleasantly surprised by the telephone call I received two minutes after I walked into my Dar es Salaam hotel room. It was the hotel operator. "Sister, welcome to Tanzania. . . . Please tell everyone in Harlem hello for us." The year was 1978, and people in Tanzania were wearing half-foot-high platform shoes and dancing to James Brown wherever I went.

56   Shortly before I left, I stood on a hill surrounded by a field of endless flowers in Arusha, near the border of Tanzania and Kenya. A toothless woman with a wide smile, a staff in her hand, and two young girls at her side, came toward me on a winding path. I spoke to her in fractured Swahili and she to me in broken English.

57   "I know you," she said smiling. "Wa-Negro." "Wa" is a prefix in Bantu languages meaning people. "You are from the lost tribe," she told me. "Welcome," she said, touching me, then walked down a hill that lay in the shadow of Mount Kilimanjaro.

58   I never told her my name, but when I told other Africans, they'd say: "*Emmmm* Itabari. Too long. How about I just call you Ita."

✧ Evaluating the Text

1. The variety of reactions Njeri's name elicits prompts her to make the case explaining why she changed her name to an African one. What were these reactions and how would this explain why she would want to justify her decision? Why was it ironic she met with the same responses in Tanzania as she did in Greenville, South Carolina?

2. What negative connotations did Njeri's given name have for her? By contrast, what positive associations does she have with her African name, Itabari?

✧ Exploring Different Perspectives

1. In what ways do both Njeri's essay and Gloria Anzaldúa's story "Cervicide" explore the predicament of the consequences of being marginalized in American society?

2. How do both Njeri and David R. Counts (see "Too Many Bananas") use humor to make their points?

✧ *Extending Viewpoints through Writing*

1. Evaluate Njeri's contention that the continued use of English-language names such as Jones, Scott, and Johnson perpetuates a legacy of slavery, whereas adoption of African names would allow African Americans to have their own identity?

2. Would you ever consider changing your name? If so, what would it be and what would it say about you that your present given name does not?

3. Describe the circumstances underlying the choice of your name. Do you like your given name or do you prefer to be called by a nickname you chose or others gave you?

Gloria Anzaldúa

Cervicide[1]

Gloria Anzaldúa is a Chicana poet and fiction writer who grew up in south Texas. She has edited several highly praised anthologies. This Bridge Called My Back: Writings by Radical Women of Color, *won the 1986 Before Columbus Foundation American Book Award.* Borderlands—La Frontera, the New Mestiza *was selected as one of the best books of 1987 by* Library Journal. *Her recent work includes* Making Face, Making Soul *(1990),* La Prieta *(1991), and a children's book,* Friends from the Other Side *(1993). She has been a contributing editor for* Sinister Wisdom *since 1984 and has taught Chicano studies, feminist studies, and creative writing at the University of Texas at Austin, San Francisco State University, and the University of California, Santa Cruz. "Cervicide" first appeared in* Labyris *(vol. 4, no. 11, Winter 1983). In it, Anzaldúa tells the poignant story of a Mexican-American family living on the Texas border who are forced to kill a pet deer whose detection by the game warden would result in an unaffordable fine or the father's imprisonment.*

Before You Read

Consider how Anzaldúa enhances the sense of urgency in what proves to be a no-win situation for Prieta.

1   *La venadita.* The small fawn. They had to kill their pet, the fawn. The game warden was on the way with his hounds. The penalty for being caught in possession of a deer was $250 or jail. The game warden would put *su papí en la cárcel.*[2]

2   How could they get rid of the fawn? Hide it? No, *la guardia's*[3] hounds would sniff Venadita out. Let Venadita loose in the *monte?* They had tried that before. The fawn would leap away and seconds later return. Should they kill Venadita? The mother and Prieta looked toward *las carabinas* propped against the wall behind the kitchen door—the shiny barrel of the .22, the heavy metal steel of the 40-40.

---

[1]*Cervicide*—the killing of a deer. In archetypal symbology the Self appears as a deer for women.
[2]*su papí en la cárcel*—her father in jail.
[3]*monte*—the woods.

No, if *they* could hear his pickup a mile and a half down the road, he would hear the shot.

3   Quick, they had to do something. Cut Venadita's throat? Club her to death? The mother couldn't do it. She, Prieta,[4] would have to be the one. The game warden and his *perros*[5] were a mile down the road. Prieta loved her *papi*.

4   In the shed behind the corral, where they'd hidden the fawn, Prieta found the hammer. She had to grasp it with both hands. She swung it up. The weight folded her body backwards. A thud reverberated on Venadita's skull, a wave undulated down her back. Again, a blow behind the ear. Though Venadita's long lashes quivered, her eyes never left Prieta's face. Another thud, another tremor. *La guardia* and his hounds were driving up the front yard. The *venadita* looked up at her, the hammer rose and fell. Neither made a sound. The tawny, spotted fur was the most beautiful thing Prieta had ever seen. She remembered when they had found the fawn. She had been a few hours old. A hunter had shot her mother. The fawn had been shaking so hard, her long thin legs were on the edge of buckling. Prieta and her sister and brothers had bottle-fed Venadita, with a damp cloth had wiped her skin, had watched her tiny, perfectly formed hooves harden and grow.

5   Prieta dug a hole in the shed, a makeshift hole. She could hear the warden talking to her mother. Her mother's English had suddenly gotten bad—she was trying to stall *la guardia*. Prieta rolled the fawn into the hole, threw in the empty bottle. With her fingers raked in the dirt. Dust caked on her arms and face where tears had fallen. She patted the ground flat with her hands and swept it with a dead branch. The game warden was strutting toward her. His hounds sniffing, sniffing, sniffing the ground in the shed. The hounds pawing pawing the ground. The game warden, straining on the leashes *les dio un tirón, sacó los perros*.[6] He inspected the corrals, the edge of the woods, then drove away in his pickup.

✦ Evaluating the Text

1. To what pressures is the family subject because they are illegal immigrants?

2. Discuss the consequences for the narrator of having to make such a choice and perform such an action. In your opinion, how will she be different from then on? In what sense might the deer symbolize the self that can no longer exist?

---

[4]*Prieta*—literally one who is dark-skinned, a nickname.
[5]*perros*—dogs.
[6]*les dio un tirón, sacó los perros*—jerked the dogs out.

3. How does being forced to choose between a deer she loves and her loyalty to her father, illustrate the kind of predicament in which those without power find themselves?

✧ *Exploring Different Perspectives*

1. Compare Anzaldúa's story with Albert Camus's story "The Guest" in terms of the existential dilemma the protagonists face.

2. In what ways is the protagonist, Prieta, in Anzaldúa's story at the mercy of the powers that be in a strange land in much the same way as is David R. Counts (see "Too Many Bananas") albeit to a lesser extent?

✧ *Extending Viewpoints through Writing*

1. What actions did a pet of yours take that led you to believe it showed evidence of consciousness, motivation, and intelligence? What could your pet say about you that no human being knows?

2. Describe your search for a name for your pet. What character traits important to you or your family does this name reveal?

Albert Camus

The Guest

◆

Albert Camus (1913–1960) was born in Mondavi, Algeria (then a colony of France), in 1913 to Breton and Spanish parents. Despite the hardships of poverty and his bouts with tuberculosis, Camus excelled as both an athlete and scholarship student at the University of Algiers. Camus lived and worked as a journalist in Algeria until 1940 when he traveled to France and became active in the Resistance, serving as editor of the clandestine paper Combat. *Internationally recognized for his essays and novels, Camus received the Nobel Prize for Literature in 1957, a few years before he was killed in an automobile accident. Camus was closely associated with Jean-Paul Sartre and the French existentialist movement, but broke with Sartre and developed his own concept of the absurd that asserts the importance of human solidarity as the only value capable of redeeming a world without meaning. Although Camus began as a journalist, his work soon extended far beyond journalism to encompass novels, such as* The Stranger *(1942), the play* Caligula *(1944), and a lengthy essay defining his concept of the "absurd" hero, in* The Myth of Sisyphus *(1942). Camus's second novel,* The Plague *(1947), uses the description of a plague in a quarantined city to depict the human struggle against physical and spiritual evil in all its forms, a position Camus outlined in great detail in his nonfiction work* The Rebel *(1951). "The Guest," translated by Justin O'Brien, is drawn from his last collection of short stories,* Exile and the Kingdom *(1957). In this story, Camus returns to the landscape of his native Algeria to depict the poignant dilemma of his protagonist, Daru, a rural schoolteacher who resists being forced into complicity with the French during the war between France and Algeria, which lasted from 1954 to 1962. Set against the background of the Algerian struggle for independence, the story masterfully explores all the important themes of the burdens of freedom, brotherhood, responsibility, moral ambiguity, and the inevitability of choice that Camus grappled with throughout his life.*

Algeria is a republic in northwest Africa bordered to the north by the Mediterranean Sea, to the east by Tunisia and Libya, to the south by Niger and Mali, and to the west by Mauritania and Morocco. Algeria was colonized by France in the nineteenth century and only gained its independence after a long and bloody battle with France in the 1960s under circumstances reflected in Albert Camus's "The Guest." After a round of elections in 1991 that were won by the Islamic Party but subsequently nullified by a court order, a movement toward Moslem fundamentalism was launched that resulted in the assassination of the head of state in July of 1992. In 1996, a new constitution excluding religious parties from politics was endorsed by a referendum. The country's first free presidential election was held in 1999 and the current head of state is Abdelaziz Bouteflika.

Before You Read

Consider the reasons why the main character, Daru, tries, but is unable to straddle the rift between native Algerians and the French.

◆

1   The schoolmaster was watching the two men climb toward him. One was on horseback, the other on foot. They had not yet tackled the abrupt rise leading to the schoolhouse built on the hillside. They were toiling onward, making slow progress in the snow, among the stones, on the vast expanse of the high, deserted plateau. From time to time the horse stumbled. Without hearing anything yet, he could see the breath issuing from the horse's nostrils. One of the men, at least, knew the region. They were following the trail although it had disappeared days ago under a layer of dirty white snow. The schoolmaster calculated that it would take them half an hour to get onto the hill. It was cold; he went back into the school to get a sweater.

2   He crossed the empty frigid classroom. On the blackboard the four rivers of France, drawn with four different colored chalks, had been flowing toward their estuaries for the past three days. Snow had suddenly fallen in mid-October after eight months of drought without the transition of rain, and the twenty pupils, more or less, who lived in the villages scattered over the plateau had stopped coming. With fair weather they would return. Daru now heated only the single room that was his lodging, adjoining the classroom and giving also onto the plateau to the east. Like the class windows, his window looked to the south too. On that side the school was a few kilometers from the point where the plateau began to slope toward the south. In clear weather could be seen the purple mass of the mountain range where the gap opened onto the desert.

3   Somewhat warmed, Daru returned to the window from which he had first seen the two men. They were no longer visible. Hence they must have tackled the rise. The sky was not so dark, for the snow had stopped falling during the night. The morning had opened with a dirty light which had scarcely become brighter as the ceiling of clouds lifted. At two in the afternoon it seemed as if the day were merely beginning. But still this was better than those three days when the thick snow was falling amidst unbroken darkness with little gusts of wind that rattled the double door of the classroom. Then Daru had spent long hours in

his room, leaving it only to go to the shed and feed the chickens or get some coal. Fortunately the delivery truck from Tadjid, the nearest village to the north, had brought his supplies two days before the blizzard. It would return in forty-eight hours.

4 Besides, he had enough to resist a siege, for the little room was cluttered with bags of wheat that the administration left as a stock to distribute to those of his pupils whose families had suffered from the drought. Actually they had all been victims because they were all poor. Every day Daru would distribute a ration to the children. They had missed it, he knew, during these bad days. Possibly one of the fathers or big brothers would come this afternoon and he could supply them with grain. It was just a matter of carrying them over to the next harvest. Now shiploads of wheat were arriving from France and the worst was over. But it would be hard to forget that poverty, that army of ragged ghosts wandering in the sunlight, the plateaus burned to a cinder month after month, the earth shriveled up little by little, literally scorched, every stone bursting into dust under one's foot. The sheep had died then by thousands and even a few men, here and there, sometimes without anyone's knowing.

5 In contrast with such poverty, he who lived almost like a monk in his remote schoolhouse, nonetheless satisfied with the little he had and with the rough life, had felt like a lord with his whitewashed walls, his narrow couch, his unpainted shelves, his well, and his weekly provision of water and food. And suddenly this snow, without warning, without the foretaste of rain. This is the way the region was, cruel to live in, even without men—who didn't help matters either. But Daru had been born here. Everywhere else, he felt exiled.

6 He stepped out onto the terrace in front of the schoolhouse. The two men were now halfway up the slope. He recognized the horseman as Balducci, the old gendarme he had known for a long time. Balducci was holding on the end of a rope an Arab who was walking behind him with hands bound and head lowered. The gendarme waved a greeting to which Daru did not reply, lost as he was in contemplation of the Arab dressed in a faded blue jellaba, his feet in sandals but covered with socks of heavy raw wool, his head surmounted by a narrow, short *chèche*. They were approaching. Balducci was holding back his horse in order not to hurt the Arab, and the group was advancing slowly.

7 Within earshot, Balducci shouted: "One hour to do the three kilometers from El Ameur!" Daru did not answer. Short and square in his thick sweater, he watched them climb. Not once had the Arab raised his head. "Hello" said Daru when they got up onto the terrace. "Come in and warm up." Balducci painfully got down from his horse without letting go the rope. From under his bristling mustache he smiled at the schoolmaster. His little dark eyes, deep-set under a tanned forehead,

and his mouth surrounded with wrinkles made him look attentive and studious. Daru took the bridle, led the horse to the shed, and came back to the two men, who were now waiting for him in the school. He led them into his room. "I am going to heat up the class-room," he said. "We'll be more comfortable there." When he entered the room again, Balducci was on the couch. He had undone the rope tying him to the Arab, who had squatted near the stove. His hands still bound, the *chèche* pushed back on his head, he was looking to-ward the window. At first Daru noticed only his huge lips, fat, smooth, almost Negroid; yet his nose was straight, his eyes were dark and full of fever. The *chèche* revealed an obstinate forehead and, under the weathered skin now rather discolored by the cold, the whole face had a restless and rebellious look that struck Daru when the Arab, turning his face toward him, looked him straight in the eyes. "Go into the other room," said the schoolmaster, "and I'll make you some mint tea." "Thanks," Balducci said. "What a chore! How I long for retire-ment." And addressing his prisoner in Arabic: "Come on, you." The Arab got up and, slowly, holding his bound wrists in front of him, went into the classroom.

8   With the tea, Daru brought a chair. But Balducci was already en-throned on the nearest pupil's desk and the Arab had squatted against the teacher's platform facing the stove, which stood between the desk and the window. When he held out the glass of tea to the prisoner, Daru hesitated at the sight of his bound hands. "He might perhaps be untied." "Sure," said Balducci, "that was for the trip." He started to get to his feet. But Daru, setting the glass on the floor, had knelt beside the Arab. Without saying anything, the Arab watched him with his fever-ish eyes. Once his hands were free, he rubbed his swollen wrists against each other, took the glass of tea, and sucked up the burning liq-uid in swift little sips.

9   "Good," said Daru. "And where are you headed?"

10   Balducci withdrew his mustache from the tea. "Here, son."

11   "Odd pupils! And you're spending the night?"

12   "No. I'm going back to El Ameur. And you will deliver this fellow to Tinguit. He is expected at police headquarters."

13   Balducci was looking at Daru with a friendly little smile.

14   "What's this story?" asked the schoolmaster. "Are you pulling my leg?"

15   "No, son. Those are the orders."

16   "The orders? I'm not . . ." Daru hesitated, not wanting to hurt the old Corsican. "I mean, that's not my job."

17   "What! What's the meaning of that? In wartime people do all kinds of jobs."

18   "Then I'll wait for the declaration of war!"

19   Balducci nodded.

20   "O.K. But the orders exist and they concern you too. Things are brewing, it appears. There is talk of a forthcoming revolt. We are mobilized, in a way."

21   Daru still had his obstinate look.

22   "Listen, son," Balducci said. "I like you and you must understand. There's only a dozen of us at El Ameur to patrol throughout the whole territory of a small department and I must get back in a hurry. I was told to hand this guy over to you and return without delay. He couldn't be kept there. His village was beginning to stir; they wanted to take him back. You must take him to Tinguit tomorrow before the day is over. Twenty kilometers shouldn't faze a husky fellow like you. After that, all will be over. You'll come back to your pupils and your comfortable life."

23   Behind the wall the horse could be heard snorting and pawing the earth. Daru was looking out the window. Decidedly, the weather was clearing and the light was increasing over the snowy plateau. When all the snow was melted, the sun would take over again and once more would burn the fields of stone. For days, still, the unchanging sky would shed its dry light on the solitary expanse where nothing had any connection with man.

24   "After all," he said, turning around toward Balducci, "what did he do?" And, before the gendarme had opened his mouth, he asked: "Does he speak French?"

25   "No, not a word. We had been looking for him for a month, but they were hiding him. He killed his cousin."

26   "Is he against us?"

27   "I don't think so. But you can never be sure."

28   "Why did he kill?"

29   "A family squabble, I think. One owed the other grain, it seems. It's not at all clear. In short, he killed his cousin with a billhook. You know, like a sheep, *kreezk!*"

30   Balducci made the gesture of drawing a blade across his throat and the Arab, his attention attracted, watched him with a sort of anxiety. Daru felt a sudden wrath against the man, against all men with their rotten spite, their tireless hates, their blood lust.

31   But the kettle was singing on the stove. He served Balducci more tea, hesitated, then served the Arab again, who, a second time, drank avidly. His raised arms made the jellaba fall open and the schoolmaster saw his thin, muscular chest.

32   "Thanks, kid," Balducci said. "And now, I'm off."

33   He got up and went toward the Arab, taking a small rope from his pocket.

34   "What are you going?" Daru asked dryly.

35   Balducci, disconcerted, showed him the rope.

36   "Don't bother."

37   The old gendarme hesitated. "It's up to you. Of course, you are armed?"

38   "I have my shotgun."

39   "Where?"

40   "In the trunk."

41   "You ought to have it near your bed."

42   "Why? I have nothing to fear."

43   "You're crazy, son. If there's an uprising, no one is safe, we're all in the same boat."

44   "I'll defend myself. I'll have time to see them coming."

45   Balducci began to laugh, then suddenly the mustache covered the white teeth.

46   "You'll have time? O.K. That's just what I was saying. You have always been a little cracked. That's why I like you, my son was like that."

47   At the same time he took out his revolver and put it on the desk.

48   "Keep it; I don't need two weapons from here to El Ameur."

49   The revolver shone against the black paint of the table. When the gendarme turned toward him, the schoolmaster caught the smell of leather and horseflesh.

50   "Listen, Balducci," Daru said suddenly, "every bit of this disgusts me, and first of all your fellow here. But I won't hand him over. Fight, yes, if I have to. But not that."

51   The old gendarme stood in front of him and looked at him severely.

52   "You're being a fool," he said slowly. "I don't like it either. You don't get used to putting a rope on a man even after years of it, and you're even ashamed—yes, ashamed. But you can't let them have their way."

53   "I won't hand him over," Daru said again.

54   "It's an order, son, and I repeat it."

55   "That's right. Repeat to them what I've said to you: I won't hand him over."

56   Balducci made a visible effort to reflect. He looked at the Arab and at Daru. At last he decided.

57   "No, I won't tell them anything. If you want to drop us, go ahead; I'll not denounce you. I have an order to deliver the prisoner and I'm doing so. And now you'll just sign this paper for me."

58   "There's no need. I'll not deny that you left him with me."

59   "Don't be mean with me. I know you'll tell the truth. You're from hereabouts and you are a man. But you must sign, that's the rule."

60   Daru opened his drawer, took out a little square bottle of purple ink, the red wooden penholder with the "sergeant-major" pen he used for making models of penmanship, and signed. The gendarme carefully folded the paper and put it into his wallet. Then he moved toward the door.

61   "I'll see you off," Daru said.

62 "No," said Balducci. "There's no use being polite. You insulted me."

63 He looked at the Arab, motionless in the same spot, sniffed peevishly, and turned away toward the door. "Good-by, son," he said. The door shut behind him. Balducci appeared suddenly outside the window and then disappeared. His footsteps were muffled by the snow. The horse stirred on the other side of the wall and several chickens fluttered in fright. A moment later Balducci reappeared outside the window leading the horse by the bridle. He walked toward the little rise without turning around and disappeared from sight with the horse following him. A big stone could be heard bouncing down. Daru walked back toward the prisoner, who, without stirring, never took his eyes off him. "Wait," the schoolmaster said in Arabic and went toward the bedroom. As he was going through the door, he had a second thought, went to the desk, took the revolver, and stuck it in his pocket. Then, without looking back, he went into his room.

64 For some time he lay on his couch watching the sky gradually close over, listening to the silence. It was this silence that had seemed painful to him during the first days here, after the war. He had requested a post in the little town at the base of the foothills separating the upper plateaus from the desert. There, rocky walls, green and black to the north, pink and lavender to the south, marked the frontier of eternal summer. He had been named to a post farther north, on the plateau itself. In the beginning, the solitude and the silence had been hard for him on these wastelands peopled only by stones. Occasionally, furrows suggested cultivation, but they had been dug to uncover a certain kind of stone good for building. The only plowing here was to harvest rocks. Elsewhere a thin layer of soil accumulated in the hollows would be scraped out to enrich paltry village gardens. This is the way it was: bare rock covered three quarters of the region. Towns sprang up, flourished, then disappeared; men came by, loved one another or fought bitterly, then died. No one in this desert, neither he nor his guest, mattered. And yet, outside this desert neither of them, Daru knew, could have really lived.

65 When he got up, no noise came from the classroom. He was amazed at the unmixed joy he derived from the mere thought that the Arab might have fled and that he would be alone with no decision to make. But the prisoner was there. He had merely stretched out between the stove and the desk. With eyes open, he was staring at the ceiling. In that position, his thick lips were particularly noticeable, giving him a pouting look. "Come," said Daru. The Arab got up and followed him. In the bedroom, the schoolmaster pointed to a chair near the table under the window. The Arab sat down without taking his eyes of Daru.

66 "Are you hungry?"

67 "Yes," the prisoner said.

68   Daru set the table for two. He took flour and oil, shaped a cake in a frying-pan and lighted the little stove that functioned on bottled gas. While the cake was cooking, he went out to the shed to get cheese, eggs, dates, and condensed milk. When the cake was done he set it on the window sill to cool, heated some condensed milk diluted with water, and beat the eggs into an omelette. In one of his motions he knocked against the revolver stuck in his right pocket. He set the bowl down, went into the classroom, and put the revolver in his desk drawer. When he came back to the room, night was falling. He put on the light and served the Arab. "Eat," he said. The Arab took a piece of the cake, lifted it eagerly to his mouth, and stopped short.

69   "And you?" he asked.

70   "After you. I'll eat too."

71   The thick lips opened slightly. The Arab hesitated, then bit into the cake determinedly.

72   The meal over, the Arab looked at the schoolmaster. "Are you the judge?"

73   "No, I'm simply keeping you until tomorrow."

74   "Why do you eat with me?"

75   "I'm hungry."

76   The Arab fell silent. Daru got up and went out. He brought back a folding bed from the shed, set it up between the table and the stove, perpendicular to his own bed. From a large suitcase which, upright in a corner, served as a shelf for papers, he took two blankets and arranged them on the camp bed. Then he stopped, felt useless, and sat down on his bed. There was nothing more to do or to get ready. He had to look at this man. He looked at him, therefore, trying to imagine his face bursting with rage. He couldn't do so. He could see nothing but the dark yet shining eyes and the animal mouth.

77   "Why did you kill him?" he asked in a voice whose hostile tone surprised him.

78   The Arab looked away.

79   "He ran away. I ran after him."

80   He raised his eyes to Daru again and they were full of a sort of woeful interrogation. "Now what will they do to me?"

81   "Are you afraid?"

82   He stiffened, turning his eyes away.

83   "Are you sorry?"

84   The Arab stared at him openmouthed. Obviously he did not understand. Daru's annoyance was growing. At the same time he felt awkward and self-conscious with his big body wedged between the two beds.

85   "Lie down there," he said impatiently. "That's your bed."

86   The Arab didn't move. He called to Daru:

87   "Tell me!"

88 The schoolmaster looked at him.

89 "Is the gendarme coming back tomorrow?"

90 "I don't know."

91 "Are you coming with us?"

92 "I don't know. Why?"

93 The prisoner got up and stretched out on top of the blankets, his feet toward the window. The light from the electric bulb shone straight into his eyes and he closed them at once.

94 "Why?" Daru repeated, standing beside the bed.

95 The Arab opened his eyes under the blinding light and looked at him, trying not to blink.

96 "Come with us," he said.

97 In the middle of the night, Daru was still not asleep. He had gone to bed after undressing completely; he generally slept naked. But when he suddenly realized that he had nothing on, he hesitated. He felt vulnerable and the temptation came to him to put his clothes back on. Then he shrugged his shoulders; after all, he wasn't a child and, if need be, he could break his adversary in two. From his bed he could observe him, lying on his back, still motionless with his eyes closed under the harsh light. When Daru turned out the light, the darkness seemed to coagulate all of a sudden. Little by little, the night came back to life in the window where the starless sky was stirring gently. The schoolmaster soon made out the body laying at his feet. The Arab still did not move, but his eyes seemed open. A faint wind was prowling around the schoolhouse. Perhaps it would drive away the clouds and the sun would reappear.

98 During the night the wind increased. The hens fluttered a little and then were silent. The Arab turned over on his side with his back to Daru, who thought he heard him moan. Then he listened for his guest's breathing, become heavier and more regular. He listened to that breath so close to him and mused without being able to go to sleep. In this room where he had been sleeping alone for a year, this presence bothered him. But it bothered him also by imposing on him a sort of brotherhood he knew well but refused to accept in the present circumstances. Men who share the same rooms, soldiers or prisoners, develop a strange alliance as if, having cast off their armor with their clothing, they fraternized every evening, over and above their differences, in the ancient community of dream and fatigue. But Daru shook himself; he didn't like such musings, and it was essential to sleep.

99 A little later, however, when the Arab stirred slightly, the schoolmaster was still not asleep. When the prisoner made a second move, he stiffened, on the alert. The Arab was lifting himself slowly on his arms with almost the motion of a sleepwalker. Seated upright in bed, he waited motionless without turning his head toward Daru, as if he were

listening attentively. Daru did not stir, it had just occurred to him that the revolver was still in the drawer of his desk. It was better to act at once. Yet he continued to observe the prisoner, who, with the same slithery motion, put his feet on the ground, waited again, then began to stand up slowly. Daru was about to call out to him when the Arab began to walk, in a quite natural but extraordinarily silent way. He was heading toward the door at the end of the room that opened into the shed. He lifted the latch with precaution and went out, pushing the door behind him but without shutting it. Daru had not stirred. "He is running away," he merely thought. "Good riddance!" Yet he listened attentively. The hens were not fluttering; the guest must be on the plateau. A faint sound of water reached him, and he didn't know what it was until the Arab again stood framed in the doorway, closed the door carefully, and came back to bed without a sound. Then Daru turned his back on him and fell asleep. Still later he seemed, from the depths of his sleep, to hear furtive steps around the schoolhouse. "I'm dreaming! I'm dreaming!" he repeated to himself. And he went on sleeping.

100   When he awoke, the sky was clear; the loose window let in a cold, pure air. The Arab was asleep, hunched up under the blankets now, his mouth open, utterly relaxed. But when Daru shook him, he started dreadfully, staring at Daru with wild eyes as if he had never seen him and such a frightened expression that the schoolmaster stepped back. "Don't be afraid. It's me. You must eat." The Arab nodded his head and said yes. Calm had returned to his face, but his expression was vacant and listless.

101   The coffee was ready. They drank it seated together on the folding bed as they munched their pieces of the cake. Then Daru led the Arab under the shed and showed him the faucet where he washed. He went back into the room, folded the blankets and the bed, made his own bed and put the room in order. Then he went through the classroom and out onto the terrace. The sun was already rising in the blue sky; a soft, bright light was bathing the deserted plateau. On the ridge the snow was melting in spots. The stones were about to reappear. Crouched on the edge of the plateau, the schoolmaster looked at the deserted expanse. He thought of Balducci. He had hurt him, for he had sent him off in a way as if he didn't want to be associated with him. He could still hear the gendarme's farewell and, without knowing why, he felt strangely empty and vulnerable. At that moment, from the other side of the schoolhouse, the prisoner coughed. Daru listened to him almost despite himself and then, furious, threw a pebble that whistled through the air before sinking into the snow. That man's stupid crime revolted him, but to hand him over was contrary to honor. Merely thinking of it made him smart with humiliation. And he cursed at one and the same time his own people who had sent him this Arab and the Arab too who had dared to kill and not managed to get away. Daru got

up, walked in a circle on the terrace, waited motionless, and then went back into the schoolhouse.

102   The Arab, leaning over the cement floor of the shed, was washing his teeth with two fingers. Daru looked at him and said: "Come." He went back into the room ahead of the prisoner. He slipped a hunting-jack on over his sweater and put on walking-shoes. Standing, he waited until the Arab had put on his *chèche* and sandals. They went into the classroom and the schoolmaster pointed to the exit, saying: "Go ahead." The fellow didn't budge. "I'm coming," said Daru. The Arab went out. Daru went back into the room and made a package of pieces of rusk, dates, and sugar. In the classroom, before going out, he hesitated a second in front of his desk, then crossed the threshold and locked the door. "That's the way," he said. He started toward the east, followed by the prisoner. But, a short distance from the schoolhouse, he thought he heard a slight sound behind them. He retraced his steps and examined the surroundings of the house; there was no one there. The Arab watched him without seeming to understand. "Come on," said Daru.

103   They walked for an hour and rested beside a sharp peak of lime-stone. The snow was melting faster and faster and the sun was drinking up the puddles at once, rapidly cleaning the plateau, which gradually dried and vibrated like the air itself. When they resumed walking, the ground rang under their feet. From time to time a bird rent the space in front of them with a joyful cry. Daru breathed in deeply the fresh morning light. He felt a sort of rapture before the vast familiar expanse, now almost entirely yellow under its dome of blue sky. They walked an hour more, descending toward the south. They reached a level height made up of crumbly rocks. From there on, the plateau sloped down, eastward, toward a low plain where there were a few spindly trees and, to the south, toward outcroppings of rock that gave the land-scape a chaotic look.

104   Daru surveyed the two directions. There was nothing but the sky on the horizon. Not a man could be seen. He turned toward the Arab, who was looking at him blankly. Daru held out the package to him. "Take it," he said. "There are dates, bread, and sugar. You can hold out for two days. Here are a thousand francs too." The Arab took the pack-age and the money but kept his full hands at chest level as if he didn't know what to do with what was being given him. "Now look," the schoolmaster said as he pointed in the direction of the east, "there's the way to Tinguit. You have a two-hour walk. At Tinguit you'll find the administration and the police. They are expecting you." The Arab looked toward the east, still holding the package and the money against his chest. Daru took his elbow and turned him rather roughly toward the south. At the foot of the height on which they stood could be seen a faint path. "That's the trail across the plateau. In a day's walk from here you'll find pasturelands and the first nomads. They'll take

you in and shelter you according to their law." The Arab had now turned toward Daru and a sort of panic was visible in his expression. "Listen," he said. Daru shook his head: "No, be quiet. Now I'm leaving you." He turned his back on him, took two long steps in the direction of the school, looked hesitantly at the motionless Arab, and started off again. For a few minutes he heard nothing but his own step resounding on the cold ground and did not turn his head. A moment later, however, he turned around. The Arab was still there on the edge of the hill, his arms hanging now, and he was looking at the schoolmaster. Daru felt something rise in his throat. But he swore with impatience, waved vaguely, and started off again. He had already gone some distance when he again stopped and looked. There was no longer anyone on the hill.

105   Daru hesitated. The sun was now rather high in the sky and was beginning to beat down on his head. The schoolmaster retraced his steps, at first somewhat uncertainly, then with decision. When he reached the little hill, he was bathed in sweat. He climbed it as fast as he could and stopped, out of breath, at the top. The rock-fields to the south stood out sharply against the blue sky, but on the plain to the west a steamy heat was already rising. And in that slight haze, Daru, with heavy heart, made out the Arab walking slowly on the road to prison.

106   A little later, standing before the window of the classroom, the schoolmaster was watching the clear light bathing the whole surface of the plateau, but he hardly saw it. Behind him on the blackboard, among the winding French rivers, sprawled the clumsily chalked-up words he had just read: "You handed over our brother. You will pay for this." Daru looked at the sky, the plateau, and, beyond, the invisible lands stretching all the way to the sea. In his vast landscape he had loved so much, he was alone.

✧ *Evaluating the Text*

1. What do you know about Daru's background that would explain why in his present circumstances he does not wish to step outside of his role as teacher to enforce the rulings of the authorities? Between what conflicting loyalties is Daru torn?

2. What can you infer about Daru's past relationship with Balducci from his reaction to Balducci's request?

3. What is the crime of which the Arab has been accused? How is it related to the food shortage afflicting the community?

4. How do the descriptions of the physical environment (the stones, the sudden snow and melting that follows) underscore the human drama?

5. How does Daru's feeling of common humanity make it increasingly difficult for him to turn the Arab over to the authorities? How does Daru try to avoid the responsibility for turning in the Arab?

6. How are Daru's actions toward the Arab misunderstood by the local populace who are spying on him? What is the significance of the message written on the blackboard?

7. What outside sources of knowledge about historical and literary contexts would be useful in interpreting this story? Why would it be helpful to know something about existentialism, the history of the Algerian revolt, or Camus's own childhood growing up as a non-Arab French citizen in Algeria?

8. Why, in your opinion, does the Arab choose to go to the place where he will be imprisoned or even executed although he now has money, food, and the freedom to go wherever he wants?

✦ Exploring Different Perspectives

1. How do the stories by Camus and Gloria Anzaldúa (see "Cervicide") dramatize the dehumanizing effect of politics on personal relationships?

2. How do both "The Guest" and the autobiographical account by Palden Gyatso dramatize the existential predicament of the exile?

✦ Extending Viewpoints through Writing

1. Describe the last time a guest stayed with you or your family, or a time when you were a guest in someone else's home. What insight did these experiences give you into Camus's story?

2. Just as the protagonist in the story finds he cannot live a private life outside of public events, do you remember where you were and what you thought immediately before and after you heard the news of an historical event, such as September 11, 2001?

3. Describe your expectations about what constitutes a good story. For example, do you want a story that will surprise you or one that is predictable? What are some of your favorite works of fiction, and how do they fulfill your expectations?

Connecting Cultures

---◆---

George Carlin, "A Place for Your Stuff"

Do upwardly striving Americans equate the accumulation of stuff with a rise in social class comparable to that described by Gayatri Devi in "A Princess Remembers" (see Chapter 1)?

Napoleon A. Chagnon, "Doing Fieldwork among the Yanomamö"

Compare Chagnon's study of the Yanomamö with Colin M. Turnbull's study of the Mbuti pygmies (see "The Mbuti Pygmies" in Chapter 1) in terms of cooperation versus aggression as key principles around which each culture is organized.

David R. Counts, "Too Many Bananas"

Compare the way sex and money solidify social ties in modern cultures, according to Raymonde Carroll (see "Sex, Money, and Success" in Chapter 5) with the way the reciprocal exchange of food and goods functions in tribal cultures such as in New Guinea, described by David R. Counts.

Palden Gyatso, "Autobiography of a Tibetan Monk"

Compare the overlapping perspectives of Palden Gyatso and Rae Yang (see "At the Center of the Storm," Chapter 6) on Chinese communism.

Jesse W. Nash, "Confucius and the VCR"

How is the conflict between the Asian emphasis on respect for parents and the American desire for independence an important theme in Jesse W. Nash's article and in Kazuo Ishiguro's story "A Family Supper" (Chapter 1)?

Poranee Natadecha-Sponsel, "Individualism as an American Cultural Value"

Discuss Natadecha-Sponsel's essay in relationship to the picture of American society portrayed in sitcoms as described by Anita Gates (see "America Has a Class System. See 'Frasier'" in Chapter 5).

Itabari Njeri, "What's in a Name?"

Compare Njeri's analysis with Gayle Pemberton's account (see "Antidisestablishmentarianism" in Chapter 1) in terms of how important it is to African Americans to achieve their own sense of self-worth in a white society.

Gloria Anzaldúa, "Cervicide"

How do the stories by Gloria Anzaldúa and Mahdokht Kashkuli (see "The Button," Chapter 5) dramatize the predicament of families faced with dehumanizing choices?

Albert Camus, "The Guest"

How do the stories by Camus and Panos Ioannides (see "Gregory," Chapter 6) dramatize the conflict between loyalty to the state and compassion for another human being?

8

Customs, Rituals,
and Entertainment

♦

In the customs, rituals, and entertainment that a society embraces, we can see most clearly the hidden cultural logic and unconscious assumptions people in that society rely on to interpret everything that goes on in their world. Customs, rituals, and even entertainment that may seem bizarre or strange to an outsider appear entirely normal and natural to those within the culture. Unfortunately, the potential for conflict exists as soon as people from different cultures whose "natural" ways do not coincide make contact with each other.

As communications, immigration, and travel make the world smaller, the potential for cross-cultural misunderstanding accelerates. Correspondingly, the need to become aware of the extent to which our own and other people's conclusions about the world are guided by different cultural presuppositions grows. Analysis of the customs of culture other than our own allows us to temporarily put aside our taken-for-granted ways of seeing the world, even if we are normally unaware of the extent to which we rely on these implicit premises—to understand that the meanings we give to events, actions, and statements are not their only possible meanings.

The range and diversity of the selections in this chapter will allow you to temporarily replace your own way of perceiving the world and become aware, perhaps for the first time, of your own cultural assumptions that govern your interpretations of the world.

The cultural value placed on having good teeth in America, provided Slavenka Drakulić (as told in "On Bad Teeth") with a means to understand crucial differences between Americans and her fellow East Europeans. Gino Del Guercio's "The Secrets of Haiti's Living Dead" reveals that, in contrast to its stereotyped image, voodoo is part of a cohesive system of social control in Haiti. Octavio Paz, in "Fiesta," explores the important role fiestas play in Mexican culture and their relationship to the Mexican national character. According to Ilan Stavans, in "Santa

Selena," the Hispanic pop singer has become an icon in popular culture since her death in 1995. Valerie Steele and John S. Major in "China Chic: East Meets West" explain the unsuspected political and social meanings of the custom of foot binding in the context of Chinese culture. Liza Dalby, the first non-Japanese to live as a geisha, tells us in "Kimono" that the garment constitutes "a social code" replete with meanings about the wearer's social class and marital status, and is an eloquent expression of Japanese values.

The Egyptian writer, Nabil Gorgy, in "Cairo Is a Small City," dramatizes how a ruthless engineer is held accountable to the traditional Bedouin concept of justice in modern-day Egypt. Based on real events, "Looking for a Rain God" by Bessie Head reveals how a family in drought-plagued Botswana came to sacrifice their children in exchange for rain.

Liza Dalby

Kimono

◆————

*Liza Dalby received a doctorate in anthropology from Stanford Univer-
sity. Dalby, who is fluent in Japanese, became the only non-Japanese ever
accepted by geishas during a yearlong residence in Kyoto. The profession
of geisha originated in the eighteenth century. As their popularity grew,
geisha became society's fashion arbiters, and their sophisticated style had
a great impact on the art, music, and literature of nineteenth-century
Japan. The world of the geisha offers a unique glimpse into a disciplined
and glamorous way of life that is quintessentially Japanese. Dalby is the
author of* Kimono: Fashion in Culture *(1993). Her latest work is* The
Tale of Murasaki *(2000). This piece, a chapter drawn from her book*
Geisha *(1998), provides insight into the social codes embodied in the kimono, the traditional costume worn by geisha.*

Before You Read

Consider what you know about the kimono and what it suggests about
Japanese cultural values to you.

————◆————

1   A month after I returned to the United States, I was invited to appear on the "To Tell the Truth" television show because of my odd distinction of being the only non-Japanese ever to have become a geisha.
The object for the panelists would be to guess the identity of the real
"geisha anthropologist," so I had dressed myself and the two women
pretending to be me in cotton kimono. As we walked through the program's format during rehearsal, each of us was to announce, "My
name is Liza Crihfield," then step ten paces to our seats facing the
panel at stage left. The director shook her head in dismay before we
even took our places. "Stop," she called. "You've just given it away."

2   After my year-long training as a geisha, the technique of walking
gracefully in a kimono had become second nature. The two poseurs,
though they had diligently studied my research proposal in order to
anticipate questions from the panel, could not, in an afternoon, master
the art of walking. It was quite obvious who was who before we even
opened our mouths.

3   Repeatedly I showed them the technique of sliding one foot,
pigeon-toed, in front of the other with knees slightly bent. I tried to
convey how the shoulders should have a barely perceptible slope, how

the arms should be carried gracefully, close to the body. We tried to minimize the contrast. They made great efforts to mimic an authentic movement, while I attempted to recreate the clumsiness of my own first experience in wearing kimono. Even so, on the show the next day, none of the panelists except Bill Cullen was fooled a bit. I am convinced that our body language had "told the truth."

4   Learning to wear kimono properly was one of the most difficult aspects of my geisha training. But it was essential so that I could fit without awkwardness into a group of geisha. No one gives geisha formal lessons in how to wear kimono. Most of them have learned how to move gracefully in kimono by virtue of their practice of Japanese dance. Awkward gestures are noticed immediately by the watchful mothers, who seldom fail to utter a reproof to a fidgety maiko.

5   When I lived in Pontochō, the sardonic old auntie who worked at the Mitsuba invariably had some critical remark when I checked in for okāsan's approval of my outfit before going off to a teahouse engagement. I usually managed to put together a feasible color combination of kimono, obi, and *obi-age* (the sheer, scarf-like sash that is tied so as to be barely visible above the obi), but it was many months before I could proceed on my way to a party without something having to be untied and retied properly. Only when I reached the point where I could put on the entire outfit in less than twenty minutes by myself did I finally win the grudging respect of the old auntie who tended the inn.

The Language of Kimono

6   Wearing kimono is one of the things that distinguishes geisha from other women in Japan. Geisha wear their kimono with a flair just not seen in middle-class ladies who, once or twice a year, pull out their traditional dress to attend a wedding, a graduation, or perhaps a retirement ceremony. They are uncomfortable in the unaccustomed garment, and it shows.

7   To the untutored eye, the kimono a geisha chooses are much the same as those any other Japanese woman might wear. The resplendent trailing black robe with deep reverse décolletage is the geisha's official outfit, but she actually wears it infrequently. Her usual garment is an ankle-length, medium-sleeve silk kimono in slightly more subdued colors than those other women wear. The subtle differences in sleeve openings, in color, or in the manner of tying the obi that set a geisha apart are not immediately obvious, even to many Japanese. But together with her natural way of wearing the outfit, such cues are visible to an observer who is sensitive to the language of kimono. A connoisseur will know the wide vocabulary of elements that varies according to the region, class, age, and profession of the wearer. He or she will be able to recognize a geisha easily.

8   The elements of the kimono costume in fact constitute a social code. This was revealed to me when I inadvertently mixed up some of them early in my geisha career, before I had acquired an appropriate wardrobe from the taller geisha in the neighborhood. In the beginning, the only kimono I owned was one that Yuriko, my well-to-do middle-aged friend in Tokyo, had given me. It was a lovely burnt orange color with a pattern of weeping willow branches in brown shot with gold. She had worn it a few times many years ago, before she had married. Now the colors were inappropriate to her age, and besides, she told me, she never wore kimono any more. She doubted she could even tie the obi by herself.

9   When okāsan first asked me to help her out at a party at the Mitsuba so I could see the geisha's side of the affair, I gladly agreed and planned to wear my only kimono. As she helped me put it on, she remarked that, lovely as it was, it would be entirely unsuitable in the future. It was the sort of thing a stylish bourgeois young lady might wear, not a geisha. It would have to do for that evening, though. She loaned me a tea-green obi with a pale cream orchid dyed into the back and gave me an old obi-age sash that she had worn as an apprentice many years ago.

10   The obi-age was of sheer white silk with a pattern of scattered fans done in a dapple-effect tie-dying technique called *kanoko*. Okāsan slipped it over the pad that held the back loop of the obi secure, and as she tied it in the front she said, "Here is a trick for keeping the front knot in place. All the geisha tie their obi-age this way." She made a little loose slipknot in one end, making sure the red fan pattern showed at the front of the knot, then drew the other end through. The effect was of a simply knotted sash, but without the bulk of both ends tied together. She smoothed and tucked this light sash down behind the top of the obi, so that only a glimpse of the red and white was visible. At the time, I was reminded of letting a bit of lace show at the neckline of a blouse. Since the obi-age is technically considered part of the "kimono underwear," my thought was more apt than I first realized.

11   Still wearing this outfit, I went out after the party. Later that evening I met a pair of college teachers at a nearby bar. We struck up a conversation, and I told them a bit about the circumstances of my being in Japan. The bartender, half listening in, finally exclaimed, "Aha, now I realize what was bothering me about you. You said you were a student, and I could tell that you're an unmarried young lady from a proper family. Your kimono is perfectly appropriate. But I think it's your sash, something about the way it's tied, that struck me as odd for a young lady—something too much like a geisha about it." As I had not yet said anything about the precise subject of my study, I was astounded at the acuity of the man's eye.

12   Incongruent as it was, my outfit that evening expressed my odd position rather well. Not exactly an *ojōsan*, a demure young lady, not yet a geisha, I was attired in disparate elements of each style, so I presented an odd aspect to someone with a perspicacious eye for dress. The bartender had received all the messages my outfit conveyed but was puzzled at the totality, as well he might have been.

Kimono Wearers

13   *Mono* means "thing," and with *ki-* from *kiru,* "to wear," kimono originally meant simply "a garment." Not all things to wear are kimono, however. Today, the relevant distinction is between *yōfuku,* "Western apparel," and *wafuku,* "native apparel": kimono. Western clothes, following all the latest fashion trends, are what most Japanese women wear most of the time. Some women don't even own a kimono, and many, like my friend Yuriko in Tokyo, have forgotten how to wear those they have tucked away in the Japanese equivalent of cedar chests. Few if any social occasions in Japan now would exclude a woman because she was not dressed in kimono.

14   Most women own a black kimono dyed with the family crest that they will pull out of a drawer for a few highly formal occasions. This garment was probably the main item in their wedding trousseaux. Families are encouraged to buy their young daughters the gaudy, long-sleeved *furisode*-style kimono for New Year, so a woman often has one of these packed away from her girlhood as well. Such occasional use means that most Japanese women are nearly as unaccustomed to the proper manner of wearing kimono as a foreigner would be. They sigh with relief when they can finally unwind the stiff obi from around their waists and slip back into comfortable Western clothes.

15   As my eye became educated to the niceties of kimono, I was more and more struck by how many women who put one on fail to achieve a graceful demeanor. A good time to view masses of kimono is the New Year holiday. Young girls, who trudge to school in loafers all year, suddenly mince about in traditional zōri that match their long-sleeved kimono. Arms swinging, knees pumping up and down as they do in skirts, the girls flock on the streets like pinioned flamingos. Colorful and clumsy, they brighten the bleak January streets briefly before donning their familiar blue and white school uniforms again at the end of holidays. Women over fifty generally feel more at home than this in kimono. They probably wore the traditional dress as children and feel a pang of nostalgia when they put it on.

16   Middle-class women of means are now rediscovering the conspicuous display afforded by kimono. The wearing of wafuku, as opposed to the Cacharel skirts and Dior blouses of their friends, has become a fashionable hobby. A woman who would blanch at spending two hundred

dollars on a dress could easily justify spending five times as much on a kimono. After all, a kimono is an investment. It won't go out of style, it can accommodate thickening midriffs without alteration, and it can be passed on to one's daughters. In the status game, it is difficult to spend more than a thousand dollars on even the most skillfully tailored Western dress. But with kimono, one can easily wear thousands of dollars on one's back without looking too obvious. The expensive yet understated possibilities of kimono are ideally suited to this aspect of fashion one-upmanship.

17   Yet the wearing of kimono is not without problems in modern Japan. Aside from the matter of expense, kimono inherently belong to a different style and pace of life. That life still thrives here and there, but usually under special circumstances—as are found, for example, in the geisha world. Few would call the beautiful kimono a practical garment for modern living.

Floors versus Chairs

18   The kimono was once part of a cultural totality that embraced every aspect of daily life. The garment was influenced by, and in turn it influenced, canons of feminine beauty that enhanced some parts of the body (nape, ankle, and hip) and concealed others (waist, legs, and bosom). Not surprisingly, the kimono flatters a figure found most often in Japanese women: a long waist and long thigh but small bust and short calf. Cultural notions of ideal beauty seem to influence actual physical characteristics, however; as Western notions of long-legged, big-bosomed glamour have affected postwar Japan, amazingly, such physical types seem to have blossomed. The cultivation of this new type of figure does not bode well for the kimono.

19   The wearing of kimono was also perfectly integrated into the arrangement of living space in the traditional Japanese home. Much of the activity of daily life was conducted close to the floor, on low tables where people knelt, not sat, to accomplish tasks. To Japanese, a shod foot treading the floor inside the house would be as gauche as shoes on a Westerner's dining room table. Floors were clean enough to permit trailing garments, and the wives of wealthy men let their robes swirl about their feet as they glided down polished halls from one tatami mat room to another. The trailing hem contributed to the overall balance of the outfit, creating an effect of elegance. Again, nowadays one must look to the geisha's formal kimono to see what that style was like. Ordinary modern kimono are adjusted, by a fold at the waist, to reach only the ankle. The line, rather than flowing, is somewhat stiff and tubular.

20   The integration of cultural elements that formed the whole of which kimono was a part has now fragmented. The single most nefari-

ous artifact in this respect is the chair. Chairs are antithetical to kimono, physically and aesthetically.

21　　　Women who wear kimono of course sit on chairs, but the garment
is poorly adapted to this posture; it is designed for sitting on the floor.
When Americans sit on the floor, this implies a greater degree of relaxation than does sitting on a chair. Not so in Japan. A chair is comfortable and relaxed compared to the straight-spine posture required to sit
properly on the tatami floor. There are two different verbs meaning "to
sit" in Japanese, depending on whether it is on the floor or in a chair. If
in a chair, then one literally "drapes one's hips" there.

22　　　When, out of determination to show the Japanese that we understand etiquette, we Westerners endure a tea ceremony or traditional
banquet sitting on the floor, after thirty minutes our knees are jelly and
our legs so benumbed they refuse to obey our brain's directive to
stand. We are consoled that young Japanese have much the same problem. Part of the exhaustion we feel is due to the gradual slumping of
our unsupported backs. Skirts ride up, pants become constricting, narrow belts bite into our waists. But the kimono that became disheveled
and kept us perched uncomfortably at the edge of a chair now offers
back support with the obi, and it turns out to be almost comfortable in
the posture for which it was designed.

23　　　The back view of a kneeling kimono-clad woman shows off the
garment to its best advantage. The obi often has a large single design
woven or painted on the back part, which forms a large, flat loop in the
common style of tying known as *taiko* (drum). This flat drum, not quite
a square foot in area, is framed by the contrasting color of the kimono.
I have often been struck by the artfulness of a seated figure, Japanese
style. In a chair, the drum of the obi is not only hidden from view, it is
a positive nuisance, as it prevents one from sitting back.

24　　　The fact that the back view of a kimono-clad figure is such an aesthetic focus has to do, I think, with the way a traditional Japanese room
is arranged and how a woman in public (such as a geisha) moves and
is viewed on a social occasion. At a banquet, low, narrow tables are laid
end to end, forming a continuous row that parallels three sides of the
room. People sit on individual flat square cushions along the outer
edge of this U-shaped arrangement. In effect, everyone sits next to
someone, but nobody sits across from anyone else.

25　　　The seating positions are hierarchical: the places of highest status
are in front of the alcove, and the lowest are those closest to the entrance. People usually have a keen sense of where they stand vis-à-vis
one another's status in Japan, so the problem of where they sit is
solved with a minimum of polite protestation. When everyone has
taken a seat, the banquet can begin. After it has started, however, people leave their original places to wander across the center of the room,
squatting temporarily in front of different personages to make a toast

or have a short conversation. This center space is a no-man's-land, ringed as it is by the prescribed statuses of the proper seats on the other side of the tables. Here more relaxed conviviality can occur.

26   When geisha attend upon a banquet, they often move into the center free space, kneeling for a few minutes across from one guest after another. As they do so, their backs are turned toward an entire row of tables on the other side of the room. The first time I was a guest at a traditional banquet, I noticed the beauty of the backs of the geisha as they talked with other guests. Upon reflection, it hardly seems accidental that the view from that particular vantage point was so striking.

✧ Evaluating the Text

1. In what way does the kimono serve as a complex signaling system that embodies and communicates traditional Japanese values?

2. Dalby says that "chairs are antithetical to kimono, physically and aesthetically." What does she mean by this, and how does this insight provide a glimpse into a traditional world that modern Japanese remember somewhat nostalgically?

3. What insights do you gain from this account as to why Dalby went to Japan to learn to be a geisha?

✧ Exploring Different Perspectives

1. Compare and contrast the constraints the wearing of kimono imposes with the lotus foot described by Valerie Steele and John S. Major in "China Chic" as symbols of femininity and status.

2. Compare and contrast the meanings that veiling has in Middle Eastern societies, as alluded to by Nabil Gorgy in his story "Cairo Is a Small City," with that of the kimono in Japanese culture as described by Dalby.

✧ Extending Viewpoints through Writing

1. To what extent do elegant outfits such as a ball gown or white tie and tails perform the same function in Western culture that the kimono does in Japan?

2. To what extent does the kimono enforce a very specified gender role for women? What physical and psychological constraints does it impose? Why would it be unlikely to catch on in the United States?

Slavenka Drakulić

On Bad Teeth

◆

Slavenka Drakulić is a leading Croatian journalist and novelist. Her insightful commentary on East European affairs first appeared in her columns in the magazine Danas, *published in Zagreb. She is a regular contributor to* The Nation, The New Republic, *and* The New York Times Magazine. *Her novel,* Holograms of Fear *(1992), received the* Independent *Foreign Fiction Award. Her nonfiction works include* How We Survived Communism and Even Laughed *(1992) and* Balkan Express: Fragments from the Other Side of War *(1993) and have been translated into eleven languages. "On Bad Teeth" is drawn from her chronicle of obvious and less obvious aspects of daily life under communism in the country formerly known as Yugoslavia. This essay first appeared in* Cafe Europa: Life After Communism *(1996). Recently, she has written* S: A Novel about the Balkans *(2000).*

Croatia is about the size of West Virginia and is situated along the eastern coast of the Adriatic Sea, extending inland to the slopes of the Julian Alps in Slovenia and into the Pannonian Valley to the banks of the Drava and Danube rivers. The capital, Zagreb, lies on the Sava River, and many famous cities, including the medieval port of Dubrovnik, are found along the extended coastline. Although Slavs began settling the Balkan peninsula as early as the sixth century A.D., Croatians were first united into a single state by King Tomislav in 925. The Croats accepted Roman Catholicism in the eleventh century, and by the 1500s, Croatia and Hungary became part of the Hapsburg Empire. In 1914 the assassination of Austria's crown prince in Sarajevo (Bosnia) embroiled the entire Balkans into World War I. For decades, Croatia was part of Yugoslavia under the socialist federation led by Josip Broz Tito. When Tito died in 1980, his authority was transferred to a collective state presidency, which had a rotating chairman. With the fall of communism and the weakening of the federation, Yugoslavia declared its independence in June 1991 and was recognized by the international community in January 1992. Opposition from the Yugoslav Army and the Serbian government, which strongly opposed independence, led to fierce fighting and the destruction of entire cities, which created a serious refugee problem. Various cease-fires brokered by the United Nations produced an uneasy peace that did not last long, as fighting between the Croats, Serbs, and Muslims broke out again in 1993. Additionally, Croatian irregulars became involved in the more serious civil war in Bosnia–Hercegovina. The most recent president of Croatia was

Franjo Tudjman. United Nations peacekeeping forces played an active role in creating circumstances under which elections could take place in 1996. In 1997 Tudjman was reelected to a second five-year term. Tudjman died in December 1999, and his nationalist party was defeated by the center-left coalition in the parliamentary elections of 2000.

Before You Read

Observe how the shift in political values in Eastern Europe is reflected in the attitude toward one's personal appearance.

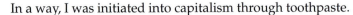

1   In a way, I was initiated into capitalism through toothpaste.

2   When I first visited the States in 1983, I loved to watch TV commercials. This is when I noticed that Americans were obsessed by their teeth. Every second commercial seemed to be for a toothpaste. Where I come from, toothpaste is toothpaste. I couldn't believe there were so many different kinds. What were they all *for*? After all the purpose of it is just to clean your teeth. In my childhood there were two kinds, mint flavour and strawberry flavour, and both of them had the same brand name, Kalodont. For a long time I was convinced that Kalodont was the word for toothpaste, because nobody at home used the generic word. We never said, "Do you have toothpaste?" we said, "Do you have Kalodont?" It is hardly surprising, then, that such a person would react with nothing short of disbelief when faced with the American cosmetic (or is it pharmaceutical?) industry and its endless production line. Toothpaste with or without sugar, with or without flour, with or without baking soda, calcium, vitamins. . . .

3   Over the years, on subsequent visits I continued to be fascinated by this American obsession with toothpaste, from the common varieties all the way up to Rembrandt, the most snobbish brand, if there could be such a thing as snobbishness about toothpaste. I soon learned that there could: in one women's magazine I saw it recommended as a Christmas present! Needless to say, in every commercial for toothpaste at least one bright, impressively beautiful set of teeth flashes across the screen, but this image is not confined to selling toothpaste. As we all know, beautiful teeth are used to advertise beer, hair shampoo, cars, anything. Indeed, they are an indispensable feature of any American advertisement. The foreigner soon learns that they stand not only as a symbol for both good looks and good health, but for something else as well.

4   If you think that such advertising might be part of the Americans' national obsession with health in general, you are not far from the truth. Americans seem to be passionate about their health and their looks, which appear to be interchangeable qualities. Health and good looks are essential badges of status among the middle classes. Nothing but narcissism, you could retort, but it is more than that. This connection

between teeth and social status is not so evident to an Eastern European. I personally had some doubts about those TV teeth, I thought that they must be artificial, some kind of prosthesis made out of plastic or porcelain. They were just too good to be true. How could people have such fine teeth? Intrigued, I decided to take a good look around me.

5   I noticed that the people I met, that is mostly middle-class urban professionals, generally, do have a set of bright, white teeth of their own, not unlike the TV teeth. It was even more surprising to me that I could detect no cavities, no missing teeth, no imperfections. I was astonished. The secret was revealed to me when a friend took her son to the dentist. When they returned, the little boy's upper teeth were fixed with a dreadful-looking kind of iron muzzle: a brace, I learned. It was obviously painful for him. "Poor little thing!" I exclaimed, but his mother showed no mercy. Moreover, she was proud that she could afford this torture device. I was puzzled. When she explained to me that the brace cost between $2,000 and $3,000, her attitude seemed even more sinister. I eventually realised that the mystery of beautiful teeth is not only about hygiene, but about money. She had money enough to get her son's teeth fixed, and the little boy was brave enough to stand the pain, because somehow he understood that this was a requirement of his social status. All the other boys from his private school had braces, too. He was going to grow up being well aware of the fact that his healthy, beautiful teeth were expensive and, therefore, an indication of prestige. Moreover, his mother could count on him to brush them three times a day, with an electric toothbrush and the latest toothpaste promising even healthier and more beautiful teeth, as if that were possible. In the long run, all the discomfort would be worth it.

6   Seeing the boy's brace, the connection between health and wealth in America became a bit clearer to me. Clean, healthy teeth feature so much in advertising because Americans have no free dental care, and neither is it covered by any medical insurance. Therefore, if you invest money and educate your child early enough (a bit of suffering is needed, too), you will save a lot later. But how much money did this take? I got my answer when I had to visit a dentist myself. On one of my last visits my filling fell out, and just to have it refilled with some temporary white stuff, whatever it was, I had to pay $100. This would be a minor financial catastrophe for any Eastern European citizen used to free dental care in his own country; it was expensive even by American standards. Only then did I become fully aware of what it means not to have free dental care.

7   Predictably enough, I was outraged. How was it possible for dental work to be so expensive in this country? For $100 back home I could have coated my tooth in pure gold! And why was it that such an affluent country did not provide its citizens with basic services like free

dental work? This was one of the very few areas in which we from former communist countries had some advantage over Americans—and we would like to keep it.

8   On my way home, I thought what a blessing it was that we did not have to worry about our teeth, or about whether we could afford to look after them—or at least, we did not have to worry yet, in my country, anyway. However, immediately upon my arrival in Zagreb, I realized that I could allow myself such rose-tinted thoughts only as long as I was on the other side of the Atlantic, from where everything at home looked a bit blurred, especially the general state of people's teeth. Back at home, I was forced to adjust my view. It was as if I had been myopic before and now I had got the right pair of glasses and could finally see properly. And what I saw did not please me at all.

9   On the bus from the airport I met one of my acquaintances, a young television reporter. For the first time I noticed that half of his teeth were missing and that those which remained looked like the ruins of a decayed medieval town. I had known this guy for years, but I had never thought about the state of the inside of his mouth before, or if I had, I'd considered it totally unimportant. Now I also noticed that, in order to hide his bad teeth, he had grown a moustache and developed a way of laughing which didn't involve him opening his mouth too wide. Even so, his bad teeth were still obvious.

10   This encounter did not cheer me up. Sitting next to the young reporter, I wondered how he managed to speak in front of a TV camera without making a mistake that would reveal his terrible secret. Without smiling, perhaps? This would be perfectly acceptable, because he reports on the war, but wasn't he tired of this uncomfortable game of hide-and- seek? Wouldn't it be much more professional and make life easier if he visited a good dentist and got it all over with? But this is not something we are supposed to talk about. How do you say such a thing to a person if he is not your intimate friend? You can't just say, "Listen, why don't you do something about your teeth?" Perhaps I should have pulled out my toothpaste and handed it to him, or casually dropped the name of my dentist, something like what my friend did last summer. A woman standing next to her in a streetcar emanated an extremely unpleasant odour from her hairy armpits. My friend could not stand it. She pulled her own deodorant stick out of her handbag and gave it to the woman. The funny thing is that the woman accepted it without taking offence. I, on the other hand, could not risk offending my acquaintance.

11   I continued my investigations at home. Yes, I admit that I looked into the mouths of friends, relatives, acquaintances, neighbours—I could not help it. I discovered that the whole nation had bad teeth, it was just that I had not been able to see it before. I concluded that the guy on the bus was only a part of the general landscape, that he was

no exception, and that therefore his failure to attend to his teeth was perfectly normal. I tried to explain this attitude to myself: perhaps people were afraid of drilling? Of course. Who isn't? But if nothing else, there must be an aesthetic drive in every human being, or one would at least think so. Yet, for some reason, aesthetics and communism don't go well together and though we might call our current state post-communism, we still have a communist attitude in such matters.

12   You could also argue that dentists, being employed by the state, are not well paid. Consequently, they don't put much effort into their job. You can claim as well that the materials they use are not of good quality. That is all probably true. But, I still believe that having your teeth repaired to a mediocre standard is preferable to treasuring the medieval ruins in your mouth or being toothless altogether.

13   There is no excuse that sounds reasonable enough for such negligence. The problem is that the condition of your teeth in Eastern Europe is regarded as a highly personal matter, not a sign of your standard of living or a question for public discussion. Having good teeth is simply a matter of being civilised and well mannered. Strangely enough, however, dirty shoes, dirty fingernails or dandruff are no longer tolerated: these are considered impolite, even offensive. Yet like such matters of personal hygiene, good teeth are not only a question of money. Dental work has been free for the last forty years. At present there co-exists a mixture of both state-run general medical care, which includes dental care, and private dentists. If you want, you can have excellent dental work done. I know people who travel from Vienna to Bratislava, Budapest, Ljubljana or Zagreb to have their teeth repaired more cheaply. But if you asked people in Eastern Europe who can afford it why they don't go to a private dentist for a better service, they would probably tell you that this is not their priority at the moment. Instead they want to fix their car, or buy a new carpet.

14   It is clear that leaders and intellectuals here certainly don't care about such a minor aspect of their image. They are preoccupied with the destiny of their respective nations, they do not have time for such trivial matters. The American idea that it is not very polite for a public figure to appear with bad teeth, just as it would be inappropriate to make a speech in your pyjamas, is not understood here. You can meet exquisitely dressed politicians or businessmen, but wait until they open their mouths! If these public figures are not worried about this aspect of their looks, why should ordinary people be concerned about theirs? They too have more important things to do, for example surviving. There is also that new breed, the *nouveau riche* of post-communism. Previously everything was valued by one's participation in politics; now it is slowly replaced by money. The arrogance of these people originates there. Unfortunately, money does not guarantee good manners, or a regular visit to the dentist for that matter.

15   I can only try to imagine the horrors when free dental work is replaced by private dentists whose prices nobody can afford. How many
decades will we have to wait until our teeth look like American ones? It
is a question of perception. In order to improve your looks, you have to
be convinced that it is worth the trouble. In other words, we are dealing
with a problem of self-esteem, with a way of thinking, rather than a superficial question. Bad teeth are the result of bad dentists and bad food,
but also of a specific culture of thinking, of not seeing yourself as an individual. What we need here is a revolution of self-perception. Not only
will that not come automatically with the new political changes, but I
am afraid that it will also take longer than any political or economic developments. We need to accept our responsibilities towards both others
and ourselves. This is not only a wise sort of investment in the future,
as we can see in the case of Americans, it also gives you the feeling that
you have done what you can to improve yourself, be it your teeth, your
health, your career, education, environment or society in general.

16   Individual responsibility, including the responsibility for oneself,
is an entirely new concept here, as I have stated many times elsewhere.
This is why the revolution of self-perception has a long way to go. As
absurd as it may sound, in the old days one could blame the Communist Party even for one's bad teeth. Now there is no one to blame, but it
takes time to understand that. If you have never had it, self-respect has
to be learned. Maybe our own teeth would be a good place to start.

17   But I can see signs of coming changes. Recently a good friend borrowed some money from me in order to repair her apartment. When
the time came to give it back, she told me that I would have to wait, because she needed the money for something very urgent. She had finally decided to have her teeth fixed by a private dentist. No wonder
she was left without a penny. But what could I have said to that? I said
the only thing I could say: "I understand you, this must come first."

18   Finally, I guess it is only fair that I should declare the state of my
own teeth. I am one of those who much too often used the free dental
work so generously provided by the communist state for the benefit of
its people. I was afraid of the dentist, all right, but also brave enough
to stand the pain because I had overcome the psychological barrier at
an early age.

19   When I was in the third grade a teacher showed us a cartoon depicting a fortress—a tooth—attacked by bad guys—bacteria. They
looked terribly dangerous, digging tunnels and ditches with their
small axes until the fortress almost fell into their hands. Then the army
of good guys, the white blood cells, arrived and saved it at the last moment. The teacher explained to us how we could fight the bad guys by
brushing our teeth regularly with Kalodont and by visiting a dentist
every time we spotted a little hole or felt pain. I took her advice literally—I was obviously very impressed by the cartoon, just as I was

impressed by the American TV commercials thirty years later. The result is that today I can say that I have good teeth, although six of them are missing. How did that happen? Well, when I spotted a little cavity, I would immediately go to the dentist all by myself. This was mistake number one. You could not choose your own dentist at that time, and my family had to go to a military hospital. A dentist there would usually fill the cavity, but for some reason the filling would soon fall out. Then he would make an even bigger hole and fill it again, until eventually there was not much tooth left.

20   Those "dentists" were in fact young students of dentistry drafted into the army. For them, this was probably an excellent chance to improve their knowledge by practising on patients. When they'd finished practising on me a more experienced dentist would suggest I had the tooth out. What could I, a child, do but agree? This was mistake number two, of course. I had to learn to live with one gap in my jaw, then another, and another. Much later I had two bridges made by a private dentist. He didn't even ask me why I was missing six of my teeth; he knew how things had worked in those days. My only consolation was that I did not have to pay much for my bridgework.

21   Like everyone else in the post-communist world, I had to learn the meaning of the American proverb "There is no such thing as a free lunch." The Americans are right. You don't get anything properly done if you don't pay for it sooner or later.

✧ Evaluating the Text

1. What connection did Drakulić discover between the importance placed on impressive teeth in American culture and social status? As she became further acquainted with American society, how did this feature provide a key to unlock many aspects of the culture for her?

2. Once sensitized to what, in America, is so pervasive and important, how did Drakulić react upon her return to Zagreb? What did she conclude about the role that bad teeth play in East European culture?

3. How does Drakulić tie together her discussion of teeth with life in a postcommunist society?

✧ Exploring Different Perspectives

1. Compare the ways in which straight white teeth exemplify beauty in America, according to Drakulić, with the way bound feet did in traditional China, as explored in "China Chic: East Meets West" by Valerie Steele and John S. Major.

2. In what sense do fiestas in Mexico, as described by Octavio Paz in "Fiesta," convey some of the same values that having good teeth do in America, as discussed by Drakulić?

✧ Extending Viewpoints through Writing

1. If you were faced with a choice of fixing your car, buying a new carpet, or fixing your teeth (a choice mentioned by Drakulić), which would you choose and why?

2. When Drakulić returned to East Europe, she was appalled by the pervasiveness of bad teeth, something she had not previously noticed. To what extent do you let your assessment of other people depend on the state of their teeth?

Gino Del Guercio

The Secrets of Haiti's Living Dead

◆

Gino Del Guercio is a national science writer for United Press International and was a MACY fellow at Boston's television station WGBH. He is currently a documentary filmmaker, specializing in scientific and medical subjects, for Boston Science Communications, Inc. "The Secrets of Haiti's Living Dead" was first published in Harvard Magazine *(January/February 1986). In 1982, Wade Davis, a Harvard-trained ethnobotanist, whose exploits formed the basis for this article, traveled into the Haitian countryside to investigate accounts of Zombies—the infamous living dead of Haitian folklore. Davis's research led him to obtain the poison associated with the process. His findings were first presented in* The Serpent and the Rainbow *(1988), a work that served as the basis for the movie of the same name, directed by Wes Craven, and later in* Passage of Darkness *(1988).*

The republic of Haiti in the West Indies occupies the western third of the island of Hispaniola, which it shares with the Dominican Republic. French rule of Haiti lasted from 1697 until Toussaint l'Ouverture, a former slave, led Haiti to become the second independent nation in the Americas, in 1804. For the most part, Haiti's history has been fraught with intrigue and violence. In 1957, François "Papa Doc" Duvalier established a dictatorship and was succeeded by his son Jean Claude ("Baby Doc"), who fled the country in 1986. In December 1990, the Reverend Jean Bertrand Aristide, a champion of the poor, was elected head of the government in Haiti's first democratic elections. Aristide was subsequently forced into exile, and the government was placed under military control. After the expulsion of the United Nations and the Organization of American States (OAS) missions by a military junta in July 1994, fifteen thousand American troops moved into Haiti in September. President Aristide briefly returned to office in October of 1994. His associate Rene Preval took over following the elections of 1996, but disputes with parliament led to a state constitutional crisis in 1999. Del Guercio's report reveals the extent to which Haitian life is controlled by voodoo, a religious belief, West African in origin, that is characterized by induced trances and magical rituals. Until this century, voodoo was the state religion and continues to flourish despite opposition from Roman Catholicism, the other major religion in Haiti.

Before You Read

Consider the extent to which your concept of zombies is influenced by films and television.

———————◆———————

1   Five years ago, a man walked into l'Estére, a village in central Haiti, approached a peasant woman named Angelina Narcisse, and identified himself as her brother Clairvius. If he had not introduced himself using a boyhood nickname and mentioned facts only intimate family members knew, she would not have believed him. Because, eighteen years earlier, Angelina had stood in a small cemetery north of her village and watched as her brother Clairvius was buried.

2   The man told Angelina he remembered that night well. He knew when he was lowered into his grave, because he was fully conscious, although he could not speak or move. As the earth was thrown over his coffin, he felt as if he were floating over the grave. The scar on his right cheek, he said, was caused by a nail driven through his casket.

3   The night he was buried, he told Angelina, a voodoo priest raised him from the grave. He was beaten with a sisal whip and carried off to a sugar plantation in northern Haiti where, with other zombies, he was forced to work as a slave. Only with the death of the zombie master were they able to escape, and Narcisse eventually returned home.

4   Legend has it that zombies are the living dead, raised from their graves and animated by malevolent voodoo sorcerers, usually for some evil purpose. Most Haitians believe in zombies, and Narcisse's claim is not unique. At about the time he reappeared, in 1980, two women turned up in other villages saying they were zombies. In the same year, in northern Haiti, the local peasants claimed to have found a group of zombies wandering aimlessly in the fields.

5   But Narcisse's case was different in one crucial respect; it was documented. His death had been recorded by doctors at the American-directed Schweitzer Hospital in Deschapelles. On April 30, 1962, hospital records show, Narcisse walked into the hospital's emergency room spitting up blood. He was feverish and full of aches. His doctors could not diagnose his illness, and his symptoms grew steadily worse. Three days after he entered the hospital, according to the records, he died. The attending physicians, an American among them, signed his death certificate. His body was placed in cold storage for twenty hours, and then he was buried. He said he remembered hearing his doctors pronounce him dead while his sister wept at his bedside.

6   At the Centre de Psychiatrie et Neurologie in Port-au-Prince, Dr. Lamarque Douyon, a Haitian-born, Canadian-trained psychiatrist, has been systematically investigating all reports of zombies since 1961. Though convinced zombies were real, he had been unable to find a scientific explanation for the phenomenon. He did not believe zombies

were people raised from the dead, but that did not make them any less interesting. He speculated that victims were only made to *look* dead, probably by means of a drug that dramatically slowed metabolism. The victim was buried, dug up within a few hours, and somehow reawakened.

7   The Narcisse case provided Douyon with evidence strong enough to warrant a request for assistance from colleagues in New York. Douyon wanted to find an ethnobotanist, a traditional-medicines expert, who could track down the zombie potion he was sure existed. Aware of the medical potential of a drug that could dramatically lower metabolism, a group organized by the late Dr. Nathan Kline—a New York psychiatrist and pioneer in the field of psychopharmacology— raised the funds necessary to send someone to investigate.

8   The search for that someone led to the Harvard Botanical Museum, one of the world's foremost institutes of ethnobiology. Its director, Richard Evans Schultes, Jeffrey professor of biology, had spent thirteen years in the tropics studying native medicines. Some of his best-known work is the investigation of curare, the substance used by the nomadic people of the Amazon to poison their darts. Refined into a powerful muscle relaxant called D-tubocurarine, it is now an essential component of the anesthesia used during almost all surgery.

9   Schultes would have been a natural for the Haitian investigation, but he was too busy. He recommended another Harvard ethnobotanist for the assignment, Wade Davis, a 28-year-old Canadian pursuing a doctorate in biology.

10   Davis grew up in the tall pine forests of British Columbia and entered Harvard in 1971, influenced by a *Life* magazine story on the student strike of 1969. Before Harvard, the only Americans he had known were draft dodgers, who seemed very exotic. "I used to fight forest fires with them," Davis says. "Like everybody else, I thought America was where it was at. And I wanted to go to Harvard because of that *Life* article. When I got there, I realized it wasn't quite what I had in mind."

11   Davis took a course from Schultes, and when he decided to go to South America to study plants, he approached his professor for guidance. "He was an extraordinary figure," Davis remembers. "He was a man who had done it all. He had lived alone for years in the Amazon." Schultes sent Davis to the rain forest with two letters of introduction and two pieces of advice: wear a pith helmet and try ayahuasca, a powerful hallucinogenic vine. During that expedition and others, Davis proved himself an "outstanding field man," says his mentor. Now, in early 1982, Schultes called him into his office and asked if he had plans for spring break.

12   "I always took to Schultes's assignments like a plant takes to water," says Davis, tall and blond, with inquisitive blue eyes. "Whatever

Schultes told me to do, I did. His letters of introduction opened up a whole world." This time the world was Haiti.

13   Davis knew nothing about the Caribbean island—and nothing about African traditions, which serve as Haiti's cultural basis. He certainly did not believe in zombies. "I thought it was a lark," he says now.

14   Davis landed in Haiti a week after his conversation with Schultes, armed with a hypothesis about how the zombie drug—if it existed— might be made. Setting out to explore, he discovered a country materially impoverished, but rich in culture and mystery. He was impressed by the cohesion of Haitian society; he found none of the crime, social disorder, and rampant drug and alcohol abuse so common in many of the other Caribbean islands. The cultural wealth and cohesion, he believes, spring from the country's turbulent history.

15   During the French occupation of the late eighteenth century, 370,000 African-born slaves were imported to Haiti between 1780 and 1790. In 1791, the black population launched one of the few successful slave revolts in history, forming secret societies and overcoming first the French plantation owners and then a detachment of troops from Napoleon's army, sent to quell the revolt. For the next hundred years Haiti was the only independent black republic in the Caribbean, populated by people who did not forget their African heritage. "You can almost argue that Haiti is more African than Africa," Davis says. "When the west coast of Africa was being disrupted by colonialism and the slave trade, Haiti was essentially left alone. The amalgam of beliefs in Haiti is unique, but it's very, very African."

16   Davis discovered that the vast majority of Haitian peasants practice voodoo, a sophisticated religion with African roots. Says Davis, "It was immediately obvious that the stereotypes of voodoo weren't true. Going around the countryside, I found clues to a whole complex social world." Vodounists believe they communicate directly with, indeed are often possessed by, the many spirits who populate the everyday world. Vodoun society is a system of education, law, and medicine; it embodies a code of ethics that regulates social behavior. In rural areas, secret vodoun societies, much like those found on the west coast of Africa, are as much or more in control of everyday life as the Haitian government.

17   Although most outsiders dismissed the zombie phenomenon as folklore, some early investigators, convinced of its reality, tried to find a scientific explanation. The few who sought a zombie drug failed. Nathan Kline, who helped finance Davis's expedition, had searched unsuccessfully, as had Lamarque Douyon, the Haitian psychiatrist. Zora Neale Hurston, an American black woman, may have come closest. An anthropological pioneer, she went to Haiti in the Thirties, studied vodoun society, and wrote a book on the subject, *Tell My Horse*, first published in 1938. She knew about the secret societies and was convinced zombies were real, but if a powder existed, she too failed to obtain it.

18   Davis obtained a sample in a few weeks.

19   He arrived in Haiti with the names of several contacts. A BBC reporter familiar with the Narcisse case had suggested he talk with Marcel Pierre. Pierre owned the Eagle Bar, a bordello in the city of Saint Marc. He was also a voodoo sorcerer and had supplied the BBC with a physiologically active powder of unknown ingredients. Davis found him willing to negotiate. He told Pierre he was a representative of "powerful but anonymous interests in New York," willing to pay generously for the priest's services, provided no questions were asked. Pierre agreed to be helpful for what Davis will only say was a "sizable sum." Davis spent a day watching Pierre gather the ingredients—including human bones—and grind them together with mortar and pestle. However, from his knowledge of poison, Davis knew immediately that nothing in the formula could produce the powerful effects of zombification.

20   Three weeks later, Davis went back to the Eagle Bar, where he found Pierre sitting with three associates. Davis challenged him. He called him a charlatan. Enraged, the priest gave him a second vial, claiming that this was the real poison. Davis pretended to pour the powder into his palm and rub it into his skin. "You're a dead man," Pierre told him, and he might have been, because this powder proved to be genuine. But, as the substance had not actually touched him, Davis was able to maintain his bravado, and Pierre was impressed. He agreed to make the poison and show Davis how it was done.

21   The powder, which Davis keeps in a small vial, looks like dry black dirt. It contains parts of toads, sea worms, lizards, tarantulas, and human bones. (To obtain the last ingredient, he and Pierre unearthed a child's grave on a nocturnal trip to the cemetery.) The poison is rubbed into the victim's skin. Within hours he begins to feel nauseated and has difficulty breathing. A pins-and-needles sensation afflicts his arms and legs, then progresses to the whole body. The subject becomes paralyzed; his lips turn blue for lack of oxygen. Quickly—sometimes within six hours—his metabolism is lowered to a level almost indistinguishable from death.

22   As Davis discovered, making the poison is an inexact science. Ingredients varied in the five samples he eventually acquired, although the active agents were always the same. And the poison came with no guarantee. Davis speculates that sometimes instead of merely paralyzing the victim, the compound kills him. Sometimes the victim suffocates in the coffin before he can be resurrected. But clearly the potion works well enough often enough to make zombies more than a figment of Haitian imagination.

23   Analysis of the powder produced another surprise. "When I went down to Haiti originally," says Davis, "my hypothesis was that the formula would contain *concombre zombi*, the 'zombie's cucumber,' which is a *Datura* plant. I thought somehow *Datura* was used in putting people

down." *Datura* is a powerful psychoactive plant, found in West Africa as well as other tropical areas and used there in ritual as well as criminal activities. Davis had found *Datura* growing in Haiti. Its popular name suggested the plant was used in creating zombies.

24   But, says Davis, "there were a lot of problems with the *Datura* hypothesis. Partly it was a question of how the drug was administered. *Datura* would create a stupor in huge doses, but it just wouldn't produce the kind of immobility that was key. These people had to appear dead, and there aren't many drugs that will do that."

25   One of the ingredients Pierre included in the second formula was a dried fish, a species of puffer or blowfish, common to most parts of the world. It gets its name from its ability to fill itself with water and swell to several times its normal size when threatened by predators. Many of these fish contain a powerful poison known as tetrodotoxin. One of the most powerful nonprotein poisons known to man, tetrodotoxin turned up in every sample of zombie powder that Davis acquired.

26   Numerous well-documented accounts of puffer fish poisoning exist, but the most famous accounts come from the Orient, where *fugu* fish, a species of puffer, is considered a delicacy. In Japan, special chefs are licensed to prepare *fugu*. The chef removes enough poison to make the fish nonlethal, yet enough remains to create exhilarating physiological effects—tingles up and down the spine, mild prickling of the tongue and lips, euphoria. Several dozen Japanese die each year, having bitten off more than they should have.

27   "When I got hold of the formula and saw it was the *fugu* fish, that suddenly threw open the whole Japanese literature," says Davis. Case histories of *fugu* poisoning read like accounts of zombification. Victims remain conscious but unable to speak or move. A man who had "died" after eating *fugu* recovered seven days later in the morgue. Several summers ago, another Japanese poisoned by *fugu* revived after he was nailed into his coffin. "Almost all of Narcisse's symptoms correlated. Even strange things such as the fact that he said he was conscious and could hear himself pronounced dead. Stuff that I thought had to be magic, that seemed crazy. But, in fact, that is what people who get *fugu*-fish poisoning experience."

28   Davis was certain he had solved the mystery. But far from being the end of his investigation, identifying the poison was, in fact, its starting point. "The drug alone didn't make zombies," he explains. "Japanese victims of puffer-fish poisoning don't become zombies, they become poison victims. All the drug could do was set someone up for a whole series of psychological pressures that would be rooted in the culture. I wanted to know why zombification was going on," he says.

29   He sought a cultural answer, an explanation rooted in the structure and beliefs of Haitian society. Was zombification simply a random criminal activity? He thought not. He had discovered that Clairvius Narcisse

and "Ti Femme," a second victim he interviewed, were village pariahs. Ti Femme was regarded as a thief. Narcisse had abandoned his children and deprived his brother of land that was rightfully his. Equally suggestive, Narcisse claimed that his aggrieved brother had sold him to a *bokor*, a voodoo priest who dealt in black magic; he made cryptic reference to having been tried and found guilty by the "masters of the land."

30   Gathering poisons from various parts of the country, Davis had come into direct contact with the vodoun secret societies. Returning to the anthropological literature on Haiti and pursuing his contacts with informants, Davis came to understand the social matrix within which zombies were created.

31   Davis's investigations uncovered the importance of the secret societies. These groups trace their origins to the bands of escaped slaves that organized the revolt against the French in the late eighteenth century. Open to both men and women, the societies control specific territories of the country. Their meetings take place at night, and in many rural parts of Haiti the drums and wild celebrations that characterize the gatherings can be heard for miles.

32   Davis believes the secret societies are responsible for policing their communities, and the threat of zombification is one way they maintain order. Says Davis, "Zombification has a material basis, but it also has a societal logic." To the uninitiated, the practice may appear a random criminal activity, but in rural vodoun society, it is exactly the opposite—a sanction imposed by recognized authorities, a form of capital punishment. For rural Haitians, zombification is an even more severe punishment than death, because it deprives the subject of his most valued possessions: his free will and independence.

33   The vodounists believe that when a person dies, his spirit splits into several different parts. If a priest is powerful enough, the spiritual aspect that controls a person's character and individuality, known as *ti bon ange*, the "good little angel," can be captured and the corporeal aspect, deprived of its will, held as a slave.

34   From studying the medical literature on tetrodotoxin poisoning, Davis discovered that if a victim survives the first few hours of the poisoning, he is likely to recover fully from the ordeal. The subject simply revives spontaneously. But zombies remain without will, in a trancelike state, a condition vodounists attribute to the power of the priest. Davis thinks it possible that the psychological trauma of zombification may be augmented by *Datura* or some other drug; he thinks zombies may be fed a *Datura* paste that accentuates their disorientation. Still, he puts the material basis of zombification in perspective: "Tetrodotoxin and *Datura* are only templates on which cultural forces and beliefs may be amplified a thousand times."

35   Davis has not been able to discover how prevalent zombification is in Haiti. "How many zombies there are is not the question," he says.

He compares it to capital punishment in the United States: "It doesn't really matter how many people are electrocuted, as long as it's a possibility." As a sanction in Haiti, the fear is not of zombies, it's of becoming one.

36   Davis attributes his success in solving the zombie mystery to his approach. He went to Haiti with an open mind and immersed himself in the culture. "My intuition unhindered by biases served me well," he says. "I didn't make any judgments." He combined this attitude with what he had learned earlier from his experiences in the Amazon. "Schultes's lesson is to go and live with the Indians as an Indian." Davis was able to participate in the vodoun society to a surprising degree, eventually even penetrating one of the Bizango societies and dancing in their nocturnal rituals. His appreciation of Haitian culture is apparent. "Everybody asks me how did a white person get this information? To ask the question means you don't understand Haitians— they don't judge you by the color of your skin."

37   As a result of the exotic nature of his discoveries, Davis has gained a certain notoriety. He plans to complete his dissertation soon, but he has already finished writing a popular account of his adventures. To be published in January by Simon and Schuster, it is called *The Serpent and the Rainbow,* after the serpent that vodounists believe created the earth and the rainbow spirit it married. Film rights have already been optioned; in October Davis went back to Haiti with a screenwriter. But Davis takes the notoriety in stride. "All this attention is funny," he says. "For years, not just me, but all Schultes's students have had extraordinary adventures in the line of work. The adventure is not the end point, it's just along the way of getting the data. At the Botanical Museum, Schultes created a world unto itself. We didn't think we were doing anything above the ordinary. I still don't think we do. And you know," he adds, "the Haiti episode does not begin to compare to what others have accomplished—particularly Schultes himself."

✧ Evaluating the Text

1. To what extent does Del Guercio's account gain credibility because he begins with the mysterious case of Clairvius Narcisse? How is Narcisse's identification by his sister intended to put the case beyond all doubt and leave the process of zombification as the only possible explanation for his otherwise inexplicable "death"?

2. Why is it important to Guercio's account that he mentions physicians from the United States as well as Haitian doctors who certified the "death" of Clairvius Narcisse? What is Del Guercio's attitude toward this phenomenon? How is this attitude revealed in the way he constructs his report?

3. How does the threat of zombification serve as a preventative measure that ensures social control in deterring crimes against the community? How did it operate in the cases of Clairvius Narcisse and "Ti Femme"? In what way is the reality of the social mechanism of zombification quite different from how it has been presented in movies and popular culture?

4. What kind of independent confirmation of the effects of tetrodotoxin, a potent neurotoxin that drastically reduces metabolism and produces paralysis, did Davis discover in his research on the effects of Japanese victims of *fugu* fish poisoning?

✦ Exploring Different Perspectives

1. How does the concept of death and resurrection enter into the account by Del Guercio and Bessie Head's story, "Looking for a Rain God"?

2. How do both Del Guercio and Nabil Gorgy, in his story "Cairo Is a Small City," provide insight into the means by which justice is obtained for those who are marginalized?

✦ Extending Viewpoints through Writing

1. If you are familiar with or interested in the processes by which various religious cults enlist and program their members, you might compare their methods to those of the vodoun priests in terms of positive and negative reinforcement of psychological, sociological, and physiological conditioning.

2. If you have had the opportunity to see the movie *The Serpent and the Rainbow* (1988), directed by Wes Craven, you might wish to compare its representation of the events described in this article with Wade Davis's book *The Serpent and the Rainbow* (1985). For further research on this subject, you might consult Wade Davis, *Passage of Darkness: The Ethnobiology of the Haitian Zombie* (1988), an in-depth study of the political, social, and botanical mechanisms of zombification.

Octavio Paz

Fiesta

◆

Octavio Paz (1914–1998), born in Mexico City, was a poet, essayist, and unequaled observer of Mexican society. He served as a Mexican diplomat in France and Japan and as Ambassador to India before resigning from the diplomatic service to protest the Tlatelolco Massacre (government massacre of 300 students in Mexico City) in 1968. His many volumes of poetry include Sun Stone *(1958), a new reading of the Aztec myths;* Marcel Duchamp *(1968);* The Children of the Mire *(1974); and* The Monkey Grammarian *(1981). In 1990, Paz was awarded the Nobel Prize for Literature. As an essayist whose works have helped redefine the concept of Latin American culture, Paz wrote* The Other Mexico *(1972) and* The Labyrinth of Solitude, *translated by Lysander Kemp (1961), from which "Fiesta" is taken. In the following essay, Paz offers insight, conveyed with his typical stylistic grace and erudition, into the deep psychological needs met by fiestas in Mexican culture.*

Before You Read

While you read, evaluate how the noncompetitive and communal nature of Mexican fiestas differs from their American counterparts.

◆

1   The solitary Mexican loves fiestas and public gatherings. Any occasion for getting together will serve, any pretext to stop the flow of time and commemorate men and events with festivals and ceremonies. We are a ritual people, and this characteristic enriches both our imaginations and our sensibilities, which are equally sharp and alert. The art of the fiesta has been debased almost everywhere else, but not in Mexico. There are few places in the world where it is possible to take part in a spectacle like our great religious fiestas with their violent primary colors, their bizarre costumes and dances, their fireworks and ceremonies and their inexhaustible welter of surprises: the fruit, candy, toys and other objects sold on these days in the plazas and open-air markets.

2   Our calendar is crowded with fiestas. There are certain days when the whole country, from the most remote villages to the largest cities, prays, shouts, feasts, gets drunk and kills, in honor of the Virgin of Guadalupe or Benito Juaréz. Each year on the fifteenth of September, at

eleven o'clock at night, we celebrate the fiesta of the *Grito*[1] in all the plazas of the Republic, and the excited crowds actually shout for a whole hour . . . the better, perhaps, to remain silent for the rest of the year. During the days before and after the twelfth of December,[2] time comes to a full stop, and instead of pushing us toward a deceptive tomorrow that is always beyond our reach, offers us a complete and perfect today of dancing and revelry, of communion with the most ancient and secret Mexico. Time is no longer succession, and becomes what it originally was and is: the present, in which past and future are reconciled.

3   But the fiestas which the Church and State provide for the country as a whole are not enough. The life of every city and village is ruled by a patron saint whose blessing is celebrated with devout regularity. Neighborhoods and trades also have their annual fiestas, their ceremonies and fairs. And each one of us—atheist, Catholic, or merely indifferent—has his own saint's day, which he observes every year. It is impossible to calculate how many fiestas we have and how much time and money we spend on them. I remember asking the mayor of a village near Mitla, several years ago, "What is the income of the village government?" "About 3,000 pesos a year. We are very poor. But the Governor and the Federal Government always help us to meet our expenses." "And how are the 3,000 pesos spent?" "Mostly on fiestas, señor. We are a small village, but we have two patron saints."

4   This reply is not surprising. Our poverty can be measured by the frequency and luxuriousness of our holidays. Wealthy countries have very few: there is neither the time nor the desire for them, and they are not necessary. The people have other things to do, and when they amuse themselves they do so in small groups. The modern masses are agglomerations of solitary individuals. On great occasions in Paris or New York, when the populace gathers in the squares or stadiums, the absence of people, in the sense of *a* people, is remarkable: there are couples and small groups, but they never form a living community in which the individual is at once dissolved and redeemed. But how could a poor Mexican live without the two or three annual fiestas that make up for his poverty and misery? Fiestas are our only luxury. They replace, and are perhaps better than, the theater and vacations, Anglo-Saxon weekends and cocktail parties, the bourgeois reception, the Mediterranean café.

5   In all of these ceremonies—national or local, trade or family—the Mexican opens out. They all give him a chance to reveal himself and to converse with God, country, friends or relations. During these days the

[1]Padre Hildalgo's call-to-arms against Spain, 1810.—*Tr.*
[2]Fiesta of the Virgin of Guadalupe.—*Tr.*

silent Mexican whistles, shouts, sings, shoots off fireworks, discharges his pistol into the air. He discharges his soul. And his shout, like the rockets we love so much, ascends to the heavens, explodes into green, red, blue, and white lights, and falls dizzily to earth with a trail of golden sparks. This is the night when friends who have not exchanged more than the prescribed courtesies for months get drunk together, trade confidences, weep over the same troubles, discover that they are brothers, and sometimes, to prove it, kill each other. The night is full of songs and loud cries. The lover wakes up his sweetheart with an orchestra. There are jokes and conversations from balcony to balcony, sidewalk to sidewalk. Nobody talks quietly. Hats fly in the air. Laughter and curses ring like silver pesos. Guitars are brought out. Now and then, it is true, the happiness ends badly, in quarrels, insults, pistol shots, stabbings. But these too are part of the fiesta, for the Mexican does not seek amusement: he seeks to escape from himself, to leap over the wall of solitude that confines him during the rest of the year. All are possessed by violence and frenzy. Their souls explode like the colors and voices and emotions. Do they forget themselves and show their true faces? Nobody knows. The important thing is to go out, open a way, get drunk on noise, people, colors. Mexico is celebrating a fiesta. And this fiesta, shot through with lightning and delirium, is the brilliant reverse to our silence and apathy, our reticence and gloom.

6   According to the interpretation of French sociologists, the fiesta is an excess, an expense. By means of this squandering the community protects itself against the envy of the gods or of men. Sacrifices and offerings placate or buy off the gods and the patron saints. Wasting money and expending energy affirms the community's wealth in both. This luxury is a proof of health, a show of abundance and power. Or a magic trap. For squandering is an effort to attract abundance by contagion. Money calls to money. When life is thrown away it increases; the orgy, which is sexual expenditure, is also a ceremony of regeneration; waste gives strength. New Year celebrations, in every culture, signify something beyond the mere observance of a date on the calendar. The day is a pause: time is stopped, is actually annihilated. The rites that celebrate its death are intended to provoke its rebirth, because they mark not only the end of an old year but also the beginning of a new. Everything attracts its opposite. The fiesta's function, then, is more utilitarian than we think: waste attracts or promotes wealth, and is an investment like any other, except that the returns on it cannot be measured or counted. What is sought is potency, life, health. In this sense the fiesta, like the gift and the offering, is one of the most ancient of economic forms.

7   This interpretation has always seemed to me to be incomplete. The fiesta is by nature sacred, literally or figuratively, and above all it is the advent of the unusual. It is governed by its own special rules, that set

it apart from other days, and it has a logic, an ethic and even an economy that are often in conflict with everyday norms. It all occurs in an enchanted world: time is transformed to a mythical past or a total present; space, the scene of the fiesta, is turned into a gaily decorated world of its own; and the persons taking part cast off all human or social rank and become, for the moment, living images. And everything takes place as if it were not so, as if it were a dream. But whatever happens, our actions have a greater lightness, a different gravity. They take on other meanings and with them we contract new obligations. We throw down our burdens of time and reason.

8   In certain fiestas the very notion of order disappears. Chaos comes back and license rules. Anything is permitted: the customary hierarchies vanish, along with all social, sex, caste, and trade distinctions. Men disguise themselves as women, gentlemen as slaves, the poor as the rich. The army, the clergy, and the law are ridiculed. Obligatory sacrilege, ritual profanation is committed. Love becomes promiscuity. Sometimes the fiesta becomes a Black Mass. Regulations, habits and customs are violated. Respectable people put away the dignified expressions and conservative clothes that isolate them, dress up in gaudy colors, hide behind a mask, and escape from themselves.

9   Therefore the fiesta is not only an excess, a ritual squandering of the goods painfully accumulated during the rest of the year; it is also a revolt, a sudden immersion in the formless, in pure being. By means of the fiesta society frees itself from the norms it has established. It ridicules its gods, its principles, and its laws: it denies its own self.

10   The fiesta is a revolution in the most literal sense of the word. In the confusion that it generates, society is dissolved, is drowned, insofar as it is an organism ruled according to certain laws and principles. But it drowns in itself, in its own original chaos or liberty. Everything is united: good and evil, day and night, the sacred and the profane. Everything merges, loses shape and individuality and returns to the primordial mass. The fiesta is a cosmic experiment, an experiment in disorder, reuniting contradictory elements and principles in order to bring about a renascence of life. Ritual death promotes a rebirth; vomiting increases the appetite; the orgy, sterile in itself, renews the fertility of the mother or of the earth. The fiesta is a return to a remote and undifferentiated state, prenatal or presocial. It is a return that is also a beginning, in accordance with the dialectic that is inherent in social processes.

11   The group emerges purified and strengthened from this plunge into chaos. It has immersed itself in its own origins, in the womb from which it came. To express it in another way, the fiesta denies society as an organic system of differentiated forms and principles, but affirms it as a source of creative energy. It is a true "re-creation," the opposite of the "recreation" characterizing modern vacations, which do not entail

any rites or ceremonies whatever and are as individualistic and sterile as the world that invented them.

12   Society communes with itself during the fiesta. Its members return to original chaos and freedom. Social structures break down and new relationships, unexpected rules, capricious hierarchies are created. In the general disorder everybody forgets himself and enters into otherwise forbidden situations and places. The bounds between audience and actors, officials and servants, are erased. Everybody takes part in the fiesta, everybody is caught up in its whirlwind. Whatever its mood, its character, its meaning, the fiesta is participation, and this trait distinguishes it from all other ceremonies and social phenomena. Lay or religious, orgy or saturnalia, the fiesta is a social act based on the full participation of all its celebrants.

13   Thanks to the fiesta the Mexican opens out, participates, communes with his fellows and with the values that give meaning to his religious or political existence. And it is significant that a country as sorrowful as ours should have so many and such joyous fiestas. Their frequency, their brilliance and excitement, the enthusiasm with which we take part, all suggest that without them we would explode. They free us, if only momentarily, from the thwarted impulses, the inflammable desires that we carry within us. But the Mexican fiesta is not merely a return to an original state of formless and normless liberty: the Mexican is not seeking to return, but to escape from himself, to exceed himself. Our fiestas are explosions. Life and death, joy and sorrow, music and mere noise are united, not to re-create or recognize themselves, but to swallow each other up. There is nothing so joyous as a Mexican fiesta, but there is also nothing so sorrowful. Fiesta night is also a night of mourning.

14   If we hide within ourselves in our daily lives, we discharge ourselves in the whirlwind of the fiesta. It is more than an opening out: we rend ourselves open. Everything—music, love, friendship—ends in tumult and violence. The frenzy of our festivals shows the extent to which our solitude closes us off from communication with the world. We are familiar with delirium, with songs and shouts, with the monologue . . . but not with the dialogue. Our fiestas, like our confidences, our loves, our attempts to reorder our society, are violent breaks with the old or the established. Each time we try to express ourselves we have to break with ourselves. And the fiesta is only one example, perhaps the most typical, of this violent break. It is not difficult to name others, equally revealing: our games, which are always a going to extremes, often mortal; our profligate spending, the reverse of our timid investments and business enterprises; our confessions. The somber Mexican, closed up in himself, suddenly explodes, tears open his breast and reveals himself, though not without a certain complacency, and not without a stopping place in the shameful or terrible mazes of his intimacy. We are not frank, but our sincerity can reach extremes

that horrify a European. The explosive, dramatic, sometimes even suicidal manner in which we strip ourselves, surrender ourselves, is evidence that something inhibits and suffocates us. Something impedes us from being. And since we cannot or dare not confront our own selves, we resort to the fiesta. It fires us into the void; it is a drunken rapture that burns itself out, a pistol shot in the air, a skyrocket.

✧ Evaluating the Text

1. What factors contribute to the popularity of fiestas in Mexico, especially in relationship to the Mexican national character, as described by Paz? In what way are people's experiences of time during the fiesta period qualitatively different from their experience of time during the rest of the year?

2. How does Paz's use of economic information as to the cost and frequency of fiestas help explain the extraordinary importance they play in Mexican life?

3. In what sense does a fiesta provide an opportunity for the solitary individual to be "at once resolved and redeemed"? What do you think Paz means by this?

4. How do Paz's comparisons between Mexican attitudes toward celebrations, life, and death with those of Europeans and North Americans make it easier for his readers to understand his analysis?

✧ Exploring Different Perspectives

1. Discuss the psychology of sacrificing what normally would be conserved to placate the gods and attract abundance, as revealed in Paz's essay and Bessie Head's story "Looking for a Rain God."

2. Discuss the theme of expenditure of material possessions for a desired purpose as explored by Paz and Slavenka Drakulić in "On Bad Teeth."

✧ Extending Viewpoints through Writing

1. Have you ever been at a party that came close in spirit to the Mexican fiesta, when people use the occasion to renew friendships, get drunk together, and discover kinships? If so, describe your experiences and discuss the similarities and differences in terms of the emotional transformation that such celebrations encourage.

2. To what extent do celebrations such as weddings, baptisms, bar mitzvahs, Mardi Gras in New Orleans, and vacations serve much the same function in the United States as fiestas do in Mexico?

Ilan Stavans

Santa Selena

◆

Ilan Stavans was born in Mexico City in 1961 and received a master's degree in 1987 from the Jewish Theological Seminary and a Ph.D. from Columbia University in 1990. He is currently a professor of Latin American and Latino Culture at Amherst College, Massachusetts, and the editor of Hopscotch: A Cultural Review. *His recent published works include* Essential Ilan Stavans *(2000) in which the following essay first appeared,* The Inveterate Dreamer *(2001),* On Borrowed Words: A Memoir of Language *(2001), and* Octavio Paz: A Meditation *(2002). This essay was first published in* Transition 70 *(Summer 1996) and was reprinted in* The Riddle of Cantinflas: Essays on Hispanic Popular Culture *(1998).*

Before You Read

Think about Selena's image in popular culture and the values she represents as a Hispanic performer.

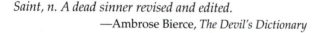

> *Saint, n. A dead sinner revised and edited.*
> —Ambrose Bierce, *The Devil's Dictionary*

1   During a recent trip to South Texas, a dignified old man told me Selena had died because heaven was desperate for another cherub. He described her to me as "a celestial beauty whose time on earth was spent helping the poor and unattended." In San Antonio, a mother of four has placed Selena's photograph in a special altar in her home, surrounded by candles and flowers, just beneath the image of the Virgin of Guadalupe. "Please, Selena," her prayer goes, "let me remain a virgin . . . just like you." (This despite the fact that, at the time of her death, Selena was married to Chris Pérez, her guitar player.) The collective imagination is stronger than anything reality has to offer: A young lady from Corpus Christi who spends a good portion of her days singing "selenatas" swears she sees the singer's ghost appear on her TV screen every night—after she's switched the set off. And a Spanish teacher I know in Dallas who recently lost her job has begun selling a poem of her own creation, "Adiós mi linda estrella," to make money. She sent me a copy of the poem, a tribute to the pop star she considers her angel protector:

Do not cry for me, do not suffer for me
Remember I love you with all my heart
I know if you listen and do as I ask
I will be content because
I have completed my mission here on my beautiful earth and
I can continue to sing to Our Father in Heaven.
Listen, Heaven does not thunder
The sun begins to hide
Our father has given us a new light
Look up to Heaven
The light comes from a divine star
That lights up all of Heaven
It is the Angel Selena
The most beautiful star of the world
and now of Heaven.
Goodbye, my lovely Star.

2   Welcome to *la frontera*, the painful wound dividing Mexico and the United States, a land of kitsch and missed opportunities where outlandish dreams and work-a-day life intertwine. Encompassing 12 million people, its capital is Tijuana, where *el día de los muertos* is the most popular holiday: an opportunity for the living to spend a wild night carousing in the cemetery at the side of their dearly departed. The flag of the region is red, white, and blue, but at its heart is an eagle devouring a writhing snake. *La frontera* is where NAFTA and Kafka cohabit, where English isn't spoken but broken, and where *yo* becomes *I*, and where *I* becomes *Ay, carajo*—a free zone, autonomous and self-referential, perceived by Mexicans as *el fin del mundo* and by Anglo-Americans as a galaxy of bad taste.

3   Since her tragic death, Selena has become omnipresent in *la frontera*, the focal point of a collective suffering—a patron saint, of sorts. Tender *señoritas* cannot bring themselves to accept the idea that she is no longer with us. On radio call-in shows, her followers bemoan the injustice of her disappearance. A movie is in the works, several instant biographies have already been published (in Spanish and English), and more are on their way to the printer. Countless imitators mimic her style, her idiosyncratic fashion, her smile: An upcoming national contest in Corpus Christi will soon crown the girl who impersonates Selena most perfectly, who loses herself in Selena's chaste yet sexy persona. In fact, the whole of Lake Jackson, Texas, Selena's hometown, has already become a kind of Graceland: Pilgrims come to weep at her birthplace and to pay homage at the places she graced with her presence: her home, the neighborhood rodeos where she sang at intermission, the arenas where she entertained the masses. Her grave at Seaside Memorial Park is inundated daily with flowers, candles,

and mementos, and the cemetery keeper has trouble disposing of the colorful offerings. Amalia González, a radio host in Los Angeles, says Selena had sojourned on earth in order "to unite all creeds and races."

4   Elvis, John Lennon, Kurt Cobain, and Jerry Garcia . . . roll over: There's a new kid in the pop star firmament, one who gives voice to the silenced and the oppressed. This until-yesterday unknown *tejana*, née Selena Quintanilla Pérez—awarded the Grammy for Best Mexican American Performance for an album titled, ironically, *Selena Live*—has instantly become the unquestioned queen of *mestizo* pop, part wetback and part *gabacha*.

5   Selena's life may have been tragically short, but death has given her an imposing stature. At 1:05 P.M. on Friday, March 31, 1995, she became immortal: Just short of her twenty-fourth birthday, she ceased to exist as a pop singer of modest means but high ambitions, poised to cross over to a mainstream market, and became not only Madonna's most fearsome competitor (her album *Dreaming of You*, which included a handful of songs in English, sold 175,000 copies in a single day), but also a cult hero, a Hispanic Marilyn Monroe, an object of relentless adoration and adulation. Magically, she has joined Eva Perón in the pantheon of mystical and magical *hispanas*, protectors of the *descamisados*, immaculate personification of eternal love.

6   How many of us from outside *la frontera* had heard of her before the murder? Not many. But even if we had heard some of her songs on the radio, we could not have fathomed her appeal: Her music is *cursi*—melodramatic, cheesy, overemotional. Tejano rhythms, which Selena was in the process of reinventing, are a jumbled fusion of rock, jazz, pop, and country, seasoned with a hint of rap—an endless addition resulting in a subtraction. She was beginning to master them all when she died. But that's not the point: Her *conjunto* pieces, as well as the mental imbalances of Yolanda Saldívar, the administrator of her fan club and her killer, are only props in a theatrical act in which Selena is the star regardless of her talents. She was a symbol, not a genius.

7   Selena's father, Abraham Quintanilla, Jr., whose family has been in South Texas for a least a hundred years, forced her to learn Spanish in order to further her career. She debuted at age five with Los Dinos, her father's group. (He was a vocalist.) Less than twenty years later, with a sexy public persona built around a halter top and tight pants, she was worth more than $5 million. Since she passed just as her crossover dreams were beginning to materialize, her legend was never—will never—be forced to confront the conundrum of assimilation: She will go down as a brave, courageous chicana—perhaps ambivalent toward, but never ashamed of, her background. "You'd see her shopping at the mall," people in South Texas say, wistfully. "And you'd see her working at home. A real sweetheart." Some even recalled how accessible she was—*una de nosotros*: Selena never turned up her nose at Mexican popular entertainment, performing in variety shows like *Siempre en Domingo*

and the melodramatic soap *Dos mujeres, un camino*, starring Erik Estrada. Small parts, no doubt, but the real *sabor*. Had Selena been visited by the angel of death only a few years later, it would have been a very different story: she would have been an American star, and her tragedy would not serve to highlight the plight of *la frontera*.

8 Now Selena is ubiquitous: on TV screens and CDs, on book covers and calendars, on velvet slippers and plastic bracelets, on shampoo bottles and make-up advertisements, on designer clothes and *piñatas*. She is a present-day Frida Kahlo: a martyr whose afterlife *en el más allá* promises to be infinitely more resonant than whatever she managed to achieve *en el más acá*. In *la frontera*, she has been made into a heroine, an ethnic mass-market artifact. "Thanks to her *tejanos* are being heard," a disk jockey from Houston told me. "She put us in the news—and on the front page." And so she did: Rosa López was merely a bit of Hispanic seasoning in the O. J. Simpson mix, but Selena has turned *la frontera*—whose children, adopted and otherwise, include film director Robert "El Mariachi" Rodriguez, performance artist Guillermo Gómez-Peña, and novelists Laura Esquivel and Cormac McCarthy— into a banquet of possibilities for the media. The trial and sentencing of Saldívar alone has catapulted Selena to eternity, winning more newspaper columns for Latinos that the Zapatista rebellion. Even Texas Governor George W. Bush, whose knowledge of *tejano* culture is close to nil, was quick enough to declare April 16, 1995—Selena's birthday and Easter Sunday—*el día de Selena*. There's even a motion to put her face on a postage stamp.

9 Selena's was a life quilted by sheer coincidence but which, studied in retrospect, shows the deliberate design of a well-patterned tapestry. The murder itself (which, strangely, took place on César Chávez's birthday) is already legendary, rivaling the Crucifixion for pathos and histrionics: Saldívar—whose much-lauded punishment is life in prison— comes out of Room 158 of the Corpus Christi Days Inn on Navigation Boulevard with a .38-caliber revolver. Selena stumbles ahead of her, wounded, bleeding, and crying for help. She names her assassin and then dies, in close-up. Cut! Roll the commercial. The next scene takes place minutes later, as Saldívar seals herself in a pickup truck and, holding the pistol to her temple à la O. J., threatens to commit suicide and keeps the police at a standstill for nine and a half hours. Blood, tears, desperation—the recipe lacks not a single ingredient. Saldívar had been a good friend of the singer and her business partner in Selena, Inc., the company that managed the singer's boutiques and beauty salons in Corpus Christi and San Antonio. So what went wrong?

10 You might find the answer in cyberspace, where a Selena home page on the World Wide Web has kept her *admiradores* up to date since a few weeks after her death. Or simply tune in to *El Show de Cristina*, the Spanish-speaking Oprah Winfrey, which was among the first TV programs to capitalize on Selena's tragedy by devoting several episodes to

her family's sorrows. Or you might give up on investigating the logic and become a *selenomaníaco* and start building up your pile of collectibles: nightgowns, hats, purses, money holders, sleepers, umbrellas and a lot more—all sporting her beautiful photograph. Or, if you are ready for a deeper investment, keep in mind the seventy-six-page special issue of *People*, which retailed at $3.95 and now sells for more than two hundred dollars. There is also, of course, the notorious April 17, 1995, issue of the same magazine, which appeared in two different versions: 442,000 copies with Selena on the cover, for sale in Texas, and 3 million issues (featuring the cast of the TV show *Friends*) for the rest of the country. A single copy of *that* Selena issue has auctioned for over $500. My own favorite item is the advertisement for the colorful T-shirt on sale at Selena, Inc. ($10.99), which is marketed as a sign of loyalty: "Tell the world of your love for Selena and her music with one of several full-color designs." One size fits all.

11   For those inclined to read more about it, an illustrated tribute to *La Virgen Selena* is now available, complete with photos of her grave, third-grade class, and mourning mother, plus a snapshot of the singer and her killer cavorting at a fan club appreciation party at the Desperado's Club in San Antonio during the Tejano Music Awards in 1993. Or you might want to bring home the most complete of Selena's thirteen biographies (at this writing), titled *Selena: Como la Flor* and written by Joe Nick Patoski, a senior editor at *Texas Monthly* and co-author of the bestseller *Stevie Ray Vaughan: Caught in the Crossfire*. Patoski's definitive report on the life of *la reina* will tell you how many hours a day she exercised to keep up her figure, the names of her favorite stores, the shoes she was wearing at the time of her death, and all the skinny you will never find in *The National Enquirer*. The newspaper's anti-Hispanic bias has forced its editors to ignore Selena's story from A to Z.

12   Never fear: Selena will survive all aggressions, and her apotheosis is not yet complete. That apex will most surely be reached with the release of the Hollywood movie by director Gregory Nava (who brought you *El Norte*, a film about the plight of poor Guatemalan immigrants in *el otro lado*, as well as *La Familia*, a transgenerational melodrama to end all melodramas). From the moment Selena's body hit the hotel floor, a pitched battle has raged over securing the movie rights to her story. (Patoski devotes several pages of his biography to the wrangling.) By all accounts, her father is firmly in command of choosing the screenwriter and, more important, who gets to play his daughter. (He also chooses who gets to play himself; unidentified sources claim that he rejected Edward James Olmos as too ugly.) Selena will surely do wonders for Nava's career. She has already granted so many miracles—one more shouldn't be a problem. Victor Villaseñor is next in line for redemption, a Chicano writer known for his *Roots*-esque family epic, *Rain of Gold*, who is under contract to write the "official" companion to the film.

Although the second book of his family saga was almost unreadable, it will be hard to go wrong with Selena for inspiration.[1]

13   Inspiration is what she is all about. Just when Latinos were convinced no one cared for them, along came Selena. As long as *la frontera* remains a hybrid territory, hidden from the sight of Anglo America and ignored by the Mexican government, people north and south of the Rio Grande will continue to pray to their new Madonna. They have realized that the best way to conquer the mainstream culture of the United States is by media storm, a subversion from within. They are confident that sooner rather than later all *gringos* will make room for Latino extroversion and sentimentality. Sooner, rather than later, *The National Enquirer* will publish a report on her return to earth in a UFO. A new, darker-complected Elvis is here to capture the imagination of a nation: SELENA IS ALIVE.

✦ Evaluating the Text

1. In what ways has Selena become an icon since her death in 1995? What examples does Stavans present that best illustrate her transformation?

2. What insights does Stavans provide into the *la frontera* culture between Mexico and the United States and the importance that Selena has for this borderline territory?

✦ Exploring Different Perspectives

1. What aspects of Selena's appeal overlap with the Mexican's celebration of saints on All Souls' Night as described by Octavio Paz in "Fiesta"?

2. How does Selena exemplify beauty for *la frontera* culture as did the women with bound feet in ancient China as described by Valerie Steele and John S. Major (see "China Chic: East Meets West")?

✦ Extending Viewpoints through Writing

1. What aspects of Selena's persona make it likely she will become a crossover icon for American culture as well?

2. Rent the film *Selena* (1997) and write an analysis comparing your observations with those of Stavans.

---

[1]As it turned out, Olmos did get to play the father and Villaseñor was eliminated as screenwriter. *Selena*, the movie released in 1997, was so saccharine it didn't even have a murder sequence.

Valerie Steele and John S. Major

China Chic: East Meets West

Valerie Steele is chief curator of the Museum at the Fashion Institute of Technology (FIT). Steele organized a major exhibition at FIT to coincide with the 1999 publication of China Chic: East Meets West. *She is the editor of* Fashion Theory: The Journal of Dress, Body, and Culture *and has also written* Paris Fashion: A Cultural History *(1998) and* Fashion and Eroticism *(2000). John S. Major is director of the China Council of the Asia Society. He is the author of* Heaven and Earth in Early Han Thought *(1993) and* The Silk Route: 7,000 Miles of History *(1996). The following essay, from* China Chic, *examines foot binding in the context of China's political, economic, and cultural history and its correspondence to fashions in the West.*

Before You Read

Consider how foot binding in China (accomplished through dwarfing the foot by dislocating its bones) was a symbol of fashion just as high-heeled shoes are in the West today.

1   Foot binding lasted for a thousand years. It apparently began in the declining years of the Tang dynasty and it persisted in remote areas of China until the middle of the twentieth century. Yet despite its manifest significance within Chinese history, foot binding has been the subject of surprisingly little scholarly research. Recently, however, scholars such as Dorothy Ko have begun to explore the subject—with surprising results. As Ko points out, "It is natural for modern-day reformers to consider footbinding a men's conspiracy to keep women crippled and submissive, but this is an anachronistic view that finds no support in the historical records."[1]

2   Many of the sources on which our understanding of foot binding are based are themselves highly problematic. Western missionaries attacked the "barbaric" practice of foot binding, but they did so within the context of a prejudiced and ignorant denunciation of many other aspects of Chinese civilization. Most of the Chinese literature on the subject was written by men, who often emphasized the erotic appeal of foot binding. For a better understanding of foot binding, it is necessary to

search for evidence of what Chinese women themselves thought about the practice. It is also necessary to place foot binding within its (changing) historical context. As Ko puts it, "Foot binding is not one monolithic, unchanging experience that all unfortunate women in each succeeding dynasty went through, but is rather an amorphous practice that meant different things to different people . . . It is, in other words, a situated practice."[2]

3   What did foot binding signify to the Chinese, and why did they maintain the practice for so long? Although historians do not know exactly how or why foot binding began, it was apparently initially associated with dancers at the imperial court and professional female entertainers in the capital. During the Song dynasty (960–1279) the practice spread from the palace and entertainment quarters into the homes of the elite. "By the thirteenth century, archeological evidence shows clearly that foot-binding was practiced among the daughters and wives of officials," reports Patricia Buckley Ebrey, whose study of Song women reproduces photographs of shoes from that period. The Fujian tomb of Miss Huang Sheng (1227–43), for example, contained shoes measuring between 13.3 and 14 cm. (5¼ to 5½ inches), while the Jiangxi tomb of Miss Zhou (1240–74) contained shoes that were 18 to 22 cm. (7 to 8⅝ inches) long.[3] Over the course of the next few centuries foot binding became increasingly common among gentry families, and the practice eventually penetrated the mass of the Chinese people.

4   Foot binding generally began between the ages of five and seven, although many poorer families delayed beginning for several years, sometimes even until the girl was an adolescent, so they could continue to benefit from her labor and mobility. First-person accounts of foot binding testify that the procedure was extremely painful. The girl's feet were tightly bound with bandages, which forced the small toes inward and under the sole of the foot, leaving only the big toe to protrude. Then the heel and toe were drawn forcefully together, breaking the arch of the foot.

5   This was the most extreme type of foot binding. However, many girls apparently had their feet "bound in less painful styles that 'merely' kept the toes compressed or limited the growth of the foot, but did not break any bones."[4] Nevertheless, there is no doubt that foot binding was a radical form of body modification. As early as the Song dynasty, Che Ruoshui made perhaps the first protest against foot binding. He wrote: "Little children not yet four or five *sui* [i.e. five to seven years old], who have done nothing wrong, nevertheless are made to suffer unlimited pain to bind [their feet] small. I do not know what use this is."[5]

6   In fact, foot binding served a number of uses. To begin with, as Ebrey suggests, by making the feet of Chinese women so much smaller than those of Chinese men, it emphasized that men and women were

different. Then, too, since only Chinese women bound their feet, the practice also served to distinguish between Chinese and non-Chinese. An investigation of the political situation suggests why this might have been thought desirable. At the time when foot binding began (in the late Tang) and spread (in the Song), China was in bad shape. Various foreign peoples who lived along the frontiers repeatedly raided and invaded China, sometimes conquering sizeable portions of Chinese territory and establishing their own dynasties on land that the Chinese regarded as properly theirs—as the Khitans did in the northeast when they defeated the Tang and established the Liao dynasty (907–1125), as the Tanguts did in the west when they established the XiXia Kingdom, and again as the Jürchens did in the north when they established the Jin dynasty (1115–1260) to succeed the Khitan Liao.

7   Although the Chinese managed to establish the Song dynasty in 960, after the turmoil that accompanied the fall of the Tang, it occupied only a portion of what had been Chinese territory, and even that portion decreased dramatically. Chinese men must often have been reminded of their military inferiority in the face of the aggressive "barbarians" encroaching from the north. Did they, perhaps, feel reassured about their strength and masculinity when they compared themselves to their crippled female counterparts? It may be possible to infer something of the sort when we analyze Song erotic poetry, devoted to the charms of tiny feet and a hesitant gait.

8   The suggestion that the spread of foot binding in the Song may have been related to the perceived need on the part of the Chinese gentry to emphasize the distinctions between men and women, Chinese and non-Chinese is strongly supported by Ebrey's analysis. "Because the ideal upper-class man was by Sung times a relatively subdued and refined figure, he might seem effeminate unless women could be made even more delicate, reticent, and stationary," she writes. In other words, anxieties about masculinity and national identity, rather than the desire to oppress women, *per se*, contributed to the spread of foot binding. "But," Ebrey adds, "we must also come to grips with women's apparently eager participation." A crucial element here, she argues, was the competition between wives and concubines. Chinese mothers may have become enthusiastic proponents of foot binding because small feet were regarded as sexually attractive, yet unlike the other tricks used by courtesans and concubines, there was nothing "forward" or "immodest" about having bound feet.[6]

9   The spread of foot binding during the Song dynasty also coincided with a philosophical movement known as Neo-Confucianism, which placed a pronounced ideological emphasis on female inferiority. (In Neo-Confucian metaphysics, the *yang* male principle was seen as su-

perior to the *yin* female principle in both a cosmological and a moral sense.) Moreover, as already seen, political developments in the Song contributed to the demise of the great aristocratic families and the corresponding proliferation of gentry families, whose social and economic position was much more insecure, and whose predominant social function was to serve as bureaucrats. Members of this new class may have been especially receptive to foot binding, because the practice simultaneously provided reassurance about their social status, proper gender relations, and Chinese identity.

10   Foot binding may have been reassuring to the Chinese, but it did not prevent the Mongols from becoming the first foreigners to conquer all of China. Genghiz Khan unified the Mongols, and Kublai Khan established the Yuan dynasty (1279–1368). Similar anxieties about sexual and racial boundaries appeared again several centuries later toward the end of the Ming dynasty, when the Chinese began to be threatened by the Manchus. Moreover, when the Manchus succeeded in conquering China and establishing the Qing dynasty in the mid-seventeenth century, they passed edicts ordering Chinese men to shave their foreheads and Chinese women to cease foot binding.

11   The resulting "hysterical atmosphere" was "full of sexual overtones," since both cutting men's hair and unbinding women's feet were perceived by Chinese males almost as a symbolic mutilation or castration, which might even be worse than death. As Ko points out, "Although no one openly advocated footbinding, the very establishment of the Manchu dynasty created a need to reemphasize the differences between 'we' and 'they' and between 'he' and 'she.' The ban on footbinding, thus doomed from the start, was rescinded in 1668, four years after its promulgation."[7]

12   Contrary to popular belief, it was not only the wealthy who bound their daughters' feet. By the Qing dynasty, the majority of Chinese women had bound feet—peasants included—although there did exist variations in the degree and type of foot binding. According to one Qing observer, "The practice of footbinding is more widespread in Yangzhou than in other places. Even coolies, servants, seamstresses, the poor, the old, and the weak have tiny feet and cramped toes."[8] Manchu women, however, did not bind their feet, nor did members of other ethnic minority groups. Indeed, under the Qing, Manchu women were specifically forbidden to bind their feet, which is intriguing, since it implies a desire to do so.

13   Because foot binding is usually interpreted today as a gruesome example of women's oppression, it is important to stress that women who experienced the practice rarely perceived it in those terms. Indeed, Ko has unearthed considerable evidence that many Chinese women felt proud of their bound feet, which they regarded as beautiful and

prestigious. Foot binding was a central part of the women's world. The rituals surrounding foot binding were female-exclusive rituals, presided over by the women of the family, especially the girl's mother, who prayed to deities such as the Tiny Foot Maiden and the goddess Guanyin. According to Ko, these rituals "and the beliefs behind them help explain the longevity and spread of the custom."

> For all its erotic appeal to men, without the cooperation of the women concerned, footbinding could not have been perpetuated for a millennium. In defining the mother–daughter tie in a private space barred to men, in venerating the fruits of women's handiwork, and in the centrality of female-exclusive religious rituals, footbinding embodied the essential features of a woman's culture documented by the writings of the women themselves.[9]

Women wrote poems about lotus shoes and they exchanged them with friends. Proverbs emphasized women's control over foot binding: "A plain face is given by heaven, but poorly bound feet are a sign of laziness."[10]

14   Good mothers were supposed to bind their daughters' feet tightly so they could make advantageous marriages, just as they made their sons study hard so they could pass their examinations. The Victorian traveler Isabella Bird visited China and reported that "The butler's little daughter, aged seven, is having her feet 'bandaged' for the first time, and is in torture, but bears it bravely in the hope of 'getting a rich husband' . . . The mother of this suffering infant says, with a quiet air of truth and triumph, that Chinese women suffer less in the process of being crippled than foreign women do from wearing corsets!"[11]

15   Indeed, Chinese and westerners alike not infrequently compared foot binding with corsetry, debating their relative injuriousness and irrationality. Yet measurements of existing corsets and lotus shoes indicate that both the sixteen-inch waist and the three-inch golden lotus were only achieved by a minority of women. Writing at the turn of the century, the sociologist Thorstein Veblen used foot binding (as well as such western fashions as corsets and long skirts) as examples of what he called "conspicuous leisure," because they supposedly indicated that the wearer could not perform productive labor. Yet, contrary to popular belief, neither bound feet nor corsets prevented women from working and walking; most Chinese women worked very hard, albeit usually at home. Moreover, although foot binding was believed to ensure female chastity by, literally, preventing women from straying, in fact women were far more restricted by social and legal constraints.

16   Although for many centuries most Chinese men and women approved of foot binding, the practice eventually ceased to be valorized as a way of emphasizing the beauty and virtue of Chinese women and/or the virility and civility of Chinese men. Writing in the early nineteenth century, the novelist Li Ruzhun attacked foot binding on the grounds that it oppressed women. His novel *Flowers in the Mirror* included a satirical sequence about a country where women ruled and men had their feet bound.

17   Missionary efforts undoubtedly played a role in the demise of foot binding, as the Chinese were made aware that Westerners thought the practice was "barbaric," unhealthy, and oppressive to women. The Chinese girls who attended mission schools were taught that foot binding was bad. More significantly, however, growing numbers of young Chinese men (and a few educated Chinese women) began to reinterpret foot binding as a "backward" practice that hindered national efforts to resist western imperialism.

18   Chinese reformers began to discuss whether China could be strengthened *vis-à-vis* the West, if only Chinese women became stronger physically. This, in turn, seemed to depend on the elimination of what was increasingly regarded by progressive Chinese as the "feudal" practice of foot binding. Organizations such as the Natural Foot Society were founded, and struggled to change the idea that unbound female feet were "big" and ugly. Indeed, it was apparently difficult to convince the Chinese that foot binding was any more "unnatural" than other kinds of bodily adornment, such as clothing, jewelry, hairstyles, or cosmetics.[12]

19   There is even some evidence that the introduction of western high-heeled shoes, which give the visual illusion of smaller feet and produce a swaying walk, may have eased the transition away from the bound foot ideal. Manchu shoes were another alternative to lotus shoes in the early years of the anti-foot-binding movement, although with the rise of anti-Manchu nationalism at the time of the 1911 Revolution, this style disappeared.

20   Foot binding had never been mandated by any Chinese government. Indeed, various Qing rulers had sporadically attempted to abolish foot binding, without success. After the Qing dynasty was overthrown and a republic was declared, foot binding was outlawed. Laws alone would not have sufficed to end the practice, however, had it not already ceased to claim the allegiance of significant segments of the Chinese population, but once foot binding began to be regarded as "backward," modern-thinking Chinese increasingly attacked the practice.

21   Older brothers argued that their sisters should not have their feet bound, or should try to let their feet out—a process that was itself painful and only partly feasible. Sometimes husbands even abandoned

wives who had bound feet, and looked for new, suitably modern brides. Obviously, these developments took place within the context of broader social change. The new generation of educated, urban Chinese increasingly argued that many aspects of traditional Chinese culture should be analyzed and improved. Women, as well as men, should be educated and should participate in athletic activities. Arranged marriages should be replaced by love matches. The Chinese nation should modernize and strengthen itself.

NOTES

1. Dorothy Ko, *Teachers of the Inner Chambers: Women and Culture in Seventeenth-Century China* (Stanford: Stanford University Press, 1994), p. 148.
2. Dorothy Ko, "The Body as Attire: The Shifting Meanings of Footbinding in Seventeenth Century China," *Journal of Women's History* 8.4 (1997), p. 15.
3. Patricia Buckley Ebrey, *The Inner Quarters: Marriage and the Lives of Chinese Women in the Sung Period* (Berkeley: University of California Press, 1993), pp. 38–39.
4. Feng Jicai, *The Three-Inch Golden Lotus*, trans. David Wakefield (Honolulu: University of Hawaii Press, 1994), p. 236.
5. Cited in Ebrey, *The Inner Quarters*, p. 40.
6. Ebrey, *The Inner Quarters*, pp. 42–43.
7. Ko, *Teachers of the Inner Chambers*, p. 149.
8. Ibid., p. 263.
9. Ibid., p. 150.
10. Ibid., p. 171.
11. Isabella Bird, *The Golden Chersonese and the Way Thither* (first published London, 1883; reprinted, Singapore: Oxford University Press, 1990), p. 66.
12. Ko, "The Body as Attire," pp. 17–19.

✧ Evaluating the Text

1. What is the practice of foot binding? What political and social meanings did it communicate within the context of Chinese culture at the time it was practiced?

2. Why do Steele and Major draw a distinction between Western condemnation of foot binding and what the practice meant to Chinese women at the time?

✧ Exploring Different Perspectives

1. How did foot binding as described in "China Chic" solidify an endangered cultural identity for the Chinese as Selena does for the *la frontera* region?

2. How do bound feet symbolize desirable cultural qualities in ancient China as straight white teeth do in America today, according to Slavenka Drakulić?

✧ *Extending Viewpoints through Writing*

1. What do the kind of shoes you wear say about you? What are your favorite styles, heel heights, and colors? Given the choice between a pair of fashionable or comfortable shoes, which would you buy? Alternatively, compare the meanings communicated by various traditional shoe types—including moccasins, sandals, mules, boots, and clogs—and their modern variants.

2. The so-called "lotus foot" (named because the walk of a woman whose foot was bound was thought to resemble the swaying of the lotus plant in the wind) captivated the Chinese imagination such that the foot took on the role of a sexual object. In what way do "shoes that have no relationship to the natural foot shape" (high heels) communicate the same psychological meaning in the West?

Nabil Gorgy

Cairo Is a Small City

———————◆———————

Nabil Gorgy was born in Cairo in 1944 and studied civil engineering at Cairo University. After working as an engineer in New York City, he returned to Cairo, where he now runs his own art gallery. His interests in mysticism, Egyptology, and Sufi traditions are reflected in his novel The Door *(1981). His most recent collection of short stories is* The Slave's Dream and Other Stories *(1991). In "Cairo Is a Small City," translated by Denys Johnson-Davies (1983), an upper-class Egyptian engineer falls victim to an age-old Bedouin tradition.*

Egypt is an Arab republic in northeastern Africa, bordered by the Mediterranean in the north, Israel and the Red Sea to the east, the Sudan to the south, and Libya to the west. Egypt was the site of one of the earliest civilizations that developed in the Nile valley more than 5,000 years ago and flourished until it became part of the Roman Empire in 30 B.C. As always, Egypt depends on the Nile River for maintaining arable lands, and its economy, although weakened in the 1980s by earlier Arab–Israeli wars, remains primarily agricultural. Under the leadership of Anwar Sadat, in 1979 Egypt became the first Arab nation to sign a peace treaty with Israel. In 1981, Sadat was assassinated by Muslim fundamentalists, and his successor, Hosni Mubarak, has faced the difficult task of dealing with the resurgence of Islamic fundamentalism while moving Egypt into a position of leadership in the Arab world. Egypt joined the United States and other nations in sending troops to Saudi Arabia after the August 1990 invasion of Kuwait by Iraq. In October 1993, Hosni Mubarak was sworn in for a third six-year term as president. Since 1997, the government instituted a policy designed to promote more efficient farming methods.

Before You Read

Notice the way Gorgy begins to infuse the story with ancient cultural traditions before we find out what happens.

———————◆———————

1 On the balcony of his luxury flat Engineer Adil Salim stood watching some workmen putting up a new building across the wide street along the centre of which was a spacious garden. The building was at the foundations stage, only the concrete foundations and some

of the first-floor columns having been completed. A young iron-worker with long hair was engaged in bending iron rods of various dimensions. Adil noticed that the young man had carefully leant his Jawa motorcycle against a giant crane that crouched at rest awaiting its future tasks. "How the scene has changed!" Adil could still remember the picture of old-time master craftsmen, and of the workers who used to carry large bowls of mixed cement on their calloused shoulders.

2   The sun was about to set and the concrete columns of a number of new constructions showed up as dark frameworks against the light in this quiet district at the end of Heliopolis.

3   As on every day at this time there came down into the garden dividing the street a flock of sheep and goats that grazed on its grass, and behind them two bedouin women, one of whom rode a donkey, while the younger one walked beside her. As was his habit each day, Adil fixed his gaze on the woman walking in her black gown that not so much hid as emphasized the attractions of her body, her waist being tied round with a red band. It could be seen that she wore green plastic slippers on her feet. He wished that she would catch sight of him on the balcony of his luxurious flat; even if she did so, Adil was thinking, those bedouin had a special code of behaviour that differed greatly from what he was used to and rendered it difficult to make contact with them. What, then, was the reason, the motive, for wanting to think up some way of talking to her? It was thus that he was thinking, following her with his gaze as she occasionally chased after a lamb that was going to be run over by a car or a goat left far behind the flock.

4   Adil, who was experienced in attracting society women, was aware of his spirit being enthralled: days would pass with him on the balcony, sunset after sunset, as he watched her without her even knowing of his existence.

5   Had it not been for that day on which he had been buying some fruit and vegetables from one of the shopkeepers on Metro Street, and had not the shopkeeper seen another bedouin woman walking behind another flock, and had he not called out to her by name, and had she not come, and had he not thrown her a huge bundle of waste from the shop, after having flirted with her and fondled her body—had it not been for that day, Adil's mind would not have given birth to the plan he was determined, whatever the cost, to put through, because of that woman who had bewitched his heart.

6   As every man, according to Adil's philosophy of life, had within him a devil, it was sometimes better to follow this devil in order to placate him and avoid his tyranny. Therefore Engineer Adil Salim finally decided to embark upon the terrible, the unthinkable. He remembered

from his personal history during the past forty years that such a temporary alliance with this devil of his had gained him a courage that had set him apart from the rest of his colleagues, and through it he had succeeded in attaining this social position that had enabled him to become the owner of this flat whose value had reached a figure which he avoided mentioning even in front of his family lest they might be upset or feel envy.

7   Thus, from his balcony on the second floor in Tirmidhi Street, Engineer Adil Salim called out in a loud voice "Hey, girl!" as he summoned the one who was walking at the rear of the convoy. When the flock continued on its way without paying any attention, he shouted again: "Hey, girl—you who sell sheep," and before the girl moved far away he repeated the word "sheep." Adil paid no attention to the astonishment of the doorman, who had risen from the place where he had been sitting at the entrance, thinking that he was being called. In fact he quietly told him to run after the two bedouin women and to let them know that he had some bread left over which he wanted to give them for their sheep.

8   From the balcony Adil listened to the doorman calling to the two women in his authoritative Upper Egyptian accent, at which they came to a stop and the one who was riding the donkey looked back at him. Very quickly Adil was able to make out her face as she looked towards him, seeking to discover what the matter was. As for the young girl, she continued on behind the flock. The woman was no longer young and had a corpulent body and a commanding look which she did not seek to hide from him. Turning her donkey round, she crossed the street separating the garden from his building and waited in front of the gate for some new development. Adil collected up all the bread in the house and hurried down with it on a brass tray. Having descended to the street, he went straight up to the woman and looked at her. When she opened a saddlebag close by her leg, he emptied all the bread into it.

9   "Thanks," said the woman as she made off without turning towards him. He, though, raising his voice so that she would hear, called out, "And tomorrow too."

10   During a period that extended to a month Adil began to buy bread which he did not eat. Even on those days when he had to travel away or to spend the whole day far from the house, he would leave a large paper parcel with the doorman for him to give to the bedouin woman who rode the donkey and behind whom walked she for whom the engineer's heart craved.

11   Because Adil had a special sense of the expected and the probable, and after the passing of one lunar month, and in his place in front of the building, with the bread on the brass tray, there occurred that which he

had been wishing would happen, for the woman riding the donkey had continued on her way and he saw the other, looking around her carefully before crossing the road, ahead of him, walking towards him. She was the most beautiful thing he had set eyes on. The speed of his pulse almost brought his heart to a stop. How was it that such beauty was to be found without it feeling embarrassed at ugliness, for after it any and every thing must needs be so described? When she was directly in front of him, and her kohl-painted eyes were scrutinizing him, he sensed a danger which he attributed to her age, which was no more than twenty. How was it that she was so tall, her waist so slim, her breasts so full, and how was it that her buttocks swayed so enticingly as she turned away and went off with the bread, having thanked him? His imagination became frozen even though she was still close to him: her pretty face with the high cheekbones, the fine nose and delicate lips, the silver, crescent-shaped earrings, and the necklace that graced her bosom? Because such beauty was "beyond the permissible," Adil went on thinking about Salma—for he had got to know her name, her mother having called her by it in order to hurry her back lest the meeting between the lovers be prolonged.

12   Adil no longer troubled about the whistles of the workers who had now risen floor by floor in the building opposite him, being in a state of infatuation, his heart captured by this moonlike creature. After the affair, in relation to himself, having been one of boldness, to end in seeing or greeting her, it now became a matter of necessity that she turn up before sunset at the house so that he might not be deprived of the chance of seeing her. So it was that Engineer Adil Salim fell in love with the beautiful bedouin girl Salma. And just as history is written by historians, so it was that Adil and his engineering work determined the history of this passion in the form of a building each of whose columns represented a day and each of whose floors was a month. He noted that, at the completion of twenty-eight days and exactly at full moon, Salma would come to him in place of her mother to take the bread. And so, being a structural engineer, he began to observe the moon, his yearning increasing when it was in eclipse and his spirits sparkling as its fullness drew near till, at full moon, the happiness of the lover was completed by seeing the beloved's face.

13   During seven months he saw her seven times, each time seeing in her the same look she had given him the first time: his heart would melt, all resolution would be squeezed out of him and that fear for which he knew no reason would be awakened. She alone was now capable of granting him his antidote. After the seventh month Salma, without any preamble, had talked to him at length, informing him that she lived with her parents around a spring at a distance of an hour's

walk to the north of the airport, and that it consisted of a brackish spring alongside which was a sweet one, so that she would bathe in the first and rinse herself clean in the other, and that there were date palms around the two springs, also grass and pasturage. Her father, the owner of the springs and the land around them, had decided to invite him and so tomorrow "he'll pass by you and invite you to our place, for tomorrow we attend to the shearing of the sheep."

14   Adil gave the lie to what he was hearing, for it was more than any stretch of the imagination could conceive might happen.

15   The following day Adil arrived at a number of beautifully made tents, where a vast area of sand was spread out below date palms that stretched to the edge of a spring. Around the spring was gathered a large herd of camels, sheep and goats that spoke of the great wealth of the father. It was difficult to believe that such a place existed so close to the city of Cairo. If Adil's astonishment was great when Salma's father passed by him driving a new Peugeot, he was yet further amazed at the beauty of the area surrounding this spring. "It's the land of the future," thought Adil to himself. If he were able to buy a few *feddans* now he'd become a millionaire in a flash, for this was the Cairo of the future. "This is the deal of a lifetime," he told himself.

16   On the way the father asked a lot of questions about Adil's work and where he had previously lived and about his knowledge of the desert and its people. Though Adil noticed in the father's tone something more than curiosity, he attributed this to the nature of the Bedouin and their traditions.

17   As the car approached the tents Adil noticed that a number of men were gathered under a tent whose sides were open, and as the father and his guest got out of the car the men turned round, seated in the form of a horse-shoe. With the father sitting down and seating Engineer Adil Salim alongside him, one of the sides of the horse-shoe was completed. In front of them sat three men on whose faces could be seen the marks of time in the form of interlaced wrinkles.

18   The situation so held Adil's attention that he was unaware of Salma except when she passed from one tent to another in the direction he was looking and he caught sight of her gazing towards him.

19   The man who was sitting in a squatting position among the three others spoke. Adil heard him talking about the desert, water and sheep, about the roads that went between the oases and the *wadi*, the towns and the springs of water, about the bedouin tribes and blood ties; he heard him talking about the importance of protecting these roads and springs, and the palm trees and the dates, the goats and the milk upon which the suckling child would be fed; he also heard him talk about how small the *wadi* was in comparison to this desert that stretched out endlessly.

20 In the same way as Adil had previously built the seven-storey building that represented the seven months, each month containing twenty-eight days, till he would see Salma's face whenever it was full moon, he likewise sensed that this was the tribunal which had been set up to make an enquiry with him into the killing of the man whom he had one day come across on the tracks between the oases of Kharga and Farshout. It had been shortly after sunset when he and a friend, having visited the iron ore mines in the oases of Kharga had, instead of taking the asphalt road to Assiout, proceeded along a rough track that took them down towards Farshout near to Kena, as his friend had to make a report about the possibility of repairing the road and of extending the railway line to the oases. Going down from the high land towards the *wadi*, the land at a distance showing up green, two armed men had appeared before them. Adil remembered how, in a spasm of fear and astonishment, of belief and disbelief, and with a speed that at the time he thought was imposed upon him, a shot had been fired as he pressed his finger on the trigger of the revolver which he was using for the first time. A man had fallen to the ground in front of him and, as happens in films, the other had fled. As for him and his friend, they had rushed off to their car in order to put an end to the memory of the incident by reaching the *wadi*. It was perhaps because Adil had once killed a man that he had found the courage to accept Salma's father's invitation.

21 "That day," Adil heard the man address him, "with a friend in a car, you killed Mubarak bin Rabia when he went out to you, Ziyad al-Mihrab being with him."

22 This was the manner in which Engineer Adil Salim was executed in the desert north-west of the city of Cairo: one of the men held back his head across a marble-like piece of stone, then another man plunged the point of a tapered dagger into the spot that lies at the bottom of the neck between the two bones of the clavicle.

✦ Evaluating the Text

1. How is the engineer, Adil Salim, characterized? What incidents reveal these character traits most clearly? How does he see himself? To what does he attribute his success and affluence?

2. Under what circumstances does the engineer first meet the Bedouin girl? What is his attitude toward her?

3. After reading the story, discuss the significance of the title, especially as it sheds light on the surprising consequences for the engineer. To what extent does the title suggest that the Cairo of the Bedouins and the Cairo of the engineer, although seemingly very different, are basically the same?

✧ *Exploring Different Perspectives*

1. In both Gorgy's story and Gino Del Guercio's account (see "The Secrets of Haiti's Living Dead"), the protagonists living in modern times come into contact with much older ways of perceiving the world. How does this operate as a theme in both works?

2. How does the psychology of sacrifice enter into both Gorgy's and Bessie Head's stories (see "Looking for a Rain God")? In what sense are both titles ironic?

✧ *Extending Viewpoints through Writing*

1. In a short essay, discuss Gorgy's attitude toward ancient cultural traditions as they emerge in the story.

2. Adil's actions and reactions indicate that he is in love. What actions and reactions of your own or someone you know serve as sure-fire signs of being in love?

Bessie Head

Looking for a Rain God

———————◆———————

Bessie Head (1937–1986) was born in Pietermaritzburg, South Africa, the daughter of a black father and a white mother. She suffered the child-hood trauma of being "reclassified"; she was taken from her mother at birth and brought up by foster parents as a Coloured. Her mother was treated as insane because of her relationship with a black man. Head was raised by her foster parents until she was thirteen, when she was placed in a mission orphanage. The emotional scars of her childhood are power-fully recorded in the widely acclaimed A Question of Power *(1973), a fictional study of madness produced by the violence of the apartheid sys-tem. After completing her education, she taught grammar school and wrote fiction for a local newspaper. In 1963, Head moved to a farm com-mune in Serowe, Botswana, with her son. She lived there, working as a teacher and a gardener in a local village until her death.*

Head's writing grows directly out of her experience of village life. Her first novel, When Rain Clouds Gather *(1968), presents the epic struggle of a village trying to survive a devastating drought. Her next two novels,* Maru *(1971) and* A Question of Power *(1973), depict women strug-gling to overcome oppression in their societies and earned her the distinc-tion of being one of Africa's major female writers. As a chronicler of vil-lage life, Head wrote two histories,* Serowe: Village of the Rain Wind *(1981) and* A Bewitched Crossroad *(1985). "Looking for a Rain God," from* The Collector of Treasures and Other Botswana Tales *(1977), is based on a shocking local incident revealing how an ancient tribal ritual resurfaced after years of drought in modern-day Botswana.*

The conditions of drought so graphically described by Bessie Head in this 1977 story were again confronted by the country during six succes-sive years of drought between 1981 and 1987.

Before You Read

As you read Head's story, consider how traditional rituals have been over-laid, but not extinguished by Christianity, in Botswana.

———————◆———————

1   It is lonely at the lands where the people go to plough. These lands are vast clearings in the bush, and the wild bush is lonely too. Nearly all the lands are within walking distance from the village. In some parts of the bush where the underground water is very near the

567

surface, people made little rest camps for themselves and dug shallow wells to quench their thirst while on their journey to their own lands. They experienced all kinds of things once they left the village. They could rest at shady watering places full of lush, tangled trees with delicate pale-gold and purple wildflowers springing up between soft green moss and the children could hunt around for wild figs and any berries that might be in season. But from 1958, a seven-year drought fell upon the land and even the watering places began to look as dismal as the dry open thornbush country; the leaves of the trees curled up and withered; the moss became dry and hard and, under the shade of the tangled trees, the ground turned a powdery black and white, because there was no rain. People said rather humorously that if you tried to catch the rain in a cup it would only fill a teaspoon. Toward the beginning of the seventh year of drought, the summer had become an anguish to live through. The air was so dry and moisture-free that it burned the skin. No one knew what to do to escape the heat and tragedy was in the air. At the beginning of that summer, a number of men just went out of their homes and hung themselves to death from trees. The majority of the people had lived off crops, but for two years past they had all returned from the lands with only their rolled-up skin blankets and cooking utensils. Only the charlatans, incanters, and witch doctors made a pile of money during this time because people were always turning to them in desperation for little talismans and herbs to rub on the plough for the crops to grow and the rain to fall.

2   The rains were late that year. They came in early November, with a promise of good rain. It wasn't the full, steady downpour of the years of good rain but thin, scanty, misty rain. It softened the earth and a rich growth of green things sprang up everywhere for the animals to eat. People were called to the center of the village to hear the proclamation of the beginning of the ploughing season; they stirred themselves and whole families began to move off to the lands to plough.

3   The family of the old man, Mokgobja, were among those who left early for the lands. They had a donkey cart and piled everything onto it, Mokgobja—who was over seventy years old; two girls, Neo and Boseyong; their mother Tiro and an unmarried sister, Nesta; and the father and supporter of the family, Ramadi, who drove the donkey cart. In the rush of the first hope of rain, the man, Ramadi, and the two women, cleared the land of thornbush and then hedged their vast ploughing area with this same thornbush to protect the future crop from the goats they had brought along for milk. They cleared out and deepened the old well with its pool of muddy water and still in this light, misty rain, Ramadi inspanned two oxen and turned the earth over with a hand plough.

4   The land was ready and ploughed, waiting for the crops. At night, the earth was alive with insects singing and rustling about in search of

food. But suddenly, by mid-November, the rain flew away; the rain clouds fled away and left the sky bare. The sun danced dizzily in the sky, with a strange cruelty. Each day the land was covered in a haze of mist as the sun sucked up the last drop of moisture out of the earth. The family sat down in despair, waiting and waiting. Their hopes had run so high; the goats had started producing milk, which they had eagerly poured on their porridge, now they ate plain porridge with no milk. It was impossible to plant the corn, maize, pumpkin, and watermelon seeds in the dry earth. They sat the whole day in the shadow of the huts and even stopped thinking, for the rain had fled away. Only the children, Neo and Boseyong, were quite happy in their little-girl world. They carried on with their game of making house like their mother and chattered to each other in light, soft tones. They made children from sticks around which they tied rags, and scolded them severely in an exact imitation of their own mother. Their voices could be heard scolding the day long: "You stupid thing, when I send you to draw water, why do you spill half of it out of the bucket!" "You stupid thing! Can't you mind the porridge pot without letting the porridge burn!" And then they would beat the rag dolls on their bottoms with severe expressions.

5   The adults paid no attention to this; they did not even hear the funny chatter; they sat waiting for rain; their nerves were stretched to breaking-point willing the rain to fall out of the sky. Nothing was important, beyond that. All their animals had been sold during the bad years to purchase food, and of all their herd only two goats were left. It was the women of the family who finally broke down under the strain of waiting for rain. It was really the two women who caused the death of the little girls. Each night they started a weird, high-pitched wailing that began on a low, mournful note and whipped up to a frenzy. Then they would stamp their feet and shout as though they had lost their heads. The men sat quiet and self-controlled; it was important for men to maintain their self-control at all times but their nerve was breaking too. They knew the women were haunted by the starvation of the coming year.

6   Finally, an ancient memory stirred in the old man, Mokgobja. When he was very young and the customs of the ancestors still ruled the land, he had been witness to a rain-making ceremony. And he came alive a little, struggling to recall the details which had been buried by years and years of prayer in a Christian church. As soon as the mists cleared a little, he began consulting in whispers with his youngest son, Ramadi. There was, he said, a certain rain god who accepted only the sacrifice of the bodies of children. Then the rain would fall; then the crops would grow, he said. He explained the ritual and as he talked, his memory became a conviction and he began to talk with unshakable authority. Ramadi's nerves were smashed by the nightly wailing of the women and soon the two men began whispering with the two women. The children

continued their game: "You stupid thing! How could you have lost the money on the way to the shop! You must have been playing again!"

7   After it was all over and the bodies of the two little girls had been spread across the land, the rain did not fall. Instead, there was a deathly silence at night and the devouring heat of the sun by day. A terror, extreme and deep, overwhelmed the whole family. They packed, rolling up their skin blankets and pots, and fled back to the village.

8   People in the village soon noted the absence of the two little girls. They had died at the lands and were buried there, the family said. But people noted their ashen, terror-stricken faces and a murmur arose. What had killed the children, they wanted to know? And the family replied that they had just died. And people said amongst themselves that it was strange that the two deaths had occurred at the same time. And there was a feeling of great unease at the unnatural looks of the family. Soon the police came around. The family told them the same story of death and burial at the lands. They did not know what the children had died of. So the police asked to see the graves. At this, the mother of the children broke down and told everything.

9   Throughout that terrible summer the story of the children hung like a dark cloud of sorrow over the village, and the sorrow was not assuaged when the old man and Ramadi were sentenced to death for ritual murder. All they had on the statute books was that ritual murder was against the law and must be stamped out with the death penalty. The subtle story of strain and starvation and breakdown was inadmissible evidence at court; but all the people who lived off crops knew in their hearts that only a hair's breadth had saved them from sharing a fate similar to that of the Mokgobja family. They could have killed something to make the rain fall.

✧ Evaluating the Text

1. How does the author lay the psychological groundwork for what otherwise would come as a shock—the choice of the two young girls in the family as sacrificial victims? Look carefully at how the girls must appear to everyone else in the family, especially in a culture where everyone, to survive, must contribute to the welfare of all. Looked at in this way, how do details such as their sloppiness (spilling food or water) and disobedience contribute to the family's decision to kill them in exchange for rain? How do the games Neo and Boseyong play provide further insight into how they are already being treated by the adults?

2. How does overwhelming stress reactivate a belief in rituals that lie just below the surface of collective tribal memory? From the de-

tails concerning the slaughter and dismemberment of the girls, how, in your opinion, was this ritual supposed to have worked?

3. Even though the police respond, as representatives of the social order, and execute Mokgobja and Ramadi for killing their children, why is it significant that Head ends the story with the statement that the other villagers "could have killed something to make the rain fall"? What does this tell you about Head's attitude toward the events in the story?

✧ Exploring Different Perspectives

1. In both this story set in Botswana and Gino Del Guercio's account of voodoo in Haiti (see "The Secrets of Haiti's Living Dead"), how are officially unsanctioned rituals resorted to in times of extreme political, environmental, and psychological stress?

2. How is the theme of ritual murder used in Head's story and in Nabil Gorgy's story "Cairo Is a Small City"?

✧ Extending Viewpoints through Writing

1. To what extent does this story give you insight into the lives of people who live in colonized nations where Western Christian values are superimposed on tribal customs and beliefs? As a follow-up research project you might wish to investigate the practice of Santéria, a religion originating in Africa, brought to the United States by Cuban émigrées. See Joseph M. Murphy's *Santéria: An African Religion in America* (1988), Judith Gleason's *Santéria, Bronx* (1975), Migene Gonzalez-Wippler's *The Santéria Experience* (1982), and *Rituals and Spells of Santéria* (1984).

2. Did your family have a secret that they kept either from someone in the family or from the outside world? If it can now be revealed, tell what it was. Does the secret seem as significant as it did at the time?

Connecting Cultures

Liza Dalby, "Kimono"

What assumptions about the autonomy of women emerge from Dalby's account and from Elizabeth W. Fernea and Robert A. Fernea's analysis of *hijab* (covering one's face, head, and body) for Muslim women in "A Look behind the Veil" in Chapter 3?

Slavenka Drakulić, "On Bad Teeth"

Discuss the level of tolerance extended by Americans toward those who look different as revealed in Slavenka Drakulić's article and in Sucheng Chan's "You're Short, Besides!" (Chapter 2).

Gino Del Guercio, "The Secrets of Haiti's Living Dead"

Explore the similarities in social conditioning that results in the concept of a "pariah" (see Viramma's "A Pariah's Life" in Chapter 5) with those that voodoo priests in Haiti use to control their victims.

Octavio Paz, "Fiesta"

Discuss the role that excess and violence play in such forms of ritualized public theater as described by Paz and in Stephen Chapman's description of Eastern forms of punishment (Chapter 6).

Ilan Stavans, "Santa Selena"

How does Stavans's analysis and Pat Mora's narrative (see "Remembering Lobo" in Chapter 1) illuminate aspects of Mexican culture?

Valerie Steele and John S. Major, "China Chic: East Meets West"

In your opinion, will female circumcision as discussed by Nawal El Saadawi in "Circumcision of Girls" (Chapter 2) go the way of foot binding as an antiquated cultural custom? Why or why not?

Nabil Gorgy, "Cairo Is a Small City"

How does the concept of reciprocity organize societies in Gorgy's story and in David R. Counts's narrative "Too Many Bananas"?

Bessie Head, "Looking for a Rain God"

How do Bessie Head's story and Ngũgĩ wa Thiong'o's account (see "Decolonising the Mind," Chapter 6) reveal the dual nature of tribal society in Botswana and Kenya? What attitude do both works reveal about superimposed colonial "civilization"?

Pronunciation Key

◆

The pronunciation of each of the following names is shown in parentheses according to the following pronunciation key.

1. A heavy accent ′ is placed after a syllable with the primary accent.
2. A lighter accent ´ is placed after a syllable with the secondary accent.
3. The letters and symbols used to represent given sounds are pronounced as in the examples below.

a	bat, nap	o	box, hot
ā	way, cape	ō	boat, go
â	dare, air	ô	ought, order
ä	art, far	oi	voice, joy
		oo	ooze, rule
b	cabin, back	ou	loud, out
ch	beach, child		
d	do, red	p	pot, paper
		r	read, run
e	bet, merry	s	see, miss
ē	equal, beet	sh	show, push
ė	learn, fern		
		t	tell, ten
f	fit, puff	th	thin, path
g	give, go	t͟h	that, smooth
h	how, him		
		u	up, butter
i	pin, big	u̇	put, burn
ī	deny, ice	ü	rule, ooze
j	jam, fudge		
k	keep, kind	v	river, save
		w	west, will
l	love, all	y	yes, yet
m	my, am	z	zeal, lazy
n	in, now	zh	vision, measure
ng	sing, long		

ə occurs only in unaccented syllables and indicates the sound of

a	in alone
e	in taken
i	in pencil
o	in gallop
u	in circus

FOREIGN SOUNDS

a   as in French *ami*
Y   as in French *do;* or as in German *über*
œ   as in French *feu;* or as in German *schön*
N   as in French *bon*
H   as in German *ach;* or as in Scottish *loch*
R   as in Spanish *pero;* or as in German *mare*

EXAMPLES

Hanan al-Shaykh   (hä´ nän´ al shāk´)
Napoleon A. Chagnon   (nə pō´lē ən shan'yən´)
Gayatri Devi   (gā a´ trē de´ vē)
Mahasweta Devi   (mä´ hə swe´ tə de´ vē)
Slavenka Drakulić   (slə ven´ kə dra kül´ ik)
Nawal El Saadawi   (na´ wäl´ əl sä dou´ wē)
Kazuo Ishiguro   (kä zü´ ō ish i gür´ ö)
Tomoyuki Iwashita   (tō mō yü´ kē i wä shē´ tä)
Mahdokht Kashkuli   (mə dōkt´ käsh kü´ lē)
Milorad Pavić   (mil´ ôr əd pä´ vich)
Tepilit Ole Saitoti   (te´ pə lit ō´ le sī tō´ tē)
Tayeb Salih   (täy´ eb sa´ la)
Ngũgĩ wa Thiong'o   (nə gōo´ gē wä tē ong´ō)

Credits

———————————◆———————————

Hanan al-Shaykh, "The Persian Carpet" from *Modern Arabic Short Stories,* translated by Denys Johnson-Davies (Washington, DC: Three Continents Press, 1988). Copyright © 1988 by Denys Johnson-Davies. Reprinted with the permission of the translator.

Gloria Anzaldúa, "Cervicide" from *Borderlands/La Frontera: The New Mexico.* Copyright © 1987 by Gloria Anzaldúa. Reprinted with the permission of Aunt Lute Books.

Machado de Assis, "A Canary's Ideas" from *The Devil's Church and Other Stories,* translated by Jack Schmitt and Lorie Ishimatsu. Copyright © 1977. Reprinted with the permission of the University of Texas Press.

Ann Louise Bardach, excerpt from "The Stealth Virus: AIDS and Latinos" from *The New Republic* (June 1995). Copyright © 1995 by The New Republic, Inc. Reprinted with the permission of *The New Republic.*

Susan Bordo, "Never Just Pictures" from *Twilight Zones: The Hidden Life of Cultural Images from Plato to O. J.* Copyright © 1993 by The Regents of the University of California. Reprinted with the permission of the author and the University of California Press.

Christy Brown, "The Letter 'A'" from *My Left Foot.* Copyright © 1955 by Christy Brown. Reprinted with the permission of Martin Secker & Warburg, Ltd.

Albert Camus, "The Guest" from *Exile and the Kingdom,* translated by Justin O'Brien. Copyright © 1957, 1958 by Alfred A. Knopf, Inc. Reprinted with the permission of the publisher.

George Carlin, "A Place for Your Stuff" from *Brain Droppings.* Copyright © 1997 by Comedy Concepts, Inc. Reprinted with the permission of Hyperion.

Raymonde Carroll, "Money and Seduction" from *Cultural Misunderstandings: The French-American Experience.* Copyright © 1988 by The University of Chicago. Reprinted with the permission of the author and The University of Chicago Press.

Napoleon A. Chagnon, "Doing Fieldwork Among the Yąnomamö" from *Yąnomamö: The Fierce People, Second Edition.* Copyright © 1977 by Holt, Rinehart & Winston, Inc. Reprinted with the permission of International Thomson Publishing.

Rhetorical Index

◆

INTERVIEWS

Lawrence Metzger   "Irony Square"
Alonso Salazar   "The Lords of Creation"

FICTION

Hanan al-Shaykh   "The Persian Carpet"
Gloria Anzaldúa   "Cervicide"
Machado de Assis   "A Canary's Ideas"
Albert Camus   "The Guest"
Kate Chopin   "Désirée's Baby"
Mahasweta Devi   "Giribala"
Nabil Gorgy   "Cairo Is a Small City"
Bessie Head   "Looking for a Rain God"
Liliana Heker   "The Stolen Party"
Panos Ioannides   "Gregory"
Kazuo Ishiguro   "A Family Supper"
Mahdokht Kashkuli   "The Button"
Catherine Lim   "Paper"
Milorad Pavić   "The Wedgwood Tea Set"
Tayeb Salih   "A Handful of Dates"
Wakako Yamauchi   "And the Soul Shall Dance"

Geographical Index

Index of Authors and Titles

◆

(U.S.)

Canada

United States

Atlantic Ocean

Mexico

Puerto Rico

Haiti

Colombia

Pacific Ocean

Brazil

Chile

Only countries mentioned in
selections are labeled on this map.

Argentina